What Is a Thesaurus?

"A Thesaurus is the opposite of a dictionary. You turn to it when you have the meaning already but don't yet have the word. It may be on the tip of your tongue, but what it is you don't yet know. It is like the missing piece of a puzzle. You know well enough that the other words you try out won't do. They say too much or too little. They haven't the punch or have too much. They are too flat or too showy, too kind or too cruel. But the word which just fills the bill won't come, so you reach for the *Thesaurus*."

—From the Introduction by I. A. RICHARDS

D1115910

ROGET'S

Pocket Thesaurus

BASED ON
*ROGET'S International Thesaurus
of English Words and Phrases*

Edited by
C. O. SYLVESTER MAWSON

Assisted by
KATHARINE ALDRICH WHITING

PUBLISHED BY POCKET BOOKS NEW YORK

POCKET BOOKS, a Simon & Schuster division of
GULF & WESTERN CORPORATION
1230 Avenue of the Americas, New York, N.Y. 10020

ISBN: 0-671-83472-X

First Pocket Books printing September, 1946

125 124 123 122 121 120 119 118

POCKET and colophon are trademarks of Simon & Schuster.

Printed in the U.S.A.

INTRODUCTION

A *Thesaurus*, says the dictionary, is "a treasury or storehouse; hence a repository, especially of words, as a dictionary." But, in a sense, this book is the opposite of a dictionary. You turn to a dictionary when you have a word but are not sure enough what it means—how it has been used and what it may be expected to do. You turn to the *Thesaurus* when you have your meaning already but don't yet have the word. It may be on the tip of your tongue, or in the back of your mind or the hollow of your thought, but what it is you don't yet know. It is like the missing piece of a puzzle. You know well enough that the other words you try out won't do. They are not the right shape. They say too much or too little. They haven't the punch or have too much. They are too flat or too showy, too kind or too cruel. But the word which just fills the bill won't come, so you reach for the *Thesaurus*.

Like the dictionary, it is a dangerous book in all sorts of ways. Sometimes you wake up—after half an hour—and realize that the problem of the missing word is still where it was. You have just been wandering happily about in the treasure house looking its riches over, forgetting what you came in for. It has worse dangers. Sometimes the words you find start new streams of thought which wash everything out.

Then not the word only but the idea too will be missing. In this "Lost Chord" situation, the best thing to conclude is that so evanescent an idea was hardly worth keeping. Sometimes, worse still, Temptation assails you. Instead of the right word—the word your thought was yearning for as its mysterious predestined mate—some

brazen hussy or wastrel of a vocable, never met and
never thought of before, seizes your regard.

> *O these encounterers*
> *That give a coasting welcome ere it comes*

Beware! As Confucius' pupil said, "For one word a man
is often deemed to be wise and for one word he is often
deemed to be foolish. We ought to be careful indeed
what we say."

A big vocabulary is a grand thing when well understood and resourcefully used. But all grandeurs have
their penalties. It is the business of a *Thesaurus* to take
us into all verbal company—to introduce us to every sort
and condition of word, with no guarantee, expressed or
implied, as to what they may not do to us if we trust
them without proper inquiry.

> *Who hath given man speech*
> *Or who hath set therein*
> *A thorn for peril and a snare for sin*

cries the Chorus in *Atalanta in Calydon.*

The great Railway strike in England turned upon the
phrase "definitive terms." One side took it to mean "unchangeable"; the other explained too late that they only
meant "full and detailed." Well does Peter Mark Roget
observe, "A misapplied or misapprehended term is sufficient to give rise to fierce and interminable disputes; a
misnomer has turned the tide of popular opinion; a verbal
sophism has decided a party question; an artful watchword, thrown among combustible materials has kindled
the flame of deadly warfare and changed the destiny of
an empire."

That is the tragic side. The comic possibilities more
concern us here. People who swagger about in borrowed
words may, like Porthos in *The Three Musketeers*, im-

press the inexperienced. They bring the wrong sorts of smiles to the lips of the discerning.

To know the words without the things is perilous indeed. "How often," said the lecturer, "have I dallied by the shores of Lac Leman or strolled on the delightful slopes overlooking Lake Geneva." "Pardon me," said a member of the audience, "but are they not synonymous?" "You may think so, Sir," replied the speaker, "but for my part I consider Lac Leman by far the more synonymous of the two." Awful warnings of this sort abound. "I always tell my children to look it up in the dictionary or the encyclopedia," said the Sea Captain. "That is what they are there for. Always be exact . . . No, I don't wear my ribbons in public places. Seems to me they are a bit promiscuous."

But when is a word our own? What is a mastery of language? How in fact do we acquire a vocabulary worthy of the name?

The answer of course is: By experience with words, by living with great books and good talkers, by watching their words at work and at play—in brief, by becoming *familiar* with words. Mere acquaintanceship with them is not profitable here. An acquaintance is one whose name and face you know, without more than a rough idea of his being and business. A familiar is one about whom you know as much as possible. Words are astonishingly like people. They have characters, they almost have personalities—are honest, useful, obliging . . . or treacherous, vain, stubborn . . . They shift, as people do, their conduct with their company. They are an endless study in which we are studying nature and ourselves at that meeting point where our minds are trying to give form to or take it from the world.

Peter Mark Roget a century ago had high hopes of the help his arrangement of words might be to thought and to the construction of a common second language such

as Basic English may become. There is nothing fantastic
about such hopes. In drawing up his scheme of divisions
his model was biological classification. He was a physician
and Secretary of the Royal Society. But we need not take
Roget's actual categories too seriously. To criticize them
would be to bring up all the hardest problems there are.
They serve their purpose—which is to remind us systematically of all that we know about words. "It is not suf-
ficiently considered," said Dr. Johnson, "that men require more often to be reminded than to be informed."
For information about words we go to the dictionary—
the bigger it is the better. We go to the *Thesaurus* in the
hope that something we really know already will come
back to us in our need. How vast is the realm of our current oblivion. "I know," said Benjamin Paul Blood, "as
having known, the secret of existence." Nothing will better make us realize how nearly true this is than an hour
spent in the treasury. How incredibly much we understand if only we can mobilize our understanding. Roget's
Thesaurus is one of the greatest of all *memoria technica*.
It is an astonishing thought that we can carry it in the
pocket.

I. A. RICHARDS

CONTENTS

POCKET THESAURUS AND WORD FINDER

ABBREVIATIONS USED IN THIS BOOK

abbr. abbreviated, abbreviation
adj. adjective, adjectival expression
adv. adverb, adverbial expression
Am. *or* Amer. America, American
Am. hist. American history
Am. Ind. American Indian
anat. anatomy
anon. anonymous
Ar. Arabic
arch. architecture
archæol. archæology
arith. arithmetic
astrol. astrology
astron. astronomy
Bib. Biblical
biol. biology
bot. botany
Brit. British
Can. Canada, Canadian
chem. chemistry
Chin. Chinese
class. classical
colloq. colloquial
com. commerce, commercial
conj. conjunction
Du. Dutch
Dan. Danish
dial. dialect, dialectal
dim. diminutive
E. East
eccl. ecclesiastical
Eng. English, England
erron. erroneous, -ly
esp. especially
exc. except
F. French
fem. feminine
fig. figurative, -ly
G. *or* Ger. German
Gr. Greek
Gr. Brit. Great Britain
her. heraldry
Hind. Hindustani
hist. history, historical
Icel. Icelandic
Ind. Indian
Ir. Irish, Ireland
int. interjection
It. Italian

Jap. Japanese
joc. jocular
L. Latin
l.c. lower case
masc. masculine
math. mathematics
mil. military
Moham. Mohammedan
myth. mythology
n. noun
naut. nautical
neut. neuter
Norw. Norwegian
obs. obsolete
opp. opposed
orig. original, -ly
parl. parliamentary
path. pathology
Pg. Portuguese
pharm. pharmacy
philos. philosophy
physiol. physiology
pl. plural
pol. *or* polit. political
pop. popular, -ly
prep. preposition
prov. proverb, provincial
psychol. psychology
R. C. Ch. Roman Catholic Church
relig. religion
rhet. rhetoric, rhetorical
Russ. Russian
S. Am. South American
Scand. Scandinavian
Scot. Scottish, Scotland
sing. singular
Skr. Sanskrit
Sp. Spanish
surg. surgery
Sw. Swedish
tech. technical
theat. theatrical
theol. theology
typog. typography
Univ. University
U. S. United States
v. verb
zool. zoology

HOW TO USE THE BOOK

I. To find a synonym or antonym for any given WORD:

Turn to the Index* and find the particular word or any term of kindred meaning; then refer to the category indicated (the numbers printed in bold face at the top outer corner of each page). There in its proper grouping, the indexed word will be found, together with a wide selection of related terms. Synonyms and antonyms are placed in adjoining positions. For example, suppose a synonym is wanted for the word "cold" in the sense of "indifferent." Turn to the Index, where the following references will be found:

> cold, *adj.*
> *frigid* **383**
> *insensible* **823**
> *indifferent* **866**

The italicized words give the general sense of the synonyms in the respective categories. The bold-faced figures denote that the indexed word is itself the heading or keyword of a distinct group. Thus, in this example, under **383** we find a list of adjectives grouped under the word "cold" in the literal sense of the term.

Turning to No. **866** (the sense required), we read through the varied list of synonyms ("indifferent, frigid, lukewarm," etc.) and select the most appropriate expression. To widen the selection, suggested references are given to allied lists; while in the adjoining category (No. **865**) are grouped the corresponding antonyms ("eager, keen, burning, ardent," etc.). The groups are arranged, not merely to supply synonyms for some special word, but also to suggest new lines of thought and to stimulate the imagination.

II. To find suitable words to express a given IDEA:

Find in the Index some word relating to the idea, and the categories referred to will supply the need.

For example, suppose a writer wishes to convey the idea of "rest." Turning to No. **265**, he will find *nouns* giving such associated senses as "quiet," "pause," "resting place," or *verbs* with the sense of "be still," "remain," "quell," or *adjectives* such as "quiescent," "still," "silent," and the like. The mere reading of the entire list will help to crystallize the idea and give it utterance.

III. To find appropriate words or new ideas on any given SUBJECT:

Turn up the subject or any branch of it. The Index itself will frequently suggest various lines of thought, while reference to the indicated groups will provide many words and phrases that should prove helpful.

Thus, suppose "poetry" is the theme, No. **597** will be found most suggestive. Or again, the subject may be "the drama" (**599**), "music" (**415**), "the vegetable kingdom" (**367**), "national legislatures" (**696**), "psychical research" (**992a**), or "mythology" (979). The writer may perhaps be hazy about the titles of the ruling chiefs of India. Reference to 875 will prevent his applying a Hindu title to a Mohammedan prince. He may wish to know the term for a "plain" in different parts of the world; No. 344 will tell him exactly. The subject may be such an everyday one as "food" (298), "automobiles" (272), "aviation" (267 and 269a), or various kinds of "amusements" (840); whatever it is, the search will not prove altogether unprofitable.

N.B.—To grasp the underlying principle of the classification, study the *Tabular Synopsis of Categories* (pp. xiv-xxviii).

The guide numbers always refer to the *section* numbers in the text, and *not* to pages.

PLAN OF CLASSIFICATION

TABULAR SYNOPSIS OF CATEGORIES

CLASS I. ABSTRACT RELATIONS

I. EXISTENCE

1. Existence	2. Nonexistence
3. Substantiality	4. Unsubstantiality
5. Subjectiveness	6. Objectiveness
7. State	8. Circumstance

II. RELATION

9. Relation	10. Irrelation
11. Consanguinity	
12. Correlation	
13. Identity	14. Contrariety
	15. Difference
16. Uniformity	16a. Want of Uniformity
17. Similarity	18. Dissimilarity
19. Imitation	20. Nonimitation
	20a. Variation
21. Copy	22. Prototype
23. Agreement	24. Disagreement

III. QUANTITY

25. Quantity	26. Degree
27. Equality	28. Inequality
	29. Mean
	30. Compensation
31. Greatness	32. Smallness
33. Superiority	34. Inferiority
35. Increase	36. Decrease
37. Addition	38. Deduction
39. Adjunct	40. Remainder
	40a. Decrement
41. Mixture	42. Simpleness
43. Junction	44. Disjunction
45. Vinculum	
46. Coherence	47. Incoherence
48. Combination	49. Decomposition
50. Whole	51. Part
52. Completeness	53. Incompleteness
54. Composition	55. Exclusion (from a compound)
56. Component	57. Extraneousness

IV. ORDER

58. Order	59. Disorder
60. Arrangement	61. Derangement
62. Precedence	63. Sequence
64. Precursor	65. Sequel

xiv

VII. CHANGE

VIII. CAUSATION

Class II.   SPACE

I. SPACE IN GENERAL

II. DIMENSIONS

Class III. MATTER

I. MATTER IN GENERAL

II. INORGANIC MATTER

(1) Solids

(2) Fluids

469. Qualification

470. Possibility	471. Impossibility
472. Probability	473. Improbability
474. Certainty	475. Uncertainty
476. Reasoning	477. Intuition. Sophistry
478. Demonstration	479. Confutation
480. Judgment	481. Misjudgment
480a. Discovery	
482. Overestimation	483. Underestimation
484. Belief	485. Unbelief. Doubt
486. Credulity	487. Incredulity
488. Assent	489. Dissent
490. Knowledge	491. Ignorance
492. Scholar	493. Ignoramus
494. Truth	495. Error
496. Maxim	497. Absurdity
498. Intelligence. Wisdom	499. Imbecility. Folly
500. Sage	501. Fool
502. Sanity	503. Insanity
	504. Madman
505. Memory	506. Oblivion
507. Expectation	508. Nonexpectation
	509. Disappointment
510. Foresight	
511. Prediction	
512. Omen	
513. Oracle	
514. Supposition	
515. Imagination	

II. COMMUNICATION OF IDEAS

516. Meaning	517. Unmeaningness
518. Intelligibility	519. Unintelligibility
	520. Equivocalness
521. Figure of Speech	
522. Interpretation	523. Misinterpretation
524. Interpreter	
525. Manifestation	526. Latency
527. Information	528. Concealment
529. Disclosure	530. Ambush
531. Publication	
532. News	533. Secret
534. Messenger	
535. Affirmation	536. Negation
537. Teaching	538. Misteaching
	539. Learning
540. Teacher	541. Learner
	542. School
543. Veracity	544. Falsehood

Class V. VOLITION

I. INDIVIDUAL VOLITION

600. Will	601. Necessity
602. Willingness	603. Unwillingness
604. Resolution	605. Irresolution
604a. Perseverance	
606. Obstinacy	607. Apostasy
	608. Caprice
609. Choice	609a. Absence of Choice
	610. Rejection
611. Predetermination	612. Impulse
613. Habit	614. Desuetude
615. Motive	615a. Absence of Motive
617. Plea	616. Dissuasion
618. Good	619. Evil
620. Intention	621. Chance
622. Pursuit	623. Avoidance
	624. Relinquishment
625. Business	
626. Plan	
627. Method	
628. Mid-course	629. Circuit
630. Requirement	
631. Instrumentality	
632. Means	
633. Instrument	
634. Substitute	
635. Materials	
636. Store	
637. Provision	638. Waste
639. Sufficiency	640. Insufficiency
641. Redundance	
642. Importance	643. Unimportance
644. Utility	645. Inutility
646. Expedience	647. Inexpedience
648. Goodness	649. Badness
650. Perfection	651. Imperfection
652. Cleanness	653. Uncleanness
654. Health	655. Disease
656. Healthiness	657. Unhealthiness
658. Improvement	659. Deterioration
660. Restoration	661. Relapse
662. Remedy	663. Bane
664. Safety	665. Danger
666. Refuge	667. Pitfall
668. Warning	
669. Alarm	
670. Preservation	

II. INTERSOCIAL VOLITION

CLASS VI. AFFECTIONS

I. AFFECTIONS IN GENERAL

II. PERSONAL AFFECTIONS

V. RELIGIOUS AFFECTIONS

ROGET'S POCKET THESAURUS AND WORD FINDER

CLASS I

Words Expressing ABSTRACT RELATIONS

I. EXISTENCE

1. EXISTENCE. — *N.* **existence,** being, entity, subsistence, presence, omnipresence, ubiquity.

reality, actuality, fact, matter of fact, truth, verity.

essence, inner reality, vital principle.

Science of existence: ontology.

V. **exist,** be, subsist, live, breathe; vegetate; happen, take place; occur, prevail.

consist in, lie in; be comprised in.

abide, continue, endure, last, remain.

Adj. **existent,** subsistent, extant; afloat, on foot, current, prevalent.

real, actual, positive, absolute; veritable, true; substantial, essential.

well founded, well grounded, authentic.

Adv. **actually,** in fact, in reality; indeed.

2. NONEXISTENCE. — *N.* **nonexistence,** inexistence; nonentity; nullity; nihilism; blank; absence, emptiness, void, vacuum; nothingness.

annihilation, extinction, destruction, abolition, extirpation, nirvana, obliteration.

V. **not exist,** be null and void; cease to exist; pass away, perish, be *or* become extinct; die out; disappear, vanish, fade, melt away, dissolve, be no more; die, etc., 360.

annihilate, nullify; abrogate, etc., 756; destroy, etc., 162; remove, displace, vacate; obliterate, extirpate.

Adj. **inexistent,** nonexistent; negative, blank; null, missing, absent, etc., 187.

unreal, baseless, unsubstantial, shadowy, spectral, visionary.

unborn, uncreated, unbegotten.

extinct, gone, lost, departed; defunct, etc. (*dead*), 360.

fabulous, ideal, etc. (*imaginary*), 515.

3. SUBSTANTIALITY.—*N.* substantiality; person, thing, object, article; something, a being, creature, body, substance, matter, etc., 316; groundwork, materiality.

Adj. **substantial,** essential; personal, bodily, corporeal, tangible, etc. (*material*), 316.

4. UNSUBSTANTIALITY.—*N.* unsubstantiality, nothingness, nihility; bubble, etc., 353.

nothing, naught, *nil* [L.], nullity, zero, cipher; blank, void, hollowness.

thing of naught, man of straw, lay figure; nonentity.

phantom, apparition, specter, shadow, dream, vision, will-o'-the-wisp, *ignis fatuus* [L.].

V. **vanish,** evaporate, fade, sink, fly, dissolve, melt away; die away, die out; disappear, etc., 449.

Adj. **unsubstantial;** baseless, groundless; ungrounded; without foundation.

visionary, imaginary, immaterial, spectral, etc., 980*a*; dreamy; shadowy; ethereal, airy, gaseous, imponderable, tenuous, vague, vaporous, dreamlike, illusory, unreal.

vacant, vacuous; empty, void, blank, hollow.

5. SUBJECTIVENESS.—*N.* subjectiveness, intrinsicality, inherence, immanence, indwelling; ego; essence, quintessence, elixir; gist, pith, core, kernel, marrow, backbone, heart, soul, life, substance.

principle, nature, constitution.

temper, temperament; spirit, humor, quality, disposition.

aspect, mood, feature, peculiarity, idiosyncrasy.

Adj. **intrinsic,** subjective; fundamental, implanted, inherent, essential, natural; innate, inborn, inbred, ingrained, indwelling, immanent, inwrought; radical, incarnate, hereditary, inherited, congenital, indigenous, native; in the grain, bred in the bone, instinctive; characteristic, ineradicable, fixed.

Adv. **practically,** virtually, substantially, in effect.

6. OBJECTIVENESS.—*N.* objectiveness, extraneousness, extrinsicality.

Adj. **extrinsic,** objective; extraneous, external, incidental, accidental, nonessential, unessential, accessory; contingent, fortuitous, casual.

implanted, ingrafted; inculcated, infused.

7. STATE.—*N.* state, condition, category; estate, lot, mood, temper.

dilemma, pass, predicament, quandary, corner, fix [*colloq.*], plight.

frame, fabric, stamp, mold; constitution.

form, shape; tone, tenor, trim, guise, fashion, mode, style, character.

8. CIRCUMSTANCE.—*N.* circumstance, situation, phase, position; footing, standing, status.

occasion, juncture, contingency.

predicament, emergency; exigency, crisis, pinch, pass, plight.

Adj. circumstantial, conditional, provisional; contingent, incidental; adventitious.

Adv. thus, in such wise; in *or* under the circumstances (*or* conditions).

accordingly, that being the case; since, seeing that.

conditionally, provided, if, in case; if so, unless, in the event of; provisionally.

II. RELATION

9. RELATION.—*N.* relation, bearing, relativity, reference, connection, concern; analogy; similarity; homogeneity, affinity, alliance, nearness, association; consanguinity, etc., 11; relationship, relevancy.

ratio, proportion; comparison.

link, tie, bond.

V. relate to, refer to; bear upon, regard, concern, touch, affect, pertain to, belong to; correlate.

associate, connect; link, bind.

Adj. relative, relating to, referable to; belonging to.

related, connected, associated, affiliated; allied, collateral, cognate, affinitive.

relevant, applicable, in the same category.

Adv. as regards, concerning, with relation to, with regard to; by the way, in the matter of.

10. [Want or absence of relation] IRRELATION.—*N.* irrelation, dissociation; inapplicability; disconnection, disjunction; inconsequence, disagreement, heterogeneity; irrelevancy.

V. have no relation to, have no bearing upon, have nothing to do with.

Adj. unrelated, irrespective, unallied, disconnected, unconnected, heterogeneous; isolated.

extraneous, strange, alien, foreign, outlandish, exotic.

irrelevant, inapplicable, not pertinent, unessential, inapposite, beside the mark.

remote, farfetched, out-of-the-way, forced, detached, apart.
incidental, parenthetical, episodic.

Adv. parenthetically, by the way, by the by; incidentally, without regard to.

11. [Relations of kindred] CONSANGUINITY.—*N.* consanguinity, relationship, kindred, blood; parentage, paternity; lineage, connection, alliance; people [as, *my people*], family, ties of blood, blood relation.

kinsman, kinsfolk; kith and kin; relative, relation; connection; next of kin; near relation, distant relation.

family, fraternity; brotherhood, sisterhood.

race, stock, generation; clan, tribe; strain, breed.

V. be related to, claim kinship with.

Adj. related, akin, consanguineous, allied, affiliated; kindred.

12. [Double or reciprocal relation] CORRELATION.—*N.* correlation, interdependence, reciprocity, mutuality, correspondence, interchange, exchange, barter.

alternation, seesaw, to-and-fro.

V. reciprocate, alternate, interact; interchange, exchange; correlate.

Adj. reciprocal, mutual, correlative; correspondent, corresponding; alternate; interchangeable; equivalent, complementary.

13. IDENTITY.—*N.* identity, sameness, unity, convertibility; equality, etc., 27; homogeneity; self, oneself.

monotony, repetition, etc., 104.

facsimile, etc. (*copy*), 21; similarity, etc., 17; exactness, fidelity; same, selfsame, counterpart.

V. coincide, coalesce.

treat as identical (*or* the same), render identical; identify.

Adj. identical, self, selfsame, ditto.

coincident, coinciding, coalescent, indistinguishable; one; equivalent, convertible, equal.

14. CONTRARIETY.—*N.* contrariety, contrast, foil, antithesis, counterpart, complement; oppositeness; antagonism, opposition, clashing, repugnance; antipathy.

inversion, subversion, reversal, the opposite, the reverse, the inverse, the converse, antipodes.

V. be contrary, contrast with, oppose, differ from.

invert, reverse, turn topsy-turvy, turn upside down, transpose.
contradict, contravene; antagonize, etc., 708.

Adj. contrary, opposite, counter, adverse, averse, converse, reverse; opposed, antithetical, contrasted, antipodean, diametrically opposite; antagonistic, conflicting, inconsistent, contradictory; hostile, inimical.

15. DIFFERENCE.—*N.* difference, dissimilarity, variance, variation, variety; diversity, divergence, heterogeneity, contrast, antithesis; disagreement, disparity, inequality, distinction, contradiction, contrariety.

nice (*or* fine, subtle) distinction, discrimination; modification.

V. differ, vary; mismatch, contrast; diverge from, depart from, deviate from; modify, change, alter.

discriminate, distinguish, etc., 465.

Adj. different, diverse, heterogeneous; varied, variant, divergent, incongruous, modified; diversified, various.

other, another, not the same; unequal, etc., 28; unmatched, widely apart.

distinctive, characteristic, discriminative, distinguishing; diagnostic.

16. UNIFORMITY.—*N.* uniformity; homogeneity, stability, continuity, permanence, consistency, accordance, conformity; agreement, etc., 23; consonance.

regularity, constancy, evenness, sameness, unity, even tenor, routine.

V. accord with, etc., 23; conform to; assimilate; level, smooth.

Adj. uniform, homogeneous, of a piece, consistent; even, equable, constant, level; invariable, regular, unvaried, undiversified, unvarying, singsong, dreary, monotonous.

Adv. always, ever, evermore, perpetually, forever, everlastingly, invariably.

16a. WANT OF UNIFORMITY.—*N.* diversity, irregularity, unevenness; uncomformity, dissimilarity, dissimilitude, divergence, heterogeneity.

Adj. diversified, varied, irregular, checkered, uneven; multifarious, of various kinds.

17. SIMILARITY.—*N.* similarity, resemblance, likeness, semblance, affinity, approximation, parallelism; agreement, etc., 23; analogy, correspondence; brotherhood, family likeness.

repetition, etc., 104; sameness, etc. (*identity*), 13; uniformity, etc., 16.

the like; match, fellow, companion, pair, mate, twin, double, counterpart, brother, sister; one's second self, *alter ego* [L.]; chip of the old block, birds of a feather.

simile, parallel, type, image, etc. (*representation*), 554.

V. resemble, look like, favor [*colloq.*], follow, echo, reproduce, bear resemblance; savor of, smack of; approximate; parallel, match, rhyme with; take after; imitate, etc., 19.

Adj. similar, resembling, like, alike; twin.

analogous, parallel, of a piece; such as.

akin to, etc. (*consanguineous*), 11; correlative, corresponding, cognate, allied to.

approximate, near, close, something like, near [as, *near* silk, *colloq.*], mock, pseudo, simulating, representing.

exact, etc. (*true*), 494; lifelike, faithful, true to life; the very image of, cast in the same mold.

Adv. as if, so to speak; as it were, as if it were; *quasi* [L.], just as.

18. DISSIMILARITY.—*N.* dissimilarity, dissimilitude; unlikeness, diversity, disparity, divergence, variation; difference, etc., 15; novelty, originality.

V. vary, etc. (*differ*), 15; differ from; diversify.

Adj. dissimilar, unlike, disparate; divergent, nonidentical, unique, new, novel, unprecedented, original; diversified, etc., 16a.

Adv. otherwise, alias.

19. IMITATION.—*N.* imitation, copying; repetition, duplication; quotation; reproduction.

mockery, aping, mimicry.

simulation, impersonation; parrotism, parrotry; representation, etc., 554; semblance, pretense; copy, etc., 21.

paraphrase; parody, etc., 21.

plagiarism; forgery, etc., 544.

imitator, echo, cuckoo, parrot, ape, monkey, mimic; copyist.

V. imitate, copy, mirror, reflect, reproduce, repeat; do like, echo, re-echo, catch; match, parallel; forge, counterfeit.

mimic, ape, simulate, impersonate, act, etc. (*drama*), 599; represent, etc., 554; parody, travesty, caricature, burlesque, take off, mock; borrow.

follow in the steps (*or* wake) of, take pattern by, follow suit [*colloq.*], follow the example of, walk in the shoes of, take after, model after; emulate.

Adj. imitative, modeled after; molded on, borrowed, counterfeit, imitation, false, pseudo, near [as, *near* silk, *colloq.*]; mock, mimic.

Adv. literally, verbatim, word for word, exactly, precisely.

20. NONIMITATION.—*N.* nonimitation, originality, creativeness.

Adj. unimitated, uncopied; unmatched, unparalleled; inimitable, etc., 33; unique, original, primordial, creative; exceptional, rare, uncommon, unexampled, out-of-the-way, unwonted.

20a. VARIATION.—*N.* variation, alteration, change, imitation; modification; discrepancy.

divergency, deviation, deflection; aberration; innovation.

V. vary, etc. (*change*), 140; deviate, etc., 279; diverge; alternate.

Adj. **varied,** modified; diversified, etc., 16*a*; dissimilar, etc., 18.

21. [Result of imitation] COPY.—*N.* copy, facsimile, counterpart, effigy, form, likeness, similitude, semblance, cast, tracing; imitation, etc., 19; model, representation, study; portrait, etc., 554; duplicate, transcript, transcription; reflection, shadow, echo; reprint, replica, transfer, reproduction, repetition.

servile copy, counterfeit, forgery.

parody, caricature, burlesque, travesty, paraphrase; cartoon.

Adj. **faithful,** lifelike, similar, close, exact.

22. [Thing copied] PROTOTYPE.—*N.* prototype, original, model, pattern, precedent, standard; type; archetype, exemplar, example.

copy, text, design; keynote.

die, mold; matrix, last, mint, seal, punch, stamp, intaglio, negative.

V. be an example, set an example.

23. AGREEMENT.—*N.* agreement, accord, accordance, unison, harmony, concord, union, unity, unanimity; understanding, *entente cordiale* [F.], concert [as, the *concert* of Europe].

conformity, uniformity, consistency; correspondence, parallelism, apposition.

fitness, aptness, relevancy; pertinence, aptitude, propriety, applicability, admissibility, compatibility.

adaptation, adjustment, accommodation; assimilation.

consent, etc. (*assent*), 488; concurrence, consensus; co-operation.

V. **agree,** accord, harmonize; correspond, tally, consent, etc. (*assent*), 488; suit, fit, befit; square with, dovetail, match, resemble, parallel.

adapt, accommodate, graduate; adjust, etc. (*render equal*), 27; regulate, reconcile.

Adj. **agreeing,** accordant, correspondent, congenial; coherent; harmonious, reconcilable, conformable; consistent, compatible; in accordance with, in harmony with, in keeping with.

apt, apposite, pertinent, pat; to the point; happy, felicitous, germane, applicable, relevant, admissible.

fit, adapted, appropriate, suitable; meet, etc. (*expedient*), 646.

24. DISAGREEMENT.—*N.* disagreement, discord, dissonance, disunion, discrepancy, unconformity, incongruity, dissension, conflict, opposition, antagonism, difference, misunderstanding.

disparity, disproportion; inequality, variance, divergence.

unfitness, inaptitude, impropriety, inapplicability, irrelevancy.

V. **disagree,** clash, conflict, dispute, quarrel, jar, interfere.

Adj. **disagreeing,** discordant, inharmonious; hostile, antagonistic, repugnant, clashing, jarring, factious, dissentient, incompatible, irreconcilable, inconsistent with; incongruous; repugnant to.

inapt, inept, inappropriate, improper, unsuited, unsuitable, inapplicable; unfit, unbefitting, unbecoming; ill-timed, unseasonable, ill-adapted, infelicitous, irrelevant.

uncongenial, unsympathetic, ill-assorted, mismatched.

Adv. in defiance of, in contempt of, in spite of.

III. QUANTITY

25. [Absolute quantity] QUANTITY.—*N.* quantity, magnitude; size, bulk, volume, mass, amount, measure, measurement, substance, strength.

[Science of quantity] mathematics.

[Definite quantity] armful, handful, mouthful, spoonful, stock, batch, lot, dose; quota, pittance, driblet.

Adj. quantitative, some, any, more or less.

26. [Relative quantity] DEGREE.—*N.* degree, grade, step, extent, measure, amount, ratio, standard, height, pitch; reach, mark, stage, rate, range, scope, caliber; gradation, shade; tenor, compass; sphere, station, rank, standing; interval, space [*music*]; intensity, strength.

V. graduate, calibrate, measure.

Adj. comparative, gradual, shading off.

Adv. by degrees, gradually, step by step, little by little, inch by inch, drop by drop; to some extent.

27. [Sameness of quantity or degree] EQUALITY.—*N.* equality, parity, symmetry, balance, poise; evenness, monotony, level; equivalence, equipoise, equilibrium; par, quits; distinction without a difference, identity, similarity.

tie, dead heat; drawn game, drawn battle; neck-and-neck race.

match, peer, compeer, equal, mate, fellow, brother; equivalent.

V. equal, match, keep pace with, run abreast; come up to; balance.

equalize, level, dress [*mil.*], balance, handicap, trim, adjust, poise; strike a balance; restore equilibrium.

Adj. equal, even, level, monotonous, symmetrical, co-ordinate; on a par with, on a level with, up to the mark.

equivalent, tantamount; quits; synonymous; convertible; all one, all the same; drawn [as, *a game*].

Adv. equally, to all intents and purposes.

28. [Difference of quantity or degree] INEQUALITY.—*N.* inequality, disparity, odds; difference, etc., 15; unevenness, shortcoming; superiority, etc., 33; inferiority, deficiency, inadequacy.

V. **be unequal,** have the advantage, turn the scale; overmatch, etc., 33; fall short of.

Adj. **unequal,** uneven, partial, inadequate, deficient; overbalanced, unbalanced, top-heavy, lopsided.

unequaled, unparalleled, unrivaled, unique, matchless, inimitable, peerless.

29. MEAN.—*N.* **mean,** medium, average, balance, rule, run, golden mean, middle; compromise, neutrality.

V. **average,** split the difference, strike a balance, pair off.

Adj. **mean,** intermediate; middle, etc., 68; average, normal, standard; neutral.

mediocre, middle class, bourgeois, commonplace.

Adv. **on an average,** in the long run; in round numbers.

30. COMPENSATION.—*N.* **compensation,** equation; indemnification; compromise, measure for measure, retaliation, equalization.

setoff, offset; makeweight, counterpoise, ballast; indemnity, equivalent, *quid pro quo*[L.]; amends, counterbalance, counterclaim.

pay, payment, reward, etc., 973.

V. **compensate,** indemnify; counterpoise, balance, counterbalance, offset, set off; square, make up for, equalize, etc., 27; recoup, redeem; pay, reward, etc., 973.

Adj. **compensating,** compensatory, equivalent, equal.

Adv. **notwithstanding,** but, however, yet, still, nevertheless, although, though; howbeit, albeit; at all events, in spite of, despite, on the other hand, at the same time.

31. GREATNESS.—*N.* **greatness,** vastness, magnitude; size, etc., 192; multitude; immensity, enormity, might, strength, intensity, fullness.

great quantity, quantity, deal [*colloq.*], volume, bulk, mass, heap; stock, store, load, shipload; abundance, sufficiency.

fame, distinction, grandeur, dignity; importance, etc., 642.

V. **be great,** soar, tower, loom, rise above, transcend; bulk, bulk large.

enlarge, etc. (*increase*), 35; wax, magnify, grow, expand, swell, dilate.

Adj. **great,** large, considerable, big, bulky, huge, etc., 192; titanic; voluminous, ample, abundant; many, etc., 102; full, intense; signal.

goodly, noble, precious, mighty; extraordinary; important, etc., 642; supreme, etc., 33; complete, etc., 52; arrant, downright; uttermost; profound, intense, consummate; rank, unmitigated, glaring, flagrant.

world-wide, widespread, far-famed, extensive.

august, grand, dignified, sublime, majestic.

vast, immense, enormous, extreme; inordinate, excessive, extravagant, monstrous, crass, gross; towering, stupendous, prodigious.

unlimited, etc. (*infinite*), 105; unutterable, indescribable, ineffable, unspeakable, inexpressible, fabulous.

absolute, positive, stark, decided, unequivocal, essential, perfect.

remarkable, notable, noticeable, noteworthy, renowned.

Adv. in a great or high degree: greatly, much, indeed, very, very much, most; pretty, enough, in a great measure, passing, richly; on a large scale; by wholesale; mightily, powerfully; extremely, exceedingly, intensely, indefinitely, immeasurably, incalculably, infinitely.

in a positive degree: truly, etc. (*truth*), 494; decidedly, unequivocally, absolutely, essentially, fundamentally, radically, downright, in all conscience.

in a complete degree: entirely, completely, wholly; abundantly, amply, fully, widely.

in a supreme degree: pre-eminently, superlatively, supremely, incomparably.

in a too great degree: immoderately, monstrously, preposterously, exorbitantly, excessively, enormously, out of all proportion.

in a marked degree: particularly, remarkably, singularly, curiously, uncommonly, unusually, peculiarly, notably, signally, strikingly, pointedly, chiefly; famously, egregiously, prominently, glaringly, emphatically, incredibly.

in a violent degree: furiously, violently, severely, desperately, tremendously, extravagantly.

in a painful degree: painfully, sadly, sorely, bitterly, piteously, grievously, miserably, cruelly, woefully, lamentably, shockingly, frightfully, dreadfully, fearfully, terribly, horribly, distressingly, balefully.

32. SMALLNESS.—*N.* smallness, littleness, paucity; fewness, sparseness, scarcity, insignificance, unimportance.

small quantity, modicum, minimum; atom, particle, trifle, electron, molecule, corpuscle, point, speck, dot, mote, jot, iota; minutiæ, details; tittle, spark; grain, scruple, minim; drop, sprinkling, dab, dash, tinge, dole, mite, bit, morsel, crumb, scrap, shred, tag, splinter, rag; snip, sliver, paring, shaving, hair; thimbleful, handful, capful, mouthful; fragment, fraction.

V. be small, lie in a nutshell.

diminish, etc. (*decrease*), 36; contract, shrink, dwindle, wane.

Adj. small, little, stunted; diminutive, etc. (*small in size*), 193; minute, miniature, inconsiderable, paltry, etc. (*unimportant*), 643; scanty, scant, limited, meager, sparing; few, etc., 103; moderate, modest.

inappreciable, infinitesimal, atomic, microscopic, molecular.

mere, simple, sheer, stark, bare.

Adv. **in a small degree:** to a small extent, on a small scale; a little, slightly, imperceptibly; miserably, wretchedly; insufficiently, imperfectly, faintly, feebly, passably.

in a certain or limited degree: partially, in part, in a certain degree, to a certain degree *or* extent; comparatively, rather, in some degree *or* measure; somewhat; simply, only, purely, merely; at least, at most, ever so little, thus far, after a fashion.

almost, nearly, well-nigh, not quite, all but, near upon, close upon, near the mark; within an ace (*or* inch) of, on the brink of; scarcely, hardly, barely, only just, no more than.

in an uncertain degree: about, thereabouts, somewhere about, nearly.

in no degree: noway, nowise, not at all, not in the least, not a bit, not a jot, in no wise, in no respect, by no means, on no account.

33. SUPERIORITY.—*N.* superiority, majority, plurality; advantage; preponderance, prevalence.

nobility, etc. (*rank*), 875; superman, overman.

supremacy, supremeness, primacy, pre-eminence, lead; maximum, record; crest, climax, culmination, summit, peak, transcendence; lion's share, excess, surplus, overweight, redundance.

V. **exceed,** excel, transcend, outdo, outbalance, overbalance, outweigh, outrank, outrival, out-Herod Herod; pass, surpass, overtop, overmatch; cap, culminate, beat, cut out [*colloq.*]; beat hollow [*colloq.*], outstrip, eclipse, throw into the shade; predominate, prevail; precede, take precedence, come first, bear the palm, break the record.

Adj. **superior,** greater, major, higher, exceeding; distinguished, ultra.

supreme, greatest, maximum, utmost, paramount, pre-eminent, foremost, crowning, excellent, peerless, matchless; unrivaled, unparalleled, unequaled, unapproached, unsurpassed; superlative, incomparable, transcendent.

Adv. **beyond,** more, over; over and above; at its height.

in a superior or supreme degree: eminently, pre-eminently, surpassing, superlatively, supremely, principally, especially, particularly, peculiarly.

34. INFERIORITY.—*N.* inferiority, shortcoming, deficiency; minimum; imperfection; meanness, poorness, baseness, shabbiness.

Personal inferiority: the people, etc., 876; subordination.

V. **be inferior,** fall short of, come short of, not come up to; become smaller, decrease, yield the palm, play second fiddle.

Adj. inferior, smaller; less, lesser, deficient, reduced, lower, subordinate, secondary, junior, minor, humble; second rate; unimportant, etc., 643.

Adv. less, short of, under.

35. INCREASE.—*N.* increase, augmentation, addition, enlargement, extension, expansion, growth, increment, accretion, development, accumulation, inflation, enhancement, aggravation, exaggeration.

gain, produce, product, profit, advantage, booty, plunder.

V. increase, augment, add to, enlarge, etc., 31; advance, rise, mount, ascend.

aggrandize, raise, exalt; deepen, heighten, lengthen, thicken; inflate, intensify, enhance, magnify, redouble, double; aggravate, exaggerate.

Adj. increasing, growing, crescent, multiplying, intensifying, intensive.

Adv. crescendo, increasingly.

36. DECREASE.—*N.* decrease, diminution, lessening, subtraction, reduction, abatement, declension; shrinkage, contraction, curtailment, abridgment.

subsidence, wane, ebb, decline; ebb tide, neap tide, ebbing.

V. decrease, diminish, lessen; abridge, shorten, shrink, contract; dwindle, fall away, waste, wear; wane, ebb, decline, subside, languish, decay, crumble.

discount, belittle, minimize, depreciate, extenuate, lower, weaken, attenuate; dwarf, reduce, shorten, subtract; mitigate, ease, moderate.

Adv. decrescendo, decreasingly.

37. ADDITION.—*N.* addition, annexation, accession, re-enforcement; increase, etc., 35; increment.

affix, codicil, tag, appendage, postscript, adjunct, supplement; accompaniment, insertion.

V. add, annex, affix, subjoin, tack to, append, tag, attach; interpose, introduce, insert.

compute, total, cast (*or* sum, count) up.

re-enforce, strengthen, augment.

Adj. additional, supplemental, supplementary; extra, spare, further, fresh, more, other, auxiliary, contributory, accessory.

Adv. in addition, more; and, also, likewise, too, furthermore, further; besides, to boot; over and above, moreover; as well as, together with, along with, in conjunction with.

38. DEDUCTION.—*N.* deduction, subtraction, retrenchment; abstraction, mutilation, amputation, curtailment, abbreviation.

rebate, etc. (*decrement*), 40*a*; minuend, subtrahend; decrease, etc., 36.

V. deduct, subtract, retrench; withdraw; take from, take away; detract, reduce, eliminate, diminish, curtail, shorten; deprive of, etc. (*take*), 789; weaken.

mutilate, amputate, cut off, cut away, excise.

pare, thin, prune, scrape, file.

Adv. less; short of; minus, without, except, excepting, with the exception of, save, exclusive of.

39. [Thing added] ADJUNCT.—*N.* adjunct, addition, affix, suffix, appendage, annex, augmentation, increment, re-enforcement, accessory, accompaniment, etc., 88; addendum (*pl.* addenda); complement, supplement, sequel.

rider, offshoot, episode, side issue, corollary, codicil, etc. (*addition*), 37.

V. add, annex, etc., 37.

Adj. additional, etc., 37.

40. [Thing remaining] REMAINDER.—*N.* remainder, residue, remains, remnant, rest, relic; leavings, odds and ends, residuum, dregs, refuse, stubble, ruins, wreck, skeleton, fossil, stump, rump.

surplus, excess; balance [*commercial slang*], result; superfluity, redundance; survival.

V. remain, survive, be left; exceed.

Adj. remaining, left, residual, residuary; over, odd; surviving; net; superfluous, etc. (*redundant*), 641.

40a. [Thing deducted] DECREMENT.—*N.* decrement, discount, rebate, defect, loss, deduction; waste.

41. MIXTURE.—*N.* mixture, admixture, junction, etc., 43; amalgamation, combination, etc., 48; infusion, transfusion; infiltration; interlarding, interpolation, etc., 228; adulteration.

Thing mixed: tinge, tincture, touch, dash, smack, spice, seasoning, infusion.

Compounds: alloy, amalgam; brass, pewter; miscellany, medley, mess, hash, hodgepodge, patchwork, jumble; potpourri, mosaic.

half-blood, half-breed, half-caste, crossbreed; mulatto, quadroon, octoroon, Eurasian; mule, cross, hybrid, mongrel.

V. mix, join, etc., 43; combine, etc., 48; mingle, commingle, intermingle, interlard, interpolate, intertwine, interweave; associate with.

imbue, infuse, diffuse, suffuse, transfuse, instill, infiltrate, dash, tinge, tincture, season, blend, cross; alloy, amalgamate, compound, adulterate.

Adj. mixed, composite, half-and-half, hybrid, mongrel, heterogeneous; motley, variegated, miscellaneous, promiscuous, indiscriminate.

Adv. among, amid, with; in the midst of.

42. [Freedom from mixture] SIMPLENESS.—*N.* simpleness, purity, homogeneity.

elimination, sifting, purification, etc. (*cleanness*), 652.

V. render simple, simplify.

sift, winnow, bolt, eliminate; exclude, get rid of; clear, purify, etc. (*clean*), 652.

Adj. simple, uniform, homogeneous, single, pure, clear; elemental, elementary.

43. JUNCTION.—*N.* junction, joining, union; connection, conjunction, annexation, attachment; marriage, wedlock; confluence, communication, meeting, reunion; assemblage, etc., 72; coherence, etc., 46; combination, etc., 48.

joint, joining, juncture, pivot, hinge, articulation; seam, gore, gusset, link, bond.

contingency, emergency, predicament, crisis, concurrence.

V. join, unite, connect; associate; put together, piece together, embody.

attach, fix, fasten, bind, secure, tighten, clinch, tie, strap, sew, lace, stitch, knit, button, buckle, hitch, lash, splice, gird, tether, moor, picket, chain; fetter, hook, link, yoke, bracket; marry; bridge over, span.

pin, nail, screw, bolt, hasp, clasp, clamp, rivet; solder, cement, etc., 46.

entwine, interlace, intertwine, interweave; entangle.

Adj. joined, joint; corporate, compact.

firm, fast, close, tight, taut, secure, inseparable, indissoluble.

Adv. jointly, in conjunction with, etc. (*in addition to*), 37; fast, firmly.

44. DISJUNCTION.—*N.* disjunction, disconnection, disunion, disengagement, dissociation, discontinuity, etc., 70; isolation, insularity, insulation, separateness; dispersion.

separation, parting; detachment, segregation; divorce; cæsura, division, subdivision, break, fracture, rupture; dismemberment, dissection, disintegration, severance, disruption, cleavage.

fissure, breach, rent, rift, crack, slit, cut, incision.

V. disjoin, disconnect, disengage, disunite, dissociate, divorce, part, detach, unfasten, separate, disentangle, cut off, segregate; set apart, keep apart; insulate, isolate; cut adrift, loose, set free, liberate.

divide, sunder, subdivide, sever, dissever, cut, chop, saw, snip, nip, cleave, rive, rend, slit, rip, split, splinter, chip, crack, snap, break, tear, burst; wrench, rupture, hack, hew, slash, slice, carve, quarter, dissect, anatomize; partition, parcel.

disintegrate, dismember, disband; disperse, etc., 73; dislocate, break up.

part, part company; separate, leave; alienate, estrange.

Adj. disjoined, discontinuous, disjunctive; isolated, insular; separate, apart, asunder, loose, free, adrift.

Adv. separately, one by one, severally, apart, asunder.

45. [Connecting medium] VINCULUM.—*N.* vinculum, link; connective, connection; junction, etc., 43; hyphen; bracket; bridge, steppingstone; bond, cord; rope, line, cable, hawser, painter; chain; string, etc. (*filament*), 205.

fastening, tie; ligament, ligature; strap; tackle, rigging; yoke, band, headband, fillet, snood, brace, thong, girdle, noose, lariat, lasso, knot, girth, cinch.

cement, glue, gum, paste, size, solder, mortar, plaster, putty.

shackle, rein, etc. (*means of restraint*), 752.

V. bridge over, span; connect, etc., 43.

46. COHERENCE.—*N.* coherence, cohesion, cohesiveness, adherence, adhesion, adhesiveness; conglomeration, aggregation, consolidation, soldering, connection; relativity.

tenacity, toughness; stickiness; inseparability.

conglomerate, concrete, etc., 321.

V. cohere, adhere, coagulate, stick, cling, cleave, hold, close with, clasp, hug.

glue, agglutinate, cement, paste, gum; solder, weld; cake, consolidate, solidify, agglomerate.

Adj. adhesive, cohesive, adhering, tenacious, tough; sticky, etc., 352.

47. INCOHERENCE.—*N.* incoherence, nonadhesion; looseness, laxity, relaxation; loosening, disjunction, etc., 44.

V. loosen, make loose, slacken, relax; unglue, etc., 46; detach, etc., 44.

Adj. nonadhesive, noncohesive, incoherent, detached, loose, baggy, slack, lax, relaxed, segregated, unconsolidated; uncombined, etc., 48.

48. COMBINATION.—*N.* combination, mixture, etc., 41; junction, etc., 43; union, unification, synthesis, incorporation, amalgamation, coalescence, fusion, brew, blend, blending; centralization.

alloy, compound, amalgam, composition, resultant.

V. **combine,** unite, incorporate, alloy, intermix, interfuse, interlard, amalgamate, embody, absorb, blend, merge, fuse, consolidate, coalesce, solidify, impregnate, centralize.

league, federate, confederate, fraternize, club, associate, amalgamate, couple, pair, ally.

Adj. **combined,** conjoint; ingrained, imbued.

allied, amalgamated, federate, confederate, corporate, leagued.

49. DECOMPOSITION.—*N.* **decomposition,** analysis, dissection, dissolution, breakup; disjunction, etc., 44; disintegration.

decay, rot, putrefaction, putrescence, putridity, caries, corruption.

V. **decompose,** analyze, dissolve; resolve into its elements, dissect, disintegrate, disperse; crumble into dust.

rot, decay, consume, putrefy.

50. [Principal part] WHOLE.—*N.* **whole,** totality, integrity, entirety, completeness; integer, integral.

all, the whole, total, aggregate, sum, sum total.

bulk, mass, lump, tissue, staple, body, greater part, main part; lion's share.

V. **form a whole,** embody, amass; aggregate, assemble; amount to.

Adj. **whole,** total, gross, entire; complete, etc., 52; wholesale, sweeping; comprehensive.

indivisible, indissoluble, indissolvable.

Adv. **wholly,** altogether; as a whole, totally, completely, entirely, all, all in all, wholesale, in a body, collectively, in the aggregate, in the main, on the whole, bodily, substantially.

51. PART.—*N.* **part,** portion; item, particular; aught, any; division; sector, segment; fraction, fragment; detachment, subdivision.

section, chapter, verse; article, clause.

piece, lump, bit, cut, cutting; chip, chunk, slice, scrap, crumb, morsel, moiety, particle; installment, dividend; share.

member, limb, arm, wing, scion, branch, bough, joint, link, offshoot, ramification, twig, spray, spring; runner, tendril; leaf, leaflet; stump.

V. **part,** divide, disjoin, etc., 44; partition, etc. (*apportion*), 786.

Adj. **fractional,** fragmentary, sectional; incomplete, partial.

divided, broken, cut, cropped, shorn.

divisible, dissoluble, dissolvable.

Adv. **partly,** in part, partially; piecemeal, by installments, in detail.

52. COMPLETENESS.—*N.* **completeness,** intactness, completion, etc., 729; fill, saturation, entirety; totality, integrity; perfection, etc., 650; solidarity, unity, all, high tide, flood tide, spring tide.

V. **complete,** etc. (*accomplish*), 729; fill, charge, load, replenish; make up, eke out, supply deficiencies; fill up, fill in, satiate; saturate.

Adj. **complete,** entire, whole, intact, perfect, full, absolute, thorough; solid, undivided.

brimful, brimming, chock-full; saturated, crammed; replete, etc. (*redundant*), 641; fraught, laden.

exhaustive, radical, sweeping, thoroughgoing.

regular, unmitigated, sheer, unqualified, unconditional, free, abundant, etc. (*sufficient*), 639.

completing, supplemental, supplementary.

Adv. **completely,** altogether, outright, wholly, totally, utterly, quite; effectually, fully, in all respects, in every respect; out and out; throughout, from first to last, from head to foot, from top to toe, every whit, every inch.

53. INCOMPLETENESS.—*N.* **incompleteness,** deficiency, shortcoming, want, lack, insufficiency, imperfection, etc., 651; immaturity.

Part wanting: defect, deficit, omission; shortage; break, etc. (*discontinuity*), 70; missing link.

V. **be incomplete,** fall short of, lack, etc. (*be insufficient*), 640.

Adj. **incomplete,** uncompleted, imperfect, unfinished; defective, deficient, wanting, failing, in arrear, short, short of; perfunctory, sketchy, crude, immature.

mutilated, garbled, hashed, mangled, butchered, docked, truncated.

in progress, in hand; going on, proceeding.

54. COMPOSITION.—*N.* **composition,** constitution; make-up; combination, etc., 48; embodiment; formation.

authorship, compilation, composition, production, invention; writing.

painting, etching, design, etc. (*painting*), 556; relief, etc. (*sculpture*), 557.

typesetting, typography, etc., 591.

V. **be composed of,** consist of.

include, etc., 76; contain, hold, comprehend, admit, embrace, embody.

compose, constitute, form, make; fabricate, weave, construct; compile, scribble, draw, write.

55. EXCLUSION.—*N.* **exclusion,** omission, exception, rejection, repudiation; exile, seclusion, lockout, ostracism, prohibition.

separation, segregation, elimination, expulsion.

V. **exclude,** bar; leave out, shut out; reject, repudiate, black-ball, ostracize; lay aside, put aside, set apart; relegate, segregate; strike off, strike out; neglect, banish, etc. (*seclude*), 893; separate, etc. (*disjoin*), 44.

pass over, omit; eliminate, weed out.

Adj. **exclusive,** inadmissible, preclusive, preventive, prohibitive.

Adv. **except,** exclusive of, save.

56. COMPONENT.—*N.* **component,** integral part, element, constituent, ingredient, contents; feature; member, etc. (*part*), 51; personnel.

V. **enter into,** be *or* form part of, etc., 51; merge in, share in, participate; belong to, appertain to; combine, unite.

form, make, constitute, compose, fabricate, etc., 54.

Adj. **inherent,** intrinsic, essential.

inclusive, all-embracing, comprehensive.

57. EXTRANEOUSNESS.—*N.* **extraneousness,** extrinsicality; exclusion; alienism.

foreign body (substance *or* element).

alien, stranger, intruder, interloper, foreigner, newcomer; immigrant, emigrant; outsider, barbarian, tenderfoot [*slang*].

Adj. **extraneous,** foreign, alien, exterior, external; outlandish, barbaric, barbarian.

excluded, inadmissible; exceptional.

Adv. **abroad,** in foreign parts, in foreign lands; oversea, overseas.

IV. ORDER

58. ORDER.—*N.* **order,** regularity, uniformity, symmetry, harmony; course, routine; method, disposition, arrangement, array, system, economy, discipline, orderliness, subordination.

gradation, progression; series, etc. (*continuity*), 69.

rank, place, etc. (*term*), 71.

V. **adjust,** regulate, systematize, standardize; time.

Adj. **orderly,** regular; in order, in trim, neat, tidy, methodical, uniform, symmetrical, shipshape, businesslike, systematic, normal, habitual.

Adv. **in order,** methodically, in turn, in its turn; step by step; systematically, by clockwork.

59. DISORDER.—*N.* **disorder,** derangement; irregularity; untidiness; anomaly, etc. (*unconformity*), 83; anarchy, anarchism; disunion; discord.

confusion, disarray, jumble, botch, litter, farrago, mess, muddle, hodgepodge, imbroglio, chaos, clutter, medley.

complexity, complication, entanglement, intricacy; perplexity; network, maze, labyrinth; wilderness, jungle; tangled skein.

turmoil, ferment, etc. (*agitation*), 315; trouble, disturbance, convulsion, tumult, uproar, riot, rumpus [*colloq.*], fracas, pandemonium, Babel, saturnalia.

V. disorder, botch, disturb, derange, etc., 61; entangle, ravel, ruffle, rumple.

Adj. disorderly, out of order, out of place, irregular, desultory; anomalous, etc. (*unconformable*), 83; disorganized; straggling; unmethodical, unsystematic; untidy, slovenly, messy [*colloq.*], indiscriminate, chaotic, confused; deranged, etc., 61; topsy-turvy, disjointed, out of joint.

complex, intricate, complicated, perplexed, involved, entangled, knotted, tangled, inextricable.

troublous, tumultuous, turbulent; riotous, etc. (*violent*), 173.

60. [Reduction to Order] ARRANGEMENT.—*N.* arrangement, plan, etc., 626; preparation, provision; disposal, disposition; distribution, sorting, assortment, allotment, apportionment, graduation, organization, groupings; analysis, classification, division, systematization, codification.

Result of arrangement: orderliness, form, array, digest; synopsis, etc. (*compendium*), 596; table; register, etc. (*record*), 551; organism; stipulation, settlement.

V. arrange, dispose, fix, place; form; set in order, set out; compose, space, range, graduate, marshal, array, rank, group, parcel out, allot, apportion, distribute, assign the parts; dispose of, assort, sort; tidy [*colloq.*].

classify, class, file, list; register, etc. (*record*), 551; catalogue, tabulate, index, alphabetize, grade, codify.

methodize, regulate, systematize, co-ordinate, organize; unravel, disentangle.

Adj. arranged, embattled, in battle array; cut and dried; methodical, orderly, regular, systematic, on file; tabular.

61. [Bringing into disorder] DERANGEMENT.—*N.* derangement, muss [*colloq.* U. S.], mess; disorder, etc., 59; discomposure, disturbance; disorganization, dislocation; inversion, etc., 218; insanity, etc., 503.

V. derange, disarrange, discompose, displace, misplace; mislay, disorder; disorganize; embroil, convulse, unsettle, disturb, confuse, trouble, perturb, disconcert, jumble; muddle; unhinge, dislocate, put out of joint, throw out of gear.

turn topsy-turvy, etc. (*invert*), 218; bedevil; complicate, involve, perplex, confound; tangle, entangle; tousle [*colloq.*], dishevel, ruffle; rumple, etc. (*fold*), 258; become insane, etc., 503.

litter, scatter; mix, etc., 41.

62. [Consecutive Order] **PRECEDENCE.**—*N.* **precedence,** the lead, superiority, etc., 33; importance, consequence; premise; antecedence, precursor, etc., 64; priority, preference.

prefix, affix; preamble; prelude, overture, voluntary.

V. **precede,** forerun, come before, come first; head, lead, lead the way; introduce, usher in; rank, outrank; take precedence.

prefix; premise, prelude, preface; affix.

Adj. **preceding,** precedent, antecedent; anterior; prior, etc., 116; before; former, foregoing, aforesaid, said; introductory, etc., 64.

Adv. **before;** in advance, etc. (*precession*), 280.

63. SEQUENCE.—*N.* **sequence,** train; following, succession; afterclap, afterglow, aftermath, afterpiece, aftertaste.

continuation, prolongation; order of succession.

V. **succeed,** come after, ensue, come next.

follow, tag [*colloq.*], heel, dog, shadow, hound, hunt; trace, retrace.

append, place after, subjoin.

Adj. **succeeding,** sequent; subsequent; proximate, next; consecutive, etc. (*continuity*), 69.

latter, posterior, etc., 117.

Adv. **after,** subsequently; behind, etc. (*rear*), 235.

64. PRECURSOR.—*N.* **precursor,** antecedent, precedent, predecessor; forerunner, pioneer; outrider; leader, bellwether; herald, harbinger.

prelude, preamble, preface, prologue, foreword, proem, exordium, introduction; heading, frontispiece, groundwork; preparation, etc., 673; overture, voluntary; premises.

prefigurement, etc., 511; omen, etc., 512.

Adj. **introductory,** preludial, prefatory, precursory, inaugural, preliminary.

65. SEQUEL.—*N.* **sequel,** suffix, tail, queue, train, wake, trail, rear; retinue, suite; appendix, postscript, postlude, conclusion, epilogue; peroration; codicil; continuation; appendage, tag, aftergrowth, afterpiece, afterthought, second thoughts; outgrowth.

follower, successor, pursuer, adherent, partisan, disciple, client; sycophant, parasite.

66. BEGINNING.—*N.* **beginning,** commencement, opening, outset, incipience, inception; introduction, etc. (*prelude*), 64; initial; inauguration, embarkation, rising of the curtain; curtain raiser, maiden speech; exordium; outbreak, onset, brunt; initiative, first move; start, starting point; dawn, etc. (*morning*), 125.

origin, etc. (*cause*), 153; source, rise; bud, germ, egg, embryo, rudiment; genesis, birth, nativity, cradle, infancy.

head, heading; title page; van, etc. (*front*), 234.

entrance, entry; inlet, orifice, mouth, porch, portal, portico, door; gate, gateway; postern, wicket, threshold, vestibule; border, frontier.

rudiments, elements, outlines, grammar, alphabet, ABC.

V. **begin,** commence; rise, arise; originate, initiate, open, start; dawn, set in, take its rise, enter upon; set out, etc. (*depart*), 293; embark in; make one's debut; institute; set about, set to work; make a start; break ground, cross the Rubicon; undertake, etc., 676.

usher in, lead the way, take the lead *or* initiative; inaugurate, head; lay the foundations, etc. (*prepare*), 673; found, etc. (*cause*), 153; set up, set on foot, launch, broach; open up, open the door to.

come into existence, take birth; burst forth, break out; spring up, crop up.

recommence; begin at the beginning, begin again, start afresh.

Adj. **initial,** prime, introductory, incipient; inaugural; embryonic, rudimentary; primal, primary, primeval, etc. (*old*), 124; aboriginal; natal.

first, maiden, foremost, front, head, leading.

Adv. **first,** in the first place, in the bud, in embryo, from the beginning, formerly.

67. END.—*N.* **end,** close, termination, conclusion, finish, completion, finis, finale, period, term, terminus, last, extreme, extremity; fag end, tip, nib, point, tail, tag, peroration, appendix, epilogue; consummation, denouement, fall of the curtain; goal, destination, terminal, limit, stoppage; expiration; dissolution, death, etc., 360; doomsday.

last stage, evening (*of life*); *coup de grâce* [F.], deathblow; knockout.

V. **end,** close, finish, terminate, conclude; expire, die, etc., 360; come to a close, perorate; run out, pass away.

bring to an end, put an end to, make an end of; achieve, etc. (*complete*), 729; stop, etc., 142.

Adj. **final,** terminal; conclusive; crowning, etc. (*completing*), 729; last, ultimate; hindermost; rear, etc., 235.

ended, settled, decided, over.

Adv. **finally,** in fine; at the last; once for all.

68. MIDDLE.—*N.* **middle,** midst, thick, midmost; mean, etc., 29; medium, middle term; center, core, kernel, nucleus, hub, heart, bull's-eye; mid-course, neutrality, compromise.

equidistance, bisection; equator, diaphragm, midriff.

Adj. **middle,** medial, mid, midmost; intermediate, equidistant, central, pivotal, mediterranean, equatorial.

Adv. **midway,** halfway, in the middle; amidships.

69. [Uninterrupted sequence] CONTINUITY.—continuity, continuousness, succession, round, suite, progression, series, train, chain; scale; gradation, course; perpetuity.

procession, cavalcade, parade; column; retinue, cortege, funeral, ovation.

pedigree, genealogy, lineage, history, family tree, race; ancestry, descent, family, house; line, line of ancestors; strain.

rank, file, line, row, range, tier.

V. **arrange in a series,** string together, file, list, thread, tabulate.

Adj. **continuous,** continued; consecutive, progressive, gradual, serial, successive; uninterrupted, unbroken, entire; linear; perennial, constant.

Adv. **continuously,** in a line, in succession, in turn; running, gradually, in file, in single file, in Indian file.

70. [Interrupted sequence] DISCONTINUITY.—*N.* discontinuity, disconnectedness; disconnection, etc., 44; interruption, break, fracture, flaw, fault, crack, cut; gap, etc. (*interval*), 198; intermission, alternation.

V. **alternate,** interchange, intermit.

discontinue, pause, interrupt, intervene; break, break off; interpose, etc., 228; disconnect, etc. (*disjoin*), 44; dissever.

Adj. **discontinuous,** disconnected, broken, interrupted, fitful, irregular, spasmodic, desultory; intermittent, alternate, recurrent, periodic.

Adv. **at intervals,** by snatches, by jerks, by fits and starts.

71. TERM.—*N.* term, rank, station, stage, step; degree, etc., 26; scale, grade, status, state, position, standing, footing, place, mark, period, range.

72. [Collective Order] ASSEMBLAGE.—*N.* assemblage, collection, levy, gathering, ingathering, mobilization, meet, forgathering, muster, team; concourse, conflux, congregation.

meeting, levee, reunion, drawing room, at home; social gathering, 892; assembly, congress, house, senate, legislature, etc., 696; convocation, caucus, convention.

company, platoon, faction, caravan, posse, watch, squad, corps, troop, troupe; army, regiment.

miscellany, miscellanea, compilation; symposium; library, etc. (*store*), 636.

crowd, throng; flood, rush, deluge; rabble, mob, host, etc. (*multitude*), 102; rout, press, crush, horde, body, tribe; crew, gang, knot, squad, force, band, party; bunch, drive, roundup.

clan, brotherhood, association, etc. (*party*), 712.

group, cluster, clump, set, batch, lot, pack; budget, assortment, bunch; parcel, packet, bundle, package, bale, fagot, wisp, truss, tuft, shock, clump; grove, thicket; rick, stack, sheaf, swath; volley, shower, storm, cloud.

accumulation, etc. (*store*), 636; heap, lump, pile, mass, pyramid; drift, snowball, snowdrift; amassment; conglomeration, aggregation, concentration, convergence, congestion, quantity, etc. (*greatness*), 31.

V. **be** *or* **come together,** assemble, collect, muster; meet, unite, join, rejoin; cluster, flock, swarm, surge, stream, herd, crowd, huddle, throng, associate; congregate, concentrate, resort, forgather.

bring together, assemble, muster, collect, gather; hold a meeting, convene, convoke; rake up, dredge, heap, mass, pile; pack, cram, lump together; compile, group, concentrate, unite, amass, accumulate, hoard, store.

Adj. **dense,** serried, teeming, swarming, populous.

73. DISPERSION.—*N.* **dispersion,** disjunction, etc., 44; divergence, radiation, broadcast, spread, dissemination, diffusion, dissipation, distribution; apportionment, allotment.

V. **disperse,** scatter, sow, disseminate, sow broadcast, diffuse, radiate, broadcast, shed, spread, bestrew, dispense, disband, dismember, distribute; apportion, etc., 786; dispel, cast forth, draft off; strew, cast, sprinkle; issue, deal out, retail, utter.

Adj. **scattered,** disseminated, strown, strewn, dispersed, diffuse, diffusive, sparse, broadcast, sporadic, widespread; epidemic, etc. (*general*), 78; adrift, stray; disheveled.

74. [Place of meeting] FOCUS.—*N.* **focus,** center, gathering place, rendezvous, rallying point, headquarters, resort, haunt, retreat, club; tryst, trysting place, place of meeting.

V. **focus,** bring to a point, bring to a focus; rally, meet.

75. [Distributive Order] CLASS.—*N.* **class,** division, subdivision, category, head, order, section; department, province, domain, sphere.

kind, sort, type, estate, genus, species, variety, family, race, tribe, caste, clan, breed, kin; clique, coterie, set; sect, gender, sex.

description, denomination, persuasion, connection, designation, character, stamp; selection, specification.

76. INCLUSION.—*N.* **inclusion,** admission, incorporation, comprisal, reception.

composition, embodiment, formation.

V. **include,** comprise, comprehend, contain, admit, embrace, receive, inclose, etc. (*circumscribe*), 229; incorporate, cover, embody, encircle; reckon among, number among; refer to; place under, arrange under, take into account.

Adj. inclusive, included, including; comprehensive, sweeping, all-embracing.

77. EXCLUSION [from a class].—*N.* exclusion, rejection; *see* exclusion (*from a compound*), 55.

78. GENERALITY.—*N.* generality, universality, catholicity, miscellany, miscellaneousness; common run, prevalence, rifeness.

everyone, everybody, all hands [*colloq.*], all the world and his wife [*humorous*], anybody.

V. be general, prevail.

render general, spread, broaden, universalize, generalize.

Adj. general, generic, collective; current, wide, broad, comprehensive, sweeping; encyclopedic, panoramic; widespread, etc. (*dispersed*), 73; common, prevalent, prevailing, rife, epidemic.

universal, catholic, world-wide.

every, all, unspecified, miscellaneous, indefinite.

Adv. generally, always, in general, generally speaking; for the most part.

79. SPECIALTY.—*N.* specialty, speciality, individuality, peculiarity; personality, characteristic, mannerism, idiosyncrasy, singularity, originality; trait, distinctive feature.

particulars, details, items, counts; minutiæ.

V. specify, particularize; individualize, specialize; designate, determine; denote, indicate, point out, select, differentiate; itemize, enter into detail.

Adj. special, especial, particular, individual, specific, proper, personal, original, private, respective, definite, minute, certain, peculiar, marked, appropriate, characteristic, exclusive, restricted; singular, exceptional; typical, representative.

Adv. each, apiece, one by one, severally, respectively, in detail. namely, that is to say, viz.; to wit.

80. RULE.—*N.* regularity, uniformity, constancy, clockwork precision; punctuality, etc. (*exactness*), 494; even tenor, rut; system; routine, custom; formula; canon, convention, maxim, rule, regulation; standard, model, precedent; conformity, etc., 82.

law, order of things; normality, normalcy, normal state, ordinary condition, standing order; hard and fast rule.

Adj. regular, uniform, symmetrical, constant, steady; according to rule, etc., 82; normal, habitual, customary, etc., 613; methodical, orderly, systematic.

81. MULTIFORMITY.—*N.* multiformity, variety, diversity.

Adj. multiform, multifold, multifarious, multiplex; manifold, many-sided; protean, heterogeneous, motley, mosaic.

indiscriminate, irregular, diversified, diverse; of every description.

82. CONFORMITY.—*N.* conformity, observance; conventionality, etc. (*custom*), 613; agreement, accord.

example, instance, exemplification, illustration, specimen, sample.

conventionalist, formalist, bromide [*slang*], Philistine.

V. **conform to,** adapt oneself to.

be regular, travel in a rut; obey rules; agree with, comply with, fall in with; be guided by, harmonize, conventionalize, follow the fashion; do at Rome as the Romans do; swim with the stream.

exemplify, illustrate, cite, quote.

Adj. **conformable to rule,** adaptable, consistent, agreeable, compliant; regular, etc., 80; according to rule, well regulated, orderly, uniform, symmetric.

conventional, etc. (*customary*), 613; ordinary, common, habitual, usual; strict, rigid; uncompromising.

typical, normal, formal; canonical, orthodox, exemplary, illustrative, in point.

Adv. **conformably,** by rule; in accordance with, in keeping with; according to; as usual, as a matter of course.

invariably, etc. (*uniformly*), 16.

83. UNCONFORMITY.—*N.* nonconformity, unconformity, nonobservance, unconventionality, informality; anomaly, anomalousness, exception, peculiarity; breach *or* violation of custom; eccentricity, oddity, rarity.

individuality, singularity, originality, idiosyncrasy, mannerism.

aberration, irregularity; singularity; exemption; qualification, proviso.

nonconformist, Bohemian, nondescript character, original, freak, prodigy, wonder, miracle, curiosity.

mongrel, half-caste, etc., 41.

outcast, outlaw, Ishmael, pariah.

V. **be uncomformable,** leave the beaten path; break (*or* violate) a law *or* custom; stretch a point.

Adj. **uncomformable,** exceptional, eccentric; abnormal, unnatural, anomalous, misplaced, out of order, irregular, arbitrary, lawless; informal, stray, eccentric, peculiar, exclusive, egregious.

unusual, unaccustomed, unwonted, uncommon; rare, singular, unique, curious, odd, extraordinary, strange, monstrous; wonderful, etc., 870; remarkable, noteworthy, queer, quaint, nondescript, original, unorthodox, unconventional, Bohemian, unprecedented, unparalleled, unexampled, unheard of; fantastic, newfangled, eccentric, grotesque, bizarre; unfamiliar, outlandish.

heterogeneous, amorphous, mongrel, hybrid; unsymmetric, etc., 243.

Adv. unconformably; except, unless, save.

V. NUMBER

84. NUMBER.—*N.* **number,** symbol, numeral, figure, cipher, digit, integer, round number; series.

sum, product, total, aggregate, difference.

ratio, proportion, percentage; progression; arithmetical progression.

power, root, exponent, index, logarithm.

85. NUMERATION.—*N.* **numeration,** numbering; tale, tally, enumeration, reckoning, computation, calculation, calculus; measurement, etc., 466; statistics.

arithmetic, algebra, differential calculus, calculus of differences.

muster, poll, census, roll call; account, etc. (*list*), 86.

Instruments: abacus, calculating machine, adding machine, cash register.

arithmetician, calculator, algebraist, geometrician, trigonometrician, mathematician, actuary, statistician.

V. **number,** count, enumerate; call over, run over; take an account of, call the roll, muster, poll; sum up, cast up; tell off, cipher, reckon, reckon up, estimate, compute, calculate.

check, prove, demonstrate, balance, audit, overhaul, take stock.

total, amount to, come to.

Adj. **numeral,** numerical; arithmetical, analytic, algebraic, statistical, computable, calculable, commensurable, commensurate.

86. LIST.—*N.* **list,** catalogue, card index; inventory, schedule; register, etc. (*record*), 551; account; bill, bill of costs; tally, file, index, table, contents; book, ledger; synopsis, syllabus; scroll, screed, invoice, manifest, bill of lading; prospectus, program; bill of fare, menu; score, bulletin, census, statistics, returns; directory, atlas, gazetteer; calendar, almanac.

dictionary, lexicon, glossary, vocabulary, wordbook, thesaurus.

roll; muster roll; roll of honor; roster, slate, poll, panel.

V. **list,** enroll, schedule, inventory, register, catalogue, invoice, bill, book, slate, post, docket; empanel, tally, file, index, tabulate, enter, census.

87. UNITY.—*N.* **unity,** oneness; individuality; unification, etc., 48; completeness, completion.

one, unit; individual.

V. **isolate,** insulate.

render one; unite, etc. (*join*), 43, (*combine*), 48.

Adj. **one, sole, lone, single, solitary;** individual, apart, alone; unaccompanied, unattended, singlehanded; singular, odd, unique, isolated; insular.

88. ACCOMPANIMENT.—*N.* **accompaniment,** adjunct, accessory; context; appendage, appurtenance; attribute.

company, association, partnership; companionship.

attendant, companion, associate, colleague, partner; consort, spouse; satellite, hanger-on, shadow; escort, suite, train, retinue, convoy, follower, etc., 65.

V. **accompany,** attend, convoy, chaperon; associate with, couple with.

Adj. **accompanying,** fellow, twin, joint; associated with, coupled with; accessory, attendant.

Adv. **with,** withal; together with, along with, in company with; therewith, herewith; and, etc. (*addition*), 37.

together, in a body, collectively, in conjunction.

89. DUALITY.—*N.* **duality,** dualism; duplicity; polarity.

two, deuce, couple, couplet, both, twain, brace, pair, twins, Castor and Pollux, gemini, fellows; yoke, span; distich.

V. **pair,** mate, couple, bracket, yoke.

Adj. **two,** twain, both; dual, twin; duplex, etc., 90; tête-à-tête.

90. DUPLICATION.—*N.* **duplication,** doubling, reduplication; iteration, etc. (*repetition*), 104; renewal.

duplicate, facsimile, copy, replica, counterpart, etc. (*copy*), 21.

V. **double;** redouble, reduplicate; repeat, etc., 104; renew, renovate.

Adj. **double;** doubled; twofold, two-sided, duplex; double-faced, double-headed; twin, duplicate, second; dual.

Adv. **twice,** once more; over again, etc. (*repeatedly*), 104.

91. [Division into two parts] BISECTION.—*N.* **bisection,** halving, bifurcation, forking, branching, ramification, dichotomy.

half, moiety.

V. **bisect,** halve, divide, separate, split, cut in two, cleave.

fork, bifurcate, branch off *or* out, ramify.

Adj. **bisected,** cloven, cleft; bifurcated; semi-, demi-, hemi-.

92. TRIALITY.—*N.* **triality** [*rare*], trinity,[1] triunity.

three, triad, triplet, trio; triangle, trident, tripod, trireme, triumvirate.

third power, cube.

Adj. **three;** triform, tertiary.

93. TRIPLICATION.—*N.* **triplication,** triplicity; trilogy.

V. **treble,** triple; cube.

Adj. **treble,** triple; threefold; third.

[1]*Trinity* is hardly ever used except in a theological sense; *see* Deity, 976.

Adv. three times, thrice; in the third place, thirdly; threefold, triply, trebly.

94. [Division into three parts] TRISECTION.—*N.* trisection, tripartition, third, third part.

V. trisect, divide into three parts, third.

95. QUATERNITY.—*N.* quaternity [*rare*], four, quartet, quadruplet; square, quadrilateral; quadrangle.

V. square, biquadrate, reduce to a square.

Adj. four; quadratic; quadrangular, quadrilateral.

96. QUADRUPLICATION.—*N.* quadruplication.

V. quadruplicate, multiply by four.

Adj. fourfold, quadruple; fourth.

Adv. four times, in the fourth place, fourthly.

97. [Division into four parts] QUADRISECTION.—*N.* quadrisection, quadripartition; quartering; fourth; quart, quarter; farthing; quarto.

V. quarter, divide into four parts, quadrisect.

98. FIVE, ETC.—*N.* five, quintet, pentagon, pentameter.

six, half a dozen; hexagon, hexameter, sextet.

seven, heptagon, heptameter, heptarchy.

eight, octave, octagon, octameter, octavo, octet.

nine, nonagon.

ten, decade, decagon, decasyllable, decemvir, decemvirate, decennium.

twelve, dozen; thirteen, long dozen, baker's dozen; twenty, score; fifty, half a hundred; sixty, threescore; seventy, threescore and ten; eighty, fourscore; ninety, fourscore and ten.

hundred, centenary, century; bicentenary, tercentenary.

thousand, millennium; myriad.

V. quintuplicate, sextuple; centuplicate.

Adj. five, fifth, quintuple; pentangular, pentagonal. sixth, sextuple, hexagonal, hexangular. seventh, septuple, heptagonal, heptangular. eight, octuple, octagonal, octangular. tenth, tenfold, decimal, decagonal, decasyllabic. eleventh, undecennial, undecennary. twelfth, duodenary, duodenal. sixtieth, sexagesimal. seventieth, septuagesimal.

centuple, centuplicate, centennial, centenary; hundredth; thousandth, millenary, millennial, etc.

99. QUINQUESECTION, ETC.—*N.* quinquesection, division by five, etc., 98; decimation; tithe; fifth, etc.

Adj. decimal, tenth; duodecimal, twelfth; sexagesimal, sexagenary; hundredth, centesimal; millesimal, etc.

100. [More than one] PLURALITY.—*N.* plurality, one or two, two or three, etc.; a few, several; multitude, etc., 102; majority.

Adj. plural, more than one, upwards of, some, certain.

100a. [Less than one] FRACTION.—*N.* fraction, fractional part; part, portion, fragment, etc., 51.

Adj. fractional, fragmentary, inconsiderable, partial.

101. ZERO.—*N.* zero, nothing; naught, nought; cipher; none, nobody.

102. MULTITUDE.—*N.* multitude, multitudinousness, multiplicity; profusion, etc. (*plenty*), 639; legion, host, array, army, galaxy; numbers, scores; heap, power, sight, lot, lots [*all five colloq.*], swarm, bevy, cloud, flock, herd, drove, shoal, school, flight, covey, hive, brood, litter, farrow, fry, nest; mob, crowd, etc. (*assemblage*), 72.

V. be numerous, swarm with, teem with, be alive with, crowd, swarm, outnumber, multiply; people.

Adj. many, several, sundry, various, alive with; numerous; profuse, manifold, multitudinous, teeming, populous, outnumbering, crowded, thick, galore [*colloq.*]; thick-coming, endless, etc. (*infinite*), 105.

103. FEWNESS.—*N.* fewness, paucity, scarcity, sparseness, sparsity; handful; small quantity, etc., 32; rarity, infrequency; minority.

Diminution of number: reduction, weeding, elimination; decimation; eradication.

V. render few, reduce, diminish, weed out, eliminate, thin, decimate.

Adj. few, scant, scanty; thin, rare, scarce, sparse, few and far between; exiguous; infrequent.

104. REPETITION.—*N.* repetition, iteration, recapitulation, reiteration; monotone; duplication, reduplication, monotony, harping, recurrence; reappearance, reproduction; periodicity, etc., 138; succession, run; alliteration; rhythm, tautology; diffuseness, redundancy.

echo, encore, burden of a song, refrain, undersong.

cuckoo, etc. (*imitation*), 19; reverberation, vibration, resonance; drumming, etc. (*roll*), 407; renewal, etc. (*restoration*), 660.

V. repeat, iterate, reiterate, redouble, reproduce, echo, re-echo, drum, harp upon, hammer; rehearse; resume, return to, recapitulate.

recur, revert, return, reappear; renew, etc. (*restore*), 660.
duplicate, reduplicate.

Adj. repeated, repetitious, recurrent, recurring; frequent, incessant; redundant, tautological; another.

monotonous, harping, iterative, unvaried; habitual, etc., 613.
aforesaid, aforenamed; said.

Adv. **repeatedly,** often, again, anew, afresh, once more; ditto, encore, again and again; over and over, frequently, etc., 136.

105. INFINITY.—*N.* **infinity,** infinitude, infiniteness; perpetuity, immortality; inexhaustibility, immensity, boundlessness.

V. **be infinite,** have no limits (*or* bounds), go on forever.

Adj. **infinite,** immense; numberless, countless, measureless, innumerable, immeasurable, incalculable, illimitable, interminable, unfathomable; without limit, without end, limitless, endless, boundless; untold, unnumbered, unmeasured, unbounded, unlimited; perpetual, etc., 112.

VI. TIME

106. TIME.—*N.* **time,** duration; period, term, stage, space, span, spell, snap, season; course.

intermediate time, while, interim, interval; intermission, interregnum, interlude; respite.

era, epoch, eon, cycle, age, reign, dynasty, administration.

V. **continue,** last, endure, stay, go on, remain, persist, abide, stand, stick [*colloq.*], hold out; intervene; elapse, etc., 109.

pass time, spend *or* while away time, tide over; employ time; seize an opportunity; linger on, drag on; tarry, etc., 110; waste time, etc. (*be inactive*), 683; procrastinate, etc., 133.

Adj. **permanent,** etc. (*durable*), 110; timely, opportune, seasonable.

Adv. **while,** whilst, during; in the course of; in the time of, when; meantime, meanwhile, in the meantime, in the interim; from day to day; for a time, for a season; till, until, up to, yet; the whole time, all the time; throughout; for good, permanently, always.

then, hereupon, thereupon, whereupon.

107. Absence of time.—*N.* **no time.**

Adv. **never,** ne'er; at no time, at no period; on no occasion, nevermore.

108. [Definite duration or portion of time] PERIOD.—*N.* **period;** octave, semester, quarter, moon, year, decennial, decennium; decade, lifetime, generation; epoch, era, century, age, millennium.

109. [Indefinite duration] COURSE.—*N.* **corridors** (*or* sweep, vista, halls, progress, process, lapse, flow, tide, march, flight) of time; duration, etc., 106.

Indefinite time: eon, age.

V. **elapse,** lapse, flow, run, proceed, advance, pass; fly, slip, slide, glide; crawl, drag; expire, go by, pass by, be past.

Adv. **in time,** in due time (*or* season, course); in course of time, in the fullness of time.

110. [Long duration] DURABILITY.—*N.* durability, durableness, permanence, continuance, persistence, lastingness, standing; immutability, stability; survival; longevity, etc. (*age*), 128; delay, etc. (*lateness*), 133; slowness.

an age, a long time, eon, century, an eternity; perpetuity, etc., 112.

V. **last,** endure, stand, remain, abide, continue, etc., 106.

tarry, etc., 133; drag on, protract, prolong; spin out, eke out, draw out; temporize, gain time.

outlast, outlive, survive.

Adj. **permanent,** durable, lasting; chronic, long-standing; persistent; lifelong, livelong; endless, fixed, long-lived, perennial; perpetual, etc., 112.

prolonged, protracted, spun out; lingering, long-winded; slow, etc., 275.

Adv. **long,** for a long time; long ago, etc. (*in a past time*), 122; all the day long, the livelong day; all the year round; permanently.

111. [Short duration] TRANSIENCE.—*N.* transience, transiency, evanescence, impermanence; changeableness, etc., 149; mortality; span; nine days' wonder, bubble; interregnum, interim.

velocity, etc., 274; suddenness, abruptness.

V. **be transient,** flit, pass away, fly, gallop, vanish, sink, melt, fade, evaporate.

Adj. **transient,** transitory, passing, evanescent, fleeting, fugitive; temporal, temporary, provisional, provisory; cursory; short-lived, ephemeral; deciduous; perishable, mortal; precarious; impermanent.

brief, quick, brisk, fleet; meteoric, volatile, summary; pressed for time, etc. (*haste*), 684; sudden, momentary, spasmodic, instantaneous.

Adv. **temporarily,** for the moment, for a time; awhile, soon, etc. (*early*), 132; briefly.

112. [Endless duration] PERPETUITY.—*N.* perpetuity, eternity, aye; immortality, perpetuation.

V. **eternalize,** immortalize, eternize, perpetuate.

Adj. **perpetual,** eternal, everlasting, continual, endless, unending; ceaseless, incessant, uninterrupted, unceasing; interminable; unfading, never-ending, deathless, immortal, undying, imperishable.

Adv. **perpetually,** always, ever, evermore, aye; forever, in all ages, without end, to the end of time; till doomsday; constantly, etc. (*very frequently*), 136.

113. [Point of time] INSTANTANEITY.—*N.* instantaneity, instantaneousness; suddenness, abruptness.

moment, instant, second, twinkling, flash, breath.

V. be instantaneous; flash.

Adj. instantaneous, momentary, extempore, sudden, abrupt.

Adv. instantaneously, in no time; presto, instanter, in a trice, in a jiffy [*colloq.*], suddenly, in the same breath; at once, plump; immediately, etc. (*early*), 132; extempore, on the spur of the moment; slapdash, etc. (*haste*), 684.

114. [Estimation, measurement, and record of time] CHRONOMETRY.—*N.* chronometry, chronology, horology.

almanac, calendar; register, registry; chronicle, annals, journal, diary.

timekeeper, clock, watch, repeater; chronometer, timepiece; dial, sundial, hourglass.

V. register, date, chronicle; measure time, beat time, mark time.

Adj. chronologic *or* chronological, temporal.

115. [False estimate of time] ANACHRONISM.—*N.* anachronism, error in time, error in chronology, misdate; anticipation; disregard (*or* neglect, oblivion) of time.

V. misdate; antedate, postdate, anticipate; take no note of time.

Adj. misdated; undated; overdue; out of date, anachronistic, behind time, ahead of time.

116. PRIORITY.—*N.* priority, predecessor, precedence, pre-existence; precursor, antecedent, forerunner; the past, etc., 122.

V. precede, come before; pre-exist, forerun; go before, lead, head; presage, herald, usher in, introduce, announce.

be beforehand, etc. (*be early*), 132; anticipate, forestall.

Adj. prior, previous, preceding, anterior, antecedent; pre-existent; former, aforementioned, foregoing, before-mentioned, aforesaid, said; introductory, etc. (*precursory*), 64.

Adv. before, prior to; earlier; previously, ere, already, yet, beforehand; on the eve of.

117. POSTERIORITY.—*N.* posteriority; succession, sequence; following, continuance, prolongation; futurity, future; successor; sequel, etc., 65; remainder.

V. follow after, pursue, come after, go after; succeed, supervene; ensue, result.

Adj. subsequent, posterior, following, after, later, succeeding, successive, ensuing, posthumous; future, etc., 121; after-dinner.

Adv. subsequently, after, afterward, since, later; next, close upon, thereafter, thereupon.

118. PRESENT TIME.—*N.* the present time, the present juncture *or* occasion; the times, time being; twentieth century.

Adj. present, actual, instant, current, latest, existing.

Adv. at this time, at this moment, etc., 113; now, at present; today, nowadays; already; even now, but now, just now; for the time being.

119. DIFFERENT TIME.—*N.* different time, other time.

Adv. then, at that time (*or* moment, instant); on that occasion.

when; whenever, whensoever; whereupon, upon which; at various times.

once, formerly, once upon a time.

120. SIMULTANEOUSNESS.—*N.* simultaneousness, synchronism, coexistence, coincidence, concurrence.

contemporary, coeval.

V. coexist, concur, accompany, keep pace with; synchronize.

Adj. simultaneous, coexisting, coincident, synchronous, concomitant, concurrent; coeval; contemporary, contemporaneous.

Adv. simultaneously, together, in concert; in the same breath.

121. THE FUTURE.—*N.* future, futurity, hereafter, time to come; morrow, tomorrow, by and by, doomsday, day of judgment, crack of doom.

approach of time, advent; destiny, etc., 152.

heritage, heirs, posterity, descendants.

prospect, anticipation, expectation; foresight, etc., 510.

V. anticipate, expect, await, foresee; forestall, etc. (*be early*), 132.

approach, await, threaten; impend, etc. (*be destined*), 152; come on, draw near.

Adj. future, to come; coming, impending, overhanging, imminent; next, near, close at hand; eventual, ulterior; prospective, in prospect.

Adv. prospectively, hereafter, in future; in course of time, eventually, ultimately, sooner or later.

soon, early; on the eve of, on the point of, about to.

122. THE PAST.—*N.* the past, past time, days of yore, days of old, times past, former times, yesterday, the olden time; retrospection, memory, priority.

antiquity, antiqueness, time immemorial, history, remote time; remote past; paleontology, archeology, antiquarianism.

antiquary, antiquarian, archeologist.

ancestry, lineage, forefathers.

V. pass, lapse, blow over.

Adj. past, gone, gone by, over, passed away, bygone, elapsed,

lapsed, expired, extinct, exploded, forgotten, irrecoverable; obsolete, antiquated, outworn.

former, pristine, quondam, late; ancestral.

foregoing, last, latter; recent.

looking back, retrospective, retroactive; archeological.

Adv. **formerly,** of old, of yore, time was, ago; anciently, long ago; lately, latterly, of late; ere now, before now, hitherto, heretofore; already, yet, up to this time.

123. NEWNESS.—*N.* **newness,** novelty; youth, juvenility, immaturity.

innovation; renovation, restoration.

upstart, *nouveau riche* [F.], parvenu.

modernism, modernness, modernity; modernization; latest fashion.

V. **renew,** renovate; rejuvenate; modernize.

Adj. **new,** novel, recent, fresh, green; young, etc., 127; raw, immature; virgin, untried; **modern,** late; newborn, new-fashioned, newfangled, newfledged; just out [*colloq.*], unhandled; brand-new, up-to-date [*colloq.*], renovated, spick-and-span.

Adv. **newly,** afresh, anew, lately, just now, latterly, of late.

124. OLDNESS.—*N.* **oldness,** age, antiquity.

maturity, matureness, ripeness.

decline, decay; senility, superannuation, dotage.

archaism, antiquarianism; thing of the past, relic of the past.

tradition, custom, immemorial usage, common law; folklore.

V. **be old,** have had its day, have seen its day.

become old, age, fade.

Adj. **old,** ancient, antique; time-honored, venerable, hoary; elder, eldest; firstborn; senile, etc., 128.

primitive, prime, primeval, aboriginal; antediluvian, prehistoric, dateless, patriarchal, archaic, classic, medieval; ancestral.

immemorial, traditional, unwritten, inveterate, rooted.

antiquated, of other times, of the old school, old world; obsolete, out-of-date, out-of-fashion, gone by, stale, old-fashioned, exploded, extinct, timeworn, crumbling, secondhand.

125. MORNING. [Noon]—*N.* **morning,** morn, forenoon, antemeridian, A.M., prime, dawn, daybreak; dayspring, peep of day, break of day, aurora, sunrise, daylight, cockcrow.

noon, midday, noonday, noontide, meridian, prime; nooning, noontime.

spring, springtide, springtime, seedtime; vernal equinox.

summer, summertide, summertime, midsummer.

Adj. **matin,** matutinal.

noon, noonday, midday.

spring, vernal.

summer, estival.

126. EVENING. [Midnight]—*N.* evening, eve, decline of day, close of day, eventide, vespers, nightfall, curfew, dusk, gloaming, twilight, sunset, sundown, bedtime.

afternoon, post meridiem [L.], P.M.

midnight; dead of night, witching time.

autumn, fall; harvesttime; autumnal equinox; Indian summer.

winter.

Adj. vesper, nightly, nocturnal; autumnal.

wintry, winterly.

127. YOUTH.—*N.* youth; juvenility; infancy, babyhood; childhood; boyhood, girlhood; rising generation; minority, immaturity, teens, tender age, bloom.

cradle, nursery.

flower of life, springtide of life, seedtime of life, golden season of life; heyday of youth, school days.

Adj. young, youthful, juvenile, green, callow, sappy, beardless, underage, in one's teens; younger, junior; newfledged, unfledged, unripe.

128. AGE.—*N.* age; oldness, old age, advanced age, senility, years, gray hairs, declining years, decrepitude, superannuation, second childhood, dotage; vale of years, decline of life; green old age, ripe age; longevity.

seniority, eldership, primogeniture; elders, etc. (*veteran*), 130; dean, father.

V. age, grow old, decline, wane.

Adj. aged; old, etc., 124; elderly, senile; ripe, mellow, declining, waning, past one's prime; gray, gray-headed, hoar, hoary, venerable, patriarchal, timeworn, antiquated, effete, decrepit, superannuated; advanced in life (*or* years); stricken in years; doting, etc. (*imbecile*), 499.

older, elder, oldest, eldest; senior; firstborn.

129. INFANT.—*N.* infant, babe, baby; nursling, suckling.

child, tot, mite, chick, kid [*slang*], little one, brat, pickaninny [*colored child*], urchin, elf.

youth, boy, lad, laddie, slip, sprig, stripling, youngster, cub, whippersnapper [*colloq.*], schoolboy, hobbledehoy, young hopeful, cadet, minor.

girl, lass, lassie, wench, damsel; maid, maiden, virgin; nymph, colleen, flapper, minx, schoolgirl; hoyden, tomboy, romp.

Adj. infantile, infantine, puerile, boyish, girlish, childish, babyish, kittenish; boylike, girllike, newborn; young, etc., 127.

130. VETERAN.—*N.* veteran, old man, patriarch, graybeard;

grandfather, sexagenarian, octogenarian, nonagenarian, centenarian; Methuselah; elders, forefathers; dotard, etc., 501.

granny, crone, hag, beldam.

Adj. veteran; aged, etc., 128.

131. ADOLESCENCE.—*N.* adolescence, majority, adulthood, womanhood, manhood, virility; flower of age; full bloom; spring of life.

man, etc., 373; woman, etc., 374; adult.

middle age, maturity, full age, prime of life, meridian of life.

V. come of age, come to man's estate, come to years of discretion; attain majority; come out [*colloq.*].

Adj. adolescent, pubescent, of age, of full age, of ripe age; out of one's teens, grown up, full-grown, manly, manlike, virile, adult; womanly; marriageable.

middle-aged, mature, in one's prime; matronly.

132. EARLINESS.—*N.* earliness, punctuality, promptitude, readiness, expedition, quickness, haste, etc. (*velocity*), 274; suddenness.

prematurity, precocity, precipitation, anticipation.

V. be early, be beforehand.

anticipate, forestall, take time by the forelock, steal a march upon; bespeak, secure, engage, pre-engage.

accelerate, expedite, etc. (*quicken*), 274; make haste, etc. (*hurry*), 684.

Adj. early, timely, seasonable, punctual, forward; prompt, etc. (*active*), 682.

premature, precipitate, precocious, anticipatory.

sudden, instantaneous, immediate; unexpected, etc., 508.

imminent, impending, near.

Adv. early, soon, anon, betimes, ere long, before long; punctually, in time; on time, on the dot [*slang*].

beforehand; prematurely, too soon; precipitately, hastily; in anticipation; unexpectedly, unawares.

suddenly, etc. (*instantaneously*), 113; at short notice, extempore; on the spur of the moment, at once; on the spot, on the instant, at sight, offhand, straight, straightway; forthwith, immediately, quickly, speedily, apace; presently, by and by, directly.

133. LATENESS.—*N.* lateness; tardiness, etc. (*slowness*), 275.

delay, procrastination, postponement, adjournment, prorogation, retardation; protraction, prolongation; moratorium; aftertime; respite, truce, reprieve, stop, stay, suspension, remand.

V. be late, tarry, wait, stay, bide, take time; dawdle, etc. (*be inactive*), 683; linger, loiter, gain time; hang fire; stand over, lie over; hang.

put off, defer, delay, lay over, suspend; stave off; retard, postpone, adjourn, prorogue, procrastinate; dally, prolong, protract, spin out, draw out, table, lay on the table, shelve; reserve, temporize, filibuster, stall [*slang*].

be kept waiting, dance attendance; cool one's heels [*colloq.*]; await, expect, wait for.

Adj. late, tardy, dilatory; slow, leisurely, behindhand, backward, unpunctual; overdue, belated, delayed; posthumous.

Adv. late; backward, at the eleventh hour, at length, at last, ultimately; behind time; too late.

slowly, deliberately, at one's leisure.

134. TIMELINESS.—*N.* timeliness, opportunity, opening, occasion, show [*colloq.*]; suitable time *or* season, high time; nick of time; golden opportunity, clear stage, fair field; spare time, leisure.

crisis, turn, emergency, juncture, conjuncture; turning point.

V. improve the occasion; seize an opportunity; use (*or* profit by) an opportunity; give (*or* grant) an opportunity; suit the occasion, etc. (*be expedient*), 646; strike the iron while it is hot, make hay while the sun shines.

Adj. timely, well timed, opportune, seasonable; appropriate, suitable.

lucky, providential, fortunate, happy, favorable, propitious, auspicious.

occasional, accidental, extemporaneous, extemporary; contingent, provisional.

Adv. opportunity, in due time; for the nonce; in the nick of time, just in time; at the eleventh hour, now or never.

by the way, by the by; while on this subject, speaking of; extempore; on the spur of the moment.

135. UNTIMELINESS.—*N.* untimeliness, unseasonableness, unsuitable time, improper time; evil hour; intrusion; anachronism.

V. be ill-timed, mistime, intrude, come amiss, break in upon; be busy, be occupied, be engaged.

lose an opportunity; neglect an opportunity; allow *or* suffer the opportunity to pass (*or* slip, go by, escape); waste time; let slip through the fingers.

Adj. ill-timed, mistimed, ill-fated, ill-omened, ill-starred; untimely, unseasonable, out of season; inopportune, inconvenient, untoward, unlucky, inauspicious, unpropitious, unfortunate, unfavorable, unsuited; inexpedient.

unpunctual, etc. (*late*), 133; premature, etc. (*early*), 132.

136. FREQUENCY.—*N.* frequency, repetition, iteration, reiteration.

V. keep on; reiterate, repeat, recur, etc., 104; do nothing but.

Adj. frequent, not rare, thick-coming, incessant, perpetual, continual, constant, habitual, etc., 613.

Adv. often, oft, ofttimes, frequently; repeatedly, in quick succession; daily, every day; habitually, commonly.

perpetually, continually, constantly, incessantly, at all times.

sometimes, occasionally, at times, now and then, again and again.

137. INFREQUENCY.—*N.* infrequency, infrequence, rarity; uncommonness.

Adj. infrequent, uncommon, sporadic; rare, few, scant, scarce; unprecedented.

Adv. seldom, rarely, scarcely, hardly; not often, infrequently, uncommonly, sparsely, scarcely ever, hardly ever.

138. REGULARITY [of recurrence].—*N.* periodicity, intermittence; oscillation, vibration; beat, pulse, pulsation; rhythm, alternation; round, revolution, rotation, regularity, bout, turn; routine; cycle.

anniversary, biennial, triennial, quadrennial, quinquennial, sextennial, septennial, octennial, decennial; tricennial, jubilee, centennial, centenary, bicentennial, bicentenary, tercentenary; birthday, natal day, fete day, saint's day, feast, festival, fast, holiday.

Christmas, Yuletide, New Year's Day, Ash Wednesday, Maundy Thursday, Good Friday, Easter; Halloween, All Saints' Day; All Souls' Day; Candlemas; Memorial *or* Decoration Day, Independence Day, Labor Day, Thanksgiving, ground-hog day, woodchuck day, leap year, St. Swithin's Day, Midsummer Day; May Day.

V. return, revolve, recur, come round again; beat, pulsate; alternate; intermit.

Adj. periodic, periodical; serial, recurrent, cyclic, cyclical, rhythmic, recurring, intermittent; alternate, every other; every.

regular, steady, constant, methodical, punctual.

Adv. by turns, in turn, in rotation, alternately, off and on, round and round.

139. IRREGULARITY [of recurrence].—*N.* irregularity, uncertainty, unpunctuality; fitfulness, capriciousness.

Adj. irregular, uncertain, unpunctual, capricious, erratic, desultory, fitful, flickering; rambling, spasmodic; unmethodical, unsystematic, unequal, uneven, variable.

Adv. by fits and starts.

VII. CHANGE

140. CHANGE.—*N.* change, alteration, mutation, permutation, variation, modification, modulation, inflection, mood, qualification, innovation, deviation, shift, turn; diversion, variety, break.

conversion, etc. (*gradual change*), 144; revolution, etc., 146; inversion, reversal; displacement, transposition, removal, transference.

transformation, metamorphosis, transfiguration, transmutation; transubstantiation; transmigration, metempsychosis; avatar.

changeableness, etc., 149.

V. change, alter, vary, modulate, diversify, qualify, tamper with; turn, shift, veer, jibe, jib, tack, chop, warp, swerve, deviate, dodge; turn aside; take a turn, turn the corner.

modify, work a change, patch, piece, transform, transfigure, transmute, convert, revolutionize; metamorphose, ring the changes; innovate, introduce new blood, shuffle the cards; shift the scene, turn over a new leaf.

recast, remodel; reverse, etc., 218; convert into, etc., 144.

Adj. changed, newfangled; changeable, changeful, variable, devious, transitional.

141. PERMANENCE.—*N.* permanence, fixity, persistence, endurance; durability; standing, *status quo* [L.]; maintenance, preservation, conservation; conservatism; stability, constancy; quiescence, etc., 265; obstinacy, inflexibility.

V. endure, persist, remain, stay, tarry, rest, hold, last, bide, abide, dwell, maintain, keep; stand fast, subsist, live, outlive, survive; hold one's ground (*or* footing).

Adj. permanent, stable, fixed, settled, established, irremovable, durable; unchanged, intact, inviolate; persistent; conservative; unfailing, unfading.

Adv. for good, at a stand, at a standstill, as you were!

142. CESSATION.—*N.* cessation, discontinuance; intermission, remission; suspense, suspension; interruption; stop; hitch [*colloq.*]; stoppage, halt.

pause, rest, lull, respite, truce, armistice, stay; interregnum. In debate: closure, cloture.

deadlock, checkmate, dead center, dead stand, dead stop; end.

punctuation: comma, semicolon, colon, period, full stop; cæsura.

V. cease, discontinue, desist, stay; break off, leave off; hold, stop, pull up, stop short; check, stick, hang fire; halt, pause, rest; come to a stand; arrive, etc., 292; go out, die away, wear away, pass away, lapse; be at an end.

have done with, give over; give up, etc. (*relinquish*), 624.

interrupt, suspend, intermit, remit; put an end to, bring to a stand (*or* standstill), stop, cut short, arrest.

143. CONTINUANCE [in action].—*N.* continuance, continuation; pursuance, maintenance, extension, perpetuation, prolongation; persistence, perseverance; repetition.

V. **continue,** persist, go on, keep on, hold on; abide, pursue; stick to; maintain its course; keep up, drag on, stick [*colloq.*], persevere, endure, carry on; keep the field, keep the ball rolling.

sustain, uphold, hold up, follow up, perpetuate, prolong, maintain; preserve.

Adj. **continuing,** uninterrupted, unvarying, persistent, unceasing, unvaried, sustained, chronic; undying, immortal, perpetual.

144. [Gradual change to something different] CONVERSION. —*N.* **conversion,** reduction, transmutation, assimilation; chemistry, alchemy; growth, progress; naturalization; transportation.

passage, transit, transition, transmigration; shifting, flux; phase.

convert, neophyte, proselyte; pervert, renegade, apostate, turncoat.

V. **be converted into;** become, turn to *or* into; turn out, lapse, shift; pass into, grow into, merge into; melt, grow, wax, mature, mellow.

convert into, resolve into; make, render; mold, form, remodel, reform, reorganize; bring to, reduce to.

145. REVERSION.—*N.* **reversion,** return; revulsion; turning point, turn of the tide; alternation, rotation; inversion, etc., 218; recoil, reaction; retrospection, retrogression; restoration, relapse, atavism, throwback.

V. **revert,** reverse, return, turn back; relapse; invert; recoil; retreat; restore; undo, unmake; turn the scale.

146. [Sudden or violent change] REVOLUTION.—*N.* **revolution,** revolt; breakup; destruction, etc., 162; clean sweep, debacle, overturn, overthrow, rebellion, rising, uprising, mutiny, counterrevolution, bolshevism.

spasm, convulsion, throe, revulsion; earthquake, eruption, upheaval, cataclysm, explosion.

V. **revolutionize,** revolt, rebel, rise; remodel, recast.

Adj. **revolutionary,** catastrophic, cataclysmic, cataclysmal, insurgent, Red, insurrectionary, mutinous, rebellious; bolshevistic *or* bolshevik.

147. [Change of one thing for another] SUBSTITUTION.—*N.* **substitution,** commutation, supplanting.

substitute, scapegoat; alternative; makeshift, temporary expedient, shift, apology, stopgap; alternate; dummy, double; changeling; representative, deputy.

price, purchase money, consideration, equivalent.

V. **substitute,** put in the place of, change for, give place to; take the place of, supplant, supersede, replace, cut out [*colloq.*]; commute, redeem, compound for.

Adj. substituted, vicarious.

Adv. instead; by proxy; in place of, in lieu of.

148. [Double or mutual change] INTERCHANGE.—*N.* interchange, exchange; commutation, permutation; transposition, shuffle; alternation, reciprocity; swap [*colloq.*], barter, exchange; retaliation, reprisal; retort, requital, cross fire.

V. interchange, exchange, bandy, barter, transpose, swap [*colloq.*], reciprocate, commute; give and take, retaliate; retort; requite.

Adj. reciprocal, mutual; interchangeable.

international, interstate, interurban, interdenominational; interscholastic, intercollegiate.

Adv. in exchange, vice versa, conversely, by turns, turn about.

149. CHANGEABLENESS.—*N.* changeableness, mutability, inconstancy; versatility, mobility; instability, vacillation, irresolution, indecision; fluctuation, vicissitude; alternation, oscillation.

Comparisons: moon, kaleidoscope, chameleon, quicksilver, shifting sands, weathercock, vane, weathervane, harlequin, turncoat; wheel of fortune.

restlessness, fidgets, disquiet; disquietude, unrest; agitation, etc., 315.

V. fluctuate, vary, waver, flicker, flutter, shift, shuffle, shake, totter, tremble, vacillate, shift to and fro; oscillate, pulsate, vibrate; alternate.

Adj. changeable, changeful; changing, mutable, variable, kaleidoscopic; protean, versatile, mobile.

inconstant, unsteady, unstable, unfixed, unsettled; fluctuating, wavering, vibratory, restless, tremulous; erratic, fickle; mercurial, irresolute, indecisive; capricious, fitful, spasmodic; vagrant, wayward; desultory, transient, etc., 111.

150. STABILITY.—*N.* stability, immutability, unchangeableness, constancy; immobility; soundness, vitality, stabilization; stiffness, solidity; permanence, etc., 141; obstinacy, obduracy.

fixture, establishment; leopard's spots.

standpatter [*politics*].

V. be firm, stick fast; stand firm, remain firm; stand pat [*colloq.*].

establish, settle, fix, set, stabilize; retain, keep hold; make good, make sure; fasten, etc. (*join*), 43; perpetuate.

settle down; strike root, take root.

Adj. unchangeable, immutable; unaltered, unalterable, constant; permanent, persistent, invariable, undeviating; stable, durable, perennial; irretrievable, irrevocable, indissoluble, indestructible, imperishable, indelible.

fixed, steadfast, firm, solid; deep-rooted, ineradicable; fast, steady, confirmed, inveterate; immovable, rooted; settled, stereotyped, established, vested; obstinate, etc., 606; incontrovertible, valid.

stuck fast, transfixed, aground, stranded.

151. PRESENT EVENTS.—*N.* eventuality, event, occurrence, incident, affair, transaction, proceeding, fact; phenomenon.

circumstance, particular; happening, adventure; crisis, pass, emergency, contingency; concern, business.

consequence, issue, result, termination, conclusion.

affairs, matters; the world, life, things, doings; the times.

V. happen, occur; take place, come to pass, take effect; present itself; fall out, turn out, befall, betide; turn up, crop up, arrive; ensue, result; arise, start; take its course, pass off.

experience; meet with; fall to the lot of; be one's lot; find, encounter; undergo, pass through, go through, endure, bear, suffer, abide, stand, brook.

Adj. eventful, stirring, full of incident; memorable, momentous, signal; current, on foot, at issue, in question; incidental.

Adv. eventually, ultimately, finally; in the event of, in case.

152. FUTURE EVENTS.—*N.* destiny, fatality, fate, lot, doom, fortune; future, future state; future existence, hereafter; next world, world to come; life to come; prospect.

V. impend, hang over, threaten, loom, await, approach; foreordain, preordain; destine, predestine, doom.

Adj. impending, destined; coming, in store, to come, instant, at hand, near, imminent; in the wind, in prospect.

Adv. in time, in the long run; all in good time; eventually.

VIII. CAUSATION

153. CAUSE.—*N.* cause, origin, source, principle, element; prime mover, ultimate cause; author, producer, creator, determinant; mainspring, agent; leaven; groundwork, foundation, support.

causality, causation; origination; production, etc., 161.

spring, fountain, well; fountainhead, reservoir, wellspring; genesis; derivation; remote cause; influence.

pivot, hinge, turning point; heart, hub, focus.

reason, reason why; ground, occasion; final cause; undercurrents.

rudiment, egg, germ, nucleus, seed.

nest, cradle, nursery, birthplace, hotbed.

V. cause, originate, give rise to, occasion, sow the seeds of; bring to pass, bring about; produce; create, develop; set on foot, entail; found, institute.

procure, induce, draw down, superinduce, evoke, elicit, provoke.

contribute, conduce to, have a hand in, influence; determine, decide, turn the scale.

Adj. **causal,** original; primary, originative, generative, productive, creative; formative; radical; in embryo, embryonic.

Adv. **from the beginning,** in the first place; because, etc., 155.

154. EFFECT.—*N.* effect, consequence; aftergrowth, afterclap, aftermath; derivative; derivation; result; resultant; upshot, issue, outcome, conclusion; catastrophe, end; development, outgrowth; fruit, crop, harvest, product.

production, work, handiwork, fabric, performance; creature, creation; offspring, offshoot; first fruits.

V. **be the effect of,** be due to, be owing to; originate in *or* from; rise from, spring from, emanate from, come from, issue from, flow from, result from; depend upon, hang upon, hinge upon, turn upon.

Adj. **owing to;** resulting from; due to; caused by; derived from, evolved from; derivative; hereditary.

Adv. **consequently,** it follows that, as a consequence, in consequence; necessarily, eventually.

155. [Assignment of cause] ATTRIBUTION.—*N.* attribution, theory, assignment, reference to, accounting for; imputation; derivation.

explanation, interpretation, reason why.

V. **attribute to,** ascribe to, impute to, refer to, lay to, trace to; blame; saddle; account for, derive from; theorize.

Adj. **attributed;** attributable, referable; due to; owing to.

Adv. **hence,** thence, therefore, for, since, on account of, because, owing to; forasmuch as; whence.

why? wherefore? whence? how comes it? how is it? how so?

156. [Absence of assignable cause] CHANCE[1].—*N.* chance, accident, fortune, hazard, luck, fluke [*cant*], casualty, hit; fate, lottery, tossup [*colloq.*]; throw of the dice; heads or tails, wheel of fortune.

probability, possibility, contingency, odds, run of luck; main chance.

gamble, speculation, gaming, game of chance.

V. **chance,** turn up; fall to one's lot; be one's fate; stumble on, light upon; blunder upon, hit, hit upon.

Adj. **casual,** fortuitous, accidental, chance, haphazard, random, incidental, unintentional, unpremeditated.

---

[1]The word *chance* has two distinct meanings: the first, the absence of assignable *cause*, as above; and the second, the absence of *design*—for the latter see 621.

Adv. **by chance,** by accident; at random, casually; perchance, etc. (*possibly*), 470.

157. POWER.—*N.* **power;** potency, efficacy, puissance, might, energy, vigor, force; ascendancy, sway, almightiness, omnipotence; authority, weight, control; influence, predominance.

ability, competence, efficiency, efficacy; validity, cogency; vantage ground.

capability, capacity; faculty, quality, attribute, endowment, virtue, gift, property, qualification.

V. **empower;** give *or* confer power; invest, endue; endow, arm; strengthen, etc., 159.

electrify, magnetize, energize, galvanize.

Adj. **powerful,** puissant, potent, capable, able; cogent, valid, effective, effectual, efficient, efficacious, adequate, competent; predominant; mighty, omnipotent, almighty.

forcible, energetic; influential; productive.

electric, magnetic, galvanic, dynamic, potential.

Adv. **by virtue of,** by dint of.

158. IMPOTENCE.—*N.* **impotence;** inability, disability, incapacity, incapability; ineptitude; inefficiency, incompetence, disqualification; inefficacy, etc. (*inutility*), 645; failure, etc., 732.

helplessness, prostration, paralysis, collapse, exhaustion, senility, superannuation, decrepitude, imbecility, inanition.

mollycoddle, old woman, milksop, sissy [*colloq.*], mother's darling.

collapse, faint, swoon, drop; go by the board; end in smoke, etc. (*fail*), 732.

render powerless, disable, disarm, incapacitate, disqualify, unfit, invalidate, undermine, deaden, cramp, tie the hands; prostrate, paralyze, muzzle, cripple, maim, lame, throttle, strangle, silence, spike the guns; unhinge, unfit; put out of gear.

unman, unnerve, devitalize, attenuate, enervate.

shatter, exhaust; weaken, enfeeble.

Adj. **powerless,** impotent, helpless; incapable, incompetent, inefficient, ineffective, unfit, unfitted, unqualified, disqualified; crippled, disabled; senile, decrepit, superannuated; paralytic, paralyzed, nerveless, out of joint, out of gear; unnerved, unhinged; done up [*colloq.*], done for [*colloq.*], dead-beat [*colloq.*], exhausted, shattered, prostrate, demoralized, harmless; unarmed, weaponless, defenseless.

nugatory, null and void, inoperative, good for nothing, ineffectual, inadequate, inefficacious, etc. (*useless*), 645.

159. STRENGTH.—*N.* **strength;** power, etc., 157; energy, vigor, force; main (*or* physical, brute) force; spring, elasticity.

vitality, virility, lustihood, stamina, nerve, muscle, sinews, physique; grit.

athletics, athleticism; gymnastics, calisthenics.

athlete, gymnast, acrobat; Atlas, Hercules.

strengthening, invigoration, refreshment.

Science of forces: dynamics, statics.

V. strengthen, invigorate, brace, nerve, fortify, buttress, sustain, harden, steel; gird, set up, gird up one's loins; recruit, set on one's legs [*colloq.*]; vivify; refresh, reinforce, restore.

Adj. strong, mighty, vigorous, forcible; hard, stout, robust, sound, sturdy, husky [*colloq.*], hardy, powerful, potent, puissant.

resistless, irresistible, invincible, impregnable, unconquerable, indomitable, incontestable, valid; overpowering, overwhelming, all-powerful.

able-bodied; athletic, Herculean, muscular, brawny, wiry, well knit, sinewy, strapping, stalwart, lusty.

manly, manful; masculine, male, virile, in the prime of manhood.

Adv. strongly, by force, by main force.

160. WEAKNESS.—*N.* weakness, debility, relaxation, languor, enervation; impotence, etc., 158; infirmity, effeminacy; fragility; inactivity, etc., 683.

anemia, bloodlessness, deficiency of blood, poverty of blood.

loss of strength, delicacy; decrepitude; invalidism.

V. be weak; drop, crumble, give way; totter, dodder; tremble, shake; halt, limp; fade, languish, decline, flag, fail.

weaken, enfeeble, debilitate, shake, relax, sap, enervate, unnerve; cripple, unman; cramp, reduce, sprain, strain, dilute, impoverish.

Adj. weak, faint, feeble, infirm; impotent; relaxed, unnerved, unstrung, limp, strengthless, powerless; weakly, sickly, flaccid.

soft, effeminate, womanish.

frail, fragile; flimsy, sleazy, papery, unsubstantial, gimcrack, rickety, jerry-built; broken, decrepit, lame, shattered, shaken, crazy, shaky, tumbledown.

unsound, spent, effete; decayed, rotten, worn, seedy, languishing, wasted, laid low, the worse for wear; on its last legs.

161. [Power in operation] PRODUCTION.—*N.* production, creation, construction, formation, fabrication, manufacture; building, architecture, erection; organization; establishment; workmanship, performance; achievement; flowering, efflorescence, fruition; genesis, birth; evolution, development, growth; breeding; propagation.

publication; works, opus (*pl.* opera) [L.]; authorship.

structure, building, edifice, fabric, erection, pile.

V. **produce,** perform, operate, do, make, form, construct, fabricate, frame, contrive, manufacture; build, raise, rear, erect; establish, constitute, compose, evolve, coin, organize, institute; achieve, accomplish.

flower, blossom, bear fruit, bear, bring forth, give birth to, usher into the world; generate, propagate, engender, create; breed, develop, bring up.

induce, superinduce; cause, etc., 153.

Adj. **productive;** prolific, etc., 168; creative, formative, constructive; generative; teeming.

162. [Nonproduction] **DESTRUCTION.—***N.* destruction; waste, dissolution, breaking up, disruption; disorganization; demolition, overthrow, subversion, suppression; abolition, etc., 756; sacrifice; ravage, devastation, incendiarism; revolution, etc., 146; road to ruin; sabotage.

fall, downfall, ruin, perdition; breakdown, breakup; cave-in [*colloq.*]; wreck, shipwreck, cataclysm.

extinction, extermination, annihilation; doom, crack of doom.

V. **perish,** fall, fall to the ground, tumble, topple; fall to pieces, break up, crumble, go to wrack and ruin; go by the board, be all over with, go to pieces, totter to its fall.

destroy, do (*or* make) away with, waste; nullify, annul, sacrifice, demolish, overturn, overthrow, overwhelm; upset, subvert, put an end to; do for [*colloq.*], undo, break down, cut down, pull down, dismantle, mow down, blow down; suppress, quash, put down, crush, blot out, efface, obliterate, cancel, erase, strike out, expunge, delete; dispel, dissipate, dissolve; consume.

smash, crash, quell, squash [*colloq.*], shatter, shiver, batter; tear (*or* pull, crush) to pieces; ruin, fell; sink, swamp, scuttle, wreck, shipwreck, engulf, submerged; lay in ruins, raze, level; deal destruction, lay waste, ravage, gut; devour, desolate, devastate, blast, exterminate, eradicate, annihilate.

Adj. **destructive,** subversive, cataclysmic, ruinous, incendiary, suicidal, deadly, all-destroying, all-devouring.

163. REPRODUCTION.—*N.* reproduction, renovation; restoration, etc., 660; renewal, revival, regeneration, revivification; apotheosis; resuscitation, reanimation, resurrection, reappearance.

V. **reproduce,** restore, etc., 660; revive, renovate, renew, repeat, regenerate, revivify, resuscitate, reanimate, refashion, multiply.

Adj. **reproductive,** resurgent, reappearing; renascent; Hydra-headed.

164. PRODUCER.—*N.* producer, originator, inventor, author, founder, generator, mover, architect, grower, raiser, introducer, creator; maker, etc. (*agent*), 690; prime mover.

165. DESTROYER.—*N.* destroyer, wrecker, annihilator; cankerworm, etc. (*bane*), 663; assassin, etc. (*killer*), 361; executioner, etc. (*punish*), 975; iconoclast, vandal, nihilist.

166. PATERNITY.—*N.* paternity, fathership, fatherhood; parentage.

parent, father, sire, dad [*colloq.*], papa, pater [*colloq.*], daddy [*colloq.*], paterfamilias; ancestor.

motherhood, maternity, mother, dam, mamma, mammy, mam [*colloq.*], matriarch, materfamilias.

stem, trunk, tree, stock, pedigree, house, lineage, line, family, race, tribe, clan; genealogy, family tree, descent, extraction, birth, ancestry; forefathers, forebears.

Adj. parental; paternal; maternal; ancestral, linear, patriarchal; racial.

167. POSTERITY.—*N.* posterity, progeny, breed, issue, offspring, brood, family, children, heirs; rising generation.

descendant, scion, offshoot, chip of the old block, heir, heiress, heir apparent, heir presumptive.

child, son, daughter, baby, kid [*colloq.*], imp, brat, cherub, tot, innocent, urchin, chit [*colloq.*]; infant, etc., 129.

lineage, line, straight descent, heredity, sonship, primogeniture.

Adj. hereditary, lineal.

filial, sonlike, daughterly, dutiful.

168. PRODUCTIVENESS.—*N.* productiveness, fecundity, fertility, luxuriance; multiplication, propagation, fructification.

V. fructify; generate, impregnate; teem, spawn, multiply; produce, etc., 161; conceive.

Adj. productive, prolific, copious; teeming, fertile, fruitful, plenteous, luxuriant; generative, life-giving; originative.

169. UNPRODUCTIVENESS.—*N.* unproductiveness, infertility, sterility, barrenness, unfruitfulness; unprofitableness, etc. (*inutility*), 645.

waste, desert, Sahara, wild, wilderness.

V. be unproductive; hang fire, flash in the pan, come to nothing.

Adj. unproductive, barren, unfertile, arid, sterile, unfruitful, fruitless, useless, fallow; unprofitable, etc. (*useless*), 645.

170. AGENCY.—*N.* agency, operation, force, function, office, maintenance, exercise, work, swing, play.

causation, impelling force; mediation, intervention, instrumentality; influence, etc., 175; action, etc. (*voluntary*), 680; method, procedure.

V. **operate,** work; act, perform, play, support, sustain, maintain, take effect, quicken, strike; have play, have free play; bring to bear upon.

Adj. **operative,** efficient, efficacious, practical, effectual; at work, on foot; acting, in operation, in force, in action.

171. ENERGY.—*N.* **energy,** force; intensity, vigor, strength, backbone [*colloq.*], vim [*colloq.*], mettle, pep [*slang*], fire, go [*colloq.*], high pressure; human dynamo.

activity, agitation, effervescence, ferment, fermentation, ebullition, stir, bustle; voluntary, energy, etc., 682; mental energy, etc., 604; resolution, stimulation; exertion, etc. (*effort*), 686.

V. **give energy,** energize, stimulate, strengthen, invigorate, kindle, excite, inflame, exert; sharpen, intensify.

Adj. **energetic,** strong, forcible, active, strenuous, brisk, forceful, mettlesome, enterprising, go-ahead [*colloq.*]; potent, etc. (*powerful*), 157; intense, keen, sharp, acute, incisive, trenchant.

poignant, virulent, caustic, corrosive, mordant; harsh, stringent, drastic.

172. INERTNESS.—*N.* **inertness,** inertia, inactivity, torpor, languor, quiescence, inaction, passivity, stagnation.

mental inertness; sloth; inexcitability, etc., 826; irresolution, indecision, vacillation; obstinacy, etc., 606.

V. **be inert,** hang fire, be inactive; smolder.

Adj. **inert,** inactive, passive; torpid, etc., 683; sluggish, logy, stagnant, dull, heavy, slack, tame, slow, lifeless, dead.

latent, dormant, smoldering, unexerted.

Adv. in suspense, in abeyance.

173. VIOLENCE.—*N.* **violence,** vehemence, might, impetuosity, boisterousness, disorder, effervescence, ebullition; turbulence, bluster; uproar, riot, row [*colloq.*], rumpus [*colloq.*].

ferocity, rage, fury, exasperation; malignity; severity, etc., 739; force, brute force; outrage.

fit, paroxysm, spasm, convulsion, throe; hysterics, passion, etc., 825.

outbreak, outburst, discharge, volley, explosion, blast, detonation, eruption, volcano, earthquake, thunderstorm.

fury, berserk, dragon, demon, tiger, wild beast; fire-eater [*colloq.*], etc. (*blusterer*), 887.

V. **be violent;** ferment, effervesce; rampage; run wild, run amuck, rage, roar, riot, storm; boil, boil over; fume, foam, ride roughshod, out-Herod Herod.

explode, go off, detonate, fulminate, let off, let fly, discharge, thunder, blow up, flash, flare, burst.

render violent; stir up, quicken, excite, incite, urge, lash, stimulate; irritate, inflame, kindle, foment, exasperate, convulse, infuriate, madden, lash into fury.

Adj. **violent,** vehement, acute, sharp; rough, tough [*colloq.*], rude, bluff, brusque, abrupt, boisterous, wild, impetuous, rampant; savage, fierce, ferocious.

turbulent, tumultuous; disorderly, raging, troublous, riotous, obstreperous, uproarious; frenzied, mad, insane; desperate, rash; infuriate, furious, frantic, outrageous; stormy, etc. (*wind*), 349.

fiery, flaming, scorching, hot, red-hot.

unbridled, unruly; headstrong, ungovernable, uncontrollable, irrepressible.

spasmodic, convulsive, explosive; detonating; volcanic, meteoric.

Adv. **violently,** amain; by storm, by force, by main force, with might and main, at one fell swoop; in desperation, with a vengeance.

174. MODERATION.—*N.* **moderation;** lenity, etc., 740; temperateness, temperance, gentleness, mildness, quiet, sobriety; mental calmness, composure, etc. (*inexcitability*), 826.

alleviation, assuagement, mitigation, relaxation, tranquilization, pacification.

moderator; sedative, lenitive, palliative; opiate, balm.

V. **moderate,** slacken, soften, mitigate, palliate, alleviate, allay, assuage, appease, temper, mollify, lull, soothe, compose, still, calm, cool, quiet, tranquilize, hush, quell, sober, pacify, smooth, deaden, smother; blunt, subdue, chasten; weaken, etc., 160; lessen, decrease; check, tame, curb, restrain.

Adj. **moderate,** gentle, mild; cool, sober, temperate, reasonable, lenient, measured; calm, unruffled, quiet, tranquil, still, halcyon; peaceful, peaceable, pacific.

Adv. in moderation, within bounds.

175. [Indirect Power] INFLUENCE.—*N.* **influence;** importance, etc., 642; weight, pressure, pull [*colloq. or slang*]; interest; preponderance, prevalence, sway; predominance, upper hand, ascendancy; dominance, reign; control, domination, hold; authority, power, potency, capability, spell, magic, magnetism.

footing; purchase, support; play, leverage, vantage ground, advantage.

patronage, protection, auspices; patron, etc. (*auxiliary*), 711; tower of strength.

V. **be influential,** carry weight, sway, bias, actuate, weight, tell; magnetize, work upon; take root, take hold; pervade, run through; be rife.

dominate, subject; predominate, outweigh; override, overbear; have *or* gain the upper hand, prevail.

lead, control, rule, manage, master, get control of, make one's influence felt; take the lead, pull the strings; turn the scale; set the fashion.

Adj. **influential,** effective, potent; important, etc., 642; weighty; prevalent, rife, rampant; dominant, predominant, authoritative, recognized.

Adv. with telling effect, with authority.

176. TENDENCY.—*N.* **tendency,** aptness, aptitude, proneness, proclivity, bent, turn, tone, bias, set, warp, leaning (*with* to *or* toward), predisposition, inclination, liability, propensity, susceptibility; quality, nature, temperament; idiosyncrasy; cast, vein, grain, humor, mood, trend, drift.

V. **tend,** contribute, conduce, lead, influence, dispose, incline, verge, bend to, warp, turn, work toward, gravitate toward, trend; affect; carry, redound to, bid fair to; promote, etc. (*aid*), 707.

Adj. **tending;** conducive, working toward, in a fair way to, likely to, calculated to; liable, etc., 177; subservient, instrumental, useful; subsidiary, accessory.

177. LIABILITY.—*N.* **liability,** susceptibility; possibility, contingency.

V. **be liable,** incur, lay oneself open to, be subjected to, run the chance, stand a chance; lie under, expose oneself to, open a door to.

Adj. **liable,** subject, in danger, open to, exposed to; answerable, responsible, accountable, amenable; apt to; dependent on.

contingent, incidental, possible, on the cards, within range of, at the mercy of.

178. CONCURRENCE.—*N.* **concurrence,** co-operation, collaboration; conformity, agreement, accord; alliance; complicity, collusion, partnership, union.

V. **concur,** conduce, conspire, contribute; agree, unite, harmonize, combine; hang *or* pull together, co-operate; keep pace with, run parallel.

Adj. **concurrent,** conformable, joint, co-operative, concordant; harmonious, in alliance with, of one mind, at one with.

179. COUNTERACTION.—*N.* **counteraction,** opposition; contrariety, contradiction; antagonism, polarity; clashing, collision, interference, resistance, friction; reaction, recoil; counterblast, neutralization, check, hindrance; repression, restraint.

V. **counteract,** clash, cross, interfere with, conflict with; contravene; jostle; militate against, stultify, antagonize, frustrate, oppose, overcome, overpower, withstand, resist, impede, hinder, repress, restrain; recoil, react.

neutralize, offset, undo, cancel; counterpoise, counterbalance.
Adj. antagonistic, conflicting, reactionary; contrary, etc., 14.
Adv. although, notwithstanding; in spite of; against.

CLASS II

Words Relating To SPACE

I. SPACE IN GENERAL

180. [Indefinite space] **SPACE.**—*N.* space, extension, extent, proportions, expanse, stretch; room, accommodation, capacity; scope, compass, range, latitude, field; sweep, play, swing; spread, expansion.

elbowroom, leeway, seaway, headway; margin; sphere, arena,

open space, free space, void, waste, desert, wild, wilderness; moor, down, downs, upland, moorland; prairie, steppe, llano, campagna.

unlimited space; heavens, ether, infinity; world, wide world.

Adj. spacious, roomy, extensive, extended, expansive, capacious, ample; widespread, vast, world-wide, wide, far-flung, boundless, limitless, endless, infinite; shoreless, trackless, pathless.

Adv. extensively; by and large; everywhere, far and near (*or* wide), here, there, and everywhere; from pole to pole, from the four corners of the earth, from all points of the compass; to the four winds, to the uttermost parts of the earth.

181. [Definite space] **REGION.**—*N.* region, sphere, ground, soil, area, realm, hemisphere, quarter, orb, circuit, circle; pale, etc. (*limit*), 233; tract, clearing; domain.

county, shire, canton, province, department, parish, diocese, township, commune, ward, bailiwick; principality, duchy, palatinate, archduchy, dukedom, dominion, colony, commonwealth, territory, country; fatherland, motherland; kingdom, empire.

precinct, arena, district, beat; patch, plot, inclosure, close, enclave, field, paddock, etc. (*inclosure*), 232; street.

clime, climate, zone, meridian, latitude.

Adj. territorial, provincial, regional, insular; local, parochial.

182. [Limited space] **PLACE.**—*N.* place, spot, whereabouts, point; niche, nook, corner, hole, pigeonhole, etc. (*receptacle*), 191; compartment; premises, courtyard, square, place, piazza, plaza, forum; hamlet, village, etc. (*abode*), 189; pen, etc. (*inclosure*), 232; location, site, locality, situation.

Adv. somewhere, in some place, here and there, in various places.

183. SITUATION.—*N.* situation, position, locality, latitude and longitude; footing, status, standing; standpoint; stage; aspect, attitude, posture, pose.

place, site; station, post, seat, whereabouts; environment, ground; bearings, direction, spot, etc. (*limited space*), 182.

topography, geography; map, plan, chart.

V. be situated, be situate, be located; lie; have its seat in.

Adj. situate, situated; local, topical, topographical.

Adv. hereabouts, thereabouts, whereabouts; in place, here, there.

184. LOCATION.—*N.* location, situation; lodgment; stowage; packing, lading; establishment, settlement, installation; insertion, etc., 300.

anchorage, roadstead, mooring.

settlement, plantation, colony; habitation, etc. (*abode*), 189.

domestication; colonization; naturalization.

V. place, situate, locate, localize, put, lay, set, seat; station, park (as, *an automobile*), lodge, quarter, post, install; house, stow, pack; load, lade; establish, fix, root; graft; plant, etc. (*insert*), 300; deposit, store, store away.

billet on, quarter upon, saddle with.

settle, domesticate, colonize, found, people; take root, strike root; anchor, cast anchor, moor, tether, picket; settle down; take up one's abode, establish *or* locate oneself; keep house; squat, burrow, get a footing; bivouac, encamp, pitch one's tent; inhabit, etc., 186.

Adj. placed; situate, ensconced, imbedded, rooted; moored, at anchor.

185. DISPLACEMENT.—*N.* displacement, misplacement, dislocation, derangement, transposition.

ejection, expulsion, eviction; exile, banishment, ostracism.

removal, etc. (*transference*), 270; transshipment, moving, shift.

V. displace, dislodge, disestablish; misplace, unseat, disturb; set aside, remove, take away, cart away, draft off; exile, etc. (*seclude*), 893.

unload, empty, etc. (*eject*), 297; transfer, etc., 270; dispel.

vacate, depart, evacuate.

Adj. displaced; unplaced, unhoused, unsettled; houseless, homeless, out of place; out of a situation.

186. PRESENCE.—*N.* presence, attendance; occupancy, occupation; ubiquity, omnipresence.

permeation, pervasion; diffusion.

bystander, etc. (*spectator*), 444.

V. be present, make one of; look on, attend, remain; find *or* present oneself; lie, stand.

inhabit, occupy, dwell, reside; stay, sojourn; live, abide; lodge, tenant; people.

frequent, resort to, haunt; revisit.
pervade, permeate; overspread; fill, run through.
Adj. **present;** situate, moored, at anchor; resident, domiciled; ubiquitous, omnipresent.
peopled, inhabited, populous.
Adv. here, there, everywhere; aboard, on board, at home, afield; on the spot; in presence of, before.

187. ABSENCE.—*N.* absence, nonresidence, absenteeism; nonattendance, cut [*colloq.*]; alibi.
emptiness; void, vacuum, vacancy.
interval, hiatus, interruption; interregnum.
truant, absentee.
V. **be absent;** keep away, play truant, absent oneself, stay away, hold aloof.
withdraw, retreat, retire; go away.
Adj. **absent,** not present, away, nonresident, gone, from home; missing; lost; wanting; omitted.
empty, void; vacant, vacuous, blank; untenanted, unoccupied, uninhabited, tenantless; desert, deserted, uninhabitable.
Adv. without, minus, nowhere; elsewhere; in default of; sans.

188. INHABITANT.—*N.* inhabitant; resident, dweller, indweller, addressee, occupier, occupant, householder; inmate; tenant, incumbent; settler, squatter, backwoodsman, planter, habitant, colonist; islander; denizen, citizen; burgher, townsman, burgess; villager; cottager, cotter; boarder, lodger.
native, aborigine, aboriginal.
people, etc. (*mankind*), 372; population; colony, settlement; household.
V. **inhabit,** dwell, etc., 186.
Adj. **indigenous,** native, domestic; domiciled; naturalized; vernacular.

189. HABITATION.—*N.* habitation, abode, dwelling, lodging, domicile, residence, address, berth, housing, quarters, headquarters.
home, fatherland, motherland, country; homestead, hearth, chimney corner; roof, household, housing, native soil, native land.
county, parish, etc. (*region*), 181.
retreat, haunt, habitat, resort; nest, arbor, bower, grotto; lair, den, cave, hole, hiding place, cell, sanctum sanctorum, eyrie, rookery, hive; covert, perch, roost.
anchorage, roadstead, roads; dock, basin, wharf, quay, port, harbor.
camp, bivouac, encampment, cantonment, barracks, quarters; tent, wigwam, tepee; igloo.

farm, farmhouse, grange.

cot, cabin, hut, hovel; shanty, dugout, chalet, log cabin, log house; shack [*colloq*], shed, booth, stall, pen, fold; stable, barn; kennel, sty, cote, dovecote, coop, hutch; cowhouse, cowshed.

house, mansion, place, villa, cottage, hermitage, rotunda, tower, château, castle, pavilion, hotel, court, manor house, hall, palace; kiosk, bungalow, country seat; apartment (*or* brownstone, duplex, frame, shingle, flat, tenement) house; three-decker; building, buildings.

hamlet, village, dorp [Dutch], rancho [Sp. Amer.].

town, borough, city, capital, metropolis; suburb; province, country; county town, county seat.

street, place, terrace, parade, esplanade, boardwalk, embankment, road, row, lane, alley, court, quadrangle, close, yard, passage.

square, polygon, circus, crescent, block, arcade, colonnade, cloister; market place.

assembly room, auditorium, concert hall, armory, gymnasium; cathedral, church, chapel, meetinghouse, etc. (*temple*), 1000; parliament, etc. (*council*), 696.

inn, hotel, tavern, caravansary, alehouse, saloon, club, clubhouse; grill room, chophouse, coffeehouse, eating house; canteen, restaurant, buffet, café, cabaret.

sanatorium, health resort, sanitarium; spa, watering place.

V. inhabit, etc., 186; take up one's abode, etc. (*locate oneself*), 184.

Adj. urban, metropolitan; cosmopolitan; suburban.

provincial, rural, rustic, country, countrified.

190. [Things contained] CONTENTS.—*N.* contents; cargo, lading, freight, shipment, load, bale, burden; cartload, shipload; stuffing.

V. load, lade, ship, pile, fill, stuff.

191. RECEPTACLE.—*N.* receptacle, container; inclosure, etc., 232; recipient, receiver; compartment, cell; hole, corner, niche, recess, nook, crypt; stall; pigeonhole; mouth.

stomach, paunch, belly, crop, craw, maw.

bag, sack, wallet, pocket, pouch; purse; knapsack, haversack, satchel, reticule; saddlebags; portfolio; valise, grip [*colloq.*], suitcase, handbag, schoolbag, brief case, traveling bag, Gladstone bag.

case, chest, box, coffer, caddy, casket; reliquary, shrine; caisson; desk, bureau; trunk, portmanteau, bandbox.

vessel, utensil; vase, canister, jar; basket, pannier, hamper; crate; creel; cradle, bassinet.

For liquids: cistern, reservoir; vat, caldron, barrel, cask, keg, tun, butt, firkin, tub; bottle, jar, decanter, ewer, carafe, canteen, flagon; demijohn; flask, vial, phial; cruet, caster; urn, percolator, coffeepot, teapot, samovar; bucket, pail; pot, tankard, jug, pitcher, mug, porringer; receiver, retort, alembic, crucible; can, kettle; bowl, basin; punch bowl, cup, goblet, beaker, chalice, tumbler, glass.

plate, platter, dish, tray, waiter, salver.

ladle, dipper; shovel, trowel, spatula.

cupboard, closet; locker, bin; buffet, sideboard; drawer, chest of drawers, chiffonier; till, safe; bookcase, cabinet.

chamber, apartment, room, cabin; office, court, hall, suite of rooms, apartment, flat, tenement; parlor, living (*or* sitting, drawing, reception) room; best room [*colloq.*]; boudoir; sanctum; bedroom, dormitory; refectory, dining room; nursery, schoolroom; library, study; studio; smoking room, den.

attic, loft, garret; cellar, vault, hold, cockpit; cubbyhole; basement, kitchen, pantry, scullery; storeroom, lumber room; dairy, laundry; garage; hangar; outhouse, penthouse; lean-to, shed.

portico, porch, stoop, veranda, piazza.

bower, arbor, summerhouse; grotto; conservatory, greenhouse.

II. DIMENSIONS

192. SIZE.—*N.* size, dimensions, proportions; magnitude, bulk, volume; largeness, greatness; expanse, amplitude, mass; capacity; tonnage; cordage; caliber.

lump, block, mass; clod, mountain, mound; heap, etc. (*assemblage*), 72.

corpulence, obesity, plumpness.

immensity, hugeness, monstrosity, enormity.

giant, Titan, Hercules, Gargantua; monster, mammoth, whale, behemoth, leviathan, elephant, jumbo [*colloq.*]; colossus.

V. be large, become large, etc. (*expand*), 194.

Adj. large, big, great, considerable, bulky, voluminous, ample, massive; capacious, comprehensive, spacious; mighty, towering.

stout, corpulent, fat, plump, chubby; portly, burly, brawny, fleshy.

unwieldy, hulky, hulking, lumpish, overgrown; puffy, swollen, bloated.

huge, immense, enormous, titanic, mighty; vast; stupendous; monster, monstrous; gigantic; elephantine, mammoth; giant, colossal, cyclopean, Gargantuan.

193. LITTLENESS.—*N.* littleness, smallness; epitome; microcosm; vanishing point.

dwarf, pygmy, midget; Lilliputian, elf; doll, puppet, manikin; Tom Thumb.

mite, insect, arthropod, ephemerid, ephemera, bug [*pop.*], larva.
atom, monad, animalcule, animalculum (*pl.* animalcula); molecule, microbe, germ, micro-organism, bacterium (*pl.* bacteria), amoeba.

particle, speck, dot, mote; scrap; spark; scintilla; fragment, fraction; grain, powder, dust; minutiæ, etc. (*unimportance*), 643.

V. belittle, lie in a nutshell; become small, decrease; contract, etc., 195.

Adj. little, small, minute, diminutive, microscopic; inconsiderable, petty; limited, cramped; puny, runty, tiny, wee [*colloq.*], elfin, miniature, pocket; undersized, stunted, dwarf, dwarfed, dwarfish, pygmy; Lilliputian; invisible, infinitesimal, homeopathic.

Adv. in a small compass, in a nutshell; on a small scale.

194. EXPANSION.—*N.* expansion, dilation; growth, increase, enlargement, amplification; extension, augmentation, aggrandizement; spread, increment, development, swell, dilatation; obesity, corpulence; dropsy, swelling, distension, puffiness, inflation.

V. enlarge, expand, widen, extend, grow, increase, swell, fill out; dilate, stretch, spread; wax; bud, shoot, sprout, germinate, put forth, open, burst forth; outgrow; overrun.

spread, augment, aggrandize; distend, develop, amplify, spread
out, widen, magnify; inflate, blow up; stuff, fatten, pad, cram,
bloat; exaggerate.

Adj. expanded, larger; swollen, expansive, widespread, overgrown, exaggerated, bloated, fat, tumid, dropsical; corpulent,
obese; puffy, distend, bulbous; full-blown, full-grown; big, etc.,
192.

195. CONTRACTION.—*N.* contraction, reduction, diminution; decrease, etc., 36; lessening, shrinking; atrophy; emaciation,
attenuation.

compression, condensation, constraint, compactness; compendium, abstract, epitome; strangulation; astringency.

V. decrease, lessen, grow less, dwindle, shrink, contract, narrow, shrivel, collapse, wither, fall away, waste, wane, ebb.

diminish, boil down; deflate, exhaust, empty; constrict, condense, compress, squeeze, crush; pinch, tighten, strangle; cramp;
dwarf; shorten, etc., 201; circumscribe, limit, bound, confine.

pare, reduce; attenuate; rub down, scrape, file, grind, chip,
shave, shear.

Adj. contracting, astringent; shrunk, shrunken, contracted;
strangulated; wizened; stunted; waning; compact.

196. DISTANCE.—*N.* distance, remoteness; space, etc., 180;
far cry to; elongation; drift, offing, background; remote region;
reach, span.

outpost, outskirt; horizon, skyline; foreign parts, antipodes.

V. be distant; extend to, stretch to, reach to, spread to, stretch
away to; range, outreach.

Adj. distant, far, far off, far away, remote; telescopic; yon,
yonder; ulterior; transatlantic, transalpine; ultramundane, antipodean; inaccessible, out-of-the-way; unapproachable.

Adv. far off, far away, afar, afar off; away; beyond range, aloof;
wide of, clear of; abroad, yonder, farther, further, beyond; far and
wide, from pole to pole; out of range, out of hearing.

apart, asunder; at arm's length.

197. NEARNESS.—*N.* nearness, proximity, propinquity; vicinity, vicinage, neighborhood, contiguity, etc., 199.

short distance, short cut; earshot, close quarters, range, stone's
throw; gunshot, hair's breadth, span.

purlieus, neighborhood, vicinage, environs, suburbs, confines.
bystander, spectator; neighbor.
approach, approximation, access; convergence, meeting.

V. be near, adjoin, abut, neighbor, trench on; border upon,
verge upon; approximate; stand by, hang about; cling to, clasp,
hug; huddle; hover over.

bring *or* draw near; converge, etc., 290; crowd, pack, huddle.

Adj. near, nigh, close (*or* near) at hand, close, neighboring, bordering upon, contiguous, adjacent, adjoining; proximate, approximate; at hand, handy; intimate.

Adv. near, nigh, hard by, close to, close upon; hard upon; at the point of; next door to; within reach (*or* call, hearing, earshot, range); on the verge of; in sight of; at close quarters; beside, alongside, side by side; in juxtaposition; at the heels of.

about; thereabouts; roughly, in round numbers; approximately, as good as, well-nigh.

198. INTERVAL.—*N.* interval, space; separation, division; hiatus, cæsura; interruption; interregnum; interstice.

parenthesis; void, vacuum; incompleteness, deficiency.

cleft, break, gap, opening; hole, puncture; chasm, mesh, crevice, chink, cranny, crack, slit, fissure, rift, fault, flaw, breach, fracture, rent, gash, cut.

gorge, defile, pass, ravine, canyon, crevasse; abyss, abysm; gulf; inlet, strait; furrow, etc., 259; gully, gulch, notch.

V. gape, yawn; separate, etc., 44.

199. CONTACT.—*N.* contact, contiguity, contiguousness, proximity, apposition, abuttal, abutment, juxtaposition, touching, meeting; conjunction; adhesion, etc., 46.

borderland; frontier, etc. (*limit*), 233.

V. adjoin, join, abut on, neighbor, border, march with; graze, touch, meet; coincide; coexist; adhere, etc., 46.

Adj. contiguous, touching, in contact, conterminous, end to end; close, etc. (*near*), 197.

200. [Linear Dimensions] LENGTH.—*N.* length, longitude, extent, span; mileage.

line, bar, rule, stripe, streak.

lengthening, prolongation, production, protraction; tension, extension.

Measures of length: line, nail, inch, hand, palm, foot, cubit, yard, ell, fathom, rood, pole, furlong, mile, knot, league; chain; meter, kilometer, centimeter, etc. pedometer, odometer, odograph, viameter, log [*naut.*], speedometer, telemeter, scale.

V. be long, stretch out, sprawl; extend to, reach to, stretch to.

lengthen, let out, extend, elongate; stretch; prolong, protract; draw out, spin out.

Adj. long, elongate, lengthy, outstretched, extended; lengthened, interminable.

linear, lineal; longitudinal.

lanky, lank, slab-sided [*slang*], rangy; tall; long-limbed.

Adv. lengthwise, at length, longitudinally, along; tandem; in a line; from end to end, from stem to stern, from head to foot, from top to toe; fore and aft; over all.

201. SHORTNESS.—*N.* shortness, brevity, littleness, etc., 193; a span.

abridgment, shortening, abbreviation, retrenchment, curtailment, epitomization, condensation; reduction, etc. (*contraction*), 195; epitome, etc. (*compendium*), 596.

elision, ellipsis; conciseness, brevity.

V. shorten, curtail, retrench, abridge, abbreviate; take in, reduce; compress, contract; epitomize, abstract, summarize, condense; cut, pare down, clip, dock, lop, prune, shear, shave, mow, crop, stunt; nip, check the growth of, foreshorten [*drawing*].

Adj. short, brief, curt; compendious, compact; stubby, pudgy, squatty; stumpy [*colloq.*], thickset, chunky, scrub, stocky, squat, dumpy; pug, turned up; little, etc., 193; concise, etc., 572; summary.

202. BREADTH, THICKNESS.—*N.* breadth, width, latitude, amplitude.

diameter, bore, caliber; radius.

thickness; corpulence, etc. (*size*), 192; expansion, dilatation.

V. expand, etc., 194; thicken, widen.

Adj. broad, wide, ample, extended, outspread, outstretched.

thick, dumpy, squat, thickset, stubby, etc., 201.

203. NARROWNESS, THINNESS.—*N.* narrowness, slenderness; closeness.

line; hair's breadth.

thinness, tenuity; leanness, lankiness, emaciation.

shaving; strip, etc. (*filament*), 205; thread, skeleton, shadow, scrag, mere skin and bone.

narrowing, tapering; contraction, etc., 195.

V. narrow, taper; contract, etc., 195.

Adj. narrow, close; slender, thin, fine, delicate, threadlike, finespun, taper, slim; scant, scanty, spare; contracted.

lean, emaciated, skinny, scrawny, meager, gaunt, rawboned, lank, lanky, weedy [*colloq.*]; starved, starveling; attenuated, shriveled, pinched, spindle-legged, spindle-shanked, spindling; worn to a shadow; hatchet-faced; lantern-jawed.

204. LAYER.—*N.* layer, stratum, course, bed, coping, substratum, floor, stage, story, tier.

leaf, sheet, flake, scale, coat, peel, membrane, film, slice, shaving, wafer.

stratification, lamination, foliation; scaliness.

V. slice, shave, pare, peel.

plate, coat, veneer; cover, etc., 223.

Adj. scaly, filmy, membranous, flaky, foliated, stratified.

205. FILAMENT.—N. filament, line; fiber, vein, hair, cobweb, capillary, strand, tendril, gossamer.

thread, yarn, packthread, cotton.

string, twine, twist, cord, rope, tape, ribbon, wire.

strip, shred, slip, band, fillet, lath, splinter.

Adj. fibrous, threadlike, wiry, stringy, ropy; capillary, wire-drawn; hairy, etc. (*rough*), 256.

206. HEIGHT.—N. height, altitude, elevation, eminence, pitch; loftiness, sublimity.

tallness, stature; prominence, etc., 250; apex, zenith, culmination.

colossus, etc. (*size*), 192; giant.

height, mount, mountain, hill; headland, foreland, promontory; ridge, dune, rising ground, down, uplands, highlands; knoll, hummock, hillock, mound; bluff, cliff, peak.

tower, pillar, column, obelisk, monument, belfry, steeple, spire, minaret, campanile, turret, dome, cupola; pyramid, pagoda.

pole, pikestaff, Maypole, flagstaff; mast, mainmast, topmast.

high water; high (*or* flood, spring) tide.

V. tower, soar, hover; cap, culminate; overhang, surmount, rise above, command, overtop, rise, ascend.

heighten, uprear, uplift, upraise, elevate.

Adj. high, elevated, eminent, exalted, lofty, sublime; tall, gigantic, big, colossal; towering, beetling, soaring, elevated; higher, superior, upper, supernal; highest, etc. (*topmost*), 210.

lanky, etc. (*thin*), 203.

upland, hilly, mountainous, alpine, heaven-kissing, cloud-capped.

overhanging, impending, incumbent, overlying; superimposed.

Adv. on high, high up, aloft, up, above, overhead; in the clouds.

207. LOWNESS.—N. lowness, levelness, flatness; debasement, prostration; depression, hollow; lowlands.

basement, cellar, vault, crypt, cavern; hold; base, etc., 211.

low water, low (*or* ebb, neap) tide.

V. be low, lie low, underlie; crouch, wallow, grovel; lower, etc. (*depress*), 308.

Adj. low, low-lying, level; flat; crouched, squat, prostrate, depressed, debased.

lower, inferior, under, nether.

lowest, nethermost, lowermost.

Adv. under, beneath, underneath, below, down, downward; underfoot, underground; downstairs, belowstairs; at a low ebb; below par.

208. DEPTH.—N. depth, profundity, depression, hollow.

pit, shaft, well, crater, chasm, crevasse, deep, abyss, bowels of the earth, bottomless pit.

soundings, draft, submersion, plunge, dive; plummet, lead.

V. **deepen,** sink, excavate, mine, sap, dig, burrow.

sound, heave the lead, take soundings.

Adj. **deep,** deep-seated, profound, buried; sunk, submerged, subaqueous, submarine, subterranean, underground.

bottomless, fathomless, unfathomed, unfathomable, abysmal, down-reaching, yawning.

Adv. **out of one's depth,** beyond one's depth; over head and ears.

209. SHALLOWNESS.—*N.* **shallowness,** superficiality; shoals.

Adj. **shallow,** slight, superficial; skin-deep, ankle-deep, knee-deep, shoal.

210. SUMMIT.—*N.* **summit,** top, vertex, apex, zenith, pinnacle, acme, crown; height, pitch, maximum; goal, consummation; climax, turning point; culmination; turn of the tide, fountainhead.

tip, tiptop; crest, crow's-nest, cap, peak; brow, head.

architrave, frieze, cornice, coping, coping stone, capital, headpiece, capstone, pediment, entablature; attic, loft, garret, housetop, upper story, roof (*covering*), 223.

V. **crown,** top, cap, crest, surmount, overtop; culminate.

Adj. **highest** (high, etc., 206), top, topmost, overmost, uppermost, tiptop; capital, head, polar; supreme, supernal.

211. Base.—*N.* **base,** basement; plinth, dado, wainscot; baseboard, mopboard; bedrock, hardpan; foundation, substructure, substratum, ground, earth, pavement, floor, paving; footing, groundwork, basis.

bottom, nadir, foot, sole, toe, hoof, root; keel.

Adj. **bottom,** undermost, nethermost; fundamental; founded on, based on.

212. VERTICALITY.—*N.* **verticality,** perpendicularity, erectness.

cliff, steep, crag, bluff, palisades; wall, precipice.

V. **be vertical,** stand erect *or* upright, stick up, cock up.

render vertical, set up, raise up, erect, rear, raise, pitch.

Adj. **vertical;** upright, erect, perpendicular, plumb, bolt upright.

Adv. **on end;** endwise; at right angles.

213. HORIZONTALITY.—*N.* **horizontality;** flatness; level, plane, stratum.

recumbency; lying down, reclination, proneness, supination, prostration.

V. **be horizontal,** lie, recline, lie flat; sprawl, loll.

render horizontal, lay, level, flatten, even, raze, smooth, align.

prostrate, knock down, floor, fell, ground, cut (*or* hew) down, mow down.

Adj. horizontal, level, even, plane, flush; flat, smooth.

recumbent, prone, supine, prostrate.

Adv. on one's back; on all fours; on its beam ends.

214. PENDENCY.—*N.* pendency, dependency; suspension, hanging.

pendant, drop, eardrop, tassel, lobe; tail, train, queue, pigtail; pendulum.

chandelier, gaselier.

V. be pendent; hang, depend, swing, dangle, lower, droop; flap, trail, beetle, jut, overhang.

suspend, hang, sling, hook up, hitch, fasten to, append.

Adj. pendent, pendulous, hanging; dependent; beetling, jutting over, overhanging; lowering; suspended.

215. SUPPORT.—*N.* support, ground, foundation, base, basis, fulcrum, purchase, footing, hold; stage, platform; rest, resting place; groundwork, substratum; floor.

supporter; aid, etc., 707; prop, truss, stand, stalk; bracket; ledge, shelf, table, trestle; rung, round; staff, stick, crook, crutch.

post, pillar, column, pediment, pedestal; caryatid; buttress, jamb, mullion, stile, abutment.

frame, framework; scaffold, skeleton, beam, rafter, girder, lintel, joist; keystone; arch; mainstay.

seat, throne, dais; divan, ottoman, sofa, davenport, couch, daybed; stall; chair, wing chair, armchair, easy chair, elbowchair, rocking chair, Morris chair; settee, form, bench; saddle, sidesaddle, pillion; packsaddle; pommel, horn.

stool, hassock, footstool.

bed, bedstead, four-poster; pallet; cot; hammock, shakedown; crib, trundle bed, cradle; litter, stretcher; bunk, berth; mat, rug, cushion; lap.

V. support, bear, carry, hold, sustain, shoulder; hold up, back up, bolster up, shore up, uphold, brace, truss, stay, prop; maintain; aid, etc., 707.

Adj. supporting, supported; fundamental.

216. PARALLELISM.—*N.* parallelism, equidistance, concentricity.

V. be parallel, parallel, equal.

Adj. parallel, coextensive, equidistant; collateral, concentric, concurrent; abreast, equal, even, alongside.

Adv. alongside, abreast, broadside on.

217. OBLIQUITY.—*N.* obliquity, inclination, incline, slope, slant; leaning, tilt; bias, diagonal, zigzag, list, twist, sag, cant, lurch; distortion, etc., 243; bend, curve.

acclivity, steepness; rise, ascent, pitch, grade, rising ground, hill, bank; cliff, precipice, etc. (*vertical*), 212; shelving beach; declivity, dip, fall.

V. be oblique; slope, slant, lean, cant, incline, shelve, decline, descend, bend; heel over, careen; sag, slouch, sidle, skid.

render oblique; sway, bias; slope, slant, tilt; incline, bend, crook; distort, etc., 243; zigzag, stagger [*mech.*].

Adj. oblique, inclined; sloping, tilted; askew, asquint, bias, aslant, diagonal, transverse, athwart; indirect, wry, awry, crooked; sinuous, zigzag; knock-kneed, etc. (*distorted*), 243.

uphill, rising, ascending; steep, abrupt, precipitous.

downhill, falling, descending; declining, shelving, declivitous.

Adv. obliquely; on one side, askew, askance, awry, edgewise, at an angle; sidelong, sidewise, slantwise.

218. INVERSION.—*N.* inversion, subversion, reversion; opposition, polarity; contrariety, contradiction, reversal, transposition, transposal; turn of the tide; overturn, revolution; somersault; revulsion.

V. be inverted, turn (*or* go, wheel) about, turn (*or* tilt, topple) over; capsize, turn turtle.

invert, subvert; reverse; upturn, overturn, upset, overset, turn topsy-turvy; transpose.

Adj. inverted, wrong side out (*or* up); inside out, upside down; on one's head, topsy-turvy.

inverse; reverse, etc. (*contrary*), 14; opposite.

Adv. inversely, conversely; heels over head, head over heels.

219. CROSSING.—*N.* crossing; intersection, grade crossing.

network, reticulation; net, web, mesh, netting, lace, plait; sieve, screen; wicker; mat, matting; trellis, lattice, grating, grille, gridiron, tracery, fretwork, filigree; entanglement.

crucifix, cross, rood, crisscross.

V. cross, intersect, interlace, intertwine, intertwist, interweave, interlink, crisscross; twine, entwine, weave, twist, wreathe; dovetail, mortise, splice, link.

plait, pleat, plat, braid; entangle, ravel; net, knot.

Adj. crossed, matted, transverse, intersected, cross; cross-shaped, cruciform; netlike, retiform, latticed, grated, barred, streaked.

Adv. cross, athwart, thwart, transversely; at grade; crosswise, across.

220. EXTERIORITY.—*N.* exteriority; outside, exterior; surface, superficies; skin, covering; face, facet.

V. be exterior, lie around, environ, encircle.

externalize, objectify, visualize, envisage, actualize.

Adj. exterior, external, extraneous; outer, outermost; outward, outlying, outside, outdoor.

outstanding; extrinsic, incidental; superficial, skin-deep.

Adv. externally, out, without, over, outwards, out of doors, in the open air.

221. INTERIORITY.—*N.* interiority; inside, interior; interspace, subsoil.

contents, etc., 190; substance, pith, marrow; heart, bosom, breast; recesses, innermost recesses; cave, etc. (*concavity*), 252.

inmate, intern, inhabitant, etc., 188.

V. inclose, etc. (*circumscribe*), 229; intern; embed, etc. (*insert*), 300; place within, keep within.

Adj. interior, internal; inner, intimate, inside, inward, inmost, innermost; deep-seated, inherent, ingrained, innate, inborn, in-bred, intrinsic.

home, inland, domestic, family, indoor.

Adv. internally; inwards, within, indoors, withindoors; at home.

222. CENTRALITY.—*N.* centrality; centralization, concentration; center; middle, midst; focus; center of gravity.

core, kernel, nucleus; heart, pole, axis, bull's-eye, nave, hub; marrow, pith; metropolis.

V. centralize, concentrate; bring to a focus; converge, etc., 290.

Adj. central; middle, axial, pivotal, nuclear, focal, concentric; middlemost; metropolitan.

223. COVERING.—*N.* covering, cover; canopy, awning, tent, marquee, wigwam, tepee; umbrella, parasol, sunshade; veil; shield, etc. (*defense*), 717.

roof, ceiling, thatch, tiles, slates, leads, shingles; dome, cupola.

coverlet, counterpane, sheet, quilt, blanket, rug; eiderdown quilt, comforter; pillowcase, pillowslip; linoleum, oilcloth; tarpaulin.

integument: skin, pellicle, fleece, fur, leather, lambskin, sable, beaver, ermine, hide, coat, buff, pelt, peltry [*collective noun*]; cuticle, cutis, epidermis; clothing, etc., 225.

peel, rind, crust, bark, husk, shell.

sheath, sheathing, capsule, pod, casing, case, wrapping, wrapper; envelope; cornhusk, corn shuck.

veneer, facing; scale, layer; incrustation, coating, paint, stain, varnish, enamel, whitewash, plaster, stucco.

V. cover, superimpose, overlay, overspread; wrap, incase, face, case, veneer, paper; clapboard, shingle; conceal, etc., 528.

coat, paint, stain, varnish, incrust, crust, cement, stucco, plaster; smear, daub, besmear, bedaub; gild, plate, japan, lacquer, enamel, whitewash.

Adj. covered, hooded, cowled, armored, armor-plated; iron-clad; scaly.

224. LINING.—*N.* lining, coating, inner coating; filling, stuffing, wadding, padding; facing, bushing; sheathing.

V. line, stuff, incrust, wad, pad, fill, face, ceil, bush, wainscot, sheathe.

225. CLOTHING.—*N.* clothing, dress; covering, etc., 223; raiment, costume, attire, toilet, habiliment; vesture, vestment;

garment, garb, wardrobe, apparel, wearing apparel, clothes, finery, etc. (*ornament*), 847.

outfit, equipment, trousseau; uniform, khaki; livery, gear, harness, turnout, accouterment, caparison, suit, trappings.

dishabille, undress, tea gown, wrapper, negligee, dressing gown, kimono; rags, tatters, old clothes.

robe, habit, gown, dress, frock; blouse, middy blouse, waist, shirtwaist; suit; coat; toga, tunic, smock.

dress suit, dress clothes, evening dress, dinner coat, dinner jacket; Tuxedo [*colloq.*]; glad rags [*slang*].

cloak, mantle, shawl, veil; cape, plaid [Scot.], muffler, overcoat, greatcoat; oilskins, slicker, mackintosh, waterproof, ulster; poncho; pea-jacket; sweater, blazer, cardigan, jersey; Mackinaw coat.

jacket, vest, waistcoat; gaberdine.

skirt, petticoat, kilt; bloomers.

trousers, breeches, pants [*colloq.*]; overalls; shorts; tights; drawers; knickers [*colloq.*].

headdress, headgear, coiffure [F.], crush hat, opera hat; tam-o'-shanter, topee [India], sombrero; cap, hat, bonnet, panama, leghorn; derby; nightcap, skullcap; hood, coif; wimple; snood; crown, etc., 247; wig, front, peruke, periwig; turban, fez, tarboosh, shako, busby, bearskin; kepi, helmet; mask, domino.

body clothes, underclothing, linen; shirt, undervest, undershirt; smock, shift, chemise; nightgown, nightshirt, pajamas; bedgown.

tie, neckerchief, neckcloth; ruff, collar, cravat, stock, handkerchief, scarf; bib, tucker; boa; girdle, cummerbund [India].

shoe, Oxford shoe, Oxford tie, pump, sneakers, boot, slipper, moccasin, sandal, galosh, arctic, overshoe, rubber; patten, clog; snowshoes, ski.

stocking, hose, sock; hosiery.

glove, gauntlet; mitten, mitt.

V. clothe, array, dress, accouter, rig, fit out, deck, drape, robe, enrobe, gown, attire, apparel, equip; harness, caparison; cover, wrap, shroud, swathe, swaddle.

wear; don; put on, slip on; mantle.

Adj. clothed, clad, invested, habited.

226. DIVESTMENT.—*N.* divestment; nudity, bareness, nakedness; dishabille, etc., 225.

baldness, hairlessness.

V. divest, uncover, expose, lay open, lay bare, denude, bare, strip; undress, disrobe, dismantle; put off, take off, doff.

peel, bare, slough, excoriate, skin, scalp, flay, bark, husk.

Adj. naked, nude, bare, stark-naked, exposed; undressed, undraped, unclad, ungarmented, unclothed.

bald, hairless, beardless; shaven, clean-shaven.

227. ENVIRONMENT.—*N.* environment, encompassment; surroundings, outskirts, suburbs, purlieus, precincts, environs, entourage, neighborhood, vicinage, vicinity.

V. environ, surround, beset, compass, encompass, inclose, encircle, circle, girdle, hedge, embrace, gird, belt, engird; skirt, hem in; circumscribe, etc., 229; beleaguer, invest, besiege, beset, blockade.

Adj. surrounding, begirt; suburban.

Adv. **around,** about: without; on every side, on all sides.

228. INTERLOCATION.—*N.* **interlocation,** interjacence, interpenetration; interjection, interpolation, interlineation, interspersion, intercalation.

intervention, interference, interposition, intrusion; insinuation; insertion.

intermediary, go-between, interagent, middleman, medium.

partition, diaphragm, midriff; wall, party wall; panel, bulkhead.

V. **intervene,** come between, get between, interpenetrate.

introduce, import; throw in, edge in, run in, work in; interpose, insinuate, interject, interpolate, insert, intersperse, interlard, dovetail, splice, mortise.

interfere, intrude, obtrude; thrust in, etc. (*insert*), 300.

Adj. **intervening,** parenthetical, episodic; intrusive; embosomed.

Adv. **between,** among; amid, amidst; in the thick of; betwixt and between [*colloq.*]; parenthetically.

229. CIRCUMSCRIPTION.—*N.* **circumscription,** limitation, inclosure; confinement, etc. (*restraint*), 751; envelope, case.

V. **circumscribe,** limit, bound, confine, inclose; surround, etc., 227; hedge in, rail in, fence round, hedge round; picket; corral; imprison, restrain.

enfold, bury, incase, enshrine, enclasp; clothe, 225; embosom.

Adj. **circumscribed,** begirt, girt; lapped; buried in, immersed in; embosomed, imbedded, mewed up; imprisoned, etc., 751; landlocked.

230. OUTLINE.—*N.* **outline,** circumference; perimeter, periphery; circuit, lines, contour, profile, silhouette, lineaments, relief, bounds; coast line, horizon.

zone, belt, girdle; girth; band; baldric, zodiac; tire, pale, etc. (*inclosure*), 232; circlet, etc., 247.

V. **outline,** delineate, silhouette, block, sketch, circumscribe, etc., 229.

231. EDGE.—*N.* **edge,** verge, brink, brow, brim, margin, border, confine, skirt, rim, side; lip.

threshold, door, porch; portal. etc. (*opening*), 260.

shore, coast, strand, bank; quay, wharf, dock, mole, landing.

fringe, flounce, frill, furbelow; valance; trimming, edging, skirting, hem, selvage, welt; frame.

V. **edge,** coast, border, skirt; fringe, flounce, hem.

232. INCLOSURE.—*N.* **inclosure,** envelope; case, etc. (*receptacle*), 191; wrapper; girdle, etc., 230.

pen, fold; sty, paddock, pasture; pound; corral, yard; net, seine.

fence, pale, paling, balustrade, rail, railing, wall; hedge, hedgerow.

barrier, barricade, cordon, stockade; gate, gateway; weir; door, hatch, prison, etc., 752.

dike, ditch, trench, drain, moat.

V. **inclose**, circumscribe, etc., 229.

233. LIMIT.—*N.* limit, boundary, bounds, pale, confine, term, bourn, verge; termination, terminus, terminal; stint; frontier, border, marches.

boundary line, landmark; turning point.

V. **limit**, bound, compass, confine, define, circumscribe.

Adj. **definite**; terminal; frontier, bordering, border, boundary.

Adv. **thus far**, thus far and no further.

234. FRONT.—*N.* front, foreground, forefront; face, frontage, façade, proscenium, frontispiece; priority; obverse (*of a medal*).

van, vanguard, advanced guard; front rank; outpost; first line; scout.

brow, forehead; visage, physiognomy, features, countenance; bow, stem, prow; jib; bowsprit.

pioneer, etc. (*precursor*), 64.

V. **front**, face, confront, brave, dare, defy, oppose; breast; come to the front *or* fore.

Adj. **fore**, foremost, headmost; forward, anterior, front, frontal.

Adv. **before**, in front, in the van, in advance; ahead; in the foreground.

235. REAR.—*N.* rear, back; rear rank, rearguard; background, hinterland.

tail, scut (*as of a hare*), brush (*of a fox*).

afterpart; stern, poop; postern door; tailpiece, crupper.

wake; train, retinue, suite, cortege.

reverse; other side of the shield.

V. **be behind**; fall astern; bring up the rear; heel, tag, shadow, follow, pursue.

Adj. **back**, rear, hindmost; posterior; after.

Adv. **behind**, in the rear *or* background; at the heels of; after, aft, abaft, astern, rearward, backward.

236. SIDE.—*N.* side, flank, quarter, lee; wing; profile; gable, gable end; broadside.

points of the compass; East, sunrise, Orient, Levant; West, Occident, sunset.

V. **flank**, skirt, outflank; sidle; border; be on one side.

Adj. **lateral**, sidelong; collateral; flanking, skirting.

eastern, eastward, east, Orient, Oriental, auroral, Levantine. **western**, west, westerly, westward, Occidental.

Adv. **sidewise**, sidelong, sideling, broadside on; abreast, alongside, beside; aside; by, by the side of; side by side; to windward, to leeward; laterally; right and left.

237. OPPOSITE.—*N.* opposite, opposite side, reverse, inverse; counterpart, antithesis; opposition, polarity; inversion, etc., 218.

antipodes, opposite poles; North and South.

Adj. opposite, reverse, converse; antipodal, diametrical, antithetic, counter; fronting, facing.

northern, north, northerly, northward, hyperborean, boreal, polar, arctic.

southern, south, southerly, southward, austral, antarctic.

Adv. over, over the way, over against; against; face to face, vis-à-vis [F.].

238. RIGHT.—*N.* right, right hand; offside, starboard.

Adj. dextral, dexterous, right-handed, dexter.

ambidexter, ambidextrous.

239. LEFT.—*N.* left, left hand, south paw [*slang*]; near side; larboard, port.

Adj. left-handed, sinistral.

III. FORM

240. FORM.—*N.* form, figure, shape, make, formation, frame, construction, cut, build, contour, outline, stamp, type, cast, mold, fashion; structure, etc., 329; sculpture, architecture.

feature, lineament, turn; phase, etc. (*aspect*), 448; posture, attitude, pose.

V. form, shape, figure, fashion, carve, cut, chisel, hew, cast; roughhew, sketch, block out; trim, model, knead, mold, sculpture; cast, stamp; build, etc. (*construct*), 161.

Adj. structural; plastic, formative, impressible; creative.

shapely, well proportioned, symmetrical, well made, well formed, trim, neat.

241. ABSENCE OF FORM.—*N.* formlessness, shapelessness, misproportion, uncouthness; rough diamond; disorder, etc., 59; deformity, etc., 243; disfigurement, defacement; mutilation.

V. deface, disfigure, deform, mutilate, derange, etc., 61; blemish, mar.

Adj. formless, shapeless, amorphous, unshapely, misshapen, unsymmetrical, malformed, unformed; anomalous.

rough, rude, barbarous, rugged, scraggy; in the rough.

242. [Regularity of form] SYMMETRY.—*N.* symmetry, shapeliness, finish; beauty, etc., 845; proportion, eurythmics, uniformity, parallelism; centrality; radiation; branching, ramification; regularity, evenness.

Adj. symmetrical, shapely, well set, finished; beautiful, etc., 845; classic, chaste, severe.

regular, uniform, balanced; equal, even, parallel.

243. [Irregularity of form] **DISTORTION.**—*N.* distortion, contortion; knot, warp, buckle, screw, twist; crookedness, obliquity; grimace, deformity, malformation; monstrosity, misproportion, ugliness, disfigurement.

V. distort, contort, twist, warp, buckle, screw, wrench, wrest, writhe, deform, misshape.

Adj. distorted, out of shape, irregular, unsymmetric, awry, wry, askew, crooked, gnarled; not true, not straight; deformed; misshapen, misproportioned, ill-proportioned; ill-made; humpbacked, hunchbacked; bandy-legged, bow-legged; knock-kneed.

244. ANGULARITY.—*N.* angularity, bifurcation; fold, etc., 258; notch, etc., 257; fork, crotch, angle, bend, elbow, knee, knuckle; zigzag; right angle, acute angle, obtuse angle; obliquity, etc., 217.

corner, nook, recess, niche.

triangle; rectangle, square; lozenge, diamond; rhomb, rhombus, rhomboid; quadrangle, quadrilateral; parallelogram; polygon, pentagon, hexagon, heptagon, octagon, oxygon, decagon; cube, prism, pyramid.

V. fork, branch, ramify, bifurcate, bend hook.

Adj. angular, bent, crooked, aquiline, jagged, serrated; forked, bifurcate, crotched, zigzag, hooked; akimbo; oblique, etc., 217.

245. CURVATURE.—*N.* curvature, curvedness, incurvature, bend; flexure, crook, hook, bending; deflection, turn; deviation, detour; sweep; curl; sinuosity, etc., 248.

curve, arc, arch, arcade, vault, bow, cresent, half-moon, horseshoe, loop, festoon; parabola, hyperbola; tracery.

V. be curved, sweep, sag; deviate, etc., 279; turn; re-enter.

render curved, bend, curve, deflect, inflect; crook; turn, round, arch, arch over, bow, coil, curl, recurve.

Adj. curved, curvate, devious; recurved, arched, vaulted; oblique, etc., 217; circular, etc., 247; bell-shaped; bow-shaped, embowed; crescent, crescent-shaped, horned; heart-shaped, cordate; hook-shaped, hooked, hooklike; moon-shaped, lunar, sickle-shaped.

246. STRAIGHTNESS.—*N.* straightness, directness; inflexibility; straight (*or* bee, right, direct) line; short cut.

V. be straight, have no turning, go straight, steer for.

render straight, straighten, rectify; set *or* put straight; unbend, unfold, uncurl, uncoil, unravel.

Adj. straight, rectilinear; direct, even, right, true, in a line; undeviating, unswerving, straight as an arrow; inflexible.

perpendicular, plumb, vertical, upright, erect.

247. [Simple circularity] CIRCULARITY.—*N.* circularity, roundness; rotundity, etc., 249.

circle, circlet, ring, hoop; bracelet, armlet; loop, wheel, cycle, orb, orbit, disk, circuit, zone, belt, cordon, band; hub, nave; sash, girdle, cestus, cincture, baldric, wreath, garland; crown, coronet, chaplet, snood, fillet; necklace, collar; noose, lasso.

ellipse, oval; ellipsoid, cycloid.

V. round; ring, encircle, etc., 227.

Adj. round, rounded, circular, oval, elliptic, elliptical, egg-shaped.

248. [Complex circularity] CONVOLUTION.—*N.* convolution, involution, winding, wave, undulation, sinuosity, sinuousness, meandering, twist, twirl; contortion.

coil, roll, curl, spiral, corkscrew, worm, tendril, scallop, kink; serpent, snake, eel; maze, labyrinth.

V. wind, twine, twirl, wreathe, entwine; wave, undulate, meander; twist, coil, roll; wrinkle; curl, friz, indent, scallop; wring, contort.

Adj. winding, twisted, convoluted; circling, snaky, serpentine, sinuous, undulating, undulated, wavy.

involved, intricate, mazy, tortuous, labyrinthine; circuitous, kinky, curly.

spiral, coiled, screw-shaped.

Adv. in and out, round and round.

249. ROTUNDITY.—*N.* rotundity, roundness, sphericity, globularity.

cylinder, barrel, drum; roll, roller, rolling pin, column.

sphere, globe, ball, spheroid, globule; bulb, bullet, pellet, pill, marble, pea, knob.

V. sphere, form into a sphere, roll into a ball, give rotundity, round.

Adj. rotund; round, etc. (*circular*), 247; cylindrical, conical, spherical, globular, bulbous; egg-shaped, ovoid, ovate; bell-shaped, etc., 245.

250. CONVEXITY.—*N.* convexity, prominence, projection, swelling, swell, bulge, protuberance, protrusion, excrescency.

excrescence, hump; bow; clump, bunch; bulb, bump, knob; knot; boss; tooth, peg; ridge, rib, snag; peak, etc. (*sharpness*), 253; growth, tumor; pimple, wart, wen; fungus, blister; nipple, teat, dug, breast.

proboscis, nose, beak, snout, nozzle.

belly, paunch; abdomen.

arch, cupola, dome, vault.

relief, cameo; low relief, bas-relief, high relief.

point of land, hill, mount, mountain; cape, promontory; fore-land, headland; hummock, ledge, spur.

V. project, bulge, protrude; bag, belly, pout, bunch; jut out, stand out, stick out, stick up; hang over, beetle.

raise, etc., 307; emboss.

Adj. prominent, protuberant, projecting; bossed, bossy, con-vex, bunchy, hummocky, bulbous; bloated, swollen, distended; bowed, arched; bold; bellied; gibbous; club-shaped, knobby, gnarled; salient, in relief, raised.

251. FLATNESS.—*N.* flatness; smoothness.

plane; level, plain, tableland, plateau; stratum; plate, table, tablet, slab.

V. flatten; level, etc., 213; fell.

Adj. flat, plane, even, smooth; flush; level, horizontal; recum-bent, supine, prostrate.

Adv. flat, flatwise, lengthwise, horizontally.

252. CONCAVITY.—*N.* concavity, depression, dip; hollow, hollowness; indentation, intaglio, cavity, dent, dint, dimple; honeycomb.

excavation, pit, sap, mine, shaft; caisson; trough, etc. (*furrow*), 259; bay, etc. (*of the sea*), 343.

cup, basin, crater; punch bowl; cell, etc.(*receptacle*), 191; socket.

valley, vale, dale, dell, dingle, glen.

cave, cavern, cove; grot, grotto; hole, burrow, kennel, tunnel; gully, etc., 198.

excavator, sapper, miner.

V. render concave; depress, hollow, gouge; stave in; scoop, scoop out; dig, delve, excavate, dent, dint, perforate; mine, sap, undermine, burrow, tunnel.

Adj. concave, hollow; funnel-shaped; retreating; cavernous; porous, perforated; honeycombed.

253. SHARPNESS.—*N.* sharpness, acuteness; saliency.

point, spike, spine, spit, needle, pin; prick, barb; spur; horn, antler; snag; tag; thorn, bristle; tooth, tusk; tine.

beard, porcupine, hedgehog, brier, bramble, thistle, bur; curry-comb, comb.

peak, crag, crest, cone, sugar loaf; spire, pyramid, steeple.

cutting edge, knife edge, blade, edge tool, cutlery, knife, pen-knife, razor; scalpel, lancet; plowshare, colter; hatchet, ax, pick, cleaver, scythe, sickle, scissors, shears; sword, etc. (*arms*), 727; bodkin, etc. (*perforator*), 262.

sharpener; hone, strop; grindstone, whetstone, steel, emery, carborundum.

V. be sharp; taper to a point; bristle with; cut, etc., 44.

sharpen, whet, point, barb, set, strop, grind.

Adj. **sharp,** keen; acute, pointed; tapering; spiked, spiky, studded, peaked, salient; prickly, spiny, thorny, bristling, barbed, spurred, bearded, thistly, briery; craggy, jagged, snaggy; cone-shaped, conical.

keen-edged, cutting; sharp-edged, knife-edged; sharpened.

254. BLUNTNESS.—*N.* **bluntness,** dullness.

V. **be** *or* **render blunt,** dull; take off the point *or* edge; blunt, turn.

Adj. **blunt,** dull, dullish, obtuse, pointless, unpointed; unsharpened.

255. SMOOTHNESS.—*N.* **smoothness;** polish, gloss; lubrication.

smoother; roller, steam roller; sandpaper, emery paper; flat-iron, sadiron; burnisher.

V. **smooth;** plane; file; mow, shave; level, roll; macadamize; polish, burnish, sleek, iron, press, mangle; lubricate, oil, grease, wax, anoint.

Adj. **smooth;** polished; even; sleek, glossy, silken, silky; velvety; slippery, glassy, oily.

256. ROUGHNESS.—*N.* **roughness,** asperity; corrugation.

hair, mat, thatch, mop; scalp lock; tress, lock, curl, ringlet; shag; mane; eyelashes, lashes; beard, whiskers; mustache; imperial, goatee; fringe; hair shirt.

plumage; plume, crest; feather, tuft.

nap, pile, grain, texture.

V. **roughen,** rough, rough up, crinkle, ruffle, crumple, rumple; corrugate; stroke the wrong way, rub the fur the wrong way.

Adj. **rough,** uneven; rugged, jagged; cross-grained, gnarled, gnarly, knotted, scraggly, scraggy; craggy, cragged; unkempt, unpolished, roughhewn; prickly, etc. (*sharp*), 253.

hairy, bristly, hirsute, tufted, bushy; nappy, bearded, shaggy.

Adv. **against the grain;** in the rough; on edge.

257. NOTCH.—*N.* **notch,** dent, nick, cut, indent, indentation; embrasure, battlement.

saw, tooth, scallop; jag.

V. **notch,** nick, mill, score, cut, dent, indent, jag, scarify, scallop.

Adj. **notched,** dentate, toothed, serrate *or* serrated.

258. FOLD.—*N.* **fold,** crease, flexure, pleat, plait, tuck, gather; joint, elbow, double; wrinkle, pucker, crow's-feet; crinkle, crumple; dog's-ear; ruffle, flounce; corrugation.

V. **fold,** double, pleat, plait, crease, wrinkle, cocker, crinkle, curl, shrivel, rumple, corrugate, ruffle, crumple, pucker; dog's-ear, tuck, ruck, hem, gather.

259. **FURROW.**—*N.* furrow, groove, rut, scratch, streak, crack, score, incision, slit.

trench, ditch, dike, moat, trough, channel, gutter, ravine, etc., 198; depression.

V. furrow, flute, groove, carve, corrugate, cut, chisel, plow; incise, engrave, etch, grave.

Adj. furrowed, ribbed, striated, fluted, corduroy.

260. **OPENING.**—*N.* opening, aperture, yawning; chasm, etc., 198.

outlet, inlet; pore; vent, venthole, blowhole, airhole; orifice, mouth, sucker, muzzle, throat, gullet, nozzle.

window, casement, lattice; embrasure; light; skylight, fanlight; bay window, bow window, oriel, dormer.

portal, porch, gate, postern, wicket, trapdoor, hatch, door; cellarway, driveway, gateway, doorway, hatchway, gangway.

way, path, etc., 627; thoroughfare; channel, gully; passage, passageway.

alley, lane, mall, aisle, glade, vista.

tube, pipe, main; water pipe, etc., 350; air pipe, etc., 351; vessel, canal, gut, fistula; smokestack, chimney, flue; bore, caliber.

tunnel, mine, pit, shaft; gallery.

hole, puncture, perforation; pinhole, loophole, peephole, eye, eyelet; slot.

sieve, strainer, colander, riddle, screen.

opener, key, master key; open-sesame.

V. open, gape, yawn, fly open.

perforate, pierce, tap, bore, drill; transpierce, transfix; enfilade, impale, spike, spear, gore, spit, stab, pink, puncture, lance; stick, prick, riddle.

uncover, unclose; punch, stave in; mine, etc. (*scoop out*), 252.

Adj. open; perforated, wide-open, agape, ajar, unclosed; gaping, yawning; patent.

tubular; pervious, permeable; porous, honeycombed.

261. **CLOSURE.**—*N.* closure, blockade, shutting up, sealing, obstruction; contraction, constipation; impermeability; blind alley; cul-de-sac [F.].

V. close, plug, block up, stop up, fill up, cork up, button up, stuff up, dam up; blockade; obstruct, bar, bolt, stop, seal; choke, throttle; ram down, dam, cram; clinch; shut, slam, snap.

Adj. closed, shut, unopened; unpierced, impervious, impermeable; impenetrable; impassable, pathless, wayless; untrodden.

tight, unventilated, airtight, watertight, hermetically sealed; snug.

262. **PERFORATOR.**—*N.* perforator, piercer, borer, auger,

chisel, gimlet, drill, awl, scoop, corkscrew, dibble, trepan, lancet, probe, bodkin, needle, stiletto; punch, gouge; spear, etc. (*weapon*), 727; puncher; punching machine, punching press.

263. STOPPER.—*N.* stopper, stopple; plug, cork, bung, spike, spill, stopcock, tap, faucet; valve, spigot; rammer; ram, ramrod; piston; stopgap; wadding, stuffing, padding, sponge [*surg.*], tourniquet.

doorkeeper, gatekeeper, janitor, concierge [F.], porter, warder, beadle, usher, guard, sentinel; watchdog.

IV. MOTION

264. MOTION.—*N.* motion, movement; move; mobility, movableness, motive power; mobilization.

stream, flow, flux, run, course, stir.

rate, pace, tread, footfall, step, stride, gait; velocity, clip [*colloq.*]; progress, locomotion.

journey, etc., 266; voyage, sail, cruise, passage; transit, etc., 270. unrest, restlessness, etc., 149.

V. move, go, hie, budge, stir, pass, flit; hover around *or* about; shift, slide, glide, roll, flow, stream, run, drift, sweep along; wander, etc. (*deviate*), 279; walk, etc., 266.

put in motion, set in motion; impel, etc., 276; propel, etc., 284; mobilize.

Adj. moving, in motion, traveling; transitional, shifting, movable, mobile, motive, motor; mercurial; restless, etc. (*changeable*), 149; nomadic, etc., 266; erratic, etc., 279; evolutionary.

Adv. under way; on the move (*or* wing, fly, tramp, march).

265. REST.—*N.* rest; stillness, quiescence; stagnation, stagnancy, fixity, immobility, catalepsy; quietism.

quiet, tranquility, calm; repose, relaxation; dead calm; silence, peace, hush; sleep, etc. (*inactivity*), 683.

pause, lull, etc. (*cessation*), 142; stand, standstill; deadlock, dead stand; full stop; embargo.

resting place; bivouac; home, abode; bed, etc. (*support*), 215; haven, etc. (*refuge*), 666; goal, destination, bourn.

V. be still, stand still, stand fast, stand firm, lie still, keep quiet, repose, rest; vegetate, stagnate.

remain, stay; stand, tarry, mark time; pull up, draw up; hold, halt, stop, discontinue, stop short, pause; bring to, heave to, lay to; anchor, cast anchor, come to anchor, ride at anchor, lie to; rest on one's laurels, take breath.

dwell, etc., 186; settle, settle down; alight, dismount, arrive.

quell, becalm, hush, calm, still, tranquilize, stay, lull to sleep, lay an embargo on.

Adj. quiescent, still; silent, hushed, quiet; motionless, moveless; fixed; stationary; at rest, at a stand, at a standstill, at anchor; stock-still; sedentary, untraveled, stay-at-home; becalmed, stagnant, quiet; unmoved, calm, restful; immovable, stable; sleeping, etc. (*inactive*), 683.

266. [Locomotion by land] **JOURNEY.**—*N.* travel, traveling, wayfaring; campaigning.

excursion, journey, expedition, tour, trip, circuit, pilgrimage, march, walk, promenade, constitutional [*colloq.*], stroll, saunter, ramble, hike [*colloq.*], tramp, turn, stalk, perambulation; outing, ride, drive, airing, jaunt.

riding, equitation, horsemanship.

roving, vagrancy, nomadism; vagabondism, hoboism; migration; emigration, immigration. *Wanderlust*, [Ger.].

itinerary, route, guide; handbook; roadbook; Baedeker.

procession, parade, cavalcade, caravan, file, cortege, column.

vehicle, etc., 272.

traveler, etc., 268.

station, stop, stopping place, terminal, terminus, depot, railway station.

V. travel, journey, flit, take wing; migrate, emigrate, immigrate; trek; tour, peregrinate.

motor, bicycle, cycle [*colloq.*], spin, speed; trolley [*colloq.*].

motorize, electrify.

wander, roam, range, prowl, rove, jaunt, ramble, stroll, saunter, perambulate, meander, straggle; gad, gad about.

take horse, ride, drive, trot, amble, canter, gallop, prance, frisk, caracole.

walk, march, step, tread, pace; plod, trudge, wend; promenade; track; hike [*colloq.*], tramp; stalk, stride; strut, bowl along, toddle; paddle; peg on, jog on, shuffle on.

glide, slide, coast, skim, skate.

file off, march in procession, defile.

go to, repair to, resort to, hie to, betake oneself to.

Adj. traveling, journeying; itinerant, peripatetic, roving, rambling, vagrant, migratory, nomadic.

self-moving, automobile, automotive, locomotive.

wayfaring, wayworn; travel-stained.

267. [Locomotion by water or air] **NAVIGATION.**—*N.* voyage, cruise, sail, passage, aquatics; boating, yachting, cruising; ship, etc., 273.

headway, sternway, leeway; fairway.

oar, scull, sweep, pole; paddle, screw, propeller, turbine; sail, canvas.

aeronautics, aerial navigation, balloonery; balloon, etc., 273; ballooning; aviation, airmanship; flying, flight, volplaning, planing [*colloq.*], hydroplaning, volplane, glide, dive, nose-dive, spin, looping the loop; wing; pinion, aileron.

mariner, etc., 269; aviator, etc., 269*a*.

V. sail; embark, etc., 293; spread sail, gather way, make sail, carry sail; ride the waves, ride out the storm.

navigate, scud, boom, drift, course, cruise, steam; coast, hug the shore.

row, paddle, pull, scull, punt.

float, swim, skim, dive, wade.

Aeronautics: fly, soar, drift, hover, aviate; volplane, plane [*colloq.*], glide, dive, fly over, nose-dive, spin, loop the loop, land; take wing, take a flight.

Adj. nautical, maritime, naval; seafaring, seagoing; coasting; afloat; navigable.

aeronautic, aeronautical, aerial.

aquatic, natatory, natatorial.

Adv. under way (*or* sail, canvas, steam), in motion, in progress, on the wing; afloat.

268. TRAVELER.—*N.* traveler, wayfarer, voyager, passenger; commuter, straphanger [*colloq.*].

tourist, excursionist, globe-trotter [*colloq.*]; explorer, adventurer, mountaineer; wanderer, rover, straggler, rambler; landsman, landlubber, vagrant, loafer, tramp, hobo, vagabond, Bohemian, gypsy, nomad, Arab; pilgrim, palmer; immigrant; emigrant.

fugitive, refugee; runaway; renegade.

courier, messenger, runner; Mercury.

pedestrian, walker, foot passenger, hiker [*colloq.*], tramper.

rider, horseman, equestrian, cavalier; jockey, trainer, breaker, roughrider; huntsman, whip; postilion, postboy.

driver, coachman, charioteer, carter, wagoner, drayman, truckman; cabman, cab driver.

Railroad: engineer; fireman, stoker; conductor, motorman.

Automobile: driver, chauffeur, automobilist, motorist.

269. MARINER.—*N.* mariner, navigator; sailor, seaman, seafarer, seafaring man, sea dog [*colloq.*]; tar, bluejacket, gob [*slang*]; marine; midshipman, middy [*colloq.*]; able seaman, hand; crew; captain, commander, master mariner, skipper; mate, boatswain; boatman, ferryman, waterman, lighterman, longshoreman; gondolier; oar, oarsman, rower.

steersman, coxswain, cox [*colloq.*], helmsman, pilot.

269a. **AERONAUT.**—*N.* aeronaut, aviator, airman, flier, aviatress *or* aviatrix, pilot, observer, spotter [*mil. cant*], scout, bomber, ace; balloonist.

270. **TRANSFERENCE.**—*N.* **transfer,** transference; removal; deportation, extradition; conveyance, carriage; contagion, infection; transfusion; transfer, etc. (*of property*), 783.

transit, transition; passage, ferry; portage, carry; carting, cartage; shipment, freight; transmission, transport, transportation; translation; transposition, transposal.

deposit, moraine, drift, alluvium.

gift, bequest, legacy, deed, lease; quitclaim.

freight, cargo, mail, baggage, luggage, goods.

V. **transfer,** transmit, transport, transplant, transfuse; convey, carry, bear; hand, pass, forward; shift; bring, fetch, reach; conduct, convoy.

send, delegate, consign, relegate, deliver; ship, freight, embark; transpose; drag, etc., 285; mail, post.

Adj. **transferable,** assignable, negotiable, transmissible, movable, portable; contagious, infectious.

271. **CARRIER.**—*N.* **carrier,** porter, redcap, bearer, freighter, expressman; stevedore; coolie; conductor, chauffeur, truck driver; letter carrier, postman; pigeon post, carrier pigeon.

beast of burden, beast, cattle, horse, steed; charger, war horse; hunter; race horse, racer, courser; Arab, barb; blood horse, thoroughbred; palfrey, cob; nag, jade, hack; pack (*or* draft, cart, dray) horse; mare, filly, colt, foal.

pony, Shetland; broncho, cow pony, mustang.

ass, donkey, jackass, burro; mule.

reindeer; camel, dromedary, llama, elephant.

vehicle, etc., 272; ship, etc., 273.

Adj. equine, asinine; electric, motor, express.

272. **VEHICLE.**—*N.* **vehicle,** conveyance, carriage, caravan, car, van.

wagon, dray, cart, lorry, truck.

tumbrel, barrow, wheelbarrow, handbarrow; dump cart; baby carriage, gocart, perambulator; wheel chair; police van, patrol wagon, Black Maria [*colloq.*]; Conestoga wagon, prairie schooner; jinrikisha, ricksha [*colloq.*].

equipage, coach, chariot, phaeton, wagonette, break, drag, landau, barouche, victoria, brougham; sulky, runabout.

post chaise, mail stage, diligence, stage, stagecoach; horsecar, omnibus, bus [*colloq.*]; cab, hansom, four-wheeler, hack; dogcart, trap [*colloq.*], buggy, chaise. team, pair, span, tandem, four-in-hand.

litter, palanquin, sedan; stretcher, hurdle; ambulance.

sled, bob, bobsled; toboggan; sledge, sleigh; ski, snowshoes, skates, roller skates.

cycle, bicycle, tricycle, tandem; machine [*colloq.*], wheel [*colloq.*], motorcycle; velocipede, hobbyhorse.

automobile, motorcar, limousine, sedan, touring car, roadster, coupé, motor [*colloq.*], machine [*colloq.*], car, auto [*colloq.*], autocar, runabout; truck, tractor; taxicab, taxi [colloq.], motorbus; flivver [slang], jitney [colloq.].

Allied automobile terms: tonneau, chassis, hood, top, ignition, spark plug, generator, distributor, magneto, self-starter, gear, gear box, differential, cylinder, manifold, intake, exhaust, carburetor, ammeter, speedometer, oil gauge, primer, clutch, universal joint, crank shaft, transmission, tire, rim; gasoline; trailer; garage; chauffeur, etc., 268.

train; express, mail; car, coach; baggage car; rolling stock; trolley, electric car, electric [colloq.].

Adj. vehicular; traveling, etc., 266.

273. SHIP.—*N.* ship, vessel, boat, sail; craft, bottom.

navy, marine, fleet, flotilla.

shipping, man-of-war, etc., 726; merchant ship, merchantman; packet, liner; whaler; slaver; collier; coaster, freight steamer, freighter, lighter; trawler, fishing boat; pilot boat; yacht.

ship, sailing vessel, clipper ship, windjammer [colloq.], bark; brig, brigantine, schooner; fore-and-after [colloq.]; sloop, cutter, revenue cutter, yawl, ketch, smack, lugger, barge, scow, cat, catboat.

steamer, steamboat, steamship; tug.

boat, rowboat; shallop, skiff, pinnace; launch; lifeboat, longboat, jolly boat, gig, cockboat, tender, cockleshell; dory, canoe, dugout, dinghy, punt, outrigger; float, raft, iceboat.

coracle, gondola, galley, argosy, galleon; junk, sampan [both Chinese]; dhow [Arab.]; trireme; derelict.

Aeronautics: aircraft; balloon, airship, dirigible, zeppelin, air-plane, monoplane, biplane, triplane; air cruiser, flying boat, hydroplane; kite, parachute.

Allied aeronautical terms: fuselage, gondola, wings, controls, aileron, lifting power, rudder; tail, hangar.

Adj. marine, maritime, naval, nautical, seafaring, ocean-going; seaworthy.

aeronautic, aerial; airworthy.

Adv. afloat, aboard; on board, on shipboard.

274. VELOCITY.—*N.* velocity, speed, celerity, swiftness, rapidity; expedition, etc. (*activity*), 682; acceleration; haste, etc., 684.

spurt, sprint, rush, dash, race, steeplechase; round pace; flight.

pace, gallop, canter, trot, round trot, run, hand gallop.

V. speed, hie, hasten, spurt, sprint, scamper, scuttle, trip, post; scud, scurry, whiz; run, dart, swoop, fly, race, shoot, tear, whisk, sweep, skim, scorch [colloq.], rush, dash; bolt, run away; ride hard; hurry, hasten, haste; accelerate, quicken; carry sail, crowd sail.

Adj. fast, speedy, swift, rapid, quick, fleet; nimble, agile, expeditious; express; active, brisk, light-footed, nimble-footed; winged.

Adv. apace; at full speed, full gallop; posthaste; in double-quick time; whip and spur; by leaps and bounds; in high (gear *or* speed) [*automobiling*].

275. SLOWNESS.—*N.* slowness, tardiness; languor, etc. (*inactivity*), 683; drawl.

jog trot, dogtrot; amble, rack, pace, single-foot, walk; mincing steps; dead march, slow march.

retardation; slackening; delay, etc. (*lateness*), 133.

slow goer, slowpoke [*colloq.*]; loiterer, sluggard, dawdler; tortoise, snail.

V. move slowly; creep, crawl, lag, walk, linger, loiter, saunter; plod, trudge, lumber; trail, drag; dawdle, etc., 683; worm one's way, inch, inch along, jog on, toddle, waddle, slouch, shuffle, halt, hobble, limp, shamble; flag, falter, totter, stagger; mince, take one's time.

retard, relax, slacken, check, moderate, rein in, curb; reef, shorten *or* take in sail; brake, slacken speed, backwater, back pedal.

Adj. slow, slack; tardy; dilatory, etc. (*inactive*), 683; leisurely; deliberate, gradual; languid, sluggish, apathetic, phlegmatic, lymphatic; moderate.

dull, slow [*colloq.*], prosaic, boring, wearisome, uninteresting, humdrum.

Adv. at half speed, in slow time; with clipped wings; in low (gear *or* speed) [*automobiling*].

gradually, by degrees, step by step, bit by bit.

276. [Motion conjoined with force] IMPULSE.—*N.* impulse, impetus; momentum; push, thrust, shove, boom, boost, explosion, etc. (*violence*), 173; propulsion, etc., 284.

clash, collision, encounter, shock, brunt, crash, bump; impact; charge, onset; percussion, concussion.

blow, stroke, knock, tap, rap, slap, smack, pat, dab; fillip; bang; hit, whack, thwack, cuff, buffet, punch, thump, kick, cut, thrust, lunge; carom, cannon; jab.

Science of mechanical forces: mechanics, dynamics.

V. impel, push; start, set going; drive, urge; boom, boost; thrust, prod; elbow, shoulder, jostle, hurtle, shove, butt, jog, jolt; throw, etc. (*propel*), 284.

strike, knock, thump, beat, bang, slam, dash, punch, thwack, whack; batter, tamp, buffet, cudgel, belabor; lunge, jab, kick; hit, tap, rap, slap, pat.

collide, foul; telescope; bump, butt.

Adj. impulsive, propulsive, dynamic.

277. RECOIL.—*N.* recoil, rebound, ricochet, backlash, boomerang: kick; elasticity, etc., 325; reflex, reflux; reverberation, resonance, repulse; reaction, revulsion.

reactionary, recalcitrant.

V. recoil, react; balk, jib; rebound, reverberate, echo; ricochet.

Adj. refluent, recalcitrant, reactionary.

278. DIRECTION.—*N.* direction, bearing, course, set, trend, run, drift, tenor; tendency, etc., 176; dip, tack, aim.

points of the compass, cardinal points.

line, path, road, range, line of march, alignment; airline, beeline.

V. tend toward, conduct to, go to; point to, bend, verge, incline, dip; steer for, make for, aim at, level at; take aim; hold a course; be bound for; make a beeline for.

Adj. bound for; direct, straight; undeviating, unswerving.

directable, steerable, dirigible, guidable.

Adv. toward, on the road to; hither, thither, whither; directly; straight, point-blank; in a bee (*or* direct, straight) line to, as the crow flies; windward, in the wind's eye.

through, via, by way of.

279. DEVIATION.—*N.* deviation; warp, refraction; sweep; deflection, zigzag.

diversion, digression, aberration, drift, sheer, divergence, ramification, forking; detour.

Oblique motion: tack, yaw [*both naut.*]; echelon [*mil.*]; knight's move [*chess*].

V. deviate, alter one's course, turn, bend, curve, swerve, heel, bear off; jibe, yaw, wear, sheer, tack [*all naut.*]; sidle, edge, veer, diverge; wind, twist; turn aside, wheel, steer clear of; dodge, step aside, shy, jib; glance off.

deflect; divert, shift, switch, shunt; sidetrack.

stray, straggle; digress, wander, meander; go astray, ramble, rove, drift.

Adj. deviating, errant; excursive, discursive; devious, desultory, rambling; stray, vagrant, circuitous, roundabout, sidelong, indirect, crooked, zigzag; oblique.

280. PRECEDING.—*N.* preceding, leading, heading, precedence, priority, the lead, van, front; precursor, etc., 64.

V. precede, go before, forerun; introduce, herald; head, take the lead; lead, steal a march, get ahead, outstrip; take precedence.

Adv. in advance, before, ahead, in the van, in front.

281. FOLLOWING.—*N.* following, attendance; pursuant; sequence, sequel.

follower, attendant, satellite, pursuer, shadow, dangler, train.

V. follow; pursue, etc., 622; go after; attend, dance attendance on, dog; shadow; hang on the skirts of; camp on the trail.

lag, loiter, linger, fall behind.

Adv. behind; in the rear; after, etc. (*order*), 63 (*time*), 117.

282. [Motion forward] PROGRESSION.—*N.* progression, progress, progressiveness; advance, advancement, headway; march, etc., 266; rise, improvement, etc., 658.

V. advance; proceed, go, go on, progress, get on, gain ground, forge ahead, press onward, step forward, make progress (*or* head, headway); go ahead, shoot ahead; distance.

Adj. progressive, advanced, up-to-date; enterprising, go-ahead [*colloq.*].

Adv. forward, onward; forth, on, ahead, under way.

283. [Motion backward] REGRESSION.—*N.* regression, retrogression, retreat, retirement, recession, withdrawal.

reflux, refluence, backwater, ebb, return; reflexion, recoil.

countermotion, countermovement, countermarch; tergiversation, backsliding, fall; deterioration, relapse, reversion.

V. recede, return, revert, retreat, retire; retrograde, back, back out [*colloq.*], back down [*colloq.*], balk; withdraw; recoil, rebound; turn back, fall back, put back; lose ground; drop astern; backwater, put about [*naut.*], veer, shy, double, wheel, countermarch; ebb, regurgitate.

Adj. retrograde, retrogressive; regressive, refluent, reflex, contraclockwise, counterclockwise; balky, perverse, reactionary.

284. PROPULSION.—*N.* propulsion, projection; push, etc. (*impulse*), 276; ejection; throw, fling, toss, shot, discharge, shy.

Science of propulsion: gunnery, ballistics.

missile, projectile; gun, etc. (*arms*), 727.

marksman, rifleman, good shot, dead shot, crack shot; sharpshooter, etc. (*combatant*), 726; gunner; archer, bowman.

V. propel, project, throw, fling, cast, pitch, toss, jerk, heave, shy, hurl.

dart, lance, tilt; drive, sling, pelt, pitchfork.

send; let off, fire off, discharge, shoot; launch, send forth, let fly; dash.

start, put *or* set in motion, set going, trundle, bundle off; impel, etc., 276; expel, eject.

Adj. propulsive, projectile, ballistic.

285. TRACTION.—*N.* traction, draft, pull, haul.

V. draw, pull, haul, lug, rake, trawl, draggle, drag, tug, tow, trail, train; take in tow.

Adj. tractile, tractional, ductile.

286. [Motion toward] APPROACH.—*N.* approach, approximation; access; advent.

pursuit, chase, hunt.

V. **approach,** converge, near, get (*or* draw) near; move toward, drift; gain upon; pursue, etc., 622; make land.

Adj. approximate, convergent; impending, imminent.

287. [Motion from] RECESSION.—*N.* **recession,** retirement, withdrawal; retreat; regression, etc., 283; departure, etc., 293; flight.

V. **recede,** go, go back, move back, retire, withdraw, ebb; shrink; drift away; depart, etc., 293; retreat, retire, fall back; run away, fly, flee.

288. ATTRACTION.—*N.* **attraction,** attractiveness; pull, magnetism, gravity.

loadstone, lodestar, polestar, magnet.

lure, bait, charm, decoy.

V. **attract,** pull, drag, draw, magnetize, bait, trap, decoy, charm, lure, allure.

Adj. attractive, attracting, seductive.

289. REPULSION.—*N.* **repulsion;** antipathy; repulse, abduction.

V. **repel,** push *or* drive from, etc., 276; chase, dispel; abduct; send away; repulse; keep at arm's length, turn one's back upon.

Adj. repellent, repulsive.

290. [Motion nearer to] CONVERGENCE.—*N.* **convergence,** confluence, concourse, concurrence, concentration; meeting.

assemblage, etc., 72; resort, etc., 74.

V. **converge,** concur; come together, unite, meet, close in upon; center, concentrate.

Adj. convergent, confluent, concurrent; centripetal.

291. [Motion farther off] DIVERGENCE.—*N.* **divergence,** ramification, forking; separation, detachment, dispersion, deviation, etc., 279.

V. **diverge,** ramify, branch off, fly off; spread, scatter, disperse, etc., 73; part, sever, separate, sunder.

Adj. divergent, radial, centrifugal.

Adv. broadcast.

292. ARRIVAL.—*N.* **arrival,** advent; landing; debarkation, disembarkation.

destination, bourn, goal; harbor, haven, port; terminus, terminal; home, journey's end; anchorage, refuge.

meeting, joining, encounter, rejoining; return, re-entry.

V. **arrive,** get to, come to; come; reach, attain; overtake; make, fetch; join, rejoin; return; enter, appear, drop in, visit.

alight, light, dismount, detrain.

land, cast anchor, put in, debark, disembark.

meet, encounter, come across; come (*or* light) upon.

Adv. here, hither.

293. DEPARTURE.—*N.* departure, embarkation; outset, start; removal; exit, etc. (*egress*), 295; exodus, hegira, flight.

leave-taking, adieu, farewell, good-by, Godspeed; valediction, valedictory, valedictorian.

V. depart; go, go away, go off, set out, start, issue, march out, debouch, sally forth; sally, go forth; retire, withdraw, remove; cut [*colloq. or slang*], take flight, take wing; fly, flit; strike tents, decamp, break camp, take leave; disappear, etc., 449; entrain; saddle, bridle, harness up, hitch up [*colloq.*].

quit, vacate, evacuate, abandon.

embark, go abroad; set sail, put to sea, sail, take ship; get under way, weigh anchor.

Adv. hence, whence, thence.

294. [Motion into] INGRESS.—*N.* ingress; entrance, entry; influx, inroad, incursion, invasion, irruption; penetration, infiltration; insinuation, insertion, etc., 300.

immigration, incoming, foreign influx.

import [*used esp. in pl.*], importation.

immigrant, incomer, newcomer, colonist.

inlet; mouth, door, etc. (*opening*), 260; path, etc., 627; conduit, etc., 350.

V. enter; come in, pour in, flow in; set foot on; burst *or* break in upon, invade; penetrate, infiltrate.

Adj. incoming, inbound, inward.

295. [Motion out of] EGRESS.—*N.* egress, exit, issue; emergence; outbreak; outburst, eruption; emanation; evacuation; leakage, percolation, oozing, drain, drainage; gush, outpour, effluence, outflow, discharge.

export [*used esp. in pl.*], exportation; shipment.

emigration, exodus, departure.

emigrant, migrant, colonist.

outlet, vent, spout, faucet, tap, sluice, floodgate; mouth, opening, door; pathway; conduit.

V. emerge, emanate, issue; go (*or* come, pass, pour, flow) out of.

exude, discharge, leak; run through, percolate; strain, distill; perspire, sweat; drain, seep, ooze, filter, infiltrate, gush, spout, flow out; pour, trickle; find vent; escape, etc., 671.

Adj. eruptive, porous, pervious, leaky; outgoing, outbound, outward bound.

296. [Motion into, actively] RECEPTION.—*N.* reception; admission, admittance, entree; importation; initiation, introduction, absorption; suction, sucking; eating, drinking, etc. (*food*), 298; insertion, etc., 300.

V. give entrance to, introduce, usher, admit, initiate; receive, import, bring in; absorb, imbibe, instill, implant, induct, inhale; let in, take in.

swallow, gulp; eat, drink, etc., 298.

Adj. introductory, initiatory, preliminary.

297. [Motion out of, actively] EJECTION.—*N.* ejection, rejection, expulsion, eviction, dislodgment, banishment, exile, deportation, expedition; discharge, evacuation, eruption, eruptiveness; tapping, drainage; emetic; vomiting.

V. eject, reject; expel, discard; ostracize, boycott; banish, exile, fire [*slang*], throw away *or* aside, push out *or* off, send off *or* away; discharge, dismiss, turn *or* cast adrift; turn out, throw overboard.

evict, oust, dislodge; turn out of doors, deport, expatriate.

emit, send out, pour out, dispatch, shed, void, evacuate; give vent to; tap, draw off; pour forth; squirt, spurt, spill; breathe, blow, exhale.

empty; drain, sweep off; clear off, draw off; clean out, purge; tap, broach.

root out, root up, unearth, eradicate; weed out, get out; eliminate, get rid of, do away with, shake off.

vomit, spew; cast up, bring up; disgorge.

unpack, unlade, unload, unship; dump.

298. [Eating] FOOD.—*N.* eating, mastication, rumination; gastronomy, carnivorousness, vegetarianism, gluttony, etc., 957.

mouth, jaws, mandible [*esp. of birds*], chops.

drinking, potation, draft, libation; carousal, etc. (*amusement*), 840; drunkenness, etc., 959.

food, meat, nourishment, nutriment, sustenance, nurture, subsistence, provender, corn, feed, fodder, provision, ration, board; commissariat, etc. (*provisions*), 637; prey, forage, pasture, pasturage; fare, cheer; diet, dietary; regimen; staff of life, bread.

eatables, victuals, edibles, grub [*slang*], meat; bread, viands, delicacy, dainty, creature comforts, ambrosia; good cheer, good living.

table, cuisine [F.], bill of fare, menu, table d'hôte [F.], à la carte [F.].

meal, repast, feed [*colloq.*], spread [*colloq.*]; mess; refreshment, entertainment; refection, collation, picnic, feast, banquet, potluck.

mouthful, tidbit, morsel.

drink, beverage, liquor, potion, dram, draft.

restaurant, café, eating house.

V. eat, feed, fare, devour, swallow, take; gulp, bolt; fall to; dispatch; tuck in [*slang*], dine, banquet, gormandize, etc., 957; crunch, chew, masticate, nibble, gnaw, mumble.

live on; feed upon; browse, graze, crop; bite, champ, munch, ruminate.

drink, quaff, sip, sup; lap; tipple, guzzle, carouse.

cater, purvey, etc., 637.

Adj. eatable, edible, esculent; dietetic; culinary; nutritive, nutritious; succulent.

underdone, rare; well done; overdone; high [*of game*]; ripe [*of cheese*].

drinkable, potable; bibulous.

omnivorous, carnivorous, flesh-eating, herbivorous, graminivorous, piscivorous.

299. EXCRETION.—*N.* excretion, discharge, emanation, exhalation, secretion, effusion, perspiration, sweat.

hemorrhage, bleeding; outpouring, etc. (*egress*), 295; diarrhea.

saliva, spittle, sputum (*pl.* sputa), spit; catarrh; lava.

V. excrete, etc. (*eject*), 297; secrete; exhale, emanate, etc. (*come out*), 295.

300. [Forcible ingress] INSERTION.—*N.* insertion, implantation, introduction; interpolation, interlineation, insinuation, etc. (*intervention*), 228; injection, inoculation, infusion; ingress, etc., 294; immersion; submersion, dip, plunge.

V. insert, introduce, put in (*or* into), run into; inject; imbed, inlay, inweave; interject, etc., 228; infuse, instill, inoculate, impregnate, imbue.

graft, ingraft, bud, plant, implant.

obtrude; thrust in, stick in, ram in, stuff in, tuck in, press in, drive in; pierce, etc. (*make a hole*), 260.

immerse, merge; bathe, soak, etc. (*water*), 337; dip, plunge, etc., 310.

301. [Forcible egress] EXTRACTION.—*N.* extraction; removal, elimination, extrication, eradication, extirpation, extermination; ejection, etc., 297; export, etc. (*egress*), 295; wrench.

V. extract, draw; take out, draw out, pull out, tear out, pluck out, pick out, get out; wring from, wrench; extort; root up, weed out; eradicate, uproot, pull up, extirpate.

elicit, evolve, bring forth, draw forth; extricate.

eliminate, etc. (*eject*), 297; remove.

express, squeeze out, press out, distill.

302. [Motion through] PASSAGE.—*N.* passage, transmission; permeation, penetration; infiltration; ingress; egress, exit, issue; path, road, way; conduit, opening; journey, voyage, sail, cruise.

V. pass, pass through; perforate, penetrate, permeate, thread, cut across; ford, cross; make (*or* work, thread, worm, force) one's way; find a way (*or* vent); transmit, make way, traverse.

303. [Motion beyond] OVERRUNNING.—*N.* overrunning, overrun, inroad, advance, infraction, transgression, encroachment, infringement; transcendence; redundance, etc., 641.

V. overrun, pass, go beyond, go by, shoot ahead of; steal a march upon, gain upon.

outstrip, override, overshoot the mark; outrun, outride, outrival, outdo; beat; distance; throw into the shade; exceed, transcend, surmount; tower above, surpass.

encroach, overstep, transgress, trespass, infringe, intrude, invade.

Adv. ahead, beyond the mark.

304. [Motion short of] SHORTCOMING.—*N.* shortcoming, failure, falling short; default, defalcation; delinquency; fizzle [*colloq.*], slump [*colloq.*]; flash in the pan.

incompleteness, deficiency; defect, imperfection, fault; insufficiency, etc., 640; noncompletion, nonfulfillment; failure, etc., 732.

V. fall short, come short of, not reach; want; keep within bounds (*or* the mark, compass).

collapse, fail, break down, flat out [*colloq.*], come to nothing; fall down, slump, fizzle out [*all colloq.*]; fall through, fall to the ground; cave in [*colloq.*], end in smoke, miss the mark.

Adj. deficient; at fault; short, short of; out of depth; perfunctory, remiss.

305. [Motion upward] ASCENT.—*N.* ascent, ascension; rising, rise, upgrowth, upward flight; upgrade; leap, etc., 309; grade, ramp, acclivity, hill, etc., 217.

stairway, staircase, stairs; flight of steps *or* stairs; ladder, scaling ladder; companionway [*naut.*]; escalator, elevator.

V. ascend, rise, mount, arise, uprise; go up, get up, work one's way up, start up, spring up, shoot up; aspire, aim high.

climb, shin [*colloq.*], swarm [*colloq.*], clamber, scramble, escalade, surmount, wind upward, scale.

tower, soar, spire, go aloft, fly aloft; surge; leap, etc., 309.

Adj. rising; ascendant; upcast; buoyant.

Adv. up, upward, skyward, heavenward; upturned; uphill.

306. [Motion downward] DESCENT.—*N.* descent, inclination, declension, declination; drop; cadence; subsidence, lapse; downcome, comedown, setback, fall; slump [*colloq.*], downfall, tumble, stumble, slip, tilt, trip, lurch.

avalanche, landslide, slide, snowslide, glissade.

declivity, dip, decline, pitch, drop, downgrade.

V. descend, go (*or* drop, come) down, fall, gravitate, drop, slip, skid, slide, settle; decline, sink, subside, droop, slump [*colloq.*].

get down, dismount, alight, light; swoop; stoop, etc., 308; fall prostrate, precipitate oneself; let fall.

tumble, trip, stumble, lurch, pitch, topple; tilt, sprawl.

Adj. steep, sloping, declivitous; beetling, overhanging; bottomless, fathomless, abysmal.

descending; down, downcast, descendent; deciduous.

Adv. downward, downhill.

307. ELEVATION.—*N.* elevation; raising; erection, lift; upheaval; sublimation, exaltation; prominence, relief.

lever, crowbar, crane, derrick, windlass, capstan, winch; dredge, dredger.

elevator, dumbwaiter; escalator.

V. elevate, raise, heighten, lift, erect; set up, tilt up; rear, hoist, heave; uplift, upraise, uprear; buoy, mount, exalt; sublimate.

take up, drag up, fish up; dredge.

Adj. elevated, upturned, stilted, rampant.

308. DEPRESSION.—*N.* depression, lowering; dip, etc. (*concavity*), 252.

overthrow, overturn; upset; prostration, reduction, abasement, subversion.

bow, curtsy, dip [*colloq.*], bob, duck, genuflexion, kowtow, obeisance, salaam.

V. depress, lower, cast down, let drop, let fall; sink, debase, bring low, abase, reduce, precipitate.

overthrow, overturn, overset, upset, prostrate, level, fell; down [*colloq.*], cast (*or* throw, fling, dash, pull, knock, hew) down, raze.

sit, sit down, squat; recline, sprawl.

crouch, stoop, bend, cower.

bow, curtsy, genuflect, kowtow, duck, bob, dip, kneel; incline, make obeisance, salaam, prostrate oneself, bow down.

Adj. depressed; at a low ebb; prostrate, horizontal.

309. LEAP.—*N.* leap, jump, hop, spring, bound, vault.

caper, dance, gambol, frisk, prance, curvet, caracole, buck; hop, skip, and jump.

V. leap, jump, hop, spring, bound, vault, clear, ramp, skip.

prance, dance, caper; buck; curvet, caracole, bob, bounce, flounce; frisk, jump about, romp, frolic, gambol; cavort, cut capers [*colloq.*].

Adj. leaping, saltatorial; frisky, lively, frolicsome.

Adv. on the light fantastic toe.

310. PLUNGE.—*N.* plunge, dip, dive, nose-dive [*aviation*], header [*colloq.*]; submergence, submersion, immersion.

diver; diving bird.

V. plunge, dip, souse, duck; dive, plump; take a header [*colloq.*]; make a plunge; bathe; pitch.

submerge, submerse; immerse; douse, sink, engulf, send to the bottom.

founder,welter,wallow; get out of one's depth; go to the bottom.

Adj. submergible, submersible.

311. CIRCULAR MOTION.—*N.* circulation, turn, excursion, circumnavigation, circumflexion; wheel, compass, lap, circuit; turning, evolution; coil, spiral.

V. turn, bend, wheel; go about, put about [*both naut.*]; go (*or* turn) round, round, turn a corner; double a point [*naut.*]; make a detour.

circle, encircle, circumscribe, circuit, describe a circle, circumnavigate; go the round.

wind, circulate, meander; whisk, twirl, twist, coil.

wallow, welter, roll.

Adj. circuitous, roundabout, devious.

312. ROTATION—*N.* rotation, revolution, gyration, circulation, roll; pirouette, convolution.

eddy, vortex, whirlpool, maelstrom; swirl, surge; whir, whirl; cyclone, tornado; vertiginousness, vertigo.

V. rotate, roll, revolve, spin, turn, turn round, encircle, circulate, swirl, gyrate,wheel,whirl, twirl, roll up, furl; box the compass.

Adj. rotating, rotary; vertiginous.

313. UNFOLDMENT.—*N.* unfoldment, unfolding, development; evolvement, evolution; inversion.

V. evolve; unfold, unroll, unwind, uncoil, untwist, unfurl, untwine, unravel; disentangle; develop.

Adj. evolutional, evolutionary.

314. [Motion to and fro] OSCILLATION.—*N.* oscillation, vibration, undulation, pulsation; pulse, beat, throb.

alternation; coming and going; ebb and flow, flux and reflux, systole and diastole; ups and downs.

fluctuation; vacillation, irresolution, indecision.

swing, wave, beat, shake, wag, seesaw, teeter.

V. oscillate, vibrate, undulate, wave; rock, teeter, sway, swing, dangle; pulsate, beat; wag, waggle; nod, bob, curtsy; wobble.

fluctuate, reel, quake; quiver, quaver, shake, flicker; wriggle; roll, toss, pitch; flounder, stagger, totter.

alternate, pass and repass, shuttle, ebb and flow, come and go; vacillate.

Adj. oscillating; undulatory, vibratory; pendulous.

Adv. to and fro, up and down, back and forth, in and out, seesaw, zigzag, from side to side, shuttlewise.

315. [Irregular motion] AGITATION.—*N.* agitation, stir, tremor, shuffling, shake, ripple, jog, jolt, jar, jerk, shock, trepidation, quiver, quaver, dance; tarantella; twitter, flicker, flutter.

disquiet, perturbation, commotion, turmoil, turbulence; tumult, hubbub, rout, bustle, fuss, racket.

twitching, chorea, St. Vitus' dance; staggers, blind staggers; epilepsy, fits.

spasm, throe, throb, palpitation, convulsion, paroxysm, seizure, grip, cramp.

disturbance, disorder; restlessness, changeableness, instability.

ferment, fermentation, ebullition, effervescence, hurly-burly; tempest, storm, whirlpool, vortex, etc., 312; whirlwind, tornado, cyclone, typhoon.

V. be agitated; shake, tremble, flutter, flicker; quiver, quaver, quake; shiver, writhe, toss; shuffle, tumble, stagger, bob, reel, sway; wag, waggle, wriggle; stumble, shamble, flounder, totter, flounce, flop, dance, curvet, prance, cavort; squirm; twitch; bustle.

throb, pulsate, beat, palpitate, go pitapat.

ferment, effervesce, foam, boil, boil over, bubble, bubble up; simmer.

agitate, shake, convulse, toss, tumble, wield, brandish, flap, flourish, whisk, jerk, jolt, jog, joggle, disturb, stir, shake up, churn.

Adj. agitated, shaking, tremulous; convulsive, jerky; effervescent, unquiet, restless.

Adv. by fits and starts; in convulsions, in fits, in a flutter.

CLASS III

Words Relating to MATTER

I. MATTER IN GENERAL

316. MATERIALITY.—*N.* materiality, corporality; substantiality, material existence; incarnation, flesh and blood.

matter, body, substance, brute matter, protoplasm, stuff, element, principle, material, substratum.

object, article, thing, something; still life; materials, etc., 635. Science of matter: physics; natural philosophy; physical science. materialist, physicist.

V. materialize, substantiate, incorporate, embody, incarnate.

Adj. material, bodily, corporeal, corporal, physical, incarnate, materialized, embodied; sensible, tangible, ponderable, palpable, substantial; unspiritual, materialistic.

objective, impersonal, nonsubjective.

317. IMMATERIALITY.—*N.* immateriality, insubstantiality, incorporality, unsubstantiality, spirituality; astral plane.

personality; I, myself, me.

ego, spirit, etc. (*soul*), 450; astral body, etheric double, subliminal self, subconscious self, higher self.

spiritualism, spiritism; animism.

spiritualist, spiritist; animist.

V. dematerialize, disembody, spiritualize.

Adj. immaterial, incorporeal, incorporate, unsubstantial; spiritistic, animistic; discarnate, bodiless, disembodied; extramundane, unearthly; spiritual, etc. (*psychical*), 450.

subjective, personal, nonobjective.

318. WORLD.—*N.* world, creation, nature, universe; earth, globe, sphere, wide world; cosmos, macrocosm.

heavens, sky, empyrean, starry cope (*or* host); firmament.

heavenly bodies, luminaries, stars, asteroids; galaxy, Milky Way; constellations, planets, satellites; comet, meteor, falling (*or* shooting) star; solar system.

sun, orb of day, daystar [*poetic*], Helios, Apollo, Phoebus, etc. (*sun god*), 423.

moon, Diana, Luna, Phoebe, Cynthia, Selene, silver-footed queen.

Adj. cosmic, mundane, terrestrial, earthly, sublunary.

celestial, empyreal, heavenly, solar; lunar; starry, stellar, sidereal, astral; nebular.

Adv. in all creation, on the face of the globe, here below, under the sun.

319. GRAVITY.—*N.* gravity, gravitation; weight, heft, heaviness, ponderousness, specific gravity, pressure, load, burden, ballast, counterpoise; mass.

Weighing instrument: balance, scales, steelyard, beam, weighbridge.

Science of gravity: statics.

V. weigh, load, press; counterweigh, poise; gravitate.

Adj. weighty, heavy, ponderous, ponderable; cumbersome, burdensome, cumbrous, unwieldy, massive; static.

320. LEVITY.—*N.* levity, lightness, imponderability, buoyancy, volatility.

ferment, leaven, yeast, pepsin.

V. be light, float, swim.

render light, lighten.

ferment, work, raise, leaven.

Adj. light, subtle, imponderous, imponderable, ethereal, airy, feathery, gossamery; volatile, vaporous, buoyant, floating, foamy, frothy; portable.

fermenting, fermentative, yeasty.

II. INORGANIC MATTER

(1) Solids

321. DENSITY.—*N.* density, solidity, solidness; impenetrability, impermeability; costiveness, constipation.

condensation; solidification, consolidation, concretion, coagulation; cohesion, etc., 46; petrifaction, etc. (*hardening*), 323; thickening, crystallization, precipitation.

solid body, mass, block, lump; concretion, concrete, conglomerate; stone, rock, cake; card.

sediment, lees, dregs, settlings.

V. **be dense**, compress, squeeze, ram down; solidify; cement, set, consolidate, condense, congeal, coagulate, curd, curdle; fix, clot, thicken, cake, candy, precipitate, deposit, cohere, crystallize; petrify, harden, stiffen.

compress, squeeze, ram down.

Adj. **dense**, solid, solidified; coherent, cohesive, compact; close, serried, thickset; substantial, massive, impenetrable, concrete, hard; crystalline, thick, stodgy.

undissolved, unmelted, unliquefied, unthawed.

indivisible; indissoluble, insoluble.

322. RARITY.—*N.* rarity, tenuity; subtlety.

rarefaction, attenuation, expansion, inflation; ether, etc. (*gas*), 334.

V. **rarefy**, expand, dilate, attenuate, thin.

Adj. **rare**, subtle, thin, fine, tenuous, compressible, flimsy, slight, light, porous; rarefied, unsubstantial.

323. HARDNESS.—*N.* hardness, firmness, rigidity, inflexibility, temper, callosity; induration, petrifaction, ossification; crystallization.

V. **harden**, render hard, temper, stiffen, cement, indurate, petrify, ossify.

Adj. **hard**, rigid, stubborn, stiff, firm; stark, unbending, unyielding, inflexible, tense.

adamantine, stony, granitic, rocky, horny, callous, bony, cartilaginous.

324. SOFTNESS.—*N.* softness, pliableness, flexibility, pliancy, pliability, malleability, ductility, tractility, plasticity, flaccidity, laxity, flabbiness, mollification, softening.

V. soften, render soft, mollify, mellow; mash; knead, massage. bend, give, yield, relent, relax.

Adj. soft, tender; mollified; supple, pliant, pliable, flexible, lithe, lithesome, limber; plastic; ductile, malleable, tractable; yielding; flabby, flaccid, lax, limp, flimsy; mellow; spongy.

downy, woolly, fluffy, feathery.

325. ELASTICITY.—*N.* elasticity, springiness, spring, resilience *or* resiliency, buoyancy; recoil, rebound, reflex.

V. be elastic; spring back, recoil.

Adj. elastic, springy, resilient, buoyant.

326. INELASTICITY.—*N.* inelasticity, flaccidity, laxity; want of elasticity, etc., 325.

Adj. inelastic, flaccid, yielding; not elastic.

327. TENACITY.—*N.* tenacity, toughness, strength; cohesiveness, cohesion, adhesion; stubbornness, etc. (*obstinacy*), 606; gumminess, glutinousness, viscidity.

Adj. tenacious, cohesive, tough, strong, resisting; adhesive, stringy, viscid, gummy, glutinous, gristly, cartilaginous; stubborn, etc. (*obstinate*), 606.

328. BRITTLENESS.—*N.* brittleness, fragility; frailty; shortness.

V. break, crack, snap, split, shiver, splinter, crumble, crash, crush, burst, give way; fall to pieces; crumble to dust.

Adj. brittle, breakable, delicate, fragile, frail; splintery; crisp, short [*as of pastry*].

329. STRUCTURE.—*N.* structure, organization, constitution, organism, anatomy, frame, mold, fabric, construction; framework, architecture; stratification.

texture, contexture; tissue, grain, web, surface, nap; roughness; warp and woof (*or* weft); fineness (*or* coarseness) of grain.

Adj. structural, organic; anatomic *or* anatomical.

textile; fine-grained, coarse-grained, ingrained; ingrain; fine, delicate, subtile, subtle, gossamer, gossamery, filmy; coarse; homespun, linsey-woolsey.

330. POWDERINESS.—*N.* powderiness, grittiness, sandiness, friability.

powder, dust, sand, shingle; sawdust; grit; meal, bran, flour, rice, spore; crumb, seed, grain; particle.

Reduction to powder: pulverization, comminution, granulation, disintegration, abrasion, detrition; mill, grater, rasp, file, pestle and mortar, grindstone, quern, millstone.

V. pulverize, powder, comminute, granulate, reduce to powder; scrape, file, abrade, grind, grate, rasp, pound, bruise, beat, crush, craunch, crunch, crumble, disintegrate.

Adj. powdery, granular, mealy, floury, farinaceous, branny, dusty, sandy, gritty.

pulverable *or* pulverizable, friable, crumbly, shivery.

331. FRICTION. *-N.* friction, rubbing, abrasion, rub; massage; erasure; elbow grease [*colloq.*].

eraser, rubber, India rubber.

V. rub, abrade, scratch, scrape, scrub, fray, rasp, graze, curry, scour, polish, rub out, erase, file, grind, etc. (*pulverize*), 330; massage.

332. [Absence or prevention of friction] LUBRICATION.—*N.* lubrication, anointment, oiling.

smoothness, polish, gloss; unctuousness.

lubricant, lubricator; ointment, salve, balm, unguent.

V. lubricate, oil, grease; lather, soap; wax; anoint.

(2) Fluids

333. FLUIDITY.—*N.* fluidity, liquidity, liquidness; liquefaction; solubility; gaseity, etc., 334.

solution; fluid; liquid; juice, sap, lymph, serum.

Science of liquids at rest: hydrostatics, hydrodynamics, hydrokinetics.

V. be fluid; run; flow, etc. (*water in motion*), 348; liquefy, etc., 335.

Adj. liquid, fluid; juicy, succulent, sappy; rheumy; fluent, flowing; liquefied, uncongealed; soluble.

334. GASEITY.—*N.* gaseity, gaseousness, vaporousness; volatility; aeration; gasification; flatulence.

elastic fluid, gas, air, vapor, ether, steam, fume, effluvium; cloud, etc., 353.

Science of elastic fluids: pneumatics, aerostatics, aerodynamics, aerography, aeromechanics.

V. gasify, render gaseous; aerate; vaporize, etc., 336.

Adj. gaseous, ethereal, aery, aerial, airy, vaporous, volatile, flatulent.

335. LIQUEFACTION.—*N.* liquefaction, liquescence; deliquescence; melting, fusion; thaw; solubleness; solution.

mixture, decoction, infusion, solution.

V. dissolve, liquefy; run; melt, thaw, fuse; hold in solution; percolate.

Adj. liquefied; soluble, dissolvable; solvent, dissolvent.

336. VAPORIZATION.—*N.* vaporization, atomization; fumigation, steaming; distillation; gasification; evaporation.

vaporizer, atomizer, spray, evaporator, still, retort.

V. vaporize, gasify, atomize; spray; distill, sublimate, evaporate; exhale, emit vapor; fumigate; fume, smoke, reek, steam.

Adj. volatile, vapory, vaporous, gaseous; volatilized.

337. WATER.—*N.* water, lymph; aqua [L.], *eau* [F.]; fluid, etc., 333.

washing, bathing, bath, immersion; dilution; infiltration, irrigation, seepage.

deluge, etc. (*water in motion*), 348; high water, flood tide, spring-tide.

sprinkler, shower *or* shower bath; nozzle; atomizer, etc., 336.

water, dilute, add water; moisten, etc., 339; steep, soak, drench, wet, dip, immerse, submerge; duck; drown; wash, lave, bathe, sprinkle, dabble; inundate, deluge; irrigate; infiltrate, percolate, seep.

inject; gargle, syringe.

Adj. watery, aquatic, lymphatic; infiltrative, seepy; drenching; diluted, weak; wet, etc. (*moist*), 339.

338. AIR.—*N.* air, etc. (*gas*), 334; atmosphere; ventilation. the open, open air; sky, blue sky.

weather, climate; rise and fall of the barometer (*or* mercury).

Science of air: aerology, aerometry, aerography; meteorology, climatology; pneumatics; aeronautics, etc., 267.

aeronaut, etc., 269a.

barometer, aneroid, weatherglass, weather gauge.

weather vane, weathercock, vane.

V. air, ventilate, fan, etc. (*wind*), 349.

fly, soar, drift, hover; aviate, etc. (*aeronautics*), 267.

Adj. containing air, flatulent, effervescent; windy, etc., 349. atmospheric, airy; aerial, aeriform; aery, pneumatic.

meteorological, barometric, aerographic, weatherwise.

Adv. in the open air, in the open, under the stars, out of doors, outdoors; alfresco [It.].

339. MOISTURE.—*N.* moisture; moistness, humidity; dew; marsh, etc., 345.

V. moisten, wet, sponge, damp, bedew; infiltrate, saturate; soak, sodden, seethe, sop; drench, etc. (*water*), 337.

perspire, etc. (*exude*), 295.

Adj. moist, damp; watery, etc., 337; undried, humid, wet, dank, muggy; dewy; juicy.

sodden, soppy, soggy, dabbled; reeking, dripping, soaking, saturated, soft, sloppy, muddy: swampy, etc. (*marshy*), 345; irriguous.

340. DRYNESS.—*N.* dryness, aridness, aridity, drought. desiccation, evaporation; drainage.

V. dry, dry up, soak up; sponge, swab, wipe, drain, parch, sear; desiccate, evaporate.

Adj. dry, rainless, fair, pleasant, fine; arid, sear, droughty, waterless, dried, desiccated; juiceless, sapless; corky; husky, parched; waterproof, watertight.

341. OCEAN—*N.* ocean, sea, main, high seas, deep, salt water; waters, waves, billows; tide, etc. (*water in motion*), 348; offing, watery waste, pond [*humorous for Atlantic*], the seven seas; ocean lane, steamer track.

Neptune, Poseidon, Oceanus, Thetis, Triton, naiad, Nereid; sea nymph, siren, mermaid, merman; trident, dolphin.

oceanography; oceanographer.

Adj. oceanic, marine, maritime; seaworthy, seagoing.

342. LAND.—*N.* land, earth, ground, soil, dry land, terra firma [L.].

continent; mainland, main; peninsula, chersonese; delta; neck of land, isthmus; oasis; promontory, etc. (*projection*), 250; highland, etc. (*height*), 206; plain, etc., 344.

realty, real estate, property, acres.

coast, shore, strand, beach; bank; seaboard, seaside, seacoast, seashore; reclamation, made land.

fatherland, home, country, native land; region, etc., 181.

soil, glebe, clay, loam, marl, gravel, mold, subsoil, clod.

rock, crag, cliff, boulder.

landsman, landlubber, tiller of the soil; agriculturist, etc., 371.

V. land, disembark, debark, come to land, come (*or* go) ashore.

Adj. earthy; continental, midland; earthly, terrestrial; littoral, alluvial; landed, territorial; geographic *or* geographical.

Adv. ashore, on shore, on land, on dry land, on terra firma.

343. GULF, LAKE.—*N.* gulf, bay, inlet, bight, estuary, bayou, fiord, frith *or* firth; mouth; lagoon, cove, creek; natural harbor; roads; sound, strait, narrows.

lake, loch [Scot.], mere, tarn, pond, pool; well, artesian well; ditch, dike, dam, race, millrace; tank, reservoir.

344. PLAIN.—*N.* plain, open country; basin, downs, waste, desert, wild, steppe [*Russia*], grassland; tundra [*Arctic*], pampas [*esp. in Argentina*], savanna [*as in Brazil; also, a treeless plain, as in Florida*], campo [*S. Amer.*], llano [*S. Amer.*], prairie, heath, common, moor, moorland; bush; plateau, tableland, mesa; uplands; reach, stretch, expanse; alkali flat.

meadow, mead, pasture, lea, pasturage, field.

lawn, green, plot, grassplot.

greensward, sward, turf, sod, grass; heather.

grounds; estate, park, common, campus.

345. MARSH.—*N.* marsh, swamp, morass, peat bog, fen, bog, quagmire, slough; mud, slush.

Adj. marsh, marshy, fenny, swampy, boggy, soft; muddy, squashy, spongy.

346. ISLAND.—*N.* island, isle, islet; reef, atoll; archipelago; islander.

V. insulate, island.

Adj. insular, seagirt; archipelagic.

347. [Fluid in motion] STREAM.—*N.* stream, etc. (*of water*), 348 (*of air*), 349.

V. flow, etc., 348; blow, etc., 349.

348. [Water in motion] RIVER.—*N.* running water, jet, squirt, spout, splash, rush, gush, sluice.

waterspout, waterfall; fall, cascade, Niagara; cataract, inundation, deluge; chute, washout.

rain, rainfall; drizzle, shower; downpour, cloudburst; rains, rainy season, monsoon.

stream, course, flux, flow, current, tide, race, millrace, tiderace.

spring; fount, fountain; rill, rivulet, streamlet, brooklet; branch; brook, river; reach; tributary.

body of water, torrent, rapids, flood; spring (*or* high, flood, full) tide; bore, eagre; ebb, reflux; undercurrent, undertow; eddy, vortex, whirlpool, maelstrom.

wave, billow, surge, swell, ripple; tidal wave; comber, rollers, ground swell, surf, breakers, white horses.

Science of fluids in motion: hydrodynamics; hydraulics, hydrostatics, hydrokinetics, hydromechanics.

V. flow, run; meander; gush, pour, spout, roll, jet, well, issue; drop, drip, dribble, plash, trickle, distill, percolate; stream, surge, swirl, overflow, inundate, deluge, flow over, splash, swash; murmur, babble, purl, gurgle, spurt, ooze, flow out, etc. (*egress*), 295.

flow into, fall into, open into, drain into; discharge itself, disembogue.

Cause a flow: pour; pour out, etc. (*emit*), 297; shower down; irrigate, drench, etc. (*wet*), 337; spill, splash.

Stop a flow: stanch; dam, plug, stop up, cork, dam up, obstruct, choke, cut off.

rain; pour; shower, sprinkle, drizzle; set in.

Adj. flowing, fluent, meandering, flexuous; choppy, rolling; tidal.

rainy, showery, drizzly, drizzling, wet.

349. [Air in motion] WIND.—*N.* wind, draft, air; breath, puff, whiff, zephyr, blow, stream, current.

gust, blast, breeze, squall, half a gale, gale.

trade wind, trades, monsoon.

storm, tempest, hurricane, whirlwind, tornado, cyclone, typhoon, simoom [*as in Asia Minor*], harmattan [*W. coast of Africa*], sirocco [*as in W. Africa, Texas, and Kansas*], khamsin [*Egypt*], mistral [*Mediterranean*]; blizzard, norther, northeaster, northeast gale.

wind gauge, anemometer, anemograph; weathercock, weather vane, vane.

breathing, respiration, inspiration, inhalation, expiration, exhalation; blowing, fanning, inflation; ventilation.

V. blow, waft; storm.

respire, breathe, inhale, exhale; inspire, expire; puff, gasp, wheeze; snuff, snuffle; sniff, sniffle; sneeze, cough, hiccup.

inflate, pump, blow up.

whistle, scream, roar, howl, sing, sing in the shrouds, growl.

Adj. windy, breezy, gusty, squally.

stormy, tempestuous, blustering, cyclonic, typhonic; boisterous, violent.

350. [Channel for the passage of water] CONDUIT.—*N.* conduit, channel, duct, watercourse, canyon, coulee, water gap, gorge, ravine, chasm; race; aqueduct, canal; flume, dike, main: arroyo, gully, gulch; moat, ditch; gutter, drain, sewer, culvert; scupper; funnel, trough, siphon, pump, hose; pipe, tube; artery; spout, gargoyle; weir, floodgate, water gate, sluice, lock, valve.

Anatomy: artery, vein, blood vessel, pore; aorta; intestines, bowels; esophagus, gullet; throat.

351. [Channel for the passage of air] AIR PIPE—*N.* air pipe, airhole, blowhole, breathing hole, touchhole, venthole, spilehole, bung, bunghole; shaft, air shaft, smoke shaft, flue, chimney, funnel, vent, ventilator.

nostril, nozzle, throat; windpipe, trachea.

352. SEMILIQUIDITY.—*N.* semiliquidity; stickiness, pastiness, adhesiveness; thickening, jellification.

mud, slush, slime, ooze; moisture, humidity; marsh, etc., 345.

V. thicken, coagulate, gelatinize; jellify, jelly, jell [*colloq.*]; emulsify; mash, squash [*colloq.*], churn, beat up.

Adj. semifluid, semiliquid; half-melted, half-frozen; milky, muddy, curdled; thick, gelatinous, mucilaginous, glutinous, sticky; ropy; clotted.

353. [Mixture of air and water] BUBBLE, CLOUD.—*N.* bubble; foam, froth, spray, surf; spume, scum; lather, suds, yeast.

effervescence, babbling, fermentation; evaporation.

cloud, vapor, fog, mist, haze, steam; scud, rack, cumulus; nebula, cirrus, curl cloud; thunderhead; stratus.

V. bubble, boil, foam, spume, froth; effervesce, ferment, fizz; aerate.

cloud, overcast, overcloud, befog, becloud, mist, fog, overshadow, shadow.

Adj. bubbling, frothy, effervescent, sparkling, fizzy, heady. cloudy, nebulous; vaporous; overcast.

354. PULPINESS.—*N.* pulpiness; fleshiness; pulp, paste, dough, sponge, batter, curd, pap, jam, poultice.

V. pulp, mash, squash [*colloq.*], macerate; coagulate, etc., 352.

Adj. pulpy; [*of fruit*] fleshy, succulent.

355. UNCTUOUSNESS.—*N.* unctuousness, oiliness; lubrication; unguent, salve, cerate; ointment, etc. (*oil*), 356; anointment; lubricant.

V. oil, anoint, lubricate, etc., 332; smear, salve, grease, lard.

Adj. unctuous, oily, oleaginous, fat, fatty, greasy; waxy, soapy, slippery.

356. OIL.—*N.* oil, fat, butter, cream, grease, tallow, suet, lard, dripping, blubber; glycerin; coconut butter; soap, soft soap; wax; paraffin, benzine, kerosene, naphtha, gasoline, petroleum; ointment, pomade, unguent, liniment.

356a. RESIN.—*N.* resin, rosin, gum; shellac, varnish, mastic, lacquer, sealing wax; amber, ambergris; bitumen, pitch, tar, asphalt.

V. varnish, etc. (*overlay*), 223; rosin, resin.

Adj. resinous, lacquered, tarred, tarry, pitched, pitchy, gummed, gummy, waxed; bituminous, asphaltic.

III. ORGANIC MATTER

(1) Vitality

357. ORGANIZATION.—*N.* organization, structure, organized nature, animated nature; living beings; organic remains; organism; animal and plant life, fauna and flora.

fossils; fossilization, petrifaction; paleontology; paleontologist.

Science of living beings: biology, natural history;[1] zoology, etc., 368, botany; physiology, anatomy, organic chemistry; evolution, Darwinism.

protoplasm, bioplasm; cell, proteid, protein, albumen, germinal matter, germ plasm, germ cell; amoeba, protozoan.

naturalist, biologist, zoologist, botanist, bacteriologist, embryologist.

[1]The term *natural history* is also used as relating to all the objects in nature whether organic or inorganic, and including, therefore, *mineralogy, geology, meteorology*, etc.

V. organize, systematize, form, arrange, construct.
fossilize, petrify, mummify.

Adj. organic, organized, structural; cellular, protoplasmic.
fossilized, petrified.

358. INORGANIZATION.—*N.* mineral kingdom, mineral
world; unorganized (*or* inorganic) matter.

Science of the mineral kingdom: mineralogy, geology, metallurgy.

V. mineralize; pulverize, turn to dust.

Adj. inorganic, inanimate, unorganized, mineral.

359. LIFE.—*N.* life; vitality; existence, etc.; animation.
vital spark, vital flame, lifeblood; respiration, breath, breath of
life.

vivification; oxygen; life force; vitalization; revival; revivification, etc., 163; life to come, etc. (*destiny*), 152.

Science of life: physiology, biology, embryology.

nourishment, nutriment, etc. (*food*), 298.

V. live, be alive, breathe, subsist, exist, walk the earth.

be born, see the light, come into the world; quicken; revive;
come to life.

give birth to, etc. (*produce*), 161; bring to life, put life into,
vitalize; vivify, reanimate, restore, resuscitate.

Adj. living, alive; in life, in the flesh, breathing, quick, animated; lively, etc. (*active*), 682; vital, vivifying.

360. DEATH.—*N.* death, decease, demise; mortality; dying,
dissolution, departure, release, rest, eternal rest; loss, bereavement.
cessation (*or* loss, extinction) of life.

river of death; Jordan, Stygian shore; the great adventure.
angel of death, death's bright angel; death, doom, fate, destiny.
death song, dirge, requiem, elegy, threnody.

V. die, expire, perish; breathe one's last; lose *or* lay down one's
life; die a violent death; give (*or* yield) up the ghost.

die for one's country, make the supreme sacrifice, go West
[*First World War euphemism*].

Adj. dead, lifeless, inanimate; deceased, late; departed, defunct; gone, no more; bereft of life.

deadly, mortal, fatal.

dying, moribund, at the point of death, at death's door, at the
last gasp.

361. [Destruction of life; violent death] KILLING.—*N.* killing; homicide, manslaughter; murder, assassination; effusion of
blood; bloodshed, slaughter, carnage, butchery, massacre.

war, warfare, organized murder; battle; war to the death, etc.
(*warfare*), 722; Armageddon; deadly weapon, etc. (*arms*), 727.

deathblow, finishing stroke, *coup de grace* [F.], quietus; execution, etc. (*capital punishment*), 972; martyrdom.

suffocation, strangulation, garrote; hanging, etc., *v.*

slayer, butcher, murderer, Cain, assassin, cutthroat, garroter, thug, gallows, executioner, etc. (*punishment*), 975; apache, gunman [*colloq.*], bandit.

regicide, parricide, fratricide [*these words refer to both doer and deed*].

suicide, self-murder, self-destruction, hara-kiri [Jap.], suttee; immolation, holocaust.

fatal accident, violent death, casualty, disaster, calamity.

Destruction of animals: slaughtering; sport; the chase, venery; hunting, coursing, shooting, fishing; pigsticking.

sportsman, huntsman, hunter, Nimrod; fisherman, angler.

shambles, slaughterhouse.

V. kill, put to death, slay, shed blood; murder, assassinate, butcher, slaughter, immolate; massacre, decimate; put an end to; dispatch, do to death, do for [*colloq.*]; hunt, shoot, saber, stab, bayonet, put to the sword.

strangle, garrote, hang, throttle, choke, stifle, suffocate; smother, asphyxiate, drown.

execute; behead, guillotine; hang; electrocute.

die a violent death; commit suicide; kill (*or* make away with, put an end to) oneself.

Adj. murderous, slaughterous, sanguinary, bloody-minded, bloodthirsty; homicidal; red-handed, bloody, bloodstained, gory.

mortal, fatal, deadly, lethal; mutually destructive, internecine; suicidal.

362. CORPSE.—*N.* corpse, carcass, skeleton, relics, remains, dust, ashes, earth, clay; mummy; carrion.

ghost, shade, phantom, specter, apparition, spirit, revenant, spook [*colloq.*].

363. INTERMENT.—*N.* interment, burial, sepulture, entombment; obsequies, funeral, funeral rite, wake; knell, passing bell, death bell, tolling; dirge, etc. (*lamentation*), 839; dead march, muffled drum; pall, bier, litter, hearse, catafalque.

cremation, burning; pyre, funeral pile.

undertaker, funeral director.

mourner, mute; pallbearer, bearer.

graveclothes, shroud, winding sheet; cerecloth, cerements.

coffin, casket; urn; sarcophagus.

burial place, grave, pit, sepulcher, tomb, vault, crypt, catacomb, mausoleum; cemetery, burial ground, graveyard, churchyard; God's acre; potter's field; barrow, tumulus; charnel house, dead-house; morgue, mortuary; burning ghat [India]; crematorium, crematory.

gravedigger, sexton.

monument; gravestone, headstone, tombstone; hatchment, stone, marker, cross; epitaph, inscription.

autopsy, post-mortem examination *or* post mortem [L.].

disinterment, exhumation.

V. **inter,** bury, entomb; inurn; cremate.

disinter, exhume, unearth.

Adj. **funereal,** funeral, mortuary, sepulchral, cinerary; burial; elegiac.

364. ANIMAL LIFE.—*N.* animal life, animalism.

human system; breath; flesh, flesh and blood; physique, strength, power, vigor, force; spring, elasticity, tone.

V. **incarnate,** incorporate.

Adj. **fleshly,** carnal, human, corporeal.

365. VEGETATION.—*N.* vegetation, vegetable life, growth, herbage, flowerage.

V. **vegetate,** germinate, sprout, grow, shoot up, luxuriate, grow rank, flourish, flower, blossom; cultivate.

Adj. **vegetative,** vegetal, vegetable; leguminous, etc., 367.

luxuriant, rank, dense, lush, wild.

366. ANIMAL.—*N.* animal kingdom, fauna, brute creation.

animal, creature, created being, living thing; dumb animal, dumb friend, dumb creature; brute, beast.

mammal, quadruped, bird, reptile, fish, crustacean, shellfish, mollusk, worm, insect, zoophyte; animalcule, etc., 193.

beasts of the field, fowls of the air; flocks and herds, livestock, domestic animals, wild animals, game.

Domestic animals: horse, etc. (*beast of burden*), 271; cattle, ox; bull, bullock; cow, milch cow, Jersey, calf, heifer, shorthorn, yearling, steer; sheep; lamb, ewe, ram; pig, swine, boar, hog, sow; yak, zebu, buffalo.

dog, hound, canine; pup, puppy; whelp, cur [*contemptuous*], mongrel.

cat, feline, puss, pussy, tabby; tomcat *or* tom; mouser; Angora, Persian, Maltese, tortoise-shell; kitten, kitty.

Wild animals: deer, buck, doe, fawn, stag, hart, hind, roe, roebuck, caribou, elk, moose, reindeer, wapiti *or* American elk, fallow deer, red deer.

antelope, gazelle, American antelope *or* pronghorn, chamois.

ape, monkey, gorilla, marmoset, chimpanzee, lemur, baboon, orangutan.

fox, reynard, vixen [*fem.*]; dingo, coyote; wildcat, lynx, bobcat; skunk.

lion, tiger, etc. (*wild beast*), 913.

rat, mouse.

lizard, saurian, iguana, newt, chameleon, Gila monster, dragon; crocodile, alligator.

whale, shark, porpoise, walrus, seal, octopus, devilfish; swordfish; pike; salmon, trout, etc.

Birds: feathered tribes, singing bird, warbler, dickybird [*colloq.*].

canary, vireo, linnet, finch, goldfinch, siskin, crossbill, chewink, peewee, titmouse *or* chickadee, nightingale, lark; magpie, cuckoo, mocking bird, catbird, starling; robin, sparrow, swallow, etc.

swan, cygnet, goose, gander, duck, drake, wild duck, mallard.

gull, sea gull, albatross, petrel, stormy petrel *or* Mother Carey's chicken; owl, bird of night; hawk, vulture, buzzard; eagle, bird of freedom.

game, ruffed grouse, grouse, blackcock, duck, plover, rail, snipe, pheasant.

poultry, fowl, cock, rooster, chanticleer, barndoor fowl, barnyard fowl, hen, chicken, chick; guinea fowl, guinea hen; peafowl, peacock, peahen.

Insects: bee, honeybee, queen bee, drone; ant, white ant, termite; wasp, locust, grasshopper, cicada, cicala, cricket; dragonfly; beetle; butterfly, moth; fly, mosquito; earwig; bug, buffalo bug, gypsy moth, weevil.

vermin, lice, cooties [*slang*], flies, fleas, cockroaches *or* roaches, water bugs, bugs, bedbugs, mosquitoes; rats, mice, weasels.

snake, serpent, viper; asp, adder, coral snake *or* harlequin snake, krait [India], cobra, cobra de capello, king cobra, rattlesnake *or* rattler, copperhead, constrictor, boa constrictor, boa, python.

Mythological: basilisk, cockatrice, salamander; griffin; chimera; Python, Hydra, Cerberus.

Adj. animal; zoological; equine; bovine; canine; feline; fishy, piscatorial; ophidian, reptilian, snakelike.

367. VEGETABLE.—*N.* vegetable, vegetable kingdom; flora.

organism, plant, tree, shrub, bush, creeper, vine; herb, seedling; exotic; annual, perennial; pulse, greens.

foliage, leafage, verdure; branch, bough, stem, trunk; leaf, spray, leaflet, frond, pad, flag, petal, needle, sepal; spray, runner, shoot, tendril.

flower, blossom, bud, floweret, flowering plant.

tree, sapling, seedling; oak, elm, beech, birch, timber tree, pine, palm, spruce, fir, hemlock, yew, larch, cedar, juniper, chestnut, maple, alder, ash, myrtle, magnolia, walnut, teak, acacia, deodar, fig tree, eucalyptus, gum tree.

woodlands, virgin forest, forest primeval, forest, wood, timberland, timber, wood lot; weald, park, greenwood, grove, copse, coppice, thicket, chaparral, jungle, bush.

undergrowth, underwood, brushwood, brake, scrub, heath, heather, fern, bracken, furze, gorse, broom, sedge, rush, bulrush, bamboo; weed, moss, lichen, turf, grass, herbage.

grassland, plain, etc., 344.

seaweed, alga (*pl.* algae), dulse, kelp, rockweed, sea lettuce, gulfweed, sargasso, sargassum; Sargasso Sea.

V. vegetate, grow, flourish, bloom, flower, blossom; bud, etc. (*expand*), 194; timber, retimber, plant, trim, graft, prune, cut.

Adj. vegetable, vegetative, vegetarian; leguminous, herbaceous, herbal, botanic *or* botanical; arboreous, arboreal, sylvan; grassy, verdant, verdurous; floral; ligneous, wooden, woody; bosky, copsy; mossy, turfy; deciduous, evergreen.

native, domestic, indigenous, native-grown, home-grown.

368. [Science of animals] ZOOLOGY.—*N.* zoology, zoography, morphology, anatomy, histology, embryology; comparative anatomy, animal physiology, comparative physiology, anthropology, ornithology, ichthyology, entomology, paleontology.

zoologist, zoographer, zoographist, anatomist, anthropologist, ornithologist, ichthyologist, entomologist, paleontologist.

Adj. zoological, zoologic; zoographical.

369. [Science of plants] BOTANY.—*N.* botany, phytology, phytobiology, vegetable chemistry; vegetable physiology, dendrology; flora; botanic garden, etc. (*garden*), 371.

botanist, phytologist, phytobiologist, dendrologist; horticulturist, etc., 371; herbalist, herbist, herbarian.

V. botanize, herborize.

Adj. botanic *or* botanical, dendroid, dendriform, herby, herbal; horticultural.

370. MANAGEMENT OF ANIMALS.—*N.* domestication, domesticity, manège, veterinary art; breeding, taming.

menagerie, zoological garden, zoo [*colloq.*]; bear pit; aviary; apiary, beehive, hive; aquarium, fishery, fish hatchery, fish pond; hennery, incubator.
Keeper: herder, cowherd, grazier, drover, cowkeeper; shepherd, shepherdess; gamekeeper; trainer, breeder; cowboy, cowpuncher; horse trainer, bronchobuster [*slang*]; beekeeper, apiarist, apiculturist.

veterinarian, veterinary surgeon, vet [*colloq.*], horse doctor, horseshoer.

inclosure, stable, barn; sheepfold, sty; cage, hencoop.

V. tame, domesticate; corral, round up; break in, gentle, break, bust [*slang*], break to harness, train; ride, drive; spur, prick, lash, goad, whip; yoke, harness, harness up [*colloq.*], hitch, hitch up [*colloq.*], cinch.

groom, tend, rub down, brush, currycomb; water, feed, fodder; bed down, litter.

tend stock, milk, shear; water, etc. (*groom*), *v.*; herd; raise, bring up.

hatch, incubate, sit, brood, cover.

Adj. tame, domestic, domesticated, housebroken, broken, gentle, docile.

371. MANAGEMENT OF PLANTS.—*N.* agriculture, cultivation, husbandry, farming; tillage, gardening, vintage; horticulture, arboriculture, forestry; floriculture; landscape gardening.

husbandman, horticulturist, gardener, florist; agriculturist, yeoman, farmer, granger, cultivator, tiller of the soil, plowman; logger, lumberman, lumberjack, forester, woodcutter, pioneer, backwoodsman.
garden; botanic (*or* flower, kitchen, market, truck) garden; nursery; greenhouse, hothouse, conservatory; grassplot, lawn; shrubbery, arboretum, orchard; vineyard, orangery.

field, meadow, mead, green, common.

V. cultivate, till, till the soil, farm, garden, sow, plant; reap, mow, cut; manure, dress the ground; dig, spade, delve, hoe, plow, harrow, rake, weed; force, seed, turf; transplant, thin out, bed, prune, graft.

Adj. **arable**, plowable, tillable.

rural, rustic, country, agrarian, pastoral, bucolic, Arcadian.

372. MANKIND.—*N.* **mankind**, man; human race (*or* species, kind, nature); humanity, mortality, generation.

Science of man: anthropology, ethnology, ethnography.

human being; person, personage; individual, creature, fellow creature, mortal, body, somebody, one, someone; soul, living soul; party [*slang or vulgar*].

people, persons, folk, public, society, world; community, general public; nation, state, realm, republic; commonweal, commonwealth; body politic; the masses, etc. (*commonalty*), 876; population; lords of creation; ourselves.

Adj. **human**, mortal, personal, individual; national, civic, public social.

373. MAN.—*N.* **man**, male; gentleman, sir, master; yeoman, chap [*colloq.*], swain, fellow, blade, beau; husband, etc. (*youth*), 129.

mister, Mr., *monsieur* (*abbr.* M., *pl.* Messrs.) [F.], *Herr* [Ger.], *signor* [It., *used before name*], *signore* [It.], *signorino* [It., *dim. of signore*], *señor* [Sp.], *senhor* [Pg.].

Male animal: cock, drake, gander, dog, boar, stag, hart, buck, horse, stallion, gelding; tom, tomcat; he-goat, billy goat [*colloq.*]; ram; bull, bullock; capon; ox, steer.

Adj. **male**, masculine, manly, virile; unwomanly, unfeminine.

374. WOMAN.—*N.* **woman**, female, petticoat.

womankind, womanhood; the sex, fair sex, softer sex.

dame [*archaic except as an elderly woman or as slang*], madam, lady, donna, belle, matron, dowager, good woman, squaw; wife.

spinster, old maid, bachelor girl, new woman, girl, etc. (*youth*), 129.

mistress, Mrs., *madame* (*pl.* mesdames) [F.], *Frau* [Ger.], *signora* [It.], *señora* [Sp.], *senhora* [Pg.]; miss, *mademoiselle* (*pl.* mesdemoiselles) [F.], *Fräulein* [Ger.], *signorina* [It.], *señorita* [Sp.], *senhorita* [Pg.].

Effeminacy: betty, molly, mollycoddle, old woman, tame cat [*all contemptuous*].

Female animal: hen; bitch, slut; sow, doe, roe, mare; she-goat, nanny goat [*colloq.*], nanny [*colloq.*]; ewe, cow; lioness, tigress; vixen.

harem, seraglio, purdah [India].

Adj. **female**, feminine, womanly, ladylike, matronly, girlish, maidenly; womanish, effeminate, unmanly.

(2) Sensation

375. PHYSICAL SENSIBILITY.—*N.* sensibility, sensitiveness, feeling, impressibility, susceptibility.

sensation, impression; consciousness.

V. feel, perceive, be sensitive to.

render sensitive, sharpen, refine, excite, stir, cultivate, tutor.

cause sensation, impress, excite (*or* produce) an impression.

Adj. sensitive, sensuous; perceptive, sentient, sensible; conscious, alive, alive to impressions, impressionable, responsive.

acute, sharp, keen, vivid, lively.

Adv. to the quick; on the raw [*slang*].

376. PHYSICAL INSENSIBILITY.—*N.* insensibility, obtuseness, paralysis, anesthesia, hypnosis, stupor, coma, sleep.

anesthetic; opium, ether, chloroform, chloral; nitrous oxide, laughing gas; cocaine, novocain; refrigeration.

V. render insensible, blunt, cloy, satiate; benumb, numb, deaden, freeze, paralyze; anesthetize; put to sleep, hypnotize, stupefy, stun.

Adj. insensible, unfeeling, senseless, callous, hard, hardened, casehardened, proof, obtuse, dull; paralytic, palsied, numb, dead.

377. PHYSICAL PLEASURE.—*N.* pleasure, bodily enjoyment, animal gratification, gusto, relish, delight, sensual delight, sensuality; luxuriousness, dissipation, round of pleasure; comfort, ease, luxury, lap of luxury; creature comforts; purple and fine linen; bed of roses.

treat; diversion, entertainment, banquet, refreshment, feast.

happiness, felicity, bliss, beatitude, etc. (*mental enjoyment*), 827.

V. enjoy, relish; luxuriate in, revel in, bask in, wallow in; feast on, gloat over, smack the lips.

please, charm, delight, enchant, etc., 829.

Adj. comfortable, cosy, snug, luxurious, in comfort, at ease, in clover [*colloq.*].

agreeable, etc., 829; grateful, refreshing, comforting, cordial, genial; gratifying, sensuous; palatable, delicious, sweet; fragrant; melodious, harmonious; lovely, etc. (*beautiful*), 845.

Adv. in comfort, on a bed of roses, on flowery beds of ease.

378. PHYSICAL PAIN.—*N.* pain, suffering, dolor, ache, smart; shoot, shooting, twinge, pang, gripe, hurt, cut; sore, soreness; discomfort.

spasm, cramp; crick, stitch; convulsion, throe; throb, colic, gripes.

torment, torture, agony, anguish, rack, crucifixion, martyrdom.

V. **suffer,** feel (*or* suffer, undergo) pain; ache, smart, bleed, tingle, shoot, twinge; writhe, wince.

pain, give pain, inflict pain; lacerate; hurt, chafe, sting, bite, gnaw, stab, grate, gall, fret, prick, pierce, wring, convulse; torment, torture; rack, agonize; crucify; flog, etc. (*punish*), 972.

Adj. **painful,** aching, poignant, excruciating, biting; on the rack; sore, raw.

(1) *Touch*

379. [Sensation of pressure] TOUCH.—*N.* touch, contact, tangency, impact, feeling; graze, glance, brush, lick; manipulation, rubbing, kneading, massage.

V. **touch,** feel, handle, finger, thumb, paw, fumble, grope; stroke, massage, rub, knead, manipulate, wield; throw out a feeler.

Adj. **tactual,** tangible, palpable, tangent, lambent.

380. SENSATIONS OF TOUCH.—*N.* itching, tickling, titillation.

itch, scabies; mange.

V. **itch,** tingle, creep, thrill, sting; prick, prickle.

tickle, titillate.

Adj. **ticklish,** titillative.

itchy, mangy; creepy, crawly.

381. [Insensibility to touch] NUMBNESS.—*N.* numbness; physical insensibility, etc., 376; anesthesia.

V. **benumb,** etc., 376; stupefy, drug, deaden, paralyze.

Adj. **numb,** benumbed, insensible, unfeeling, deadened; intangible, impalpable; dazed, comatose, narcotic.

(2) *Heat*

382. HEAT.—*N.* heat, caloric; temperature, warmth, incandescence.

summer, dog days, heat wave, broiling sun; sun, etc. (*luminary*), 423.

flush, glow, blush, redness; fever.

fire, spark, scintillation, flash, flame, blaze; bonfire; wildfire; sheet of fire, lambent flame.

hot springs, geysers; thermae, hot baths, Turkish bath; steam.

V. **be hot,** glow, flush, sweat, swelter, bask, smoke, reek, stew, simmer, seethe, boil, burn, singe, scorch, scald, broil, blaze, flame; smolder, parch, pant.

heat, etc. (*make hot*), 384; incandesce.

thaw, fuse, melt, liquefy.

Adj. **warm**, mild, genial; tepid, lukewarm.

hot, heated, fervid, fervent, baking, ardent, sunny, sunshiny, torrid, tropical, thermal.

close, sultry, stifling, stuffy, suffocating, oppressive, sweltering.

fiery; incandescent, ebullient, glowing, aglow, reeking, smoking; live; on fire, blazing, in flames, in a blaze; alight, afire, ablaze, smoldering.

feverish, febrile, inflamed, burning; in a fever.

383. COLD.—*N.* **cold**, coldness, frigidity, inclemency.

winter; depth of winter; hard winter; arctic, antarctic.

ice; sleet; hail, hailstone; frost, rime, hoarfrost; icicle, thick-ribbed ice; iceberg, floe, berg, ice field, ice pack, glacier.

snow, snowflake, snowball, snowdrift, snowstorm, snowslip, snow avalanche.

chill, chilliness, shivering, goose flesh, chilblains, frostbite, chattering of teeth.

V. **be cold**, shiver, quake, shake, tremble, shudder, chill, freeze.

Adj. **cold**, cool, chill, chilly, frigid; fresh, keen, bleak, raw, inclement, bitter, biting, cutting, nipping, piercing, pinching; shivering, anguish; frostbitten.

icy, glacial, frosty, freezing, wintry, boreal, arctic, snowbound, icebound, frost-bound, frozen.

Adv. with chattering teeth.

384. CALEFACTION.—*N.* **calefaction**, tepefaction, heating, melting, fusion, liquefaction, combustion; cremation; calcination; incineration; carbonization; cauterization.

ignition, kindling, inflammation, conflagration; incendiarism, arson; auto-da-fé [Pg.], the stake, burning at the stake; suttee.

incendiary, arsonist, pyromaniac, fire bug.

boiling, ebullition, ebullience, decoction; hot spring, geyser.

crematory, crematorium, incinerator; furnace, etc., 386.

wrap, blanket, flannel, wool, fur; wadding, lining, interlining; clothing, etc., 225.

Products of combustion: cinder, ash, embers, slag, clinker; coke, carbon, charcoal.

V. **heat**, warm, chafe, foment; make hot; sun oneself, bask in the sun.

fire, set fire to, set on fire; kindle, enkindle, light, ignite; rekindle.

melt, thaw, fuse; liquefy, dissolve.

burn, scorch; inflame; roast, toast, fry, grill, singe, parch, bake; brand, cauterize, sear, burn in; corrode, char, carbonize, calcine, incinerate, smelt; reduce to ashes.

take *or* **catch fire**; blaze, etc. (*flame*), 382.

boil, stew, cook, seethe, scald, parboil, simmer.

Adj. heated, warmed; burnt, scorched; molten; volcanic. inflammable, inflammatory, combustible.

385. REFRIGERATION.—*N.* refrigeration, cooling, congelation, glaciation; solidification; ice; icebox, ice chest; refrigerator.

fire extinguisher, asbestos; fireman, fire brigade, fire department, fire engine.

V. cool, fan, refresh; ice, refrigerate, congeal, freeze, benumb, chill, petrify, pinch, nip, cut, pierce, bite.

extinguish, put out, stamp out; damp, slack, quench.

Adj. incombustible, asbestic, unflammable, uninflammable; fireproof.

386. FURNACE.—*N.* furnace, stove; cookstove, cooker, oven, brick oven, tin oven, Dutch oven, range, fireless cooker; forge, fiery furnace; volcano; kiln, brickkiln, limekiln.

brasier, tripod, salamander, heater, warming pan, footstove, foot warmer; radiator, register, coil; boiler, caldron, pot; urn, kettle; chafing dish; retort, crucible, alembic, still; flatiron, sadiron; toasting fork, toaster.

galley, caboose; hothouse, conservatory; bakehouse; washhouse, laundry.

fireplace, hearth, grate, firebox; andiron, firedog, fire irons; poker, tongs, shovel, hob, trivet; damper, crane, pothooks, chains, turnspit, spit, gridiron.

hot bath; thermae; Turkish (*or* Russian, vapor, electric, sitz, hip, shower) bath; bathroom, lavatory.

387. REFRIGERATOR.—*N.* refrigerator, icebox, ice chest; cold storage; refrigerating plant; icehouse; ice-cream freezer, freezer; ice bag, ice pack, cold pack; ice pail, cooler, wine cooler.

refrigerant, freezing, mixture, ice, ammonia.

388. FUEL.—*N.* fuel, firing, combustible, coal, anthracite, bituminous coal; carbon, slack, cannel coal *or* cannel, lignite, coke, charcoal; turf, peat; oil, gas, natural gas, electricity; ember, cinder, ash, slag, clinker; tinder, touchwood; punk.

log, backlog, yule log, firewood, fagot, kindling wood, kindlings, brushwood. fumigator, incense, joss stick; smudge; disinfectant.

brand, firebrand, torch; fuse, wick; spill, match, light.

V. coal, stoke; feed, fire, etc., 384.

Adj. carbonaceous; combustible, inflammable; slow-burning, free-burning.

389. THERMOMETER.—*N.* thermometer, thermometrograph, thermostat, thermoscope; differential thermometer, telethermometer, pyrometer.

(3) *Taste*

390. TASTE.—*N.* taste, flavor, gusto, savor, relish; smack, tang; aftertaste.

palate; tongue; tooth; stomach.

V. taste, flavor, savor, smack; tickle the palate, etc. (*savory*), 394.

Adj. tasty, savory, flavored, spiced; palatable, etc., 394.

391. INSIPIDITY.—*N.* insipidity; tastelessness, unsavoriness.

Adj. insipid; tasteless, unsavory, unflavored, jejune, savorless; weak, stale, flat, vapid, wishy-washy [*colloq.*].

392. PUNGENCY.—*N.* pungency, piquancy, poignancy, tang, nip.

sharpness, acridity; sourness, unsavoriness.

dram, cordial, nip, bracer [*colloq.*], pick-me-up [*colloq.*], potion, liqueur.

tobacco, nicotine; smoke, cigar, cheroot, stogy; cigarette, fag [*slang*], Havana, Cuban tobacco; weed [*colloq.*]; snuff.

V. season, spice, bespice, salt, pepper, pickle, brine, devil, curry.

Adj. pungent, strong, high-flavored, full-flavored, high-seasoned; gamy, high; sharp, piquant, racy; biting, mordant; spicy; seasoned, spiced; hot, peppery; acrid, bitter; sour, acid, etc., 397; unsavory, etc., 395.

salt, saline, brackish, briny.

393. CONDIMENT.—*N.* condiment, flavoring, seasoning, sauce, spice, relish; pickle; chutney; appetizer.

V. season, etc. (*render pungent*), 392.

394. SAVORINESS.—*N.* savoriness, tastiness, palatability; delectability; relish, zest.

appetizer, hors d'oeuvre [F.].

delicacy, titbit, dainty, ambrosia, nectar.

V. be savory; tickle the palate (*or* appetite); tempt the appetite, taste good.

relish, like, smack the lips.

Adj. savory, tasty; good, palatable; pleasing, nice, dainty, exquisite, delicate; delectable, toothsome, appetizing, delicious; rich, luscious, ambrosial, nectareous; distinctive.

395. UNSAVORINESS.—*N.* unsavoriness; acridness, sourness, etc., 397; acerbity; gall and wormwood.

V. be unpalatable, sicken, disgust, nauseate, pall, turn the stomach.

Adj. unsavory, unpalatable, ill-flavored; bitter, acrid, acrimonious.

offensive, repulsive, nasty, sickening, nauseous; loathsome; unpleasant, etc., 830.

396. SWEETNESS.—*N.* sweetness, saccharinity.

sugar, saccharin; preserve, jam, sugar candy, sugarplum.

sweets, confectionery, caramel, lollipop, bonbon, jujube, comfit, sweetmeat, confection; honey, manna; glucose, sirup, treacle, molasses, maple sirup, maple sugar; taffy, butterscotch.

Sweet beverages: nectar; mead, liqueur, sweet wine.

pastry, cake, pie, tart, puff, pudding.

V. **sweeten,** sugar, sugar off [*local*]; candy.

Adj. **sweet,** sugary, saccharine, candied, honied, luscious, cloying, honey-sweet, nectareous; dulcet, mellifluous.

397. SOURNESS.—*N.* **sourness,** acerbity, acidity; acid.

V. **render sour,** acidify, acidulate, acetify; ferment.

Adj. **sour;** acid, acidulated; subacid; tart, crabbed; hard, unripe, green; astringent, styptic.

(4) *Odor*

398. ODOR.—*N.* **odor,** smell, scent; effluvium; emanation, exhalation; fume, trail, redolence.

V. **have an odor** (*or* **scent**); smell, exhale; give out a smell (*or* odor); scent.

smell, scent, snuff, sniff, inhale.

Adj. **odorous,** odoriferous; strong-scented, redolent, pungent.

Relating to the sense of smell: olfactory; quick-scented, keenscented.

399. INODOROUSNESS.—*N.* **inodorousness,** absence (*or* want) of smell.

deodorization; deodorizer, deodorant.

V. **be inodorous** (*or* **scentless**); not smell.

Adj. **inodorous,** scentless; without smell (*or* odor).

400. FRAGRANCE.—*N.* **fragrance,** aroma, redolence, perfume, bouquet; sweet smell (*or* odor), scent.

perfumery; incense, frankincense; musk, myrrh, attar, bergamot, balm, civet, potpourri, tuberose, hyacinth, heliotrope, rose, jasmine, lily, lily of the valley, violet, pomander; toilet water; eau de cologne [F.], cologne, cologne water.

bouquet, nosegay, posy [*colloq.*], boutonniere [F.], buttonhole [*colloq.*].

spray; wreath, garland, chaplet.

Scent containers: smelling bottle, scent bottle, vinaigrette; scent bag, sachet; thurible, censer, incense burner, atomizer, spray.

V. **be fragrant** (*or* **scented**); have a perfume (*or* aroma); smell sweet, scent, perfume; embalm.

Adj. **fragrant,** aromatic, redolent, spicy, balmy, scented; sweetsmelling, sweet-scented; perfumed; incense-breathing, ambrosial.

401. FETOR—*N.* **fetor,** bad smell (*or* odor), stench, stink, fetidness, fustiness, mustiness; rancidity; foulness.

V. **have a bad smell,** smell, stink, smell strong, smell offensively.

Adj. **fetid;** strong-smelling; high, bad, strong, offensive, noisome, rank, rancid, moldy, tainted, musty; smelling, stinking; putrid, rotten, foul; suffocating.

(5) Sound

402. SOUND.—*N.* sound, noise; sonority, sonorousness; strain; accent, twang, intonation; tune, cadence; audibility; resonance, vibration; voice, etc., 580.

Science of sound: acoustics, phonetics, phonology, phonography; telephony, radiophony.

V. sound, make a noise; give out sound, emit sound; resound.

Adj. sounding, sonorous, resonant, audible, distinct; auditory, acoustic.

phonetic, phonic, sonant.

403. SILENCE.—*N.* silence, stillness, quiet, peace, hush, lull; rest [*music*]; muteness; silence of the tomb (*or* grave).

V. silence, still, hush, stifle, muffle, gag, stop; muzzle, put to silence.

Adj. silent; still, stilly; noiseless, quiet, calm, soundless, hushed; speechless; aphonic, surd, mute.

solemn, soft, awful, deathlike.

Adv. in dead silence.

404. LOUDNESS.—*N.* loudness, power, vociferation, uproariousness.

din, loud noise, clang, clangor, clatter, noise, roar, uproar, hubbub, racket, hullabaloo, pandemonium; fracas; outcry, etc., 411; explosion, detonation.

blare, trumpet blast, flourish of trumpets, fanfare, blast; peal, swell, alarum, boom; resonance, etc., 408.

V. be loud (*or* deafening); peal, swell, clang, boom, thunder, roar; deafen, stun, rend the air, awake the echoes; resound, etc., 408; speak up, shout, etc. (*vociferate*), 411; bellow, etc. (*cry as an animal*), 412.

Adj. loud, sonorous, deep, full, powerful; noisy, blatant; clangorous, thundering, deafening, earsplitting, piercing; shrill, etc., 410; obstreperous, uproarious; clamorous, vociferous, fullmouthed, stentorian.

Adv. loudly, noisily; aloud; at the top of one's lungs, lustily, in full cry.

405. FAINTNESS.—*N.* faintness, inaudibility; faint sound, whisper, breath; undertone; murmur, hum, buzz, purr, lap [*of waves*], plash; sough, moan, rustle; tinkle.

hoarseness, huskiness.

silencer, muffler; soft pedal, damper, mute, sordine [*all music*].

V. whisper, breathe; mutter, etc. (*speak imperfectly*), 583.

murmur, purl, hum, gurgle, ripple, babble, flow; rustle; tinkle.

muffle, deaden, mute, subdue.

Adj. **faint,** low, dull; stifled, muffled; inaudible; hoarse, husky; gentle, soft; floating; purling, flowing; muttered; whispered; liquid; soothing; dulcet, etc. (*melodious*), 413.

Adv. **in a whisper,** with bated breath, *sotto voce* [It.]; between the teeth; aside; piano, pianissimo [*both music*]; out of earshot; inaudibly, faintly.

406. [**Sudden and violent sounds**] **SNAP.**—*N.* **snap,** etc., *v.;* toot, shout, yell, yap [*dial.*], yelp, bark.

report, thump, knock, clap, thud; burst, thunderclap, thunderburst, eruption, blowout [*tire*], explosion, discharge, detonation, firing, salvo, volley.

V. **snap,** rap, tap, knock; click; clash; crack, crackle; crash; pop; slam, bang, clap; thump, toot, yelp, bark, fire, explode, rattle, burst on the ear.

407. [**Repeated and protracted sounds**] **ROLL.**—*N.* **roll,** etc., *v.;* drumming, rumbling, howl, dingdong; ratatat, rubadub, tattoo; pitapat; quaver, clutter, charivari, racket; peal of bells, devil's tattoo; drumfire, barrage; whir, rattle, drone; reverberation.

V. **roll,** drum, boom; whir, rustle, tootle, roar, drone, rumble, rattle, clatter, patter, clack.

hum, trill, shake; chime, peal, toll; tick, beat.

408. RESONANCE.—*N.* **resonance;** ring, chime, ringing, clangor, bell note, tintinnabulation, vibration, reverberation.

bass; basso [It.], basso profundo [It.]; baritone, contralto; pedal point, organ point; snoring, snore.

V. **resound,** reverberate, re-echo; ring, sound; chink, clink; jingle, tinkle; chime; gurgle, mutter, murmur; plash, echo, ring in the ear.

Adj. **resonant,** reverberant, resounding, reverberating; deep-toned, deep-mouthed; hollow, sepulchral; gruff, etc. (*harsh*), 410.

408a. NONRESONANCE.—*N.* **nonresonance,** dead sound; thud, thump, muffled drums, cracked bell; damper, sordine, mute; muffler, silencer.

V. **muffle,** deaden, mute; sound dead; stop (*or* deaden) the sound.

Adj. **nonresonant,** dead, mute; muffled, deadened.

409. [**Hissing sounds**] **SIBILATION.**—*N.* **sibilation,** hissing; zip; hiss, buzz; sneezing, sternutation.

V. **hiss,** buzz, whiz; rustle; fizz, fizzle; wheeze, whistle, sizzle, swish.

Adj. **sibilant;** hissing; rustling; wheezy.

410. [**Harsh or high sounds**] **STRIDENCY.**—*N.* **stridency;** stridor, harshness, raucousness; sharpness; creak, jar; creaking, grating; discord, dissonance.

high note, shrill note; soprano, treble, tenor, alto, falsetto; head voice, head tone; shriek, yell, cry, wail, pipe.

V. **grate,** creak, saw, snore, jar, burr, pipe, twang, jangle, clank; scream, etc. (*cry*), 411; set the teeth on edge, pierce (*or* split) the ears; yelp, etc. (*animal sound*), 412; buzz, etc. (*hiss*), 409.

Adj. **grating,** creaking, jangling, jarring, strident, harsh, coarse, hoarse, raucous; metallic; rough, rude; gruff, grum, sepulchral, hollow.

high, sharp, acute, shrill; piercing, high-pitched; cracked; discordant.

411. CRY.—*N.* **cry,** shout; shriek; hubbub; bark, etc. (*animal*), 412.

outcry, vociferation, ejaculation, hullabaloo, chorus, clamor, hue and cry, plaint; lungs; stentor.

V. **cry,** roar, shout, bawl; halloo, halloa, yo-ho, whoop; yell, bellow, hoot, boo; howl, scream, screech, shriek; shrill, squeak, squeal, squall; whine, pipe.

cheer, huzza, hurrah, yell.

moan, grumble, groan.

snort, snore; grunt, etc., 412.

vociferate, raise (*or* lift) the voice; yell out, call out, sing out, cry out; exclaim, give cry, clamor; rend the air; make the welkin ring; shout at the top of one's voice.

Adj. **clamorous,** clamant, vociferous; stentorian, etc. (*loud*), 404; open-mouthed; full-mouthed.

412. [Animal sounds] ULULATION.—*N.* **ululation,** howling, cry, roar; call, note, howl, bark, yelp, bowwow, belling; woodnote; insect cry; twittering, drone.

V. **ululate,** howl; cry, roar, bellow; bark, yelp; bay, bay the moon; yap, growl, snarl, howl; grunt, snort, squeak; neigh, bray; mew, purr, caterwaul; bleat, low, moo; crow, screech, croak, caw, coo, gobble, quack, cackle, cluck; chirp, cheep, chirrup, peep, sing, twitter; chatter, hoot, wail; hum, buzz; hiss; blat [*colloq.*].

413. MELODY. CONCORD.—*N.* **melody,** rhythm, measure; rhyme, etc. (*poetry*), 597; euphony.

Musical terms: pitch, timbre, intonation, tone, overtone.
orchestration, harmonization, modulation, phrasing.
staff *or* stave, line, space, brace; bar, rest; passage, phrase; trill *or* shake, turn, arpeggio [It.].
note, musical note, notes of a scale; sharp, flat, natural; high note, etc., 410; low note, etc., 408; interval; semitone.
breve, semibreve *or* whole note, minim *or* half note, crotchet *or* quarter note, quaver *or* eighth note, semiquaver *or* sixteenth note, demisemiquaver *or* thirty-second note; sustained note, drone.
scale, gamut; diapason; key, clef, chord.
harmony, concord; tonality; consonance; part; unison; chime.
Science of harmony: harmony, harmonics; thorough bass, counterpoint; composer.

opus (*pl. opera*) [L.], piece of music, etc., 415.

V. harmonize, chime, symphonize, transpose, orchestrate; blend, put in tune, tune, accord, string.

Adj. harmonious, harmonic, in concord, in tune, in concert, in unison.

melodious, musical, tuneful, tunable; sweet, dulcet, mellow, mellifluous; soft; clear, silvery; euphonious; enchanting, etc. (*pleasure-giving*), 829; fine-toned, silver-toned, full-toned, deep-toned.

414. DISCORD.—*N.* discord, dissonance, want of harmony; harshness, etc., 410; charivari, racket; Babel, pandemonium.

V. be discordant (*or* harsh); jar, etc. (*sound harshly*), 410.

Adj. discordant, dissonant, out of tune, tuneless; unmusical, untunable; unmelodious, inharmonious; singsong; harsh, etc., 410; jarring.

415. MUSIC.—*N.* music; minstrelsy; strain, tune, air, melody; piece of music; rondo, rondeau, pastoral; cavatina, fantasia, toccata [It.]; fugue, canon; potpourri, medley; incidental music; variations, roulade, cadenza, cadence, trill; serenade, nocturne.

instrumental music; orchestral score, full score; composition, opus (*pl. opera*) [L.]; concert piece; concerto [It.]; symphony, sonata, symphonic poem, tone poem; chamber music; movement; overture, prelude, voluntary; string quartet (*or* quintet).

lively music, polka, reel, etc. (*dance*), 848; ragtime, jazz; syncopation, martial music, march; allegro, presto.

slow music, Lydian measures; adagio, largo, andante; lullaby, cradle song, berceuse [F.]; dirge, etc. (*lament*), 839; dead march; minuet.

vocal music, vocalism; chant; psalm, psalmody, hymnology; hymn; canticle; oratorio; opera, operetta; cantata; song, lay, ballad, ditty, carol; recitative, aria.

solo, duet, trio, quartet, quintet, sestet, septet, double quartet, chorus; part song, descant, glee, madrigal, catch, round, chorale; antiphon; accompaniment; inside part, second, alto, tenor, bass; score, piano score, vocal score.

concert, musicale, recital, chamber concert, popular concert *or* pop [*colloq.*], open-air concert; serenade; community singing, singsong [*colloq.*].

method, solfeggio [It.], tonic sol-fa, sight singing, sight reading.

V. compose, write, etc., 416; attune, tune.

perform, execute, play, etc., 416.

Adj. musical; instrumental, vocal, choral, lyric, melodic; operatic; classic, modern, orchestral, symphonic, contrapuntal; program, imitative; harmonious, etc., 413.

416. MUSICIAN. [Performance of music]—*N.* musician, virtuoso, performer, player, minstrel; bard, etc. (*poet*), 597; accompanist, instrumentalist, organist, pianist, violinist, fiddler; flutist, harpist, fifer, trumpeter, cornetist, piper, drummer.

orchestra; strings, woodwind, brass; band, brass band, military band, German band, jazz band; street musicians.

vocalist, singer, warbler; songbird; songster, songstress; chorister; chorus singer; choir, chorus.

Orpheus, Apollo, the Muses, Polyhymnia, Erato, Euterpe, Terpsichore.

conductor, choirmaster, bandmaster, concertmaster, drum major, song leader, precentor.

performance, execution, touch, expression.

V. play, tune, tune up, pipe, pipe up, strike up, sweep the chords, fiddle, strike the lyre, beat the drum; blow (*or* wind) the horn; twang, pluck, pick; pound, thump; drum, thrum, strum, beat time; execute, perform; accompany.

compose, set to music; arrange, harmonize, orchestrate.

sing, troll, chant, intone, hum, warble, twitter, carol, chirp, chirrup, lilt, quaver, trill, shake.

Adj. musical; lyric, dramatic; bravura, florid, brilliant.

417. MUSICAL INSTRUMENTS.—*N.* musical instruments; orchestra (*including* strings, woodwind, brass, and percussive instruments); band; string band, military band, brass band.

418. [Sense of sound] HEARING.—*N.* hearing, audition; audibility; acoustics; ear for music.

ear; eardrum, tympanum.

Instruments: ear trumpet, audiophone, dentiphone, speaking trumpet; phonograph, gramophone, graphophone, microphone, victrola; stethoscope; telephone, radiophone, wireless telephone, radio.

hearer, auditor, audience, listener; eavesdropper.

V. hear, overhear; hark, hearken; list, listen; strain one's ears, attend to, give attention, prick up one's ears; give ear, give a hearing to.

Adj. hearing, auditory, acoustic, phonic; auricular; auditive.

419. DEAFNESS—*N.* deafness, hardness of hearing, inaudibility; deaf-mute; deaf-and-dumb alphabet.

V. deafen, render deaf, stun, split the ears (*or* eardrum).

Adj. deaf, hard (*or* dull) of hearing; stunned, deafened; stone-deaf; inattentive.

inaudible, out of earshot (*or* hearing).

(6) *Light*

420. LIGHT.—*N.* light, ray, beam, stream (*of light*), gleam, streak; sunbeam, moonbeam; aurora, dawn, daylight, day, sunshine; glint, glare, glow, afterglow; sun, etc., 423.

reflection, refraction, dispersion.

halo, glory, nimbus, aureole, aura.

spark, scintilla, scintillation, flash, blaze, coruscation; flame, glare, blaze; lightning; phosphorescence.

luster, sheen, shimmer, gloss, brightness, brilliancy, splendor, effulgence; illumination, radiance, radiation.

Science of light: optics, radiometry; photography; phototelegraphy, radiotelegraphy; actinic rays, radioactivity; Röntgen rays, X rays, ultraviolet rays.

illuminant, gas, etc., 423.

V. shine, glow, beam, glitter, glisten, gleam; flare, blaze, glare, shimmer, glimmer, flicker, sparkle, scintillate, coruscate, flash.

daze, dazzle, bedazzle.

lighten, enlighten, light, irradiate, illume, illumine, illuminate; kindle, etc., 384.

Adj. luminous, lucent; light, sunny, bright, vivid, splendid, resplendent, refulgent, lustrous, brilliant, radiant, lambent; aglow.

shiny, glossy, burnished, glassy.

clear, cloudless, unclouded.

421. DARKNESS.—*N.* darkness, duskiness; blackness, swarthiness; obscurity, gloom, murk, murkiness; dusk; dimness, etc., 422.

night; midnight; dead of night.

shadow, shade; obscuration, adumbration; eclipse; radiograph.

V. darken, obscure, shade, dim; lower, overcast, overshadow, cloud, becloud, bedim.

extinguish, put out, blow out, snuff out.

Adj. dark, darkling, obscure; black, etc. (*color*), 431; nocturnal.

somber, dusky; dingy, lurid, gloomy, murky; shady, umbrageous; overcast, etc. (*dim*), 422; cloudy, etc., 426.

422. DIMNESS.—*N.* dimness, paleness, dullness, duskiness, mistiness.

twilight, dusk, nightfall, gloaming; dawn, daybreak, break of day, Aurora; moonlight, moonshine [*poetic*], starlight.

V. cloud over, gloom, lower.

twinkle, glimmer, flicker.

pale, fade, grow dim.

dim, bedim, obscure, shade, shadow, darken, cloud, becloud.

Adj. dim, dull, dingy, dusky, lackluster; cloudy, misty, hazy.

leaden, lurid, dun; overcast, dirty.

423. [Source of light] LUMINARY.—*N.* luminary; light, ray, beam; flame, etc. (*fire*), 382; spark, scintilla; phosphorescence.

Heavenly bodies: sun, orb of day, daystar [*poetic*]; star; constellation; galaxy, Milky Way; polestar, Polaris; morning star, Lucifer; evening star, Venus; moon, etc., 318.

sun god, Helios, Phoebus, Apollo, Hyperion, Ra [*Egypt*].

phosphorus; *ignis fatuus* [L.]; Jack-o'-lantern, will-o'-the-wisp.

polar lights, northern lights, aurora borealis [L.], aurora australis [L.]; aurora.

Artificial light: gas, gaslight, electric light, electric torch; headlight, searchlight; spotlight, flashlight, limelight, calcium light; lamplight, lamp, lantern, dark lantern, bull's-eye; candle, taper, rushlight; torch, flambeau, brand; gaselier, chandelier; candelabrum, sconce, luster, candlestick; fireworks, pyrotechnics.

signal light, rocket, balefire, beacon fire; lighthouse.

V. illuminate, etc. (*light*), 420.

Adj. self-luminous; phosphorescent; radiant, etc. (*light*), 420.

424. SHADE.—*N.* shade; awning, etc. (*cover*), 223.

screen, curtain, portiere [F.]; shutter, blind.

veil, mantle, mask.

cloud, mist, shadow; smoke screen [*mil.*].

blinkers, blinders; smoked glasses, colored spectacles.

V. veil, draw a curtain; cast a shadow, etc. (*darken*), 421.

Adj. shady, umbrageous, shadowy.

425. TRANSPARENCY.—*N.* transparency, transparence, translucence, diaphanousness; lucidity, limpidity; fluorescence; translumination.

V. be transparent (*or* pellucid); transmit light.

Adj. transparent, pellucid, lucid, diaphanous; translucent, limpid, clear, serene, crystalline.

426. OPACITY.—*N.* opacity, opaqueness; cloudiness; film; cloud, etc., 353.

V. be opaque; obstruct the passage of light.

Adj. opaque, impervious to light; dim, etc., 422; turbid, thick, muddy, cloudy, foggy, vaporous; smoky, murky, smeared, dirty.

427. SEMITRANSPARENCY.—*N.* semitransparency, opalescence, milkiness, pearliness; mist, haze, steam.

V. cloud, frost, cloud over, frost over.

Adj. semitransparent, semidiaphanous, semiopaque; opalescent, opaline; pearly, milky; frosted, hazy, misty.

428. [Specific Light] COLOR.—*N.* color, hue, tint, tinge, dye, complexion, shade, tincture; coloration; glow, flush; tone, key.

primary color, complementary color; coloring, keeping, tone, value.

spectrum, spectrum analysis; prism, spectroscope, kaleidoscope.

pigment, coloring matter, paint, dye, wash, distemper, stain; medium.

V. color, dye, tinge, stain, tint, tone; paint, wash, distemper, ingrain, grain, illuminate, emblazon.

Adj. colored, dyed; chromatic, prismatic; double-dyed.

bright, vivid, intense, deep; fresh, rich, gorgeous; bright-colored, gay.

gaudy, florid; garish; showy, flaunting; flashy; many-colored, parti-colored, variegated; raw, crude; glaring, flaring.

mellow, harmonious, pearly, sweet, delicate, subtle, tender.

dull, sad, somber, sad-colored, grave, gray, dark.

429. ABSENCE OF COLOR.—*N.* decoloration, discoloration; pallor, paleness, sallowness.

neutral tint, monochrome, black and white.

V. lose color, fade, become colorless, turn pale; pale, fade out.

deprive of color, decolor, wash out, tone down; whiten, bleach, blanch.

Adj. colorless, uncolored, hueless, pale, pallid; pale-faced, anemic; faint, dull, cold, muddy, leaden, dun, wan, sallow, dingy, ashy, ashen, ghastly, cadaverous, glassy, lackluster; discolored.

light-colored, fair, blond, ash-blond; white, etc., 430; towheaded.

430. WHITENESS.—*N.* whiteness, showiness, hoariness.

whitewash, whiting, whitening, calcimine.

V. whiten, bleach, blanch, silver, frost.

whitewash, calcimine, white.

Adj. white, snow-white, snowy, frosted, hoar, hoary; silvery, silver, milk-white, milky.

whitish, creamy, pearly, ivory, fair, blond, ash-blond; blanched; light.

431. BLACKNESS.—*N.* blackness, darkness, obscurity; swarthiness, swartness; lividness.

Negro, Negress, blackamoor, man of color, colored man, colored woman, nigger [*colloq., usually contemptuous*], darky [*colloq.*], black, Ethiop, Ethiopian, Hottentot, Pygmy, Bushman, African.

V. black, blacken, blot, blotch, smut, smudge, smirch; darken, etc., 421.

Adj. black, sable, somber, livid, dark, inky, ebon, pitchy, sooty; swart, swarthy, dusky, dingy, murky; blotchy, smudgy; low-toned.

432. GRAY.—*N.* gray, etc., *adj.*; grayness; neutral tint, silver, dove color, pepper and salt, chiaroscuro [It.].

V. render gray, gray.

Adj. gray; iron-gray, dun, drab, dingy, leaden, pearly, dove-colored, silver, silvery, silvered; dapple-gray; ashen, ashy; grizzly, grizzled.

433. BROWN.—*N.* brown, etc., *adj.*; brownness.

V. render brown, brown, tan, embrown, bronze.

Adj. brown, nut-brown, seal-brown, mahogany, chocolate; fawn, ecru, tawny; tan, fawn-colored, snuff-colored, liver-colored.

reddish-brown, terra cotta, russet, foxy, bronze, coppery, copper-colored, maroon; bay, roan, sorrel; chestnut, henna, auburn, hazel.

sunburned; tanned, etc., *v.*

434. RED.—*N.* red, etc., *adj.*; flesh color, flesh tint, color, warmth; redness, ruddiness, blush.

V. redden, rouge, crimson, incarnadine; ruddle, rust.
blush, flush, color, color up, mantle, redden.

Adj. red, scarlet, cardinal, vermilion, carmine, crimson, pink, rose, cerise, cherry, salmon, maroon, carnation, magenta, solferino, damask.

reddish; sanguine, bloody, gory; coral, coralline, rosy, roseate; blood-red, wine-red, wine-colored, ruby, rufous, bricky, reddish-brown, etc., 433; rose (*or* ruby, cherry, claret, flame, flesh, peach, salmon, brick, rust) -colored.

red-complexioned, red-faced, florid, burned, rubicund, ruddy, red, high-colored, glowing, sanguine, blooming, rosy, hectic, flushed, inflamed.

Of hair: sandy, carroty, brick-red, Titian, auburn, chestnut.

435. GREEN.—*N.* green, etc., *adj.*; greenness, verdancy, verdure.

Adj. green, verdant, olive; verdurous; emerald (*or* pea, grass, apple, sea, leaf, bottle, Irish, Kelly) green; greenish, aquamarine, blue-green.

436. YELLOW.—*N.* yellow, etc., *adj.*; yellowness; jaundice.
V. render yellow, yellow, gild.
Adj. yellow, aureate, golden, gold, gilt, gilded, lemon, fallow; sallow, jaundiced; tawny, cream, creamy; flaxen, yellowish, buff; gold (*or* saffron, citron, lemon, amber, straw, primrose, cream) -colored.

437. PURPLE.—*N.* purple, etc., *adj.*; royal purple; gridelin, amethyst; damson, heliotrope.
V. render purple, purple, empurple.
Adj. purple, violet, plum-colored, lavender, lilac, puce, mauve, purplish, amethystine, magenta, solferino, heliotrope; livid; purplish.

438. BLUE.—*N.* blue, etc., *adj.*; azure [*her.*]; indigo; sapphire, blueness, bluishness; bloom.
Adj. blue, azure, cerulean, sky-blue, navy-blue, midnight-blue, cadet-blue, robin's-egg-blue, baby-blue, ultramarine, aquamarine, electric-blue, steel-blue; bluish; cold.

439. ORANGE.—*N.* orange, old gold; gold color, etc., *adj.*
Adj. orange, orange (*or* gold, brass, apricot) -colored; warm, hot, glowing, flame-colored.

440. VARIEGATION.—*N.* variegation; iridescence, play of colors, spottiness; tricolor.

check, plaid, tartan, patchwork; marquetry, parquet, parquetry, mosaic, checkerwork; chessboard, checkers; harlequin.

V. variegate, stripe, streak, checker, fleck, speckle, besprinkle,

sprinkle; stipple, dot, tattoo, inlay, tessellate; damascene; embroider, quilt.

Adj. variegated, many-colored, many-hued, divers-colored, parti-colored, polychromatic; kaleidoscopic.

iridescent, opaline, opalescent, prismatic, pearly, shot, tortoiseshell.

mottled, pied, piebald, skewbald; motley, marbled, pepper-and-salt, dappled.

checkered, checked, plaid, mosaic, tessellated.

spotted, spotty; powdered; speckled, freckled, flea-bitten, studded; flecked.

barred, veined, brindled, tabby, watered.

441. [Perception of light] VISION.—*N.* vision, sight, optics, eyesight.

view, look, glance, ken, glimpse, glint, peep, peek; gaze, stare, leer; contemplation, regard, survey; inspection, reconnaissance, watch, espionage, autopsy; sight-seeing, globe-trotting [*colloq.*].

viewpoint, standpoint, point of view; loophole, watchtower.

field of view; theater, amphitheater, arena, vista, horizon; bird's-eye view, panoramic view.

eye, visual organ, organ of vision, naked eye; clear (*or* sharp, quick, eagle) sight.

V. see, behold, discern, perceive, descry, sight, make out; discover, distinguish, recognize, spy, espy, command a view of; witness, contemplate, look on, see at a glance.

look, view, eye, survey, scan, inspect; reconnoiter, glance, cast a glance; observe, etc. (*attend to*), 457; watch, keep watch; watch for, etc. (*expect*), 507; peep, peek, peer, pry, take a peep.

look intently; strain one's eyes; rivet the eyes upon; stare, gaze; pore over, gloat on, gloat over; leer, ogle, glare; goggle; squint, gloat, look askance.

Adj. ocular, visual, optic *or* optical; ophthalmic; visible, etc., 446.

clear-sighted, clear-eyed, farsighted; eagle-eyed, hawk-eyed, lynx-eyed, keen-eyed, Argus-eyed.

Adv. at sight, at first sight, at a glance, at the first blush.

442. BLINDNESS.—*N.* blindness, sightlessness, benightedness, cataract; dim-sightedness, etc., 443; Braille.

V. be blind, not see; lose one's sight; grope in the dark.

blind, blindfold, hoodwink, dazzle; put one's eyes out; throw dust into one's eyes; screen, hide.

Adj. blind, eyeless, sightless, visionless; dark; stone-blind, stark-blind, undiscerning; dim-sighted, etc., 443.

Adv. blindly, blindfold; darkly.

443. DIM-SIGHTEDNESS.—*N.* **Imperfect vision:** dim (*or* short, near, long) -sightedness; purblindness, blearedness, myopia, astigmatism; color blindness, snow blindness; ophthalmia; cataract.

squint, cross-eye, cast in the eye, swivel eye, cockeye, goggle-eyes.

Limitation of vision: blinker, blinder; screen, curtain, veil.

Fallacies of vision: refraction, distortion, illusion, mirage, phantasm, phantom; vision; specter, apparition, ghost; will-o'-the-wisp, etc., 423.

V. **be dim-sighted,** see double; see through a glass darkly; wink, blink, squint, look askance, screw up the eyes, glare, glower.

dazzle, glare, swim, blur.

Adj. **dim-sighted,** myopic, nearsighted, shortsighted, astigmatic; blear-eyed, goggle-eyed, one-eyed; half-blind, purblind; cockeyed [*colloq.*], dim-eyed, mole-eyed.

444. SPECTATOR.—*N.* **spectator,** beholder, observer, looker-on, onlooker, witness, eyewitness, bystander, passer-by; sightseer; rubberneck [*slang*].

spy, scout; sentinel, etc. (*warning*), 668.

grandstand [*fig.*], bleachers [*fig.*], gallery.

V. **witness,** behold, etc. (*see*), 441; look on, etc. (*be present*), 186.

445. OPTICAL INSTRUMENTS.—*N.* **optical instruments;** lens, magnifier, microscope; spectacles, glasses, goggles, eyeglass, pince-nez; periscope; telescope, glass, lorgnette, binocular; spyglass, opera glass, field glass; burning glass, convex lens; prism.

camera, hand camera, kodak [*trade name*]; moving-picture machine, magic lantern, stereopticon; stereoscope, kaleidoscope.

mirror, reflector, speculum; looking glass, pier glass, cheval glass.

optics, optician; photography, photographer; optometry, optometrist; microscopy, microscopist.

446. VISIBILITY.—*N.* **visibility,** perceptibility, conspicuousness, distinctness, appearance, etc., 448; exposure; manifestation, etc., 525; ocular demonstration; field of view, vista, horizon.

V. **appear,** open to the view; catch the eye; present (*or* show, manifest, reveal, expose, betray) itself; stand forth, stand out; materialize; show; arise; peep out, peer out; start up, spring up; gleam, glimmer; glitter, glow, loom; glare; burst forth; burst upon the view; heave in sight [*naut. or colloq.*]; come into view, come out, come forth, come forward; attract the attention, etc., 457.

expose to view, show, display.

Adj. **visible,** perceptible, discernible, apparent; in view, in full view, in sight; exposed to view.

distinct, plain, clear, definite; obvious, etc. (*manifest*), 525; recognizable; glaring, palpable, staring, conspicuous.

Adv. before one, under one's very eyes, in sight of.

447. INVISIBILITY.—*N.* invisibility, imperceptibility; indistinctness; mystery; latency, obscurity; concealment, mystification.

V. **be invisible** (*or* imperceptible); be hidden, etc. (*hide*), 528; escape notice.

render invisible; conceal, etc., 528; put out of sight.

Adj. **invisible**, imperceptible; out of sight, not in sight, unseen; viewless; inconspicuous; covert, latent.

indistinct; dim; mysterious, dark, obscure; confused, indistinguishable, shadowy, indefinite, undefined, ill-defined, blurred, out of focus; misty, veiled, concealed.

448. APPEARANCE.—*N.* **appearance**, phenomenon, sight, show, scene, view; lookout, outlook, prospect, vista, perspective, bird's-eye view, scenery, landscape, seascape, picture, tableau; display, exposure, rising of the curtain.

spectacle, pageant; peep show, magic lantern, biograph, cinematograph, cinema [*colloq.*], moving pictures, movies [*colloq.*], photoplay, photodrama; panorama.

aspect, angle, phase, shape, form, guise, look, complexion, color, image, mien, air, cast, carriage, port, demeanor; presence, expression, point of view, light.

lineament, feature, trait, lines; outline, outside; contour, silhouette, face, countenance, visage, profile; physiognomy.

V. **appear**, be visible, seem, look, show; cut a figure, figure; present to the view; show, etc. (*make manifest*), 525; look like, resemble.

Adj. **apparent**, seeming, ostensible; on view.

Adv. to all appearance, ostensibly, seemingly, on the face of it, at the first blush, at first sight, to the eye.

449. DISAPPEARANCE.—*N.* **disappearance**, evanescence, eclipse; departure, exit; vanishing point.

V. **disappear**, vanish, dissolve, fade, melt away, pass, go, depart, be gone, leave no trace; be lost to view (*or* sight), pass out of sight.

efface, etc., 552.

Adj. **disappearing**, evanescent; missing, lost; lost to sight.

CLASS IV

Words Relating to the INTELLECTUAL FACULTIES

I. FORMATION OF IDEAS

450. INTELLECT.—*N.* **intellect,** mind, understanding, reason; rationality; intellectual faculties (*or* powers); senses, consciousness, observation, intellectuality, mentality, intelligence; conception, judgment, wits, brains, parts, capacity, genius; wit; ability; wisdom; ideality, idealism.

ego, soul, spirit; heart, breast, bosom; subconscious self, subliminal consciousness.

seat of thought, brain; head, headpiece; skull, cranium.

Science of mind: psychology, psychoanalysis; psychophysics; metaphysics; philosophy.

psychical research; telepathy, thought transference, thought reading; clairaudience; clairvoyance, mediumship; spiritualism, etc., 992a.

V. **reason,** understand, think, reflect, cogitate, conceive, judge, contemplate, meditate; ruminate, etc. (*think*), 451.

note, notice, mark; take notice of; be aware of, realize; appreciate.

Adj. **intellectual,** mental, rational; psychological; conscious, percipient, brainy [*colloq.*].

hyperphysical, subconscious, subliminal; telepathic, clairvoyant; psychic *or* psychical, spiritual, metaphysical, transcendental.

450a. ABSENCE OF INTELLECT.—*N.* want of intellect (*or* mind, understanding); unintellectuality; imbecility, etc., 490.

Adj. unendowed with (*or* void of) reason; unintelligent, etc. (*imbecile*), 499.

451. THOUGHT.—*N.* **thought;** reflection, cogitation, consideration, meditation, study, speculation, deliberation, brainwork, cerebration; close study, application.

mature thought; afterthought, reconsideration, second thoughts; retrospection, examination.

abstraction, abstract thought, contemplation, musing; reverie, etc., 458; depth of thought.

V. **think,** reflect, cogitate, consider, reason, deliberate: contemplate, meditate, ponder, muse, dream, ruminate, speculate; brood over, con over, study; bend (*or* apply) the mind; digest, discuss, hammer at, hammer out; weigh, realize, appreciate; fancy.

harbor, cherish, entertain, nurture (*as an idea*), imagine; bear in mind; reconsider.

suggest itself, present itself, occur to; come into one's head; strike one, come uppermost; enter (or cross, flash across, occupy) the mind.

Adj. thoughtful, pensive, meditative, reflective, cogitative, contemplative, speculative, deliberative, studious, introspective, philosophical.

absorbed, rapt; lost in thought; engrossed in, intent.

Adv. all things considered, taking everything into consideration (or account).

452. ABSENCE OF THOUGHT.—*N.* vacancy of mind, poverty of intellect; thoughtlessness, etc. (*inattention*), 458; inanity, fatuity, vacuity.

V. put away thought; relax (or divert) the mind; make the mind a blank, let the mind lie fallow; indulge in reverie, etc. (*be inattentive*), 458.

Adj. vacant, inane, unintellectual, unoccupied, unthinking, irrational, unreasoning, thoughtless, inattentive; diverted; bigoted, narrow-minded.

453. [Object of thought] IDEA.—*N.* idea, notion, conception, thought; apprehension, impression, perception; sentiment, reflection, observation, consideration; abstract idea.

view, opinion, theory; conceit, fancy; fantasy, etc., 515.

viewpoint, point of view; aspect, angle; field of view.

454. [Subject of thought] TOPIC.—*N.* subject, subject matter; matter, motif, theme, topic, thesis, text, business, affair, matter in hand, argument; motion, resolution, case, point; proposition, theorem; field of inquiry; moot point, point at issue; problem, etc. (*question*), 461.

V. enter the mind, etc., 451.

Adv. under consideration, under advisement; in question, in the mind; at issue, before the house, on foot, on the carpet.

455. [Desire of knowledge] CURIOSITY.—*N.* curiosity; inquisitiveness; interest, thirst for knowledge, mental acquisitiveness; inquiring mind.

investigator, inquirer, etc., 461.

busybody, newsmonger; Peeping Tom, Paul Pry, eavesdropper; gossip.

V. be curious; take an interest in, investigate; stare, gape; see the sights.

pry, nose, search, ferret out.

Adj. curious, inquiring, etc., 461; inquisitive, burning with curiosity, overcurious, prying; inquisitorial; agape, expectant.

456. [Absence of curiosity] INCURIOSITY.—*N.* incuriosity; incuriousness; apathy, unconcern, indifference.

V. be incurious (*or* indifferent); have no curiosity, etc., 455; be bored by, take no interest in.

Adj. incurious, uninquisitive, indifferent; impassive, etc., 823; uninterested, bored.

457. ATTENTION.—*N.* attention; intentness, alertness; thought, etc., 451; observance, observation; consideration, reflection; heed; heedfulness; notice, regard; circumspection, etc. (*care*), 459; study, scrutiny; inspection, revision, revisal.

minuteness, circumstantiality, attention to detail.

V. attend, watch, observe, look, see, view, notice, regard, take notice, mark; pay attention to, give heed to; occupy oneself with; contemplate, etc. (*think of*), 451, look to, see to; heed, mind, take cognizance of, entertain, recognize; make (*or* take) note of; note.

examine, scan, scrutinize, consider; overhaul, revise, pore over; inspect, review.

revert to, hark back to; come to the point.

meet with attention; attract notice, fall under one's notice; be under consideration.

call attention to, bring under one's notice; point out (*or* to, at), indicate; direct attention to; show; bring forward.

Adj. attentive, mindful, heedful, observant, regardful; alive to, awake to, on the job [*colloq.*], alert; taken up with, occupied with; engrossed in, wrapped in, absorbed, rapt; watchful; intent on, open-eyed; on the watch.

458. INATTENTION.—*N.* inattention, inconsideration, want of consideration, inconsiderateness; oversight; inadvertence, disregard; want of thought; heedlessness, etc. (*neglect*), 460; unconcern.

abstraction; absence of mind, absorption, preoccupation, distraction, reverie, brown study [*colloq.*], woolgathering.

V. be inattentive (*or* unobservant); overlook, disregard; pass by, neglect; think little of; pay no attention to; dismiss from one's mind; drop the subject, think no more of; turn a deaf ear to.

confuse, disconcert, discompose, perplex, bewilder, fluster, flurry; call off *or* distract the attention (thoughts, mind); put out of one's head.

Adj. inattentive, unobservant, undiscerning, unmindful, unheeding, regardless; listless, apathetic; blind, deaf; volatile, scatter-brained, flighty, giddy; unreflecting; inconsiderate, thoughtless; wild, harum-scarum [*colloq.*], heedless, careless, neglectful.

abstracted, absent, distrait [F.], woolgathering, dreamy; dazed, absent-minded; lost in thought; rapt, in the clouds, daydreaming; preoccupied, engrossed; in a reverie; off one's guard; caught napping.

459. CARE. [Vigilance]—*N.* **care,** solicitude, anxiety; heed, concern, heedfulness; scruple.

vigilance; watchfulness, surveillance, watch, vigil, lookout, watch and ward; espionage, reconnoitering; watching.

alertness, attention, prudence, forethought, circumspection, precaution, caution; accuracy, exactness; minuteness, attention to detail.

watcher, watchman, watchdog.

V. **be careful,** take care, be cautious; take precautions; pay attention to, etc., 457; take care of; look *or* see to, look after, keep an eye upon; chaperon, matronize, keep watch, mount guard, watch.

Adj. **careful,** regardful, heedful; prudent, discreet, cautious; considerate, thoughtful; provident; alert; sure-footed.

guarded, on one's guard; on the alert (*or* watch, lookout); awake, vigilant; watchful, wakeful, Argus-eyed, lynx-eyed.

scrupulous, punctilious, conscientious; tidy, orderly; clean; accurate, exact.

Adv. **carefully,** with care, gingerly.

460. NEGLECT.—*N.* **neglect;** carelessness; negligence; omission, procrastination; supineness, apathy; inattention, etc., 458; imprudence, improvidence, recklessness; slovenliness, untidiness; dirt; inexactness, inaccuracy.

trifler, waiter on providence; Micawber; slacker.

V. **neglect,** take no care of, let slip, let go; lose sight of.

delay, defer, procrastinate, postpone, adjourn, pigeonhole, shelve, table, lay on the table.

overlook, disregard; pass over, pass by; let pass; wink at, connive at.

scamp; trifle, slight, slur; skim, skip, take a cursory view of, run over, dip into; slur *or* slip over; push aside, throw into the background, sink; ignore; forget.

Adj. **neglectful,** negligent, remiss; heedless, careless; thoughtless, inconsiderate; perfunctory, offhand.

unwary, unwatchful, unguarded, off one's guard.

supine, apathetic; inattentive, etc., 458; nonchalant, indifferent; imprudent, reckless; slovenly, disorderly; dirty; inexact, inaccurate; improvident, unthrifty.

neglected, unheeded, uncared for, unattended to; abandoned, shunted, shelved.

461. INQUIRY. [Subject of inquiry. QUESTION.]—*N.* **inquiry;** request, etc., 765; search, research, quest; pursuit, prosecution.

examination, review, scrutiny, investigation; inquest, inquisi-

tion; trial; exploration; exploitation, ventilation; sifting; calculation, analysis, dissection; study, consideration.

reconnoitering, reconnaissance, espionage.

questioning, interrogation, interrogatory; challenge, examination, third degree [*colloq.*], cross-examination; discussion; catechism.

question, query, problem, poser, desideratum, point (*or* matter)
in dispute; moot point; issue, question at issue; bone of contention, enigma, etc. (*secret*), 533; knotty point.

inquirer, investigator, inquisitor, inspector, querist, examiner,
catechist; scrutator, scrutinizer; analyst.

V. **inquire,** seek, search, make inquiry, look for, scan, reconnoiter, explore, sound, rummage, ransack, pry, peer, look round;
overhaul; look behind the scenes; nose, nose out, trace up; hunt
out, fish out, ferret out; unearth.

track, seek a clue; hunt, trail, shadow, mouse, dodge, trace,
pursue, experiment, etc., 463.

examine, study, consider, calculate; dip *or* dive into, probe,
sound, fathom, scrutinize, analyze, anatomize, dissect, parse,
resolve, sift, winnow, thresh out; investigate, look into, discuss,
canvass, subject to examination, quiz, pose; audit, tax, pass in
review.

question, ask, demand; interrogate, catechize, pump; cross-
question, cross-examine; grill [*colloq*], put through the third
degree [*colloq.*].

Adj. **inquiring,** inquisitive, catechetical, inquisitorial, analytic;
interrogative.

undetermined, undecided, tentative; in question, in dispute, in
issue, under consideration; moot, proposed; doubtful, etc. (*uncertain*), 475.

462. ANSWER.—*N.* answer, response, reply, rejoinder; retort,
repartee; antiphon, acknowledgment; password; echo; counter-
statement, countercharge, contradiction.

[Law] defense, plea, reply, rejoinder, rebutter, surrebutter, surrejoinder.

solution, explanation; discovery, disclosure; cause; clue.

oracle, etc., 513.

V. **answer,** respond, reply, rebut, retort, rejoin; give answer;
acknowledge, echo.

[Law] defend, reply, surrejoin, surrebut, plead, rebut.

explain, interpret; solve, etc. (*unriddle*), 522; discover, fathom,
hunt out, inquire; satisfy, set at rest, determine.

Adj. **responsive,** respondent, antiphonal; oracular; conclusive.

463. EXPERIMENT.—*N.* experiment, essay, trial, attempt;

analysis, investigation; verification, probation, proof, criterion, diagnosis, test, crucial test; assay, ordeal.

speculation, random shot, leap in the dark; feeler, pilot balloon.

experimenter, experimentalist, assayer, analyst; prospector, adventurer; speculator, gambler, stock gambler, plunger [*slang*].

V. experiment, essay, try, venture, make an experiment, make trial of; rehearse; put to the test, prove, verify, test.

grope, grope for, feel one's way, fumble, throw out a feeler; send up a pilot balloon; see how the land lies (*or* wind blows); feel the pulse; fish for, angle, trawl, cast one's net.

Adj. experimental, probationary; analytic, speculative, tentative, empirical.

on trial, on examination, on *or* under probation, under suspicion; on one's trial.

464. COMPARISON.—*N.* comparison, contrast, parallelism, balance; identification; simile, similitude, allegory, etc. (*metaphor*); 521.

V. compare, collate, confront, contrast, balance; parallel.

Adj. comparative, relative, contrastive; metaphorical, etc., 521.

Adv. relatively; as compared with.

465. DISCRIMINATION.—*N.* discrimination, distinction, differentiation, diagnosis, nice perception; estimation; nicety, refinement, taste, judgment; tact, discernment, acuteness, penetration.

V. discriminate, distinguish, separate; draw the line, sift; estimate, etc. (*measure*), 466; sum up, criticize; take into account, weigh carefully.

Adj. discriminating, critical, diagnostic, perceptive, discriminative, distinctive; nice, acute.

465a. INDISCRIMINATION.—*N.* indiscrimination, indistinction; want of discernment; uncertainty, etc. (*doubt*), 475.

V. confound, confuse, jumble, heap indiscriminately; swallow whole.

Adj. indiscriminate, indistinguishable, lacking distinction, undistinguished, undistinguishable; promiscuous, undiscriminating.

466. MEASUREMENT.—*N.* measurement, mensuration, survey, valuation, appraisement, assessment, estimate, estimation; dead reckoning [*naut.*]; reckoning, gauging; horsepower, candle power.

measure, gauge; yard measure, standard, rule, foot rule, spirit level, plumb line; square, T-square, steel square, compass, dividers, calipers; log, log line, patent log [*naut.*]; meter, line, rod, check.

flood mark, high-water mark, load-line mark.

scale; graduation, graduated scale; vernier, quadrant, theodolite; beam, steelyard, weighing machine, balance.

latitude and longitude, altitude and azimuth.

geometry; topography, cartography; surveying, land surveying.

surveyor, land surveyor, topographer, cartographer.

V. **measure,** meter; value, assess, rate, appraise, estimate, form an estimate; standardize; span, pace, step, inch, divide, gauge, balance, poise, weigh; plumb; probe, sound, fathom; survey, plot, block in, block out, rule, draw to scale.

Adj. **metrical,** metric; measurable; topographic *or* topographical, cartographic *or* cartographical.

467. [Materials for reasoning] EVIDENCE.—*N.* **evidence;** facts, premises, data, grounds, proof; confirmation, corroboration, ratification, authentication.

testimony, attestation; affirmation, declaration; deposition.

authority, warrant, credential, diploma, voucher, certificate, document, deed, warranty; autograph, handwriting, signature, seal, countersign; exhibit; citation, reference, quotation; admission, etc. (*assent*), 488.

witness, eyewitness, deponent [*law*]; sponsor.

writ, summons, etc. (*lawsuit*), 696.

V. **evince,** show, betoken, indicate, denote, imply, involve, argue, bespeak.

have weight, carry weight; tell, speak volumes, speak for itself.

testify, bear witness, give evidence, depose, witness, vouch for; certify, attest, acknowledge.

confirm, ratify, corroborate, indorse, support, bear out, vindicate, uphold, warrant.

adduce, evidence, cite, quote; refer to, call, call to witness; bring forward, bring into court; allege, plead.

establish, make out a case; authenticate, substantiate, verify, make good.

Adj. **evidential,** indicative, deducible, inferential, firsthand, authentic, documentary; cumulative, corroborative, confirmatory; significant, weighty, overwhelming, conclusive.

oral, hearsay, circumstantial, presumptive.

Adv. **by inference;** according to, in corroboration of.

468. COUNTEREVIDENCE.—*N.* **counterevidence,** rejoinder, disproof, refutation, negation, denial; plea, etc., 617; vindication.

V. **refute,** rebut, oppose; confute, etc. (*refute*), 479; subvert; destroy, check, weaken; contravene; contradict, deny, alter the case; turn the tables; prove a negative.

Adj. **contradictory,** conflicting; unattested, unauthenticated, unsupported, supposititious, trumped up.

Adv. **on the other hand** (*or* side), in opposition; in rebuttal.

469. QUALIFICATION.—*N.* **qualification,** limitation, modification, coloring; allowance, consideration, extenuating circumstances; mitigation.

condition, proviso, exception; exemption; saving clause.

~V. qualify, limit, modify, affect, give a color to, narrow, temper; allow for, take into account.

Adj. qualifying, extenuating, palliative; conditional; exceptional; hypothetical, contingent.

Adv. provided, if, unless, but, yet; according as; conditionally, admitting, supposing; even, although, though.

470. POSSIBILITY.—*N.* possibility, potentiality, practicability, feasibility, workableness; potency; compatibility, etc. (*agreement*), 23.

contingency, chance, etc., 156.

V. be possible, stand a chance; admit of, bear.

render possible, put in the way of, bring to bear, bring together.

Adj. possible, conceivable, imaginable, credible; compatible, etc., 23; likely.

practicable, feasible, workable, achievable; within reach, accessible, surmountable; attainable, obtainable.

Adv. possibly, perhaps, perchance, peradventure, haply.

471. IMPOSSIBILITY.—*N.* impossibility, impracticability, incredibility, hopelessness, infeasibility; discrepancy.

V. attempt impossibilities; square the circle, find the elixir of life, discover the philosopher's stone, discover the grand panacea, find the fountain of youth, discover the secret of perpetual motion; make bricks without straw; weave a rope of sand; be in two places at once; gather grapes from thorns.

Adj. impossible, not possible, absurd, contrary to reason, unlikely, unreasonable, incredible, visionary, impractical, inconceivable, improbable, unimaginable, unthinkable.

impracticable, unachievable, infeasible; insuperable, insurmountable, inaccessible, unattainable, unobtainable; out of the question; incompatible, etc., 24; impassable, impervious, self-contradictory.

472. PROBABILITY.—*N.* probability, likelihood, likeness, verisimilitude, plausibility; color, semblance, show of; presumption; credibility; prospect; chance, etc., 156.

V. be probable, lend color to; point to; imply, bid fair, promise, stand (*or* run) a good chance.

presume, infer, venture, suppose, take for granted, flatter oneself; expect, etc., 507; count upon, etc. (*believe*), 484.

Adj. probable, likely, hopeful, presumable, presumptive, apparent.

plausible, specious, ostensible, colorable, reasonable, credible.

Adv. in all probability, most likely, apparently, seemingly, to all appearance.

473. IMPROBABILITY.—*N.* improbability, unlikelihood; bare possibility; long odds; incredibility.

V. be improbable, go beyond reason, strain one's credulity; have a small chance.

Adj. improbable, unlikely, rare, unheard of, inconceivable; unimaginable, incredible.

474. CERTAINTY.—*N.* certainty; necessity, etc., 601; certitude, sureness, surety, assurance; infallibility, reliability, inevitableness; fact; positive fact, matter of fact.

bigotry, positiveness, dogmatism, dogmatization; fanaticism.

dogmatist, doctrinaire, bigot; zealot, fanatic.

V. render certain, insure, assure; clinch, make sure; determine, decide; know, etc. (*believe*), 484.

Adj. certain, sure, inevitable, assured, solid, well founded.

unqualified, absolute, positive, definite, clear, unequivocal, categorical, unmistakable, decisive.

conclusive, undeniable, unquestionable; indisputable, incontestable, indubitable; irrefutable; final; undoubted, unquestioned, undisputed; questionless.

authoritative, authentic, official.

evident, manifest; self-evident, axiomatic.

infallible, unerring; unchangeable, etc., 150; trustworthy, reliable.

dogmatic, opinionated, dictatorial, doctrinaire; fanatical, bigoted.

Adv. certainly, undoubtedly, indubitably; for certain, surely, no doubt, doubtless, to be sure, of course, as a matter of course, in truth, truly, without fail.

475. UNCERTAINTY.—*N.* uncertainty, incertitude, doubt, doubtfulness, dubiousness.

hesitation, suspense, perplexity, embarrassment, dilemma, bewilderment; puzzle, quandary; timidity, etc. (*fear*), 860; vacillation, wavering, indetermination.

vagueness, haze, fog, obscurity, ambiguity, open question, blind bargain, pig in a poke, leap in the dark.

fallibility, unreliability, untrustworthiness; precariousness.

V. hesitate, flounder, miss one's way, wander aimlessly, beat about; lose oneself, lose one's head.

perplex, pose, puzzle, confuse, confound, bewilder, nonplus.

doubt, etc. (*disbelieve*), 485.

Adj. uncertain, unsure; casual, random, aimless, doubtful, dubious; insecure, unstable, indecisive, irresolute; unsettled, undecided, undetermined, in question; experimental, tentative.

vague, indefinite, ambiguous, equivocal, undefined, confused; mysterious, cryptic, veiled, obscure, undefinable; oracular.

perplexing, enigmatic, paradoxical, apocryphal, problematical.

fallible, questionable, debatable, untrustworthy, unreliable.

puzzled, perplexed; lost, astray, adrift, at sea, at fault, at a loss, at one's wit's end, distracted, distraught.

476. REASONING.—*N.* reasoning, ratiocination; inference, induction, generalization.

logic, art of reasoning, dialectics; deduction, induction; synthesis, analysis; syllogism.

discussion, comment; ventilation; inquiry, etc., 461.

argumentation, controversy, debate; polemics, wrangling, contention.

argument, case, plea, proposition, terms, premises, data, principle.

arguments, reasons, pros and cons.

reasoner, logician, dialectician, casuist; disputant, controversialist; wrangler, arguer, debater.

V. reason, argue, discuss, debate, dispute, contend, wrangle; chop logic; controvert, deny; canvass; consider, examine.

Adj. reasoning, rational; argumentative, controversial, dialectic, polemical; disputatious.

logical, syllogistic, inductive, deductive, synthetic *or* synthetical, analytic *or* analytical; relevant, germane.

Adv. for, because, hence, whence, seeing that, since, then, thence, so; whereas, considering, therefore, wherefore; consequently, *ergo* [L.], thus, accordingly.

finally, in conclusion, in fine, after all, on the whole.

477. [Absence of reasoning] INTUITION. [Specious reasoning] SOPHISTRY.—*N.* intuition; instinct, association of ideas; rule of thumb; presentiment.

sophistry, casuistry, equivocation, evasion, mental reservation, chicanery; perversion, mystification; speciousness; nonsense, etc., 497; hairsplitting, quibbling; begging of the question.

sophism, quibble, quirk, fallacy, subterfuge, shift, subtlety; inconsistency; claptrap.

V. pervert, quibble, equivocate, mystify, evade, elude; gloss over, varnish; misteach, etc., 538; mislead, etc. (*error*), 495; misrepresent, etc. (*lie*), 544; cavil, refine, split hairs; misjudge, etc., 481; beg the question, reason in a circle.

Adj. intuitive, instinctive, impulsive.

illogical, unreasonable, false, unsound, invalid; unwarranted, gratuitous; incongruous, inconsequent, inconsequential; unconnected; inconsistent; unscientific; untenable, inconclusive, incorrect, fallacious, groundless, unproved.

specious, sophistic *or* sophistical, casuistic; deceptive, illusive, illusory, hollow, plausible; evasive; irrelevant, inapplicable.

weak, feeble, poor, flimsy, loose, vague, irrational; nonsensical, absurd, foolish, etc. (*imbecile*), 499; frivolous; pettifogging, quibbling.

478. DEMONSTRATION.—*N.* demonstration, proof; conclusiveness; evidence, etc., 467; verification, etc., 462.

V. **demonstrate,** prove, establish, make good; show, evince, verify, etc., 467; settle the question.

follow; stand to reason; hold good, hold water [*colloq.*].

Adj. **demonstrative;** demonstrable; unanswerable, conclusive, decisive, convincing; irresistible, irrefutable, undeniable.

demonstrated, proved; unconfuted, unanswered, unrefuted; evident, self-evident, axiomatic.

deducible, inferential, following.

Adv. **of course,** in consequence, consequently, as a matter of course.

479. CONFUTATION.—*N.* confutation, refutation; answer, disproof, conviction, invalidation; exposure, exposé [F.], retort.

V. **confute,** refute, parry, negative, disprove, expose, show up; rebut, defeat, demolish, upset, subvert, overthrow, overturn, confound; invalidate; convince, silence; clinch an argument.

Adj. **confutable,** refutable; capable of refutation.

480. [Results of reasoning] JUDGMENT.—*N.* judgment, decision, determination, finding, verdict, sentence, decree; opinion, etc. (*belief*), 484; good judgment.

result, conclusion, upshot; deduction, inference, corollary.

estimation, valuation, appreciation; arbitrament, arbitration; assessment.

estimate, award; review, criticism, critique, notice, report.

plebiscite, voice, casting vote; vote, suffrage, election.

arbiter, arbitrator; judge, umpire; assessor, referee; inspector; censor.

reviewer, critic; connoisseur; commentator, annotator.

V. **judge,** conclude, opine; come to (*or* arrive at) a conclusion; ascertain, determine.

deduce, derive, gather, collect, infer.

estimate, form an estimate, appreciate, value, count, assess, rate, rank, account; regard, consider, think of; size up [*colloq.*].

decide, settle; try, pronounce, rule; find, pass judgment, sentence, doom, decree; give (*or* deliver) judgment; adjudge, adjudicate; arbitrate, award; confirm.

review, comment, criticize; examine, etc., 457; investigate, etc., 461.

Adj. **judicious,** judicial; determinate, conclusive, confirmatory.
critical, hypercritical, hairsplitting, censorious.

Adv. on the whole, all things considered, therefore, wherefore.

480a. [Result of search or inquiry] DISCOVERY.—*N.* discovery, detection, disclosure, find, revelation.

V. discover, find, determine, evolve; fix upon; find (*or* trace, make, root) out; spot [*colloq.*], fathom, bring out, draw out, educe, elicit, bring to light, dig up, unearth, disinter.

solve, resolve; unriddle, unravel, find a clue to; interpret; disclose; see through, detect; catch; scent, smell out.

recognize, realize, verify, make certain of, identify.

481. MISJUDGMENT.—*N.* misjudgment, obliquity of judgment, warped judgment; miscalculation, misconception, misinterpretation, etc., 523; hasty conclusion.

preconception, prejudgment, foregone conclusion; presumption, preconceived idea; prejudice, predilection, prepossession; presentiment, foreboding; fixed idea, obsession.

partisanship, clannishness; *esprit de corps* [F.], prestige, party spirit, class prejudice, class consciousness, race prejudice, provincialism.

quirk, shift, quibble, equivocation, evasion, subterfuge.

bias, warp, twist; hobby, whim, craze, cult, fad, crotchet, partiality.

V. misjudge, misconjecture, misconceive, misunderstand; miscalculate, misreckon; overestimate, etc., 482; underestimate, etc., 483.

prejudge, dogmatize; have a bias, run away with the notion; jump to a conclusion; blunder, etc., 699.

bias, warp, twist; prejudice, prepossess.

Adj. misjudging, ill-judging, wrong-headed; superficial; prejudiced, prepossessed; shortsighted, purblind; partial, one-sided; warped.

narrow, narrow-minded, provincial, parochial, insular; mean-spirited, confined, illiberal, intolerant, infatuated, fanatical, positive, dogmatic, dictatorial, pragmatic; egotistical, conceited, opinionated; bigoted, etc. (*obstinate*), 606; unreasonable, stupid, etc., 499; credulous, gullible.

482. OVERESTIMATION.—*N.* overestimation, exaggeration, hyperbole; optimism, much ado about nothing; tempest in a teacup; fine writing, rodomontade, gush [*colloq.*], hot air [*slang*].

egoism, egotism, bombast, conceit; vanity; megalomania.

egoist, egotist, megalomaniac; optimist; braggart, boaster, braggadocio, swaggerer.

V. overestimate, overrate, overpraise; strain, magnify; exaggerate, etc., 549.

eulogize, gush over [*colloq.*], boost; puff [*colloq.*]; extol.

Adj. **inflated,** puffed up; grandiose, stilted, pompous, pretentious, bombastic.

483. UNDERESTIMATION.—*N.* **underestimation,** undervaluation; depreciation, etc. (*detraction*), 934; pessimism; self-detraction, self-depreciation; modesty, etc., 881.

pessimist, depreciator, knocker [*slang*], crapehanger [*slang*].

V. **underrate,** underestimate, undervalue; depreciate; disparage, detract, decry, ridicule, deride; slight, etc. (*despise*), 930; neglect; slur over.

make light (*or* little) of, belittle, run down [*colloq.*], minimize, set no store by, set at naught, disregard.

Adj. **depreciating,** depreciative, depreciatory; pessimistic.

depreciated, unappreciated, unvalued, unprized.

484. BELIEF.—*N.* **belief,** credence; credit; assurance; faith, trust, confidence, presumption; hope.

conviction, principle; persuasion, certainty, opinion, view, conception, impression, surmise; conclusion.

doctrine, tenet, dogma, articles, canons; view, gospel; article (*or* declaration, profession) of faith, creed; assent, avowal, confession; propaganda.

credibility, probability; plausibility.

V. **believe,** credit, give faith (*or* credit, credence) to; realize; assume, take it; consider, presume; count (*or* depend, rely, build) upon; take for granted.

confide in, believe in, put one's trust in, place reliance on, trust.

think, hold, opine, conceive; have (*or* hold, entertain, adopt, embrace, foster, cherish) a belief *or* an opinion.

persuade, assure, convince, satisfy, bring to reason, convert, indoctrinate; wean, bring round, bring (*or* win) over; carry conviction.

Adj. **certain,** sure, assured, positive, cocksure [*colloq.*], satisfied, confident, unhesitating, convinced, secure.

confiding, trustful, unsuspecting, unsuspicious; credulous, gullible.

believed, trusted, unsuspected, undoubted.

credible, reliable, trustworthy, accredited, satisfactory; probable.

485. UNBELIEF. DOUBT.—*N.* **unbelief,** disbelief, incredulity; infidelity, etc. (*irreligion*), 989; wrangling, nonconformity; dissent, change of opinion; retractation, etc., 607.

doubt, uncertainty, skepticism, misgiving, demur; discredit; distrust, mistrust; misdoubt, suspicion, jealousy, scruple, qualm.

incredibility, incredibleness, unbelievability.

agnostic, skeptic; unbeliever, etc., 487.

V. **disbelieve,** discredit, misbelieve, dissent; refuse to believe.

doubt, distrust, mistrust; question, challenge, dispute; deny, etc., 536; cavil, wrangle; suspect, scent, smell, smell a rat [*colloq.*], harbor suspicions; have one's doubts.

demur, stick at, pause, hesitate, shy at, scruple; waver.

stagger, startle; shake one's faith, stagger one's belief.

Adj. **unbelieving,** skeptical, incredulous; distrustful of, suspicious of.

doubtful, etc. (*uncertain*), 475; disputable, questionable, suspicious; incredible, unbelievable, inconceivable.

Adv. with caution, with grains of allowance.

486. CREDULITY.—*N.* **credulity,** credulousness, gullibility; infatuation; self-delusion, self-deception; superstition; bigotry.

credulous person, dupe, gull.

V. **be credulous;** follow implicitly; swallow, swallow whole, gulp down; take on faith.

impose upon, etc. (*deceive*), 545.

Adj. **credulous,** gullible, easily deceived *or* convinced; simple, silly, childish; infatuated, superstitious; confiding, trustful, unsuspicious.

487. INCREDULITY.—*N.* **incredulity,** incredulousness; skepticism, doubt, disbelief, etc., 989; unbelief, etc., 485.

unbeliever, skeptic, doubting Thomas, disbeliever, agnostic, infidel, misbeliever; heretic, etc. (*heterodox*), 984.

V. **be incredulous,** distrust, doubt, suspect, refuse to believe; turn a deaf ear to.

Adj. **incredulous,** skeptical, suspicious; dissenting, unbelieving; heterodox.

488. ASSENT.—*N.* **assent,** acquiescence, admission; nod; consent, compliance; agreement, understanding; affirmation; recognition, acknowledgment, avowal, confession.

unanimity, common consent, consensus, acclamation, chorus; public opinion; concurrence, accord.

ratification, confirmation, corroboration, approval, acceptance; indorsement.

consenter, indorser, subscriber; upholder, etc. (*auxiliary*), 711.

V. **assent,** give assent, acquiesce, agree, accept, accede, accord, concur, consent, coincide, echo, reciprocate, go with; recognize; subscribe to, conform to, defer to; go with the stream; be in the fashion, join in the chorus.

acknowledge, own, admit, confess; concede, yield; abide by; permit, etc., 760.

confirm, ratify, approve, indorse, countersign; corroborate, etc., 467.

Adj. assenting, of one accord (*or* mind); of the same mind, at one with, agreed, acquiescent.

uncontradicted, unchallenged, unquestioned, unanimous.

Adv. yes, yea, aye, true; granted; even so, just so; to be sure, as you say; surely, assuredly; exactly, precisely, certainly, of course, unquestionably, no doubt, doubtless.

unanimously, by common consent, to a man, as one man; with one consent (*or* voice, accord).

489. DISSENT.—*N.* dissent, nonconsent, discordance, disagreement.

nonconformity, heterodoxy, protestantism, schism; disaffection, secession, recantation.

dissension, discord, caviling, wrangling; discontent, etc., 832.

protest, contradiction, denial; noncompliance, rejection.

dissentient, dissenter, nonconformist; sectary; separatist, protestant; heretic, etc., 984.

V. dissent, demur, call in question, disagree, refuse to admit; cavil, wrangle, protest, repudiate; contradict, deny.

secede; recant, etc., 607.

Adj. dissenting, negative; contradictory; dissentient; unconvinced, unconverted.

sectarian, denominational, schismatic; heterodox; intolerant.

Adv. at variance with, at issue with; under protest.

490. KNOWLEDGE.—*N.* knowledge; cognizance; cognition, acquaintance, experience, ken, insight, familiarity; comprehension, apprehension; recognition; appreciation, judgment, etc., 480; intuition, consciousness, perception.

enlightenment, light; impression, perception, discovery, revelation.

learning, erudition, lore, scholarship; letters, literature; book learning, bookishness, general information; education, culture, cultivation, attainments, acquirements, accomplishments, proficiency.

V. know, be aware of; conceive, apprehend, comprehend; realize, understand, appreciate; fathom, make out; recognize, discern, perceive, see, experience.

learn, imbibe knowledge; discover, evolve.

Adj. aware of, cognizant of, conscious of; acquainted with, privy to, in the secret; alive to; apprized of, informed of; undeceived.

educated, erudite, instructed, learned, lettered, well informed, well versed, well read, well grounded, well educated; high-brow [*slang*], bookish, scholastic, profound, deep-read, book-learned, accomplished; self-taught, self-educated, knowing, shrewd.

known, ascertained, well known, recognized, noted, received, notorious, proverbial; familiar, hackneyed, trite, commonplace.

Adv. to the best of one's knowledge; as every schoolboy knows.

491. IGNORANCE.—*N.* ignorance, illiteracy, unlearnedness, unacquaintance, unconsciousness, darkness, blindness; incomprehension, simplicity.

sealed book; virgin soil, unexplored ground; dark ages.

Imperfect knowledge: smattering, superficiality, half learning, shallowness, glimmering; incapacity.

Affectation of knowledge: pedantry, charlatanry, charlatanism.

V. be ignorant (*or* uninformed); be uneducated; know nothing of; ignore, be blind to.

Adj. ignorant; unknowing, unaware, unacquainted, uninformed, uninitiated, unwitting, unconscious; witless, unconversant.

illiterate, unread, low [*slang*], uncultivated, uninstructed, untaught, untutored, unschooled, uneducated, unlearned, unlettered, empty-headed.

shallow, superficial, green, rude, empty, half-learned, half-baked [*colloq.*], unscholarly.

in the dark; benighted, blinded, blindfold, hoodwinked; misinformed.

unknown, unapprehended, unexplained, uninvestigated, unexplored, unheard of; concealed, etc., 528.

Adv. unawares; for aught one knows; not that one knows.

492. SCHOLAR.—*N.* scholar, savant [F.], pundit [India], schoolman, professor, academician, doctor, fellow, don [Eng.], graduate, postgraduate, classicist, philosopher, scientist, linguist, etymologist, philologist, lexicographer; man of learning.

bookworm, bibliophile, bibliomaniac, bluestocking [*colloq.*], high-brow [*slang*].

pedant, doctrinaire; pedagogue, Dr. Pangloss; instructor, etc., 540.

student, learner, pupil, schoolboy, etc. (*learner*), 541.

Adj. learned, etc., 490.

493. IGNORAMUS.—*N.* ignoramus, illiterate, dunce, duffer, numskull [*colloq.*]; no scholar.

smatterer, dabbler, half scholar; charlatan; wiseacre.

novice, greenhorn, plebe [*West Point cant*]; tyro, etc. (*learner*), 541.

Adj. bookless, shallow, simple, dull, dumb [*colloq.*], dense, crass; illiterate, etc., 491.

494. [Object of knowledge] TRUTH.—*N.* truth, verity; fact, reality, authenticity, gospel; veracity, etc., 543.

accuracy, exactitude, exactness, preciseness, precision, regularity, fidelity, nicety.

V. hold true, stand the test, have the true ring, hold good.

trace, solve, etc. (*discover*), 480a.

Adj. true, real, actual, veritable; certain, etc., 474; unimpeachable; veracious, etc., 543.

pure, sound, sterling, true-blue; natural, unsophisticated, unadulterated, simon-pure [*colloq.*], unvarnished, undisguised.

exact, accurate, definite, concrete, precise, well defined, just, right, correct, strict, severe, rigid, rigorous, scrupulous, literal, punctilious, mathematical, scientific, unromantic; faithful, constant, unerring; particular, nice, meticulous, delicate, fine; clean-cut, clear-cut.

authentic, genuine, legitimate; orthodox, etc., 983a; official.

valid, well grounded, well founded, solid, substantial, tangible.

Adv. truly, verily, indeed, in reality; in very truth, in fact, as a matter of fact, beyond doubt.

495. ERROR.—*N.* error, fallacy, misconception, misapprehension, misunderstanding; aberration, inexactness, laxity; misconstruction, misinterpretation; misjudgment, heresy, misstatement, anachronism; fable, etc. (*untruth*), 546.

mistake, fault, blunder, oversight, misprint, erratum (*pl.* errata), slip, blot, flaw, trip, stumble, bungle; slip of the tongue, slip of the pen, clerical error; bull, etc. (*absurdity*), 497; spoonerism, malapropism.

delusion, illusion, false impression; bubble; self-deceit, self-deception; hallucination, mirage, etc., 443; dream, etc. (*fancy*), 515.

V. mislead, misguide, lead astray, beguile, misinform, delude; falsify, misstate; deceive, etc., 545; lie, etc., 544.

err, be in error, be mistaken, be deceived; mistake, deceive oneself, blunder, misapprehend, misconceive, misunderstand, miscalculate, misjudge.

trip, stumble, lose oneself, go astray; fail, etc., 732; take the shadow for the substance.

Adj. erroneous, untrue, false, faulty, erring, fallacious, unreal, ungrounded, groundless, unsubstantial, unsound, inexact, inaccurate, incorrect.

illusive, illusory, delusive; mock, imaginary, spurious, etc., 545; deceitful, etc., 544; untrustworthy.

exploded, refuted, discarded.

mistaken, in error, deceived, out in one's reckoning; wide of the mark, at fault, at cross-purposes, at sea, bewildered.

496. MAXIM.—*N.* **maxim,** aphorism, dictum, saying, adage, saw, proverb, motto, epigram, sentence, mot [*Gallicism*], commonplace, moral.

axiom, theorem, formula, truism.

principle, profession of faith, conclusion, etc. (*judgment*), 480.

Adj. **aphoristic,** proverbial, axiomatic; hackneyed, trite.

Adv. as the saying is, as they say.

497. ABSURDITY.—*N.* **absurdity,** absurdness, imbecility, etc., 499; nonsense, paradox, inconsistency.

blunder, muddle, Irish bull; anticlimax, bathos.

farce, burlesque, parody, limerick; farrago, extravagance.

pun, sell [*colloq.*], catch [*colloq.*], verbal quibble, joke.

jargon, gibberish, balderdash, bombast, claptrap, twaddle, moonshine, stuff.

tomfoolery, mummery, monkeyshine [*slang*], monkey trick, frisk, practical joke, escapade.

V. **play the fool,** blunder, muddle; be guilty of absurdity; romance, talk nonsense, exaggerate; be absurd, frisk, caper, joke, play practical jokes.

Adj. **absurd,** nonsensical, farcical, burlesque, preposterous, egregious, senseless, inconsistent, ridiculous, extravagant, self-contradictory, paradoxical; foolish, etc., 499; meaningless, fantastic, bombastic, high-flown.

498. [Faculties] INTELLIGENCE. WISDOM.—*N.* **intelligence,** capacity, comprehension, understanding; intellect, etc., 450; brains, parts, sagacity, mother wit, wit, gumption [*colloq.*], acuteness, acumen, longheadedness, subtlety, penetration, perspicacity, discernment, good judgment; discrimination, cunning, refinement.

wisdom, sapience, sense, common sense, clear thinking, rationality, reason; reasonableness, judgment, solidity, depth, profundity, caliber.

genius, inspiration, talent, etc., 698.

Wisdom in action: prudence, etc., 864; vigilance, etc., 459; tact, etc., 698; foresight, etc., 510; sobriety, self-possession, ballast, mental poise, balance.

V. **have all one's wits about one;** be brilliant, scintillate, coruscate; understand, etc. (*intelligible*), 518.

penetrate, see through, see at a glance, discern; foresee, etc., 510; discriminate.

Adj. **Applied to persons: intelligent,** quick of apprehension, keen, acute, alive, awake, bright, quick, sharp, quick-witted, wide-awake; shrewd, astute; clearheaded, long-sighted, calculating, thoughtful, farsighted, discerning, perspicacious, penetrating, piercing; sharp as a needle; alive to, etc. (*cognizant*), 490; clever, etc. (*apt*), 698.

wise, sage, sapient [*often in irony*], sagacious, rational, sensible, judicious, strong-minded; worldly-wise, sophisticated.

impartial, unprejudiced, unbiased, unbigoted, equitable, fair.

prudent, etc. (*cautious*), 864; sober, staid, solid; watchful; provident, prepared, etc., 673.

Applied to actions: wise, sensible, judicious, well judged, well advised; prudent, politic; expedient, etc., 646.

499. IMBECILITY, FOLLY.—*N.* imbecility, want of intelligence (*or* intellect), shallowness, silliness, foolishness, stupidity, stolidity; incompetence.

simplicity, puerility; senility, dotage, second childhood; fatuity; idiocy.

folly, frivolity, irrationality, trifling, ineptitude, inconsistency, giddiness; eccentricity, etc., 503; extravagance, etc. (*absurdity*), 497; rashness, etc., 863.

V. trifle, drivel, dote; ramble, play the fool, fool, stultify oneself, talk nonsense.

Adj. Applied to persons: unintelligent, unintellectual, unreasoning; mindless, brainless; half-baked [*colloq.*], bovine, thick [*colloq.*], blockish, unteachable; ungifted, unenlightened, unwise; thick-skulled, muddleheaded, addleheaded, weak-minded, feeble-minded.

stupid, dull, heavy, obtuse, blunt, stolid, asinine, inapt.

childish, childlike; infantine, infantile, babyish, puerile, senile, anile; simple, credulous.

imbecile, fatuous, idiotic, driveling; vacant, bewildered.

foolish, silly, senseless, irrational, insensate, nonsensical, maudlin.

narrow-minded, bigoted, etc., 606; rash, etc., 863; eccentric, odd.

Applied to actions: foolish, unwise, injudicious, improper, unreasonable, ill-advised, ridiculous, silly, stupid, asinine; inconsistent, irrational; extravagant, nonsensical, frivolous, trivial; useless, etc., 645; inexpedient, etc., 647.

500. SAGE.—*N.* sage, wise man; master mind, thinker, philosopher, savant [F.], pundit, etc. (*scholar*), 492; wiseacre [*ironical*]; expert, etc., 700.

authority, oracle, mentor, Solon, Solomon, Buddha, Confucius.

Adj. venerable, venerated, reverenced, revered, honored; authoritative, oracular; wise, erudite, etc., 490.

501. FOOL.—*N.* fool, idiot, tomfool, wiseacre, simpleton,

Simple Simon; donkey, ass, owl, goose, dolt, booby, noodle, imbecile, nincompoop [*colloq.*], oaf, lout, blockhead, bonehead [*slang*], calf [*colloq.*], colt, numskull [*colloq.*], clod, clodhopper; soft or softy [*colloq. or slang*], mooncalf, saphead [*slang*], gawk, rube [*slang*].

greenhorn, etc. (*dupe*), 547; dunce, etc. (*ignoramus*), 493; lubber, etc. (*bungler*), 701; madman, etc., 504; dotard, driveler, old fogy [*colloq.*].

502. SANITY.—*N.* sanity, soundness, rationality, sobriety, lucidity, senses, common sense, horse sense [*colloq.*], sound mind.

V. become sane, come to one's senses, sober down, cool down, see things in proper perspective.

render sane, bring to one's senses, sober, bring to reason.

Adj. sane, rational, normal, wholesome, right-minded, reasonable, sound, sound-minded, in possession of one's faculties.

Adv. sanely, in reason, within reason, within bounds.

503. INSANITY.—*N.* insanity, lunacy; madness, mania, dementia, idiocy; delirium tremens, d.t.'s, the horrors [*colloq.*]; frenzy, raving, wandering, delirium, delusion, obsession, hallucination, derangement, unsoundness of mind.

vertigo, dizziness, swimming, sunstroke.

oddity, eccentricity, twist, monomania; fanaticism, infatuation, craze.

V. be *or* become insane, lose one's senses (*or* reason), go mad, rave, dote, ramble, wander; lose one's head, drivel.

derange, render *or* drive mad, madden, infatuate, obsess, befool; turn the brain, turn one's head.

Adj. insane, mad, lunatic; crazy, crazed, crackbrained, cracked [*colloq.*], touched; bereft of reason; unhinged, insensate, beside oneself, demented, maniacal, daft, frenzied, deranged, maddened, moonstruck, off one's head.

giddy, vertiginous, wild, flighty, distracted, distraught, bewildered.

odd, fanatical, infatuated, eccentric.

delirious, lightheaded, rambling, wandering, frantic, raving, stark mad.

504. MADMAN.—*N.* madman, lunatic, maniac; crank [*colloq.*], nut [*slang*].

dreamer, visionary, rhapsodist, seer, enthusiast, fanatic; Don Quixote, Ophelia.

idiot, etc., 501.

505. [The Past] MEMORY.—*N.* memory, remembrance; retention, retentiveness; retentive (*or* tenacious, trustworthy, ready) memory.

recollection, retrospect, reminiscence; recognition; afterthought.

reminder, hint, suggestion, memorandum (*pl.* memoranda), token, memento, souvenir, keepsake, relic; memorial, monument; commemoration, jubilee.

mnemonics; art of memory, artificial memory; Mnemosyne.

fame, celebrity, renown, reputation; repute, notoriety.

V. **remember,** retain the memory of, keep in mind; bear in mind, haunt one's mind (*or* thoughts); rankle; keep the wound open, brood over.

recollect, recall, call up, conjure up, retrace; look back upon, review; call (*or* bring) to mind.

remind, suggest, hint, prompt; put (*or* keep) in mind; bring to mind, call up, summon up, renew; redeem from oblivion; commemorate.

memorize, commit to memory; con, con over; fix in the mind, engrave upon the memory; learn by heart, know by rote, have at one's fingers' ends.

make a note of, put down, record.

Adj. **remembering,** mindful, reminiscent; fresh, still vivid; enduring, unforgotten; never to be forgotten, indelible; within one's memory; memorable, suggestive.

Adv. **by heart,** by rote, without book, word for word.

506. OBLIVION.—*N.* **oblivion;** forgetfulness; Lethe; obliteration of the past; short (*or* treacherous, untrustworthy, slippery, failing) memory; decay (*or* failure, lapse) of memory; amnesia.

amnesty, general pardon.

V. **forget,** be forgetful; fall (*or* sink) into oblivion; have a short memory; lose, lose the memory of, lose sight of.

efface, from the memory; unlearn; consign to oblivion, think no more of; let bygones be bygones.

Adj. **forgotten,** unremembered, out of mind; buried (*or* sunk) in oblivion.

forgetful, oblivious; heedless, deaf to the past; Lethean.

507. [The Future] EXPECTATION.—*N.* **expectation,** expectancy, anticipation, prospect, contingency, reckoning, calculation; foresight; suspense; abeyance.

assurance, confidence, reliance, hope, trust, presumption; prognostication; prediction, etc., 511.

V. **expect;** look for, look out for, look forward to; hope for, anticipate; have in prospect, keep in view; contemplate; wait for, watch for, await; foresee, prepare for, forestall.

predict, prognosticate, forecast.

Adj. **expectant;** expecting, in expectation, vigilant; open-eyed, open-mouthed; agape, gaping, on tenterhooks, on tiptoe; ready, prepared, provided for, provident.

expected, foreseen; in prospect, prospective, provisional; future, coming; in view, on the horizon; impending.

Adv. expectantly, on the watch, with muscles tense, on edge [*colloq.*], with eyes (*or* ears) strained, with bated breath.

soon, shortly, forthwith, presently.

508. NONEXPECTATION.—*N.* nonexpectation, unforeseen contingency, the unforeseen; miscalculation, false expectation; disappointment; disillusion.

surprise, blow, shock; bolt out of the blue; astonishment, amazement; wonder, bewilderment.

V. be unexpected, come unawares, turn up, burst *or* flash upon one; take by surprise, catch unawares.

surprise, startle, stun, stagger, astound; throw off one's guard; spring upon, astonish, etc. (*strike with wonder*), 870.

Adj. nonexpectant, surprised; unwarned, unaware; off one's guard.

unexpected, unanticipated, unlooked for, unforeseen; unheard of; startling; sudden.

Adv. unexpectedly, abruptly, suddenly, unawares; without notice *or* warning.

509. DISAPPOINTMENT.—*N.* disappointment, blighted hope, disillusion, balk; blow, false (*or* vain) expectation; miscalculation; fool's paradise.

V. be disappointed; look blank, look *or* stand aghast; find to one's cost.

disappoint, crush (*or* dash, blight) one's hope, balk *or* disappoint one's expectation, balk, tantalize; dumfounder, dumfound, disconcert, disillusionize; dissatisfy; disgruntle.

Adj. aghast; disgruntled; out of one's reckoning.

510. FORESIGHT.—*N.* foresight, prevision, long-sightedness, farsightedness; anticipation; prudence; forethought.

foreknowledge, prescience; presentiment, foreboding; second sight.

prospect; foregone conclusion; forecast.

V. foresee; look forward to, look ahead *or* beyond; look into the future; see one's way; see how the land lies.

anticipate, expect, surmise, contemplate; predict; forewarn.

Adj. foreseeing, prescient, anticipatory; farseeing, farsighted, long-sighted; provident; weatherwise; prospective; expectant.

Adv. against the time when; for a rainy day.

511. PREDICTION.—*N.* prediction, announcement; program;

platform; premonition, presage, foreboding; phophecy, prognostication, augury, forecast; omen, etc., 512; horoscope; soothsaying,
fortunetelling, divination; oracle, etc., 513.

astrology; spell, charm, etc., 993; sorcery, magic, etc., 992.

V. predict, forecast, prognosticate, prophesy, divine, foretell;
tell fortunes, cast a horoscope (*or* nativity); forewarn.

presage, augur, bode, forebode; foretoken, betoken; portend,
signify, point to.

herald, usher in, announce; lower; threaten.

Adj. prophetic, oracular, sibylline; weatherwise.

ominous, portentous; auspicious, premonitory, significant of.

512. OMEN.—*N.* omen, portent, presage, augury; sign, token;
harbinger; bird of ill omen; halcyon birds; signs of the times;
warning, etc., 668.

Adj. auspicious, favorable, halcyon, of good omen.

inauspicious, ill-boding, ill-omened, ill-starred.

513. ORACLE.—*N.* oracle; prophet, seer, soothsayer, proph-
etess, witch, sibyl; augur, haruspex; medium, clairvoyant, palm-
ist; fortuneteller; sorcerer, etc., 994; interpreter, etc., 524.

Delphic oracle; Cumaean Sibyl, Sibyl, Cassandra, Witch of
Endor, Sphinx.

weather prophet, weather bureau.

514. [Creative Thought] SUPPOSITION.—*N.* supposition,
assumption, presumption, condition, hypothesis, postulate,
theory, data; thesis, theorem; conjecture, guess, guesswork, speculation; surmise, suspicion, inkling, suggestion, hint.

theorist, theorizer, doctrinaire, doctrinarian.

V. suppose, conjecture; surmise, suspect, guess, divine; theorize, speculate; presume, presuppose, assume, predicate; believe,
take for granted.

propound, propose, put forth; put a case, submit; move, make a
motion; hazard *or* put forward a suggestion (*or* supposition); suggest, allude to, hint.

Adj. assumed, given; conjectural, presumptive, hypothetical;
theoretical, academic.

suggestive, allusive, stimulating.

Adv. if, if so be; on the supposition, in case, in the event of; as
if, provided; perhaps, for aught one knows.

515. IMAGINATION.—*N.* imagination, originality, invention;
fancy; inspiration.

ideality, idealism; romanticism, utopianism, castle-building,
dreaming; frenzy, rhapsody, ecstasy, reverie, daydream.

conception; flight of fancy; creation of the brain; imagery;
word painting.

fantasy, conceit; figment, myth; romance, extravaganza; dream, vision; shadow, chimera, phantasm, illusion, phantom, fancy, whim, vagary; bugbear, nightmare; flying Dutchman, great sea serpent, man in the moon, castle in the air, castle in Spain, Utopia, fairyland; land of Prester John.

Creative works: work of fiction, etc. (*novel*), 594; poetry, etc., 597; drama, etc., 599; music, etc., 415; painting, sculpture, architecture; art.

idealist, romanticist, visionary, romancer, daydreamer, dreamer, castle-builder; creative artist.

V. imagine, fancy, conceive; idealize, realize; dream, dream of; indulge in reverie; fancy (*or* represent, picture, figure) to oneself.

create, originate, devise, invent, make up, coin, fabricate; improvise.

Adj. imaginative, original, inventive, creative, productive.

extravagant, romantic, high-flown, flighty, preposterous; unreal; unsubstantial.

ideal; intellectual, impracticable, imaginary, visionary, utopian, quixotic.

fanciful; fantastical; fictitious; fabulous, legendary, mythic *or* mythical, mythological, chimerical; whimsical; fairy, fairylike.

II. COMMUNICATION OF IDEAS

516. MEANING.—*N.* meaning [*idea to be conveyed*], signification, significance; sense, import, purport; pith, essence; force; drift, bearing, tenor, spirit; allusion; suggestion, interpretation; acceptation.

Thing signified: matter, subject, subject matter, substance, gist, argument.

V. mean, signify, denote, express; import, purport; convey, imply, indicate; tell of, speak of; touch on; point to, allude to; drive at; involve; declare; affirm, state.

paraphrase, state differently; express by a synonym.

Adj. meaning, expressive, significant, pithy; intelligible, explicit, clear; suggestive; allusive.

literal, word-for-word, verbatim; exact, real.

synonymous; tantamount, equivalent.

implied; understood, tacit.

Adv. to that effect; that is to say.

517. UNMEANINGNESS.—*N.* unmeaningness, absence of meaning, drivel, senselessness; empty sound.

nonsense, jargon, gibberish, mere words, rant, bombast, balderdash, babble, inanity, twaddle, trash, rubbish; absurdity; imbecility, folly; ambiguity, vagueness, etc., 519.

V. mean nothing; be unmeaning; gibber; jabber, twaddle, rant, babble.

scribble, scrawl, scratch.

Adj. unmeaning, meaningless, senseless; nonsensical; inexpressive; vague; not significant.

trashy, inane, trumpery, trivial, insignificant.

518. INTELLIGIBILITY.—*N.* intelligibility; comprehensibility; clearness, clarity, explicitness, lucidity, perspicuity; precision; plain speaking.

V. render intelligible, popularize, simplify, elucidate, explain, interpret.

understand, comprehend; take in, catch, grasp, follow; master.

Adj. intelligible; clear, lucid; perspicuous, transparent.

plain, distinct, clear-cut, hard-hitting, to the point, explicit; positive; definite, precise; unequivocal, legible, obvious, etc., 525.

graphic, telling, vivid; expressive.

519. UNINTELLIGIBILITY.—*N.* unintelligibility, incomprehensibility, vagueness, obscurity, ambiguity, confusion; mystification; jargon.

enigma, riddle; sealed book.

V. render unintelligible, conceal, darken, confuse, mystify, perplex.

Adj. unintelligible, incomprehensible, unaccountable, undecipherable, unfathomable, inexplicable, inscrutable, insoluble, impenetrable; puzzling, enigmatic; indecipherable, illegible.

obscure, crabbed, dark, muddy, dim, nebulous, mysterious, hidden, latent, occult; abstruse; indefinite, vague, loose, ambiguous.

inexpressible, unutterable, ineffable.

520. [Having a double sense] EQUIVOCALNESS.—*N.* equivocalness, equivocation, double meaning; ambiguity; quibble; conundrum, riddle; pun, word play; sphinx, Delphic oracle.

equivocation, etc. (*duplicity*), 544; white lie, mental reservation, etc., 528.

V. equivocate, etc. (*palter*), 544; prevaricate; have a double meaning.

Adj. equivocal, ambiguous; double-tongued; enigmatical; indeterminate, doubtful.

521. FIGURE OF SPEECH.—*N.* figure, trope, phrase, expression; euphemism; image, imagery; personification, metaphor; simile, satire, irony.

allegory, apologue, parable, fable.

V. employ figures of speech; personify, allegorize, fable, shadow forth, allude to.

Adj. figurative, metaphorical, euphuistic, allusive; allegoric *or* allegorical, ironic, ironical, satiric *or* satirical; euphemistic.

522. INTERPRETATION.—*N.* interpretation, definition, explanation; elucidation, diagnosis; solution, answer; meaning, etc., 516; clue.

translation; rendering, rendition; metaphrase, literal (or word-for-word) translation; free translation; key; crib, horse, pony, trot [school cant].

comment, commentary; exegesis, exposition; inference, deduction; illustration, exemplification; gloss, annotation, note, construction, version, reading.

equivalent, equivalent meaning, synonym; paraphrase, convertible terms.

dictionary, etc., 562.

prediction, etc., 511; chiromancy, palmistry; astrology.

V. interpret, explain, define, construe, translate, render; decipher, make out, unravel, disentangle, solve; read between the lines.

elucidate, account for, throw or shed light upon; clear up, popularize, simplify; illustrate, exemplify; unfold, expound, comment upon, annotate.

Adj. explanatory, expository; interpretative, elucidative, inferential, illustrative.

equivalent, convertible, synonymous.

metaphrastic, literal, word-for-word.

Adv. in explanation; that is to say, to wit, namely.

literally, strictly speaking; in plain terms (or words).

523. MISINTERPRETATION.—N. misinterpretation, misapprehension, misconception, misunderstanding, misconstruction; misapplication; cross-purposes; mistake, etc., 495.

misrepresentation, perversion, misstatement, exaggeration; abuse of terms; play upon words, pun, parody, travesty; falsification, etc. (lying), 544.

V. misinterpret, misapprehend, misunderstand, misconceive; misjudge, misspell; mistranslate, misconstrue, misapply; mistake, etc., 495.

misrepresent, pervert, misstate, garble, falsify, distort; travesty, play upon words; stretch (or strain, twist, wrest) the sense or meaning.

Adj. misinterpreted, mistranslated; confused, tangled, snarled, mixed.

dazed, perplexed, bewildered, rattled [slang], benighted.

Adv. at cross-purposes, at sixes and sevens [colloq.]; in a maze.

524. INTERPRETER.—N. interpreter, translator, expositor, expounder, exponent; demonstrator; commentator, annotator; oracle, etc., 513.

spokesman, speaker, mouthpiece, foreman of the jury, mediator, advocate, delegate, representative, diplomatic agent, ambassador, plenipotentiary.

guide, courier, cicerone, showman, barker [*colloq.*].

525. MANIFESTATION.—*N.* manifestation, indication, expression; plain speaking, candor, openness; showing, exposition, demonstration; séance, materialization; exhibition, production, display, show.

Thing shown: exhibit, exhibition, exposition, show [*colloq.*], performance.

publicity, etc., 531; disclosure, etc., 529; openness, candor; saliency, prominence.

V. **make manifest**, materialize, express, represent, set forth, evidence, exhibit, produce, show, show up, expose; hold up, show forth, unveil, display, demonstrate, lay open; draw out, bring out; manifest oneself; speak out, proclaim, publish.

indicate, point out; disclose, discover; translate, transcribe, decipher, decode; elicit, bring to light, disinter.

be manifest *or* **plain**, appear, etc., 446; transpire, come to light, be disclosed; go without saying, be self-evident.

Adj. **manifest**, apparent; salient, striking, prominent, in the foreground, ostensible, notable, pronounced.

plain, intelligible, clear, defined, definite, distinct, conspicuous, obvious, evident, unmistakable; conclusive, indubitable, palpable, self-evident; open, patent, express, explicit; naked, bare, literal, downright, unreserved, frank, plain-spoken.

barefaced, brazen, bold, shameless, daring, flaunting, loud [*colloq.*]; flagrant, arrant, notorious; glaring.

Adv. **manifestly**, openly, plainly, above board, in plain sight, in the open, in broad daylight; without reserve.

526. LATENCY.—*N.* latency, hidden meaning; obscurity, ambiguity; secret, mystery, occultism, mysticism, symbolism; reserve, reticence; concealment, mystification, suppression, evasion; Delphic oracle; undercurrent; snake in the grass.

allusion, insinuation, implication; innuendo.

latent influence, power behind the throne, friend at court, wire-puller [*colloq.*], kingmaker.

V. **lurk**, smolder, underlie, make no sign; escape observation (*or* detection, recognition); lie hid, lie in ambush.

keep back, etc. (*conceal*), 528.

involve, imply, connote, import, allude to, leave an inference; symbolize.

Adj. **latent**, lurking; dormant, secret, occult; esoteric, recondite, veiled, symbolic, cryptic, mystic, mystical.

unapparent, unknown, unseen, unsuspected; invisible; unexpressed, undisclosed, tacit.

indirect, crooked, underhand, underground; by inference, by implication; implied, implicit, understood, tacit; allusive, covert, undercover, concealed.

Adv. secretly, stealthily, incognito; in the background; behind the scenes, between the lines; below the surface.

527. INFORMATION.—*N.* information, enlightenment, acquaintance, knowledge; publicity, notoriety.

mention; instruction, communicativeness, intercommunication.

notification, intimation, communication, notice, annunciation, announcement, communiqué; representation; message, etc., 532.

report, advice, monition; news, tidings, return, record, account, description; statement, estimate, specification.

informant, authority, teller, harbinger, herald, reporter, exponent, mouthpiece; spokesman, etc. (*interpreter*), 524; spy, informer, eavesdropper, detective, sleuth [*colloq.*]; newsmonger; messenger, etc., 534.

guide, cicerone; pilot; guidebook, handbook; map, plan, chart, gazetteer; itinerary.

hint, suggestion, insinuation, innuendo, inkling, whisper, cue, byplay; gesture; word to the wise.

V. tell, inform, acquaint, impart, apprise, advise, instruct, enlighten.

mention, express, intimate, represent, communicate, make known; publish, disseminate; notify, signify, specify; retail, describe; state, declare, assert, affirm.

announce, report, bring (*or* send, leave) word; telegraph, wire [*colloq.*], telephone, phone [*colloq.*].

disclose, etc., 529; explain.

hint, insinuate, allude to, glance at, let fall, indicate; suggest, prompt, give the cue.

undeceive, set right, correct, disabuse.

Adj. informational, advisory.

expressive, explicit, plain-spoken; declaratory; expository; communicative.

528. CONCEALMENT.—*N.* concealment, mystification; reticence, reserve, reservation; mental reservation, aside; suppression, evasion, white lie; silence, closeness, secretiveness, mystery.

screen, cloak; ambush, ambuscade; stowaway; blind baggage [*slang*].

cipher, code, sympathetic ink.

stealth, stealthiness, slyness, caution, cunning.

secrecy, privacy, secretness; disguise, mask, masquerade; incognito (*fem.* incognita).

masquerader, masker, mask, domino.

V. conceal, hide, secrete; lock up; cover, screen, cloak, veil, shroud; curtain, muffle; mask, camouflage, disguise; ensconce.

keep from, keep to oneself, keep secret; bury; sink, suppress; keep in the background; stifle, hush up; withhold, reserve.

code, use a code *or* cipher, reduce to a code.

hoodwink, blind, blindfold; mystify, puzzle, deceive, lead astray.

be concealed, hide oneself, couch; lie in ambush, lurk, sneak, skulk, slink, prowl, gumshoe [*slang*].

Adj. concealed, hidden, secret, private, privy; recondite, mystic, mystical, occult, dark, cryptic; in secret, tortuous; close, inviolate, confidential, behind a screen, undercover, in ambush, in hiding, in disguise; undisclosed, untold, covert, mysterious.

furtive, stealthy, skulking, surreptitious, underhand, sly, cunning, evasive; secretive, clandestine; reserved, reticent, uncommunicative, close, taciturn.

Adv. secretly, in secret, in private, incognito.

behind closed doors, under the rose, *sub rosa* [L.]; on the sly [*colloq.*]; in a whisper.

confidentially, in strict confidence, between ourselves, between you and me.

underhand, by stealth, like a thief in the night; stealthily.

529. DISCLOSURE.—*N.* disclosure, revelation, divulgence, exposition, exposure, publication, exposé.

acknowledgment, avowal, confession, confessional.

narrator, etc., 594; talebearer, etc., 532; informant, etc., 527.

V. disclose, discover, unmask, unveil, unfold, uncover, unseal, lay bare, expose, bare, bring to light, disabuse, open the eyes of, turn informer.

divulge, reveal, let into the secret, tell, etc. (*inform*), 527; breathe, utter, peach [*slang*]; let slip *or* drop, betray; blurt out, vent, whisper about, speak out, break the news, publish, etc., 531.

acknowledge, allow, concede, grant, admit, own, confess, avow, make a clean breast, unbosom oneself; turn informer.

be disclosed, transpire, come to light, become known, escape the lips; ooze out, leak out, come to one's ears.

530. AMBUSH. [Means of concealment]—*N.* ambush, ambuscade, lurking place, trap, snare, pitfall, etc., 667.

hiding place, secret place, recess, hole, cubbyhole, crypt; safe, safe-deposit box, safety-deposit box.

screen, cover, shade, blinker; veil, curtain, blind, cloak, cloud.

mask, visor, disguise, masquerade, domino.

V. **ambush,** ambuscade, lie in ambush, lie in wait for; set a trap for, ensnare.

531. PUBLICATION.—*N.* **publication,** public announcement, promulgation, propagation, proclamation, pronouncement, edict.

publicity, notoriety, currency, flagrancy, cry, hue and cry, bruit; report, etc. (*news*), 532; telegram, etc., 532.

the press, the fourth estate, public press; newspaper, journal, gazette.

advertisement, placard, bill, flier [*cant*], leaflet, handbill, poster; circular, notice, program, manifesto.

V. **publish,** make public, broach, utter, circulate, propagate, promulgate, spread, spread abroad, rumor, diffuse, disseminate; issue; bring before the public; give to the world; report, voice, bruit; proclaim, herald, blazon, noise abroad, advertise.

telegraph, cable, wireless [*colloq.*], broadcast, wire [*colloq.*].

Adj. **published,** current; public, notorious, flagrant.

Adv. **publicly,** in public, in open court, with open doors.

532. NEWS—*N.* **news,** information, etc., 527; intelligence, tidings; beat *or* scoop [*newspaper cant*], story, copy [*cant*].

message, word, advice, communication, bulletin, broadcast, dispatch; telegram, cable [*colloq.*], wire [*colloq.*], radio, radiogram, wireless telegram, wireless [*colloq.*]; telephone, radiophone, wireless telephone.

report, rumor, hearsay, cry, bruit, fame; talk, scandal, gossip; tittle-tattle.

narrator, historian; newsmonger, scandalmonger; talebearer, telltale, gossip, tattler, tattletale; chatterer, busybody; informer.

V. **transpire,** etc. (*be disclosed*), 529; rumor, etc. (*publish*), 531.

Adj. **rumored,** rife, current, in circulation.

533. SECRET.—*N.* **secret,** mystery; problem, etc. (*question*), 461; unintelligibility, etc., 519.

enigma, riddle, puzzle, conundrum, charade, rebus.

maze, labyrinth, intricacy.

Adj. **secret,** concealed, etc., 528; involved, tortuous, circuitous, labyrinthine; enigmatic *or* enigmatical.

534. MESSENGER.—*N.* **messenger,** intermediary, go-between; envoy, emissary, legate, nuncio, delegate; angel; Gabriel, Hermes, Mercury.

courier, runner; commissionaire, errand boy; herald, crier, trumpeter, bellman.

mail, post, post office; air mail; postman, mailman, letter carrier; carrier pigeon.

telegraph, cable, wire [*colloq.*], radiotelegraph, wireless telegraph, wireless [*colloq.*], radio.

telephone, phone [*colloq.*], radiotelephone, radiophone, wireless telephone.

reporter, newspaperman, journalist; gentleman (*or* representative) of the press; special correspondent; scout, spy, informer.

535. AFFIRMATION.—*N.* affirmation, statement, allegation, profession, assertion, declaration; confirmation; asseveration, swearing, oath, affidavit, deposition; assurance, protest, protestation.

positiveness, emphasis, peremptoriness, dogmatism, weight. vote, voice; ballot, suffrage.

remark, observation, saying, dictum, sentence.

V. assert, say, affirm, declare, state; protest, profess; acknowledge; put forward; advance, allege, propose, propound; announce, enunciate, broach, set forth, maintain, contend, pronounce.

depose, aver, avow, avouch, asseverate, swear, affirm; take one's oath; make an affidavit; vow, vouch, warrant, certify, assure; attest, adjure.

emphasize, insist upon, lay stress on; lay down the law; dogmatize, repeat, reassert, reaffirm.

Adj. affirmative, declaratory, positive; unmistakable, clear; certain, etc., 474; express, explicit, absolute, emphatic, decided, insistent, dogmatic, formal, solemn, categorical, peremptory.

Adv. with emphasis, ex cathedra, without fear of contradiction.

536. NEGATION.—*N.* negation, denial; disavowal, disclaimer; contradiction, protest; dissent, etc., 489.

qualification, etc., 469; repudiation, rejection, recantation, revocation; retractation, rebuttal, confutation; refusal, etc., 764.

V. deny; contradict, contravene; controvert, gainsay, negative, give the lie to, belie.

disclaim, disown, repudiate, disaffirm, disavow, abjure, forswear, renounce; recant, revoke.

dispute, impugn, confute, rebut, join issue upon; bring (*or* call) in question, set aside, ignore; refuse, etc., 764.

Adj. contradictory; negative; recusant, dissentient, at issue upon.

Adv. no, nay, not, nowise, not at all, not in the least, quite the contrary, by no means.

537. TEACHING.—*N.* teaching, pedagogics, pedagogy, instruction, edification, education, tuition, tutorship, tutelage; direction, guidance.

preparation, qualification, training, schooling, discipline; drill, practice.

lesson, lecture, recitation, sermon, homily, harangue, disquisition; apologue, parable; discourse; explanation; exercise, task; curriculum; course.

V. teach, instruct, educate, edify, school, tutor, cram [*colloq.*], grind [*colloq.*], prime, coach; enlighten, inform, etc., 527; direct, guide.

inculcate, infuse, instill, imbue, impregnate, implant; disseminate, propagate.

expound, etc. (*interpret*), 522; lecture; hold forth, preach; sermonize, moralize.

train, discipline, form, ground, prepare, qualify, drill, exercise, practice, familiarize with, inure, initiate, graduate.

Adj. educational, scholastic, academic, disciplinary, instructive, pedagogic, didactic; cultural, humanistic, humane; pragmatic, practical, utilitarian.

538. MISTEACHING.—*N.* misteaching, misinformation, misguidance, misdirection, perversion, sophistry; the blind leading the blind.

V. misinform, misteach, misinstruct, misdirect, misguide, pervert; deceive, mislead, misrepresent, lie.

render unintelligible, bewilder, mystify, conceal.

539. LEARNING.—*N.* learning, acquisition of knowledge, acquirement, attainment; mental cultivation, scholarship, erudition; lore; wide reading; study, grind [*colloq.*]; inquiry, etc., 461.

apprenticeship, tutelage, novitiate.

V. learn, acquire (*or* gain, imbibe, pick up, obtain) knowledge *or* learning; master, grind [*college slang*], cram [*colloq.*], get up, learn by heart.

study, read, peruse; con, pore over, wade through, plunge into. burn the midnight oil; be taught.

Adj. studious; industrious, etc., 682; scholastic, scholarly, well read, widely read, erudite, learned.

540. TEACHER.—*N.* teacher, preceptor, instructor, master, tutor, schoolmaster, dominie, pedagogue; kindergartner, governess, mistress; coach [*colloq.*], crammer [*colloq.*]; professor, don [*Univ. cant*], lecturer, reader, preacher; pastor, etc. (*clergy*), 996; schoolmistress.

guide, counselor, adviser, mentor, pioneer, apostle, missionary, propagandist; example.

professorship, chair, fellowship, tutorship, mastership, instructorship.

Adj. pedagogic, tutorial, professorial; scholastic, etc., 537.

541. LEARNER.—*N.* learner, scholar, student, alumnus (*pl.* alumni; *fem.* alumna, *pl.* alumnae), pupil, schoolboy, schoolgirl;

monitor, prefect; undergraduate, freshman; graduate student, postgraduate student.

class, form, grade, room; promotion, graduation.

disciple, follower, apostle, proselyte.

classmate, fellow student, schoolmate, schoolfellow, fellow pupil.

novice, beginner, tyro, recruit, tenderfoot [*slang or colloq.*], neophyte, probationer; apprentice.

Adj. in leading strings, pupillary, probationary.

542. SCHOOL.—*N.* school, academy, lyceum, seminary, college, educational institution, institute; university, varsity [*colloq.*], alma mater [L.].

General: day (*or* boarding, preparatory, elementary, denominational, secondary, military, naval, technical, library, secretarial. business, correspondence) school; kindergarten, nursery school; Sunday (*or* Sabbath. Bible) school.

United States: district (*or* grade, parochial, public, primary, grammar, junior high, high, Latin) school; private school, normal school, kindergarten training school; summer school; military academy (West Point); naval academy (Annapolis); college, fresh-water college [*colloq. or slang*], state university; graduate school, postgraduate school.

class, division, form, etc., 541; seminar.

classroom, room, schoolroom, recitation room; lecture room, lecture hall, theater, amphitheater.

desk, reading desk, pulpit, forum, stage, rostrum, platform.

schoolbook, textbook; grammar, primer, reader.

Adj. scholastic, academic, collegiate; educational, cultural; gymnastic, athletic, physical, eurythmic.

543. VERACITY.—*N.* veracity, truthfulness, frankness, truth, sincerity, candor, honesty, fidelity, love of truth; probity, etc., 939.

V. speak the truth, tell the truth; speak on oath; speak without equivocation (*or* mental reservation), make a clean breast, disclose, etc., 529; speak one's mind.

Adj. truthful, true; veracious, scrupulous, punctilious; sincere, candid, frank, open, outspoken, straightforward, unreserved, truth-telling, honest, trustworthy; guileless, pure, truth-loving; true-blue, as good as one's word; unfeigned, ingenuous.

544. FALSEHOOD.—*N.* falsehood, falseness, falsity, falsification, misrepresentation, deception, etc., 545; untruthfulness, lying; untruth, etc., 546; mendacity, guile, perjury, false swearing; forgery, invention, fabrication; perversion, distortion, exaggeration, prevarication, equivocation, evasion, fraud; simulation, dissimulation, dissembling; deceit; sham, pretense; malingering.

duplicity, double dealing, insincerity, hypocrisy, cant, pharisaism; casuistry, Machiavellism; lip service, hollowness, mere show; quackery, charlatanism, charlatanry; humbug; cajolery, flattery; Judas kiss; perfidy, etc., 940; cunning, etc., 702; misstatement, false report.

V. **lie,** tell a lie (*or* an untruth), fib, swear falsely, forswear, perjure oneself, bear false witness.

falsify, misstate, misquote; misrepresent, etc., 523; belie; garble, gloss over, disguise, color, varnish, doctor [*colloq.*], dress up, embroider; exaggerate, etc., 549.

prevaricate, equivocate, quibble; trim, shuffle, fence, beat about the bush.

fabricate, invent; trump up; forge; coin; hatch, concoct; romance.

dissemble, dissimulate; feign, assume; pretend, make believe; play false, play a double game; coquet; act *or* play a part; affect, pose; simulate, pass off for; counterfeit, sham; malinger; deceive, etc., 545.

Adj. **false,** untrue, deceitful, mendacious, lying, untruthful, fraudulent, dishonest; faithless, forsworn; evasive, disingenuous, hollow, insincere; artful, cunning, tricky, wily, sly; perfidious, treacherous, perjured; spurious, etc., 545; falsified.

hypocritical, canting, pharisaical; Machiavellian, double-tongued, double-dealing; two-faced, double-faced; smooth-spoken, smooth-tongued; plausible, mealy-mouthed; affected, canting, insincere.

545. DECEPTION.—*N.* **deception;** falseness, etc., 544; untruth, etc., 546; imposition, imposture; fraud, deceit, guile, fraudulence, misrepresentation, bluff; trickery, knavery, sharp practice, collusion, chicanery; treachery, double-dealing.

delusion, jugglery, sleight of hand, legerdemain, conjuring.

trick, cheat, wile, blind, feint, chicane, juggle, swindle; stratagem, artifice; hoax; bunk [*slang*], gold brick [*colloq.*].

snare, trap, pitfall, gin; bait, decoy duck, stool pigeon; cobweb, net, meshes, toils; ambush, ambuscade.

disguise, false colors, camouflage, masquerade, mask, mummery, borrowed plumes; dissembler, hypocrite, etc., 548.

sham, mockery, copy, counterfeit, make-believe, forgery, fraud, untruth, etc., 546; hollow mockery; whited sepulcher, tinsel, paste.

illusion, delusion, self-deception, *ignis fatuus* [L.], mirage, etc., 443.

V. **deceive,** mislead, lead astray, take in, defraud, cheat, cozen, swindle, victimize; betray, play false; lie, etc., 544; mystify; blind, hoodwink; throw dust into the eyes; impose upon, practice upon, palm off on; bluff.

outwit, circumvent, overreach, steal a march on.

insnare, ensnare, entrap, decoy, waylay, lure, beguile, delude, inveigle, trick.

fool, befool, dupe, gull, hoax, humbug, stuff [*slang*], sell [*slang*]; trifle with, cajole, flatter; dissemble, dissimulate, sham, counterfeit.

practice chicanery, live by one's wits, juggle, conjure, play off, palm off, foist off.

Adj. deceptive, deceitful, tricky, cunning, etc., 702; elusive, insidious; delusive, illusory.

make-believe; untrue, etc., 546; mock, sham, counterfeit, pseudo, spurious, so-called, pretended, feigned, bogus [*colloq.*], fraudulent, surreptitious, illegitimate, contraband; adulterated, disguised; unsound, meretricious, jerry-built; tinsel.

Adv. under false colors, under cover of.

546. UNTRUTH.—*N.* untruth, falsehood, lie, story, fib, whopper [*colloq.*].

fabrication, forgery, invention; misstatement, misrepresentation, perversion, falsification, false coloring, exaggeration.

fiction; fable, nursery tale, fairy tale, romance, extravaganza; canard; yarn [*colloq.*], fish story [*colloq.*], traveler's tale, cock-and-bull story, myth, moonshine, bosh [*colloq.*].

half truth, white lie, pious fraud; suppression; irony.

pretense, pretext, subterfuge, evasion, shift, shuffle, make-believe, sham, etc., 545; profession, Judas kiss, cajolery, flattery; disguise, etc., 530.

V. feign, make-believe, pretend, sham, counterfeit; lie, etc., 544.

Adj. untrue, false, trumped up; unfounded, invented, fictitious, fabulous, fabricated, fraudulent, forged; evasive.

547. DUPE.—*N.* dupe, gull, victim, April fool; sucker [*slang*]; laughingstock, etc., 857; greenhorn; fool, etc., 501; puppet, cat's-paw.

V. be deceived, be the dupe of; fall into a trap; swallow *or* nibble at the bait; swallow whole; bite.

Adj. credulous, gullible, etc., 486.

mistaken, etc. (*error*), 495.

548. DECEIVER.—*N.* deceiver, dissembler, hypocrite, Pharisee; sophist; serpent, snake in the grass, Judas, wolf in sheep's clothing.

liar, storyteller, perjurer, false witness, faker [*slang*], fraud, four-flusher [*slang*], confidence man, decoy, stool pigeon; rogue, knave, cheat, swindler.

impostor, pretender, malingerer, humbug; adventurer, adventuress.

trickster, conjurer, juggler, necromancer, sorcerer, magician, wizard, medicine man, witch doctor; quack, charlatan, mountebank.

549. EXAGGERATION.—N. **exaggeration,** expansion, amplification; fringe, embroidery; extravagance, hyperbole, stretch, high coloring, caricature; yarn [*colloq.*], traveler's tale, fish story [*colloq.*]; tempest in a teacup; much ado about nothing; puffery, etc. (*boasting*), 884; rant, etc., 577.

V. **exaggerate,** magnify, pile up, aggravate; amplify, expand, overestimate, overstate, overdraw, overshoot the mark, overpraise; stretch a point; draw a long bow [*colloq.*], out-Herod Herod; overcolor, heighten; embroider, color; puff, etc. (*boast*), 884.

Adj. **exaggerated,** overwrought; bombastic, etc. (*magniloquent*), 577; hyperbolical, extravagant; preposterous, egregious.

550. [Means of communication] INDICATION.—N. **indication,** sign, symbol; index, indicator, pointer, cue, note, token, symptom; type, figure, emblem, cipher, device; motto, epitaph.

means of recognition; lineament, feature, trait, trick, earmark, characteristic.

gesture, gesticulation; pantomime; wink, glance, leer; nod, shrug, beck; touch, nudge; byplay, dumb show; deaf-and-dumb alphabet, dactylology.

track, spoor, trail, footprint, scent; clue, key.

signal, rocket, watch fire, beacon fire, watchtower; telegraph, semaphore; fiery cross; calumet, peace pipe; heliograph; searchlight, flashlight.

mark, line, stroke, score, streak, scratch, tick, dot, notch, nick, blaze; red letter, underlining, impression.

Map drawing: hachure, contour line; isobar, isopiestic line, isobaric line; isotherm, isothermal line; latitude, longitude, meridian, equator.

For identification: badge, countercheck, countersign, counterfoil, stub, duplicate, tally; label, ticket, counter, check, chip, voucher, stamp; trade-mark, hallmark; card, visiting card; credentials; handwriting, sign manual, autograph, signature; monogram, seal, signet; fingerprint; brand; caste mark; mortarboard [*colloq.*], cap and gown, hood; shibboleth; watchword, catchword, password, cue; sign, countersign, pass, grip; open-sesame.

Insignia: banner, flag, colors, streamer, pennant, pennon, ensign, standard; eagle, oriflamme, blue peter, jack, Union Jack; Old Glory [*colloq.*], Stars and Stripes.

Heraldry: crest, arms, coat of arms, armorial bearings; hatchment, escutcheon or scutcheon; shield, supporters; livery, uniform; cockade, brassard, epaulet, chevron; garland, chaplet, love knot, favor.

Of locality: beacon, flagstaff, hand, pointer, vane, cock, weathercock, weather vane; guidepost, signpost; sign, signboard; North Star, polestar; landmark, seamark; lighthouse; address, direction, name.

Of the future: warning, premonition; omen, portent, sign.

Of the past: trace, record.

Of danger: warning, alarm, fire alarm, burglar alarm.

Of authority: scepter, etc., 747.

Of triumph: trophy, etc., 733.

Of mourning: mourning, etc., 839.

Of quantity: gauge, etc., 466.

Of distance: milestone, milepost.
Of disgrace: brand, foolscap, mark of Cain, stigma, stripes, broad arrow.
call, word of command; bugle call, trumpet call; bell, alarum, battle cry, reveille, taps, last post; sacring bell, Sanctus bell, angelus; dirge.

V. **indicate,** denote, betoken, connote, signify; represent, stand for; typify, symbolize; mark, note, stamp, nick, blaze; label, ticket.

make a sign, signalize; beckon, nod, wink, glance, leer, nudge, shrug, gesticulate.

sign, seal, attest, underscore, underline; call attention to.

Adj. **indicative,** indicatory; connotative, denotative, representative, typical, individual, symbolic *or* symbolical, symptomatic, characteristic, significant, diagnostic, emblematic, armorial.

551. RECORD.—*N.* **trace,** vestige, relic, remains; scar, cicatrix; footstep, footmark, footprint; track, mark, wake, trail, scent, spoor.

monument, hatchment; escutcheon *or* scutcheon; slab, tablet, trophy, obelisk, pillar, column, monolith; memorial; memento; testimonial, medal, Congressional medal; cross, Victoria cross [Eng.], iron cross [Ger.]; ribbon, garter; commemoration, etc. (*celebration*), 883.

record, note, minute; register, registry; roll, list; entry, memorandum, endorsement, inscription, copy, duplicate, docket; mark, etc., 550; deed; document; deposition, affidavit; certificate.
notebook, memorandum book; bulletin, bulletin board, scoreboard, score sheet; card index, file, letter file, pigeonholes.
newspaper, daily, gazette, magazine, paper [*colloq.*].
calendar, diary, log, journal, daybook, ledger, cashbook.
archive, scroll, state paper, return, bluebook; almanac, gazetteer, census report; statistics; Congressional Records; minutes, chronicle, annals; legend; history, biography, etc., 594.
registration; registry, enrollment, tabulation; entry, booking; signature, sign manual; recorder, etc., 553; journalism.
mechanical record, recording instrument; phonograph, etc., 418; speedometer, pedometer, patent log [*naut.*]; ticker, tape; time clock; turnstile; cash register.

V. **record,** put *or* place upon record, chronicle, calendar, hand down to posterity; commemorate, etc. (*celebrate*), 883; report, commit to writing, note, put *or* set down; mark, etc. (*indicate*), 550; sign, etc. (*attest*), 467; enter, book, post, insert; mark off, tick off; register, list, enroll, inscroll; file.

552. [Suppression of sign] OBLITERATION.—*N.* **obliteration,** erasure, cancellation, deletion; blot; effacement, extinction.

V. **efface,** obliterate, erase, expunge, cancel; blot (*or* rub, scratch, strike, wash, wipe) out; deface, render illegible; rule out.
be effaced, leave no trace.

Adj. **obliterated,** erased; unrecorded, unregistered.

553. RECORDER.—*N.* **recorder,** notary, clerk; registrar, register; amanuensis, secretary, recording secretary, stenographer, bookkeeper, scribe.

annalist, historian, historiographer, chronicler; biographer, etc.

(*narrator*), 594; antiquary, antiquarian, archeologist; memorialist.

journalist, newspaperman, reporter, interviewer; publicist, author, editor.

554. REPRESENTATION.—*N.* representation, depiction, imitation, illustration, delineation, imagery, portraiture; design, designing; art, fine arts; painting, etc., 556; sculpture, etc., 557; engraving, etc., 558.

photography; radiography, X-ray photography, skiagraphy.
personation, impersonation; personification; drama, etc., 599.

drawing, picture, sketch, draft; tracing; copy, etc., 21.
photograph, photo [*colloq.*], daguerreotype, print, cabinet, snapshot.
image, effigy, icon, portrait, likeness, facsimile.
figure, figurehead, puppet, doll, manikin, lay figure, model, marionette, statue, statuette, bust.
map, plan, chart; diagram; ground plan, projection, elevation; atlas; outline, view.
radiograph, radiogram, skiagraph, skiagram, X-ray photograph, Xray [*colloq.*].
delineator, draftsman; artist, etc., 559; photographer, radiographer, X-ray photographer, skiagrapher, daguerreotypist.

V. **represent**, delineate, depict, portray, picture, limn, photograph, snapshot; figure, shadow forth, adumbrate; describe, etc., 594; trace, copy; mold; illustrate, symbolize; paint, etc., 556; sculpture, etc., 557; engrave, etc., 558.

personate, impersonate, dress up [*colloq.*], pose as, act; personify; play, etc. (*drama*), 559; mimic, etc. (*imitate*),19.

Adj. **representative**; illustrative; imitative, figurative; similar, like, etc., 17; descriptive, etc., 594.

555. MISREPRESENTATION.—*N.* misrepresentation, misstatement, falsification, exaggeration, distortion; bad likeness, daub, scratch.

burlesque, travesty, parody, take-off, caricature, extravaganza.

V. **misrepresent**, distort, overdraw, exaggerate, daub; falsify, understate, overstate, stretch.

burlesque, travesty, parody, caricature.

556. PAINTING. BLACK AND WHITE.—*N.* painting, depicting, drawing; design; perspective; composition; treatment; arrangement, values, atmosphere, tone, technique.

palette; easel; brush, pencil, stump, black lead, charcoal, crayons, chalk, pastel; paint, etc. (*coloring matter*), 428; water (*or* oil) colors; oils, oil paint; varnish; distemper, fresco, enamel, mosaic, encaustic painting; batik.
style, school; the grand style, high art; futurist, cubist, vorticist.
picture, painting, piece, tableau, canvas; fresco, cartoon; drawing, draft; still life, genre (*or* landscape) painting; sketch, outline, study.
portrait; head; miniature; silhouette; profile.

view, landscape, seascape, sea view, seapiece; scene, prospect; interior; panorama, bird's-eye view.

picture gallery, art gallery, art museum; studio, atelier [F.].

photograph, radiography, etc., 554; photograph, radiograph, etc., 554.

V. paint, design, limn, draw, sketch, pencil, color; stencil; depict, etc. (*represent*), 554.

Adj. pictorial, graphic; picturesque, historical; futurist, cubist, vorticist; in the grand style.

557. SCULPTURE.—*N.* **sculpture,** carving, modeling, statuary; ceramics.

marble, bronze, terra cotta; ceramic ware, pottery, porcelain, china, earthenware; cloisonné, enamel, faïence.

relief, low relief, bas-relief, high relief; intaglio; cameo; medal, medallion.

statue, statuette, bust; cast.

V. **sculpture,** carve, cut, chisel, model, mold; cast.

558. ENGRAVING.—*N.* **engraving,** etching, chiseling; plate (*or* copperplate, steel, half-tone, wood) engraving; lithography, chromolithography, photolithography.

printing; color printing, lithographic printing; type printing; three-color process. impression, print, engraving, plate; steel-plate, copperplate; etching; aquatint, mezzotint; cut, woodcut; lithograph, chromolithograph, photolithograph. illustration, illumination; half-tone; photogravure; rotogravure; vignette, initial letter, tailpiece.

V. **engrave,** grave, etch; bite; bite in; lithograph; print.

559. ARTIST.—*N.* **artist;** painter, drawer, sketcher, designer, engraver, graver, line engraver, draftsman; chaser; copyist; enameler, enamelist; cartoonist, caricaturist.

historical (*or* landscape, marine, flower, portrait, genre, miniature, scene) painter; carver, modeler, statuary, sculptor.

(1) Language generally

560. LANGUAGE.—*N.* **language;** phraseology, etc., 569; speech, etc., 582; tongue, lingo [*chiefly humorous or contemptuous*], vernacular, mother (*or* vulgar, native) tongue; king's English; dialect, brogue, patois, idiom.

confusion of tongues, Babel; universal language, Esperanto, Ido; pantomime, dumb show.

literature, letters, polite literature, belles-lettres [F.], muses, humanities, republic of letters, dead languages, classics.

linguist, etc. (*scholar*), 492.

V. **express,** say, express by words.

Adj. **lingual,** linguistic; dialectal, dialectic; vernacular, current; bilingual; polyglot; literary; colloquial, slangy.

561. LETTER.—*N.* **letter;** character; hieroglyphic; alphabet,

ABC; consonant, vowel, diphthong, mute, surd, sonant, liquid, labial, palatal, cerebral, dental, guttural.

syllable; monosyllable, dissyllable, polysyllable; prefix, suffix.

spelling, orthography; phonetic spelling, phonetics.

cipher, code; monogram, anagram; acrostic, double acrostic. *V.* spell; transliterate.

cipher, decipher; code, decode.

Adj. literal; alphabetical, syllabic.

phonetic, voiced, tonic, sonant; voiceless, surd; mute, labial, palatal, cerebral, dental, guttural, liquid.

562. WORD.—*N.* word, term, vocable; name, etc., 564; phrase, etc., 566; root, derivative; part of speech.

dictionary, lexicon, vocabulary, wordbook, index, glossary, thesaurus.

Science of language: etymology, philology; terminology; pronunciation, orthoëpy; lexicography.

verbosity, verbiage, wordiness; loquacity, etc., 584.

V. vocalize; etymologize, derive; index; translate.

Adj. verbal, literal; derivative.

verbose, wordy, etc., 573; loquacious, etc., 584.

563. NEOLOGY.—*N.* neology, neologism; barbarism; corruption.

dialect, brogue, patois, provincialism, broken English, Anglicism, Briticism, Gallicism, Americanism; gypsy lingo, Romany.

lingua franca, pidgin English, Hindustani; Esperanto, Ido.

jargon, dog Latin, gibberish; confusion of tongues, Babel; lingo, slang, cant, argot, billingsgate.

pseudonym, pen name; nickname; alias.

neologist, word coiner, coiner of words.

V. coin words; Americanize, Anglicize, Gallicize.

Adj. neologic, neological; slang, cant, barbarous.

564. NOMENCLATURE.—*N.* nomenclature; naming, nicknaming; baptism.

name, appellation, appellative, designation, denomination; nickname, etc., 565; epithet; title, head, heading; style, proper name, cognomen, patronymic, surname; title, handle to one's name; namesake.

term, expression, noun; technical term; cant.

V. name, call, term, denominate, designate, style, entitle, dub [*colloq. or humorous*], christen, baptize, nickname, characterize, specify, label.

Adj. named, yclept [*humorous*]; known as; titular, nominal.

565. MISNOMER.—*N.* misnomer; malapropism, Mrs. Malaprop.

nickname, sobriquet, pet name, assumed name, alias; stage name; *nom de guerre* [F.], nom de plume [English formation], pen name, pseudonym.

V. misname, miscall, nickname; take an assumed name.

Adj. misnamed; self-styled; so-called, quasi.

nameless, anonymous; unacknowledged; pseudo.

566. PHRASE.—*N.* **phrase,** expression, locution; sentence, paragraph; paraphrase, metaphor, euphemism, euphuism; motto, proverb; figure of speech; idiom, turn of expression; phraseology, etc., 569.

V. **express,** phrase; word, voice; put into (*or* express by) words; call, denominate, designate, dub.

Adv. in round (*or* set) terms; in set phrases; by the card.

567. GRAMMAR.—*N.* **grammar,** accidence, syntax, analysis, parts of speech; inflection, case, declension, conjugation; philology.

V. parse, analyze, conjugate, decline.

Adj. grammatical, syntactic *or* syntactical, inflectional, declensional, synthetic *or* synthetical.

568. SOLECISM.—*N.* **solecism;** grammatical blunder; error, slip; slip of the pen, slip of the tongue, bull; barbarism, impropriety.

V. **solecize,** commit a solecism; murder the king's English.

Adj. ungrammatical, incorrect, inaccurate, faulty; improper.

569. STYLE.—*N.* **style,** diction, phraseology, wording; manner, strain; composition; mode of expression, idiom, choice of words; mode of speech, literary power, command of language; authorship, artistry.

V. **word,** phrase, express by words, write; apply the file.

Various Qualities of Style

570. PERSPICUITY.—*N.* **perspicuity,** perspicacity, explicitness, lucidness, lucidity, limpidity, clearness; plain speaking, expression, definiteness, definition; exactness, etc., 494.

Adj. lucid, intelligible, etc., 518; limpid, pellucid, clear, explicit; exact, etc., 494.

571. OBSCURITY.—*N.* **obscurity,** unintelligibility, involution, confusion; hard words; ambiguity, indefiniteness, vagueness, inexactness, inaccuracy; darkness of meaning.

Adj. obscure, involved, confused.

572. CONCISENESS.—*N.* **conciseness,** terseness, brevity, laconicism, abridgment, compression, condensation, epitome, etc., 596.

Portmanteau word [Lewis Carroll]; brunch [breakfast + lunch], slithy, *adj.* [slimy + lithe], torrible, *adj.* [torrid + horrible].

V. be concise, telescope, compress, condense, abridge, abbreviate, abstract, etc., 596; come to the point.

Adj. concise, brief, short, laconic, succinct, curt, compact, summary, compendious, etc., 596; terse, to the point; compressed, condensed, pointed; pithy, crisp, trenchant, epigrammatic, sententious.

Adv. briefly, summarily; in brief, in short, in a word.

573. DIFFUSENESS.—*N.* diffuseness, profuseness, amplification, verbosity, wordiness; verbiage, flow of words, etc. (*loquacity*), 584; looseness; tautology, exuberance, redundance, prolixity, periphrase, expletive; padding [*editors' cant*]; drivel, twaddle.

V. expand, expatiate, enlarge, dilate, amplify, inflate, pad [*editors' cant*], rant; maunder, prose; harp upon, dwell on.

digress, ramble, beat about the bush, protract.

Adj. diffuse, profuse, wordy, verbose, copious, exuberant; lengthy, long, long-winded, protracted, prolix, diffusive, roundabout, digressive, discursive, loose; rambling, frothy.

574. VIGOR.—*N.* vigor, power, force; boldness, intellectual force; spirit, punch [*slang*], point, piquancy, raciness; verve, ardor, enthusiasm, glow, fire, warmth; gravity, weight.

loftiness, elevation, sublimity, grandeur.

eloquence; command of words, command of language.

Adj. vigorous, nervous, powerful, forcible, forceful; mordant, biting, trenchant, incisive; graphic, impressive.

spirited, lively, glowing, sparkling; racy, bold, pungent, piquant, pithy.

lofty, elevated, sublime, poetic, grand, weighty, ponderous; eloquent.

vehement, passionate, burning, impassioned, petulant.

575. FEEBLENESS.—*N.* feebleness, baldness, enervation, flaccidity, vapidity, poverty.

Adj. feeble, tame, meager, insipid, watery, nerveless, vapid, trashy, poor, dull, dry, languid; bald, colorless, enervated; prosy, prosaic, weak, slight; careless, slovenly, loose, lax; slipshod, inexact; puerile, childish; rambling, etc. (*diffuse*), 573.

576. PLAINNESS.—*N.* plainness, homeliness, simplicity, severity; household words.

V. speak plainly, waste no words, come to the point.

Adj. plain, simple, unornamented, unadorned, unvarnished; homely, homespun; neat; severe, chaste, pure, Saxon; commonplace, matter-of-fact, natural, prosaic, sober.

Adv. point-blank; in plain English; in common parlance.

577. ORNAMENT.—*N.* ornament, floridness, grandiloquence, magniloquence, declamation, well-rounded periods; elegance, etc., 578; flourish, trope; euphuism, euphemism.

bombast, inflation, pretension; rant, fustian, highfalutin [*slang*], buncombe, balderdash; fine writing; purple patches.

V. ornament, overcharge, overload; euphuize, euphemize.

Adj. ornate; ornamented, beautified, florid, rich, flowery; euphuistic, euphemistic; sonorous, inflated, swelling, tumid; turgid, pedantic, pompous, stilted, high-flown, sententious, rhetorical, declamatory; grandiose; grandiloquent, magniloquent, bombastic; frothy, flashy, flamboyant.

578. ELEGANCE.—*N.* elegance, distinction, clarity, purity, grace, felicity, ease; gracefulness, euphony; taste, good taste, restraint, propriety, correctness.

purist, classicist, stylist.

Adj. elegant, polished, classic *or* classical, correct, artistic; chaste, pure; graceful, easy, fluent, unaffected, natural, mellifluous, euphonious; restrained.

felicitous, happy, neat; well expressed.

579. INELEGANCE.—*N.* inelegance, impurity, vulgarity; poor diction, poor choice of words; loose construction; ill-balanced sentences; barbarism, slang; solecism, mannerism, affectation.

Adj. inelegant, graceless, ungraceful; harsh, abrupt; dry, stiff, cramped, formal, forced, labored; artificial, mannered, affected, ponderous, awkward; unpolished; turgid, barbarous, uncouth, rude, crude, halting, vulgar.

(2) Spoken Language

580. VOICE.—*N.* voice; intonation; utterance; vocalization; cry, exclamation, expletive, ejaculation; vociferation, enunciation, articulation; distinctness; clearness; delivery, attack.

accent, accentuation; emphasis, stress; pronunciation; euphony, etc. (*melody*), 413.

V. speak, utter, breathe; cry, etc. (*shout*), 411; ejaculate, rap out; articulate, enunciate, vocalize, pronounce, accentuate, deliver, emit; whisper, murmur.

Adj. vocal, phonetic, oral; ejaculatory, articulate, distinct, euphonious, melodious.

581. DUMBNESS.—*N.* dumbness; silence, etc. (*taciturnity*), 585; deaf-mutism, deaf-muteness, deaf-dumbness, mute, dummy, deaf-mute.

V. silence, muzzle, muffle, suppress, smother, gag, strike dumb, dumfound.

Adj. dumb, mute, mum; tongue-tied; voiceless, speechless, wordless; silent, etc. (*taciturn*), 585; inarticulate.

582. SPEECH.—*N.* speech, locution, talk, parlance, word of mouth, prattle.

oration, recitation, delivery, speech, address, discourse, lecture, harangue, sermon, tirade, soliloquy, etc., 589; conversation, etc., 588; salutatory; valedictory.

oratory, elocution, eloquence, rhetoric, declamation; grandiloquence.

speaker, spokesman, mouthpiece, orator, rhetorician, lecturer, preacher, elocutionist, reciter, reader; spellbinder.

V. speak, talk, say, utter, pronounce, deliver, breathe, let fall, rap out, blurt out.

soliloquize, etc., 589; tell, etc. (*inform*), 527; address, etc., 586; converse, etc., 588.

declaim, hold forth, harangue, stump [*colloq.*], spout, rant; recite, lecture, sermonize, discourse, expatiate.

Adj. oral, lingual, phonetic, unwritten, spoken.

eloquent, oratorical, rhetorical, elocutionary, declamatory, grandiloquent.

583. [Imperfect Speech] STAMMERING.—*N.* inarticulateness; stammering, hesitation, impediment in one's speech; lisp, drawl, nasal accent; twang; falsetto, brogue.

V. stammer, stutter, hesitate, falter.

mumble, mutter, maunder; mince, lisp; jabber, gabble, gibber; splutter, sputter; drawl, mouth; croak.

murder the language, murder the king's English; mispronounce.

Adj. inarticulate; stammering, guttural, throaty, nasal; tremulous.

584. LOQUACITY.—*N.* loquacity, loquaciousness, effusion; talkativeness, garrulity.

gabble, gab [*colloq.*], jaw [*low*], hot air [*slang*]; jabber, chatter; prate, prattle, twaddle, small talk.

fluency, volubility, flow of words; verbosity, etc. (*diffuseness*), 573; eloquence.

talker; chatterer, chatterbox; babbler, ranter, proser, driveler, gossip, magpie.

V. be loquacious, talk glibly, pour forth, prate, palaver, prose, maunder, chatter, blab, gush, prattle, jabber, jaw [*low*], babble, gabble; expatiate, gossip, talk at random, talk nonsense.

Adj. loquacious, talkative, garrulous, chattering, chatty, declamatory, fluent, voluble, effusive, glib, flippant.

585. TACITURNITY.—*N.* taciturnity, silence, muteness, curtness; reserve, reticence.

man of few words; Spartan.

V. be silent, keep silence; hold one's tongue, say nothing; render mute.

Adj. silent, mute, mum, still, dumb.

taciturn, laconic, concise, sententious, close, close-mouthed, curt; reserved; reticent.

586. ADDRESS.—*N.* address, allocution; speech, etc., 582; appeal, invocation, salutation, salutatory.

V. address, speak to, accost, apostrophize, appeal to, invoke; hail, salute; call to, halloo.

lecture, preach, harangue, spellbind.

587. RESPONSE, etc., *see* Answer 462.

588. CONVERSATION.—*N.* conversation, colloquy, converse, interlocution, talk, discourse, dialogue, duologue.

chat, tattle, gossip, tittle-tattle; babble.

conference, parley, interview, audience, reception; congress, etc. (*council*). 696; powwow.

debate, palaver, war of words, controversy.

talker, gossip, tattler; chatterer, etc. (*loquacity*), 584; speaker, etc., 582; conversationalist.

V. converse, talk together, hold (*or* carry on, join in, engage in) a conversation; parley; palaver; chat, gossip, tattle; prate, etc., 584.

confer with, discourse with, commune with, talk it over.

Adj. conversational, conversable; chatty, colloquial.

589. SOLILOQUY.—*N.* soliloquy, monologue, apostrophe.

V. soliloquize, monologize, talk to oneself; think aloud, apostrophize.

Written Language

590. WRITING.—*N.* writing, chirography, penmanship; typewriting; manuscript; script; character, letter, etc., 561.

shorthand, stenography, phonography; secret writing, cipher, cryptography.

handwriting; signature, mark, autograph, hand, fist [*colloq.*]; calligraphy.

composition, authorship; lucubration, production, work, screed, article, paper; book, etc., 593; essay, theme, thesis; novel, text-book; poem, book of poems (*or* verse), anthology.

writer, scribe; author, etc., 593; amanuensis, secretary, clerk, penman, copyist; stenographer, typewriter, typist.

V. **write,** pen, typewrite, type [*colloq.*]; copy, engross; transcribe; scribble, scrawl, scratch; note down, write down, record.

compose, indite, draw up, draft, formulate; dictate; inscribe.

Adj. **written,** in writing, in black and white; stenographic.

591. PRINTING.—*N.* printing, typography; type, linotype, monotype; composition, print, letterpress, text, context, matter; copy, impression, proof, galley, galley proof, page proof.

printer, compositor; reader, proofreader, corrector of the press; printer's devil; copyholder, copyeditor.

V. **print;** compose; go to press; publish, issue, bring out.

Adj. **typographical,** printed, in type.

592. CORRESPONDENCE.—*N.* correspondence, letter, epistle, missive, note, post card, postal card; dispatch; bulletin, circular.

correspondent, writer, letter writer.

V. **correspond,** write to, send a letter to; communicate, communicate by writing (*or* letter); circularize, follow up, bombard; reply.

593. BOOK.—*N.* book, booklet; writing, work, volume, tome, tract, treatise, brochure, monograph, pamphlet, libretto; handbook, manual, novel, etc. (*composition*), 590; publication; magazine, periodical.

work of reference, encyclopedia, cyclopedia, dictionary, thesaurus, concordance, anthology, compilation.

writer, author, essayist, contributor; hack writer, hack; journalist, publicist, reporter, correspondent; editor, scribe, etc., 590; playwright, etc., 599; poet, etc., 597.

publisher, bookseller; librarian; bookworm.

bookstore, bookshop, bookseller's shop, publishing house.

library, public library, lending library.

594. DESCRIPTION.—*N.* description, account, statement, report, record; brief, etc. (*abstract*), 596; delineation, sketch, pastel, vignette; monograph; narration, recital, rehearsal, relation.

   narrative, history, memoir; annals, etc., (*chronicle*), 551; journal, letters, biography, autobiography, life, adventures.

   Fiction: novel, romance, story, tale, short story, anecdote; detective story, fairy tale, fable, parable, allegory.

   narrator, historian, biographer, novelist, storyteller, romancer, anecdotist, word painter; writer, etc., 593.

V. **describe,** set forth, picture, portray, characterize, delineate, narrate, relate, recite, recount, romance, tell, report; detail, particularize.

Adj. **descriptive,** graphic, narrative, epic, romantic, historic *or* historical, biographical, autobiographical; traditional, legendary, mythical, fabulous; anecdotic, idealistic; realistic, true to life.

595. DISSERTATION.—*N.* dissertation, treatise, essay, thesis, theme; tract, discourse, memoir, disquisition, lecture, sermon, homily, investigation, study, discussion, exposition.

commentary, review, critique, criticism, article, leader, editorial.

commentator, critic, essayist, publicist, reviewer, leader writer, editor.

V. comment, explain, interpret, criticize, illuminate; treat of (*or* ventilate, discuss, deal with, go into) a subject.

596. COMPENDIUM.—*N.* compendium, abstract, précis, epitome, analysis, digest, brief, condensation, abridgment, abbreviation, etc., 201; summary, draft, minute, note; excerpt, extract; synopsis, textbook, outlines, syllabus, contents, heads, prospectus.

fragments, extracts, cuttings; fugitive pieces, anthology, miscellany, compilation.

recapitulation, résumé, review; symposium.

V. abridge, abstract, epitomize, summarize; abbreviate, etc. (*shorten*), 201; condense, etc. (*compress*), 195.

compile, etc. (*collect*), 72; note down, collect, edit.

recapitulate, review, skim, run over, sum up.

Adj. compendious, synoptic, abridged, analytic *or* analytical.

Adv. in short, in substance, in few words, in a nutshell.

597. POETRY.—*N.* poetry, poetics, poesy, muse, Apollo, Parnassus, inspiration, fire of genius.

poem; epic, ballad, lyric, ode, idyl, eclogue, pastoral, sonnet, elegy; dramatic (*or* didactic, satirical, narrative, lyric) poetry; satire; anthology.

versification, rhyming, prosody; scansion, scanning.
canto, stanza, verse, line, couplet, triplet, quatrain; refrain, chorus, burden; octave, sextet.
verse, rhyme, assonance, alliteration, meter, measure; foot, numbers, rhythm; ictus, beat, accent, accentuation, iambus, iambic, dactyl, spondee, trochee, anapest, etc.; hexameter, pentameter; Alexandrine; blank verse, heroic verse; doggerel.

poet, genius, creator; poet laureate; laureate; bard, lyrist, sonneteer, rhapsodist, satirist, troubadour; minstrel; minnesinger, Meistersinger; jongleur, versifier, rhymer, rhymester, minor poet, poetaster.

V. poetize, sing, write poetry; string verses together, versify, make verses, rhyme.

Adj. poetic *or* poetical; lyric *or* lyrical; tuneful; metrical; elegiac, iambic, dactylic, spondaic, trochaic, anapestic.

598. PROSE.—*N.* prose, prosaicness; poetic prose; narrative, etc., 594.

prose writer, essayist, novelist, etc., 594.

V. prose; write prose (*or* in prose).

Adj. prosaic, prosy, unpoetical, unrhymed, in prose.

599. THE DRAMA.—*N.* the drama, the stage, the theater, the play; theatricals, histrionic art.

play, drama, piece, tragedy, comedy, opera, vaudeville, curtain raiser, interlude, afterpiece, farce, extravaganza, harlequinade, pantomime, burlesque, ballet, spectacle, masque, melodrama; comedy of manners; charade, mystery, miracle play, morality play.

act, scene, tableau, curtain; introduction, prologue, exposition, epilogue; libretto, book, text, prompter's copy.

performance, representation, show [colloq.], stage setting, stagecraft; acting; impersonation, stage business; slapstick [slang], buffoonery.

theater, playhouse, amphitheater, moving-picture theater, moving pictures, movies [colloq.]; puppet show, marionettes, Punch and Judy.

cast, dramatis personae [L.], role, part, character; repertoire, repertory.

actor, player, performer; masker, mime, mimic; star, headliner; comedian, tragedian.

buffoon, mummer, pantomimist, clown; pantaloon, harlequin, columbine; punch.

company, first tragedian, prima donna, leading lady; lead; leading man; comedian, comedienne; juvenile lead, juvenile; villain, heavy lead, heavy, heavy father; ingenue, soubrette; character man, character woman, extra, mute, supernumerary, super [theat. cant].

dramatist, playwright, playwriter; dramatic author (*or* writer).

audience, house; orchestra, gallery.

V. act, play, perform; put on the stage, dramatize, stage, produce, set; personate, mimic, enact; rehearse, spout, rant; tread the stage (*or* boards); make one's debut, take a part, star.

Adj. **dramatic**; theatrical; scenic, histrionic, comic, tragic, farcical, tragicomic, melodramatic, operatic; stagy, spectacular.

Adv. **on the stage**, on the boards; in the limelight, in the spotlight; before the footlights, before an audience; behind the scenes.

CLASS V

Words Relating to the VOLUNTARY POWERS

I. Individual Volition

600. WILL.—*N.* will, volition, free will; freedom, etc., 748; discretion; choice, inclination, intent, purpose, option, etc. (*choice*), 609; spontaneity, spontaneousness; originality.

determination, etc. (*resolution*), 604; force of will, will power, autocracy, bossiness [colloq.].

wish, desire, pleasure, mind, disposition, etc., 602; intention, etc., 620.

V. will, see fit, think fit; determine, etc. (*resolve*), 604; enjoin; settle, etc. (*choose*), 609; volunteer; do what one chooses, etc. (*freedom*), 748; have one's own way; use one's discretion; boss, [colloq.]; originate.

Adj. **voluntary,** volitional, willful; free, etc., 748; optional, discretionary; autocratic, dictatorial, bossy [*colloq.*].

willing, etc., 602; unbidden, spontaneous; original.

Adv. **voluntarily,** at will, at pleasure.

of one's own accord, on one's own responsibility; by choice, purposely, intentionally.

601. NECESSITY.—*N.* **necessity,** obligation; compulsion, etc., 744; subjection, etc., 749; stern (*or* dire) necessity, last resort.

instinct, blind impulse, natural tendency (*or* impulse), predetermination.

destiny, fatality, fate, kismet, doom, election, predestination; lot, fortune; fatalism.

Fates, God's will, heaven, will of heaven; stars; planets; wheel of fortune.

V. **be obliged,** be forced, be driven; be fated, be doomed, be destined, have no alternative.

destine, doom, foredoom, devote; predestine, preordain; necessitate; compel, etc., 744.

Adj. **necessary,** needful, etc. (*requisite*), 630; compulsory, etc. (*compel*), 744; inevitable, unavoidable, irresistible, irrevocable, inexorable, binding.

fated; destined, fateful, set apart, devoted, elect.

involuntary, instinctive, automatic, blind, mechanical; unconscious, unwitting, unthinking; unintentional.

Adv. **necessarily,** of necessity, of course; willy-nilly.

602. WILLINGNESS.—*N.* **willingness,** disposition, inclination, liking, turn, propensity, leaning, frame of mind, humor, mood, vein, bent, aptitude.

geniality, cordiality, good will; alacrity, readiness, zeal, enthusiasm, earnestness, eagerness.

assent, etc., 488; compliance, etc., 762.

volunteer, unpaid worker, amateur, nonprofessional.

V. **be willing,** incline, lean to, mind, hold to, cling to; desire, etc., 865; acquiesce, assent, comply with; jump at, catch at; take up, plunge into, have a go at [*colloq.*].

volunteer, offer, proffer.

Adj. **willing,** fain, disposed, inclined, favorable, content, well disposed; ready, forward, earnest, eager, zealous, enthusiastic; bent upon, desirous.

docile, amenable, easily persuaded, facile, easygoing, tractable, genial, gracious, cordial.

voluntary, gratuitous, free, unconstrained, spontaneous, unasked, unforced.

Adv. willingly, fain, freely, with pleasure, of one's own accord; graciously, with a good grace, without demur.

603. UNWILLINGNESS.—*N.* unwillingness, indisposition, disinclination, aversion, averseness, reluctance; indifference, etc., 866; backwardness, slowness; obstinacy, etc., 606.

scruple, scrupulousness, delicacy, qualm, shrinking, recoil, hesitation, fastidiousness.

dissent, etc., 489; refusal, etc., 764.

V. be unwilling, dislike, etc., 867; demur, stick at, scruple, stickle; hang fire, shirk, slack, recoil, shrink, hesitate; avoid, etc., 623; oppose, etc., 708; dissent, etc., 489; refuse, etc., 764.

Adj. unwilling, loath, disinclined, indisposed, averse, reluctant, opposed, adverse, laggard, backward, remiss, slack, indifferent, scrupulous; repugnant, restive; grudging, forced, under compulsion, irreconcilable.

Adv. unwillingly, grudgingly, with an ill grace; against one's will, against the grain; under protest.

604. RESOLUTION.—*N.* determination, will, decision, resolution; backbone; clear grit, grit; sand [*slang*]; strength of mind, resolve, firmness, energy, manliness, vigor, resoluteness; zeal, devotion.

self-control, self-mastery, self-command, self-reliance, self-restraint, self-denial.

tenacity, perseverance, etc., 604a; obstinacy, etc., 606; pluck.

V. resolve, will, determine, decide, form a resolution, conclude, fix, bring to a crisis, take a decisive step, take upon oneself.

take one's stand, stand firm, insist upon, make a point of, set one's heart upon; stick at nothing, make short work of, not stick at trifles; persevere, etc., 604a.

Adj. resolved, determined; strong-willed, strong-minded; resolute, self-possessed, earnest, serious; decided, peremptory, unflinching, firm, iron, game, plucky, tenacious, gritty, indomitable, inexorable, relentless; obstinate, etc., 606; unyielding; grim, stern, inflexible, irrevocable.

Adv. resolutely, in earnest, earnestly; on one's mettle, manfully, like a man.

604a. PERSEVERANCE.—*N.* perseverance, continuance, constancy, steadiness, persistence, patience; pertinacity, industry.

grit, bottom, pluck, stamina, backbone, sand [*slang*]; tenacity, staying power, endurance; bulldog courage.

V. persevere, persist, hold on, hold out; stick to, cling to, adhere to; keep on, carry on, hold on; bear up, keep up, hold up; plod; continue, die in harness, die at one's post.

Adj. **persevering,** constant; steady, steadfast, unwavering, unfaltering, unflinching, unflagging, plodding; industrious, etc., 682; strenuous, pertinacious, persistent; indomitable, indefatigable.

Adv. **without fail,** through thick and thin, through fire and water; sink or swim, rain or shine, fair or foul.

605. IRRESOLUTION.—*N.* **irresolution,** indecision, indetermination, instability, uncertainty; demur, suspense, hesitation, hesitancy, vacillation, changeableness, fluctuation; caprice, etc., 608; lukewarmness.

fickleness, levity, pliancy, weakness, timidity; cowardice, etc., 862.

waverer, shilly-shally, turncoat, opportunist, timeserver.

V. **be irresolute,** remain neuter; dilly-dally, hesitate, hover, shilly-shally, hem and haw, demur, debate, balance; dally with, coquet with; go halfway, compromise, be afraid.

vacillate, falter, waver, fluctuate, change, alternate, shuffle, palter, shirk, trim.

Adj. **irresolute,** drifting, halfhearted; undecided, undetermined, uncertain, at a loss; fickle, unreliable, irresponsible, unstable; capricious, etc., 608.

weak, feeble-minded, frail, timid, cowardly, pliant.

Adv. **irresolutely,** in faltering accents; off and on.

606. OBSTINACY.—*N.* **obstinacy,** tenacity, cussedness; perseverance, etc., 604*a*; immovability, inflexibility, obduracy, doggedness, stubbornness, self-will, contumacy, perversity; resolution, etc., 604.

bigotry, intolerance, dogmatism; fixed idea, fanaticism, zealotry, infatuation, monomania.

bigot, dogmatist, zealot, fanatic, bitter-ender [*colloq.*]; mule.

V. **be obstinate,** stickle, take no denial, be wedded to an opinion, persist, die hard, not yield an inch, stand out.

Adj. **obstinate,** tenacious, stubborn, obdurate, inflexible, balky; immovable, unchangeable, inexorable, determined, mulish, dogged; sullen, sulky; unmoved.

arbitrary, dogmatic, positive, bigoted, opinionated, stiff-necked, hidebound, unyielding; incorrigible.

willful, self-willed, perverse; ungovernable, wayward, refractory, unruly, headstrong; contumacious; cross-grained.

Adv. **with set jaw;** no surrender.

607. APOSTASY.—*N.* **apostasy,** recantation; renunciation; abjuration, defection, retraction, withdrawal, disavowal, revocation, tergiversation, reversal; backsliding.

turncoat, apostate, renegade, pervert, deserter, backslider, crawfish [*slang*].

timeserver, trimmer, double-dealer; weathercock.

V. **apostatize,** veer round, turn round; change one's mind, abjure, renounce, relinquish, back down, shift one's ground, change sides, go over, recant, retract, revoke, rescind, forswear.

trim, shuffle, blow hot and cold, be on the fence, straddle.

Adj. **changeful,** irresolute, ductile, slippery, trimming, timeserving.

608. CAPRICE.—*N.* **caprice,** fancy, humor, whim, fit, crotchet, quirk, freak, fad, vagary, prank, escapade.

V. **be capricious,** take it into one's head, blow hot and cold, play fast and loose.

Adj. **capricious,** erratic, eccentric, fitful, inconsistent, fanciful, whimsical, crotchety, freakish, wayward, wanton; contrary, captious, unreasonable, arbitrary; fickle, etc. (*irresolute*), 605.

Adv. **by fits,** by fits and starts, without rhyme or reason.

609. CHOICE.—*N.* **choice,** option, selection, pick; discretion, alternative, preference, adoption, decision.

Scylla and Charybdis.

election, poll, ballot, vote, voice, suffrage, plebiscite, referendum; electioneering; voting, elective franchise; ticket; ballot box.

voter, elector, constituent, electorate, constituency.

V. **choose;** elect, make one's choice; make choice of, fix upon, settle, decide, make up one's mind; adopt, take up, embrace, espouse.

vote, poll, hold up one's hand, give a (*or* the) voting sign; divide.

select, pick, cull, glean, winnow; pitch upon, indulge one's fancy; set apart, mark out for.

prefer, fancy, have rather, had (*or* would) as lief; reserve.

Adj. **optional,** discretional, at choice, on approval.

chosen, choice, elect, select, popular; preferential.

Adv. **optionally,** at pleasure, at the option of.

by choice, by preference; in preference; rather, before.

609a. ABSENCE OF CHOICE.—*N.* **no choice;** Hobson's choice; first come first served; necessity, etc., 601.

neutrality, indifference; indecision, etc. (*irresolution*), 605.

V. **be neutral,** have no preference, waive, not vote.

Adj. **neutral,** neuter; indifferent; undecided, etc. (*irresolute*), 605.

610. REJECTION.—*N.* **rejection,** repudiation, exclusion; refusal, etc., 764.

V. **reject,** set (*or* lay) aside, give up; decline, etc. (*refuse*), 764; exclude, except; pluck up, spurn, cast out; repudiate, scout, disclaim, discard.

Adv. **neither,** neither the one nor the other.

611. PREDETERMINATION.—*N.* predetermination, predestination, premeditation, foregone conclusion; resolve, project; intention, etc., 620; fate, necessity.

list, schedule, calendar, docket, slate [*pol. cant*], register, roster, poll, muster, draft.

V. predetermine, predestine, premeditate, resolve beforehand.

list, schedule, docket, slate, register, poll, empanel, draft.

Adj. premeditated, predesigned, prepense [*as*, malice *prepense*], studied, designed, calculated, aforethought; foregone.

well laid, well devised, well weighed; maturely considered; cut-and-dried.

Adv. deliberately, with eyes open, in cold blood; intentionally.

612. IMPULSE.—*N.* impulse, sudden thought; impromptu, improvisation; inspiration, flash, spurt.

V. improvise, extemporize; say what comes uppermost, act on the spur of the moment, rise to the occasion; spurt.

Adj. extemporaneous, impulsive, snap, improvised, unpremeditated, unprompted, natural, unguarded; spontaneous.

Adv. extempore, extemporaneously; offhand, impromptu.

613. HABIT.—*N.* habit, addiction, wont, run, way, matter of course, beaten path, second nature; trick, knack, skill.

custom, use, usage, prescription, practice; prevalence, observance; conventionalism, conventionality, mode, fashion, vogue, etiquette.

rule, standing order, precedent, routine, red tape, rut, groove.

V. habituate, inure, harden, season, caseharden; accustom, familiarize; acclimatize.

cling to, adhere to; acquire a habit; follow the beaten track (*or* path), move in a rut.

prevail; come into use, become a habit, take root; grow upon one.

Adj. habitual, customary, accustomed, wonted, usual, general, ordinary, common, frequent, everyday, household, familiar, trite, hackneyed, commonplace, conventional, regular, set, stock, established, stereotyped; fixed, rooted, permanent, inveterate, besetting, ingrained, current.

wont; used to, given to, addicted to, in the habit of; seasoned, imbued with, devoted to, wedded to.

Adv. as usual, as things go, as the world goes; as you were [*mil.*].

as a rule, for the most part, generally, most frequently.

614. DESUETUDE.—*N.* desuetude, disusage; disuse, etc., 678; want of practice.

V. be unaccustomed, leave off (*or* break off, shake off, violate) a habit *or* custom; be weaned from; disuse, etc., 678; wear off.

Adj. unaccustomed, unused, unwonted, unseasoned, untrained; new, fresh, original; unskilled.

unconventional, unfashionable, unusual; disused, etc., 678.

615. MOTIVE.—*N.* motive, reason, ground, call, principle, mainspring, pro and con, reason why; ulterior motive; intention, etc., 620.

inducement, consideration; attraction, loadstone, magnet, magnetism, temptation, enticement, allurement, glamour, witchery; charm, spell; fascination, blandishment, cajolery; seduction.

influence, prompting, dictate, instance; impulse, incitement, press, insistence, instigation; inspiration, persuasion, encouragement, exhortation, advice, solicitation, pull [*slang*].

incentive, stimulus, spur, fillip, whip, goad, provocative, whet.

bribe, lure, sop, decoy, bait, bribery and corruption.

tempter, prompter, instigator, coaxer, wheedler, siren; firebrand.

V. induce, move, draw, inspire; put up to [*slang*], prompt; stimulate, rouse, arouse, animate, whet, incite, provoke, instigate, actuate, encourage, advocate.

influence, bias, sway, incline, dispose, predispose; lead, lobby.

persuade, prevail upon, overcome, carry, bring round, conciliate, win (*or* talk) over; enlist, engage; invite, court.

tempt, overpersuade, entice, allure, captivate, fascinate, bewitch, hypnotize, charm, magnetize, wheedle, coax, lure, inveigle.

bribe, tamper with, suborn, grease the palm, corrupt.

enforce, force, impel, propel, whip, lash, goad, spur, prick, urge, egg on, hound on, hurry on.

Adj. persuasive, inviting, tempting, suasive, seductive, attractive, fascinating; provocative.

Adv. because, therefore, for, by reason of, for the sake of, on account of; out of, from, as, forasmuch as.

615a. ABSENCE OF MOTIVE.—*N.* absence of motive; caprice, etc., 608; chance, etc. (*absence of design*), 621.

V. scruple, etc. (*be unwilling*), 603; have no motive.

Adj. aimless, capricious, without rhyme or reason.

Adv. capriciously, out of mere caprice.

616. DISSUASION.—*N.* dissuasion, expostulation, remonstrance; deprecation, etc., 766; discouragement, damper, wet blanket.

curb, restraint, constraint, check.

V. dissuade, cry out against, remonstrate, expostulate, warn.

disincline, indispose, shake, stagger; discourage, dishearten.

disenchant; deter, hold back, restrain, repel, turn aside, damp, cool, chill, blunt, calm, quiet, quench.

Adj. averse, etc. (*unwilling*), 603; repugnant, etc. (*dislike*), 867.

617. [Ostensible motive, ground, or reason] PLEA.—*N.* plea, pretext; allegation, excuse, vindication, justification; color; gloss, guise.

pretense, subterfuge, dust thrown in the eye; blind, lame excuse, makeshift, shift.

V. plead, allege, excuse, vindicate; color, gloss over, make a pretext of, use as a plea, take one's stand upon; pretend.

Adj. ostensible, alleged, pretended.

Adv. ostensibly; under the plea of, under the pretense of.

618. GOOD.—*N.* good, benefit, advantage; improvement, etc., 658; interest, service, behoof, behalf; commonweal; gain, profit, harvest; boon, etc. (*gift*), 784; good turn, blessing, prize, windfall, godsend, good fortune; happiness, etc., 827; goodness, etc., 648.

V. benefit, profit, advantage, serve, help, avail, do good to.

gain, prosper, flourish, thrive.

Adj. commendable, etc., 931; useful, etc., 644; good, beneficial, etc., 648.

Adv. well, aright, satisfactorily, favorably, in one's interest.

619. EVIL.—*N.* evil, ill, harm, hurt, mischief, nuisance, drawback, disadvantage; ills that flesh is heir to, mental suffering, pain; bane, etc., 663.

badness, etc., 649; painfulness, etc., 830; evildoer, etc., 913.

blow, buffet, stroke, scratch, bruise, wound, gash, mutilation; mortal blow (*or* wound); damage, loss.

disaster, accident, casualty, mishap, misfortune, calamity, woe, fatal mischief, catastrophe, tragedy, ruin; adversity, etc., 735.

outrage, wrong, injury, foul play; bad turn, disservice, grievance.

V. harm, injure, hurt, do disservice to.

Adj. disastrous; hurtful, etc., 649; disadvantageous, injurious, harmful.

Adv. amiss, wrong, ill; to one's cost.

620. INTENTION.—*N.* intention, intent, purpose; project, etc., 626; undertaking, design, ambition; view, proposal; contemplation.

object, aim, end; drift, tendency; destination, mark, point, goal, target, prey, quarry, game.

decision, determination, resolve; fixed purpose, resolution; ultimatum.

V. intend, purpose, design, mean, have in view, bid for, labor for, aspire to, aim at; contemplate, meditate, think of, dream of, talk of; premeditate, destine, propose; project, etc. (*plan*), 626; desire, etc., 865; pursue, etc., 622.

Adj. **intentional,** advised, express, determinate; bound for; disposed, inclined, bent upon, at stake; in prospect.

Adv. **intentionally,** advisedly, wittingly, knowingly, designedly, purposely, on purpose, by design, studiously, pointedly; deliberately.

621. [Absence of purpose] CHANCE.[1]—*N.* chance, etc., 156; lot, destiny, etc., 601; luck; hoodoo [*colloq.*], jinx [*slang*], Jonah, voodoo; wheel of chance, fortune's wheel; mascot.

speculation, venture, random shot, blind bargain, leap in the dark; fluke [*sporting cant*], flier [*slang*]; flutter [*slang*]; futures.

gambling, betting, drawing lots; wager; gamble, risk, stake, bet.

gambler, gamester, speculator; bookmaker, man of the turf.

V. **chance,** etc., 156; toss up, cast (*or* draw) lots; tempt fortune; speculate.

risk, venture, hazard, stake; wager, bet, gamble, game, play for.

Adj. **chance;** fortuitous, etc., 156; unintentional, unintended, accidental; random, undesigned, purposeless.

Adv. **at random,** at a venture, by chance, as it may happen.

622. [Purpose in action] PURSUIT.—*N.* pursuit, prosecution; pursuance, enterprise, undertaking, business, etc., 625; adventure, quest, hobby.

chase, hunt, race, steeplechase; hunting, coursing, sport, shooting, angling, fishing.

pursuer; hunter, huntsman, the field; sportsman, Nimrod; hound.

V. **pursue,** prosecute, follow, shadow; carry on, undertake, engage in, set about, endeavor, seek, trace, aim at, fish, fish for; press on, follow up, take up; go in for.

chase, give chase, stalk, course, hunt, hound.

Adj. **in quest of,** in pursuit, in full cry, on the scent.

623. [Absence of pursuit] AVOIDANCE.—*N.* avoidance, evasion, flight; escape, retreat, recoil, departure.

abstention, abstinence; forbearance; inaction, etc., 681; neutrality.

shirker, slacker [*colloq.*], shirk, quitter, truant; fugitive, refugee, runaway, deserter, renegade, backslider.

V. **abstain,** refrain, spare; eschew, keep from, let alone.

avoid, shun, steer (*or* keep) clear of; fight shy of, evade, elude, shirk.

shrink, hang (*or* hold, draw) back; recoil, retire, flinch, shy, dodge, parry.

[1] See note on 156.

beat a retreat; turn tail, take to one's heels; run, run away, cut and run [*colloq.*]; fly, flee, take flight; desert, make off, sneak off, sheer off; slip, play truant, decamp, flit, bolt, abscond; escape, etc., 671; abandon, etc., 624.

Adj. elusive, evasive; fugitive, runaway; shy, wild.

624. RELINQUISHMENT.—*N.* relinquishment, abandonment; desertion, defection, secession, withdrawal; discontinuance, renunciation, abrogation, resignation, retirement; cession, etc. (*of property*), 782.

V. relinquish, give up, abandon, desert, forsake, leave in the lurch; go back on [*colloq.*]; leave, quit, vacate, resign.

renounce, forego, have done with, drop, discard, give up the point (*or* argument), table, table the motion.

625. BUSINESS.—*N.* business, occupation, employment, undertaking, pursuit; affair, concern, matter, case.

task, work, job, chore, errand, commission, mission, charge, duty; avocation, hobby.

function, part, role, capacity, province, department, sphere, field, line; walk, round, routine; race, career.

office, place, position, post, incumbency, living; situation, berth, billet, appointment, engagement; undertaking, etc., 676.

vocation, calling, profession; cloth, faculty; craft, handicraft; trade.

V. occupy oneself with; employ oneself in *or* upon; undertake, etc., 676; turn one's hand to; be engaged in, be occupied with, be at work on; have in hand; ply one's trade.

officiate, serve, act, do duty; discharge (*or* perform) the duties of; hold (*or* fill) an office; hold a portfolio.

Adj. businesslike; workaday; professional, official, functional; busy.

in hand, on hand, afoot, on foot, going on; acting.

626. PLAN.—*N.* plan, scheme, design, project, proposal, proposition, suggestion; resolution, motion; organization, arrangement, system.

outline, sketch, skeleton, draft, rough draft, copy; forecast, program, prospectus; order of the day, memoranda, platform, plank, slate, ticket; role; policy.

contrivance, invention, expedient, receipt, nostrum, artifice, device; stratagem, trick; shift.

measure, step; stroke, master stroke; trump, trump card.

intrigue, cabal, plot, conspiracy, machination; mine.

promoter, designer, organizer, founder, projector; author, artist.

V. plan, scheme, design, frame, contrive, project, forecast, sketch, devise, invent, hatch, concoct; hit upon; map out, shape out a course; prepare, etc., 673.

systematize, organize; cast, recast, arrange; digest, mature.

plot, intrigue; counterplot, mine, countermine, lay a train.

Adj. under consideration, on the carpet, on the table.

627. METHOD. [Path]—*N.* method, way, manner, form, mode, fashion, guise; procedure.

path, road, route, course, tack; trajectory, orbit, track, beat.

means of access, entrance, approach, passage, cloister, covered way, lobby, corridor, aisle; alley, lane, avenue, artery, channel; gateway, door; secret passage; covert way.

roadway, thoroughfare; highway, turnpike, state road, causeway, king's highway; parkway, boulevard, speedway; walk, footpath, pathway, pavement, sidewalk, byroad, crossroad; railroad, railway, trolley track, tramway; towpath; street, etc. (*abode*), 189; bridge, viaduct.

Adv. how; in what way, in what manner; by what mode; so, thus; anyhow.

628. MID-COURSE.—*N.* mid-course, middle way, middle course; moderation; mean, etc., 29; golden mean.

compromise, half measures, neutrality.

V. keep the golden mean, steer a middle course; go straight.

compromise, make a compromise, concede half, go halfway.

Adj. neutral, average, even; impartial, moderate; straight.

Adv. in the mean; in moderation.

629. CIRCUIT.—*N.* circuit, roundabout way, digression, detour, loop, winding.

V. go round about, make a circuit, make a detour; meander, deviate.

Adj. circuitous, indirect, roundabout; zigzag.

Adv. in a roundabout way; by an indirect course.

630. REQUIREMENT.—*N.* requirement, need, wants, necessities; stress, exigency, pinch, case of need; desideratum; necessity, indispensability, urgency.

requisition, demand, request, claim; run, call for.

charge, command, injunction, precept, mandate, order, ultimatum.

V. require, need, want, stand in need of, lack; desire, etc., 865.

Adj. necessary, requisite, needful, imperative, essential, indispensable, called for; in demand, in request.

urgent, exigent, pressing, instant, crying.

Adv. of necessity; at a pinch.

631. INSTRUMENTALITY.—*N.* instrumentality; aid, etc., 707; subservience, mediation, intervention; pull [*slang*], influence; medium, intermediary, vehicle, tool, agency; instrument, expedient; means, etc., 632.

minister, handmaid, servant; friend at court, go-between.

V. **mediate,** minister, intervene, come (*or* go) between; interpose; use one's influence, be instrumental; subserve.

Adj. **instrumental;** useful, etc., 644; subservient, serviceable; intermediary, intermediate, intervening; conducive.

Adv. **through,** by, whereby, thereby, hereby; by the agency of, by dint of; by (*or* in) virtue of; by means of.

somehow, by fair means or foul; somehow or other; by hook or by crook.

632. MEANS.—*N.* **means,** resources, wherewithal, ways and means; capital, etc. (*money*), 800; revenue, income; stock in trade, provision, reserve, remnant, last resource, appliances, conveniences; expedients, wheels within wheels; sheet anchor; aid, etc., 707; medium, etc., 631.

V. **provide the wherewithal,** find (*or* possess) means, have powerful friends, have friends at court; have something to draw on.

Adj. **instrumental,** etc., 631; mechanical, etc., 633.

trustworthy, reliable, efficient; honorable, etc. (*upright*), 939.

Adv. **by means of,** with; wherewith, herewith, therewith; wherewithal.

633. INSTRUMENT.—*N.* **instrument,** organ, tool, implement, utensil, machine, engine, lathe, gin, mill; motor; machinery, mechanism.

equipment, gear, tackle, tackling; rigging, apparatus, appliances; plant, harness, trappings, fittings, accouterments, appointments, furniture, upholstery; chattels; paraphernalia.

mechanical powers; leverage; fulcrum, lever, crow, crowbar, jimmy, marline spike, handspike; arm, limb, wing; wheel and axle; wheelwork, clockwork; wheels within wheels; pinion, crank, winch, capstan, wheel, flywheel, turbine, water wheel, pump; pulley, crane, derrick; inclined plane; wedge; screw; jack; spring, mainspring; loom, shuttle, jenny.
handle, hilt, haft, shaft, shank; tiller, rudder, helm; treadle, pedal.

Adj. **mechanical;** propulsive, driving, hoisting, elevating, lifting.

useful, labor-saving, ingenious; well made, well fitted, well equipped.

634. SUBSTITUTE.—*N.* **substitute,** etc., 147; proxy, alternate, understudy; deputy, etc., 759.

635. MATERIALS.—*N.* **material,** raw material, stuff, stock, staple; ore.

636. STORE.—*N.* **store,** accumulation, hoard; stock, fund, mine, vein, lode, quarry; spring, fount, fountain; well; orchard, garden, farm; stock in trade, supply; treasure; reserve, reserve fund, savings.

crop, harvest, vintage, yield, product, gleaning.

storehouse, storeroom, store closet; depository, depot, cache, warehouse, magazine; garner, granary, grain elevator, silo; safe-deposit vault; armory; arsenal; stable, barn.

reservoir, cistern, tank, pond, millpond; gasometer.

V. store, put by, lay by, set by, stow away, store up, hoard up, treasure up, lay up, save, preserve, save up, bank; cache, deposit; stow, stack, load; harvest; accumulate, amass, hoard.

reserve, keep back, hold back; husband, husband one's resources.

Adj. in store, in reserve, spare, supernumerary.

Adv. for a rainy day, for a nest egg, to fall back upon; on deposit.

637. PROVISION.—*N.* provision, supply; grist, resources, etc. (*means*), 632; groceries, purveyance, commissariat.

caterer, purveyor, commissary, quartermaster, steward, purser, housekeeper; innkeeper, landlord, mine host; grocer, fishmonger, provision merchant.

V. provide, make provision, lay in, lay in a stock (*or* store).

supply, furnish; cater, victual, provision, purvey, forage; stock, make good, replenish, fill; recruit, feed.

store, etc., 636; conserve, keep, preserve, lay by, gather into barns.

638. WASTE.—*N.* consumption, expenditure, exhaustion; dispersion, leakage, loss, wear and tear, waste; prodigality.

V. consume, spend, expend, use, swallow up; exhaust, spill, drain, empty, deplete; disperse, etc., 73; waste; squander.

labor in vain, etc. (*useless*), 645; cast pearls before swine; waste powder and shot.

run to waste; ebb, leak, melt away, run dry, dry up.

Adj. wasted, gone to waste, useless, run to seed; dried up.

wasteful, etc. (*prodigal*), 818; penny wise and pound foolish.

639. SUFFICIENCY.—*N.* sufficiency, adequacy, enough, wherewithal, competence.

abundance, plenitude, plenty, copiousness, amplitude, profusion, full measure; fill; luxuriance, affluence, fat of the land.

rich man, etc. (*wealth*), 803; financier, banker, plutocrat.

V. suffice, do, just do [*both colloq.*], satisfy, pass muster; have enough, have one's fill.

abound, teem, flow, stream, rain, shower down; pour, pour in; swarm; bristle with.

Adj. sufficient, enough, adequate, up to the mark, commensurate, competent, satisfactory; ample; plenty, plentiful, plenteous; copious, abundant; replete, unstinted, inexhaustible.

rich, affluent, etc. (*wealthy*), 803; luxuriant, etc. (*fertile*), 168.

Adv. without stint; to the good.

640. INSUFFICIENCY.—*N.* insufficiency, inadequacy, incompetence, deficiency, imperfection, shortcoming; paucity, stint, bare subsistence; poverty, etc., 804.

scarcity, dearth; want, need, lack, poverty, starvation, famine, drought.

dole, mite, pittance; short allowance; half rations.

depletion, emptiness, vacancy; ebb tide; low water; insolvency, etc. (*nonpayment*), 808.

poor man, pauper, etc., 804; bankrupt.

V. want, lack, need, require; be in want, etc. (*poor*), 804; live from hand to mouth.

impoverish, drain, drain of resources; stint, etc., 819.

Adj. insufficient, inadequate, too little, not enough; incompetent, perfunctory, deficient, wanting; imperfect; ill-furnished, ill-provided, ill-stored.

short of, out of, destitute of, devoid of, bereft of, slack, at a low ebb; empty, vacant, bare; dry, drained.

unprovided, unsupplied, unfurnished; unfed; empty-handed.

meager, poor, thin, spare, stinted, starved, emaciated, undernourished, underfed, half-starved, famine-stricken, famished.

scarce, scant, not to be had, scurvy, stingy, etc., 819; at the end of one's tether; without resources, in want.

Adv. in default of, for want of; failing.

641. REDUNDANCE.—*N.* redundance, too much, too many, superabundance, superfluity, exuberance, profuseness; profusion, plenty, repletion, plethora, glut, congestion, surfeit, overdose, oversupply, overflow; excess, surplus, remainder.

V. superabound, overabound, swarm; bristle with, overflow, run over; run riot; overrun, overstock, overdose, overfeed, overload, overburden, overwhelm, overshoot the mark; gorge, glut, load, drench, inundate, deluge, flood; send (*or* carry) coals to Newcastle.

cloy, choke, suffocate; pile up, lay on thick, lavish.

Adj. redundant, turgid; exuberant, inordinate, superabundant, excess, overmuch, replete, profuse, lavish, prodigal; exorbitant, extravagant, overflowing; gorged, stuffed.

superfluous, unnecessary, needless, over and above, supernumerary, spare, duplicate, supererogatory.

Adv. over and above; over much, too much; too far; over, too; over head and ears, over one's head; up to one's eyes; extra.

642. IMPORTANCE.—*N.* importance, consequence, moment, prominence, consideration, mark; weight, influence; value, usefulness; greatness, etc., 31; superiority, etc., 33; notability.

salient point, outstanding feature; cardinal point; substance, gist, sum and substance, cream, salt, core, kernel, heart, nucleus; key, keynote; keystone.

import, significance, concern; emphasis, interest.

gravity, seriousness, solemnity; pressure, urgency, stress.

V. be important, be somebody, be something; import, signify, matter, carry weight; come to the front, lead the way, take the lead.

value, care for, set store upon *or* by.

accentuate, emphasize, lay stress on; mark, underline, under-score.

Adj. important, of importance, momentous, material, consider-able, weighty, influential, notable, prominent, salient, signal; memorable, remarkable; stirring, eventful.

grave, serious, earnest, grand, solemn, impressive, command-ing, imposing.

urgent, pressing, critical, crucial, instant.

foremost, principal, leading, chief, main, prime, primary; capital; superior, etc., 33; marked, rare; paramount, essential, vital, radical, cardinal.

significant, telling, trenchant, emphatic, pregnant.

Adv. in the main; above all, in the first place, before everything else.

643. UNIMPORTANCE.—*N.* unimportance, insignificance, nothingness, immateriality.

triviality, levity, frivolity, paltriness, smallness, matter of in-difference; no object.

nothing, small (*or* trifling) matter; joke, jest, snap of the fingers, fudge, fiddlestick, incident, mere nothing, nonentity.

toy, plaything, gewgaw, bauble, trinket, bagatelle, kickshaw, knickknack.

trumpery, trash, rubbish, stuff, frippery; chaff, dross, froth, scum, bubble, smoke; weed; refuse.

trifle, straw, pin, fig, button, feather, continental, jot, mote, rap, old song; cent, red cent; picayune [*colloq.*].

nine days' wonder, flash in the pan, much ado about nothing, tempest in a teapot.

minutiae, details, minor details.

V. be unimportant, not matter, matter (*or* signify) little, not matter a straw.

make light of, catch at straws, make mountains out of mole-hills.

Adj. unimportant, immaterial; nonessential, unessential, irrel-evant; indifferent, mediocre, passable, fair, tolerable, common-place; mere, common, ordinary, insignificant.

trifling, trivial; slight, slender, light, airy, flimsy, idle, shallow, weak, powerless, frivolous, petty, finical.

paltry, poor, pitiful, contemptible, puerile; sorry, mean, meager, shabby, miserable, wretched, vile, niggardly, scurvy, beggarly, worthless, two-by-four [*colloq.*], cheap, trashy, catchpenny, gimcrack, trumpery; one-horse [*colloq.*]

Adv. rather, somewhat, fairly, fairly well, tolerably.

644. UTILITY.—*N.* utility, usefulness, efficacy, efficiency, adequacy; helpfulness, service, use, help, aid, applicability, subservience; value, worth, productiveness, utilization.

commonweal, public good; utilitarianism.

V. avail, serve, conduce, tend, answer (*or* serve) one's turn; benefit, bear fruit, profit, remunerate.

act a part, etc. (*action*), 680; discharge a function, render a service; bestead, stand one in good stead; help, etc., 707.

Adj. useful, of use, serviceable, subservient, conducive, helpful.

advantageous, beneficial, profitable, gainful, remunerative, valuable; invaluable, beyond price; prolific.

adequate; efficient, efficacious; effective, effectual.

applicable, available, ready, handy, at hand, commodious, adaptable.

645. INUTILITY.—*N.* inutility, uselessness, inefficacy, futility; ineptitude, inadequacy, unfitness; inefficiency, incompetence, unskillfulness, labor in vain; worthlessness; triviality, etc., 643.

rubbish, junk, lumber, litter, odds and ends, shoddy; rags, leavings, dross, trash, refuse, sweepings, offscourings, waste, rubble, debris; chaff, stubble, dregs, weeds, tares.

V. **labor in vain;** seek (*or* strive) after impossibilities; use vain efforts, beat the air, pour water into a sieve, bay at the moon; cast pearls before swine, carry coals to Newcastle.

render useless, dismantle, dismast, disqualify; disable, hamstring, cripple, lame; spike guns, clip the wings; put out of gear.

Adj. useless, inutile, futile, unavailing, bootless; inoperative, inadequate, inept, inefficient, ineffectual, incompetent.

worthless, valueless, unsalable; not worth a straw, good for nothing, dear at any price; vain, empty, inane; gainless, profitless, fruitless; unserviceable, unprofitable; ill-spent; effete, barren, sterile, impotent, worn out, unproductive; uncalled for; unnecessary, unneeded, superfluous.

646. EXPEDIENCE.—*N.* expedience, desirability, fitness, propriety, utility, advantage, opportunity; opportunism; pragmatism.

V. **be expedient,** suit, befit; suit (*or* befit) the occasion.

Adj. expedient, desirable, advisable, acceptable; convenient; worth while, meet; fit, fitting, due, proper, eligible, seemly, becoming, befitting; opportune, advantageous, etc., 644; suitable.

practical, practicable, effective, pragmatic, pragmatical.

Adv. in the nick of time; in the right place.

647. INEXPEDIENCE.—*N.* inexpedience, undesirability, impropriety, unfitness, inutility, disadvantage, inconvenience, inadvisability.

V. be inexpedient, come amiss, embarrass, put to inconvenience.

Adj. inexpedient, undesirable; inadvisable, ill-advised, unsuitable, troublesome, objectionable, ineligible, inadmissible, inconvenient, discommodious, disadvantageous; inappropriate, unfit; unsatisfactory, unprofitable, inept, inopportune, improper, unseemly.

clumsy, awkward; cumbrous, cumbersome, lumbering, unwieldy, hulky.

648. [Good qualities] GOODNESS.—*N.* goodness, excellence, merit; beneficence, benevolence, etc., 906; virtue, etc., 944; value, worth, price.

perfection, quintessence; superiority, etc., 33; prime, flower, cream, elite, pick, A 1 *or* A number 1 [*colloq.*], pick of the crop, salt of the earth; prodigy, wonder; gem of the first water, treasure, one in a thousand.

good man, etc., 948.

V. be beneficial, produce (*or* do) good, profit, benefit, improve, be the making of, make a man of; do a good turn, confer an obligation.

be good, be pure gold, look good to [*colloq.*]; excel, transcend, stand the test; pass muster, pass an examination.

vie, challenge, comparison, emulate, rival.

Adj. beneficial, valuable, of value; useful, etc., 644; advantageous, profitable; edifying, salutary.

harmless, innocuous, innocent, inoffensive.

favorable; propitious, etc. (*hope-giving*), 858; fair.

good, excellent; better; superior, etc., 33; above par; nice, fine; genuine, etc. (*true*), 494.

choice, best, select, picked, elect, rare, priceless, matchless, peerless, unequaled, unparalleled, inimitable, crack [*colloq.*], crackajack [*slang*], gilt-edge [*colloq.*]; superfine, of the first water; first-rate, first-class; high-wrought, exquisite, admirable, capital, estimable, precious, priceless, invaluable, inestimable.

satisfactory, up to the mark, unexceptionable, unobjectionable.

Adv. for one's benefit.

649. [Bad qualities] BADNESS.—*N.* badness, hurtfulness, virulence; abomination, pestilence, guilt, depravity, vice, etc. 945; malignity, malevolence.

bane, etc., 663; plague spot, evil star, ill-wind; hoodoo [*colloq.*], jinx [*slang*], Jonah; snake in the grass, skeleton in the closet; thorn in the flesh.

ill-treatment, annoyance, molestation, abuse, oppression, persecution, outrage, misusage, scathe, injury.

bad man, etc., 949; evildoer, etc., 913.

V. **hurt,** harm, scathe, injure; pain, etc., 830.

wrong, aggrieve, oppress, persecute, trample upon; overburden, weigh down; victimize.

maltreat, abuse; ill-use, ill-treat; buffet, bruise, scratch, maul; smite, molest, do violence; stab, pierce.

Adj. **hurtful,** harmful, baneful, baleful, injurious, deleterious, detrimental, noxious, pernicious, mischievous, mischief-making, malignant, prejudicial; oppressive, burdensome, onerous; malign.

corrupting, virulent, venomous, corrosive; poisonous, deadly, destructive.

bad, ill, arrant, dreadful; horrid, horrible; dire; rank, foul, rotten.

unsatisfactory, indifferent, deteriorated, below par, imperfect, ill-conditioned.

deplorable, wretched, sad, grievous, lamentable, pitiful, pitiable, woeful.

evil,wrong; depraved,wicked, etc., 945; shocking; reprehensible.

hateful, abominable, vile, base, villainous, detestable, execrable, cursed, accursed, damnable, diabolic.

Adv. to one's cost; where the shoe pinches.

650. PERFECTION.—*N.* perfection; paragon, pink, pink (*or* acme) of perfection.

model, standard, pattern, mirror.

masterpiece, master stroke, prize winner, prize; superexcellence.

V. **perfect,** bring to perfection, ripen, mature; consummate, crown, put the finishing touch to (*or* upon); complete.

Adj. **perfect,** faultless, immaculate, spotless, impeccable, unblemished, sound, scathless, intact; consummate, finished.

best, model, standard; inimitable, unparalleled, beyond all praise.

Adv. clean as a whistle; with a finish; to the limit.

651. IMPERFECTION.—*N.* imperfection; deficiency, inadequacy, defection, badness, immaturity.

fault, defect, weak point; screw loose; flaw, taint, blemish, weakness, shortcoming, drawback.

V. **be imperfect,** have a defect, lie under a disadvantage; not pass muster, fall short.

Adj. **imperfect,** deficient, defective, faulty, unsound, tainted, out of order; warped, injured; inadequate, crude, incomplete, below par.

indifferent, middling, ordinary, mediocre, average, tolerable, fair, passable; decent; not bad, not amiss; admissible, bearable.

inferior, secondary, second-rate, one-horse [*colloq.*]; two-by-four [*colloq.*].

Adv. to a limited extent, pretty, moderately, considering.

652. CLEANNESS.—*N.* cleanness, purity, purification, purgation; ablution, lavation; disinfection, drainage, sewerage.

bath, bathroom, swimming pool, swimming bath, public bath, baths, bathhouse, lavatory; laundry, washhouse.

cleaner, washerwoman laundress, laundryman, washerman; scavenger, sweeper; street sweeper, white wing [*local*]; dustman.

brush; broom, vacuum cleaner, carpet sweeper; mop, swab, hose.

cathartic, purgative, aperient, laxative.

V. clean, cleanse; rinse, flush, mop, sponge, scour, swab, scrub; wash, lave, launder; purify; purge, expurgate, clarify, refine.

strain, separate, filter, filtrate, drain; percolate.

sift, winnow, sieve, bolt, screen, riddle; pick, weed.

comb, rake, scrape, rasp; card.

sweep, brush, brush up, rout out; clean house, spruce up [*colloq.*].

disinfect, fumigate, ventilate, deodorize; whitewash.

Adj. clean, cleanly, pure, immaculate, spotless, stainless, unspotted, unsoiled, unsullied, untainted, sweet.

neat, spruce, tidy, trim, cleaned.

653. UNCLEANNESS.—*N.* uncleanness, impurity; defilement, contamination, abomination; taint.

decay, putrefaction; corruption; mold, mildew, dry rot, caries [*med.*].

squalor, squalidness, slovenliness.

dirt, filth, soil, slop; dust, smoke, soot, smudge, smut, grime.

dregs, grounds, lees, sediment, heeltap; dross, ashes, cinders; scum, froth.

sty, pigsty, lair, den, Augean stable, sink of corruption; slum, rookery.

mud, mire, quagmire, silt, slime, slush.

V. rot, putrefy, fester, rankle, reek; mold, molder, go bad.

soil, smoke, tarnish, spot, smear; daub, blot, blur, smudge, smutch, smirch; drabble, besmear, befoul, splash, stain, sully.

pollute, defile, debase, contaminate, taint, corrupt.

Adj. unclean, dirty, filthy, grimy, soiled, dusty, smutty, sooty; mussy [*colloq.*].

uncleanly, slovenly, slatternly, untidy, frowzy, sluttish, unkempt, unwashed, squalid.

offensive, nasty, coarse, foul, impure, abominable, beastly, reeky, fetid; moldy, musty, rancid, bad, touched, rotten, corrupt, tainted, putrid; gory, bloody.

654. HEALTH.—*N.* health, sanity; soundness, vigor; good (*or* perfect, excellent, robust) health; bloom, convalescence, strength, poise.

V. **be in health,** bloom, flourish, enjoy good health.

return to health, recover, etc., 660; get better, convalesce, be convalescent, recruit; restore to health, cure.

Adj. **healthy,** healthful, in health, well, sound, whole, strong, blooming, hearty, hale, fresh, green, florid, hardy, robust, vigorous, in fine fettle; chipper [*colloq.*].

uninjured, unscathed, unmarred, without a scratch, safe and sound.

655. DISEASE.—*N.* disease; illness, sickness; infirmity, ailment, indisposition; complaint, disorder, malady, loss of health, delicacy, delicate health, invalidism, malnutrition, want of nourishment; prostration, decline, collapse, decay.

visitation, attack, seizure, stroke, fit, epilepsy, apoplexy, palsy, paralysis; shock; shell shock.

taint, virus, pollution, infection, contagion; epidemic, plague, pestilence.

Science of disease: pathology, therapeutics; diagnostics, diagnosis.

V. **ail,** suffer, be affected with, droop, flag, languish, sicken, pine, dwindle; waste away, fail, lose strength, be laid by the heels; lie helpless.

Adj. **sick,** ill, not well, indisposed, ailing, squeamish, poorly, seedy [*colloq.*], laid up, confined, bedridden, in hospital, on the sick list; out of health, out of sorts [*colloq.*], under the weather [*colloq.*]; valetudinary.

sickly, infirm, unsound, unhealthy, weakly, drooping, flagging, lame, halt, crippled, halting.

diseased, morbid, tainted, poisoned, septic; mangy, leprous, cankered; rotten, withered; palsied, paralytic; consumptive, tubercular, tuberculous.

656. HEALTHINESS.—*N.* healthiness, wholesomeness; healthfulness, salubrity.

Preservation of health: hygiene, pure air, exercise, nourishment, tonic; immunity; sanitarium, sanatorium.

V. **be salubrious,** make for health, conduce to health; be good for, agree with.

Adj. **healthy,** healthful; salubrious, salutary, wholesome, sanitary, prophylactic; benign, bracing, tonic, invigorating, nutritious; hygienic.

innocuous, innocent; harmless, uninjurious, immune.

657. UNHEALTHINESS.—*N.* unhealthiness, plague spot; malaria, insalubrity; contagion; poisonousness.

V. **be unhealthy,** disagree with; shorten one's days.

Adj. **unhealthy,** insalubrious, unwholesome, noxious, noisome; pestiferous, pestilential; virulent, venomous, poisonous, septic, toxic, deadly.

infectious, contagious, catching, communicable, epidemic, sporadic, endemic; epizootic [*of animals*].

658. IMPROVEMENT.—*N.* **improvement,** amelioration, betterment; recovery, mend, amendment, emendation; advancement, advance, promotion, preferment, elevation, increase.

cultivation, culture, march of intellect, civilization.

reform, reformation; revision, radical reform; correction, refinement, elaboration; purification, repair.

reformer, progressive, radical.

V. **improve,** mend, amend, better, ameliorate, relieve; correct, repair, restore.

improve upon; rectify; enrich, mellow, elaborate, fatten.

refresh, revive; invigorate, strengthen, recruit, renew, revivify, freshen.

promote, cultivate, advance, forward, enhance, bring forward, foster.

revise, edit, review, make corrections, make improvements.

reform, remodel, reorganize, reclaim, civilize, lift, uplift, inspire.

Adj. **better,** better off, all the better for; improving, progressive, improved.

corrigible, improvable, curable.

Adv. **on consideration,** on reconsideration, on second thought.

659. DETERIORATION.—*N.* **deterioration,** debasement; wane, ebb, recession, retrogradation, decrease.

degeneracy, degeneration, degradation, depravation, depravity, demoralization.

injury, damage, loss, detriment, harm, impairment, outrage, havoc, inroad, ravage, vitiation, discoloration, pollution, poisoning, contamination, canker, corruption, adulteration, alloy.

decline, declension, declination; decadence, falling off; senility, decrepitude.

decay, dilapidation, wear and tear, erosion, corrosion, rottenness; moth and rust, dry rot, blight, atrophy.

V. **deteriorate,** degenerate, fall off, wane, ebb; retrograde, decline, droop, run to seed *or* waste, lapse, break down, crack, shrivel, fade, wither, molder, rot, rankle, decay, go bad; rust, crumble, shake, totter, perish.

corrupt, taint, infect, contaminate, poison, envenom, canker, blight, rot, pollute, defile, vitiate, debase, deprave, degrade; alloy, adulterate, tamper with, prejudice; pervert, demoralize, brutalize.

embitter, exasperate, irritate.

injure, impair, damage, harm, hurt, spoil, mar, despoil, waste; overrun, ravage, pillage

wound, stab, pierce, maim, lame, cripple, hamstring, mangle, mutilate, disfigure, blemish, deface, warp.

Adj. deteriorated, unimproved, injured, degenerate, imperfect; battered, weathered, weather-beaten, stale, dilapidated, faded, worn, wasted, wilted, shabby, threadbare, frayed.

decayed, moth-eaten, worm-eaten, mildewed, rusty, moldy, seedy [*colloq.*], timeworn, effete, crumbling, moldering, rotten, cankered, blighted, tainted; decrepit, broken-down, worn-out, used up [*colloq.*].

stagnant, backward, unprogressive.

Adv. on the downgrade, on the downward track; beyond hope.

660. RESTORATION. –*N.* restoration, replacement, rehabilitation, reconstruction, reproduction, renovation, renewal, revival, resuscitation, reanimation, reorganization; redemption, restitution, relief, redress, retrieval, reclamation, recovery, convalescence, resumption.

renaissance, renascence, rebirth, new birth, regeneration, regeneracy, resurrection.

repair, repairing, reparation, mending; recruiting.

mender, repairer, tinker, cobbler.

V. recover, rally, revive; come to, come round, come to oneself; pull through, weather the storm, be oneself again; get well, survive, reappear.

restore, put back, reinstate, replace, rehabilitate, re-establish, reconstruct, rebuild, reorganize, convert, recondition, renew, renovate; regenerate; rejuvenate.

redeem, reclaim, recover, retrieve; rescue, etc. (*deliver*), 672.

cure, heal, remedy, doctor, bring round, set on one's legs.

resuscitate, revive, reanimate, revivify, reinvigorate, refresh.

repair, mend, put in repair, retouch, tinker, cobble, patch up, darn; stanch, calk, splice.

Adj. restored, convalescent, rejuvenated, renascent.

restorative, recuperative, curative, remedial.

restorable, remediable, retrievable, curable.

661. RELAPSE. –*N.* relapse, lapse; falling back, retrogradation; deterioration, etc., 659; backsliding.

V. relapse, lapse, fall (*or* slip) back, have a relapse, be overcome, be overtaken, yield again to, fall again into, return, retrograde.

Adj. backsliding, retrograde.

662. REMEDY.—*N.* remedy, help, redress, febrifuge; antipoison, antidote, emetic; stimulant, tonic; prophylactic, antiseptic, germicide, disinfectant; restorative; specific; cure, sovereign remedy, panacea.

materia medica, pharmacy, pharmaceutics; pharmacopoeia.

narcotic, opium, morphine, cocaine, hashish, dope [*slang*]; sedative.

physic, medicine, simples, drug, potion, draft, dose, pill, medicament; recipe, receipt, prescription; patent medicine, nostrum; elixir, balm, balsam, cordial.

salve, ointment, oil, lenitive, lotion, embrocation, liniment.

treatment, regimen, diet; dietary, dietetics; operation, the knife [*colloq.*], surgical operation; major operation.

healing art, practice of medicine, therapeutics; allopathy, homeopathy, osteopathy, eclecticism, surgery; faith cure, faith healing, mind cure, psychotherapy, psychotherapeutics; vocational therapy; dentistry.

hospital, surgery, infirmary, clinic, sanitarium, sanatorium; springs, baths, spa; asylum, home; Red Cross; ambulance.

dispensary, drugstore.

doctor, physician, medical man, general practitioner; specialist, consultant; surgeon.

intern, anesthetist, aurist, oculist, dentist, dental surgeon; osteopath, osteopathist; nurse, sister, nursing sister; apothecary, druggist, pharmacist, pharmaceutical chemist, Hippocrates, Galen; masseur (*fem.* masseuse), rubber.

V. apply a remedy, doctor [*colloq.*], dose, physic, nurse, minister to, attend, dress the wounds; relieve, palliate, heal, cure, remedy, restore.

Adj. remedial, restorative, corrective, palliative, healing; sanatory, sanative; prophylactic; medical, medicinal; therapeutic, surgical; tonic, sedative, lenitive; allopathic, homeopathic, eclectic; aperient, laxative, cathartic, purgative; septic; aseptic, antiseptic.

dietetic, dietary, alimentary; nutritious, nutritive; digestive, digestible.

663. BANE.—*N.* bane, curse, thorn in the flesh; bête noir [F.], bugbear; evil, scourge; fungus, mildew; dry rot; canker, cancer; poison, virus, venom; stench, fetor, poison gas.

sting, fang, thorn, bramble, brier, nettle.

Science of poisons: toxicology.

Adj. baneful, poisonous, etc. (*unwholesome*), 657.

664. SAFETY.—*N.* safety, security, surety, impregnability, invulnerability, escape, means of escape; safeguard, palladium; sheet anchor; rock, tower.

guardianship, wardship, wardenship; tutelage, custody, safekeeping, protection; auspices.

protector, guardian; warden, warder: preserver, lifesaver, custodian, duenna, chaperon.

safe-conduct, escort, convoy; guard, shield, guardian angel; tutelary deity (*or* saint).

watchman, patrolman, policeman, police officer, officer [*colloq.*]; cop, copper [*both slang*], bluecoat [*colloq.*], constable; detective, spotter [*slang*]; sheriff, deputy; sentinel, sentry, scout.

armed force, garrison, lifeguard, state guard, militia, regular army, navy; volunteer; marine, etc., 726; battleship, man-of-war, etc., 726.

judge, justice, judiciary, magistrate, justice of the peace.

V. **protect**, watch over, take care of, preserve, cover, screen, shelter, shroud, flank, ward, guard; defend, take precautions.

escort, support, accompany, convoy.

watch, mount guard, patrol, scout, spy.

Adj. **safe**, secure, sure, on terra firma [L.]; on the safe side; undercover, under lock and key; out of danger, protected; at anchor, high and dry, above-water; safe and sound.

snug, seaworthy, watertight, weatherproof, waterproof, fireproof; bombproof, shellproof.

defensible, tenable, proof against, invulnerable, unassailable, impregnable.

guardian, tutelary, protective.

Adv. with impunity.

665. DANGER.—*N.* **danger**, peril, insecurity, jeopardy, risk, hazard, venture, precariousness, instability; exposure, vulnerability, vulnerable point, heel of Achilles; forlorn hope.

Sense of danger: apprehension, etc., 860.

V. **endanger**, expose to danger, imperil, jeopardize, beard the lion in his den; sail too near the wind.

risk, hazard, venture, adventure, stake, set at hazard; run the gantlet.

Adj. **dangerous**, hazardous, perilous, unsafe, unprotected, insecure.

defenseless, guardless, unsheltered, unshielded; vulnerable, exposed; at bay.

precarious, critical, ticklish; slippery, between Scylla and Charybdis, between two fires; under fire; at stake, in question.

unsteady, unstable, shaky, tottering, top-heavy, tumble-down, ramshackle, crumbling, helpless, trembling in the balance; nodding to its fall.

threatening, ominous, ill-omened, alarming.

666. [Means of safety] REFUGE.—*N.* **refuge**, sanctuary, retreat, fastness, stronghold, fortress, castle, keep; asylum, shelter, covert, ark, home, hiding place.

anchorage, roadstead; breakwater, port, haven, harbor, pier, jetty, embankment, quay, wharf.

anchor, sheet anchor, grapnel, grappling iron, mainstay, support, safeguard.

667. [Source of danger] PITFALL.—*N*. pitfall, ambush, trap, snare, mine, spring gun.

rocks, reefs, sunken rocks, snags; sands, quicksands; breakers, shoals, shallows, lee shore, rockbound coast.

abyss, abysm, pit, void, chasm.

whirlpool, eddy, vortex, rapids, undertow; current, tiderace, maelstrom; eagre, bore, tidal wave.

pest, ugly customer, incendiary, firebug [*slang*]; firebrand; hornet's nest.

sword of Damocles; wolf at the door, snake in the grass, snake in one's bosom.

668. WARNING.—*N*. warning, caution, notice, premonition, prediction; symptom; lesson, admonition; handwriting on the wall, monitor, warning voice; stormy petrel, bird of ill omen, gathering clouds.

watchtower, beacon, signal post; lighthouse, etc., 550.

sentinel, sentry; watch, watchman; watch and ward; watchdog; patrol, picket, scout, spy, lookout, flagman.

V. warn, caution; forewarn, admonish, forbode, give warning; put on one's guard; sound the alarm.

beware, take warning, look out, keep watch and ward.

Adj. premonitory, cautionary; ominous, threatening, lowering, minatory; symptomatic.

Adv. with alarm, on guard, after due warning, with one's eyes open.

669. [Indication of danger] ALARM.—*N*. alarm; alarum, alarm bell, tocsin, beat of drum, sound of trumpet, hue and cry; signal of distress, SOS; fog signal, siren; yellow flag; danger signal; red light, red flag; fire alarm, still alarm; burglar alarm; police whistle.

V. alarm, give (*or* raise, sound) an alarm, warn, ring the tocsin.

670. PRESERVATION.—*N*. preservation, safekeeping, conservation, economy, maintenance, support, salvation, deliverance, etc., 672.

Means of preservation: prophylaxis; preserver, preservative; hygiene, hygienics; ensilage; dehydration, evaporation, drying, canning, pickling.

V. preserve, maintain, keep, sustain, support; save, rescue, make safe, take care of, guard; husband, economize.

embalm, dry, cure, salt, pickle, season, bottle, pot, tin, can; dehydrate, evaporate.

Adj. preserved, unimpaired, unbroken, uninjured, unhurt, unmarred; safe, safe and sound, intact, with a whole skin.

671. ESCAPE.—*N.* escape, flight, evasion, loophole, retreat; narrow (*or* hairbreadth) escape; close call [*colloq.*]; impunity.

refugee, etc. (*fugitive*), 623.

V. escape, make one's escape; break jail; get off, get clear off, elude, make off, give one the slip; wriggle out of; break loose, break away.

Adj. stolen away; fled; scot-free.

672. DELIVERANCE.—*N.* deliverance, extrication, rescue, ransom, reprieve, respite; armistice, truce; liberation, emancipation; redemption, salvation.

V. deliver, extricate, rescue, save, free, liberate, set free, release, emancipate, redeem, ransom; come to the rescue.

673. PREPARATION.—*N.* preparation, provision, arrangement, anticipation, precaution, forecast, rehearsal; dissemination, propaganda.

groundwork, steppingstone; foundation; scaffold, scaffolding.

elaboration, ripening, evolution; concoction, digestion; hatching, incubation.

Preparation of men: training, education, equipment, inurement; novitiate.

Preparation of food: cooking, cookery, culinary art; brewing.

Preparation of the soil: tilling, plowing, sowing, cultivation.

preparedness, readiness, ripeness, mellowness; maturity.

preparer, trainer, coach, teacher, pioneer; prophet; forerunner, etc. (*precursor*), 64; sappers and miners.

V. prepare, prime, get (*or* make) ready, arrange, make preparations, settle preliminaries, get up; prepare the ground, lay the foundations, erect the scaffolding.

elaborate, mature, ripen, mellow, season, bring to maturity; nurture; cook, brew.

equip, arm, man; fit out, fit up; furnish, rig, dress, accouter, array.

prepare for, guard against, forearm; make provision for; provide, provide against; set one's house in order, make all snug; clear decks, clear for action.

be prepared, be ready, watch and pray, keep one's powder dry, lie in wait for, anticipate, foresee.

Adj. preparatory, precautionary, provident; provisional, preliminary; in embryo, in hand, in train; afoot, afloat; on foot, brewing, hatching, forthcoming.

prepared, ready, cut and dried; available, at one's elbow, ready for use, all ready; handy.

ripe, mature, mellow; seasoned, practiced, experienced.

elaborate, labored, high-wrought, worked up.

Adv. in preparation, in anticipation of; afoot, astir, abroad.

674. NONPREPARATION.—*N.* nonpreparation, unpreparedness; improvidence.

immaturity, crudity, rawness; disqualification.

Absence of art: nature, state of nature; virgin soil, unweeded garden; rough diamond; raw material.

improvisation, etc. (*impulse*), 612.

V. be unprepared; lie fallow; live from hand to mouth.

extemporize, improvise; cook up, fix up.

surprise, drop in [*colloq.*], take (*or* catch) unawares; take by surprise.

Adj. unprepared, incomplete, premature, rudimental, embryonic, immature, unripe, callow, unfledged, unhatched; uncooked, raw, green, crude; coarse; rough, roughhewn; in the rough.

untaught, uneducated, untrained, untutored, unlicked.

fallow, unsown, untilled, uncultivated.

unfitted, disqualified, unqualified, ill-digested; unready, unorganized, unfurnished, unprovided, unequipped.

shiftless, improvident, unthrifty, thriftless, happy-go-lucky; slack, remiss.

Adv. inadvertently, by surprise, without premeditation; extempore.

675. ESSAY—*N.* essay, trial, endeavor, attempt; aim, struggle, venture, adventure, speculation, probation, experiment.

V. try, essay; experiment, etc., 463; endeavor, strive; tempt, attempt, venture, adventure, speculate, tempt fortune.

Adj. tentative, experimental, empirical, problematic, probationary.

Adv. on examination, on trial, at a venture; by rule of thumb.

676. UNDERTAKING.—*N.* undertaking, adventure, venture, engagement, compact, enterprise; pilgrimage.

V. undertake, engage in, embark in, launch (*or* plunge) into, volunteer; apprentice oneself to; engage, contract, devote oneself to, take up, take on, take in hand; tackle [*colloq.*]; set about; launch forth; betake oneself to, turn one's hand to, have in hand, begin, broach, institute.

Adj. energetic; full of pep [*slang*]; enterprising, adventurous, venturesome.

677. USE.—*N.* use, employ, exercise, application, appliance; disposal; consumption; agency, usefulness, etc., 644; benefit, recourse, resort, avail.

Conversion to use: utilization, utility, service, wear.

Way of using: usage, employment, *modus operandi* [L.].

user, consumer, market, demand.

V. use, make use of, employ, put to use, apply, put in action, set in motion, set to work; ply, work, wield, handle, manipulate; exert, exercise, practice, avail oneself of, profit by; resort to, have recourse to, recur to, take up, try.

utilize, turn to account (*or* use); exploit; administer, apply, bring into play; task, tax, put to task; devote, dedicate, consecrate.

consume, use up, devour, swallow up; absorb, expend; wear.

Adj. useful, etc., 644; instrumental, subservient, utilitarian, pragmatic.

678. DISUSE.—*N.* disuse; forbearance, abstinence; relinquishment, abandonment; desuetude, disusage.

V. not use; do without, dispense with, let alone, forbear, abstain, spare, waive, neglect; keep back, reserve.

disuse; lay up, lay by, shelve; set aside, lay aside, leave off, have done with; supersede, discard, throw aside, relinquish; destroy, make away with, cast (*or* throw) overboard; dismantle.

Adj. disused, done with, run down, worn out; unemployed, unapplied, unexercised, uncalled for, not required.

679. MISUSE.—*N.* misuse, misusage, misapplication, misappropriation; abuse, profanation, desecration; waste.

V. misuse, misemploy, misapply; exploit; misappropriate; desecrate, abuse, profane.

overtask, overtax, overwork; squander, waste.

680. ACTION.—*N.* action, performance, perpetration, exercise, movement, operation, evolution, work, employment; labor, exertion, execution; procedure, conduct; handicraft; business, agency.

deed, act, stitch, touch, transaction, job, doings, dealings, proceeding, measure, step, maneuver, bout, passage, move, stroke, blow; feat, exploit, achievement; handiwork, craftsmanship, workmanship; manufacture; stroke of policy.

doer, worker, agent, etc., 690.

V. do, perform, execute, achieve, transact, enact; commit, perpetrate, inflict; exercise, prosecute, carry on, work, labor, practice, play; employ oneself, ply one's task; officiate, have in hand; shape one's course.

act, operate, take action, take steps, take in hand, put in practice, carry into execution, act upon.

Adj. in action, acting, in harness, on duty; at work; operative.

Adv. in the act, in the midst of; red-handed.

681. INACTION.—*N.* inaction, passiveness, watchful waiting; noninterference; neglect, etc., 460; inactivity, etc., 683; stagnation, vegetation, rest, loafing, want of occupation, unemployment; sinecure; soft snap, cinch [*both slang*].

V. not do, not act, not attempt; be inactive, abstain from doing, do nothing, hold, spare; leave (or let) alone; let be, let pass, let things take their course, live and let live; rest upon one's oars; stand aloof; refrain, relax one's efforts; desist, stop, pause, wait; waste time.

undo, do away with; take down, take to pieces; destroy, etc., 162.

Adj. **passive;** unoccupied, unemployed, out of employ (or work, a job); uncultivated, fallow.

Adv. at a stand.

682. ACTIVITY.—*N.* **activity,** animation, life, vivacity, spirit, verve, pep [*slang*], dash, go [*colloq.*], energy, snap, vim.

smartness, nimbleness, agility; quickness, velocity, alacrity, promptitude; dispatch, expedition, haste, etc., 684; punctuality.

eagerness, zeal, ardor, enthusiasm, earnestness, intentness, vigor, devotion, exertion.

industry, assiduity, assiduousness, sedulousness, laboriousness, drudgery, diligence, perseverance, etc., 604a.

vigilance, etc., 459; wakefulness; sleeplessness, restlessness; insomnia.

bustle, hustle [*colloq.*], movement, stir, fuss, ado, bother, fidget, flurry.

officiousness, dabbling, meddling; interference, intermeddling; butting in [*slang*], intrusiveness, intrigue.

man of action, busy bee; new broom; devotee, enthusiast, fanatic, zealot, hustler [*colloq.*], live wire, human dynamo [*both colloq.*].

meddler, intriguer, busybody.

V. **be active,** busy oneself in; stir, stir about, bestir oneself; speed, hasten, bustle, fuss; push, go ahead, push forward; make progress; toil, moil, drudge, plod, persist, persevere, hustle [*colloq.*], push [*colloq.*], keep moving, seize the opportunity, lose no time, dash off, make haste.

have a hand in, take an active part, put in one's oar, have a finger in the pie, dabble, intrigue; agitate.

meddle, tamper with, interfere, interpose; obtrude; butt in, horn in [*both slang*].

Adj. **active,** brisk, lively, animated, vivacious, alive, frisky, spirited; nimble, agile, light-footed, nimble-footed.

quick, prompt, instant, ready, alert, spry [*colloq. and dial.*], sharp, smart; fast, etc. (*swift*), 274; capable, expeditious, awake, go-ahead [*colloq.*], live [*colloq.*], hustling [*colloq.*], wide-awake.

enterprising, eager, ardent, strenuous, zealous, resolute.

industrious, assiduous, diligent, sedulous, painstaking, intent, indefatigable, persevering, unwearied, sleepless; busy, occupied; hard at work, hard at it; plodding, hard-working, businesslike.

bustling, restless, fussy, fidgety, pottering.

meddlesome, pushing, officious.

astir, stirring, afoot, on foot, in full swing; on the alert.

Adv. with life and spirit, with might and main, full tilt.

683. INACTIVITY.—*N.* inactivity; inaction, etc., 681; inertness, lull, quiescence; rust.

idleness, remissness, sloth, indolence, dawdling, puttering, relaxation.

languor, dullness, sluggishness, procrastination, torpor, stupor, somnolence, drowsiness, heaviness, hypnotism, lethargy.

sleep, slumber; Morpheus; coma, trance, catalepsy, hypnosis, dream; nap, doze, siesta; hibernation.

idler, drone, dawdler, truant; dead one [*slang*], dummy, bum [*slang*], tramp, hobo, beggar, lounge lizard [*slang*], lounger, loafer, slow-poke, laggard, sluggard.

V. be inactive, do nothing; dawdle, drawl, lag, hang back, slouch, loll, lounge, loaf, loiter; sleep at one's post; take it easy.

dally, dilly-dally, idle (*or* fritter, fool) away time; putter, dabble.

sleep, slumber, be asleep, oversleep, hibernate; doze, drowse, nap, take a nap; fall asleep, drop asleep; get sleepy, nod, go to bed, turn in.

languish, expend itself, flag, hang fire; relax.

Adj. inactive, motionless; unoccupied, unemployed.

indolent, lazy, slothful, idle, remiss, slack, inert, torpid, sluggish, logy, languid, listless; lackadaisical, maudlin; heavy, dull, leaden; dilatory, laggard, slow, flagging; puttering.

sleeping, asleep, comatose; in the arms (*or* lap) of Morpheus.

sleepy, dozy, drowsy, somnolent, lethargic, heavy, heavy with sleep; soporific, hypnotic; dreamy.

Adv. with half-shut eyes, half asleep; in dreams, in dreamland.

684. HASTE.—*N.* haste, urgency, dispatch, acceleration, spurt, forced march, rush, scurry, scuttle, dash; velocity, etc., 274; precipitancy, precipitation, impetuosity; hurry, drive, scramble, bustle, fidget, flurry.

V. haste, hasten, make haste, dash on, push on, press on *or* forward, hurry, scurry, bustle, flutter, scramble, plunge, dash off, rush, express; bestir oneself, etc. (*be active*), 682; lose no time, make short work of; work against time, work under pressure.

quicken, accelerate, expedite, precipitate, urge, whip, spur, flog, goad.

Adj. hasty, hurried, cursory, precipitate, headlong, furious, boisterous, impetuous, hotheaded; feverish, pushing.

in haste, in a hurry, in hot haste, breathless, hard-pressed, urgent.

Adv. with haste, with speed, in haste, apace, amain; at short notice, immediately, posthaste; by cable, by telegraph, by wireless [*colloq.*], by airplane, by return mail, by forced marches.

hastily, precipitately, helter-skelter, hurry-scurry, slapdash, slap-bang; full-tilt, full-drive; heels over head, headlong.

685. LEISURE.—*N.* leisure, convenience; spare time, vacant hour; time, time to spare; holiday, ease.

V. have leisure, take one's time (*or* leisure, ease); repose, etc., 687; move slowly, while away the time, be master of one's time, be an idle man.

686. EXERTION.—*N.* exertion, effort, strain, stress, tug, pull, throw, stretch, struggle, spell, spurt; dead lift, heft [*dial.*]; trouble, pains, duty; energy, etc. [*physical*], 171.

exercise, practice, play, gymnastics, field sports; breather [*colloq.*].

labor, work, toil, manual labor, sweat of one's brow, drudgery, slavery.

worker, plodder, laborer, drudge, slave; man of action; Hercules.

V. labor, work, toil, sweat, fag, drudge, slave, strive, strain; pull, tug, ply; ply the oar; exert oneself, bestir oneself (*be active*), 682.

work hard; rough it; put forth one's strength, buckle to, set one's shoulder to the wheel, do double duty; burn the candle at both ends, work (*or* fight) one's way; do one's best, do one's utmost; take pains; strain every nerve; spare no efforts *or* pains.

Adj. laborious, elaborate; strained; toilsome, wearisome, burdensome; uphill; herculean.

hard-working, painstaking, strenuous, energetic, never idle.

Adv. with might and main, with all one's might, to the best of one's abilities, tooth and nail, hammer and tongs, heart and soul.

687. REPOSE.—*N.* repose, rest, sleep, etc., 683; relaxation, breathing time; halt, stay, pause, respite.

day of rest, Sabbath, Lord's day, Sunday; holiday, red-letter day, gala day; vacation, recess.

V. repose, rest, take rest, take one's ease; lie down, recline, go to rest (*or* bed, sleep).

relax, unbend, slacken, take breath, rest upon one's oars; pause, etc. (*cease*), 142; stay one's hand.

take a holiday, shut up shop; lie fallow.

Adj. holiday, festal; sabbatic *or* sabbatical.

688. FATIGUE.—*N.* fatigue; weariness, etc., 841; yawning, drowsiness, lassitude, tiredness, sweat.

faintness, fainting, swoon, exhaustion, collapse, prostration.

V. be fatigued, yawn, droop, sink; flag; gasp, pant, puff, blow, drop, swoon, faint, succumb.

fatigue, tire, bore, weary, flag, jade, harass, exhaust, wear out, prostrate.

tax, task, strain; overtask, overwork, overburden, overtax, overstrain, fag, fag out.

Adj. fatigued; weary, etc., 841; drowsy, haggard, toilworn, wayworn, footsore, faint; done up [*colloq.*], exhausted, prostrate, spent, ready to drop, all in [*slang*], dog-tired, tired to death, played out.

worn, worn out; battered, shattered, seedy [*colloq.*], enfeebled.

breathless, short of (*or* out of)breath, blown, puffing and blowing, short-breathed, broken-winded.

689. REFRESHMENT.—*N.* recuperation; recovery of strength, restoration, revival, etc., 660; repair, refreshment; relief, etc., 834.

V. refresh, brace, strengthen, reinvigorate; air, freshen up, recruit, regale, repair, restore, revive; get better, recover (*or* regain) one's strength, recuperate.

Adj. refreshing, recuperative.

690. AGENT.—*N.* agent, doer, actor, performer, perpetrator, operator; executor, executrix; practitioner, worker; minister, etc. (*instrument*), 631; representative, etc. (*commissioner*), 758, (*deputy*), 759; factor, steward; servant, etc., 746; factotum.

workman, artisan, craftsman, handicraftsman, mechanic, operative; workingman, laboring man; hewers of wood and drawers of water; laborer; hand, man, day laborer, journeyman, hack, drudge, roustabout.

maker, artificer, artist, wright, manufacturer, architect, contractor, builder, smith.

machinist, engineer, electrician.

workwoman, charwoman, dressmaker, modiste, seamstress, needlewoman, milliner, laundress, washerwoman.

coworker, associate, fellow worker, co-operator, colleague, confrere; force, staff, personnel.

691. WORKSHOP.—*N.* workshop, laboratory, manufactory, armory, arsenal, mill, factory, studio, atelier; hive, hive of industry, beehive; bindery; dock, dockyard, slip, yard, wharf; foundry, forge, furnace.

melting pot, crucible, caldron, mortar, alembic; matrix.

692. CONDUCT.—*N.* conduct, behavior; deportment, carriage, demeanor, guise, bearing, manner; course of conduct, line of action; role; process, ways, practice, procedure, method; dealing, transaction, business.

policy, tactics, game, generalship, statesmanship, strategy, plan.

management; government, etc., 693; stewardship, husbandry; housekeeping, ménage, regime, regimen, economy; economics, political economy.

career, life, course, walk, province, race, record; execution, treatment; campaign.

V. **transact,** execute; dispatch, proceed with, discharge; carry on (*or* through, out, into effect); work out; go through, get through; enact.

adopt a course, shape one's course, play one's part; shift for oneself, paddle one's own canoe; conduct; manage, etc. (*direct*), 693.

behave, conduct (*or* acquit, carry, comport, bear, demean) oneself.

Adj. **directive,** methodical, businesslike, practical, executive, strategic, economic.

693. DIRECTION.—*N.* **direction;** management, government, conduct, legislation, regulation, guidance, reins; steerage, pilotage, helm, rudder, needle, compass; guiding star, lodestar, polestar, cynosure.

ministry, administration; stewardship, proctorship; chair; agency.

supervision, superintendence; surveillance, oversight; eye of the master; control, charge; auspices; command, etc. (*authority*), 737.

statesmanship, statecraft, kingcraft, reins of government; director, etc., 694; seat, portfolio.

V. **direct,** manage, govern, conduct; order, prescribe, head, lead, regulate, guide, steer, pilot, take the helm, be at the helm; hold the reins, drive.

superintend, supervise; overlook, oversee, control, handle, look after, see to, administer, patronize; rule, etc. (*command*), 737; hold office.

Adj. **directing,** executive, gubernatorial, supervisory; statesmanlike.

Adv. **in charge of,** under the guidance of, under the auspices of; in control of, at the helm, at the head of.

694. DIRECTOR.—*N.* **director,** manager, governor, controller, superintendent, supervisor, overseer, supercargo, inspector, foreman, surveyor, taskmaster; master, etc., 745; leader, ringleader, agitator, demagogue, conductor, precentor, bellwether, file leader.

guide, pilot; helmsman, steersman; adviser, etc., 695.

driver, whip, charioteer; coachman, carman, cabman; postilion, muleteer, teamster; chauffeur, motorman, engine driver.

head, headman, chief, principal, president, speaker; chair, chairman; captain, etc. (*master*), 745; superior; prime minister, premier.

officer, functionary, minister, official, bureaucrat, officeholder.

statesman, strategist, legislator, lawgiver, politician, boss [*slang*], political dictator, wirepuller [*colloq.*], power behind the throne, kingmaker.

steward, factor, agent, bailiff, factotum, major-domo, seneschal, housekeeper, shepherd; proctor, curator, librarian.

695. ADVICE.—*N.* advice, counsel, word to the wise, suggestion, recommendation, advocacy; consultation; exhortation, expostulation, dissuasion, admonition; guidance.

instruction, charge, injunction, message, speech from the throne.

adviser, prompter; counsel, counselor; monitor, mentor, sage, wise man; teacher, etc., 540; physician; arbiter, referee, judge.

consultation, conference, parley, powwow; reference.

V. advise, counsel, suggest, prompt, recommend, prescribe, advocate, exhort, persuade.

enjoin, enforce, charge, instruct, call, call upon, request, dictate.

expostulate, dissuade, admonish, warn.

confer, consult, refer to, call in; follow, take (*or* follow) advice.

696. COUNCIL.—*N.* council, committee, privy council, court, chamber, cabinet, board, directorate, syndicate, bench, staff.

Ecclesiastical: convocation, synod, congregation, church, chapter, vestry. consistory, conventicle, conclave, convention.

legislature, parliament, congress, national council, states-general, diet.

Duma [Russia], Storthing *or* Storting [Norway], Rigsdag [Denmark], Riksdag [Sweden], Cortes [Spain], Reichsrath *or* Reichsrat [Austria], Volksraad [Dutch], Dail Eireann [Sinn Fein].

upper house, upper chamber, first chamber, senate, legislative council, House of Lords, House of Peers; Bundesrath *or* Bundesrat [Ger.], federal council, Lagting [Nor.], Landsthing [Den.].

lower house, lower chamber, second chamber, house of representatives, House of Commons, the house, legislative assembly, chamber of deputies; Odelsting [Nor.], Folkething [Den.], Reichstag [Ger.].

assembly, caucus, clique; meeting, sitting, séance, conference, hearing, session, palaver; council fire, powwow.

Representatives: congressman, M.C., senator, representative; member, member of parliament, M.P., assemblyman, councilor.

Adj. curule, congressional, senatorial, parliamentary; synodic *or* synodical.

697. PRECEPT.—*N.* precept, direction, instruction, charge; prescript, prescription; recipe, receipt; golden rule; maxim, etc., 496.

rule, canon, law, code, convention; unwritten law; canon law; act, statute, rubric, stage direction, regulation; model, form, formula, technicality.

order, etc. (*command*), 741.

698. SKILL.—*N.* skill, skillfulness, address, dexterity, adroitness, expertness, proficiency, competence, craft; facility, knack, trick, sleight; mastery, excellence, sleight of hand, etc. (*deception*), 545.

accomplishment, acquirement, attainment; art, science; finish, technique.

worldly wisdom, knowledge of the world, *savoir-faire* [F.]; tact; mother wit, discretion, finesse; management.

cleverness, talent, ability, ingenuity, capacity, talents, faculty, endowment, forte, turn, gift, genius, intelligence, sharpness, readiness, aptness, aptitude, resourcefulness; felicity, capability, qualification.

expert, adept, etc., 700.

masterpiece, masterwork, chef-d'oeuvre [F.].

V. **be skillful,** excel in, be master of; have a turn for.

take advantage of, make the most of, profit by, make a hit, make a virtue of necessity, make hay while the sun shines.

Adj. **skillful,** dexterous, adroit, expert, apt, handy, quick, deft, ready, smart, proficient, good at, at home in, master of, conversant with; masterly, crack [*colloq.*], crackajack [*slang*], accomplished.

experienced, practiced, skilled, up in, in practice, competent, efficient, qualified, capable, fitted, fit for, trained, initiated, sophisticated, prepared, primed, finished.

clever, able, ingenious, felicitous, gifted, talented, resourceful, inventive; shrewd, sharp, cunning; neat-handed, fine-fingered; nimble-fingered, ambidextrous, sure-footed.

technical, artistic, scientific, workmanlike, businesslike, statesmanlike.

Adv. **skillfully,** artistically, with skill, with fine technique, with consummate skill; like a machine.

699. UNSKILLFULNESS.—*N.* unskillfulness, want of skill, incompetence, inability, infelicity, clumsiness, inaptitude, inexperience; disqualification.

mismanagement, misconduct, bad policy, impolicy; maladministration; misrule, misgovernment.

blunder, act of folly, bungle, botch, bad job, sad work.

bungler, etc., 701; fool, etc., 501.

V. **bungle,** blunder, muff [*esp. baseball*], boggle, fumble, botch, mar, spoil, flounder, stumble, trip; mismanage, misdirect, misapply.

mistake, take the shadow for the substance, bark up the wrong tree; be in the wrong box [*colloq.*]; lose one's way, miss one's way; fall into a trap.

Adj. **unskillful,** unskilled, inexpert, incompetent, bungling, awkward, clumsy, gawky, unhandy, maladroit; stupid, ill-qualified, unfit; raw, green, inexperienced; rusty, out of practice.

unaccustomed, unused, untrained, uninitiated; unbusinesslike, unpractical, shiftless; unstatesmanlike.

ill-advised, misadvised; ill-devised, ill-judged, ill-contrived, ill-conducted; misguided, foolish, wild; infelicitous.

700.·EXPERT.—N. expert, adept, proficient, connoisseur, master, master hand; top sawyer; prima donna, first fiddle; past master.

picked man; medalist, prizeman.

veteran, old stager, old campaigner, man of business, man of the world.

genius; mastermind, master spirit; prodigy of learning, walking encyclopedia, mine of information.

man of cunning, diplomatist, diplomat, Machiavellian; politician, tactician strategist.

701. BUNGLER.—N. bungler, blunderer, blunderhead; fumbler, lubber, clown, lout, duffer [*colloq.*]; butter-fingers, muff, muffer [*all colloq.*]; awkward squad; novice, greenhorn.

landlubber, fresh-water sailor, fair-weather sailor, horse marine. sloven, slattern, slut.

702. CUNNING.—N. cunning, craft, subtlety, maneuvering, temporization; circumvention; chicane, chicanery; sharp practice, knavery, jugglery, concealment, guile, duplicity, foul play.

diplomacy, politics, Machiavellianism; gerrymander, jobbery, back-stairs influence.

artifice, art, device, machination; plot, maneuver, stratagem, dodge, wile, trick, trickery, ruse, finesse, subterfuge, evasion, white lie, gold brick [*colloq.*], imposture, deception, net, trap.

schemer, trickster, sly boots [*humorous*], fox, reynard; intriguer, man of cunning.

V. intrigue, live by one's wits; maneuver, gerrymander, finesse, double, temporize, circumvent, outdo, get the better of, throw off one's guard; surprise, waylay, undermine, flatter; have an ax to grind.

Adj. cunning, crafty, artful, skillful; subtle, feline, deep, profound, designing, timeserving, tricky, wily, sly, insidious, stealthy, underhand, double-faced, shifty, deceptive; deceitful, crooked; shrewd, acute; sharp, canny, astute, knowing.

703. ARTLESSNESS.—N. artlessness, unsophistication, simplicity, innocence, candor, sincerity, singleness of purpose, honesty.

rough diamond, matter-of-fact man; *enfant terrible* [F.].

V. be artless, think aloud; speak one's mind; be free with one, call a spade a spade; tell the truth, the whole truth, and nothing but the truth.

Adj. artless, natural, pure, confiding, simple, plain, unsophisticated, unaffected, naïve; sincere, frank, open, candid, ingenuous, guileless; unsuspicious, honest, childlike; innocent. straightforward, aboveboard; single-minded.

matter-of-fact, plain-spoken, outspoken; blunt, downright, direct, unflattering, unvarnished.

Adv. in plain words (*or* English); without mincing the matter.

704. DIFFICULTY.—*N.* difficulty, hardness, impracticability, uphill work, herculean task; dead weight, dead lift.

dilemma, predicament, fix [*colloq.*], quandary, embarrassment, deadlock, perplexity, intricacy, entanglement, knot, Gordian knot, maze, coil, strait, pass, pinch, rub, critical situation, exigency, crisis, trial, emergency, scrape, slough, quagmire, hot water [*colloq.*], pickle, stew, imbroglio, mess, muddle, botch, hitch, stumbling block.

vexed question, poser, puzzle, knotty point, paradox; hard nut to crack, crux.

V. be difficult, go against the grain, try one's patience, go hard with one, pose, perplex, bother, nonplus.

flounder, boggle [*local*], struggle, stick fast; come to a deadlock.

render difficult, enmesh, encumber, embarrass, entangle; spike one's guns.

Adj. difficult, hard, tough [*colloq.*]; troublesome, toilsome, irksome; laborious, onerous, arduous, herculean, formidable.

awkward, unwieldy, unmanageable, intractable, stubborn, perverse, refractory, knotted, knotty, thorny; pathless, trackless, intricate.

embarrassing, perplexing, delicate, ticklish, critical, thorny.

in difficulty, in hot water [*colloq.*], in a fix [*colloq.*], in a scrape, between Scylla and Charybdis; on the horns of a dilemma; on the rocks; reduced to straits; hard-pressed; run hard; pinched, straitened; hard up [*slang*]; puzzled, at a loss, at one's wits' end, at a standstill; nonplused, stranded, aground.

Adv. with much ado; uphill, upstream; in the teeth of; against the grain.

705. FACILITY.—*N.* facility, ease, easiness, capability, feasibility, practicability; flexibility, pliancy, smoothness, plain sailing; mere child's play; cinch, snap [*both slang*].

V. be easy, run smoothly; have full play, obey the helm, work well, work smoothly.

facilitate, smooth, ease, lighten, free, clear, disencumber, disembarrass, disentangle, extricate, unravel, unknot; humor, leave a loophole, leave the matter open; give full play, make way for, pave the way, bridge over.

Adj. easy, facile; feasible, practicable, within reach, gettable, accessible.

manageable, tractable; submissive; yielding, ductile, tractable, pliant.

unburdened, unencumbered, unloaded, unobstructed, untrammeled; unrestrained, free, at ease, light.

Adv. **easily,** readily, expertly, adroitly, smoothly, swimmingly, with no effort.

706. HINDRANCE.—*N.* **prevention,** obstruction, stoppage, interruption, interception, hindrance, embarrassment, constriction, restriction, restraint, etc., 751.

interference, interposition, obtrusion; discouragement, disapproval, disapprobation, opposition.

impediment, obstacle, obstruction, knot, snag, hitch, contretemps, stumbling block, lion in the path.

check; encumbrance; clog, brake, anchor; bit, snaffle, curb; drag, load, burden, onus, impedimenta; dead weight; lumber, pack; nightmare, incubus; stay, stop; preventive, prophylactic.

drawback, objection; difficulty, etc., 704; obstacle; ill-wind, head wind; trammel, tether.

damper, wet blanket, kill-joy, dog in the manger, usurper, interloper, opponent; filibusterer.

V. **hinder,** impede, filibuster, embarrass.

avert, keep off, stave off, ward off; obviate; turn aside, draw off, prevent, nip in the bud; retard, slacken, check, counteract, countercheck, preclude, debar, inhibit, restrict.

obstruct, stop, stay, bar, bolt, lock; block, barricade; dam up, put on the brake, put a stop to, interrupt, intercept, oppose, interfere, interpose.

encumber, cramp, hamper; clog, cumber, handicap; choke, saddle with, load with, overload, overwhelm, lumber, entrammel, trammel, incommode, discommode, discompose, corner.

thwart, frustrate, disconcert, balk, foil; circumvent, baffle, override, defeat, spoil, mar, clip the wings of, cripple, damp, dishearten, discountenance, undermine.

Adj. **obstructive,** intrusive, meddlesome; onerous, burdensome; cumbrous, cumbersome.

Adv. **in the way,** with everything against one, through all obstacles, under many difficulties.

707. AID.—*N.* **aid,** assistance, help, succor; support, lift, advance, furtherance, promotion.

patronage, auspices, countenance, favor, interest, advocacy.

sustenance, maintenance, nutrition, nourishment; manna in the wilderness, food, means, subsidy, bounty.

relief, rescue; ministry, ministration; supernatural aid; *deus ex machina* [L.].

supplies, re-enforcements, contingents, recruits, support, ally.

V. **aid,** assist, help, succor, lend a hand; contribute, subscribe to;

take by the hand, take in tow; relieve, rescue; set on one's legs, give new life to, be the making of; re-enforce, recruit; promote, further, forward, advance; speed, expedite, quicken, hasten.

support, sustain, uphold, prop, hold up, bolster.

nourish, nurture, nurse, cradle, dry-nurse, suckle, foster, cherish, cultivate.

serve; do service to, tender to, pander to, minister to; tend, attend, wait on; take care of; entertain, regale.

oblige, accommodate, consult the wishes of; humor, cheer, encourage.

second, stand by, back, back up; abet, work for, stick up for [*colloq.*], stick by, take up (*or* espouse) the cause of; advocate, countenance, patronize, smile upon, favor, befriend, side with.

Adj. aiding, auxiliary, adjuvant, helpful, subservient, accessary, accessory, subsidiary.

friendly, amicable, favorable, propitious, well disposed, neighborly, obliging, at one's beck.

Adv. in aid of, on (*or* in) behalf of, in favor of, in the name of, in furtherance of, on account of, for the sake of.

708. OPPOSITION.—*N.* opposition, antagonism, contrariness, contrariety; contravention, counteraction; resistance, etc., 719; hindrance, restraint, etc., 751.

collision, conflict, discord, want of harmony; filibuster, clashing.

competition, rivalry, emulation, race, contest; tug of war.

V. oppose, counteract, withstand, etc. (*resist*), 719; hinder, restrain; obstruct, etc., 706; antagonize, cross, thwart, pit against, face, confront, cope with; protest (*or* vote) against; disfavor; contradict, contravene, belie.

encounter, meet, stem, breast, resist, grapple with, kick against the pricks; contend with (*or* against), do battle with (*or* against).

compete, emulate, rival; force out, drive one out of business.

Adj. adverse, antagonistic, oppugnant, contrary, at variance, at issue, at war with, in opposition, at daggers drawn.

unfavorable, unpropitious, unfriendly, hostile, inimical, cross.

competitive, emulous, cutthroat; in rivalry with, in friendly rivalry.

Adv. against, counter to, in conflict with, at cross-purposes.

in spite, in despite, in defiance; in the teeth (*or* face) of; across; athwart.

709. CO-OPERATION.—*N.* co-operation, concert, concurrence, complicity, collusion; participation; union, combination.

association, alliance, joint stock, partnership, pool, gentleman's agreement; confederation, coalition, federation, fusion; logrolling; freemasonry.

unanimity, *esprit de corps* [F.], party spirit, school spirit; clanship, partisanship; concord.

V. co-operate, concur; conduce, combine, pool, unite one's efforts, pull together, stand shoulder to shoulder; act in concert, join forces, fraternize; conspire, concert.

side with, take sides with, go along with, join hands with, make common cause with, unite with, join with, take part with, cast in one's lot with; rally round.

participate, be a party to, lend oneself to; chip in [*colloq.*], bear part in, second, espouse a cause.

Adj. co-operating, in league, hand in glove with; favorable to, unopposed.

Adv. unanimously, as one man, shoulder to shoulder.

710. OPPONENT.—*N.* opponent, antagonist, adversary; opposition; assailant, enemy, etc., 891.

oppositionist, wrangler, disputant; filibuster, filibusterer, extremist, bitter-ender, irreconcilable, obstructionist.

malcontent; demagogue, reactionist; anarchist, Red.

rival, competitor, contestant; the field.

711. AUXILIARY.—*N.* auxiliary, recruit, assistant, help, helper, helpmate, helping hand; colleague, partner, confrere, cooperator, coadjutor, collaborator, associate, right hand, right-hand man.

ally; friend, etc., 890; confidant (*fem.* confidante), alter ego [L.], pal [*slang*], chum [*colloq.*], mate.

puppet, cat's-paw, creature, tool; satellite, adherent, parasite, dependent.

confederate; accomplice; accessory.

upholder, seconder, backer, supporter, abettor, advocate, partisan, champion, patron, friend at court, mediator.

friend in need, special providence, guardian angel, fairy godmother, tutelary genius.

712. PARTY.—*N.* party, faction, denomination, class, communion, side, crew, team; band, horde, posse, phalanx; caste, family, clan.

community, body, fellowship, party spirit, solidarity, freemasonry; fraternity, sodality, brotherhood, sisterhood, sorority; fraternal order.

gang, tong [Chin.], bolsheviki, bolshevists, ring, machine, junto, cabal.

clique, knot, circle, set, coterie; club, casino.

corporation, corporate body, guild, company, partnership, firm, house; combine [*colloq.*], trust; holding company, merger.

society, association; institute, institution; union; trade-union;

league, syndicate, alliance, combination, coalition, federation, confederation, confederacy.

staff; cast, dramatis personae [L.].

V. unite, join, band together, club together, co-operate, etc., 709; associate, federate, federalize.

Adj. joint, federal, corporate, confederated, organized, leagued, syndicated; fraternal, Masonic, institutional, denominational; cliquish, cliquy.

Adv. side by side, hand in hand, shoulder to shoulder, in the same boat.

713. DISCORD.—*N.* discord, dissidence, dissonance, disagreement, jar, clash, break, shock.

variance, difference, dissension, misunderstanding, cross-purposes, odds, division, split, rupture, disruption, disunion, breach, schism, feud, faction.

polemics; litigation, strife, warfare, outbreak, open rupture, declaration of war.

quarrel, dispute, tiff, bicker, squabble, altercation, words, high words, family jars.

broil, brawl, row [*colloq.*], racket, hubbub, imbroglio, fracas, scrimmage, rumpus [*colloq.*], squall, riot, disturbance, commotion.

subject of dispute, ground of quarrel, battleground, disputed point, bone of contention, apple of discord, question at issue.

V. disagree, clash, jar, conflict, misunderstand, live like cat and dog; differ; dissent, etc., 489.

quarrel, fall out, dispute, litigate; controvert, squabble, altercate, row [*colloq.*], wrangle, bicker, nag, spar, brawl.

split, break with; declare war, try conclusions, join issue, pick a quarrel; sow dissension, embroil, entangle, disunite, widen the breach; set (*or* pit) against.

Adj. discordant, dissident, out of tune, dissonant, harsh, grating, jangling, unmelodious; on bad terms, dissentient, unreconciled, unpacified; inconsistent, contradictory, incongruous.

quarrelsome, heated, unpacific, controversial, polemic, disputatious, factious.

at strife, at odds, at loggerheads, at daggers drawn, at variance, at issue, at cross-purposes, at sixes and sevens, embroiled, torn, disunited.

714. CONCORD.—*N.* concord, accord, harmony, homologue, correspondence, agreement, sympathy, response; union, unison, unity, peace, unanimity; happy family.

amity, etc. (*friendship*), 888; alliance, *entente cordiale* [F.], good understanding, conciliation, arbitration, reunion.

peacemaker, intercessor, interceder, mediator.

V. **agree,** accord, harmonize with, fraternize, go hand in hand, run parallel, concur, co-operate, pull together, sing in chorus.

side with, sympathize with; go with, chime in with, fall in with; assent, etc., 488; reciprocate.

smooth, pour oil on the troubled waters, keep in good humor, meet halfway; mediate, intercede.

Adj. **concordant,** congenial; in accord, harmonious, united, cemented, allied, friendly, fraternal, conciliatory, of one mind.

Adv. **unanimously,** with one voice, in concert with, hand in hand.

715. DEFIANCE.—*N.* **defiance,** dare, defial; challenge; threat, etc., 909; war cry, war whoop.

V. **defy,** dare, beard, brave, set at defiance, set at naught, hurl defiance at; laugh to scorn; disobey, etc., 742; threaten; challenge.

Adj. **defiant;** rebellious, bold, insolent, reckless, contemptuous, greatly daring, regardless of consequences.

Adv. in the teeth of; under one's very nose; in open rebellion.

716. ATTACK.—*N.* **attack,** assault, onset, onslaught, charge.

aggression, offense; incursion, inroad, invasion; irruption, outbreak; sally, sortie, raid, foray.

storm, storming, boarding, escalade; siege, investment, bombardment, cannonade, barrage; zero hour.

fire, volley, fusilade; sharpshooting, broadside, cross-fire.

thrust, lunge, pass, home thrust; cut.

assailant, aggressor, invader; sharpshooter, dead shot.

V. **attack,** assault, assail; set upon, pounce upon, fall upon, charge; enter the lists.

show fight, take the offensive; strike at, thrust at; aim (*or* deal) a blow at; be the aggressor, strike the first blow, fire the first shot; advance (*or* march) against, march upon, invade, harry.

close with, come to close quarters, bring to bay, come to blows.

fire upon, fire at, draw a bead on, shoot at, pop at, level at, open fire, pepper, bombard, shell, fire a volley.

besiege, beset, beleaguer, invest; sap, mine; storm, board, scale the walls, go over the top.

cut and thrust, bayonet, butt; kick, strike, etc., 276; horsewhip, whip.

Adj. **aggressive,** offensive; up in arms; amuck.

Adv. on the warpath; over the top; at bay.

717. DEFENSE.—*N.* **defense,** protection, guard, ward; guardianship.

self-defense, self-preservation; resistance, etc., 719.

safeguard, screen, fortification, bulwark, trench, mine, dugout;

moat, ditch, intrenchment; rampart, dike; parapet, battlement, bastion, redoubt, embankment, mound, bank, breastwork, earthwork, fieldwork; buttress, abutment, fence, wall, paling, palisade, stockade; barrier, barricade, boom; portcullis, barbed-wire entanglements.

stronghold, hold, fastness, asylum, keep, donjon, citadel, capitol, castle; tower, fortress, fort, barrack; blockhouse.

[protective devices] buffer, fender, cowcatcher, armor; mail, shield, buckler.

defender, protector, guardian, bodyguard, champion; knight-errant, paladin; garrison.

V. defend, guard, ward (*or* beat) off, shield, screen, shroud; garrison, man; fence, intrench, arm, accouter.

repel, parry, put to flight; hold (*or* keep) at bay; resist invasion, stand siege, stand (*or* act) on the defensive, show fight; stand one's ground, hold, stand in the gap.

Adj. defensive; armed, armed at all points (*or* to the teeth); panoplied, accoutered; iron-plated, ironclad; bulletproof, bomb-proof; protective.

Adv. on the defensive, in defense, in self-defense; at bay.

718. RETALIATION.—*N.* retaliation, reprisal, retort; counter-stroke, counterblast; retribution.

requital, desert; tit for tat, give-and-take, blow for blow, an eye for an eye; boomerang.

recrimination, accusation; revenge, etc., 919; compensation.

V. retaliate, retort, turn upon; pay, pay off, pay back; cap, match; reciprocate, turn the tables upon, return the compliment; exchange blows; give and take, be quits, be even with; pay off old scores.

Adj. retaliatory, retaliative, retributive, recriminatory, reciprocal.

719. RESISTANCE.—*N.* resistance, stand, front, opposition, recalcitrance, repugnance, repulsion.

repulse, rebuff, snub.

insurrection, revolt, etc., 742; strike, lockout; boycott; riot.

V. resist; withstand; stand, stand firm (*or* fast, one's ground), stick it out [*colloq.*].

face, confront, breast the wave, stem the tide; grapple with; show a bold front, make a stand.

oppose, etc., 708; fly in the face of; withstand an attack, rise up in arms, strike, turn out, boycott; revolt, rebel; repel, repulse.

Adj. resistant, resistive, refractory, repugnant, recalcitrant, repulsive, repellent; up in arms.

unconquerable, stubborn, unconquered; indomitable, unyielding.

720. CONTENTION.—*N.* contention, strife, contest, struggle; belligerency, pugnacity, opposition.

controversy, polemics; debate, war of words, paper war, high words, quarrel, litigation.

competition, rivalry, match, race; athletics, athletic sports; games of skill.

conflict, skirmish; encounter, rencounter, rencontre, collision, affair, brush, fracas, etc. (*discord*), 713; clash of arms; tussle, scuffle, bout, broil, fray, affray, fight, battle, combat, action, engagement, joust, tournament, tourney; pitched battle; guerrilla (*or* irregular) warfare; death struggle, Armageddon.

duel, single combat, satisfaction, passage of arms, affair of honor; hostile meeting, appeal to arms.

V. contend, contest, strive, struggle, scramble, wrestle; spar, exchange blows, tussle, tilt, box, fence; skirmish, fight; wrangle; oppose, etc., 708; join issue.

compete (*or* cope, vie, race) with, emulate, rival; run a race.

Adj. contentious, combative, bellicose, belligerent, warlike, quarrelsome, pugnacious, pugilistic.

athletic, gymnastic, competitive, rival.

721. PEACE.—*N.* peace, amity, etc. (*friendship*), 888; harmony, concord, tranquillity, truce. pipe of peace, calumet.

piping time of peace, quiet life; neutrality; pacifism.

V. be at peace, keep the peace, make peace, pacify; be a pacifist.

Adj. pacific; peaceable, peaceful; calm, tranquil, untroubled, halcyon; bloodless; neutral, pacifistic.

722. WARFARE.—*N.* warfare, fighting, hostilities; war, arms, the sword, bloodshed; Mars.

appeal to arms (*or* the sword); ordeal (*or* wager) of battle; declaration of war.

battle array, campaign, crusade, expedition; warpath.

art of war, rules of war, the war game, tactics, strategy, generalship.

battle, conflict, etc. (*contention*), 720; service, campaigning, active service, tented field; war to the death (*or* knife).

war medal, military medal, Congressional Medal, Victoria Cross, V. C. [Eng.], *Croix de guerre* [F.], *Médaille militaire* [F.], Iron Cross [Ger.].

V. war, make war, go to war, declare war, wage war, arm, take up (*or* appeal to) arms; take the field, give battle, engage, fight, combat, contend, battle with.

serve; enroll, enlist; be on service (*or* active service), campaign;

smell powder, be under fire; be on the warpath, keep the field; take by storm; go over the top [*colloq.*]; sell one's life dearly.

Adj. **armed,** in (*or* under) arms, in battle array, in the field; embattled; battled.

warlike, belligerent, combative, bellicose, martial, military, militant; soldierly, chivalrous; civil, internecine; irregular, guerrilla.

Adv. in the thick of the fray, in the cannon's mouth; at the sword's point, at the point of the bayonet.

723. PACIFICATION.—*N.* **pacification,** conciliation, reconciliation, reconcilement; accommodation, arrangement, adjustment; terms, compromise; amnesty.

peace offering; olive branch; calumet, peace pipe.

truce, armistice; suspension of arms (*or* hostilities); truce of God; flag of truce, white flag.

V. **pacify,** tranquillize, compose, allay, reconcile, propitiate, placate, conciliate, meet halfway, hold out the olive branch, heal the breach, make peace, restore harmony, bring to terms.

raise a siege, sheathe the sword, bury the hatchet, lay down one's arms, turn swords into plowshares.

Adj. **conciliatory,** pacificatory.

724. MEDIATION.—*N.* **mediation,** mediatorship, intervention, interposition, interference, intercession; parley, negotiation, arbitration, good offices.

mediator, intercessor, peacemaker, negotiator, go-between, diplomatist, propitiator; umpire, arbitrator.

V. **mediate,** intercede, interpose, interfere, intervene; step in, negotiate; meet halfway; arbitrate, propitiate.

Adj. **mediatory,** propitiatory, diplomatic.

725. SUBMISSION.—*N.* **submission,** yielding, acquiescence, compliance, submissiveness, deference, nonresistance, obedience.

surrender, cession, capitulation, resignation, backdown [*colloq.*].

obeisance, homage, kneeling, genuflection, curtsy, kowtow [Chinese], salaam [Oriental], prostration.

V. **submit,** succumb, yield, defer to; bend, stoop; accede, resign oneself.

surrender, cede, capitulate, come to terms, lay down one's arms, strike one's flag, give way (*or* ground, in, up); obey.

yield obeisance, kneel to, bow to, pay homage to, cringe to, truckle to; kneel, bow submission, curtsy, kowtow [Chinese].

Adj. **submissive,** resigned, crouching, prostrate; unresisting, humble.

untenable, indefensible, insupportable, unsupportable.

726. COMBATANT.—*N.* **combatant;** belligerent, assailant, swashbuckler, duelist, swordsman; competitor, rival.

fighter, fighting man, prize fighter, pugilist, bruiser; gladiator.

soldier, warrior, brave, man at arms, guardsman, gendarme [F.]; campaigner, veteran; military man; knight; myrmidon, mercenary, irregular, free lance, franctireur; private, Tommy Atkins [Brit.], doughboy [*slang*], rank and file; sepoy [India], spearman, pikeman; archer, bowman; musketeer, rifleman, sharpshooter, skirmisher; grenadier, fusileer, infantryman, foot soldier, chasseur, zouave, artilleryman, gunner, cannoneer, engineer; cavalryman, trooper, dragoon; cuirassier, hussar, lancer; recruit, rookie [*slang*], conscript, drafted man, enlisted man.

officer, etc. (*commander*), 745; subaltern, ensign, standard-bearer.

horse and foot; cavalry, horse, light horse; infantry, foot, rifles; artillery, horse artillery, field artillery, gunners; military train.

armed force, troops, soldiery, military, forces, the army, standing army, regulars, the line; militia, national guard, state guard, yeomanry, volunteers, minutemen [*Am. hist.*]; posse; guards, yeomen of the guard, beefeaters [Eng.], lifeguards, household troops, bodyguard.

levy, draft; raw levies, awkward squad.

army, army corps; division, column, wing, detachment, garrison, flying column, brigade, regiment, battalion, squadron, company, battery, section, platoon, squad; picket, guard, legion, phalanx, cohort.

navy, first line of defense, wooden walls, naval forces, fleet, flotilla, armada, squadron; man-of-war's man, etc. (*sailor*), 269; marines.

man-of-war, line-of-battle ship, ship of the line, battleship, warship, ironclad, war vessel, superdreadnought, dreadnought, cruiser; torpedo boat, destroyer, gunboat, submarine, submersible, U-boat [Ger.]; submarine chaser, monitor; frigate, sloop of war, corvet, flagship; privateer; troopship, transport, tender.

airplane, hydroplane, seaplane, flying boat; glider; dive-bomber, bomber, Flying Fortress; dirigible, blimp [*cant*]; zeppelin, etc. (*aeronautics*), 273.

727. ARMS.—N. arms; arm, weapon, deadly weapon; armament; armor.

side arms, sword, cold steel, naked steel, steel, blade; broadsword, saber, cutlass, scimitar, rapier, foil, dagger, poniard, dirk, stiletto, bowie knife, bayonet.

ax, battle-ax, poleax, halberd, tomahawk, bill, partisan.

spear, lance, pike, assagai, javelin, dart, arrow; harpoon, boomerang; oxgoad, ankus.

club, war club, mace, truncheon, staff, bludgeon, cudgel, shillelagh, quarterstaff; billy, life preserver, blackjack.

bow, crossbow, long bow; catapult, sling.

firearms; gun, piece; artillery, ordnance; park, battery; cannon, fieldpiece, field gun, siege gun, mortar, howitzer, pompom, seventy-five [*French rapid-fire 75-mm. field gun*]; Lewis gun.

small arms; musketry; musket, firelock, fowling piece, rifle, carbine, blunderbuss, matchlock, harquebus, shotgun, breechloader, muzzle-loader, magazine rifle, automatic pistol, automatic, revolver, repeater; shooting iron [*slang*], six-shooter [*colloq.*], gun [*colloq. for revolver or pistol*], pistol.

missile, bolt, projectile, shot, ball, slug; grape, shrapnel, grenade, shell, bomb, depth bomb, smoke bomb, gas bomb; bullet; dumdum (*or* explosive, expanding) bullet; torpedo.

ammunition; powder, powder and shot; explosive; gunpowder; dynamite, cordite; cartridge; poison gas, mustard gas, chlorine gas, tear gas, etc.

728. ARENA.—N. arena, field, platform; scene of action, theater, walk, course; hustings; stage, boards, amphitheater, coliseum, colosseum; hippodrome, circus, race course, turf, cockpit, bear garden, gymnasium, ring, lists; campus, playing field, playground.

battlefield, battleground, field of battle; no man's land [*First World War*]; theater (*or* seat) of war.

729. COMPLETION.—*N.* completion; accomplishment, achievement, fulfillment, performance, execution; dispatch, consummation, culmination; finish, conclusion; limit, close, finale, denouement, issue, upshot, result.

V. complete, perfect, effect, accomplish, achieve, compass, consummate, bring to maturity (*or* perfection); elaborate.

do, execute, make, work out, enact, dispatch, knock off [*colloq.*], finish off, dispose of, perform, discharge, fulfill, realize; carry out (*or* into effect).

do thoroughly, not do by halves, drive home; carry through, deliver the goods [*colloq.*].

finish, bring to a close, wind up, clinch, seal, put the last (*or* finishing) touch to; crown, crown all; cap.

Adj. conclusive, final, crowning, exhaustive, complete, mature, perfect, consummate, thorough.

Adv. to crown all, as a last stroke, as a fitting climax.

730. NONCOMPLETION.—*N.* noncompletion, nonfulfillment, nonperformance, neglect, etc., 460; shortcoming, incompleteness; drawn battle, drawn game.

V. leave unfinished, leave undone, neglect, etc., 460; let alone, let slip; lose sight of.

fall short of, do things by halves, hang fire; collapse.

Adj. incomplete, uncompleted, unfinished, unaccomplished, unperformed, unexecuted; sketchy; sterile.

Adv. without (*or* lacking) the final touches.

731. SUCCESS—*N.* success, successfulness; progress; advance; good fortune, prosperity, etc., 734; profit.

trump card; hit, stroke, master stroke; ten-strike [*colloq.*]; checkmate; prize.

mastery, advantage over; upper hand, whip hand; ascendancy, conquest, victory, walkover [*colloq.*], triumph.

victor, conqueror, master, champion, winner; master of the situation (*or* position).

V. succeed, be successful, gain one's end (*or* ends); crown with success; gain (*or* attain, carry, secure) a point *or* an object; get there [*slang*]; manage to, contrive to; accomplish, effect; come off successfully, take (*or* carry) by storm; gain the day (*or* prize, palm); carry all before one, score a success.

make progress, etc. (*advance*), 282; win (*or* make, work) one's way; speed; turn to account, prosper, etc., 734; strike oil [*slang*], make one's fortune.

triumph, be triumphant, gain a victory (*or* an advantage); surmount (*or* overcome) a difficulty, stem the torrent, weather the storm, master; distance, surpass, win.

defeat, conquer, discomfit, vanquish, overcome, overthrow, overpower, overmaster, outwit, outdo, outmaneuver, outgeneral, checkmate, beat, rout, floor, worst, lick to a frazzle [*colloq.*]; settle [*colloq.*], do for [*colloq.*], subdue, subjugate, reduce.

quell, silence, put down, confound, nonplus, baffle, circumvent, elude; drive to the wall.

avail, answer, answer the purpose; prevail, take effect, do, turn out well, take [*colloq.*], tell, bear fruit.

Adj. **successful**; prosperous, etc., 734; triumphant, crowned with success, victorious; unbeaten.

Adv. **successfully**, with flying colors, in triumph, swimmingly.

732. FAILURE.—*N.* **failure**, unsuccess, nonsuccess, nonfulfillment; labor in vain, no go [*colloq.*], inefficacy; vain attempt; frustration, disappointment.

blunder, error, etc., 495; fault, omission, miss, oversight, slip, trip, stumble; step, *faux pas* [F.]; scrape, mess, muddle, botch, fiasco.

mishap, etc. (*misfortune*), 735; split, collapse, smash, blow, explosion.

repulse, rebuff, defeat, rout, overthrow, discomfiture; beating, drubbing; subjugation, checkmate.

fall, downfall, ruin, perdition, wreck; deathblow; bankruptcy.

V. **fail**, be unsuccessful, make vain efforts, labor in vain; flunk [*colloq.*]; bring to naught, make nothing of, fall short of, go to the wall [*colloq.*], lick the dust; be defeated, have the worst of it, lose the day, lose; succumb.

miss, miss one's aim (*or* the mark), slip, trip, stumble, blunder, miscarry.

flounder, falter, limp, halt, hobble, fall, tumble, run aground, split upon a rock, break down, sink, drown, founder, come to grief.

come to nothing, end in smoke; flat out [*colloq.*]; fall through, hang fire, flash in the pan, collapse, go to wrack and ruin.

Adj. **unsuccessful**, successless, at fault; unfortunate, etc., 735; abortive, sterile, fruitless, bootless; ineffectual, ineffective, inefficient, lame, insufficient, unavailing.

stranded, aground, grounded, swamped, wrecked, shipwrecked, foundered, capsized.

undone, lost, ruined, broken, bankrupt, played out; done up, done for [*colloq.*]; broken down, overborne, overwhelmed; all up with [*colloq.*].

frustrated, thwarted, crossed, disconcerted; unhorsed, hard hit, stultified, befooled, dished [*colloq.*], foiled, defeated, victimized, sacrificed.

Adv. to little or no purpose, in vain.

733. TROPHY.—*N.* trophy; medal, prize, palm, laurel, laurels, bays, crown, chaplet, wreath; eulogy, citation; scholarship; garland; triumphal arch; war medal, etc., 722; Carnegie medal, Nobel prize; blue ribbon; decoration, etc., 877.

734. PROSPERITY.—*N.* prosperity, welfare, well-being; affluence, etc. (*wealth*), 803; success, etc., 731; luck, good fortune, good luck, blessings, godsend; bed of roses; fat of the land.

upstart, parvenu, *nouveau riche* [F.], mushroom.

V. prosper, thrive, flourish, swim with the tide; rise (*or* get on) in the world; light on one's feet; bask in the sunshine; have a run of luck; make one's fortune, feather one's nest, make one's pile [*slang*].

flower, blossom, bloom, fructify, bear fruit; fatten, batten.

Adj. prosperous, thriving, well off, well to do, at one's ease; rich, etc., 803; fortunate, lucky; palmy, halcyon.

auspicious, propitious, providential.

Adv. prosperously, swimmingly; as good luck would have it.

735. ADVERSITY.—*N.* adversity, evil, etc., 619; failure, etc., 732; bad (*or* ill, evil, adverse, hard) fortune *or* luck, frowns of fortune; broken fortunes; slough of despond; evil day, hard times, rainy day, cloud, gathering clouds, ill-wind; affliction, trouble, hardship, curse, blight, load, pressure, humiliation.

misfortune, mishap, mischance, misadventure, disaster, calamity, catastrophe; accident, casualty, blow, trial, sorrow, visitation, infliction, reverse, check, setback, contretemps [F.].

downfall, fall; losing game; ruin, undoing, extremity.

V. come to grief, go downhill, go to wrack and ruin, go to the dogs [*colloq.*]; fall, decay, sink, decline, go down in the world; have seen better days; be all up with [*colloq.*].

Adj. unfortunate, unblest, unhappy, unlucky, unprosperous, hoodooed [*colloq.*], luckless, hapless, out of luck; under a cloud; badly off; in adverse circumstances; poor, etc., 804; decayed, undone, on the road to ruin.

ill-fated, ill-starred, ill-omened; devoted, doomed; inauspicious, ominous, sinister, unpropitious, unfavorable.

adverse, untoward; disastrous, calamitous, ruinous, dire, deplorable.

Adv. from bad to worse, out of the frying pan into the fire.

736. MEDIOCRITY.—*N.* mediocrity, golden mean, moderation; moderate (*or* average) circumstances; respectability.

middle classes, *bourgeoisie* [F.].

V. strike the golden mean; preserve a middle course.

jog on, get along [*colloq.*], get on tolerably (*or* respectably).

Adj. middling, so-so, fair, medium, moderate, mediocre, ordinary.

Adv. with nothing to brag about.

II. INTERSOCIAL VOLITION[1]

737. AUTHORITY.—*N.* authority; influence, patronage, power, prestige, prerogative, jurisdiction.

right, divine right, authoritativeness, royalty, absolutism, despotism, tyranny.

command, empire, sway, rule; dominion, domination; sovereignty, supremacy, suzerainty, kingship; lordship, headship, leadership, mastership, government, dictation, control, hold, grasp; grip, iron sway, rod of empire.

reign, dynasty, administration; dictatorship, protectorate, presidency, presidentship, consulship, magistracy.

Governments: empire; monarchy; limited (*or* constitutional) monarchy; aristocracy; oligarchy, democracy, republic; triumvirate; autocracy; dictatorship, totalitarian state.

representative government, constitutional government, home rule, dominion rule [Brit.], colonial government; self-government, autonomy, self-determination; republicanism, federalism; socialism; communism; authoritarianism; totalitarianism; bureaucracy; martial law; feudal system, feudalism.

state, realm, commonwealth, country, power, body politic.

ruler, person in authority, lord, etc., 745; judicature, etc., 965; cabinet, etc. (*council*), 696; seat of government, headquarters.

V. authorize, empower, etc., 760; warrant, dictate.

rule, sway, command, control, administer, govern, direct, lead, preside over, be at the head of, reign.

dominate, have the upper (*or* whip) hand; preponderate, boss [*colloq.*]; override, overrule, overawe; lord it over, keep under, bend to one's will, have it all one's own way, be master of the situation, take the lead, lay down the law.

Adj. ruling, regnant, dominant, paramount, supreme, predominant, preponderant, in the ascendant, influential; imperious, dictatorial, peremptory; authoritative, executive, administrative, official, gubernatorial, bureaucratic, departmental.

sovereign; regal, royal, royalist, monarchical, kingly; dynastic, imperial, autocratic; oligarchic, democratic, republican.

[1]Implying the action of the will of one mind over the will of another.

Adv. in the name of, by the authority of, at one's command, in virtue of, under the auspices of.

738. [Absence of authority] **LAXITY.**—*N.* laxity; laxness, looseness, slackness; toleration, lenity, etc., 740; relaxation; freedom, etc., 748.

anarchy, interregnum; misrule, license, insubordination, mob rule, mob law, lynch law, nihilism, reign of violence.

Deprivation of power: dethronement, impeachment, deposition, abdication; usurpation.

V. **be lax,** hold a loose rein; give the reins to, give rope enough, give free rein to; tolerate; relax; misrule.

have one's fling, act without authority, act on one's own responsibility, usurp authority.

dethrone, depose; abdicate.

Adj. **lax,** loose; slack, remiss, negligent, etc., 460; weak.

relaxed, licensed, unbridled; anarchic *or* anarchical, nihilistic; unauthorized.

739. SEVERITY.—*N.* severity; strictness, harshness, rigor, stringency, austerity, inclemency; arrogance, etc., 885.

arbitrary power; absolutism, despotism; dictatorship, autocracy, tyranny, domination, oppression, assumption, usurpation; inquisition, reign of terror, iron rule, coercion, etc., 744; martial law.

bureaucracy, red-tapism, officialism.

tyrant, disciplinarian, martinet, stickler, despot, autocrat, oppressor, inquisitor, extortioner.

V. **arrogate,** assume, usurp, take liberties; domineer, bully, tyrannize, put on the screw, be hard upon, ill-treat, rule with a rod of iron, oppress, override, trample under foot, ride roughshod over; coerce, etc., 744.

Adj. **severe,** strict, hard, harsh, dour [Scot.], rigid, stern, rigorous, uncompromising, exacting, searching, inexorable, inflexible, obdurate, austere, relentless, stringent, strict, strait-laced, peremptory, absolute, arbitrary, imperative, coercive, tyrannical, extortionate, oppressive, cruel, arrogant; formal, punctilious.

Adv. with a high (*or* strong, tight, heavy) hand.

740. MILDNESS.—*N.* mildness, lenity, moderation, temperateness; tolerance, toleration, mildness, gentleness; favor; indulgence, clemency, mercy, forbearance, quarter, compassion, etc., 914.

V. **be lenient,** tolerate, bear with; spare the vanquished, give quarter; indulge, spoil.

Adj. **lenient,** mild, gentle, tolerant, indulgent, easy, moderate, complaisant, easygoing; clement, compassionate, forbearing; long-suffering.

741. COMMAND.—*N.* command, order, ordinance, act, fiat, bidding, word, call, beck, nod; direction, injunction, charge, instructions; dispatch, message.

demand, exaction, imposition, requisition, claim, requirement, ultimatum; request, etc., 765.

decree, dictate, dictation, mandate, precept; prescript, writ, ordination, bull, edict, dispensation, prescription, enactment, law, act; warrant, passport, summons, subpoena, citation; word of command, order of the day.

V. command, order, decree, enact, ordain, dictate, direct, give orders, issue a command; call to order; assume the command.

prescribe, set, appoint, mark out; set (*or* prescribe, impose) a task; set to work.

bid, enjoin, charge, instruct; require, demand, exact, impose, tax.

claim, lay claim to, reclaim.

cite, summon, call for, send for; subpoena; beckon.

Adj. commanding, authoritative, imperative, decisive, final.

Adv. in a commanding tone; by a stroke (*or* dash) of the pen; by order.

742. DISOBEDIENCE.—*N.* disobedience, insubordination, contumacy; infraction, infringement, violation.

revolt, rebellion, mutiny, outbreak, rising, uprising, insurrection, riot, tumult, strike.

sedition, treason; lese majesty; defection, secession, revolution; bolshevism.

insurgent, mutineer, rebel, traitor, communist, Fenian, Sinn Feiner, Red, Bolshevist, seceder, Secessionist [esp., U. S. hist.] *or* Secesh [*colloq. or slang*, U. S.]; apostate, renegade, anarchist.

V. disobey, violate, infringe; shirk, slack; defy, set at defiance, run riot, take the law into one's own hands; kick over the traces; refuse to support, bolt [*politics*].

resist, strike, rise, rise in arms; secede, mutiny, rebel.

Adj. disobedient, unruly, ungovernable; insubordinate, restive, refractory, defiant, contumacious; recusant, recalcitrant.

lawless, riotous, mutinous, seditious, insurgent, revolutionary.

743. OBEDIENCE.—*N.* obedience, observance, compliance; submission, subjection; nonresistance, passivity, resignation, submissiveness, ductility, obsequiousness, servility.

allegiance, loyalty, fealty, homage, deference, devotion; constancy, fidelity.

V. obey, submit, etc., 725; comply, do one's bidding, attend to orders, serve faithfully (*or* loyally, devotedly, without question); be resigned to, be submissive to; serve, etc., 746; play second fiddle.

Adj. obedient, law-abiding, complying, compliant; loyal, faithful, devoted; under beck and call, under control.

resigned, passive; submissive, etc., 725; unresisting, pliant.

Adv. as you please, if you please; in compliance with, in obedience to.

744. COMPULSION.—*N.* compulsion, coercion, constraint; restraint, etc., 751; enforcement, draft, conscription; eminent domain.

force; brute (*or* main, physical) force; the sword; mob law, martial law.

necessity, etc., 601; spur of necessity, Hobson's choice.

V. compel, force, make, drive, dragoon, coerce, constrain, enforce, necessitate, oblige.

extort, wring from, force upon, drag into; bind, pin down; require; tax, put in force; commandeer; restrain, etc., 751.

Adj. compelling, coercive, inexorable, compulsory, obligatory, stringent, peremptory, binding.

Adv. forcibly, by force, by force of arms; on compulsion, perforce, under protest, in spite of, in one's teeth; against one's will.

745. MASTER.—*N.* master, lord, commander, commandant, captain, chief, chieftain; paterfamilias [*Rom. law*], patriarch; sahib [India], head, senior, governor, ruler, dictator, leader, director, boss; sachem, sagamore.

potentate; liege, liege lord, suzerain, overlord, sovereign, monarch, crowned head, emperor, king, majesty, protector, president; autocrat, despot, tyrant, oligarch, dictator.

caesar, kaiser, czar, sultan, caliph, mogul, great mogul, mikado, inca; prince, duke, etc. (*nobility*), 875; archduke, doge; maharaja, raja, emir, nizam, nawab [*Indian ruling chiefs*].

empress, queen, sultana, czarina, princess, infanta, duchess, maharani, rani [both Hindu], begum [Moham.].

regent, viceroy, khedive, pasha, bey, mandarin.

the authorities, the powers that be, the government; staff, official, man in office, person in authority.

Military authorities: marshal, field marshal, generalissimo; commander in chief, general, brigadier general, brigadier, lieutenant general, major general, colonel, lieutenant colonel, major, captain, lieutenant, sublieutenant; officer, staff officer, side-de-camp, adjutant, ensign, cornet, cadet, subaltern; noncommissioned officer; sergeant, top sergeant, corporal.

Civil authorities: mayor, prefect, chancellor, magistrate, syndic; burgomaster, seneschal, alderman, warden, constable.

Naval authorities: admiral, admiralty; commodore, captain, commander, lieutenant; skipper, master, mate.

746. SERVANT.—*N.* servant, retainer, follower, henchman, servitor, domestic, menial, help [*local*], employee; attaché [F.], official.

subject, liege, liegeman.

retinue, suite, cortege, staff, court; office force, clerical staff, clerical force, workers, associate workers, employees, the help.

attendant, squire, usher, apprentice; page, buttons [*colloq.*]; trainbearer, cupbearer; waiter, butler, lackey, footman, flunky [*colloq.*]; boy [*any colored male servant, as in the Orient, South Africa, etc*]; valet, equerry, groom, jockey, hostler or ostler, orderly, messenger, caddie; secretary, stenographer, clerk, agent, underling, understrapper, man

maid, maidservant; girl, help [*local*], handmaid, lady's maid, nurse, ayah [India], nursemaid; cook, scullion, Cinderella; general servant [Brit.], general-housework maid [U. S.], general [*colloq.*]; washerwoman, laundress, charwoman.

dependent, hanger-on, satellite, parasite, protégé [F.], ward, hireling, mercenary, puppet, creature; serf, vassal, thrall, slave, Negro, helot; bondsman, bondswoman; bondslave; villein [*hist.*], churl [*hist.*].

V. **serve,** minister to, help, co-operate; wait (*or* attend, dance attendance) upon; squire, valet, tend, do for [*colloq.*].

Adj. **serviceable,** useful, helpful, co-operative; at one's call.

servile, slavish, subject, thrall, bond; subservient, obsequious, base, fawning, truckling, sycophantic, parasitic, cringing.

747. [Insignia of authority] SCEPTER.—*N.* **Regal:** scepter, orb; pall; robes of state, ermine, purple; crown, coronet, diadem; triple plume; flail [Egyptian]; signet seal.

Ecclesiastical: tiara, triple crown; ring, keys; miter, crozier, crook, staff; cardinal's hat; bishop's apron (*or* sleeves, lawn, gaiters), fillet.

Military: epaulet, star, bar, eagle, crown [Brit.], oak leaf, Sam Browne belt; chevron, stripe

caduceus; Mercury's staff (*or* rod, wand); mace, fasces, ax, truncheon, staff, baton, wand, rod; flag, etc. (*insignia*), 550; regalia; toga, mantle; decoration, title, etc., 877; portfolio.

throne, divan; woolsack [*seat of English Lord Chancellor in the House of Lords*], chair, seat, dais.

talisman, amulet, charm, sign.

748. FREEDOM.—*N.* **freedom,** liberty, independence; license, indulgence.

scope, range, latitude, play, free play (*or* scope), swing, full swing, elbowroom, margin, rope, wide berth.

franchise; prerogative, etc., 924.

freeman, freedman, citizen, denizen.

immunity, exemption; emancipation, etc., 750; right, privilege.

autonomy, self-government; free trade; self-determination, non-interference; Monroe Doctrine [U. S.].

independent, free lance, freethinker, free trader.

V. **be free,** have scope (*or* one's own way), do what one likes, go at large, feel at home, stand on one's rights.

free, liberate, set free, etc., 750; give the reins to; make free of, enfranchise.

Adj. **free,** independent, at large, loose, scot-free; unconstrained, unconfined, unchecked, unhindered, unobstructed, uncontrolled, ungoverned, unchained, unshackled, unfettered, unbridled, uncurbed, unmuzzled, unvanquished.

unrestricted, unlimited, unconditional; absolute; with unlimited power (or opportunity); discretionary.

unbiased, unprejudiced, uninfluenced; spontaneous.

free and easy, at ease, at one's ease; quite at home.

exempt, immune, freed, freeborn; autonomous, freehold.

gratuitous, gratis, etc., 815; for nothing, for love.

Adv. freely, at will, with no restraint.

749. SUBJECTION.—*N.* subjection; dependence, subordination; thrall, thralldom, subjugation, bondage, serfdom; feudalism, vassalage, slavery, enslavement; conquest.

service; servitude, employ, tutelage, constraint, yoke, submission, obedience.

V. be subject, be at the mercy of, depend upon; fall a prey to, fall under, play second fiddle; serve, etc., 746; obey, etc., 743; submit, etc., 725.

subjugate, subject, tame, break in; master, tread down, weigh down, keep under, enthrall, enslave, lead captive, rule, etc., 737; hold in bondage (or leading strings).

Adj. subject, dependent, subordinate; feudal, feudatory; under control; in leading strings, in harness; servile, slavish, enslaved, downtrodden; henpecked; under one's thumb, tied to one's apron strings, at one's beck and call; liable.

Adv. under; under orders (or command), at one's orders.

750. LIBERATION.—*N.* liberation, disengagement, release, emancipation, Emancipation Proclamation; enfranchisement, manumission; discharge, dismissal.

deliverance, etc., 672; redemption, extrication, acquittance, absolution, acquittal, escape.

V. liberate, free, set free, emancipate, release; enfranchise, manumit; demobilize, disband, discharge, dismiss; let go, let loose, let out, deliver, etc., 672; absolve, acquit.

unfetter, untie, loose, loosen, relax; unbolt, unbar, unhand, unbind, unchain, disengage, disentangle; clear, extricate; reprieve.

Adj. liberated, freed; foot-loose, one's own master.

Adv. at large, at liberty; adrift.

751. RESTRAINT.—*N.* restraint; hindrance, etc., 706; coercion, compulsion, constraint, repression; discipline, control; limitation, restriction, protection, monopoly; prohibition, economic pressure.

confinement, durance, duress; imprisonment, incarceration, thrall, thralldom, limbo, captivity; blockade.

keep, care, charge, custody, ward.

repressionist, monopolist, protectionist.

V. restrain, check, restrict, debar, hinder, constrain, coerce, compel, curb, harness, control; hold in leash, withhold, repress, suppress, keep under; smother, pull in, rein in, hold, prohibit.

fasten, enchain, fetter, shackle, trammel; bridle, muzzle, gag, pinion, manacle, handcuff, hobble, bind, swathe, swaddle; tether, picket, tie, secure.

confine, shut up (*or* in), lock up, box up, bottle up, cork up, seal up, blockade, hem in, bolt in, wall in, rail in; impound, pen, coop; inclose, cage, imprison, immure, incarcerate, entomb; put in irons, cast into prison.

arrest, take into custody; take (*or* make) prisoner, lead captive, send to prison, commit; give in charge (*or* custody).

Adj. restrained, constrained, repressive, suppressive; imprisoned, pent up, wedged in; on parole; doing time [*colloq. or slang*], in custody.

stiff, narrow, prudish, strait-laced, hidebound.

Adv. under restraint (*or* lock and key, hatches), under discipline; in prison, in jail, in durance vile, in confinement; behind bars, in captivity, under arrest.

752. [Means of restraint] PRISON.—*N.* prison, prisonhouse; jail, cage, coop, den, cell; stronghold, fortress, keep, donjon, dungeon, Bastille, penitentiary, state prison, lockup, station house, station [*colloq.*], pen [*also slang for penitentiary*], pound; penal settlement; workhouse [U. S.; *in England, a workhouse is a poorhouse*], reformatory, reform school.

Restraining devices: shackle, bond, gyve, fetter, irons, pinion, manacle, handcuff, straight jacket, stocks, pillory; vise, bandage, splint, strap; yoke, collar, halter, harness; muzzle, gag, bit, curb, snaffle, bridle; rein, reins, lines [U. S. and dial. Eng.], ribbons [*colloq.*]; tether, picket, band, chain, cord.

bar, bolt, lock, padlock; rail, paling, palisade; wall, fence, barrier, barricade.

drag, brake, check, etc. (*hindrance*), 706.

753. KEEPER.—*N.* keeper, custodian, ranger, gamekeeper, warder, jailer, turnkey, castellan, guard; watch, watchdog, watchman, concierge [F.], sentry, sentinel; coastguard.

escort, bodyguard; convoy.

guardian, protector, governor; duenna, governess, nurse.

754. PRISONER.—*N.* prisoner, convict, captive, close prisoner.

V. stand committed; be imprisoned.

Adj. imprisoned, in prison, in custody, in charge, behind bars, under lock and key, under hatches.

755. [Vicarious authority] COMMISSION.—*N.* commission,

delegation; consignment, assignment; proxy, power of attorney, deputation, legation, mission, embassy; agency.

errand, charge, brevet, diploma, permit.

appointment, nomination, charter; ordination; installation, inauguration, investiture; accession, coronation, enthronement.

V. commission, delegate, depute; consign, assign, commit, charge, intrust, authorize.

accredit, engage, hire, bespeak, appoint, name, nominate, return; ordain, install, induct, inaugurate, invest, crown; enroll, enlist; employ, empower.

Adv. instead of, in one's stead, in one's place; as proxy for.

756. ANNULMENT.—*N.* annulment, nullification, cancellation, abrogation, revocation, repeal.

dismissal, *congé* [F.], sack [*slang*], deposition, dethronement; disestablishment, disendowment.

countermand, repudiation, retractation, recantation; abolition, abolishment; dissolution.

V. annul, cancel, destroy, abolish, abrogate, revoke, repeal, rescind, reverse, retract, recall; overrule, override; set aside; disannul, dissolve, quash, nullify, nol-pros [*law, short for nolle prosequi*], disestablish; countermand, counterorder, throw overboard.

disclaim, deny, ignore, repudiate; recant, break off.

dismiss, discard; turn out, cast off (*or* adrift, aside, away); send off, send away, discharge, get rid of, bounce [*slang*]; fire, sack [*both slang*].

cashier, oust, unseat, dethrone, depose, unfrock, strike off the roll, disbar.

757. RESIGNATION.—*N.* resignation, retirement, abdication; renunciation, retractation, retraction, disclaimer, abandonment, relinquishment.

V. resign, give up, throw up, lay down, abjure, renounce, forego, disclaim, retract, deny, desert.

vacate, abdicate, retire; tender (*or* hand in) one's resignation.

758. CONSIGNEE.—*N.* consignee, trustee, nominee; committee.

functionary, curator; treasurer, etc., 801; agent, factor, steward, bailiff, clerk, secretary, attorney, solicitor, proctor, broker, underwriter, commission agent, factotum, caretaker, employee; servant, etc., 746.

negotiator, go-between; middleman.

delegate, commissioner; emissary, envoy, messenger.

diplomatist, diplomat, ambassador, plenipotentiary, diplomatic agent, representative, resident, consul, legate, etc., 534; attaché [F.].

salesman, traveler, traveling salesman, commercial traveler, drummer, traveling man.

759. DEPUTY.—*N.* deputy, substitute, proxy, delegate, representative, alternate; vice-president.

regent, vicegerent, viceroy, minister, premier, chancellor, provost, warden, lieutenant, consul, ambassador; delegate, etc., 758.

team, eight, nine, eleven; captain, champion.

V. represent, stand for, appear for, hold a brief for, answer for; stand in the shoes of; stand in the stead of.

delegate, depute, empower, commission, substitute, accredit.

Adj. acting, vice, viceregal; accredited to; delegated, representative.

Adv. in behalf of, in the place of, as representing, by proxy.

760. PERMISSION.—*N.* permission, leave, allowance, sufferance, tolerance, toleration, connivance; liberty, law, license, concession, grace; indulgence, favor, dispensation, exemption, release; authorization, accordance, admission.

permit, warrant, sanction, authority, pass, passport; license, carte blanche [F.], grant, charter, patent.

V. permit, let, allow, admit; suffer, tolerate, recognize; concede, etc., 762; accord, vouchsafe, favor, humor, gratify, indulge, wink at, connive at.

grant, empower, charter, enfranchise, privilege, license, authorize, warrant, sanction; intrust, commission.

absolve, release, exonerate, dispense with.

Adj. permitted, permissible, allowable, lawful, legitimate, legal, legalized, chartered, unforbidden.

Adv. by (*or* with) leave, under favor of, by all means.

761. PROHIBITION.—*N.* prohibition, inhibition; veto, interdict, interdiction, injunction, embargo, ban, taboo, proscription, restriction; contraband; forbidden fruit; Volstead Act, 18th amendment [all U. S.].

V. prohibit, inhibit, forbid, disallow; bar, debar, hinder, restrain, etc., 751; withhold, limit, circumscribe, clip the wings of, restrict; interdict, taboo, proscribe; exclude, shut out.

Adj. prohibitive, prohibitory; proscriptive; restrictive, exclusive.

prohibited, unlicensed, contraband, taboo, illegal, unauthorized.

762. CONSENT.—*N.* consent; assent, etc., 488; acquiescence, approval, compliance, agreement, concession, accession, acknowledgment, acceptance; permit, etc. (*permission*), 760; promise, etc., 768.

settlement, adjustment, ratification, confirmation.

V. consent; assent, etc., 488; yield assent, admit, allow, concede, grant, yield; acknowledge, give consent, comply with, acquiesce, agree to, accede, accept, close with, satisfy, settle, come to terms; deign, vouchsafe, promise.

Adj. willing, compliant, agreeable [*colloq.*], eager.

763. OFFER.—*N.* offer, proffer, tender, bid, overture, proposal, proposition; motion, invitation, offering.

V. offer, proffer, present, tender; bid; propose, move, make a motion, start, invite, place at one's disposal; make possible, put forward, press, urge upon, hold out.

volunteer, come forward, be a candidate, offer (*or* present) oneself, stand for, bid for; seek; be at one's service.

Adj. in the market, for sale, to let, disengaged, on hire; at one's disposal.

764. REFUSAL.—*N.* refusal, rejection, denial, declension, flat (*or* point-blank) refusal; repulse, rebuff; discountenance, disapprobation.

negation, abnegation, protest, renunciation, disclaimer; dissent, etc., 489; revocation, annulment.

V. refuse, reject, deny, decline, turn down [*slang*], dissent, etc., 489; negative, withhold one's assent, grudge, begrudge; stand aloof, be deaf to, turn one's back upon, discountenance, forswear, set aside.

resist, repel, repulse, rebuff, deny oneself, discard, repudiate, rescind, disclaim, protest.

Adj. uncomplying, deaf to, noncompliant, unconsenting; recusant, dissentient.

Adv. on no account, not for the world, not on your life! [*colloq.*].

765. REQUEST.—*N.* request, requisition; claim, demand, etc., 741; petition, suit, prayer, solicitation, invitation, entreaty, importunity, supplication, invocation.

motion, overture, application, canvass, address, appeal, imprecation; proposal, proposition.

V. request, ask, beg, crave, sue, pray, petition, solicit, canvass, invite, beg leave, beg a boon, apply to, call to, call for; make a request, make application, claim, demand; offer up prayers.

entreat, beseech, plead, supplicate, implore; conjure, adjure; apostrophize, cry to, kneel to, appeal to; invoke, evoke; press, urge, importune, dun, clamor for, cry aloud, cry for help.

Adj. importunate, clamorous, urgent, solicitous; cap in hand.

Adv. please, prithee, do, pray; be so good as, be good enough; have the goodness, vouchsafe, will you, I pray thee, if you please.

766. [Negative request] DEPRECATION.—*N.* deprecation, expostulation; intercession, mediation, protest, remonstrance.

V. deprecate, protest, expostulate, enter a protest, remonstrate.

Adj. **deprecatory**, expostulatory, intercessory.

unsought, unbesought; unasked.

767. PETITIONER.—*N.* petitioner, solicitor, applicant, suppliant, supplicant, suitor, candidate, claimant, aspirant, competitor, bidder; place hunter.

salesman, drummer, etc., 758; canvasser.

beggar, mendicant, panhandler [*slang*], cadger.

hotel runner, runner [*both cant*], steerer [*colloq.*], barker [*colloq.*].

sycophant, parasite, etc. (*servility*), 886.

768. PROMISE.—*N.* promise, undertaking, word, troth, plight, pledge, parole, word of honor, vow, oath, profession, assurance, warranty, guarantee, insurance, obligation, contract, stipulation.

engagement, affiance, betrothal, marriage contract (*or* vow); plighted faith.

V. **promise**, undertake, engage; make (*or* form, enter into) an engagement; bind (*or* pledge) oneself; vow, swear, give (*or* pledge) one's word; betroth, plight faith.

assure, warrant, guarantee, covenant, agree, vouch for, attest; answer for, be answerable for; secure, give security, underwrite.

Adj. **promissory**, votive, under hand and seal, upon oath, upon affirmation.

promised, affianced, pledged, bound, committed, compromised.

Adv. as true as I live; in all soberness; upon my honor; my word for it.

769. COMPACT.—*N.* compact, contract, specialty, deal [*colloq.*], agreement, bargain; pact, bond, covenant, indenture [*law*]; stipulation, settlement, convention; compromise, negotiation.

treaty, protocol, concordat, charter, Magna Charta, pragmatic sanction.

ratification, completion, signature, seal, bond.

V. **contract**, covenant, agree for; engage, etc. (*promise*), 768.

negotiate, treat, stipulate, make terms; bargain.

conclude, close, close with, complete, strike a bargain; come to terms (*or* an understanding); compromise, settle; confirm, ratify, clinch, subscribe, underwrite; indorse, sign, seal.

Adj. **contractual**, complete, agreed; signed, sealed, and delivered.

Adv. **as agreed upon**, as promised, according to the contract.

770. CONDITIONS.—*N.* conditions, terms, articles, articles of agreement; memorandum, clauses, provisions, proviso, covenant, stipulation, obligation, ultimatum.

V. **condition**, stipulate, insist upon, make a point of; bind, tie up; fence in, hedge in, make (*or* come to) terms.

Adj. conditional, provisional, guarded, fenced, hedged in.

Adv. conditionally, provisionally, on condition; with a string to it [*colloq.*], with a reservation.

771. SECURITY.—*N.* security, guaranty, guarantee; gage, bond, tie, pledge, mortgage, debenture; bill of sale, lien, collateral, bail, stake, deposit, earnest.

promissory note; bill, bill of exchange; I O U; personal security, covenant.

acceptance, indorsement, signature, execution, stamp, seal.

sponsor, surety, bail, hostage; godchild, godfather, godmother.

authentication, verification, warrant, certificate, voucher, receipt.

deed, instrument, title deed, indenture; charter, paper, parchment, settlement, will, testament, codicil.

V. give security, give bail, go bail; pawn, put in pawn, pledge, mortgage.

guarantee, warrant, assure; accept, indorse, underwrite, insure.

execute, stamp; sign, seal.

Adj. pledged, pawned, in pawn, at stake, on deposit, as earnest.

772. OBSERVANCE.—*N.* observance, performance, compliance, acquiescence, concurrence; obedience, etc., 743; fulfillment, satisfaction, discharge; acquittance, acquittal; adhesion, ackowledgment; fidelity.

V. observe, comply with, respect, acknowledge, abide by; cling to, adhere to, be faithful to, act up to; meet, fulfill, carry out, execute, perform, discharge, keep one's word (*or* pledge).

Adj. observant, faithful, true, loyal, honorable, etc., 939; punctual, punctilious, scrupulous, as good as one's word.

Adv. to the letter.

773. NONOBSERVANCE.—*N.* nonobservance, noncompliance, evasion, failure, omission, neglect, slackness, laxness, laxity, informality; lawlessness, disobedience, etc., 742; bad faith, etc., 940.

infringement, infraction; violation, transgression; piracy, literary theft.

V. evade, fail, neglect, omit, elude, cut [*colloq.*], set aside, ignore; shut (*or* close) one's eyes to.

infringe, transgress, violate, steal, pirate [*a book, etc.*].

discard, repudiate, protest, nullify, declare null and void, cancel, forfeit.

Adj. elusive, evasive, slack, lax, casual, slippery; nonobservant.

774. COMPROMISE.—*N.* compromise, composition, middle term, compensation, adjustment, mutual concession.

V. compromise, commute, compound, split the difference, meet one halfway, give and take, come to terms, submit to arbitration, patch up, arrange, straighten out, adjust, agree, make the best of, make a virtue of necessity.

Possessive Relations[1]

(1) Property

775. ACQUISITION.—*N.* acquisition, procurement; purchase, inheritance; gift, etc., 784.

recovery, redemption, salvage, find.

gain, thrift, money-making, pelf, lucre, filthy lucre, the main chance.

profit, earnings, wages, salary, emolument, income, remuneration; winnings, pickings, perquisite; proceeds, produce, product; outcome, output; return, fruit, crop, harvest; benefit; prize; wealth, etc., 803.

V. acquire, get, gain, win, earn, obtain, procure, gather; collect, pick, pick up, glean, find, light upon, come across, come at; scrape up (*or* together); get in, net, bag, secure; derive, draw, get in the harvest.

profit, turn to profit (*or* account), make capital out of, make money by, obtain a return, reap the fruits of; gain an advantage; make (*or* coin, raise) money, raise funds; realize, clear, produce, take, receive, come by, inherit.

recover, get back, regain, retrieve, redeem.

Adj. profitable, productive, advantageous, gainful, remunerative, paying, lucrative.

Adv. in the way of gain; for money; at interest.

776. LOSS.—*N.* loss, forfeiture, lapse; privation, bereavement, deprivation, riddance; damage, squandering, waste.

V. lose, incur a loss, miss, mislay, let slip, be deprived of, be without, forfeit.

squander, lavish, get rid of, waste.

Adj. bereft, bereaved, deprived of, shorn of, denuded, minus [*colloq., exc. in math.*], cut off; rid of, quit of, out of pocket, lost.

777. POSSESSION.—*N.* possession, ownership, proprietorship, occupancy, hold, holding, tenure, tenancy, dependency.

exclusive possession, monopoly, retention, corner.

future possession, heritage, inheritance, heirship, reversion; primogeniture.

V. possess, have, hold, occupy, enjoy, be possessed of, own, command, inherit.

[1]That is, relations which concern property.

monopolize, corner, engross, forestall, appropriate.

belong to, appertain to, pertain to; be in one's possession, vest in.

Adj. possessing, worth, possessed of, master of, in possession of; endowed (*or* blest, fraught, laden, charged) with.

possessed, on hand, in hand, in store, in stock; at one's command, at one's disposal.

777a. EXEMPTION.—*N.* exemption, exception, immunity, privilege, release.

V. not have, not possess, not own, be without.

Adj. devoid of, exempt from, without, unpossessed of, unblest with; immune from.

unpossessed; untenanted, vacant, without an owner.

778. [Joint possession] PARTICIPATION.—*N.* participation, joint tenancy; joint (*or* common) stock; partnership; communion; community of possessions, communism, collectivism, socialism; co-operation.

participator, sharer, partner; shareholder; joint tenant; tenants in common; coheir.

communist, communalist, collectivist, socialist.

V. participate, partake, share, share in, join in, go shares, go cahoots [*slang*], go halves; share and share alike.

communize, communalize; have (*or* possess) in common.

Adj. communistic, socialistic; co-operative, profit-sharing.

Adv. in common, share and share alike; on shares.

779. POSSESSOR.—*N.* possessor, holder, occupant, occupier, tenant, tenant at will, lessee, lodger.

owner; proprietor, proprietress, master, mistress, lord.

landholder, landowner, landlord, landlady; lord of the manor, laird [*Scot.*], landed gentry.

Future possessor: heir, heir apparent, heir presumptive; inheritor, heiress, inheritrix.

780. PROPERTY.—*N.* property, possession, tenure; ownership, etc., 777.

estate, interest, right, title, claim, demand, holding, vested interest; use, trust, benefit; term, lease, settlement; remainder, reversion.

dower, dowry, jointure, inheritance, heritage, patrimony, legacy.

assets, belongings, means, resources, circumstances; wealth, etc., 803; money, etc., 800; estate and effects.

realty, real estate, land, lands, landed (*or* real) property; tenements; plant, fixtures; ground; freehold, copyhold, leasehold.

manor, domain, demesne; farm, plantation, ranch.

territory, state, kingdom, principality, realm, empire, protectorate, dependency, sphere of influence, mandate.

personalty, personal property (or estate, effects), chattels, goods, effects, movables: stock, stock in trade, things, paraphernalia, equipage, appurtenances; income, etc., 810.

baggage, luggage [esp. in Eng.], impedimenta, bag and baggage; cargo.

V. possess, etc., 777; be the possessor, own; inherit.

Adj. landed, hereditary, entailed, real, personal.

Adv. to one's credit, to one's account; to the good.

781. RETENTION.—*N.* retention, detention, custody; tenacity, firm hold, grasp, gripe, grip, clutches, talon, claw, fang, tentacle.

captive, prisoner, bird in hand.

V. retain, keep, hold, hold fast, clinch, clench, clutch, grasp, gripe, hug; secure, withhold, detain; hold (or keep) back; husband, reserve; have (or keep) in stock; entail, tie up, settle.

Adj. retentive, tenacious.

782. RIDDANCE.—*N.* riddance, relinquishment, abandonment, renunciation, dereliction; cession, surrender, dispensation; resignation.

derelict, jetsam; abandoned farm [U. S.]; waif, foundling.

V. relinquish, give up, surrender, yield, cede; let go, let slip; spare, drop, resign, forego, renounce, abandon, give away, dispose of, part with; lay aside, set aside, discard, cast off, dismiss; maroon.

cast (or throw, fling) away, jettison.

supersede, give notice to quit, give warning; be (or get) rid of; eject.

divorce, cut off, desert, disinherit; separate.

Adj. relinquished, cast off, derelict; disowned, disinherited, divorced.

783. TRANSFER [of property].—*N.* transfer, conveyance, assignment, alienation, conveyancing, transmission, sale, lease, release, exchange, barter; succession, reversion.

V. transfer, convey, alienate, assign, grant, consign; make over, hand over, transmit, negotiate; hand down; exchange.

change hands, devolve, succeed; require, come into possession.

disinherit; dispossess, etc., 789; substitute.

Adj. transferable, alienable, negotiable, reversional, transmissive; inherited.

784. GIVING.—*N.* giving, bestowal, presentation, concession, cession; delivery, consignment, dispensation, endowment; investment, investiture; award, recompense, etc., 973.

charity, almsgiving, liberality, generosity.

gift, donation, present, boon, favor, benefaction, grant, offering, bonus, oblation, sacrifice.

allowance, contribution, subscription, subsidy, tribute.

bequest, legacy, devise, will, dot, dowry, dower.

gratuity, alms, largess, bounty, dole, help, offertory, honorarium, Christmas box, tip, baksheesh, consideration.

bribe, bait, peace offering; graft [*colloq.*].

giver, grantor, donor, testator; investor, subscriber, contributor; fairy godmother.

V. deliver, hand, pass, assign, hand (*or* make, deliver, turn) over.

pay, etc., 807; render, impart, communicate.

concede, cede, yield, part with, shed; spend, sacrifice.

give, bestow, donate, confer, grant; accord, award, assign, offer; present, give away, dispense, dispose of; give (*or* deal) out, fork out [*slang*]; allow, contribute, subscribe.

invest, endow, settle upon; bequeath, leave, devise.

furnish, supply, help, administer to, afford, spare, accommodate with, indulge with, favor with; lavish, pour on, thrust upon.

bribe, tip; grease the palm [*slang*].

Adj. charitable, eleemosynary, tributary; gratis, etc., 815; donative.

785. RECEIVING.—*N.* receiving, acquisition, etc., 775; reception, acceptance, admission.

recipient, receiver; assignee, legatee, grantee, lessee; beneficiary, pensioner.

income, etc. (*receipt*), 810.

V. receive; take, etc., 789; pocket; acquire, etc., 775; admit, take in, catch, accept.

be received; come in, come to hand, go into one's pocket; fall to one's lot (*or* share), accrue.

Adj. receiving, recipient; stipendiary, pensionary.

received, given, allowed; secondhand.

786. APPORTIONMENT.—*N.* apportionment, allotment, consignment, assignment, allocation, appropriation; distribution, division, deal; partition, administration.

portion, dividend, share, allotment, lot, measure, dose; dole, meed, pittance; ration; ratio, proportion, quota, modicum, allowance.

V. apportion, divide; distribute, administer, dispense; allot, allocate, detail, cast, share, mete; portion (*or* parcel, dole) out; deal, carve.

partition, assign, appropriate, appoint.

Adv. respectively, each to each; by lot; in equal shares.

787. LENDING.—*N.* lending, loan, advance, accommodation, mortgage, etc., 771; investment.

lender, pawnbroker, my uncle [*slang*], moneylender, usurer, Shylock.

V. **lend,** advance, accommodate with; lend on security; loan; pawn.

invest, intrust, place (*or* put) out to interest; place, put; embark, risk, venture, sink.

let, lease, sublet, sublease.

Adv. in advance; on loan, on security.

788. BORROWING.—*N.* **borrowing,** pledging, pawning.

V. **borrow,** pledge, pawn, put up the spout [*slang*], raise money, raise the wind [*slang*]; run into debt.

hire, rent, farm; take a lease.

appropriate, adopt, apply, imitate, make use of, take; plagiarize, pirate.

789. TAKING.—*N.* **taking,** reception, appropriation, capture, apprehension, seizure; abduction, abstraction.

dispossession; deprivation, bereavement, disinheritance; attachment, execution, sequestration, confiscation, eviction.

rapacity, rapaciousness, extortion, bloodsucking; theft, etc.,791.

taker, captor, capturer; extortioner *or* extortionist; vampire.

V. **take,** catch, hook, bag, sack, pocket, receive, accept.

reap, crop, cull, pluck, gather, draw.

appropriate, assume, possess oneself of; commandeer [*colloq.*]; help oneself to, make free with, lay under contribution; intercept, scramble for; deprive of.

seize, snatch, abstract, take away (*or* off), run away with; abduct, kidnap, capture, steal, pounce (*or* spring) upon; swoop down upon; take by storm; take prisoner; grapple, embrace, grip, gripe, clasp, grab [*colloq.*], clutch, collar, throttle, claw.

dispossess, take from, take away from; tear from, tear away from, wrench (*or* wrest, wring) from, extort; deprive of, bereave; disinherit, oust, evict, eject, divest; levy, distrain [*law*], confiscate; sequester, sequestrate, usurp; despoil, strip, fleece, bleed [*colloq.*].

Adj. **predatory,** wolfish, rapacious, ravening, ravenous; parasitic; all-devouring, all-engulfing.

790. RESTITUTION.—*N.* **restitution,** return, restoration, reinstatement, reinvestment, rehabilitation, reparation, atonement; compensation, indemnification; recovery.

V. **restore,** return, give back, render, give up, let go, release, remit; disgorge, recoup, reimburse, compensate, indemnify, reinvest, reinstate, rehabilitate, repair, make good.

recover, get back, retrieve, redeem; take back again.

Adj. **compensatory,** indemnificatory; reversionary, redemptive.

Adv. in full restitution; as partial compensation; to atone for.

791. STEALING.—*N.* stealing, theft, thievery, robbery, rapacity, thievishness, abstraction, appropriation, plagiarism, depredation; kidnaping.

pillage, spoliation, plunder, sack, rapine, brigandage, highway robbery, holdup [*slang*]; raid, foray, piracy, privateering, buccaneering, filibustering; burglary, housebreaking; shoplifting, blackmail.

peculation, embezzlement, fraud, forgery, larceny, pilfering; kleptomania.

V. steal, thieve, rob, purloin, pilfer, filch, bag, crib [*colloq.*], palm; abstract; appropriate, plagiarize.

abduct, convey away, carry off, kidnap, impress, make (*or* run) off with, run away with, spirit away, seize.

plunder, pillage, filibuster, rifle, sack, loot, ransack, spoil, despoil, strip, sweep, gut, forage, levy blackmail, maraud, poach, smuggle, bunko; hold up.

swindle, peculate, embezzle; sponge, pluck, fleece, defraud, obtain under false pretenses.

counterfeit, forge, coin, circulate bad money.

Adj. thievish, light-fingered, piratical; predatory, raptorial.

792. THIEF.—*N.* thief, robber, spoiler, depredator, pillager, marauder; pilferer, plagiarist; harpy, shark [*slang*], smuggler, poacher, kidnaper; crook [*slang*], shoplifter.

pirate, corsair, viking, buccaneer, privateer.

brigand, bandit, filibuster, freebooter, thug, cattle thief, bushranger, mosstrooper [*hist.*], highwayman, footpad, strong-arm man.
pickpocket, cutpurse, light-fingered gentry; sharper; cardsharper, trickster.
swindler, peculator, forger, coiner, counterfeiter; fence, receiver of stolen goods.
burglar, housebreaker, yegg [*slang*], cracksman [*slang*], sneak thief; second-story thief (*or* man).

793. BOOTY.—*N.* booty, spoil, plunder, prize, prey, loot, swag [*cant*]; perquisite, boodle [*polit. cant*], graft [*colloq.*], pork barrel [*polit. cant*], pickings; blackmail; stolen goods.

Adj. looting, plundering, spoliative.

794. BARTER.—*N.* barter, exchange, interchange, Indian gift [*colloq.*].

trade, commerce, buying and selling, traffic, business, custom, transaction, negotiation, bargain; speculation, jobbing, stock-jobbing.

free trade [*opp. to* protection].

V. barter, exchange, truck, swap *or* swop [*colloq. and dial.*]; interchange.

trade, traffic, buy and sell, give and take, carry on (*or* ply) a trade; deal in, speculate.

bargain; drive (*or* make, strike) a bargain; negotiate, bid for; haggle, stickle, dicker, cheapen, beat down, underbid; outbid.

Adj. commercial, mercantile, trading; marketable, staple, in the market, for sale; at a bargain, marked down; retail; wholesale.

Adv. across the counter; in the marts of trade.

795. PURCHASE.—*N.* purchase, buying, purchasing, shopping.
buyer, purchaser, client, customer, patron, clientele.

V. buy, purchase, invest in, procure; shop, market, go a-shopping; rent, hire, repurchase, buy in.

796. SALE.—*N.* sale, disposal; auction, custom.
salableness, salability, marketability, vendibility.
seller, vender, vendor [*law*]; merchant, auctioneer.
salesmanship, selling ability.

V. sell, vend, dispose of, make a sale, effect a sale; auction, sell at auction, put up to (*or* at) auction; hawk, dump, unload, place, undersell; dispense, offer, retail; deal in, sell off (*or* out), turn into money, realize.

Adj. salable, marketable, staple, in demand, popular.
unsalable, unpurchased, unbought, on the shelves, on one's hands.

797. MERCHANT.—*N.* merchant, trader, dealer, salesman; money-changer, shopkeeper, shopman; tradesman, tradespeople, tradesfolk.

peddler, hawker, huckster, sutler, vivandière; costermonger; canvasser, solicitor; faker [*slang*].

moneylender, usurer, banker; money-changer, money broker. jobber, broker; buyer, seller; bear, bull [*Stock Exchange*].

firm, company, house, corporation, concern, trust.

798. MERCHANDISE.—*N.* merchandise, ware, commodity, effects, goods, article, stock, produce, staple commodity; stock in trade, cargo.

799. MART.—*N.* mart, market, market place; fair, bazaar, exchange, stock exchange, Wheat Pit [*Chicago*]; bourse, curb.

shop, store, department store, chain store, warehouse, depot, emporium, establishment; stall, booth; office, chambers, counting-house, bureau; counter.

(2) Monetary Relations

800. MONEY.—*N.* money, finance, funds, treasure, capital, stock; assets, wealth, etc., 803; supplies, ways and means, wherewithal *or* wherewith, sinews of war, almighty dollar, cash.

solvency, responsibility, reliability, solidity, soundness.

sum, amount; balance, balance sheet; sum total; proceeds, receipts.

currency, circulating medium, specie, coin, piece, hard cash; dollar, sterling; pounds, shillings, and pence, £ s. d.; guinea; wallet, roll, wad [*slang*], purse, ready money.

precious metals, gold, silver, copper, bullion, ingot, bar, nugget.

petty cash, pocket money, pin money, spending money, change, small coin.

wampum.

great wealth, money to burn [*colloq.*]; power *or* mint of money [*colloq.*], good sum, millions, thousands.

Science of coins: numismatics.

paper money; bill, money order; note, note of hand; bank note, promissory note; I O U, bond; bill of exchange; draft, check, order, warrant, coupon, debenture, greenback.

V. total, amount to, come to, mount up to.

issue, utter, circulate; fiscalize, monetize.

demonetize, deprive of standard value; cease to issue.

Adj. monetary, pecuniary, fiscal, financial; sterling.

solvent, sound, substantial, good, reliable, responsible, solid, having a good rating; able to pay 100 cents to the dollar.

801. TREASURER.—*N.* treasurer, bursar, purser, banker, financier; receiver, liquidator, steward, trustee, accountant, expert accountant, almoner, paymaster, cashier, teller; money-changer.

802. TREASURY.—*N.* treasury, bank, exchequer, bursary; strongbox, stronghold, strong room; coffer, chest, safe, depository, cash register, cashbox, money box, till.

purse, moneybag, pocketbook, wallet; pocket.

securities, stocks; public stocks (*or* funds, securities); bonds, government bonds, Liberty bonds [U. S.], gilt-edged securities.

803. WEALTH.—*N.* wealth, riches, fortune, opulence, affluence; easy circumstances; independence, competence.

capital, money; great wealth, bonanza, El Dorado; philosopher's stone; the golden touch.

pelf, mammon, lucre, filthy lucre.

means, resources, substance, command of money; property, income, livelihood.

rich man, moneyed man, man of substance; capitalist, millionaire, multimillionaire, plutocrat; nabob, Croesus, Midas.

V. be rich, roll (*or* wallow) in wealth, have money to burn [*colloq.*]; afford, well afford, command money.

become rich, fill one's pocket, feather one's nest, make a fortune; make money; worship mammon, worship the golden calf.

Adj. wealthy, rich, affluent, opulent, moneyed, well-to-do, well off, rolling in riches.

804. POVERTY.—*N.* poverty, indigence, penury, pauperism, destitution, want; need, neediness; lack, necessity, privation, distress, difficulties, wolf at the door, straits; low water [*slang*], impecuniosity.

mendicancy, beggary, mendicity; broken (*or* loss of) fortune; insolvency.

poor man, pauper, mendicant, beggar.

V. be poor, want, lack, starve, live from hand to mouth, have seen better days, go to rack and ruin; beg one's bread, run into debt.

impoverish, reduce, reduce to poverty, pauperize, fleece, ruin.

Adj. poor, indigent; poverty-stricken, badly off, moneyless, penniless; impecunious, short of money, hard up, seedy [*colloq.*]; barefooted, beggarly, beggared, destitute, reduced, needy, necessitous, distressed, pinched, straitened, embarrassed, involved, insolvent.

805. CREDIT.—*N.* credit, trust, score, tally, account.

paper credit, letter of credit, circular note; duplicate; mortgage. lien, draft, securities.

creditor, lender, lessor [*law*], mortgagee; dun, usurer.

V. credit, accredit, intrust, keep (*or* run up) an account with; place to one's credit (*or* account); give *or* take) credit.

Adj. accredited; of good credit, of unlimited credit; well rated; credited.

Adv. on credit, to the account of, to the credit of.

806. DEBT.—*N.* debt, obligation, liability, debit, score.

arrears, deferred payment, deficit, default, insolvency; bad debt.

interest; premium, usury.

debtor; mortgagor, defaulter, borrower.

V. be in debt, owe; incur (*or* contract) a debt, run up a bill, (*or* an account); borrow, run into debt, be in difficulties.

answer for, go bail for; back one's note.

Adj. liable, chargeable, answerable for.

indebted, in debt, in embarrassed circumstances, in difficulties; encumbered, involved; insolvent.

unpaid; unrequited, unrewarded; owing, due, in arrear, outstanding.

807. PAYMENT.—*N.* payment, discharge, settlement, clearance, liquidation, satisfaction, reckoning, arrangement.

acknowledgment, release; receipt, voucher.

repayment, reimbursement, retribution; pay, money paid.

V. pay, defray, make payment; pay one's way, expend, put down, lay down; discharge, settle, foot the bill [*colloq.*]; settle with, satisfy, pay in full, clear, liquidate, pay up; cash, honor a bill, acknowledge; redeem.

repay, refund, reimburse, disgorge, make repayment.

Adj. out of debt, owing nothing, all clear, clear of debt, above-water; solvent.

Adv. money down, cash down, cash on delivery, C.O.D.

808. NONPAYMENT.—*N.* nonpayment; default, defalcation; protest, repudiation.

insolvency, bankruptcy, failure; run upon a bank; overdrawn account.

defaulter, bankrupt, insolvent, insolvent debtor; absconder, welsher [*slang*].

V. not pay, fail, break, stop payment; become insolvent (*or* bankrupt), swindle, run up bills.

protest, dishonor, repudiate, nullify.

Adj. in debt, behindhand, in arrear; beggared, insolvent, bankrupt, ruined.

809. EXPENDITURE.—*N.* expenditure, outgoings, outlay, expenses, disbursement; circulation.

Money paid: payment, etc., 807; pay, etc. (*remuneration*), 973; fee, footing, subsidy, tribute, ransom, bribe, donation, gift; investment; purchase.

deposit, earnest, installment.

V. expend, spend; run (*or* get) through, pay, disburse; lay out, fork out [*slang*]; invest, sink money.

reward, fee, remunerate; give, subscribe, subsidize; bribe.

Adj. lavish, free, liberal; beyond one's income.

expensive, costly, dear, high-priced, precious, high.

810. RECEIPT.—*N.* receipt, value received, income, revenue, return, proceeds; earnings.

rent, rent roll; rental.

premium, bonus, prize, drawings, handout [*slang*].

pension, annuity, pittance, jointure, alimony.

V. receive, get, be in receipt of, have coming in; take money; draw from, derive from; acquire, take.

yield, bring in, afford, pay, return; accrue.

Adj. remunerative, profitable, gainful, well paying, interest-bearing, well invested.

Adv. within one's income.

811. ACCOUNTS.—*N.* accounts, money matters, finance, budget, bill, score, reckoning, account.

bookkeeping, audit, single entry, double entry; ledger, cash-book, journal; balance sheet; receipts, assets; expenditure, liabilities; profit and loss account (*or* statement).

accountant, auditor, actuary, bookkeeper; expert accountant, certified accountant; bank examiner.

V. keep accounts, enter, post, post up, book, credit, debit, balance.

812. PRICE.—*N.* price, amount, cost, expense, charge, figure, demand, fare, hire; wages.

dues, duty, toll, tax, impost, tariff, levy; capitation, poll tax; custom, excise, assessment, taxation, tithe, ransom, salvage, towage; brokerage, wharfage, freightage.

worth, rate, value, par value, valuation, appraisement, money's worth; price current, market price, quotation.

V. price, set (*or* fix) a price, appraise, assess, charge, demand, ask, require, exact.

fetch, sell for, cost, bring in, yield, afford.

Adj. taxable, dutiable, assessable.

813. DISCOUNT.—*N.* discount, abatement, concession, reduction, depreciation, allowance, qualification, setoff, drawback, percentage, rebate.

V. discount, bate, rebate, abate, deduct, strike off, mark down, reduce, take off, allow, give, make allowance; depreciate.

Adv. at a discount, at a bargain, below par.

814. DEARNESS.—*N.* dearness, expensiveness, costliness, high price; overcharge, extravagance, exorbitance, extortion.

V. overcharge, bleed [*colloq.*], skin [*slang*], fleece, extort, profiteer.

pay too much, pay dearly, pay through the nose [*colloq.*].

Adj. dear, high, high-priced, expensive, costly, precious; extravagant, exorbitant, extortionate.

at a premium, beyond price, above price; priceless, of priceless value.

Adv. dear, dearly; at great cost, at heavy cost, at a high price.

815. CHEAPNESS.—*N.* cheapness, low price, depreciation, bargain, drug in the market.

V. be cheap, cost little; come down (*or* fall) in price, be marked down.

buy at a bargain, buy dirt-cheap, have one's money's worth; beat down, cheapen.

Adj. cheap, low-priced, low, moderate, reasonable, inexpensive, cheap at the price; dirt-cheap, catchpenny.

reduced, half-price, depreciated, shopworn, marked down, unsalable.

gratuitous, gratis, free, for nothing; costless, without charge, scot-free, complimentary, honorary.

Adv. at a bargain, for a mere song; at cost price, at prime cost.

816. LIBERALITY.—*N.* liberality, generosity, munificence;

bounty, bounteousness, hospitality, charity, open (*or* free) hand, open (*or* large) heart.

cheerful giver, free giver, patron; benefactor.

V. **be liberal**, spend freely; shower down upon, spare no expense, give with both hands; keep open house.

Adj. **liberal**, free, generous. charitable, hospitable; bountiful, bounteous, ample, handsome; unsparing, ungrudging; unselfish; open-handed, large-hearted; munificent, princely.

Adv. ungrudgingly; with open hands, with both hands.

817. ECONOMY.—*N.* **economy**, frugality; thrift, thriftiness; care, husbandry, retrenchment.

savings; prevention of waste, save-all; parsimony, etc., 819.

V. **economize**, save; retrench, cut down expenses; make both ends meet, meet one's expenses, pay one's way; husband, save (*or* invest) money; provide against a rainy day.

Adj. **economical**, frugal, careful, thrifty, saving, chary, spare, sparing; parsimonious, etc., 819; sufficient; plain.

818. PRODIGALITY.—*N.* **prodigality**, wastefulness, unthriftiness, waste; profusion, profuseness; extravagance, lavishness.

prodigal, spendthrift, waster, high roller [*slang*], squanderer, spender, prodigal son.

V. **squander**, lavish, sow broadcast, pay through the nose, spill, waste, dissipate, exhaust, drain, overdraw, spend money like water.

Adj. **prodigal**, profuse, thriftless, unthrifty, improvident, wasteful, extravagant, lavish, dissipated; penny-wise and pound-foolish.

Adv. with an unsparing hand.

819. PARSIMONY.—*N.* **parsimony**, parsimoniousness, stinginess, stint, illiberality, avarice, avidity, rapacity, extortion, venality, cupidity, selfishness.

miser, niggard, churl, screw, skinflint, curmudgeon, harpy, extortioner, extortionist, usurer.

V. **grudge**, begrudge, stint, pinch, gripe, screw, dole out, hold back, withhold, starve, famish.

drive a bargain, cheapen, beat down; have an itching palm, grasp, grab.

Adj. **parsimonious**, penurious, stingy, miserly, mean, shabby, near, niggardly, close, sparing, grudging, illiberal, ungenerous, churlish, sordid, mercenary, venal, covetous, avaricious; greedy, grasping, extortionate, rapacious.

Adv. with a sparing hand.

CLASS VI

Words Relating to the SENTIENT and MORAL POWERS

I. AFFECTIONS IN GENERAL

820. AFFECTIONS.—*N.* **character,** qualities, disposition, affections, nature, spirit, temper, temperament, idiosyncrasy, predilection, turn of mind, bent, bias, predisposition, proneness, proclivity, propensity, vein, humor, mood, sympathy.

soul, heart, bosom, inner man; inmost recesses of the heart.

passion, pervading spirit; ruling passion, fullness of the heart.

energy, fervor, fire, verve, force.

Adj. **characterized,** affected, formed, molded, cast, tempered; framed.

prone, predisposed, disposed, inclined; having a bias.

inborn, inbred, ingrained; deep-rooted, congenital, inherent.

Adv. at heart; in the vein, in the mood.

821. FEELING.—*N.* **feeling,** suffering, endurance, sufferance, response; sympathy, impression, inspiration, affection, sensation, emotion, pathos.

fervor, unction, gusto, vehemence, heartiness, cordiality, earnestness, eagerness, gush [*colloq.*], ardor, warmth, zeal, passion, enthusiasm, ecstasy.

excitement; thrill, shock, agitation, quiver, flutter, flurry, fluster, twitter, tremor, throb, throbbing, pulsation, palpitation, panting; blush, flush.

V. **feel,** receive an impression, be impressed with, respond, enter into the spirit of.

bear, suffer, support, sustain, endure, brook, brave, stand, abide, experience, taste, prove.

be agitated, be excited, glow, flush, blush, crimson, change color, mantle; darken, whiten, pale, tingle, thrill, heave, pant, throb, palpitate, tremble, quiver, flutter, shake, stagger, reel; wince.

Adj. **sentient,** sensuous, emotional; of (*or* with) feeling.

keen, sharp, lively, quick, acute, cutting, piercing, incisive, trenchant, pungent, racy, piquant, poignant, caustic.

impressive, deep, profound, indelible, deep-felt, heartfelt, soul-stirring, electric, thrilling, rapturous, ecstatic, rapt; pervading, penetrating, absorbing.

earnest, wistful, eager, fervent, fervid, gushing [*colloq.*], warm, passionate, hearty, cordial, sincere, zealous, enthusiastic, glowing, ardent.

rabid, raving, feverish, fanatical, hysterical, impetuous.

Adv. heartily, heart and soul, from the bottom of one's heart, devoutly.

822. SENSITIVENESS.—*N.* sensitiveness, sensibleness, sensibility, impressibility, susceptibility, vivacity, tenderness, sentimentality, sentimentalism.

excitability, etc., 825; physical sensibility, etc., 375.

V. be sensitive, have a tender heart; take to heart, shrink, wince, blench, quiver.

Adj. sensitive, sensible, impressible, impressionable; susceptive, susceptible; warmhearted, tenderhearted, softhearted, tender; sentimental, romantic; enthusiastic, impassioned, spirited, mettlesome, vivacious, lively, expressive, mobile, excitable, oversensitive, thin-skinned, fastidious.

Adv. to the quick, on the raw.

823. INSENSITIVENESS.—*N.* insensitiveness, insensibility, insensibleness, inertness, inertia, impassibility, impassivity, apathy, dullness, insusceptibility, lukewarmness.

coldness, coolness, frigidity, stoicism, nonchalance, unconcern, indifference, callousness, heart of stone.

torpor, torpidity, lethargy, coma, trance; sleep, stupor, stupefaction; paralysis, numbness.

stoic, Indian, man of iron.

V. be insensitive, not mind, not care, not be affected by; take no interest in; disregard.

blunt, numb, benumb, paralyze, deaden, stun, stupefy; brutalize.

inure; harden, steel, caseharden, sear.

Adj. insensitive, insensible, unconscious, impassive, insusceptible, unimpressible; passionless, spiritless, heartless, soulless, unfeeling.

apathetic, unemotional, phlegmatic; dull, frigid, cold, cold-blooded, coldhearted; inert, supine, sluggish, torpid, sleepy, languid, halfhearted; numb, numbed; comatose.

indifferent, lukewarm, careless, mindless, inattentive, unconcerned, nonchalant.

unaffected, unruffled, unimpressed, unexcited, unmoved, unstirred, untouched, unshocked, unblushing.

callous, thick-skinned, impervious, hard, hardened, inured, casehardened; imperturbable, unfelt.

Adv. in cold blood; with dry eyes.

824. EXCITEMENT.—*N.* excitement, excitation, stimulation, piquancy, provocation, inspiration, animation, agitation, perturbation; fascination, intoxication, impressiveness; irritation, passion, thrill.

emotional appeal, melodrama, sensationalism, yellow journalism.

V. **excite,** affect, touch, move, impress, strike, interest, animate, inspire, smite, infect, awake, wake; awaken, waken; call forth; evoke, provoke; raise up, summon up, call up, wake up, raise; rouse, arouse, stir, fire, kindle, enkindle, illumine, illuminate, inflame.

stimulate, inspirit; stir up, infuse life into, give new life to; introduce new blood, quicken; sharpen, whet, fillip; fan, foster, heat, warm, foment, revive, rekindle.

penetrate, pierce; go to one's heart, touch to the quick, possess the soul, rivet the attention; prey on the mind.

agitate, perturb, ruffle, fluster, flutter, flurry, shake, disturb, startle, shock, stagger, strike dumb, stun, astound, electrify, galvanize, petrify.

irritate, sting, cut, pique, infuriate, madden, lash into fury.

flare up, flash up, seethe, boil, simmer, foam, fume, flame, rage, rave.

Adj. **excited,** wrought up, overwrought, hot, red-hot, flushed, feverish; raging, flaming, ebullient, seething, foaming, fuming, stung to the quick; wild, raving, frantic, mad, distracted, beside oneself.

exciting, impressive, telling, warm, glowing, fervid, spirit-stirring, thrilling; soul-stirring, heart-stirring, agonizing, sensational, yellow [*colloq.*], melodramatic, hysterical; overpowering, overwhelming.

piquant, spicy, appetizing, stinging, provocative, tantalizing.

Adv. at a critical moment, under a sudden strain.

825. [Excess of sensitiveness] EXCITABILITY.—*N.* excitability, impetuosity, vehemence, boisterousness, turbulence; impatience, intolerance, irritability; disquiet, disquietude, restlessness, fidgets, agitation.

trepidation, perturbation, ruffle, hurry, fuss, flurry, fluster, flutter; ferment; whirl; stage fright, thrill.

passion, excitement, flush, heat, fever, fire, flame, fume, tumult, effervescence, ebullition; gust, storm, tempest; burst, fit, paroxysm, explosion, outbreak, scene, outburst; agony.

fury; violence, fierceness, rage, furor, desperation, madness, distraction, raving, delirium; frenzy, hysterics; intoxication; towering rage, anger, etc., 900.

fixed idea, monomania; fascination, infatuation; fanaticism; quixotism, quixotry.

V. fidget, fuss.

fume, rage, foam; bear ill, wince, chafe, champ the bit, lose one's temper, break out, burst out, fly out, explode, flare up, flame up, fire up, boil, rave, rant, tear, go into hysterics; run riot, run amuck; raise Cain [*slang*].

Adj. excitable, easily excited, mettlesome, high-mettled, skittish, high-strung, nervous, irritable, hasty, impatient, intolerant, moody; feverish, hysterical, delirious, mad.

restless, unquiet, mercurial, galvanic, fidgety, fussy.

vehement, demonstrative, violent, wild, furious, fierce, fiery, hotheaded; overzealous, enthusiastic, impassioned, fanatical; rabid, rampant, clamorous, uproarious, turbulent, tempestuous, boisterous.

impulsive, impetuous, passionate, uncontrolled, uncontrollable, ungovernable, irrepressible, volcanic.

Adv. in confusion, pellmell.

826. INEXCITABILITY.—*N.* inexcitability, imperturbability, even temper, tranquil mind, dispassion; toleration, tolerance, patience; passiveness, inertia, etc., 172; impassibility, etc. (*insensibility*), 823; stupefaction.

calmness, composure, placidity, *sang-froid* [F.], coolness, tranquillity, serenity, content; quiet, quietude; peace of mind.

equanimity, poise, staidness, gravity, sobriety, philosophy, stoicism, self-possession, self-control, self-command, self-restraint; presence of mind.

resignation, submission, sufferance, endurance, long-sufferance, forbearance, longanimity, fortitude, patience of Job, moderation, restraint.

V. endure, bear, go through, support, brave, disregard; tolerate, suffer, stand, bide; abide, bear with, put up with, acquiesce, submit, resign oneself to, brook, digest, eat, swallow, pocket, stomach; carry on, carry through; make light of, make the best of, put a good face on.

compose, appease, assuage, propitiate, repress, restrain, master one's feelings, set one's mind at ease (*or* rest), calm down, cool down.

Adj. inexcitable, imperturbable; unsusceptible, dispassionate, cold-blooded, enduring, stoical, philosophical, staid, sober, grave; sedate, demure, coolheaded, levelheaded.

easygoing, peaceful, placid, calm; quiet, tranquil, serene, cool, undemonstrative.

composed, collected, temperate, unstirred, unruffled, unperturbed.

meek, mild, tame, subdued, unoffended, unresisting, submissive, gentle, patient, tolerant, clement, long-suffering.

Adv. in cold blood; more in sorrow than in anger.

II. PERSONAL AFFECTIONS[1]

827. PLEASURE.—*N.* **pleasure,** gratification, enjoyment, delectation, relish, zest, gusto, satisfaction, complacency; well-being; good, etc., 618; comfort, ease, luxury; physical pleasure, etc., 377.

joy, gladness, delight, glee, cheer, sunshine; cheerfulness, etc., 836; treat, luxury; amusement, etc., 840.

happiness, felicity, bliss, beatitude, enchantment, transport, rapture, ecstasy; paradise, heaven.

V. **enjoy oneself,** joy, be in clover [*colloq.*], tread on enchanted ground; go into raptures; feel at home, breathe freely, bask in the sunshine.

enjoy, like, relish, be pleased with, derive pleasure from, take pleasure in, delight in, rejoice in, indulge in, gloat over, love; take to, take a fancy to [*both colloq.*].

Adj. **pleased,** gratified, glad, gladsome; comfortable, etc. (*physical pleasure*), 377; at ease; content, etc., 831.

happy, blessed, blissful, beatified, joyful, in raptures, in ecstasies.

overjoyed, entranced, enchanted; raptured, enraptured, ravished, transported; fascinated, captivated.

pleasing, delightful, ecstatic, beatific, painless, unalloyed, cloudless.

828. PAIN.—*N.* **pain,** mental suffering, dolor, suffering, ache; physical pain, etc., 378.

displeasure, dissatisfaction, discomfort, discomposure, disquiet; inquietude, uneasiness, discontent.

annoyance, irritation, worry; infliction, visitation; plague, bore; bother, vexation, mortification, chagrin.

care, anxiety, solicitude, concern, trouble, trial, ordeal, shock, blow, fret, burden, load.

grief, sorrow, distress, affliction, woe, bitterness, heartache, heavy (*or* aching, bleeding, broken) heart.

misery, unhappiness, infelicity, tribulation, wretchedness, desolation; despair, etc., 859; extremity, prostration, depth of misery, slough of despond; nightmare, incubus.

anguish, pang, agony, torture, torment; crucifixion, martyrdom, rack, hell upon earth; reign of terror.

sufferer, victim, prey, martyr, wretch, shorn lamb.

V. **suffer,** ail, feel (*or* suffer, undergo, bear, endure) pain, smart, ache, bleed, bear the cross; fall on evil days, come to grief.

fret, chafe, sit on thorns, wince, worry oneself, fret and fume; take to heart.

[1] Or those which concern one's own state of feeling.

grieve, mourn, lament, etc., 839; yearn, repine, pine, droop, languish, sink, despair, break one's heart.

Adj. pained, afflicted, suffering, worried, displeased, aching, griped, sore, raw, on the rack.

uneasy, uncomfortable, ill at ease; disturbed; discontented; weary, etc., 841.

unfortunate, etc., 735; doomed, devoted, accursed, undone, crushed, lost, stranded; victimized, ill-used.

unhappy, infelicitous, poor, wretched, miserable, woebegone, comfortless, cheerless, etc. (*dejected*), 837; careworn; heavy-laden, stricken.

sorry, concerned, sorrowful, cut up [*colloq.*], chagrined, horrified, horror-stricken; heartbroken, brokenhearted.

829. [Capability of giving pleasure] PLEASURABLENESS.— *N.* pleasurableness, pleasantness, agreeableness, pleasure giving, amusement, etc., 840; treat, etc. (*physical pleasure*), 377; dainty titbit, sweets, sweetmeats, nuts, salt, savor.

attraction, attractiveness, charm, fascination, captivation, enchantment, witchery, seduction, winning ways, winsomeness; loveliness, beauty, etc., 845.

V. delight, charm, gladden, bless, captivate, fascinate; enchant, entrance, enrapture, transport, bewitch, ravish.

please, satisfy, gratify, satiate, quench, indulge, humor, flatter, tickle; tickle the palate, refresh, enliven, treat, amuse, take one's fancy; attract, allure; stimulate, excite, interest.

Adj. pleasurable, pleasure-giving, pleasing, pleasant, amiable, agreeable, grateful, gratifying; acceptable; dear, beloved, welcome, favorite.

refreshing, comfortable, cordial, genial, glad, gladsome; sweet, delectable, nice, dainty, delicate, delicious.

attractive, inviting, prepossessing, engaging; winning, winsome, magnetic, fascinating, seductive; alluring, enticing, appetizing, cheering, bewitching, enchanting, entrancing.

delightful, charming, felicitous, exquisite, lovely, ravishing, rapturous; heartfelt, thrilling, ecstatic, heavenly.

Adv. to one's delight, in utter satisfaction; at one's ease; in clover [*colloq.*].

830. [Capability of giving pain] PAINFULNESS.— *N.* painfulness, trouble, care, trial, affliction, infliction, misfortune, mishap; cross, blow, stroke, burden, load, curse.

annoyance, pique, grievance, nuisance, vexation, mortification, worry, bore, bother, hornet's nest, plague, pest, wound; sore subject, skeleton in the closet; thorn in the flesh.

V. pain, hurt, wound, cause (*or* occasion, give, inflict) pain;

pierce, prick, cut, etc. (*physical pain*), 378; pierce (*or* break, rend) the heart; make the heart bleed.

sadden, make unhappy, grieve, afflict, distress; cut up [*colloq.*], cut to the heart.

annoy, incommode, displease, discompose, trouble, disturb, cross, thwart, perplex, molest; tease, tire, irk, fret, vex, mortify, worry, plague, bother, pester, bore, harass, harry, badger, heckle [*Brit.*], bait, beset, infest, persecute.

torment, wring, harrow, torture, rack, crucify, convulse, agonize.

irritate, provoke, sting, nettle, pique, fret, roil, rile [*colloq. & dial.*], chafe, gall; aggrieve, affront, enrage, ruffle, give offense.

maltreat, bite, snap at, assail, smite, etc., 972.

repel, revolt, sicken, disgust, nauseate, disenchant, offend, shock, rankle, gnaw, corrode, horrify, appall.

Adj. **painful,** hurtful, dolorous; distressing, cheerless, dismal, disheartening, depressing, dreary, melancholy, grievous, piteous, woeful, mournful, deplorable, pitiable, lamentable, sad; affecting, touching, pathetic.

unpleasant, unpleasing, displeasing, disagreeable, unpalatable, bitter, distasteful, uninviting, unwelcome, undesirable, obnoxious; unacceptable.

inauspicious, unlucky, ill-starred, unsatisfactory; untoward.

irritating, provoking, annoying, aggravating [*colloq.*], exasperating, galling, vexatious; troublesome, tiresome, irksome, wearisome.

importunate, pestering, bothering, harassing, worrying, tormenting.

insufferable, intolerable, insupportable, unbearable, unendurable.

shocking, terrific, grim, appalling, crushing; dreadful, fearful, frightful, tremendous, dire, heartbreaking, heart-rending, harrowing, rending.

odious, hateful, execrable, repulsive, repellent, horrid, horrible; offensive; nauseous, disgusting, revolting, nasty, loathsome, vile, hideous.

acute, sharp, sore, severe, grave, hard, harsh, cruel, biting, caustic; cutting, corroding, consuming, excruciating, agonizing.

cumbrous, cumbersome, burdensome, onerous, oppressive.

desolating, withering, tragical, disastrous, calamitous, ruinous.

Adv. in agony, out of the depths.

831. CONTENT.—*N.* content, contentment, contentedness; complacency, satisfaction, ease, peace of mind, serenity, cheerfulness; comfort.

patience, moderation, endurance; conciliation, reconciliation; resignation.

V. be content, rest satisfied, let well enough alone; take in good part; be reconciled to, take heart, take comfort.

content, set at ease, comfort; conciliate, reconcile, win over, propitiate, disarm, beguile; content, satisfy; gratify, etc., 836.

Adj. content, contented, satisfied, at ease, at one's ease, easy-going, not particular; conciliatory, unrepining, resigned, cheerful, serene, at rest; snug, comfortable.

satisfactory, adequate, sufficient, ample, equal to; satisfying.

Adv. to one's heart's content.

832. DISCONTENT.—*N.* discontent, dissatisfaction; disappointment, mortification; cold comfort; regret, repining, inquietude, vexation of spirit, soreness; heartburning.

malcontent, grumbler, growler, grouch [*slang*], croaker, fault-finder.

the opposition; bitter-enders [*politics*, U. S.], die-hards.

V. be discontented, repine, regret, take to heart, make a wry face, look blue, look black, look glum.

grumble, take ill, take in bad part; fret, chafe, croak; lament.

dissatisfy, disappoint, mortify, put out [*colloq.*], disconcert, dishearten.

Adj. discontented, dissatisfied, unsatisfied, regretful, dejected, etc., 837; dissentient, malcontent, exacting.

glum, sulky, in high dudgeon, in a fume, in the sulks (*or* dumps), in bad humor; sour, soured, sore; out of humor, out of temper.

833. REGRET.—*N.* regret, repining; homesickness, nostalgia; bitterness, heartburning; lamentation, penitence, etc., 950.

V. regret, deplore, bewail, lament, etc., 839; repine, rue, rue the day; repent, etc., 950; leave an aching void.

Adj. regretful, rueful; homesick.

834. RELIEF.—*N.* relief, deliverance, alleviation, mitigation, palliation, solace, consolation, comfort, unction; encouragement.

V. relieve, ease, alleviate, mitigate, palliate, soothe; salve; soften, assuage, allay; remedy, cure, restore, refresh.

cheer, comfort, console; enliven; encourage, give comfort, in-spirit, invigorate.

Adj. soothing, assuaging, balmy, lenitive, palliative, curative.

835. AGGRAVATION.—*N.* aggravation, heightening, intensification, overestimation, exaggeration.

V. aggravate, render worse, heighten, embitter, sour, intensify, enhance [*Note:* aggravate *in the sense of* provoke *is colloquial*].

Adj. aggravated, worse, unrelieved, aggravative.

Adv. from bad to worse, worse and worse.

836. CHEERFULNESS.—*N.* cheerfulness, geniality, gayety, cheer, good humor, spirits; high spirits, animal spirits, glee, high glee, light heart.

liveliness, life, alacrity, vivacity, animation, joviality, jollity, levity, jocularity.

mirth, merriment, hilarity, exhilaration, laughter, merrymaking, rejoicing, etc., 838.

optimism, hopefulness, etc., 858.

V. **be cheerful,** have the mind at ease, smile, keep up one's spirits, cheer up, take heart, cast away care, perk up; rejoice, etc., 838; carol, chirp, chirrup, lilt.

cheer, enliven, elate, exhilarate, gladden, delight, inspirit, animate, inspire.

Adj. **cheerful;** happy, etc., 827; cheery, sunny, smiling; blithe, in good spirits, chipper [*colloq.*], gay, debonair, light, lightsome, lighthearted; buoyant, bright, airy, jaunty, sprightly, spirited, lively, animated, vivacious, sparkling, sportive.

merry, joyful, joyous, jocund, jovial; jolly, blithesome, gleeful, hilarious.

winsome, bonny, hearty, buxom.

playful, tricksy, frisky, frolicsome, jocose, jocular, waggish, mirthful, rollicking.

elate, elated; exulting, jubilant, flushed, rejoicing.

cheering, inspiriting, exhilarating, pleasing, palmy, flourishing.

Adv. **cheerfully,** cheerily, with relish, with zest.

837. DEJECTION.—*N.* dejection, depression, mopishness, low (*or* depressed) spirits; heaviness, gloom, weariness, disgust of life; prostration, broken heart; despair, hopelessness.

melancholy, sadness, melancholia, blue devils [*colloq.*], blues [*colloq.*], dumps [*chiefly humorous*], doldrums, horrors, hypochondria, pessimism; despondency, slough of despond; disconsolateness, hope deferred.

gravity; demureness, solemnity; long face, grave face.

hypochondriac, self-tormentor, croaker, pessimist, damper, wet blanket.

V. **be dejected,** grieve, mourn, lament, give way, lose heart, despond, droop, sink, despair.

lower, frown, pout; look blue, lay to heart, take to heart.

mope, brood over, fret, sulk, pine, pine away; yearn, repine.

depress, discourage, dishearten, dispirit, damp, dull, deject, sink, dash, unman, prostrate, break one's heart; sadden, dash one's hopes, prey on the mind, damp the spirits.

Adj. **cheerless,** joyless, spiritless; unhappy, etc., 828; melancholy, dismal, dreary, depressing, somber, dark, gloomy, lowering, frowning, funereal, mournful, lamentable, dreadful.

downcast, downhearted, down in the mouth [*colloq.*], down on one's luck [*colloq.*], heavyhearted; sullen, mopish, moody, glum; sulky, etc. (*discontented*), 832; out of heart (*or* spirits); lowspirited; weary, etc., 841; discouraged, disheartened, despondent, crestfallen.

sad, pensive, doleful, woebegone, melancholic, bilious, jaundiced, saturnine, lackadaisical.

serious, sedate, staid, earnest, grave, sober, solemn, demure, grim, grim-faced, rueful, wan, long-faced.

disconsolate, forlorn, comfortless, desolate, sick at heart, heartsick.

overcome, broken-down, prostrate, cut up [*colloq.*], unnerved, unmanned; downfallen, downtrodden; brokenhearted; careworn.

Adv. with a long face, with tears in one's eyes.

838. [Expression of pleasure] REJOICING.—*N.* rejoicing, exultation, triumph, jubilation, heyday, flush, reveling, merrymaking, pæan, *Te Deum* [L.]; congratulation.

smile, simper, smirk, grin; broad grin, sardonic grin.

laughter, giggle, titter, snicker, snigger, crow, cheer, chuckle, shout; guffaw, burst (*or* fit, shout, roar, peal) of laughter.

cheer, huzza, hurrah, cheering; shout, yell [U. S. and Can.], college yell; tiger [*colloq.*].

V. rejoice, congratulate oneself, hug oneself, clap one's hands; skip; sing, carol, chirrup, chirp, hurrah, cry for joy, leap with joy; exult, triumph; make merry.

smile, simper, smirk, grin, laugh in one's sleeve.

laugh, giggle, titter, snigger, snicker, chuckle, cackle; burst out, shout, roar, shake (*or* split) one's sides.

Adj. rejoicing, jubilant, exultant, triumphant, flushed, elated; laughing, convulsed with laughter.

laughable, ludicrous, etc. 853.

Adv. in fits of laughter; in triumph.

839. [Expression of pain] LAMENTATION.—*N.* lamentation, lament, wail, complaint, plaint, murmur, mutter, grumble, groan, moan, whine, whimper, sob, sigh; frown, scowl.

cry, scream, howl; outcry, wail of woe.

weeping, flood of tears, fit of crying, crying; melting mood. plaintiveness; languishment; condolence, etc., 915.

mourning, weeds [*colloq.*], widow's weeds, crape, deep mourning; sackcloth and ashes; death song, dirge, requiem, elegy, threnody, jeremiad, keen [Ir.].

mourner, keener [Ir.]; Niobe.

V. lament, mourn, deplore, grieve, keen [Ir.], weep over; bewail, bemoan, condole with, etc., 915; fret.

sigh, give (*or* heave) a sigh; wail.

cry, weep, sob, blubber, snivel, whimper, shed tears, burst into tears.

scream, groan, moan, whine, yelp, howl, yell, roar; rend the air.

complain, murmur, mutter, grumble, growl, clamor, croak, grunt.

Adj. lamenting, in mourning, in sackcloth and ashes, clamorous, sorrowing, sorrowful, mournful, lamentable, tearful, lachrymose, plaintive querulous; in tears.

840. AMUSEMENT.—*N.* amusement, entertainment, diversion, recreation, relaxation, solace; pastime, sport; labor of love; pleasure, etc., 827.

fun, frolic, merriment, jollity, joviality, laughter, etc., 838; pleasantry, quip, jocoseness; drollery, buffoonery, tomfoolery; mummery, pageant.

play, game, gambol, romp, prank, antic, lark [*colloq.*], spree, skylarking, vagary, monkey trick, escapade, practical joke.

dance, hop [*colloq*]; ball, masquerade, ballet; step dance, skirt dance, folk dance, morris dance; gavot, minuet, Highland fling, reel, jig, hornpipe, sword dance, cakewalk; country dance, Scotch reel, Virginia reel, quadrille, lancers, cotillion; waltz, polka, mazurka, schottische, one-step, fox-trot.

festivity, fete, festival, merrymaking; party, etc. (*social gathering*), 892; revels, revelry, reveling, carnival, saturnalia, jollification [*colloq.*], junket, picnic.

holiday, red-letter day, play day; high days and holidays; high holiday.

place of amusement, theater; concert hall, ballroom, dance hall, assembly room; moving-picture theater; movies [*colloq.*]; music hall; vaudeville theater; circus, hippodrome.

Sports and games: athletic sports, track events, gymnastics; tournament, skating, tobogganing; cricket, tennis, lawn tennis, rackets, squash, fives; croquet, golf, curling, hockey, polo, football Rugby rugger [*colloq*]; quoits discus putting the weight (*or* shot), tug of war; baseball, basketball, pushball, lacrosse
billiards, pool pyramids bagatelle; bowls, skittles, ninepins, tenpins; chess, draughts, checkers, dominoes, dice; card games, etc.

toy, plaything, doll, bauble.

sportsman (*fem.* sportswoman), hunter, Nimrod.

gamester, sport, gambler, dicer, punter, plunger.

devotee, enthusiast, follower, fan [*slang*], rooter [*slang or cant*].

V. amuse, entertain, divert, enliven, raise a smile, excite (*or* convulse with) laughter; cheer, rejoice, solace, please, interest.

amuse oneself, sport, disport, revel, junket, feast, carouse.

banquet, make merry; frolic, gambol, frisk, romp, caper, dance.

Adj. amusing, entertaining, diverting, recreative, pleasant, laughable, etc. (*ludicrous*), 853; witty, etc., 842, festive, festal, jovial, jolly, roguish, arch, playful, sportive.

Adv. at play, in sport.

841. WEARINESS.—*N.* weariness, ennui, boredom, lassitude, fatigue, etc., 688; drowsiness, languor.

disgust, nausea, loathing, sickness; satiety, repletion.

tedium, wearisomeness, tediousness, monotony.

bore, buttonholer, proser, dry-as-dust, fossil [*colloq.*], wet blanket.

V. weary, tire, fatigue, bore, send to sleep; buttonhole.

pall, sicken, nauseate, disgust; harp on the same string.

Adj. wearying, wearing, wearisome, tiresome, irksome, uninteresting, stupid, monotonous, dull, dry, arid, tedious, humdrum, flat; prosy, prosing; slow, soporific, somniferous.

weary, tired, drowsy, sleepy, etc., 683; uninterested, flagging, used up, worn out, blasé [F.].

842. WIT.—*N.* wit, wittiness, Attic salt, Atticism; point, fancy, whim, humor, drollery, pleasantry.

buffoonery, fooling, farce, tomfoolery, broad farce, fun.

jocularity, jocoseness, facetiousness, waggishness, comicality.

smartness, ready wit, banter, persiflage, retort, repartee.

witticism, smart saying, sally, flash, scintillation, flash of wit; jest, joke, epigram, conceit.

wordplay, play upon words, pun, riddle, conundrum, quibble.

V. joke, jest, cut jokes; crack a joke, pun; make merry with.

retort, flash back, flash, scintillate; banter, etc. (*ridicule*), 856.

Adj. witty, clever, keen, keen-witted, brilliant, pungent, quick-witted, smart, jocular, jocose, funny, waggish, facetious, comic, whimsical, humorous, sprightly, sparkling epigrammatic.

843. DULLNESS.—*N.* dullness, heaviness, flatness, stupidity, want of originality, dearth of ideas; matter of fact, commonplace, platitude.

V. be dull, hang fire, fall flat, platitudinize, prose.

depress, damp, throw cold water on, lay a wet blanket on.

Adj. dull, jejune, dry, uninteresting, heavy-footed, elephantine; insipid, tasteless, unimaginative; prosy, prosaic, matter-of-fact, commonplace, platitudinous, pointless.

stupid, slow, flat, humdrum, monotonous, stolid.

844. HUMORIST.—*N.* humorist, wag, wit, epigrammatist, punster; life of the party; joker, jester, buffoon, comedian, merry-andrew, mime, tumbler, acrobat, mountebank, harlequin, pantaloon, punch, punchinello, clown; motley fool; caricaturist.

845. BEAUTY.—*N.* beauty, form, elegance, grace, symmetry, bloom, delicacy, refinement, charm, style; comeliness, fairness, polish, gloss; good effect, good looks.

brilliancy, radiance, splendor, gorgeousness, magnificence; sublimity.

beau ideal, Venus, Aphrodite, Hebe, the Graces, peri, houri, Cupid, Apollo, Hyperion, Adonis; Helen of Troy, Cleopatra; Venus de Milo, Apollo Belvedere.

loveliness, pleasurableness, etc., 829.

beautifying, decoration, ornamentation, etc., 847.

V. beautify, set off, grace; decorate, etc., 847.

Adj. beautiful, beauteous, handsome; pretty; lovely, graceful, elegant, exquisite, delicate, dainty.

comely, fair, goodly, bonny, good-looking, well favored, well formed, well proportioned, shapely, symmetrical, harmonious.

bright, bright-eyed; rosy-cheeked, rosy, ruddy, blooming, in full bloom.

trim, trig, tidy, neat, spruce, smart, jaunty, dapper.

brilliant, shining, sparkling, radiant, splendid, resplendent, dazzling, glowing, glossy, sleek; rich, gorgeous, superb, magnificent, grand, fine.

artistic, aesthetic, picturesque, pictorial, enchanting, attractive, becoming, ornamental.

perfect, unspotted, spotless, immaculate; undeformed, undefaced.

passable, presentable, tolerable, not amiss.

846. UGLINESS.—*N.* ugliness, deformity, inelegance, disfigurement, blemish, want of symmetry, distortion; squalor.

eyesore, object, figure, sight [*colloq.*], fright, scarecrow, hag, harridan, satyr, witch, monster.

V. deface, disfigure, deform, distort, blemish, injure, spoil; soil.

Adj. ugly, inartistic, unsightly, unseemly, uncomely, unshapely, unlovely; unbeautiful; coarse, plain, homely.

misshapen, misproportioned, shapeless, monstrous, gross; ill-made, ill-shaped, ill-proportioned, crooked, distorted.

unprepossessing, hard-featured, ill-favored, ill-looking; squalid, haggard; grim, grisly, ghastly, cadaverous, gruesome.

uncouth, ungainly, graceless, inelegant, ungraceful, stiff, rough, gross, rude, awkward, clumsy, gawky, lumbering, unwieldy.

repellent, forbidding, frightful, hideous, odious, repulsive; horrid, horrible, shocking.

disfigured, tarnished, smeared, besmeared, discolored, spotted, spotty.

showy, specious, pretentious, garish.

847. ORNAMENT.—*N.* ornament, ornamentation, ornateness, adornment, decoration, embellishment.

embroidery, needlework; lace, trimming, drapery; tapestry, arras; millinery.
wreath, festoon, garland, chaplet, flower, nosegay, bouquet, posy [*colloq.*].
tassel, knot; shoulder knot, epaulet, star, rosette, bow; feather, plume, fillet, snood.
jewelry: tiara, crown, coronet, diadem; jewel, gem, precious stone, trinket.

finery, frippery, tinsel, spangle, excess of ornament; pride, show, ostentation.

illustration, illumination; purple patches.

virtu, article of virtu, work of art, bric-a-brac, curio; rarity, a find.

V. ornament, embellish, enrich, decorate, adorn, beautify; garnish, furbish, polish, gild, varnish, enamel, paint.

spangle, bespangle, bead, embroider, chase, tool; emblazon, blazon, illuminate.

smarten, trim, bedizen, prink, trick up, trick out, deck, bedeck, array; spruce up [*colloq.*]; smarten up, dress, dress up.

Adj. ornamental, ornate, ornamented, rich, gilt, begilt, festooned.

smart, gay, flowery, glittering, new-spangled, fine, well groomed.

showy, gorgeous, flashy, gaudy, garish, tawdry, etc., 851.

848. BLEMISH.—*N.* blemish, disfigurement, deformity, defect, flaw, injury, eyesore.

stain, blot, spot, speck, speckle, blur, freckle, patch, blotch, smudge, birthmark, scar, mole, pimple, blister.

V. disfigure, etc. (*injure*), 659.

Adj. disfigured, imperfect, injured; discolored, specked, speckled, freckled, pitted, bruised.

849. SIMPLICITY.—*N.* simplicity, plainness, homeliness; chasteness, chastity, restraint, severity, naturalness, unaffectedness.

V. simplify, reduce to simplicity, strip of ornament, chasten, restrain.

Adj. simple, plain, homelike, homely, homespun [*fig.*], ordinary.

unaffected, natural, native; inartificial, free from affectation; chaste, severe; unadorned, unornamented.

simple-minded, childish, credulous, etc., 486.

850. [Good taste] TASTE.—*N.* taste, good (*or* refined, cultivated) taste; delicacy, refinement, fine feeling, discrimination, tact, polish, elegance, grace, culture, cultivation.

Science of taste: aesthetics.

man of taste, connoisseur, judge, critic, virtuoso, amateur, dilettante; purist, precisian.

V. display taste, appreciate, judge, criticize, discriminate.

Adj. in good taste, tasteful, unaffected, pure, chaste, classical, cultivated; graceful, attractive, charming, aesthetic, artistic.

refined, elegant, prim, precise, formal.

Adv. with quiet elegance; with elegant simplicity; without ostentation.

851. [Bad taste] VULGARITY.—*N.* vulgarity, vulgarism, barbarism, vandalism, bad taste; want of tact; ill-breeding, coarseness, indecorum, misbehavior, boorishness.

lowness, low life, brutality, blackguardism, rowdyism, ruffianism; ribaldry.

Excess of ornament: gaudiness, tawdriness, cheap jewelry; flashy clothes (*or* dress), finery, frippery, trickery, tinsel.

vulgarian, rough diamond, clown, Goth, vandal; snob, cad [*colloq.*], cub; parvenu, upstart; frump [*colloq.*], dowdy, slattern.

V. be vulgar, misbehave; show a want of tact (*or* consideration); be a vulgarian.

Adj. in bad taste, vulgar, unrefined, coarse, indecorous, ribald, gross; unseemly, unpresentable, ungraceful; dowdy, slovenly; low, extravagant, monstrous, horrid, shocking.

ill-mannered, ill-bred, underbred, snobbish, uncourtly, uncivil, discourteous, ungentlemanly, unladylike.

uncouth, unkempt, unpolished, plebeian; rude, awkward; homely, homespun, provincial, countrified, rustic; boorish, clownish; savage, brutish, blackguardly, rowdy, wild; barbarous, barbaric, outlandish; uncultivated.

antiquated, obsolete, out of fashion, old-fashioned, out of date, unfashionable.

newfangled, fantastic, fantastical, odd, affected.

tawdry, gaudy, meretricious, obtrusive, flaunting, loud, crass, showy, flashy, garish.

852. FASHION.—*N.* fashion, style, society, good (*or* polite) society, civilized life, civilization; court, high life, world, fashionable world; upper ten [*colloq.*], elite, smart set [*colloq.*], the four hundred; Vanity Fair; Mayfair.

manners, breeding, politeness; air, demeanor, *savoir-faire* [F.], gentility, decorum, propriety, Mrs. Grundy; convention, conventionality, the proprieties, punctiliousness, form, formality, etiquette.

mode, vogue, style, the latest thing, the rage, prevailing taste; custom.

V. be fashionable, be the rage, have a run, pass current, follow the fashion, go with the stream

Adj. fashionable, in fashion, *à la mode* [F.], presentable; punctilious, genteel, decorous, conventional; well bred, gentlemanly, ladylike.

polished, refined, thoroughbred, gently bred, courtly, distinguished, aristocratic, self-possessed, poised, easy, frank, unconstrained.

modish, stylish, swell [*slang*], all the rage, all the go [*colloq.*].

Adv. for fashion's sake; in the latest style (*or* mode).

853. RIDICULOUSNESS.—*N.* ridiculousness, comicality, oddity, drollery; farce, comedy, burlesque, buffoonery, bull, Irish bull, spoonerism; bombast, anticlimax, bathos; absurdity, laughingstock.

V. be ridiculous, play the fool, make a fool of oneself, commit an absurdity.

Adj. ridiculous, ludicrous, comic *or* comical, waggish, quizzical, droll, funny, laughable, farcical, seriocomic, tragicomic.

odd, grotesque, whimsical, fanciful, fantastic, queer, quaint, bizarre, eccentric, strange, outlandish, out-of-the-way.

extravagant, monstrous, preposterous, absurd, bombastic, inflated, stilted, burlesque, mock heroic.

854. FOP.—*N.* fine gentleman, fop, swell [*colloq.*], dandy, exquisite, coxcomb, beau, man about town, spark, popinjay, puppy [*contemptuous*], prig, jackanapes, carpet knight; dude [*colloq.*].

fine lady, belle, flirt, coquette, toast.

855. AFFECTATION.—*N.* affectation, affectedness, pretense, pretension, airs, pedantry, stiffness, formality, mannerism, euphuism; boasting, charlatanism, quackery.

prudery, demureness, mock modesty, false shame; sentimentalism.

foppery, dandyism, coxcombry, puppyism, conceit; coquetry.

poser, actor; pedant, pedagogue, doctrinaire, purist, euphuist, mannerist; bluestocking, prig, charlatan; prude, puritan, precisian, formalist.

V. affect, act a part, give oneself airs, boast, simper, mince, attitudinize, pose, languish; overact, overdo.

Adj. affected, pretentious, pedantic, stilted, stagy, theatrical, canting, insincere, unnatural; self-conscious, artificial; overdone, overacted.

stiff, formal, prim, smug, complacent; demure, puritanical, prudish.

priggish, conceited, foppish, finical, finicking, mincing, simpering, namby-pamby, sentimental, languishing.

856. RIDICULE.—*N.* ridicule, derision, snicker *or* snigger, grin, scoffing, mockery, banter, irony, persiflage, raillery, chaff. squib, satire, skit, quip.

burlesque, parody, travesty, farce, caricature.

buffoonery, practical joke, horseplay, roughhouse [*slang*].

V. ridicule, deride; laugh at, grin at, smile at; snicker *or* snigger; banter, chaff, joke, guy [*colloq.*], rag [*slang*], haze [*colloq.*].

burlesque, satirize, parody, caricature, travesty.

Adj. derisive, sarcastic, ironical, satirical, quizzical, burlesque, mock.

Adv. as a joke, to raise a laugh.

857. [Object and cause of ridicule] LAUGHINGSTOCK.—*N.* laughingstock, butt, game, fair game, April fool, original, oddity; queer fish [*colloq.*], figure of fun [*colloq.*]; monkey; buffoon.

858. HOPE.—*N.* hope; desire, etc., 865; trust, confidence, reliance, faith, assurance, security; reassurance.

hopefulness, buoyancy, optimism, enthusiasm, aspiration; assumption, presumption; anticipation.

optimist, utopian.

daydream, castles in the air, utopia, millennium; golden dream, airy hopes, fool's paradise, fond hope.

mainstay, anchor, sheet anchor; staff.

V. hope, trust, confide, rely, lean upon; live in hope, rest assured.

hope for, etc. (*desire*), 865; anticipate; presume, aspire; promise oneself; expect.

be hopeful, look on the bright side of, make the best of it, hope for the best; hope against hope, take heart, flatter oneself.

encourage, hearten, inspirit, hold out hope, cheer, assure, reassure, buoy up, embolden; promise, bid fair, augur well.

Adj. hopeful, confident, in hopes, secure, sanguine, buoyant, elated, flushed, exultant, enthusiastic.

fearless, unsuspecting, unsuspicious, undespairing, self-reliant; dauntless, etc. (*courageous*), 861.

propitious, promising; probable, auspicious, reassuring; encouraging, cheering, inspiriting, bright, roseate.

859. HOPELESSNESS.—*N.* hopelessness, despair, desperation; despondency, dejection, etc., 837; pessimism, hope deferred, dashed hopes.

pessimist, hypochondriac; bird of ill omen.

V. despair; lose (*or* give up, abandon) all hope, give up, give over, yield to despair; falter; despond.

Adj. hopeless, desperate, despairing, gone, in despair, forlorn, inconsolable, brokenhearted.

undone, ruined; incurable, cureless, incorrigible; irreparable, irrecoverable, irretrievable, irreclaimable, irredeemable, irrevocable.

unpropitious, unpromising, inauspicious, ill-omened, threatening, lowering, ominous.

860. FEAR.—*N.* **fear,** timidity, diffidence, apprehensiveness, fearfulness, solicitude, anxiety, care, apprehension, misgiving, mistrust, suspicion, qualm; hesitation.

trepidation, flutter, fear and trembling, perturbation, tremor, quivering, shaking, trembling, palpitation, nervousness, restlessness, disquietude, funk [*colloq.*].

fright, alarm, dread, awe, terror, horror, dismay, consternation, panic, scare; stampede [*of horses*].

intimidation, bullying; terrorism, reign of terror; terrorist, bully.

V. **fear,** be afraid, apprehend, dread, distrust; hesitate, falter, funk [*colloq.*], cower, crouch, skulk, take fright, take alarm; start, wince, flinch, shy, shrink, fly.

tremble, shake, shiver, shudder, flutter, quake, quaver, quiver, quail.

frighten, fright, terrify, inspire (*or* excite) fear, bulldoze [*colloq.*], alarm, startle, scare, dismay, astound; awe, strike terror, appall, unman, petrify, horrify.

daunt, intimidate, cow, overawe, abash, deter, discourage; browbeat, bully, threaten, terrorize.

haunt, obsess, beset, besiege; prey (*or* weigh) on the mind.

Adj. **afraid,** frightened, alarmed, fearful, timid, timorous, nervous, diffident, fainthearted, tremulous, shaky, afraid of one's shadow, apprehensive; aghast, awe-struck, awe-stricken, horror-stricken, panic-stricken.

dreadful, alarming, redoubtable, perilous, dread, fell, dire, direful, shocking, frightful, terrible, terrific, tremendous; horrid, horrible, ghastly, awful, awe-inspiring, revolting.

861. [Absence of fear] **COURAGE.**—*N.* **courage,** bravery, valor, resoluteness, boldness, spirit, daring, gallantry, intrepidity, prowess, heroism, chivalry, audacity, rashness, dash, defiance, confidence, self-reliance; manhood, manliness, nerve, pluck, mettle, grit, virtue, hardihood, fortitude, firmness, backbone, resolution, tenacity.

exploit, feat, deed, act, achievement.

brave man, man of courage, a man, hero, demigod; Hercules, Achilles, Sir Galahad.

brave woman, heroine; Amazon, Joan of Arc.

V. **dare,** venture, make bold; face (*or* front, confront, brave, defy, despise) danger; face; meet, brave, beard, defy.

nerve oneself, summon up (*or* pluck up) courage, take heart, stand to one's guns, bear up, hold out; present a bold front, show fight, face the music.

hearten, inspire courage, reassure, encourage, embolden, inspirit, cheer, nerve, rally.

Adj. courageous, brave, valiant, valorous, gallant, intrepid, spirited, high-spirited, mettlesome, plucky; manly, manful, stout-hearted, lionhearted, bold, daring, audacious, fearless, dauntless, undaunted, undismayed, unflinching, unshrinking, confident, self-reliant.

enterprising, adventurous, venturous, venturesome; dashing, chivalrous, warlike, soldierly, heroic.

fierce, savage, pugnacious, bellicose.

strong-minded, strong-willed, hardy, doughty [*archaic or humorous*]; firm, resolute, determined, dogged, indomitable.

862. [Excess of fear] COWARDICE.—*N.* cowardice, pusillanimity, cowardliness, timidity, effeminacy; baseness, abject fear, funk [*colloq.*]; fear, etc., 860; white feather, cold feet [*slang*], yellow streak [*slang*].

coward, poltroon, dastard, sneak, recreant, cur [*contemptuous*], craven.

alarmist, terrorist, pessimist.

shirker, slacker; fugitive, etc., 623.

V. quail, funk [*colloq.*], cower, skulk, sneak; flinch, shy, fight shy, slink, run away; show the white feather.

Adj. cowardly, coward, fearful, shy, timid, timorous, spiritless, soft, effeminate, fainthearted; white-livered; dastard, dastardly, base, craven, sneaking, recreant; unwarlike.

Adv. with fear and trembling, in fear of one's life, in a blue funk [*colloq.*].

863. RASHNESS.—*N.* rashness, temerity, imprudence, indiscretion; overconfidence, presumption, audacity, precipitancy, impetuosity, foolhardiness, heedlessness, thoughtlessness, carelessness, desperation.

gaming, gambling; blind bargain, leap in the dark.

desperado, madcap, daredevil; scapegrace, Don Quixote, knight-errant, adventurer; fire-eater, bully, bravo.

gambler, gamester, etc. (*chance*), 621.

V. be rash, stick at nothing, play a desperate game, run into danger, play with fire (*or* edged tools); rush on destruction, tempt providence, go on a forlorn hope.

Adj. rash, incautious, indiscreet, injudicious, imprudent, improvident, uncalculating, impulsive, heedless, careless, without ballast.

reckless, wild, madcap, desperate, devil-may-care, death-defying, hotheaded, headlong, headstrong; breakneck, foolhardy, harebrained, precipitate.

overconfident, overweening; venturesome, venturous, adventurous, quixotic.

Adv. posthaste, headforemost.

864. CAUTION.—*N.* caution, cautiousness, discretion, prudence, heed, circumspection, calculation, deliberation, foresight, etc., 510; vigilance, etc., 459; warning, etc., 668.

worldly wisdom; safety first, Fabian policy, watchful waiting.

coolness, self-possession, self-command; presence of mind, *sang-froid* [F.].

V. **be cautious,** take care, take heed, mind, be on one's guard; think twice, look before one leaps, count the cost, feel one's way, see how the land lies; pussyfoot [*colloq.*], keep out of harm's way, stand aloof; keep (*or* be) on the safe side.

warn, caution, etc., 668.

Adj. **cautious,** wary, guarded, on one's guard, suspicious, vigilant, careful, heedful, chary, sure-footed, circumspect, prudent, noncommittal, canny [Scot.], discreet, politic, strategic.

unenterprising, unadventurous, cool, steady, self-possessed; overcautious.

865. DESIRE.—*N.* desire, wish, fancy, inclination, leaning, bent, mind, whim, partiality, predilection, propensity, liking, love, fondness, relish.

longing, hankering, yearning, aspiration, ambition, eagerness, zeal, ardor, solicitude, anxiety.

need, want, exigency, urgency, necessity.

appetite, keenness, hunger, stomach, thirst, drought.

avidity, greed, greediness, covetousness, ravenousness, grasping, craving, rapacity, voracity.

mania, passion, rage, furor, frenzy, itching palm, cupidity, kleptomania, dipsomania; monomania.

Person desiring: lover, votary, devotee, aspirant; parasite, sycophant.

attraction, magnet, loadstone, lure, allurement, fancy, temptation, fascination; hobby.

V. **desire,** wish, wish for, care for, affect, like, take to, cling to, fancy; prefer, have an eye to, have a mind to; have a fancy for, have at heart, be bent upon; set one's heart (*or* mind) upon, covet, crave, hanker after, pine for, long for; hope, etc., 858.

woo, court, ogle, solicit; fish for.

want, miss, need, lack, feel the want of.

attract, allure, whet the appetite; appetize, take one's fancy, tempt, tantalize, make one's mouth water.

Adj. **desirous,** desiring, appetitive, inclined, fain, wishful, longing, wistful; anxious, solicitous, sedulous.

eager, keen, burning, fervent, ardent; agog; breathless; impatient.

ambitious, aspiring, vaulting.

craving, hungry, sharp-set, peckish [*colloq.*], ravening, famished; thirsty, athirst, dry [*colloq. when meaning thirsty*], droughty.

greedy, voracious, ravenous, omnivorous, covetous, rapacious, grasping, extortionate, exacting, sordid, insatiable, insatiate.

desirable, desired, in demand, popular, pleasing, appetizing.

Adv. fain; with eager appetite.

866. INDIFFERENCE.—*N.* indifference, neutrality; unconcern, nonchalance, apathy, supineness, disdain, inattention, coldness.

V. be indifferent, stand neuter, take no interest in, have no desire for, have no taste for, not care for, care nothing for (*or* about); not mind; spurn, disdain.

Adj. indifferent, cold, frigid, lukewarm; cool, neutral, unconcerned, phlegmatic, easygoing, careless, listless, halfhearted, unambitious, undesirous, unsolicitous.

unattractive, unalluring, undesired, undesirable, unwished.

867. DISLIKE.—*N.* dislike, distaste, disrelish, disinclination, unwillingness, reluctance, backwardness.

repugnance, disgust, nausea, loathing, aversion, abomination, antipathy, abhorrence, horror, hatred, detestation; hate, etc., 898.

V. dislike, disrelish; mind, object to, have no taste for, shudder at, turn up the nose at, look askance at; shun, avoid, eschew, shrink from.

loathe, abominate, detest, abhor; hate, etc., 898.

repel, disincline, sicken, pall, nauseate, disgust, shock, make one's blood run cold.

Adj. loath, averse; shy of, sick of, disinclined, heartsick.

repugnant, repulsive, repellent, abhorrent, insufferable, fulsome, nauseous, loathsome, offensive, disgusting.

unpopular, undesirable, uncared for, disliked, out of favor.

uneatable, inedible, unappetizing, unsavory.

Adv. to satiety, to one's disgust.

868. FASTIDIOUSNESS.—*N.* fastidiousness, nicety, hypercriticism, epicurism.

discrimination, discernment, perspicacity, keenness, sharpness, insight.

epicure, gourmet.

Excess of delicacy: prudery, prudishness, primness.

V. be fastidious, split hairs; mince the matter; turn up one's nose at, disdain.

discriminate, have nice discrimination; have exquisite taste; be discriminative.

Adj. fastidious, nice, delicate, meticulous, finicking *or* finicky, exacting, hard to please, difficult, dainty, squeamish, thin-skinned; querulous; particular, scrupulous; critical, hypercritical, overcritical.

prudish, strait-laced, prim.

discriminative, discriminating, discerning, judicious, keen, sharp, perspicacious.

869. SATIETY.—*N.* satiety, satisfaction, saturation, repletion, glut, surfeit, satiation.

V. sate, satiate, satisfy, saturate, cloy, quench, slake, pall, glut, gorge, surfeit; bore, tire, spoil.

Adj. satiated, overgorged, overfed, blasé [F.], sick of.

870. WONDER.—*N.* wonder, astonishment, amazement, wonderment, bewilderment, admiration, awe; stupor, stupefaction, fascination, surprise.

V. wonder, marvel, admire, be surprised, start, stare; gape, hold one's breath, stand aghast.

astonish, surprise, amaze, astound; dumfound, dumfounder, startle, dazzle, daze, strike, electrify, stun, stupefy, petrify, confound, bewilder, stagger, fascinate, take away one's breath, strike dumb.

Adj. astonished, surprised, aghast, breathless, agape, openmouthed, thunderstruck, spellbound; lost in amazement (*or* wonder, astonishment).

wonderful, wondrous, surprising, striking, marvelous, miraculous; unexpected, mysterious, monstrous, prodigious, stupendous, inconceivable, incredible, strange.

indescribable, inexpressible, ineffable; unutterable, unspeakable.

Adv. for a wonder, strange to say, to one's great surprise.

871. [Absence of wonder] EXPECTANCE.—*N.* expectance, expectancy, expectation, etc., 507.

calmness, imperturbability, *sang-froid* [F.], coolness, steadiness, lack of nerves, want of imagination.

V. expect, etc., 507; not wonder, make nothing of, take it coolly.

Adj. expecting, unamazed, astonished at nothing, blasé [F.], expected, foreseen.

calm, imperturbable, nerveless, cool, coolheaded, unruffled, steady, unimaginative.

common, ordinary, etc. (*habitual*), 613.

872. PRODIGY.—*N.* prodigy, phenomenon, wonder, wonderment, marvel, miracle; freak, freak of nature, monstrosity, monster; curiosity, infant prodigy, lion, sight, spectacle; sign, portent.

873. REPUTE.—*N*. repute, reputation, distinction, mark, name, figure, note, notability, éclat, vogue, celebrity, fame, renown, popularity; credit, prestige, account, regard, respect, fair name.

dignity, stateliness, solemnity, grandeur, luster, splendor, nobility, majesty, sublimity, glory, honor.

rank, standing, precedence, station, place, status, position, order, degree, caste, condition.

eminence, greatness, height, importance, pre-eminence, supereminence, elevation, exaltation.

celebrity, worthy, hero, man of mark (*or* rank), lion, notability, somebody.

scholar, savant; paragon, star; elite.

ornament, honor, feather in one's cap, halo, aureole, nimbus; laurels.

posthumous fame, memory, celebration, canonization, enshrinement, glorification, immortality, immortal name.

V. be distinguished, shine, etc. (*light*), 420; shine forth, figure, cut a figure, flourish, flaunt, play first fiddle, bear the palm, take precedence; win laurels (*or* golden opinions).

surpass, outshine, outrival, outvie, eclipse; throw into the shade, overshadow.

rival, emulate, vie with.

honor, give (*or* do, pay) honor to, accredit, dignify, glorify, pledge, toast, look up to, exalt, aggrandize, elevate, enthrone, signalize, immortalize, deify.

consecrate; dedicate to, devote to; enshrine, inscribe, blazon, lionize.

Adj. distinguished, noted, of note, honored, popular, remarkable, notable, celebrated, renowned, famous, famed, far-famed, conspicuous, foremost.

reputable, in good odor, in favor, in high favor, respectable, creditable, worthy.

imperishable, deathless, immortal, never fading, fadeless.

illustrious, glorious, splendid, brilliant, radiant; bright, etc., 420.

eminent, prominent, high, etc., 206; peerless, pre-eminent, great, dignified, proud, noble, honorable, lordly, grand, stately, august, princely, imposing, solemn, transcendent, majestic, sacred, sublime.

874. DISREPUTE.—*N*. disrepute, discredit, ill-repute, ill-favor, ingloriousness, derogation, abasement, debasement, degradation; odium, obloquy, opprobrium, ignominy, dishonor, disgrace, shame, humiliation, scandal, infamy.

stigma, brand, reproach, imputation, slur, stain, blot, spot, blur, tarnish, taint, badge of infamy.

V. be inglorious, have a bad name; disgrace oneself, lose caste; fall from one's high estate, cut a sorry figure.

shame, disgrace, put to shame, dishonor; tarnish, stain, blot, sully, taint; discredit, degrade, debase, expel.

stigmatize, vilify, defame, slur, brand, post, send to Coventry, snub, show up [*colloq.*], reprehend.

disconcert, put out [*colloq.*], upset, discompose; put to the blush.

Adj. disgraced, overcome, downtrodden, in bad repute, under a cloud, in the shade (*or* background); down in the world, down and out [*colloq.*].

inglorious, nameless, obscure, unknown to fame, unnoticed, unnoted, unhonored, unglorified.

discreditable, questionable, shameful, disgraceful, disreputable, despicable; unbecoming, unworthy, derogatory, degrading, humiliating, scandalous, infamous, opprobrious, arrant, shocking, outrageous, notorious, ignominious, base, abject, vile.

beggarly, pitiful, mean, petty, shabby.

875. NOBILITY.—*N.* nobility, rank, condition, distinction, blood, birth, high descent, order, quality.

high life, upper classes, upper ten [*colloq.*], the four hundred; elite, aristocracy, fashionable world.

celebrity, bigwig [*humorous*], magnate, great man, star, great gun [*colloq.*].

The nobility: peerage, baronage; House of Lords (*or* peers); lords, noblesse.

peer, noble, nobleman; lord, grandee, don, hidalgo; aristocrat, swell [*colloq.*], gentleman, squire, patrician.

gentry, gentlefolk, magnates.

king, etc., 745; prince, duke, marquis, earl, viscount, baron, baronet, knight, chevalier, count, esquire, laird [Scot.]; signior, seignior; *signor* [It.], *señor* [Sp.], *senhor* [Pg.]; sheik, pasha, sahib.

empress, queen, princess, duchess, marchioness, viscountess, countess; lady, *doña* [Sp.], *dona* [Pg.]; *signora* [It.], *señora* [Sp.], *senhora* [Pg.].

Hindu titles: raja, rana (*fem.* rani), maharaja, maharana (*fem.* maharani), Gaekwar [*lit.* cowherd; *Baroda*].

Mohammedan titles: nawab, sultan (*fem.* sultana), amir.

Rank or office: kingship, dukedom, marquisate, earldom; viscountship, county, lordship, baronetcy, knighthood.

Adj. noble, exalted, princely, titled, patrician, aristocratic; highborn, well born, courtly.

Adv. in high quarters.

876. THE PEOPLE.—*N.* the people, commonalty, democracy; obscurity; *bourgeoisie* [F.], the four million; lower classes (*or* orders), common herd, rank and file, the many, the general, the crowd, the ruck, the populace, the multitude, the million, the masses, the mobility [*humorous*], the peasantry, proletariat; *hoi polloi* [Gr.].

rabble, horde, canaille, dregs of society, mob, trash, riffraff, ragtag and bobtail. commoner, one of the people, democrat, plebeian, republican, bourgeois [F.]. peasant, countryman, boor, churl, serf; swain, clown, clodhopper, yokel, lout, bumpkin; plowman, hayseed [*slang*], rustic, lunkhead [*colloq.*], rube [*slang*]; tiller of the soil; hewers of wood and drawers of water; gamin, street Arab.

rough, rowdy, roughneck [*slang*], ruffian, tough [*colloq.*], scullion, low fellow, cad.

upstart, parvenu, nobody, snob, mushroom, adventurer, *nouveau riche* (*pl. nouveaux riches*) [F.].

vagabond, beggar, caitiff, ragamuffin, pariah, outcast, tramp, panhandler [*slang*], bum [*slang*], hobo.

Adj. ignoble, common, mean, low, base, vile, sorry, scrubby, beggarly; vulgar, low-minded; snobbish, parvenu, low-bred; menial, servile.

plebeian, proletarian, lowborn, baseborn, risen from the ranks, obscure, untitled.

rustic, country, uncivilized; loutish, boorish, clownish, churlish, rude.

barbarous, barbarian, barbaric.

Adv. below the salt.

877. TITLE.—*N.* title, honor; earldom, etc. (*nobility*), 875.

highness, excellency, grace, lordship, reverence; reverend; esquire, sir, master, Mr., *signor* [It.], *señor* [Sp.], etc., 373; your (*or* his) honor.

madam, etc. (*mistress*), 374; empress, queen, etc., 875.

decoration, laurel, palm, wreath, garland, bays; medal, ribbon, cordon, cross, crown, coronet, star, garter; epaulet, chevron, colors, cockade; livery; order, arms, coat of arms, shield, escutcheon *or* scutcheon, crest; handle to one's name.

878. PRIDE.—*N.* pride, haughtiness, high notions, hauteur, vainglory, arrogance, self-importance, pomposity, side [*slang*], swagger, toploftiness [*colloq.*].

dignity, self-respect, self-esteem, decorum, stateliness, seemliness.

V. be proud, presume, swagger, strut, hold one's head high, look big, carry with a high hand; ride the high horse, give oneself airs.

Adj. dignified, stately, lordly, lofty-minded, high-souled, high-minded, high-mettled, high-flown.

proud, haughty, lofty, high, mighty, swollen, puffed up, flushed, vainglorious; purse-proud, fine.

supercilious, disdainful, bumptious, magisterial, imperious, high and mighty, overweening, consequential; pompous, toplofty [*colloq.*]; arrogant.

stiff, stiff-necked; starched, stuck up [*colloq.*]; strait-laced, prim, affected, etc., 855.

Adv. with head erect, with nose in air, with nose turned up; with a sneer, with curling lip.

879. HUMILITY.—*N.* humility, humbleness, meekness, lowliness, abasement, self-abasement, submission, resignation.

modesty, timidity; confusion, humiliation, mortification.

V. be humble, deign, vouchsafe, condescend, humble oneself, stoop, submit, yield the palm, sing small [*colloq.*], hide one's face.

be humiliated, be put out of countenance, be shamed, be put to the blush, receive a snub, eat humble pie.

humble, humiliate, snub, abash, abase, strike dumb, lower, cast into the shade, put to the blush, confuse, shame, mortify, disgrace, crush.

Adj. humble, lowly, meek, modest, etc., 881; humble-minded, sober-minded; submissive, servile.

humbled, bowed down, abashed, ashamed, dashed, crestfallen, shorn of one's glory.

Adv. with downcast eyes, with bated breath, on bended knee.

880. VANITY.—*N.* vanity, conceit, conceitedness, self-conceit, self-sufficiency, self-praise, self-glorification, self-applause, self-admiration; selfishness, etc., 943.

pretension, airs, affected manner, mannerism; egoism, egotism, priggishness; vainglory, arrogance, pride, ostentation.

egoist, egotist; peacock; coxcomb.

V. be vain, pique oneself, have too high opinion of oneself, strut, put oneself forward; give oneself airs, boast, etc., 884.

render vain, inflate, puff up, turn one's head.

Adj. vain, conceited, overweening, forward, vainglorious, highflown, ostentatious, etc., 882; puffed up, inflated, flushed, elate.

self-satisfied, complacent, self-confident, self-sufficient, self-admiring, pretentious, priggish, egotistic *or* egotistical, arrogant, assured.

881. MODESTY.—*N.* modesty; humility, etc., 879; diffidence, demureness, timidity, bashfulness, retiring disposition, unobtrusiveness; blush, blushing; reserve, constraint.

V. be modest, retire, give way to, hide one's face; keep in the background; hide one's light under a bushel.

Adj. modest, diffident, retiring, humble, etc., 879; timid, timorous, bashful, shy, coy, demure, sheepish, shamefaced, blushing.

unpretending, unpretentious, unobtrusive, unassuming, unostentatious, reserved, constrained.

Adv. modestly, quietly, privately; without ceremony.

882. OSTENTATION.—*N.* ostentation, display, show, flourish, parade, pomp, magnificence, splendor, pageantry, array, state, solemnity; dash [*colloq.*], splash [*colloq.*], glitter, pomposity, pretense, pretensions.

demonstration, pageant, spectacle, exhibition, exposition, procession, turnout [*colloq.*]; fete, field day, review, march past, promenade.

ceremony, ceremonial, ritual, form, formality, etiquette, punctilio.

V. **flaunt,** show off, parade, display, exhibit, brandish, blazon forth; dangle, emblazon.

Adj. **ostentatious,** showy, dashing, pretentious, grand, pompous; garish, gaudy, flaunting, glittering, gay.

splendid, magnificent, sumptuous, palatial.

theatrical, theatric, dramatic, spectacular, scenic.

ceremonial, ceremonious, ritualistic; solemn, stately, majestic, formal, punctilious.

Adv. with flourish of trumpet, with beat of drum, with flying colors.

883. CELEBRATION.—*N.* **celebration,** solemnization, commemoration; jubilation, ovation, triumph; inauguration, installation, presentation; coronation; debut, coming out [*colloq.*].

birthday, anniversary, biennial, triennial, etc.; centenary, centennial; bicentenary, bicentennial; tercentenary, tercentennial, etc.; festivity, festival, fete, holiday.

triumphal arch; salute, salvo, salvo of artillery; flourish of trumpets, fanfare; colors flying; illuminations.

jubilee, 50th anniversary; diamond jubilee.

V. **celebrate,** keep, signalize, do honor to, commemorate, solemnize; rejoice, etc., 838; paint the town red [*colloq.*].

inaugurate, install, instate, induct, chair.

Adj. **commemorative,** celebrated, kept in remembrance; immortal.

Adv. in honor of, in commemoration of, in celebration of, in memory of, in memoriam [L.].

884. BOASTING.—*N.* **boasting,** boast, vaunt, pretensions, braggadocio, puff [*colloq.*], flourish, bluff, highfalutin, swagger, jingoism, chauvinism, brag, bounce, bluster, bravado, buncombe [*cant or slang*]; rodomontade, bombast, hot air [*slang*], tall talk [*colloq.*], exaggeration, magniloquence, heroics.

boaster, braggart, pretender, bluffer, hot-air artist [*slang*]; chauvinist, jingo, jingoist; blusterer, swaggerer.

V. **boast,** brag, vaunt, puff, show off, flourish, strut, swagger, bluff; talk big, draw the long bow, blow one's own trumpet.

exult, crow [*colloq.*], triumph, glory, rejoice, cheer; gloat, gloat over, chuckle.

Adj. **boastful,** braggart, pretentious, vainglorious, highfalutin.

elate, elated, jubilant, triumphant, exultant; in high feather.

885. [Undue assumption of superiority] INSOLENCE.—*N.* insolence, brazenness, haughtiness, arrogance, airs; bumptiousness, assumption, presumption; disdain, insult, bluster, swagger.

impertinence, cheek [*colloq. or, slang*], nerve [*slang*], sauce [*colloq.*], abuse; flippancy.

impudence, self-assertion, assurance, audacity, hardihood, gall [*slang*], shamelessness, effrontery.

V. be insolent, bluster, swagger, give oneself airs, arrogate, assume, presume; make bold, make free, take a liberty.

outface, outlook, outstare, outbrazen, brazen out; look big.

domineer, bully, dictate, hector; lord it over; snub, browbeat, intimidate; dragoon, bulldoze [*colloq.*], terrorize.

Adj. insolent, haughty, arrogant, imperious, dictatorial, arbitrary, highhanded, supercilious, overbearing, toplofty [*colloq.*], intolerant, domineering, overweening, bumptious.

pert, flippant, fresh [*slang*], saucy, forward, impertinent, assuming, impudent, audacious, presumptuous.

brazen, shameless, unblushing, unabashed; barefaced, brazenfaced; lost to shame.

blustering, swaggering, hectoring, rollicking, roistering, devil-may-care.

jingo, jingoistic, chauvinistic.

Adv. with nose in air; with arms akimbo; with a high hand.

886. SERVILITY.—*N.* servility, slavery, obsequiousness, toadying, subserviency; abasement, prostration, toadeating, fawning, flunkyism, sycophancy; humility, etc., 879.

sycophant, parasite, toady, toadeater, flunky, hanger-on, timeserver, flatterer, tool; beat [*slang*], dead beat [*slang*]; heeler, ward heeler [*both polit. cant*]; sponge, sponger, truckler.

V. cringe, bow, stoop, kneel; fawn, crouch, cower, sneak, crawl, sponge, toady, grovel; be servile.

go with the stream, follow the crowd, worship the rising sun; be a timeserver.

Adj. servile, obsequious, oily, pliant, cringing, fawning, slavish, groveling, sniveling, mealy-mouthed; sycophantic, parasitical; abject, prostrate, base, mean, sneaking, timeserving.

887. BLUSTERER.—*N.* blusterer, swaggerer, braggart; roisterer, brawler, bully, terrorist, rough, ruffian, roughneck [*slang*], tough [*colloq.*], rowdy, hoodlum [*colloq.*], hooligan [*slang*], swashbuckler; desperado, daredevil, fire-eater [*colloq.*], jingo.

dogmatist, doctrinaire, stump orator.

III. SYMPATHETIC AFFECTIONS

888. FRIENDSHIP.—*N.* friendship, amity, friendliness; harmony, concord, peace, etc., 721; cordiality, *entente cordiale* [F.], good understanding, sympathy, fellow feeling, response; affection, etc. (*love*), 897; benevolence, good will; partiality, favoritism.

brotherhood, fraternization, association; acquaintance, familiarity, intimacy, intercourse, fellowship.

fraternity, sodality; sisterhood, sorority, sorosis.

V. be friendly, be friends, be acquainted with, know; have dealings with, sympathize with, have a leaning to, bear good will, love, befriend.

become friendly, make friends with, break the ice, be introduced to, make (*or* scrape) acquaintance with, get into favor, gain the friendship of; shake hands with, fraternize.

Adj. friendly, amicable, neighborly; brotherly, fraternal, sisterly; ardent, devoted, sympathetic, harmonious, hearty, cordial, warmhearted.

friends with, at home with, on good (*or* friendly, amicable, cordial, familiar, intimate) terms, on speaking terms, on visiting terms.

acquainted, familiar, intimate, hail fellow well met, free and easy; welcome.

Adv. with open arms; arm in arm.

889. ENMITY.—*N.* enmity, hostility, antagonism, unfriendliness; discord, etc., 713; bitterness, rancor; heartburning, animosity; malevolence, etc., 907.

alienation, estrangement; dislike, aversion, hate, etc., 898.

V. be unfriendly, keep (*or* hold) at arm's length; be at loggerheads, bear malice, fall out; take umbrage; alienate, estrange.

Adj. unfriendly, inimical, hostile; at enmity, at variance, at daggers drawn, up in arms against.

on bad terms, not on speaking terms; cool, cold, estranged, alienated, disaffected, irreconcilable.

890. FRIEND.—*N.* friend, alter ego [L.], other self; intimate, confidant (*masc.*), confidante (*fem.*); best (*or* bosom, fast) friend, well-wisher; neighbor, acquaintance.

patron, backer, tutelary saint, good genius, advocate, partisan, sympathizer; ally, friend in need.

associate, comrade, mate, companion, confrere, colleague, partner, consort, chum [*colloq.*], pal [*slang*], buddy [*slang, First World War*]; playfellow, playmate, schoolma', schoolfellow, classmate; bedfellow, bunkie [*colloq.*], roommate, shopmate, shipmate, messmate; fellow (*or* boon) companion.

Famous friendships: Pylades and Orestes, Castor and Pollux, Achilles and Patroclus, Damon and Pythias, David and Jonathan; Soldiers Three, the Three Musketeers.

host, hostess (*fem.*).

guest, visitor, frequenter, habitué, protégé.

compatriot, countryman, fellow countryman; fellow townsman.

891. ENEMY.—*N.* **enemy,** antagonist, foe, foeman, open (*or* bitter) enemy, opponent; mortal aversion (*or* antipathy); snake in the grass.

public enemy, enemy to society; anarchist, seditionist, traitor, traitress (*fem.*).

892. SOCIALITY.—*N.* **sociality,** sociability, social intercourse, intercourse, companionship, comradeship, fellowship; urbanity, intimacy, familiarity, condescension, *esprit de corps* [F.]; morale.

conviviality, good fellowship, joviality, jollity, festivity, merry-making; hospitality, heartiness; cheer.

welcome, greeting; hearty (*or* warm) reception; hearty welcome (*or* greeting), the glad hand [*slang*].

social gathering, social reunion, assembly, barbecue; bee; cornhusking, corn shucking [U. S.]; husking, husking-bee [U. S.]; hen party [*colloq.*]; house raising, housewarming, hanging of the crane, smoker [*colloq.*]; Dutch treat [*colloq.*]; stag, stag party [*both colloq.*]; sociable [U. S.], party, entertainment, reception, levee, at home, soirée, matinee; garden party, coming-out party [*colloq.*], surprise party; ball, hunt ball, dance festival.

Social meals: breakfast, wedding breakfast, hunt breakfast; luncheon, lunch; picnic lunch, basket lunch, picnic; tea, afternoon tea, five-o'clock tea, cup of tea, dish of tea [esp. Brit.], coming-out tea [*colloq.*]; tea party, tea fight [*slang*]; dinner, potluck, bachelor dinner, stag dinner [*colloq.*], hunt dinner; church supper, high tea, banquet.

visit, visiting; round of visits; call, morning call, interview; tryst, appointment.

V. **be sociable,** know, be acquainted, associate with, consort with, club together, join; make advances, fraternize.

visit, pay a visit, call at, call upon, leave a card, drop in, look in.

entertain, give a party; see one's friends, keep open house, do the honors, receive, welcome; kill the fatted calf.

Adj. **sociable,** companionable, clubbable [*colloq.*], cozy, chatty, conversational; convivial, festive, festal, jovial, jolly, hospitable.

free and easy, hail fellow well met, familiar, intimate, social, neighborly.

Adv. *en famille* [F.], in the family circle; on terms of intimacy; in the social whirl.

893. SECLUSION. EXCLUSION.—*N.* **seclusion,** privacy, retirement, concealment, rustication, solitude, isolation, loneliness, voluntary exile, aloofness.

retreat, cell, hermitage, cloister, convent; sanctum sanctorum [L.], study, library, den [*colloq.*].

exclusion, excommunication, banishment, exile, ostracism, cut.

unsociability, unsociableness, inhospitality, domesticity, self-sufficiency.

recluse, hermit; caveman, cave dweller, troglodyte, cynic, Diogenes.

outcast, pariah, leper; outsider, rank outsider; castaway, foundling.

V. seclude oneself, keep aloof, shut oneself up; deny oneself, rusticate, retire, retire from the world; take the veil.

exclude, repel, cut; send to Coventry, turn one's back upon, shut the door upon; blackball, excommunicate, exile, expatriate; banish, outlaw, maroon, ostracize, keep at arm's length; boycott, embargo, blockade, isolate.

Adj. secluded, sequestered, retired, private, out of the world.

unsociable, unsocial, inhospitable; domestic, stay-at-home.

excluded, unfrequented, unvisited, uninvited, unwelcome, under a cloud.

friendless, homeless, desolate, lorn, forlorn; solitary, lonely, lonesome, isolated, single, estranged; derelict, outcast, deserted, banished.

uninhabited, unoccupied, untenanted, tenantless, abandoned.

894. COURTESY.—*N.* courtesy; respect, etc., 928; good manners (*or* behavior, breeding); manners, politeness, urbanity, gentility, breeding, gentle breeding, cultivation, culture, polish, civility, amenity, suavity; good temper, good humor, amiability, complacency, affability, complaisance, compliance, gallantry, chivalry.

pink of courtesy, pink of politeness; flower of knighthood; Chesterfield; Lancelot.

ceremonial; salutation, reception, presentation, introduction, welcome, greeting; respects, regards, remembrances; deference, love.

Forms of greeting: bow, curtsy, salaam, kowtow [China], obeisance, bowing and scraping; kneeling, genuflection; capping, pulling the forelock, nod, shaking hands; embrace, hug, squeeze, kiss; salute, accolade.

V. be courteous, show courtesy; behave oneself, conciliate, speak one fair, take in good part.

do the honors, usher, usher in, receive, greet, hail, bid welcome, welcome; bid Godspeed; speed the parting guest.

salute; nod to; smile upon; uncover, touch (*or* raise) the hat, doff the cap, bow, make one's bow, curtsy, bob a curtsy, kneel; bow (*or* bend) the knee; salaam, kowtow [China], prostrate oneself.

Adj. courteous, polite, civil, mannerly, urbane; well behaved, well mannered, well bred, gently bred, of gentle breeding; polished, cultivated, refined; gallant, chivalrous, chivalric, knightly.

tactful, ingratiating, winning; gentle, mild; good-humored,

cordial, gracious, amiable, familiar; neighborly; obliging, complacent, conciliatory.

bland, suave, affable, honey-tongued; oily, unctuous, obsequious.

Adv. with a good grace; with open arms, with outstretched arms, with perfect courtesy, in good humor.

895. DISCOURTESY.—*N.* discourtesy, ill-breeding, bad manners; tactlessness; discourteousness, rusticity, incivility, lack (*or* want) of courtesy, disrespect, impudence, misbehavior, barbarism, barbarity; vulgarity, brutality, blackguardism, conduct unbecoming a gentleman.

bad temper, ill-temper, peevishness, surliness, churlishness, perversity; moroseness, etc., 901*a*; sternness, austerity; moodishness, captiousness, tartness, acrimony, asperity.

scowl, black looks, frown; sulks, short answer, rebuff; hard words, unparliamentary language, personality.

bear, brute, blackguard, beast; unlicked cub; crosspatch [*colloq.*], grouch [*slang*].

V. be rude, insult, treat with discourtesy, make bold with, make free with; take a liberty; stare out of countenance, ogle, point at.

sulk, frown, scowl, glower, pout; snap, snarl, growl.

cut; turn one's back upon, turn on one's heel; give the cold shoulder, keep at a distance.

Adj. discourteous, uncourteous, uncourtly, ill-bred, ill-mannered, ill-behaved, unmannerly, uncivil, impolite, unaccommodating, unneighborly, ungallant, ungracious, unpolished; ungentlemanly; unladylike; vulgar.

pert, forward, obtrusive, impudent, rude, saucy, flippant.

rough, rugged, bluff, blunt, short, gruff; churlish, boorish, bearish; brutal, brusque, stern, harsh, austere; cavalier.

bad-tempered, ill-tempered, ill-humored, crusty, tart, sour, crabbed, sharp, trenchant, sarcastic, caustic, virulent, bitter, acrimonious, venomous, contumelious, snarling, surly, perverse, grim, sullen, peevish, bristling, thorny.

Adv. with a bad grace.

896. CONGRATULATION.—*N.* congratulation, felicitation, compliment; compliments of the season; good wishes, best wishes.

V. congratulate, felicitate, wish one joy, compliment, tender (*or* offer) one's congratulations; wish many happy returns of the day.

897. LOVE.—*N.* love, affection, sympathy, fellow feeling; tenderness, heart, brotherly love; charity, good will, benevolence; attachment, fondness, liking, inclination; regard, admiration, fancy.

yearning, tender passion, gallantry, passion, flame, devotion, fervor, enthusiasm, rapture, enchantment, infatuation, adoration, idolatry.

mother love, maternal love, natural affection.

attractiveness, charm; popularity; idol, favorite, etc., 899.

god of love, Cupid, Eros, Venus; myrtle.

lover, suitor, fiancé [F.], follower [*colloq.*], admirer, adorer, wooer, beau, sweetheart, swain, young man [*colloq.*], flame [*colloq.*], love, truelove.

ladylove, sweetheart, mistress, inamorata, darling, idol, angel, goddess; betrothed, fiancée [F.].

flirt, coquette.

V. love, like, fancy, care for, take an interest in, sympathize with; be in love with, regard, revere, take to, set one's affections on, adore, idolize, dote on (*or* upon), make much of, hold dear, prize; hug, cling to, cherish, caress, fondle, pet.

charm, attract, attach, fascinate, captivate, bewitch, enrapture, turn the head.

Adj. loving, affectionate, tender, sympathetic, amorous, love-sick, fond, ardent, passionate, rapturous, devoted, motherly.

loved, beloved, well beloved, dearly beloved; dear, precious, darling, pet; favorite, popular.

lovable, adorable, lovely, sweet, attractive, winning, winsome, charming, enchanting, captivating, fascinating, bewitching, amiable.

898. HATE.—*N.* hate, hatred, vials of hate; hymn of hate; disaffection, disfavor; alienation, estrangement, coolness; enmity, etc., 889; animosity, malice, implacability.

umbrage, pique, grudge, spleen, bitterness, bitterness of feeling; ill-blood, bad blood; acrimony.

repugnance, etc. (*dislike*), 867; odium, unpopularity; detestation, abhorrence, loathing, execration, abomination, aversion, antipathy.

object of hatred, an abomination, an aversion, bête noire [F.]; enemy, etc., 891; bitter pill.

V. hate, detest, abominate, abhor, loathe; recoil at, shudder at; shrink from, revolt against, execrate; dislike, etc., 867.

alienate, estrange, repel, horrify, set against, sow dissension, set by the ears, envenom, incense, irritate, ruffle, vex.

Adj. abhorrent, averse from, set against; bitter, etc. (*acrimonious*), 895; implacable.

unloved, unbeloved, unlamented, undeplored, unmourned, uncared for, unvalued; disliked.

lovelorn, jilted, crossed in love, forsaken, rejected.

hateful, obnoxious, odious, abominable, repulsive, offensive, shocking; disgusting, reprehensible.

invidious, spiteful; malicious, etc., 907.

899. FAVORITE.—*N.* favorite, pet, idol, jewel, spoiled child, apple of one's eye, man after one's own heart.

love, dear, darling, duck, honey, sweetheart, etc. (*ladylove*), 897.

general (*or* universal) favorite; idol of the people; matinee idol.

900. RESENTMENT.—*N.* resentment, displeasure, animosity, anger, wrath, ire, indignation; exasperation, vexation, wrathful, indignation.

pique, umbrage, huff, soreness, acerbity, virulence, bitterness, acrimony, asperity; irascibility, etc., 901; sulks, etc., 901a; hate, etc., 898; revenge.

irritation; warmth, ferment, excitement, ebullition; angry mood, pet, tiff, passion, fit, tantrum [*colloq.*].

rage, fury, towering rage, passion; outburst, explosion, paroxysm, storm, violence, vials of wrath; hot blood, high words.

Furies, Erinyes (*sing.* Erinys), Eumenides.

provocation, affront, offense, indignity, insult, grudge; last straw, sore subject; ill-turn, outrage; buffet, blow, box on the ear, rap on the knuckles.

V. resent, take amiss, take offense (*or* umbrage, exception); pout, frown, scowl, lower, snarl, growl, gnash, snap; redden, color; look black, look daggers.

be angry, fly into a rage, bridle up, fire up, flare up; chafe, mantle, fume, kindle, fly out, boil, boil with indignation (*or* rage); rage, storm, foam; hector, bully, bluster; lose one's temper; raise Cain [*slang*]; breathe revenge.

anger, affront, offend, give offense (*or* umbrage); hurt the feelings; insult, ruffle, heckle [Brit.], nettle, huff, pique; excite, irritate, fret, sting, provoke, chafe, wound, incense, inflame, enrage, envenom, embitter, exasperate, infuriate, madden; rankle.

Adj. angry, wroth, irate, ireful, wrathful; irascible, etc., 901; bitter, virulent, acrimonious, offended, indignant, hurt, sore.

fuming, raging, hot under the collar [*slang*]; convulsed with rage; fierce, wild, furious, fiery, rabid, savage, violent.

Adv. in the height (*or* heat) of passion; in an ecstasy of rage.

901. IRASCIBILITY.—*N.* irascibility, temper; crossness, petulance, irritability, tartness, acerbity, acrimony, asperity, pugnacity, excitability.

shrew, vixen, virago, dragon, scold, spitfire, fury.

V. be irascible, have a temper, be possessed of the devil, have the temper of a fiend; fire up, flare up.

Adj. irascible, bad-tempered, irritable, excitable; thin-skinned, sensitive; hasty, quick, warm, hot, testy, touchy, huffy, pettish, petulant, fretful, querulous, captious, moody, cross, fractious, peevish.

quarrelsome, contentious, disputatious, pugnacious, cantankerous [*colloq.*], cross-grained; waspish, peppery, fiery, passionate, choleric, shrewish.

901a. SULLENNESS.—*N.* sullenness, moroseness, spleen; churlishness, irascibility, moodiness, perversity, obstinacy, crabbedness.

sulks, dudgeon, dumps [*humorous*], doldrums; black looks, scowl; grouch [*slang*], huff.

V. sulk, frown, scowl, lower, glower, pout, grouch [*slang*].

Adj. sullen, sulky, ill-tempered, ill-humored, ill-disposed; crusty, crabbed, sour, sore, surly, moody, cross, cross-grained; perverse, wayward, refractory, restive, ungovernable, cussed [*vulgar or euphemistic*]; grumpy, glum, grum, grim, morose, grouchy [*slang*].

902. [Expression of affection] ENDEARMENT.—*N.* endearment, caress, blandishment, fondling, billing and cooing, dalliance, caressing, embrace, salute, kiss, smack, osculation.

courtship, wooing, suit, addresses, love-making; calf love [*colloq.*]; amorous glances, ogle, side glance, sheep's eyes, goo-goo eyes [*slang*].

flirting, flirtation, gallantry; coquetry, spooning [*slang*].

engagement, betrothal; marriage, etc., 903; honeymoon; love letter, billet-doux; valentine.

flirt, coquette; male flirt, philanderer; spoon [*slang*].

V. caress, fondle, pet; smile upon, coax, wheedle, coddle, make much of, cherish, foster.

clasp, hug, cuddle; fold to the heart, press to the bosom, fold in one's arms; snuggle, nestle, nuzzle; embrace, kiss, salute.

court, make love, bill and coo, spoon [*slang*], toy, dally, flirt, coquet, philander, pay court to; serenade; woo.

propose, make (*or* have) an offer, pop the question [*colloq.*]; become engaged, become betrothed; plight one's troth.

Adj. lovesick, spoony [*slang*].

903. MARRIAGE.—*N.* marriage, matrimony, wedlock, union, intermarriage; nuptial tie, nuptial knot; match; betrothment.

wedding, nuptials, Hymen, bridal, espousals; leading to the altar; honeymoon.

bridesmaid, maid of honor, matron of honor; attendant, usher, best man, bridesman, groomsman; bride, bridegroom.

married man, partner, spouse, mate, husband, man [*dial.*], consort.

married woman, wife, wedded wife, spouse, helpmeet, helpmate, better half, lady [*obs. or uncultivated*]; squaw; matron.

married couple, man and wife, wedded pair, wedded couple, Darby and Joan.

Kinds of marriage: monogamy, bigamy, polygamy, polyandry; Mormonism; morganatic (*or* left-handed) marriage, *mésalliance* [F.].

matchmaker, matrimonial agency (*or* agent, bureau).

V. **marry,** wive, take to oneself a wife; be married, be spliced [*colloq.*]; wed, espouse, lead to the altar, join, couple, be made one.

Adj. **engaged,** betrothed, plighted, affianced.

Matrimonial, marital, conjugal, connubial, wedded; nuptial, hymeneal, spousal, bridal.

904. CELIBACY.—*N.* **celibacy,** singleness, single blessedness; bachelorhood, bachelorship; misogyny.

virginity, maidenhood, maidenhead.

unmarried man, bachelor, old bachelor; misogamist, misogynist; monk, priest, celibate, religious.

unmarried woman, maid, maiden, virgin, spinster, old maid; nun, sister, vestal, vestal virgin; Diana.

Adj. **unmarried,** unwedded; wifeless, spouseless; single, celibate, virgin.

905. DIVORCE. WIDOWHOOD.—*N.* **divorce,** divorcement; separation, judicial separation, separate maintenance.

widowhood, weeds.

widow, relict, dowager; divorcée; grass widow.

widower; grass widower.

V. live separate; separate, divorce, put away.

906. BENEVOLENCE.—*N.* **benevolence,** Christian charity; God's grace; good will, philanthropy, unselfishness, kindness, kindliness, good nature, loving-kindness, benignity, brotherly love, charity, humanity, kindly feelings, fellow feeling, sympathy, goodness of heart, warmheartedness, kindheartedness, amiability, tenderness, love, friendship; tolerance, consideration; mercy.

charitableness, bounty, almsgiving; good works, beneficence, generosity, a good turn.

philanthropist, salt of the earth; good Samaritan, sympathizer, well-wisher, altruist.

V. **bear good will,** wish well, take (*or* feel) an interest in; be interested in, sympathize with, feel for; treat well, give comfort, do good, do a good turn, benefit, assist, render a service, render assistance, aid.

enter into the feelings of others, practice the golden rule, do as you would be done by.

Adj. **benevolent,** kind, kindly, well meaning, amiable, cordial, obliging, accommodating, indulgent, gracious, tender, considerate, warmhearted, kindhearted, tenderhearted, largehearted, softhearted, merciful; sympathizing, sympathetic.

full of natural affection, fatherly, motherly, brotherly, sisterly; paternal, maternal, fraternal; friendly.

charitable, beneficent, philanthropical, generous, humane, benignant, unselfish, altruistic, bountiful.

Adv. with the best intentions; out of deepest sympathy.

907. MALEVOLENCE.—*N.* **malevolence,** bad intent, bad intention, unkindness, uncharitableness, ill-nature, ill-will, enmity, hate, malice, malignance, malignity, maliciousness; spite, resentment; gall, venom, rancor, virulence, hardness of heart, heart of stone, obduracy; evil eye, cloven foot (*or* hoof).

ill-turn, bad turn; affront, indignity; tender mercies (*ironical*).

cruelty, brutality, savagery, ferocity; outrage, atrocity, illusage, persecution; barbarity, inhumanity, truculence, ruffianism; inquisition, torture.

V. **bear malice,** harbor a grudge; hurt, annoy, injure, harm, wrong, outrage, malign; molest, worry, harass, harry, bait, hound, persecute, oppress, grind, maltreat, ill-treat; give no quarter, have no mercy.

Adj. **malevolent,** ill-disposed, ill-intentioned, ill-natured, illconditioned, evil-minded, evil-disposed, venomous, malicious, malign, malignant, maleficent; rancorous, spiteful, treacherous, caustic, bitter, envenomed, acrimonious, virulent; grinding, galling, harsh; disobliging, unkind, unfriendly; ungracious, churlish, surly, sullen.

cold-blooded, coldhearted, hardhearted, stonyhearted, cold, unnatural; ruthless, pitiless, relentless.

cruel, brutal, brutish, savage, ferocious, inhuman; barbarous, fell, truculent, bloodthirsty, atrocious, fiendish, diabolic *or* diabolical, devilish, infernal, hellish.

Adv. with bad intent; with the ferocity of a tiger.

908. MALEDICTION.—*N.* **malediction,** malison, curse, imprecation, denunciation, execration; anathema, ban, proscription, excommunication, commination, fulmination; disparagement, vilification, vituperation.

abuse, evil speaking, foul (*or* bad, strong, unparliamentary) language, billingsgate, blackguardism, cursing, profane, swearing, expletive, oath, foul invective, ribaldry, scurrility, invective.

V. **curse,** imprecate, damn, swear at; execrate, vituperate, scold; anathematize, denounce, proscribe, excommunicate, fulminate, thunder against.

909. THREAT.—*N.* **threat,** menace, defiance, abuse, intimidation, denunciation, fulmination, etc., 908; gathering clouds.

V. **threaten,** threat, menace; snarl, growl, mutter, bully; defy, intimidate, shake the fist at; thunder, fulminate, bluster.

Adj. **threatening,** menacing, minatory, abusive; ominous, defiant.

910. PHILANTHROPY.—*N.* **philanthropy,** altruism, humanity, humanitarianism, benevolence; public welfare.

public spirit, patriotism, nationality, love of country.

philanthropist, altruist, etc., 906; humanitarian, patriot.

Adj. **philanthropic,** altruistic, humanitarian, public-spirited, patriotic; humane, largehearted, benevolent, etc., 906; generous, liberal, etc., 942.

911. MISANTHROPY.—*N.* **misanthropy,** hatred of mankind; selfishness, egoism, egotism; sullenness, moroseness, cynicism; want of patriotism.

misanthrope, misanthropist, egoist, egotist, cynic, man hater. woman hater, misogynist.

Adj. **misanthropic,** antisocial, unpatriotic; egoistical, egotistical, selfish; morose, sullen, cynical, etc., 901*a*.

912. BENEFACTOR.—*N.* **benefactor,** savior, protector, good genius, tutelary saint, guardian angel, good Samaritan; friend in need; salt of the earth; philanthropist, etc., 910; fairy godmother.

913. [Maleficent being] EVILDOER.—*N.* **evildoer,** evil worker, wrongdoer, etc., 949; mischiefmaker, marplot; oppressor, tyrant; incendiary, etc., 384; anarchist, nihilist, destroyer, vandal, iconoclast, terrorist.

savage, brute, ruffian, barbarian, desperado; apache, gunman, hoodlum [*colloq.*], redskin, tough [*colloq.*], bully, rough, hooligan [*slang*], dangerous classes; thief, etc., 792; cutthroat.

wild beast, tiger, leopard, panther, hyena, catamount [U. S.]; catamountain, lynx, cougar, jaguar, puma; bloodhound, hell-hound, sleuthhound; gorilla; vulture.

cockatrice, adder; snake, serpent, cobra, asp, viper, rattlesnake, boa; alligator, crocodile, octopus.

hag, hellhag, beldam, Jezebel.

monster, fiend, demon, etc., 980; devil incarnate, Franken-stein's monster; cannibal; bloodsucker, vampire, ogre, ghoul.

914. PITY.—*N.* **pity,** compassion, commiseration, sympathy, fellow feeling, tenderness, softheartedness, yearning, forbearance, humanity, mercy, clemency; leniency, lenity, charity, ruth, long-suffering; quarter, grace.

sympathizer; advocate, friend, partisan, patron, well-wisher, defender, champion.

V. pity, have (*or* take) pity, commiserate, condole, sympathize, feel for, be sorry for.

forbear, relent, relax, give quarter.

excite pity, touch, soften, melt, melt the heart; propitiate.

Adj. pitying, pitiful, compassionate, sympathetic, touched. merciful, clement, humane, humanitarian; tender, tender-hearted, softhearted, lenient, forbearing.

914a. PITILESSNESS.—*N.* pitilessness, inclemency, inexorability, inflexibility, hardness of heart; want of pity, severity, malevolence, etc., 907.

V. be pitiless, turn a deaf ear to; claim one's pound of flesh; have no mercy, give no quarter.

Adj. pitiless, merciless, ruthless, unpitying, unmerciful, inclement, grim-faced, grim-visaged; inflexible, relentless, inexorable, harsh, cruel, etc., 907.

915. CONDOLENCE.—*N.* condolence, sympathy, consolation; lamentation, etc., 839.

V. condole with, console, sympathize, express pity; afford consolation; lament with, express sympathy for, feel for, send one's condolences; share one's sorrow.

916. GRATITUDE.—*N.* gratitude, gratefulness, thankfulness; sense of obligation; acknowledgment, recognition, thanksgiving, giving thanks.

thanks, praise, benediction; paean; *Te Deum* [L.], grace, requital, thank offering.

V. be grateful, thank; give (*or* render, return, offer, tender) thanks, acknowledge, requite; lie under an obligation; never forget, overflow with gratitude.

Adj. grateful, thankful, obliged, beholden, indebted to, under obligation.

917. INGRATITUDE.—*N.* ingratitude, thanklessness, unthankfulness; thankless task, thankless office.

V. be ungrateful, feel no obligation, owe one no thanks, forget benefits, have a short memory for.

Adj. ungrateful, unmindful, unthankful; thankless, ingrate. forgotten; unacknowledged, unthanked, unrequited, unrewarded; ill-requited; ill-rewarded.

918. FORGIVENESS.—*N.* forgiveness, pardon, grace, remission, absolution, amnesty, oblivion; reprieve.

conciliation; reconciliation, forbearance, propitiation.

exoneration, excuse, quittance, release, indemnity; acquittal, exculpation.

V. forgive, pardon, think no more of, let bygones by bygones, bury the hatchet. start afresh.

remit, exculpate, exonerate, absolve, give absolution; blot out one's sins (*or* offenses, transgressions), wipe the slate clean; reprieve, acquit.

excuse, pass over, overlook; condone, wink at; bear with, allow for, make allowances for; pocket the affront.

conciliate, propitiate, placate; beg (*or* ask) pardon, make up a quarrel.

Adj. forgiving, placable, conciliatory.

919. REVENGE.—*N.* revenge, vengeance; vendetta, death feud, eye for an eye, tooth for a tooth, retaliation; day of reckoning.

rancor, vindictiveness, implacability, ruthlessness; malevolence, etc., 907.

avenger, nemesis, Eumenides.

V. revenge, avenge, take revenge, have one's revenge; breathe vengeance; give no quarter, take no prisoners.

keep the wound open, harbor revenge, bear malice; rankle, rankle in the breast.

Adj. revengeful, vengeful, vindictive, rancorous; pitiless, ruthless, rigorous, avenging, retaliative; unforgiving, unrelenting; inexorable, implacable, relentless, remorseless.

920. JEALOUSY.—*N.* jealousy, distrust, mistrust, heartburn; envy, etc., 921; doubt, suspicion; green-eyed monster.

V. be jealous, view with jealousy, grudge, begrudge.

doubt, distrust, mistrust, suspect, misdoubt.

Adj. jealous, jaundice, yellow-eyed, envious.

921. ENVY.—*N.* envy, enviousness; rivalry; ill-will, spite; jealousy, etc., 920.

V. envy, covet, grudge, begrudge, break the tenth commandment.

Adj. envious, invidious, covetous, grudging, begrudged; belittling.

IV. MORAL AFFECTIONS

922. RIGHT.—*N.* right; what ought to be, what should be; fitness.

justice, equity, equitableness, propriety, fairness, fair play, square deal [*colloq.*], impartiality; lawfulness, legality.

morals, etc. (*duty*), 926; law, etc., 963; honor, etc., 939; virtue, etc., 944.

V. be right, stand to reason.

do right, see justice done, see fair play; do justice to, recompense, hold the scales even, give everyone his due.

Adj. **right,** good; just, reasonable; fit, etc., 924; equal, equable, equitable; even-handed, fair, square.

legitimate, justifiable, rightful, as it ought to be; lawful, legal.

Adv. in justice, in equity, in reason; upon even terms.

923. WRONG.—*N.* wrong, iniquity; what ought not to be, what should not be; unreasonableness, grievance; shame.

injustice, unfairness, foul play, partiality, leaning, favor, favoritism, partisanship; undueness, unlawfulness, illegality.

dishonor, etc., 939; vice, etc., 945.

V. do wrong, be inequitable, show partiality, favor, lean toward; encroach; impose upon; reap where one has not sown.

Adj. **wrong,** wrongful, iniquitous, bad, unjust, unfair, inequitable, unequal, partial, one-sided; injurious.

unjustifiable, unreasonable, unwarrantable, objectionable, improper, unfit, unjustified; unlawful; illegal, immoral.

924. AUTHORIZATION.—*N.* authorization, sanction, authority, charter, warrant; constitution; bond.

right, dueness, due, privilege, prerogative, prescription, title, claim, pretension, legality, demand, birthright.

immunity, license, liberty, franchise; vested interest (*or* right).

deserts, merits, dues.

claimant, appellant; plaintiff, etc., 938.

V. deserve, merit, be worthy of, make good.

demand, claim, lay claim to, reclaim, exact; insist on (*or* upon), make a point of, require, assert, assume, arrogate.

entitle, give (*or* confer) a right, authorize, sanction, legalize, ordain, prescribe, allot.

Adj. **privileged,** allowed, sanctioned, warranted, authorized; ordained, prescribed, constitutional, chartered, enfranchised.

prescriptive, presumptive, absolute, inalienable, inviolable, sacrosanct.

merited, due to, deserved, condign [*archaic, except of punishment*].

right, creditable, fit, fitting, correct, square, due, proper, meet, befitting, becoming, seemly; decorous.

lawful, legitimate, legal, legalized, allowable.

Adv. by right, by divine right; on the square [*colloq.*].

925. [Want of authorization] IMPROPRIETY.—*N.* impropriety, undueness, unrightfulness, illegality, unlawfulness; falseness, invalidity of title; illegitimacy.

loss of right, disfranchisement, forfeiture.

assumption, usurpation, tort [*law*], violation, breach, encroachment, seizure, exaction, imposition.

usurper, pretender, impostor.

V. **infringe,** encroach, trench on, exact, arrogate, usurp, violate; get under false pretenses, sail under false colors.

disentitle, disfranchise, disqualify; invalidate.

Adj. **undue,** unlawful, illegal, illicit, unconstitutional, unauthorized, unwarranted, unsanctioned, unjustified; disqualified, unqualified; unprivileged, unchartered.

undeserved, unmerited, unearned.

illegitimate, bastard, spurious, false; usurped.

improper, unfit, unbefitting, unseemly, unbecoming, misbecoming; preposterous, pretentious, would-be.

926. DUTY.—*N.* **duty,** moral obligation, accountability, liability, onus, responsibility.

allegiance, fealty, tie; engagement; function, part, calling.

observance, fulfillment, discharge, performance, acquittal, satisfaction, redemption; good behavior.

morality, morals, decalogue; conscientiousness, conscience, inward monitor, still small voice within, sense of duty.

propriety, fitness, seemliness, decorum, the thing, the proper thing.

Science of morals: ethics, moral (*or* ethical) philosophy, casuistry, polity.

V. **behoove,** become, befit, beseem; belong to, pertain to; rest with, fall to one's lot, devolve on.

take upon oneself, be (*or* become) sponsor for, incur a responsibility; perform (*or* discharge) a duty *or* an obligation; act one's part, redeem one's pledge, be at one's post, do one's duty.

impose a duty, enjoin, require, exact; bind, bind over; saddle with, prescribe, assign, call upon, look to, oblige.

Adj. **obligatory,** binding, imperative, peremptory, stringent, incumbent on.

amenable, liable, accountable, responsible, answerable.

right, meet, etc. (*due*), 924; moral, ethical, conscientious.

Adv. with a safe conscience, as in duty bound, on one's own responsibility, at one's own risk.

927. DERELICTION OF DUTY.—*N.* **dereliction,** nonobservance, nonperformance, nonco-operation; indolence, neglect, infraction, violation, transgression, failure, evasion; fault, etc. (*guilt*), 947.

slacker, loafer, time killer; eyeserver, eyeservant; striker; nonco-operator.

V. **violate,** break, break through; infringe, set aside, set at naught; encroach upon, trench upon, trample on; slight, get by [*slang*], neglect, evade, escape, transgress, fail.

927a. EXEMPTION.—*N.* **exemption,** freedom, irresponsibility, immunity, liberty, license, release, discharge, excuse, dispensation, absolution, exculpation, exoneration.

V. **exempt**, release, acquit, discharge, remit; free, set at liberty, let off [*colloq.*], pass over, spare, excuse, dispense with, license; absolve, exonerate.

Adj. **exempt**, free, immune, at liberty, scot-free, released, unbound; irresponsible, not accountable, excusable.

928. RESPECT.—*N.* **respect**, regard, consideration, courtesy, attention, deference, reverence, honor, esteem, estimation, veneration, admiration; approbation, etc., 931.

homage, fealty, obeisance, genuflection, kneeling, prostration; salaam, etc., 894.

V. **respect**, regard; revere, reverence, honor, venerate, hallow; esteem, think much of, entertain respect for, look up to, defer to, pay attention to, pay respect to, do honor to; do the honors, hail, show courtesy, pay homage to.

command respect, inspire respect; awe, impose, overawe, dazzle.

Adj. **respectful**, deferential, decorous, reverential, ceremonious, bareheaded, cap in hand; prostrate.

respected, estimable; time-honored, venerable.

Adv. **in deference to**; with all respect, with due respect, with the highest respect; with submission.

929. DISRESPECT.—*N.* **disrespect**, disfavor, disrepute, want of esteem, low estimation, disparagement, detraction; irreverence, slight, indignity, contumely, affront, dishonor, insult, outrage, discourtesy, scoffing; hiss, hissing, hoot, derision; mockery.

gibe, flout, jeer, scoff, taunt, sneer, fling.

V. **slight**, disregard, undervalue, humiliate, depreciate, trifle with, pass by, push aside, overlook, be discourteous.

disparage, call names; throw mud at; point at, indulge in personalities.

dishonor, desecrate; insult, affront, browbeat, outrage.

deride, scoff, sneer, laugh at, ridicule, gibe, mock, jeer, taunt, twit, flout, roast [*colloq.*], guy [*colloq.*], rag [*dial. Eng.* and *college slang*], burlesque, scout, hiss, hoot.

Adj. **disrespectful**, disparaging, etc., 934; insulting, supercilious, rude, derisive, sarcastic, scurrilous, contemptuous, insolent, disdainful; irreverent.

unrespected, unregarded, disregarded, unenvied, unsaluted.

930. CONTEMPT.—*N.* **contempt**, disdain, scorn, contemptuousness, derision, etc. (*disrespect*), 929; contumely; slight, sneer, spurn, byword.

V. **despise**, contemn, scorn, disdain, disregard, scout, slight, pass by, look down upon, sneer at, laugh at, curl up one's lip, think nothing of, make light of, underestimate, esteem slightly, care nothing for, set no store by; pooh-pooh, damn with faint praise.

spurn, turn one's back upon, trample underfoot; kick; fling to the winds, repudiate.

Adj. contemptuous, disdainful, scornful, withering, supercilious, cynical, haughty, cavalier; derisive; with the nose in air.

contemptible, despicable, despised, pitiable, pitiful, downtrodden.

931. APPROBATION.—*N.* approbation, approval, sanction, advocacy; esteem, estimation, good opinion, admiration; love, etc., 897; appreciation, regard, account, popularity, credit, repute.

commendation, compliment, praise, laud, laudation; good word; encomium, eulogy, eulogium, panegyric, blurb [*slang*]; benediction, blessing, benison.

applause, plaudit, clap, clapping, acclaim, acclamation; cheer; paean, shout (*or* peal, chorus, thunders) of applause.

V. approve, esteem, value, prize, set great store by; honor, hold in esteem, look up to, admire, like, appreciate; stand up for, stick up for [*colloq.*], uphold, countenance, sanction, indorse, recommend.

commend, praise, laud, compliment, applaud, clap, cheer, acclaim, encore; eulogize, boost [*colloq.*], root for [*slang*], cry up, puff; extol, magnify, glorify, exalt, sing the praises of.

Adj. commendatory, complimentary, laudatory, panegyrical, eulogistic, lavish of praise, uncritical.

approved, praised, popular, in good odor; in high esteem, in favor, in high favor.

praiseworthy, commendable, worthy of praise, good, meritorious, estimable, creditable, unimpeachable.

Adv. with credit, to admiration.

932. DISAPPROBATION.—*N.* disapprobation, disapproval, disesteem, odium, dislike, black list, blackball, ostracism, boycott.

disparagement, depreciation, dispraise, detraction, etc., 934; denunciation, condemnation, stricture, objection, exception, criticism; blame, censure, obloquy, sarcasm, satire, insinuation, innuendo, sneer, taunt.

reproof, reprehension, remonstrance, expostulation, reprobation, admonition, reproach; rebuke, reprimand, lecture, curtain lecture; wigging, dressing down [*both colloq.*]; rating, scolding, correction, rebuff, home thrust, hit; frown, scowl, black look.

abuse, personalities, personal remarks, vituperation, invective, contumely, hard words; bad language.

diatribe, tirade, philippic.

clamor, outcry, hue and cry; hiss, hissing, catcall; execration.

V. disapprove, dislike, object to, take exception to, think ill of, view with disfavor, frown upon, look askance, look black upon, set one's face against.

blame, censure, reproach, reprobate, impugn, impeach, accuse, denounce, expose, brand, gibbet, stigmatize; show up [*colloq.*].

reprove, reprehend, chide, admonish, berate, take to task, overhaul, lecture, rebuke, blow up [*colloq.*], correct, reprimand, snub; chastise, castigate, lash, trounce.

remonstrate, expostulate, recriminate.

abuse, scold, rate, upbraid, fall foul of; jaw [*low*], rail, rail at, call names, execrate, revile, vilify.

decry, cry down, run down, backbite; insinuate, damn with faint praise; hiss, hoot, catcall, mob; ostracize, blacklist, boycott, blackball.

disparage, depreciate, knock [*colloq.*], dispraise, deprecate, speak ill of, condemn, scoff at, sneer at, satirize, lampoon, defame, criticize.

incur blame, scandalize, shock, revolt; get a bad name, forfeit one's good opinion, be under a cloud.

Adj. disparaging, condemnatory, denunciatory, reproachful, abusive, vituperative, defamatory.

critical, satirical, sarcastic, sardonic, cynical, dry, sharp, cutting, biting, severe, withering, trenchant, censorious, captious, hypercritical.

blameworthy, reprehensible, blamable, answerable, bad; vicious, etc., 945.

Adv. with a wry face.

933. FLATTERY.—*N.* flattery, adulation, cajolery, fawning, wheedling, obsequiousness, sycophancy, flunkeyism, toadyism.

honeyed words, flummery, buncombe [*cant or slang*]; blarney, soft soap [*both colloq.*].

V. flatter, overpraise, puff, wheedle, cajole, fawn upon, humor, pet, coquet, butter [*colloq.*], jolly [*slang or colloq.*]; truckle to, pander to, court, curry favor with.

Adj. flattering, adulatory; mealy-mouthed, honeyed, smooth, smooth-tongued; oily, unctuous, specious, plausible, servile, sycophantic, fulsome.

934. DETRACTION.—*N.* detraction, disparagement, depreciation, vilification, obloquy, scandal, defamation, slander, calumny, evil-speaking, backbiting; sarcasm, cynicism, criticism; invective.

personality, libel, lampoon, skit, squib.

V. detract, derogate, decry, depreciate, disparage, run down, cry down, belittle, criticize, pull to pieces, asperse, bespatter, blacken, vilify, brand, malign, backbite, libel, lampoon, traduce, slander, defame, calumniate.

Adj. **detracting,** defamatory, detractory, derogatory, disparaging, libelous; scurrilous, abusive, foul-mouthed; slanderous, calumnious.

935. FLATTERER.—*N.* **flatterer,** adulator, eulogist, euphemist; optimist; puffer, booster [*colloq.*], whitewasher.

toady, sycophant, parasite, hanger-on; courtier.

936. DETRACTOR.—*N.* **detractor,** censor, censurer; cynic, critic, caviler, carper.

defamer, knocker [*colloq.*], backbiter, slanderer, lampooner, satirist, traducer, libeler, calumniator, reviler, vituperator.

Adj. defamatory, etc., 934.

937. VINDICATION.—*N.* **vindication,** justification, warrant; exoneration, exculpation, acquittal; whitewashing, extenuation, palliation, softening, mitigation.

plea, apology, gloss, varnish; excuse, extenuating circumstances; allowance; reply, defense; recrimination.

apologist, vindicator, justifier; defendant, etc., 938.

V. justify, warrant, lend a color, vindicate, exculpate, acquit, clear, exonerate, whitewash.

extenuate, palliate, excuse, soften, apologize.

advocate, defend, plead one's cause; contend for, speak for; bear out, make good; support, plead, say in defense.

Adj. vindicative, vindicatory, vindicating, palliative, extenuating, exculpatory, apologetic.

excusable, defensible, pardonable; venial, plausible, justifiable.

938. ACCUSATION.—*N.* **accusation,** charge, imputation, slur, incrimination, recrimination, denunciation.

libel, challenge, citation, arraignment, impeachment, indictment, true bill, lawsuit, condemnation.

accuser, prosecutor, plaintiff, complainant, libelant, informant, informer.

accused, defendant, prisoner, respondent, litigant.

V. accuse, charge, tax, impute, twit, taunt with, reproach, stigmatize, slur; incriminate, inculpate, implicate.

inform against, indict, denounce, arraign; charge with, saddle with; impeach, show up [*colloq.*], challenge, cite, prosecute; blow upon [*colloq.*], squeal [*slang*].

Adj. accusatory, denunciatory, recriminatory.

inexcusable, indefensible, unpardonable, unjustifiable.

939. PROBITY.—*N.* **probity,** integrity, rectitude, uprightness, respectability, honesty, faith, honor, good faith; constancy, faithfulness, fidelity, loyalty, trustworthiness, truth, veracity, candor, singleness of heart.

fairness, fair play, justice, equity, impartiality, principle.

punctiliousness, punctilio, delicacy, scrupulosity, scrupulousness, scruple; point of honor.

man of honor, man of his word, gentleman, trump [*slang*], brick [*slang or colloq.*].

V. be honorable, speak the truth, draw a straight furrow, make a point of; do one's duty, play the game [*colloq.*]; redeem one's pledge, keep one's promise (*or* word), keep faith with.

Adj. upright, honest, veracious, truthful, virtuous, noble, honorable, reputable, respectable; fair, right, just, equitable, impartial, square, white [*slang*].

manly, straightforward, frank, candid, openhearted.

loyal, constant, faithful, stanch; true; trusty, trustworthy; incorruptible.

conscientious, right-minded, high-principled, high-minded, scrupulous, religious, strict; nice, punctilious.

stainless, unstained, unsullied, inviolate, untainted, incorrupt, innocent, pure, undefiled, undepraved.

chivalrous, jealous of honor, high-spirited.

Adv. on the square [*colloq.*], in good faith, in all honor, by fair means, with clean hands.

940. IMPROBITY.—*N.* improbity, dishonesty, dishonor, disgrace; fraud, lying; bad faith, infidelity, faithlessness; Judas kiss, betrayal, perfidy, treachery, double-dealing; villainy, baseness, degradation, turpitude, moral turpitude.

breach of trust (*or* faith), disloyalty, divided allegiance, hyphenated allegiance [*cant*], treason, high treason; apostasy.

knavery, roguery, rascality, foul play; jobbing, jobbery, graft [*colloq.*], venality, corruption, sharp practice.

V. play false; break one's word (*or* promise), jilt, betray, forswear; grovel, sneak, lose caste; sell oneself, squeal [*slang*], go back on [*colloq.*].

Adj. dishonest, dishonorable; unconscientious, unscrupulous; fraudulent, knavish, falsehearted; unfair, one-sided; double, double-tongued, double-faced; timeserving, crooked, slippery; fishy [*colloq.*], questionable.

infamous, arrant, foul, base, vile, low, ignominious, perfidious, treacherous, perjured; contemptible, abject, mean, shabby, paltry, dirty, sneaking, groveling, rascally, corrupt, venal.

derogatory, degrading, undignified, unbefitting, ungentlemanly, unchivalric, unmanly, recreant, inglorious.

faithless, false, unfaithful, disloyal; untrustworthy; trustless, lost to shame, dead to honor.

Adv. like a thief in the night, by crooked paths, by foul means.

941. KNAVE.—*N.* **knave,** rogue, villain, rascal, etc., 949; shyster.

traitor, betrayer, archtraitor, conspirator, Judas; reptile, serpent, snake in the grass, wolf in sheep's clothing, sneak, squealer [*slang*], telltale, mischiefmaker; renegade, recreant, slacker.

942. DISINTERESTEDNESS.—*N.* **disinterestedness,** unselfishness, generosity; liberality, altruism, benevolence, loftiness of purpose, exaltation, magnanimity; honor, chivalry, heroism, sublimity.

self-denial, self-control, stoicism, self-abnegation, self-sacrifice, devotion, self-devotion; labor of love.

Adj. **disinterested,** unselfish, self-denying, self-sacrificing, altruistic.

magnanimous, high-minded; princely, great, high, elevated, lofty, exalted, greathearted, largehearted; generous, liberal; chivalrous, heroic, sublime.

943. SELFISHNESS.—*N.* **selfishness,** self-love, self-indulgence, self-worship, self-seeking, self-interest; egotism, egoism; illiberality, meanness.

self-seeker, timeserver, fortune hunter, monopolist, dog in the manger, trimmer; hog, roadhog [*colloq.*].

V. **be selfish,** feather one's nest; have an eye to the main chance, live for oneself alone.

Adj. **selfish,** self-seeking, self-indulgent, self-interested; self-centered; egotistic, egoistic.

illiberal, mean, ungenerous, narrow-minded; mercenary, venal; covetous.

worldly, unspiritual, earthly, earthly-minded, mundane, worldly-minded, worldly-wise; timeserving, interested.

Adv. from selfish motives.

944. VIRTUE.—*N.* **virtue,** morality, moral rectitude; integrity, probity, nobleness, well-doing, good actions, good behavior, well-spent life, innocence.

merit, worth, desert, excellence, credit; self-control, self-denial.
morals; ethics, duty, etc., 926; cardinal virtues.

V. **be virtuous,** practice virtue, do one's duty, fight the good fight; acquit oneself well, keep in the right path.

Adj. **virtuous,** good, innocent, meritorious, deserving, worthy, dutiful, duteous; moral, right, righteous, right-minded; creditable, laudable, commendable, praiseworthy; sterling, pure, noble; whole-souled.

exemplary; matchless, peerless; saintly, saintlike; angelic, godlike.

945. VICE.—*N.* vice, evildoing, wrongdoing, wickedness, viciousness, iniquity, sin, immorality, want of principle, knavery, obliquity, backsliding, infamy, brutality.

depravity, demoralization, corruption, profligacy, flagrancy.

weakness, infirmity, frailty, imperfection, error; foible; failing, failure; besetting sin; defect, defection.

fault, crime; guilt, etc., 947.

reprobate; sinner, etc., 949.

V. be vicious, sin, commit sin, err, transgress; misconduct oneself, misbehave; fall, lapse, slip, trip, offend, trespass, go astray; sow one's wild oats.

demoralize, brutalize; corrupt, degrade, etc., 659.

Adj.[1] vicious, sinful; wicked, iniquitous, immoral, unrighteous, wrong, criminal; unprincipled, lawless, disorderly, disgraceful, recreant, disreputable; demoralized, corrupt, depraved, degenerate; evil-minded, heartless, graceless, shameless, abandoned.

base, sinister, foul, gross, vile, black, felonious, nefarious, shameful, scandalous, infamous, villainous, heinous; flagrant, atrocious.

diabolic *or* diabolical, devilish, fiendish, fiendlike, demoniacal, Mephistophelian, satanic, hellish, infernal, hellborn.

incorrigible, irreclaimable, obdurate, reprobate, reprehensible.

unjustifiable, indefensible, inexcusable, inexpiable, unpardonable.

improper, unseemly, indecorous, indiscreet, unworthy, blameworthy, discreditable; incorrect, undutiful, naughty.

weak, frail, lax, infirm, imperfect; spineless, invertebrate [*both fig.*].

946. INNOCENCE.—*N.* innocence; guiltlessness, incorruption, impeccability; clean hands, clear conscience.

innocent, newborn babe; lamb, dove.

Adj. innocent, not guilty, unguilty; guiltless, faultless, sinless, stainless, spotless, clear, immaculate, unerring, undefiled, inculpable, blameless, above suspicion, irreproachable, unimpeachable; virtuous, etc., 944.

harmless, inoffensive, innocuous, pure.

Adv. with clean hands; with a clear conscience.

947. GUILT.—*N.* guilt, guiltiness, culpability, criminality; vice, sinfulness, misconduct, misbehavior, misdeed; fault, sin, error, transgression; dereliction, delinquency.

indiscretion, lapse, slip, trip, flaw, blot, omission, failing, failure, blunder, break [*colloq.*].

[1]Most of these adjectives are applicable both to the act and to the agent.

offense, trespass; misdemeanor, malefaction, malversation, corruption, malpractice; crime, felony, capital crime.

enormity, atrocity, outrage; deadly sin, mortal sin.

Adj. guilty, blamable, culpable, reprehensible, blameworthy.

Adv. in the very act, red-handed.

948. GOOD MAN. GOOD WOMAN.—*N.* good man, worthy, model, paragon, pattern, good example; hero, demigod, angel, saint; benefactor, etc., 912; philanthropist, etc., 910.

salt of the earth; one in ten thousand; a man among men, white man [*slang*].

good woman, virgin, innocent; goddess, queen, Madonna, ministering angel, heaven's noblest gift.

949. BAD MAN. BAD WOMAN.—*N.* bad man, wrongdoer, worker of iniquity; evildoer, etc., 913; sinner, transgressor; bad example.

rascal, scoundrel, villain, knave, etc., 941; miscreant, wretch, reptile, viper, serpent, monster, devil, demon, devil incarnate, fallen angel, lost sheep, black sheep, castaway, prodigal.

bad woman, jade, Jezebel, hellcat.

ruffian, rowdy, bully, etc., 887; thief, murderer.

culprit, delinquent, criminal, malefactor, felon, convict, outlaw.

riffraff, scum of the earth; blackguard, loafer, sneak, vagabond.

scamp, scapegrace, ne'er-do-well, good for nothing, reprobate, scalawag [*colloq.*], limb [*colloq.*], rapscallion [*all the words in this paragraph are commonly applied jocularly or lightly*].

950. PENITENCE.—*N.* penitence, contrition, compunction, repentance, remorse, regret, self-reproach, self-reproof, self-accusation, self-condemnation, qualms of conscience.

acknowledgment, confession, apology, recantation; penance.

penitent, Magdalen, prodigal son, returned prodigal.

V. **repent,** be sorry for, rue, regret, think better of, recant; plead guilty, acknowledge, confess, humble oneself, beg pardon, apologize; turn over a new leaf.

reclaim, reform, regenerate, redeem, convert, amend, make a new man of, restore self-respect.

Adj. penitent, repentant, contrite, softened, melted, touched, conscience-stricken; self-accusing, self-convicted.

951. IMPENITENCE.—*N.* impenitence, irrepentance, recusancy, hardness of heart, heart of stone, seared conscience, obduracy.

V. **be impenitent,** steel the heart, harden the heart; die and make no sign.

Adj. impenitent, obdurate, hard, hardened, seared, recusant, unrepentant; relentless, remorseless, graceless.

lost, incorrigible, irreclaimable; unreclaimed, unreformed.

952. ATONEMENT.—*N.* atonement, reparation, compromise, composition, compensation, quittance, expiation, redemption, reclamation, conciliation, propitiation; indemnification, redress, amends, apology, satisfaction; sacrifice.

penance, fasting, sackcloth and ashes, shrift, purgation, purgatory.

V. **atone,** atone for, expiate, propitiate, make amends; reclaim, redeem, repair, ransom, absolve, purge, shrive, do penance, pay the penalty.

apologize, express regret, beg pardon, give satisfaction.

Adj. propitiatory, expiatory, sacrifice, sacrificial.

953. [Moral Practice] TEMPERANCE.—*N.* temperance, moderation, frugality, sobriety, soberness, forbearance, abnegation; self-denial, self-restraint, self-control.

abstinence, abstemiousness, asceticism; vegetarianism, prohibition, teetotalism, total abstinence.

abstainer; teetotaler, etc., 958; vegetarian, fruitarian; ascetic.

V. **be temperate,** abstain, forbear, refrain, deny oneself, spare.

Adj. **temperate,** moderate, sober, frugal, sparing, abstemious.

954. INTEMPERANCE.—*N.* intemperance, sensuality, animalism, pleasure, luxury, luxuriousness, freeliving, indulgence, high living, dissipation, self-indulgence; voluptuousness, debauchery.

revel, revels, revelry, orgy; drunkenness, debauch, carousal, drinking bout, saturnalia.

V. **be intemperate,** indulge, exceed; live high (*or* on the fat of the land), dine not wisely but too well; plunge into dissipation, revel, carouse, run riot, sow one's wild oats.

Adj. **intemperate,** excessive; sensual, self-indulgent, voluptuous, wild, dissipated, dissolute, fast.

brutish, swinish, piggish, hoggish, beastlike, beastly.

luxurious, epicurean, sybaritical; nursed in the lap of luxury; indulged, pampered; full fed, high fed.

intoxicated, drunk, etc., 959.

954a. SENSUALIST.—*N.* sensualist, sybarite, voluptuary, man of pleasure, epicure, epicurean, gourmet; gourmand, glutton, pig, hog; free liver, hard liver.

955. ASCETICISM.—*N.* asceticism, puritanism, austerity; total abstinence; mortification, sackcloth and ashes, penance, fasting; martyrdom.

ascetic, anchorite, hermit, recluse; puritan, yogi [Hindu]; dervish, fakir [both Moham.]; martyr.

Adj. **ascetic,** austere, puritanical.

956. FASTING.—*N.* fasting, famishment, starvation.

fast, fast day, Lent, spare (*or* meager) diet, lenten diet, Barmecide feast; short rations.

V. fast, starve, famish, perish with hunger.

Adj. fasting, lenten, unfed; starved, half-starved, hungry.

957. GLUTTONY.—*N.* gluttony; greed, greediness, voracity; epicurism, gastronomy; high living; guzzling.

feast, banquet, good cheer, blow out [*slang*].

glutton, gormandizer, cormorant, hog, etc. (*sensualist*), 954a.

epicure, *bon vivant* [F.], gourmand [*obs. as* glutton], gourmet.

V. gormandize, gorge; overeat, glut, satiate, indulge, eat one's fill, cram, stuff, guzzle, bolt, devour, gobble up, gulp, raven, eat out of house and home.

Adj. gluttonous, greedy, gormandizing, omnivorous, voracious, devouring, overfed, gorged.

958. SOBRIETY.—*N.* sobriety; total abstinence, teetotalism.

water drinker; prohibitionist, dry [*slang*], teetotaler, total abstainer.

V. take the pledge; abstain, etc., 953.

Adj. sober, temperate, moderate, abstemious.

959. DRUNKENNESS.—*N.* drunkenness, intemperance, drinking, inebriety, inebriation, intoxication, winebibbing; bacchanalia; libations.

alcoholism, dipsomania; delirium tremens, d.t.'s [*colloq.*].

drink, alcoholic drinks, alcohol, blue ruin [*slang*], booze [*colloq.*]; grog, punch; punchbowl, cup, rosy wine, flowing bowl; liquor, dram, beverage, beer, etc.; cocktail, highball, peg [*slang*, orig. India]; stirrup cup, parting cup.

illicit distilling; bootlegging [*slang*], moonshining, moonshine *or* moonshine whisky [*colloq.*], hooch [*slang*], home-brew; moonshiner [*colloq.*]; bootlegger [*slang*].

drunkard, sot, toper, tippler, winebibber, hard drinker, soaker [*slang*], sponge [*slang*], boozer [*colloq.*], bum [*slang*]; reveler, carouser; dipsomaniac.

V. get (*or* be) drunk, see double; take a drop (*or* glass) too much; drink, tipple, booze [*colloq.*], soak [*slang*], have a jag on [*slang*], carouse; drink hard (*or* deep, like a fish).

liquor, liquor up [*both slang*], wet one's whistle [*colloq. or humorous*]; raise the elbow, hit the booze [*slang*], crack a bottle.

inebriate, fuddle [*colloq.*], befuddle.

sell illicitly, bootleg [*slang*].

Adj. drunk, tipsy, intoxicated, inebriate, inebriated; in a state of intoxication, overcome, fuddled [*colloq.*], boozy [*colloq.*], full [*vulgar*], lit up [*slang*], elevated [*colloq.*]; groggy [*colloq.*]; screwed, tight, primed [*all slang*], muddled, maudlin; blind drunk, dead drunk.

960. PURITY.—*N.* purity; decency, decorum, delicacy; continence, chastity, virtue, modesty; virginity.

virgin, vestal, prude; Diana.

Adj. pure, undefiled, modest, delicate, clean, decent, decorous; chaste, continent, virtuous, honest.

961. IMPURITY.—*N.* impurity, uncleanness; immodesty; grossness; indelicacy, indecency, obscenity; dissipation.

Adj. impure, unclean; immodest, shameless, indelicate, indecent, coarse, gross.

962. LIBERTINE.—*N.* libertine, voluptuary, rake, roué [F.], fast man.

5. Institutions

963. LEGALITY.—*N.* legality, legitimacy, legitimateness; legitimization.

law, code, constitution, charter, act, enactment, statute, rule, canon, ordinance, institution, regulation, bylaw, decree, standing order.

equity, common law; unwritten law; law of nations, international law; constitutionality; justice, etc., 922; jurisprudence; legislation.

V. legalize, legitimize; enact, ordain, decree, authorize, pass a law, legislate; codify, formulate, regulate.

Adj. legal, legitimate; according to law; vested, constitutional, chartered, legalized, lawful, statutory; legislative; judicial, juridical.

Adv. in the eye of the law.

964. [Absence or violation of law] ILLEGALITY.—*N.* lawlessness, illicitness; breach (*or* violation) of law; disobedience, violence, brute force, despotism, tyranny, outlawry; mob (*or* lynch) law.

illegality, informality, unlawfulness, illegitimacy; smuggling.

V. violate the law, set the law at defiance, make the law a dead letter, take the law into one's own hands.

smuggle, run, poach, bootleg [*slang*].

Adj. illegal, prohibited, unlawful, illegitimate, illicit, contraband, actionable.

unchartered, unconstitutional, lawless, unwarranted, unauthorized; unofficial.

arbitrary, despotic, summary, irresponsible.

Adv. with a high hand, in violation of law.

965. JURISDICTION. [Executive]—*N.* jurisdiction, judicature, administration of justice; judge, etc., 967; tribunal, etc., 966.

city government, municipal government, commission government, Oregon plan [U. S.]; municipality, corporation; police, police force, constabulary.

executive, officer, commissioner, lord lieutenant [Brit.], city manager, mayor, alderman, councilor, selectman; bailiff, beadle; sheriff, constable, policeman, police constable, police sergeant, patrolman, gendarme [F.].

bureau, department, portfolio, secretariat.

V. judge, adjudge, adjudicate, sit in judgment; have jurisdiction over.

Adj. executive, administrative; municipal; judiciary, judicial, juridical.

966. TRIBUNAL.—*N.* tribunal, court, board, bench, judicature, court of justice (*or* law); judgment seat, mercy seat; bar, bar of justice; town hall, statehouse, townhouse, courthouse; forum; sessions.

United States courts: U. S. Supreme Court, U. S. District Court, U. S. Circuit Court of Appeal; Federal Court of Claims, Court of Private Land Claims; Supreme Court, Superior Court, court of sessions, criminal court, police court, juvenile court.

court-martial, (*pl.* courts-martial), drumhead court-martial. *Adj.* judicial, etc., 965; appellate; curial.

967. JUDGE.—*N.* judge, justice, justice (*or* judge) of assize; magistrate, police magistrate, beak [*slang*]; his worship [Eng.], his honor, his lordship [Brit.]; the court.

Lord Chancellor, Master of the Rolls, Vice-Chancellor, Lord Chief Justice [all Brit.], Chief Justice.

arbiter, arbitrator; moderator, receiver, master; umpire, referee; censor.

jury, grand jury, petty jury, inquest, panel.

juror, juryman, talesman; grand juror, grand juryman; petty juror, petty juryman.

V. adjudge, etc. (*determine*), 480; try a case, try a prisoner. *Adj.* judicial, etc., 965.

968. LAWYER.—*N.* lawyer, jurist, legal adviser, advocate; barrister, barrister-at-law [Eng.]; counsel, counselor; king's counsel [Eng.]; pleader, special pleader.

attorney, solicitor; conveyancer, notary, notary public; pettifogger, shyster.

bar, legal profession; Inns of Court [Eng.].

V. practice law; practice at (*or* within) the bar, plead; be called to (*or* within) the bar; admitted to the bar.

disbar, degrade.

Adj. learned in the law; at the bar; forensic.

969. LAWSUIT.—*N.* lawsuit, suit, action, cause; litigation; suit in law.

writ, summons, subpoena, citation; habeas corpus [L.].

arraignment, prosecution, impeachment, accusation; presentment, true bill, indictment.

arrest, apprehension, committal, commitment; imprisonment.

pleadings; declaration, bill, claim; affidavit, libel; answer, plea, demurrer, rebutter, rejoinder; surrebutter, surrejoinder.

litigant, suitor, libelant; plaintiff, defendant, etc., 938.

hearing, trial; judgment, sentence, finding, verdict; appeal, writ of error.

case, decision, decided case, precedent.

V. litigate, go to law, appeal to the law; bring to justice (*or* trial, the bar), put on trial, accuse, prefer (*or* file) a claim.

cite, summon, summons, serve with a writ, arraign; sue, prosecute, indict, impeach; attach, distrain; commit, apprehend, arrest, give in charge.

try, hear a cause; sit in judgment; adjudicate, etc., 480.

970. ACQUITTAL.—*N.* acquittal, exculpation, acquittance, clearance, exoneration, discharge, release, absolution, reprieve, respite, pardon.

Exemption from punishment: impunity, immunity.

V. acquit, exculpate, exonerate, clear; absolve, whitewash, discharge, release, liberate, reprieve, respite, pardon.

Adj. acquitted, uncondemned, unpunished; recommend to mercy.

971. CONDEMNATION.—*N.* condemnation, conviction, judgment, penalty, sentence; death warrant.

V. condemn, convict, find guilty, damn, doom, sentence, pass sentence on, attaint, confiscate, sequestrate.

proscribe, interdict; disapprove, etc., 932; accuse, etc., 938.

Adj. condemnatory, damnatory, condemned, self-convicted.

972. PUNISHMENT.—*N.* punishment, punition, chastisement, chastening, correction, castigation; discipline, infliction, trial; judgment, penalty, retribution, nemesis, retributive justice.

Forms of punishment: lash, scaffold, etc. (*instrument of punishment*), 975; imprisonment; transportation, banishment, expulsion, exile, involuntary exile, ostracism, penal servitude, hard labor, galleys; beating, flagellation, bastinado, blow, stripe, cuff, kick, buffet, pummel; torture, rack.

capital punishment, execution; hanging, shooting, electrocution, decapitation, strangling, strangulation, crucifixion, impalement, martyrdom, auto-da-fé (*pl.* autos-da-fé) [Pg.], hara-kiri [Jap.], happy dispatch [*jocular*], lethal chamber, hemlock.

V. punish, chastise, chasten, castigate, correct, inflict punishment; tar and feather; masthead, keelhaul.

visit upon, pay, settle, settle with, do for [*colloq.*], get even with, make an example of; give it one [*both colloq.*].

strike, etc., 276; smite; spank, thwack, thump, beat, buffet, thrash, pommel, drub, trounce, belabor; trim [*colloq.*], cowhide, 'ambaste [*slang*], lash, flog, scourge, whip, birch, cane, switch, horsewhip, lay about one, beat black and blue; sandbag, blackjack; pelt, stone.

execute; bring to the block (*or* gallows), behead, decapitate, guillotine; hang [*p. p.* hanged, *not* hung, *for the death penalty*], electrocute, shoot, burn, crucify, impale, lynch.

torture, agonize, rack, put on (*or* to) the rack, martyr, martyrize.

banish, exile, transport, deport, expel, ostracize; rusticate; drum out; dismiss, disbar; unfrock [*as a priest*].

Adj. punitive, penal, punitory, inflictive, castigatory.

973. REWARD.—*N.* reward, recompense, remuneration, prize, meed, guerdon, indemnity, indemnification; quittance, compensation, reparation, redress, acknowledgment, requital, amends, sop, consideration, return; atonement.

perquisite, perks [*slang*]; donation, etc., 784; tip, bribe, hush money, blackmail.

allowance, salary, stipend, wages; pay, payment, emolument; tribute; premium, fee, honorarium; hire; mileage.

V. reward, recompense, repay, requite, remunerate, compensate; fee, tip, bribe; pay, etc., 807; make amends, indemnify, redress, atone, satisfy, acknowledge.

Adj. remunerative, compensatory; retributive.

974. PENALTY.—*N.* penalty; retribution, etc. (*punishment*), 972; pain, penance.

fine, mulct, forfeit, forfeiture, damages, sequestration, confiscation.

V. penalize, fine, mulct, confiscate, sequestrate, sequester; forfeit.

975. [Instrument of punishment] SCOURGE.—*N.* scourge, whip, lash, strap, thong, cowhide, knout, cat, cat-o'-nine-tails; rope's end; black snake, bullwhack, quirt, rawhide.

rod, cane, stick, rattan, birch, birch rod; rod in pickle; switch, ferule, cudgel, truncheon.

Various instruments: pillory, stocks, whipping post, ducking stool, iron maiden; thumbscrew, boot, rack, wheel; treadmill, crank, galleys; bed of Procrustes.

scaffold; block, ax, guillotine; stake; cross, gallows, gibbet, tree; noose, rope, halter, bowstring; death chair, electric chair.

prison, jail, etc., 752; jailer.

executioner; electrocutioner, headsman, hangman; lyncher, torturer.

malefactor, criminal, culprit, felon, victim, gallows bird [*slang*].

V. RELIGIOUS AFFECTIONS

976. DEITY.—*N.* Deity, Divinity, Godhead, Omnipotence, Omniscience, Providence.

GOD, Lord, Jehovah, The King of Kings, The Lord of Lords, The Almighty, The Supreme Being, The Absolute, The First Cause, Author of all things, Creator of all things, The Infinite, The Eternal, The All-powerful, The Omnipotent, The All-wise, The All-merciful, The All-knowing, The Omniscient.

Deus [L.], *Theos* [Gr. Θεος], *Dieu* [F.], *Gott* [Ger.], *Dio* [It.], *Dios* [Sp.], *Deos* [Pg.], *Gud* [Nor., Sw., and Dan.], *God* [Du.], *Bog* [Russ.], *Brahma* [Skr.], *Deva* [Skr.], *Khuda* (Hind.), Allah (Ar.).

THE TRINITY, The Holy Trinity, The Trinity in Unity, Triunity, Threefold Unity.

I. GOD THE FATHER, The Maker, The Creator, The Preserver.

Functions: creation, preservation, divine government, thearchy.

II. GOD THE SON, Jesus Christ; The Messiah, The Anointed, The Saviour, The Redeemer, The Mediator, The Intercessor, The Advocate, The Judge; The Son of God, The Son of Man; The Only-Begotten, The Lamb of God, The Word, Logos; The Man of Sorrows; Jesus of Nazareth, King of the Jews, The Son of Mary, The Risen, Immanuel, The King of Kings and Lord of Lords, The King of Glory, The Prince of Peace, The Good Shepherd, The Way, The Door, The Truth, The Life, The Bread of Life, The Light of the World, The Vine, The True Vine.

The Incarnation, The Word made Flesh.

Functions: salvation, redemption, atonement, propitiation, mediation, intercession, judgment.

III. GOD THE HOLY GHOST, The Holy Spirit, Paraclete, The Comforter, The Consoler, The Intercessor, The Spirit of God, The Spirit of Truth, The Dove.

Functions: inspiration, regeneration, sanctification, consolation, grace.

The Deity in other religions: **Brahmanism** *or* **Hinduism:** Brahma (*neuter*), the Supreme Soul *or* Essence of the Universe; Trimurti *or* Hindu trinity *or* Hindu triad: (1) Brahma (*masc.*), the Creator; (2) Vishnu, the Preserver; (3) Siva, the Destroyer and Regenerator.

Buddhism: the Protestantism of the East; Buddha, the Blessed One, the Teacher.

Zoroastrianism: Zerâna-Akerana, the Infinite Being; Ahuramazda *or* Ormazd, the Creator, the Lord of Wisdom, the King of Light (*opposed by* Ahriman, the King of Darkness).

Mohammedanism *or* **Islam:** Allah.

V. create, fashion, make, form, mold, manifest.

preserve, uphold, keep, perpetuate, immortalize.

atone, redeem, save, propitiate, expiate; intercede, mediate.

predestinate, predestine, foreordain, preordain; elect, call, ordain.

bless, sanctify, hallow, justify, absolve, glorify.

Adj. **almighty,** all-powerful, omnipotent; omnipresent, all-wise, all-seeing, all-knowing, omniscient, supreme.

divine, heavenly, celestial; holy, hallowed, sacred, sacrosanct.

supernatural, superhuman, spiritual, ghostly, unearthly.

Adv. by God's will, by God's help, *Deo volente* [L.], God willing; in Jesus' name, in His name, to His glory.

977. [Beneficent spirits] ANGEL.—*N.* angel, archangel, messenger of God, guardian angel; ministering spirits, invisible helpers, choir invisible, heavenly host, sons of God; saint; seraphim (*sing.*, seraph, *E. pl.*), seraphs; Cherubim (*sing.*, cherub, *E. pl.*, cherubs· cherubim *or* cherubin *are often treated as* **sing.**).

Madonna, Our Lady, *Notre Dame* [F.], Holy Mary, The Virgin, The Blessed Virgin, The Virgin Mary.

Adj. **angelic,** seraphic, cherubic, archangelic.

978. [Maleficent spirits] SATAN.—*N.* Satan, the Devil, Lucifer, Belial, Beelzebub, Mephistopheles, Mephisto, Asmodeus, *le Diable* [F.], Deil [Scot.].

fallen angels, unclean spirits, devils; rulers of darkness, the powers of darkness; demon, etc.,980.

Moloch, Mammon; Belial, Beelzebub; Loki [*Norse Myth*].

diabolism, devil worship, demonism, demonology; Black Mass, black magic, demonolatry, witchcraft.

diabolist, demonologist.

V. **demonize;** bewitch, bedevil, etc. (*sorcery*), 992; possess, obsess.

Adj. **satanic,** diabolic *or* diabolical, devilish, demoniac *or* demoniacal, infernal, hellborn.

979. MYTHIC AND PAGAN DEITIES.—*N.* god, goddess; heathen gods and goddesses; pantheon.

Greek and Latin: Zeus, Jupiter *or* Jove (*King*); Apollo *or* Phoebus Apollo (*the sun*); Ares, Mars (*war*); Hermes, Mercury (*messenger*); Poseidon, Neptune (*ocean*); Hephaestus, Vulcan (*smith*); Dionysus, Bacchus (*wine*); Hades [Gr.], Pluto or Dis [L.] (*King of the lower world*); Kronos, Saturn (*time*); Eros, Cupid (*love*); Pan, Faunus (*flocks, herds, forests, and wild life*).

Hera, Juno (*Queen*); Demeter, Ceres (*fruitfulness*); Persephone, Proserpina *or* Proserpine (*Queen of the lower world*); Artemis, Diana (*the moon and hunting*); Athena, Minerva (*wisdom*); Aphrodite, Venus (*love and beauty*); Hestia, Vesta (*the hearth*); Rhea *or* Cybele ("Mother of the gods," *identified with* Ops, *wife of Saturn*); Gaea *or* Ge, Tellus (*earth goddess, mother of the Titans*).

Norse: Ymir (*primeval giant*), Odin *or* Woden (*the All-father = Zeus*); the Æsir: Thor (*the Thunderer*), Balder (**=** *Apollo*), Freyr (*fruitfulness*), Tyr (*war*), Bragi (*poetry and eloquence*), Höder (*blind god of the winter*), Heimdall (*warder of Asgard*), Loki (*evil*).

the Vanir: Njorth (*the winds and the sea*), Frey (*prosperity and love*), Freya (*goddess of love and beauty* **=** *Venus*).

Frigg or Frigga (*wife of Odin*), Hel (*goddess of death = Persephone*), Idun (*goddess of spring, wife of Bragi*), Sigyn (*wife of Loki*).

Egyptian: Ra or Amon-Ra (*the sun god*), Osiris (*judge of the dead*), Isis (*wife of Osiris*), Horus (*the morning sun; son of Osiris and Isis*), Anubis (*jackal-god, brother of Horus, a conductor of the dead*), Nephthys (*sister of Isis*), Set (*evil deity, brother of Osiris*), Thoth (*clerk of the underworld*), Bast or Bubastis (*a goddess with head of a cat*), the Sphinx (*wisdom*).

Various: Baal [Semitic]; Astarte or Ashtoreth (*goddess of fertility and love*) [Phoenician]; Bel [Babylonian]; The Great Spirit [N. Amer. Indian].

nymph, dryad, hamadryad, wood nymph; naiad, fresh-water nymph; oread, mountain nymph; nereid, sea nymph; Oceanid, ocean nymph; Pleiades, Hyades.

fairy, fay, sprite; nix (*fem.* nixie), water sprite; the good folk, brownie, pixy, elf (*pl.* elves), banshee; the Fates; kobold, troll, hobgoblin, gnome, kelpie; faun; peri, undine, sea maid, mermaid (*masc.* merman); Mab, Oberon, Titania, Ariel; Puck, Robin Goodfellow.

familiar spirit, familiar, genius, guide, good genius, daimon, demon.

mythology, mythical lore, folklore, fairyism, fairy mythology.
Adj. mythical, mythic, mythological, fabulous, legendary.
fairylike, sylphlike, elfin, elflike, elfish, nymphlike.

980. EVIL SPIRITS.—*N.* demon, fiend, devil, etc. (*Satan*), 978; evil genius, familiar, familiar spirit; bad (*or* unclean) spirit; incubus; ogre, ogress, ghoul, vampire, harpy; Fury, the Furies, the Erinyes, the Eumenides.

imp, bad fairy, sprite, jinni (*pl.* jinn), genius (*pl.* genii), dwarf.
changeling, elf child, werewolf; satyr.

elemental, sylph, gnome, salamander, nymph [*Rosicrucian*].
siren, nixie, undine, Lorelei.

bugbear, bugaboo, bogy, goblin, hobgoblin.
Adj. demoniac, demoniacal, fiendish, fiendlike, evil, ghoulish; pokerish [*colloq.*], bewitched.

980a. SPECTER.—*N.* specter, ghost, apparition, vision, spirit, sprite, shade, shadow, wraith, banshee, spook [*now humorous*], phantom, phantasm, materialization [*spiritualism*], double.

will-o'-the-wisp, etc., 423.

Adj. spectral, ghostly, ghostlike, spiritual, wraithlike, weird, uncanny, eerie, spooky [*colloq.*] haunted; unearthly, supernatural.

981. HEAVEN.—*N.* heaven; kingdom of heaven (*or* God), heavenly kingdom; heaven of heavens, God's throne, throne of God; Paradise, Eden, Zion, Holy City, New Jerusalem, Heavenly City, City Celestial, abode of the blessed.

Mythological heaven or paradise: Olympus; Elysium, Elysian fields, Islands (*or* Isles) of the Blessed, Happy Isles, Fortunate Isles, garden of the Hesperides; third heaven, seventh heaven; Valhalla [Scandinavian]; Nirvana [Buddhist]; happy hunting grounds [N. Amer. Indian].

future state, life after death, eternal home, resurrection, translation; apotheosis, deification.

Adj. heavenly, celestial, supernal, unearthly, paradisaic, beatific; Elysian, Olympian.

982. HELL.—*N.* hell, bottomless pit, place of torment; pandemonium; hell-fire, everlasting fire (*or* torment); worm that never dies.

purgatory, limbo, Gehenna, abyss.

Mythological hell: Tartarus, Hades, Avernus; infernal regions, inferno, shades below, realms of Pluto.
Pluto, Rhadamanthus, Erebus, Charon, Cerberus; Persephone, Proserpina; Minos, Osiris.
Rivers of hell: Styx, Acheron, Cocytus, Phlegethon, Lethe.

Adj. hellish, infernal, stygian.

983. [Religious Knowledge] THEOLOGY.—*N.* theology, theosophy, divine wisdom, divinity, hagiography; monotheism, theism, religion; religious persuasion (*or* sect, denomination, affiliation); creed, articles (*or* declaration, profession, confession) of faith.

theologian, scholastic, divine, schoolman, the Fathers; monotheist, theist.

Adj. theological, religious, divine, canonical; denominational; sectarian.

983a. ORTHODOXY.—*N.* orthodoxy; strictness, soundness, religious truth, true faith; truth, etc., 494; soundness of doctrine; Christianity, Catholicism.

the church, Holy Church, Church Militant, Church Triumphant; Catholic (*or* Universal, Apostolic) Church; Established (*or* State) Church; The Bride of the Lamb; temple of the Holy Ghost; Church of Christ; Christians, Christendom.

canons; thirty-nine articles; Apostles' (*or* Nicene, Athanasian) Creed.

Adj. orthodox, sound, strict, faithful, catholic, Christian, evangelical, scriptural, literal, divine, monotheistic, true, etc., 494.

984. HETERODOXY. [Sectarianism]—*N.* heterodoxy; error, false doctrine, heresy, schism, recusancy, backsliding, apostasy; materialism, atheism; idolatry, superstition.

bigotry, fanaticism, iconoclasm; precisianism; sabbatarianism, puritanism, bibliolatry.

sectarianism, nonconformity, dissent, secularism; religious sects, the clash of creeds, the isms.

[*Generally speaking, each sect is* orthodox *to itself and* heterodox *to others.*]

paganism, heathenism, heathendom; animism, polytheism, pantheism; dualism.

pagan, heathen, paynim; kafir, non-Mohammedan; gentile; pantheist, polytheist, animist.

misbeliever, heretic, apostate; backslider; antichrist; idolater; skeptic, etc., 989.

bigot, dogmatist, fanatic, dervish, iconoclast.

sectarian, sectary; seceder, separatist, recusant, dissenter, nonconformist.

materialist, positivist, deist, agnostic, atheist, etc., 989.

Adj. **heterodox,** heretical, unorthodox, unscriptural, uncanonical, unchristian, apocryphal; antichristian; schismatic, recusant, iconoclastic; sectarian, dissenting, secular; agnostic, atheistic; skeptical, etc., 989.

bigoted, dogmatical, fanatical; superstitious, credulous; idolatrous.

pagan, heathen, heathenish, gentile, paynim; polytheistic, pantheistic, animistic.

985. REVELATION. [Biblical]—*N.* **revelation,** inspiration.

The Bible, the Book, the Book of Books, The Good Book, the Word, the Word of God, Scripture, the Scriptures, Holy Writ, Holy Scriptures, inspired writings, Gospel.

Old Testament, Septuagint, Vulgate, Pentateuch; the Law, the Prophets; Apocrypha.

New Testament; Gospels, Evangelists, Acts, Epistles, Apocalypse, Revelation; Good Tidings, Glad Tidings.

inspired writers, prophet, evangelist, apostle, disciple, saint; the Fathers, the Apostolic Fathers; Holy Men of old.

Adj. **scriptural,** biblical, sacred, prophetic; evangelical, evangelistic, apostolic, apostolical; inspired, apocalyptic, revealed; ecclesiastical, canonical.

986. SACRED WRITINGS. [Non-Biblical]—*N.* The Vedas, Upanishads, Puranas, Sutras, Bhagavad Gita [all Brahmanic]; Zendavesta, Avesta [Zoroastrian]; The Koran *or* Alcoran [Mohammedan]; Tripitaka, Dhammapada [Buddhist]; Granth, Adigranth [*Sikh*]; the Kings [Chinese]; the Eddas [Scandinavian].

Non-Biblical prophets and religious founders: Gautama (Buddha); Zoroaster, Confucius, Mohammed.

987. PIETY.—*N.* **piety,** religion, theism, faith; religiousness, religiosity, holiness, saintship; reverence, humility, veneration, devotion, worship, grace, sanctity, consecration.

beatification, regeneration, conversion, sanctification, salvation, inspiration, bread of life; Body and Blood of Christ.

believer, convert, theist, Christian, devotee, pietist, saint.

V. **be pious,** have faith, believe, receive Christ; venerate, adore, worship, revere, be converted, be on God's side, stand up for Jesus, fight the good fight, keep the faith, let one's light shine.

regenerate, convert, edify, sanctify, hallow, keep holy, beatify, inspire, consecrate, enshrine.

Adj. pious, religious, devout, devoted, reverent, godly, humble, pure, pure in heart, holy, spiritual, saintly, saintlike; believing, faithful, Christian.

regenerated; inspired, consecrated, converted, unearthly.

elected, adopted, justified, sanctified.

988. IMPIETY.—*N.* impiety, sin, irreverence; profaneness, profanity, blasphemy, profanation; desecration, sacrilege; scoffing.

Assumed piety: hypocrisy, pietism, cant, pious fraud; lip devotion, lip service; formalism, austerity; sanctimony, sanctimoniousness, pharisaism, sabbatarianism; sacerdotalism; bigotry; blue laws.

apostasy, recusancy, backsliding, perversion, reprobation.

bigot, pharisee, sabbatarian, formalist, pietist, precisian, devotee, ranter, fanatic.

sinner, scoffer, blasphemer, sabbath breaker; worldling; hypocrite.

the wicked, the evil, the unjust, the reprobate.

V. profane, desecrate, blaspheme, revile, scoff, swear; commit sacrilege.

dissemble, simulate, play the hypocrite, snuffle.

Adj. impious, irreligious, etc., 989; profane, irreverent, sacrilegious, blasphemous.

unhallowed, unsanctified, unregenerate; hardened, perverted, reprobate.

hypocritical, canting, pietistical, sanctimonious, unctuous, pharisaical, overrighteous.

bigoted, fanatical, hidebound, narrow, narrow-minded, illiberal, prejudiced, little; provincial, parochial, insular.

989. IRRELIGION.—*N.* irreligion, impiety, ungodliness, laxity, apathy, indifference.

skepticism, doubt; unbelief, disbelief, incredulity, agnosticism, freethinking; materialism, rationalism, positivism; atheism, infidelity.

unbeliever, infidel, atheist, heretic, heathen, alien, gentile, Nazarene; freethinker, skeptic, rationalist; materialist, positivist, nihilist, agnostic.

V. disbelieve, lack faith; doubt, question, deny the truth.

Adj. irreligious; undevout, godless, graceless, ungodly; unholy, unsanctified, unhallowed; atheistic.

skeptical, freethinking, unbelieving, unconverted; incredulous, faithless.

worldly, mundane, earthly, carnal, worldly, worldly-minded, unspiritual.

990. WORSHIP.—*N.* worship, cult, adoration, devotion, vow, aspiration, homage, service; kneeling, genuflection, prostration.

prayer, invocation, supplication, intercession, orison, petition; collect, litany, Lord's prayer, paternoster; *Ave Maria* [L.], Hail, Mary.

thanksgiving; grace, praise, glorification, paean, benediction, doxology, hosanna, hallelujah, alleluia, *Te Deum* [L.], *Gloria* [L.]. psalm, hymn, chant, response, anthem.

offering, oblation, sacrifice, incense, libation, offertory, collection.

divine service, office, duty; exercises; morning prayer; Mass, matins, evensong, vespers, vigils, lauds.

worshiper, congregation, communicant, celebrant.

V. worship, lift up the heart, aspire; revere, adore, do service, pay homage, offer one's vows, vow; bow down and worship.

pray, invoke, supplicate; beseech; offer up prayers, say one's prayers, tell one's beads, recite the rosary.

give thanks, say grace, bless, praise, laud, glorify, magnify, sing praises.

Adj. devout, devotional, reverent, solemn, fervid.

991. IDOLATRY.—*N.* idolatry, idolatrousness, demonism, demonology, devil worship, fetishism.

idolization, deification, apotheosis, canonization; hero worship.

sacrifice, hecatomb, holocaust; human sacrifices, immolation, self-immolation, suttee.

idol, golden calf, graven image, fetish, joss [Chinese], *lares et penates* [L.]; god (*or* goddess) of one's idolatry; Baal, Moloch, Juggernaut.

idolater, idolatress, idolizer, fetishist.

V. idolize, idolatrize, worship idols, worship, put on a pedestal, prostrate oneself before; make sacrifice to, deify, canonize.

Adj. idolatrous, idolistic, prone before, prostrate before, in the dust before, at the feet of.

992. SORCERY.—*N.* sorcery, magic, black magic, the black art, necromancy, demonology, witchcraft, witchery, wizardry, fetishism, hoodoo, voodoo, voodooism; fire worship, incantation, enchantment, bewitchment, glamour; obsession, possession.

divination, etc. (*prediction*), 511; sortilege, ordeal, hocus-pocus.

V. practice sorcery, cast a nativity (*or* horoscope), conjure, charm, enchant, bewitch, bedevil, witch, voodoo, hoodoo [*colloq.*]; entrance, fascinate, hypnotize, cast a spell; call up spirits.

Adj. magic, magical, witching, weird, cabalistic, talismanic.

992a. PSYCHICAL RESEARCH.—*N.* psychical research, psychical (*or* psychic) investigation; abnormal (*or* mediumistic) phenomena; mysticism.

the subconscious, the subconscious self, the subliminal self, the higher self, ego, astral body; aura; subconsciousness, subliminal consciousness; intuition; dual personality, multiple personality, obsession, possession.

psychotherapy, psychotherapeutics, psychoanalysis; hysteria, neurasthenia, dreams, visions, apparitions, hallucinations.

mesmerism, ánimal magnetism; mesmeric trance; hypnotism; hypnosis.

Phenomena: telepathy, thought transference, thought transmission, telepathic transmission; second sight, clairvoyance, clairaudience, psychometry.

premonitions, previsions, premonitory apparition, fetch, wraith, double; death lights, ominous dreams.

automatism, automatic writing, planchette, ouija board, trance writing, spirit writing; trance speaking, inspirational speaking.

spiritualism, spiritism, spirit manifestations; trance, spirit control, spirit possession; mediumistic communications; séance; materialisation.

medium, seer, clairvoyant, clairaudient, telepathist; guide, control; mesmerist, hypnotist.

V. psychologize; investigate the abnormal (*or* supernormal, subconscious, subliminal), traverse the borderland, know oneself.

mesmerize, magnetize, hypnotize, place under control, subject to suggestion, place in a trance, induce hypnosis.

Adj. psychical, psychic, psychological; spiritistic, spiritualistic, spiritual; subconscious, subliminal, supernormal, abnormal; mystic *or* mystical.

993. SPELL.—*N.* spell, charm, incantation, exorcism, abracadabra, open-sesame; evil eye.

talisman, amulet, phylactery, philter, fetish, wishbone; mascot, rabbit's foot, hoodoo [*colloq.*], jinx [*slang*], scarabaeus *or* scarab; veronica, swastika.

wand, caduceus, rod, divining rod, witch hazel, Aaron's rod.

Magic wish-givers: Aladdin's lamp, Aladdin's casket, magic casket, magic ring, magic belt, magic spectacles, wishing cap, Fortunatus' cap; seven-league boots; magic carpet; cap of darkness.

994. SORCERER.—*N.* sorcerer, magician, wizard, necromancer, conjuror, prestidigitator; charmer, exorcist, voodoo medicine man, witch doctor; astrologer, soothsayer, etc., 513.

sorceress, witch, hag; siren, harpy.

Cagliostro, Merlin; Circe, weird sisters, witch of Endor.

995. CHURCHDOM.—*N.* churchdom; church, ministry, priesthood, prelacy, hierarchy, church government; clericalism, sacerdotalism, episcopalianism.

monasticism, monkhood, monachism; celibacy.

Ecclesiastical offices and dignities: cardinalate, cardinalship; primacy, archbishopric, archiepiscopacy; prelacy, bishopric, episcopate, episcopacy, see, diocese; benefice, incumbency, living, cure, charge, cure of souls; rectorship, vicariate, vicarship; pastorate, pastorship, pastoral charge; deaconry, deaconship; curacy; chaplaincy, chaplainship, presbytery.

holy orders, ordination, institution, consecration, induction, installation, preferment, translation, presentation.

papacy, pontificate, See of Rome, the Vatican, the apostolic see.

V. **call,** ordain, induct, install, translate, consecrate, present, elect, bestow.

Adj. **ecclesiastical,** clerical, sacerdotal, priestly, pastoral, ministerial, hierarchical, episcopal, canonical; pontifical, papal, apostolic.

996. CLERGY.—*N.* **clergy,** clericals, ministry, priesthood, presbytery, the cloth, the pulpit, the desk.

clergyman, divine, ecclesiastic, priest, pastor, shepherd, minister, preacher, clerk in holy orders, parson, sky pilot [*slang*]; father, padre, *abbé* [F.], *curé* [F.]; reverend.

Dignitaries of the church: Pope, pontiff, Holy Father; cardinal, primate, metropolitan, archbishop, bishop, prelate, dean, archdeacon, canon, rector, vicar, beneficiary, incumbent, chaplain, curate; elder, deacon.

religious, abbot, prior, monk, friar, lay brother, pilgrim, palmer.

nun, sister, priestess, abbess, prioress, canoness; mother superior, the reverend mother; novice.

Adj. **ordained,** in orders, in holy orders, called to the ministry.

997. LAITY.—*N.* **laity,** flock, fold, congregation, assembly, brethren, people; society [U. S.]; class [Methodist].

layman, parishioner, catechumen.

V. **laicize,** secularize.

Adj. **secular,** lay congregational, civil, temporal, profane.

998. RITE.—*N.* **rite,** ceremony, observance, function, duty, form, solemnity, sacrament; service, ministry, ministration.

sermon, preaching, preachment, exhortation, religious harangue, homily, lecture, discourse.

worship, etc., 990; invocation of saints, confession, the confessional; absolution, remission of sins; reciting the rosary, telling one's beads.

Seven Sacraments: (1) **baptism,** immersion, christening; baptismal regeneration; font.

(2) **confirmation,** laying on of hands.

(3) **Eucharist,** Mass, Lord's supper, communion; the sacrament, the holy sacrament; consecrated elements, bread and wine, celebration; transubstantiation, real presence.

(4) **penance,** fasting, sackcloth and ashes, flagellation.

(5) **extreme unction**, last rites, viaticum.

(6) **holy orders**, ordination, etc. (*churchdom*), 995.

(7) **matrimony**, marriage, wedlock, etc., 903.

Sacred articles: relics, rosary, beads, reliquary, host, cross, rood, crucifix; pyx, censer, thurible; prayer wheel [Buddhist]; Sangraal, Holy Grail.

ritual, liturgy, rubric, canon, ordinal, missal, breviary, Mass book, beadroll, litany, prayer book, Book of Common Prayer; psalter, psalmbook, hymnbook, hymnal.

ritualism, ceremonialism; sabbatism, sabbatarianism; ritualist, sabbatarian.

V. **perform service**, do duty, minister, officiate, celebrate.

excommunicate; ban with bell, book, and candle.

preach, sermonize, address the congregation.

Adj. **ritual**, ritualistic, ceremonial, liturgic *or* liturgical; paschal.

999. CANONICALS.—*N.* canonicals, vestments, robe, gown, surplice, etc.

1000. TEMPLE.—*N.* temple, fane, place of worship; house of God, house of prayer; cathedral, minster, church, kirk [Scot.], chapel, meetinghouse.

synagogue, tabernacle; mosque [Moham.]; pagoda, Chinese temple, joss house [*colloq.*]; pantheon, shrine.

monastery, priory, abbey, friary, convent, nunnery, cloister.

parsonage, rectory, vicarage, manse, deanery, clergy house; bishop's palace; Vatican.

Adj. **churchly**, cloistered, monastic, monasterial, conventual.

INDEX

The numbers refer to the headings under which the words or phrases occur. When the same word or phrase can be used in various senses, the several headings under which it or its synonyms will be found are indicated by *italics*.

When the word given in the Index is itself the title or heading of a category, the word is printed in capitals and the reference number in bold-faced type, thus: **ACTIVITY 682**. When the word is the keyword to a group of synonyms, the reference number is also in bold-faced type.

Derivatives likewise have been sparingly admitted, since the allied or basic term will serve as a key to the various derived forms; thus *alarm* is given, but not *alarmed* or *alarming*. Adverbs ending in *-ly* should be looked for under the adjective, if not found in the Index.

IMPORTANT NOTE

The numbers following all references in this Index Guide refer to the *section* numbers in the text, and *not* to pages.

INDEX

A

abandon 624, 782
abandoned
  forsaken 893
  vicious 945
abandonment 757, 782
abase 879
abasement 874
abash 879
abashed 879
abatement 36
abbess 996
abbey 1000
abbot 996
abbreviation 201
abdicate 757
abdomen 250
abduct repel 289
  steal 791
aberration 83
abet 707
abhor 867, 898
abhorrence 867, 898
abhorrent painful 830
  hateful 898
abide endure 1, 106
  remain 110
  dwell 186
ability 157, 698
abject vile 874
  servile 886
abjure deny 536
  renounce 607
ablaze 382
able capable 157
  skillful 698
able-bodied 159
ablution 652
abnormal 83
aboard present 186
  afloat 273
abode 189
abolish 756
abolition 2, 162, 756
abominable bad 649
  hateful 898
abominate dislike 867
  hate 898
abomination 867
aboriginal 66, 124
aborigine 188
abound 639
about nearly 32, 197
  around 227

above 206
abracadabra 993
abrade 330,331
abrasion 330,331
abreast 216, 236
abridge 36, 201
  in writing 596
abridgment 35, 201
abroad 57, 196
abrupt sudden 113
  steep 217
abscond 623
ABSENCE 187
  -of mind 458
  -of time 107
absent 187, 458
absentee 187
absent-minded 458
absolute not relative 1
  great 31
  certain 474
absolution 918
absolve 918, 952
absorb combine 48
  take in 296
absorbed 451
absorption 296
abstain refrain 623
  be temperate 953
abstainer 953, 958
abstemious 953, 958
abstention 623
abstinence 623, 953
abstract, v. take 789
abstract, n. epitome 195, 596
abstracted inattentive 458
abstraction 38, 451, 458
absurd 471, 497, 583
ABSURDITY
  impossibility 471
  nonsense 497
  ridiculousness 853
abundance 31, 639
abundant great 31
  enough 639
abuse, v. illtreat 649
  misuse 679
abuse, n. in-vective 908, 932
abusive 909, 932
abut 197
abysmal deep 208

abyss 198, 667
academic 537
academy 542
accede assent 488
  submit 725
  consent 762
accelerate 132, 274, 684
accent 402, 580
accentuate 580, 642
accept assent 488
  receive 785
acceptable
  expedient 646
  agreeable 829
acceptance security 771
access approach 286
accessible possible 470
  easy 705
accession increase 35
accessory extrinsic 6
  adjunct 37, 39
  accompanying 88
accident 151, 619, 735
accidental extrinsic 6
  occasional 134
  fortuitous 156
acclaim 931
acclamation 488, 931
acclivity 217
accommodate suit 23
  aid 707
accommodation
  adaptation 23
  space 180
ACCOMPANIMENT
  adjunct 37, 39
  coexistence 88
  musical 415
accompany
  coexist 88
  escort 664
accomplice 711
accomplish execute 161
  complete 729
accomplishment
  learning 490
  talent 698
accord
  agree 23
  assent 488
  grant 760, 784
accordance 16, 23
accordingly 8, 476

311

apathy 823
ape *monkey* 366
ape, *v. imitate* 19
aperient 652
aperture 260
apex 206, 210
aphorism 496
apiary 370
apiece 79
Apocalypse 985
Apocrypha 985
apocryphal 475
apologetic 937
apologist 937
apology *substitution* 147
 vindication 937
 penitence 950
apostasy *recantation* 607
 impiety 988
apostate *turncoat* 607
 heretic 984
apostatize 607
apostle 985
apostolic 985, 995
apostrophe 589
apostrophize 765
apothecary 662
apotheosis 981, 991
appall *pain* 830
 terrify 860
apparatus 633
apparel 225
apparent *visible* 446
 appearing 448
 probable 472
 manifest 525
apparition
 phantom 4, 362
 spirit 980a, 992a
appeal *address* 586
 request 765
appear *arrive* 292
 come in sight 446, 448
APPEARANCE 448
appease 174, 826
append 37, 63
appendage *addition* 37
 adjunct 39
 sequel 65
 accompaniment 88
appendix 65
appertain 777
appetite 865
appetizer 394
appetizing 394
applaud 931
applause 931
appliance *use* 677
appliances 632
applicable *relevant* 9, 23
 useful 644
applicant 767
application *study* 457
 request 765
apply *appropriate* 788
appoint 755, 786

appointment *business* 625
 charge 755
 interview 892
appointments *gear* 633
apportion 786
APPORTION 786
apposition 23, 199
appraise 466
appreciate *realize* 450
 know 490
apprehend *know* 490
 fear 860
 seize 969
apprehension *idea* 453
 fear 860
apprehensive 860
apprentice 541
apprenticeship 539
APPROACH 286
 of time 121
 nearness 197
 path 627
approbation 931
appropriate *fit* 23
 peculiar 79
 timely 134
 borrow 788
 take 789
appropriation
 allotment 786
 taking 789
approval *assent* 488
 commendation 931
approve 488, 931
approved 931
approximate
 related to 9
 resemble 17
 near 197
 nearing 286
appurtenance 780
apt *consonant* 23
 clever 698
aquatic 267
aqueduct 350
aquiline 244
arable 371
arbiter *critic* 480
 judge 967
arbitrament 480
arbitrary 10
 willful 606
 severe 739
 lawless 964
arbitrate 480, 724
arbitration 480
arbitrator 724
arbor 191
arboreal 367
arc 245
arcade 189
arch *curve* 245
 convexity 250
 roguish 840
archeologist 122
archeology 122

archaic *old* 124
archaism 122, 124
archangel 977
archbishop 996
archer 284, 726, 840
archetype 22
archipelago 346
architect 164, 690
architecture 161
archive 551
arctic 237, 383
arctics 225
ardent *eager* 682
 loving 897
ardor *vigor* 574
 feeling 821
arduous 704
area 181
ARENA *space* 180
 field of battle 728
argosy 273
argot 563
argue 467, 476
argument 476
argumentation 476
arid 169, 340
aright 618
arise *begin* 66
 happen 151
 mount 305
aristocracy 875
aristocrat 875
aristocratic 852
arithmetic 85
ark 666
arm *part* 51
 power 157
 prepare 673
 weapon 727
armada 726
armament 727
armchair 215
armed 722
 -force 664, 726
armful 25
armistice 142, 723
armor 727
armorial 550
armory 636
ARMS 727 [see arm]
 heraldry 550
army *collection* 72
 multitude 102
 troops 726
aroma 400
around 227
arouse *move* 615
 excite 824
arraign *accuse* 938
 indict 969
arraignment 969
arrange *set in order* 60
 organize 357
 harmonize 416
 plan 626
 compromise 774

curb 752
brake, *v. retard* 275
bramble 253
branch, *n.* 51, 367
branch, *v. ramify* 244
brand, *n. fuel* 388
  torch 423
  mark 550
  sword 727
brand, *v. sear* 384
  defame 874
brandish 315
brass *alloy* 41
bravado 884
brave, *adj.* 861
  -man **861**
  -woman **861**
brave, *v. defy* 234
  bear 826
bravery 861
brawl *discord* 713
brawny *strong* 159
brazen *unreserved* 525
  insolent **885**
breach *crack* 44
  gap 198
  quarrel 713
  violation 925
bread 298
BREADTH 202
break *fracture* 44
  discontinuity 70
  gap 198
  faux pas 947
break, *v. crumble* **328**
  train animals 370
  -in *domesticate* 370
  -out *begin* 66
  -up *disjoin* 44
  destroy 162
breakdown 162
breakers *surf* 348
breakneck
  rash 863
breast, *n.* 221
breast, *v. confront* 234
breath *breeze* 349
  life 359
breathe *exist* 1
  blow 349
breathing **349**
breathless
  out of breath **688**
  astonished 870
breeches 225
breed, *n. race* 11
breed, *v. multiply* 161
breeding *politeness* 894
breeze *wind* 349
brethren 997
brevity 201, 572
brew 48
bribe, *n. gift* **784**
bribe, *v. tempt* **615**
  buy 795
  reward 973

bribery [*see* bribe]
bric-a-brac 847
bridal 903
bride 903
bridegroom 903
bridesmaid 903
bridge *link* 45
  -over *join* 43, **45**
bridle *depart* 293
  restrain 751
brief *time* 111
  space 201
  concise 572
briefly *awhile* 111
  anon 132
  shortly **572**
brier 253
brigade 726
brigand 792
bright *shining* 420
  color **428**
  intelligent 498
  cheery 836
  beautiful 845
  cheering 848
brilliant *shining* 420
  witty 842
  beautiful **845**
  glorious 873
brim 231
brimful 52
brindled 440
brine *salt* 392
bring 270
  -about *cause* 153
  -forth *produce* 161
  -forward *adduce* 467
  -over *persuade* 484
  -round *persuade* 615
  -together *assemble* **72**
  -to mind 505
  -to terms 723
  -up *develop* 161
brink 231
briny 392
brisk *prompt* 111
  active 274, 682
bristle 253
bristling *thorny* 253
  discourteous 895
bristly *rough* 256
brittle 328
BRITTLENESS 328
broach *begin* 66
  tap 297
broad *general* 78
  space 202
broadcast
  disperse 73, 291
  publish 531
broaden 78
broadside *side* 236
  cannonade 716
broadsword 727
broil, *n. fray* 713
broil, *v. heat* 382

fry 384
broken *divided* 51
  discontinuous 70
  weak 160
  of horses 370
  -heart 837
broker 758
brokerage 812
bromide
  conventionalist 82
broncho 271
  -buster 370
bronze *brown* 433
brood *multitude* 102
  family 167
brook, *n. stream* 348
brook, *v. bear* 826
broom *undergrowth* 367
  sweeper 652
brother 17, 27
brotherhood 11, 17, **888**
brotherly 888
brow *top* 210
  front 234
browbeat 860
BROWN 433
  -study 458
brownie 979
brownness 433
browse 298
bruise *powder* 330
  injure 649
bruised *blemished* 848
brunt 66, 276
brush, *n. tail* 235
  fight 720
brush, *v. groom* 370
  touch 379
  clean 652
brushwood 367
brusque 895
brutal *savage* 907
brutalize 945
brute *animal* 366
  rude person 895
  evildoer 913
  -force 964
brutish *intemperate* **954**
BUBBLE, *n.*
  transience 111
  air 353
bubble, *v. boil* 315
bubonic *plague* 655
buccaneer 792
buck, *n. stag* 366
buck, *v. leap* 309
bucket *receptacle* 191
buckle, *n. tie* 43
buckle, *v. distort* 243
  -to *labor* 686
buckler 717
bucolic 371
bud, *n. blossom* 367
bud, *v. expand* 194
Buddhism 976
buddy *chum* 890

budge 264
budget *finance* 811
buff *color* 436
buffer 717
buffet *strike* 276
  smite 972
buffet *café* 189
  cupboard 191
buffoon *actor* 599
  humorist 844
  butt 857
buffoonery
  humor 840, 842, 853
  horseplay 856
bug 193, 366
bugaboo 980
bugbear 980
build *construct* 161
  form 240
building 189
bulb 249, 250
bulge 250
bulk, *n. quantity* 25
  whole 50
  size 192
bulk, *v.* 31
bulkhead 228
bulky 31, 192
bull *animal* 366
  absurdity 495, 497
  stock exchange 797
bulldoze 860
bullet 727
bulletin *list* 86
  news 532
bullion 800
bully, *n.* 863, 887
bully, *v. frighten* 860
  bluster 885
  threaten 909
bulwark 717
bump, *n.* 250
bump, *v.* 276

bumptious *proud* 878
bunch *collection* 72
  protuberance 250
buncombe *bombast* 577
  boast 884
  flattery 933
bundle *packet* 72
bung 263
bungle 495, 699
bungler 701
bunkum
  [see buncombe]
buoy *raises* 307
buoyant
  floating 305
  light 320
  elastic 325
  hopeful 858
bur 53
burden *clog* 706
bureau *chest* 191
  department 965
bureaucracy 737
burgess 188
burgher 188
burglar 792
burglary 791
burial 363
  -place 363
burlesque, *n.*
  travesty 555, 853
  absurdity 497
  ridicule 856
burlesque, *v. imitate* 19
  ridicule 856
burn *heat* 382
  consume 384
burnish *polish* 255
burrow *excavate* 208, 252
burst, *n. sound* 406
  paroxysm 825
burst, *v.*
  -forth *begin* 66

expand 194
be seen 446
bury 229, 363
bush *shrub* 367
bushy 256
BUSINESS 151, 625
businesslike
  orderly 58
  business 625
  practical 692
bustle *energy* 171
  agitation 315
  activity 682
bustling 682
busy 625, 682
busybody 455
but 30
butcher *kill* 361
butchered 53
butler 746
butt, *n. cask* 191
  laughingstock 857
butt, *v.* 276
butter 356
button *fasten* 43
buttonhole, *n.*
  bouquet 400
buttonhole, *v.*
  to bore 841
buttress 717
buxom 836
buy 795
buyer 795
buzz 409
by 236, 631
  -and by 132
  -means of 632
  -the by 134
  -the way 134
bygone *past* 122
byplay 550
bystander 197, 444
byword, *contempt* 930

C

cab 272
cabin *room* 189
cabinet *receptacle* 191
  council 696
cable, *n. link* 45
  dispatch 532
cable, *v.* 534
cabman 268
cackle (*of geese*) 412
  laugh 838
cad 851
cadaverous *pale* 429
  hideous 846
cadence *sound* 402
  music 415
cadet *junior* 129
  officer 745
caesura 44, 198

café 189, 298
cage, *n. prison* 752
cage, *v. restrain* 751
caisson 191, 252
cajole *flatter* 933
  [see cajolery]
cajolery *imposition* 544
  persuasion 615
  flattery 933
cake, *n.* 396
cake, *v. stick* 46
  consolidate 321
calamitous
  adverse 735, 935
  disastrous 830
calamity *killing* 361
  evil 619
  adversity 735

calcine 384
calculate 85
calculation 85
caldron 191
CALEFACTION 384
calendar *list* 86, 611
  chronicle 114
calf *animal* 366
  fool 501
caliber *measure* 26, 192
  intellectual capacity 498
calipers 466
calisthenics 159
calk 660
call *signal* 550
  name 564
  visit 892
  ordain 995

coil *convolution* 248
  circuit 311
coin, *n.* 800
coin, *v. fabricate* 161
coincide 13, 120, 488
coincidence *identity* 13
  in time 120
coincident 13, 120, 178
coiner 792
COLD, *n. frigidity* 383
cold, *adj.*
  frigid 383
  insensible 823
  indifferent 866
cold-blooded 907
cold-bloodedness 871
coldhearted
  unfeeling 823
  malevolent 907
coldness *cold* 383
  unconcern 823
  indifference 866
collaboration 178
collaborator 711
collapse, *n.*
  prostration 158
  failure 732
collapse, *v. fail* 304
collar *dress* 225
  circlet 247
collateral *relative* 9
colleague
  associate 88, 690
  friend 890
collect *assemble* 72
  compile 596
collected *calm* 826
collection *assemblage* 72
  offertory 990
collective 78
collectively 50
college 542
collide 276
collision *clash* 179
  percussion 276
  opposition 708
  encounter 720
colloquial 588
collusion *deceit* 545
  complicity 709
colonel 745
colonial 188
colonist 188, 294, 295
colonization 184
colonize 184
colony *region* 184
  settlement 188
COLOR, *n. hue* 428
color, *v. redden* 434
  be angry 900
colored 428
colorless *pale* 429
colors *ensign* 550
colossal 106, 192
colossus 206
colt *horse* 271

column *height* 206
  support 215
  monument 551
coma 683
comb, *n.* 253
comb, *v. clean* 652
combat 720
COMBATANT 726
combative 720, 722
COMBINATION 48
combine *unite* 48
  compose 56
  co-operate 709
combustible 384, 388
combustion 384
come *arrive* 292
  -after *succeed* 117
  -amiss 135
  -of age 131
  -out *come of age* 131
  -together *assemble* 72
    converge 290
  -to nothing
    fail 732
  -to pass 151
comedian 844
comedy 599, 853
comely 845
comfort *pleasure* 377
  delight 827
  relief 834
comfortable 377
Comforter 976
comforter *wrap* 223
comfortless 837
comic 842, 853
coming [*see* come]
  impending 152
  -out *debut* 883
COMMAND, *n.*
  requirement 630
  authority 737
  order 741
command, *v. tower* 206
  order 737, 741
  possess 777
commandant 745
commander 744, 789
commander
  mariner 269
  chief 745
commander-in-chief 745
commemorate 883
commemorative 883
commence 66
commend 931
commendable 944
commendatory 931
comment 522, 595
commentary 522, 595
commentator 595
commerce 794
commercial 794
commingle 41
commiserate 914
commissariat 637

COMMISSION
  task 625
  delegate 755
commissioner 745, 758
commit *do* 680
  delegate 755
  arrest 969
  -to memory 505
commitment 969
committee 696, 758
commodious 644
commodity 798
commodore 745
common, *n.* 367
common, *adj.*
  general 78
  ordinary 82
  habitual 613
  base 876
  -run 78
  -sense 498, 502
  in - *participated* 778
commonality 876
commoner 876
commonplace *mediocre* 29
  plain 576
  habit 613
  unimportant 643
commonweal
  mankind 372
  good 618
  utility 644
commonwealth *region* 181
  mankind 372
  state 737
commotion 315
commune *township* 181
commune with 588
communicate *tell* 527
communication 43, 527
communicative 527
communion
  participation 778
  sacrament 998
communist 778
communistic 778
community *party* 712
communize 778
commutation
  substitution 147
  interchange 148
commute 774
commuter 268
COMPACT *joined* 43
  compressed 195
  compendious 201
  dense 321
  bargain 769
compactness
  [*see* compact]
companion *match* 17
  accompaniment 88
  friend 890
companionable 892
companionship 892
company *assembly* 72

cottager 188
couch, n. bed 215
couch, v. lurk 528
cough 349
COUNCIL senate 696
councilor 696
counsel advice 695
   lawyer 968
count, n. item 79
   lord 875
count, v.
   compute 37, 85
   estimate 480
countenance, n. face 234
   appearance 448
   favor 707
countenance, v. approve
   931
counter, n. token 550
counter, adj. contrary 14
   reverse 237
counteract 179, 706
COUNTERACTION 179
counterbalance 30, 179
countercharge 462
counterclaim 30
COUNTEREVIDENCE
   468
counterfeit imitate 19
   copy 21
   sham 545
   swindle 791
counterfeiter 792
countermand 756
countermarch 283
countermotion 283
counterpane 223
counterpart identity 13
   complement 14
   match 17
   copy 21
counterpoise
   compensate 30
countersign n.
   evidence 467
   mark 550
countersign, v. 488
countess 875
countless 105
countrified 189
country region 181
   abode 189
   land 342
   state 737
countryman 876
county 181
coupé 272
couple, n. two 89
couple, v. unite 43
   combine 48
COURAGE 861
courageous 861
courier traveler 268
   messenger 534
COURSE order 58
   continuity 69

time 106, 109
   layer 204
   locomotion 267
   direction 278
   lesson 537
   pursue 622
courser horse 271
court, n. house 189
   hall 191
   retinue 746
court, v. invite 615
   tribunal 966
   woo 902
   flatter 933
courteous 894
COURTESY
   politeness 894
courtier 935
courtly 852
court-martial 966
courtship 902
courtyard 182
cousin 11
cove hollow 252
   bay 343
covenant compact 769
   condition 770
   security 771
cover, n. dress 225
   lid 223
cover, v. include 76
   superpose 223
   conceal 528
   keep safe 664
covered 223
COVERING 220, 223
coverlet 223
covert abode 189
   invisible 447
   latent 526
   refuge 666
coverture 903
covet desire 865
   envy 921
covetous miserly 921
covey 102
cow, n. animal 366
cow, v. intimidate 860
coward 862
COWARDICE 862
cowardly 862
cowboy 370
cower stoop 308
   fear 860
   quail 862
   fawn 886
cowherd 370
cowhide, n. whip 975
cowhide, v lash 972
coworker 690
cowpuncher 370
coxcomb 854, 880
coxcombry affectation 855
coxswain 269
coy 881
cozy 377, 892

crabbed sour 397
   unintelligible 519
   uncivil 895
crack, n. fissure 44, 198
   furrow 259
crack, v. split 44
   crush 328
   sound 406
crack, adj. excellent 648
crack-brained insane 503
cracked unmusical 410
   mad 503
crackle 406
cracksman 792
cradle beginning 66
   infancy 127
   origin 153
   bed 215
   aid 707
craft shipping 273
   calling 625
   cunning 702
craftsman 690
craftsmanship 680
crag cliff 212, 253, 342
craggy rough 256
crake 884
cram stuff 194
   choke 261
   teach 537
   learn 539
   gorge 957
cramp, n. spasm 315
cramp, v. paralyze 158
   weaken 160
   hinder 706
crane lever 307
cranium 450
crank fanatic 504
   instrument 633
cranny 198
crash, n. collision 276
   sound 406
crash, v. destroy 162
   crack 328
crass unintelligent 493
   bad taste 851
cravat 225
crave ask 765
   desire 865
craven cowardly 862
craving 865
craw 191
crawl elapse 109
   creep 275
   cower 886
crazy weak 160
   mad 503
creak 410
cream, n. 356
   important part 642
   best 648
cream, adj. yellow 436
creamy 430
crease 258
create cause 153

compress 195
shatter 328
humble 879
crushed *unhappy* 828
crust 223
crusty *discourteous* 895
crutch *support* 215
crux *difficulty* 704
CRY *stridor* 410
human 411
animal 412
weep 839
crying [see cry]
urgent 630
crypt *cell* 191
grave 207, 363
cryptic *uncertain* 475
concealed 528
crystalline *dense* 321
transparent 425
crystallization 321, 323
crystallize 321
cub *cad* 851
cubicle 191
cubist 556
cuddle 902
cudgel, *n.* 727
cudgel, *v. beat* 276
cue *hint* 527
watchword 550
cuff *blow* 276
cuirass 717
cuisine 298
cul-de-sac 261
culinary 298
cull *choose* 609
take 789
culminate *cap* 33
tower 206
crown 210
culprit 949, 975
cult 481, 990
cultivate *till* 371
improve 658, 707
cultivated *courteous* 894
cultivation *tillage* 371
knowledge 490
improvement 658
courtesy 894
cultivator 371
cultural 537, 542
culture *knowledge* 490
improvement 658
courtesy 894
cumber 706
cumbersome *heavy* 319
disagreeable 830
cumbrous 319, 830
cumulative 467
CUNNING *artfulness* 702
cup *vessel* 191

hollow 252
cupboard 191
cupidity *avarice* 819
desire 865
cupola *dome* 223, 250
cupping 662
cur *dog* 366
curable 658, 660
curate 996
curb, *n. bit* 752
curb, *v. moderate* 174
slacken 275
check 706
restrain 751
curd 321
curdle *condense* 321
cure *reinstate* 660
remedy 662
curio 847
CURIOSITY 455
phenomenon 872
curious *exceptional* 83
inquisitive 455
curl *bend* 245
convolution 248
hair 256
curly 248
currency *publicity* 531
money 800
current, *n.*
of air 349
current, *adj. existing* 1
general 78
present 118
happening 151
rife 531, 532
currycomb 253
curse, *n. bane* 663
adversity 735
curse, *v. execrate* 908
cursory *transient* 111
hasty 684
curt *short* 201
concise 572
curtail *retrench* 38
shorten 201
curtailment
decrease 36
[see curtail]
curtain *shade* 424
screen 530
curtsy 308
CURVATURE 245
curve 245, 252, 279
curved 245
curvet *leap* 309
cushion *pillow* 215
cussedness 606
custodian 753
custody 664, 751
custom, *rule* 80

habit 124, **613**
barter 794
sale 796
fashion 852
customary [see custom]
regular 80
customer 795
cut, *n. bit* 51
notch 257
blow 276
path 627
cut, *v. divide* 44
absent 187
curtail 201
form 240
depart 293
reap 371
carve 557
ignore 460
snub 895
-across 302
-adrift 44
-away 38
-off *subduct* 38
disjoin 44
bereft 776
divorce 782
-out *surpass* 33
substitute 147
-short *stop* 142
cuticle 223
cutlass 727
cutlery 253
cutter 273
cutthroat 361, 913
cutting *sharp* 253
affecting 821
painful 830
-edge 253
cuttings 596
cycle *period* 138
circle 247
vehicle 272
cyclic 138
cyclist 268
cyclone *rotation* 312
wind 349
cyclonic 349
cyclopedia 593
cylinder 249, 272
cylindrical 249
cynic *recluse* 893
misanthrope 911
detractor 936
cynical *morose* 911
contemptuous 930
censorious 932
cynicism
misanthropy 911
discourtesy 895
czar 745

D

E

F

futile 645
futility 499, 645
FUTURE 117, 121, 152

expected 507
-events **152**
-state *destiny* 152

heaven **981**
futurity 121

G

gab 584
gabble **584**
gable *side* 236
gad 266
gag 403, 581
  muzzle 751
gage *measure* 466
gain *increase* **35**
  prosper 618
  acquisition 775
  -time *protract* 110
  -upon *approach* 286
  pass 303
gainsay 536
garish [*see* garish]
gait *walk* 264
galaxy *multitude* 102
  stars 318
gale 349
gall, *n. bitterness* 395
  insolence 885
gall, *v. hurt* 378
  annoy 830
gallant *brave* 861
  courteous 894
gallantry 861, 902
gallery *room* 191
  passage 260
  spectators 444
galley *ship* 273
  cookroom 386
  printing 591
gallop 266, 274
gallows 361, 975
galore 102
galvanic *excitable* 825
galvanize 157
gamble 156, 621, 840
gambler 463, 621, 863
gambling *chance* 621
  rashness 863
gambol 309
game, *n. animal* 366
  amusement 840
game, *adj. resolute* 604
game, *v. gamble* 621
gamester 840
gaming 156
gang 72, 712
gangway 260
gaol [*see* jail]
gap 70, 198
gape, *yawn* 198, 260
  stare 455
garage 191, 272
garb 225
garble *misinterpret* 523
  falsify 544

garden 371
gardener 371
gargle 337
garish 851
garland *circle* 247
  fragrance 400
  ornament 847
garment 225
garner *store* 636
garnish 847
garret 210
garrison 717, 726
garrote 361
garrulity 584
garter *fastening* 45
gas *gaseity* 334
GASEITY 334
gaseous *unsubstantial* 4
  vaporous 334, 336
gash *cut* 44
  interval 198
gasify 334
gasoline 356
gasp 688
gastronomy 957
gate 66, 232, 260
gather *collect* 72
  fold 258
  conclude 480
gathering *assemblage* 72
gaudy 428, 851
gauge 466
gaunt 203
gauntlet *glove* 225
gawky *awkward* 699
  ugly 846
gay *bright* 428
  cheerful 836
  showy 882
gayety [*see* gay] 836
gaze 441
gazelle 366
gazette 531
gazetteer 86
gear *clothes* 225
  harness 633
gelatinous 352
gem *excellence* 648
  ornament 847
gendarme 726, 965
gender 75
genealogy 69
general, *adj. generic* 78
  habitual 613
general, *n.* 745
GENERALITY 78
generalize 78, 476
generally 16, 78

generalship 692, 722
generate 161, 168
generation
  consanguinity 11
  period 108
  production 161
generic 78
generosity *liberality* 816
  benevolence 906
  disinterestedness 942
generous [*see* generosity]
genesis *beginning* 66
  production 161
genial *cordial* 377
  warm 382
  willing 602
geniality 602
  [*see* genial]
genius *intellect* 450
  talent 498
  skill 698
  adept 700
  familiar spirit 979
genteel 852
gentile *heterodox* 984
gentility 852
gentle *moderate* 174
  lenient 740
  meek 826
  courteous 894
  -breeding 894
gentlefolk 875
gentleman 373, 939
gentleness [*see* gentle]
gentry 875
genuflexion 308
genuine *true* 494
  good 648
genus 75
geography 183
geometry 466
germ *origin* 66
  cause 153
  stem 193
  -cell 357
germane *relevant* 23
germinate 194, 365
gesticulate 550
gesture 550
get *acquire* 775
  -back *regain* 775
  -down *descend* 306
  -in 775
  -on *advance* 282
  prosper 734
gewgaw *trifle* 643
geyser 382, 384
ghastly *pale* 429

-nature 906
-offices *mediation* 724
-taste 578, 850
-turn *kindness* 906
-will *benevolence* 906
-woman **948**
-word 931
make - *restore* 790
  substantiate 924
  vindicate 937
good-for-nothing 158, 949
good-looking 845
goodly *great* 31
  handsome 845
good-natured 906
GOODNESS 648
goods *effects* 780
  merchandise 798
goose *bird* 366
gore, n. *gusset* 43
  blood 361
gore, *v.* 260
gorge, n. *ravine* 198
gorge, *v. glut* 869
  gormandize 957
gorgeous *gay* 428
  beautiful 845
gorilla 366
gormandize **957**
gorse 367
gory *murderous* 361
  red 434
gospel *doctrine* 484
  truth 494
Gospels 985
gossamer 205
gossamery 320
gossip *news* 532
  babbler 584
  conversation 588
gouge 262
gourmand *glutton* 957
gourmet 868, **954a**
govern 693, 737
governess 540
government **737**, 745, 965
governor *director* 694
  ruler 745
gown *dress* 225
grab *take* 789
grace *elegance* 845
  polish 850
  pity 914
  forgiveness 918
  worship 990
graceful *elegant* 578
  beautiful 845
  tasteful 850
graceless *inelegant* 579
  ugly 846
  impenitent 951
Graces 845
gracious *courteous* 894
  kind 906
gradation *degree* 26
  order 58

grade *degree* 26
  classify 60
  term 71
  obliquity 217
  ascent 305
  class 541
  crossing 219
gradual *degree* 26
  continuous 69
  slow 275
gradually **275**
graduate, n. 492
graduate, *v. adjust* 23
  measure 26
  arrange 60
  initiate 537
graduation 541
graft, *v. insert* 300
graft, n. *loot* 784
  improbity 940
grain *humor* 5
  tendency 176
  roughness 256
  texture 329
  powder 330
  *against the-*704
GRAMMAR 567
grammatical 567
gramophone 418
grand *august* 31
  important 642
  handsome 845
  glorious 873
  ostentatious 882
  -juror 967
grandee 875
grandeur *greatness* 31
  repute 873
grandfather 130, 166
grandmother 166
grandness [see *grand*]
granny **30**
grant *admit* 529
  permit 760
  consent 762
  confer 784
granular 330
graphic *intelligible* 518
  vigorous 574
  descriptive 594
graphophone 418
grapnel 666
grapple 789
-with
  -a question 461
  -difficulties 704
  oppose 708
  resist 719
grasp, n. *power* 737
grasp, *v. comprehend* 518
  retain 781
  -at 865
grasping *miserly* 819
  covetous 865
grass 367
  -widow 905

grassland 367
grassplot 371
grassy 367
grate, n. *fireplace* 386
grate, *v. rub* 330
  -on the ear
    harsh sound 410
grateful *enjoyable* 377
  agreeable 829
  thankful **916**
gratification 377, 827
gratify *permit* 760
  please 829
grating *lattice* 219
  stridor 410
gratis 815
GRATITUDE **916**
gratuitous
  inconsequent 477
  free **748**, 815
gratuity *gift* **784**
grave, n. 363
grave, *adj. somber* 428
  important 642
  distressing 830
  sad 837
graveclothes 363
gravedigger 363
gravestone 363
gravitate *descend* 306
  weigh 319
  -towards 176
GRAVITY *weight* **319**
  importance 642
  seriousness **837**
  [see *grave*]
GRAY *old* 128
  color 428, **432**
graybeard 130
graze *touch* 199, 379
  browse 298
  rub 331
grease *lubricate* 332
  oil 355, 356
greasy 355
great *much* **31**
  big 192
  glorious 873
greater 33
greatness 33
GREATNESS **31**
greed *desire* 865
  gluttony 957
greedy 819, **865**, 957
Greek - deities 970
GREEN, n. *lawn* 344, 371
  color **435**
green, *adj. new* 123
  young 127
  sour 397
  credulous 486
  novice 701
  immature 674
greenhorn *novice* 493
  bungler 701
greenness **435**

hunchbacked 243
hundred 98
hunger 865
hungry 865, 956
hunt *pursuit* 286, 622
  inquiry 461
hunter *horse* 271
  pursuer 622
hurl 284
hurrah 838
hurricane *tempest* 349
hurry 274, 684
hurt, n. *physical pain* 378
  evil 619
hurt, v.
  cause (physical) pain 378
  maltreat 649
  injure 659, 907
  pain 830
  more frightened than-
  860
hurtful 649
hurtle 276
hurtless 648

husband *store* 636
  director 694
  spouse 903
husbandman 371
husbandry *agriculture* 371
  conduct 692
  economy 817
hush *moderate* 174
  stop 265
  silence 403
  taciturn 585
  -up *conceal* 528
  pacify 723
husk *covering* 223
husky *strong* 159
  hoarse 405, 581
hussar 726
hustings 728
hustle 682
hustler 682
hut 189
hybrid 41
hydroplane 273
hydroplaning 267

hygiene 656
hygienic 656
hygienics 670
Hymen 903
hymeneal 903
hymn *song* 415
  worship 990
hyperbole 549
hypercriticism 868
hyperphysical 450
hyphen 45
hypnosis 376, 992*a*
hypnotic 683
hypnotism 683, 992*a*
hypnotize 615, 992
hypochondriac 837, 859
hypocrisy 544, 988
hypocrite 548
hypocritical 544, 988
hypothesis 514
hypothetical 514
hysteria 992*a*
hysterical 821
hysterics 173

I

ice 383, 387
iceberg 383
ice chest 385
icon 554
iconoclasm 984
iconoclast 165
icy 383
IDEA *notion* 453
ideal 515
idealism 450, 515
idealist 515
ideality 450, 515
idealize 515
identical 13
identification 13
IDENTITY 13, 27
idiocy 503
idiom 560, 566
idiosyncrasy 5, 79, 83
idiot 501
idiotic *foolish* 499
idle *trivial* 643
  slothful 683
idler 683
idol *favorite* 899
  fetich 991
idolater 991
IDOLATRY 991
idolize *love* 897
  idolatrize 991
idyl 597
if 8, 469, **514**
igneous 382
ignis fatuus 4, 443
ignite 384
ignition *calefaction* **384**
ignoble 876

ignominious 940
ignominy *shame* 874
  dishonor 940
IGNORAMUS **493**
IGNORANCE **491**
ignorant 491
ignore *neglect* 460
  not known 491
ill, n. *evil* 619
  badness 649
  sick 655
ill, *adj. bad* 649
  -usage 807
  -will 907, 921
ill-adapted 24
ill-advised *inexpedient* **647**
  unskillful 699
ill-assorted 24
ill-behaved 895
ill-bred *vulgar* 851
  rude 895
ill-disposed 907
illegal 964
ILLEGALITY **964**
illegible 519
illegitimate 925, 964
ill-fated 135, **735**
ill-favored 846
illiberal *stingy* 819
  selfish 943
  bigoted 988
illicit 925, 964
illiteracy 491
illiterate 491, **493**
ill-made 243
ill-mannered 851
ill-natured 907

illness 655
illogical 477
ill-omened 135, **735**
ill-proportioned 846
ill-spent 645
ill-starred 135
ill-timed 24, **135**
ill-treat 649, 907
ill-treatment 649
illuminant 420
illuminate *enlighten* 420
  comment 595
illumine *lighten* 420
  excite 824
ill-use 649
illusion
  fallacy of vision 443
  error 495
  deception 545
illusive 4, 495
illusory 4, 495
illustrate *exemplify* 82
  interpret 522
  represent 554
illustration 558
illustrious 873
image *likeness* 17
  appearance 448
  metaphor 521
imagery *fancy* 515
  metaphor 521
imaginable 470
imaginary 2, 4, 515
IMAGINATION 515
imaginative 515
imagine 515
imbecile, *adj. ignorant* 493

interchangeable 148
intercollegiate 148
intercourse 888, 892
interdependence 12
interdict 971
interest, *n. influence* 175
  curiosity 455
  advantage 618
  importance 642
  property 780
  debt 806
interest, *v.* 824, 829, 840
interested *selfish* 943
interfere *disagree* 24
  counteract 179
  intervene 228
  thwart 706
interim 106, 111
interior 221
INTERIORITY 221
interjacence 228
interject 228
interlace 43, 219
interlard *mix* 41
  interpolate 228
interlineation 228
INTERLOCATION 228
interloper 57
interlude 106
intermediary 228, 534
intermediate *mean* 29
  middle 68
  intervening 228
  -time 106
intermediation 170
INTERMENT 363
interminable
  infinite 105, 112
  long 200
intermingle 41
intermission 106, 142
intermit *interrupt* 70
  recur 138
  discontinue 142
intermittent 138
intermix 41, 48
intern 221
internal *intrinsic* 5
  interior 221
international 148
interpenetration 228
interpolation 228
interpose *intervene* 228
  hinder 706
interpret 522, 595
INTERPRETATION 522
INTERPRETER 524
interregnum 111, 187, 198
interrogate 461
interrogation 461
interrupt *suspend* 70, 142
  hinder 706
interruption
  [see interrupt]
  interval 187, 198
intersect 219

intersection 219
intersperse *diffuse* 73
interstice 198
intertwine *unite* 41, 43
  cross 219
INTERVAL *degree* 26
  -*of time* 106
  absence 187
  -*of space* 198
  at intervals 70
intervene *interrupt* 70
  -*in space* 228
  be instrumental 631
  mediate 724
intervention 228
interview 588
interviewer 553
interweave *join* 41, 43
  cross 219
inthrall *subject* 749
intimacy 888
intimate, *n.* 890
intimate, *adj. close* 197
  friendly 888
intimate, *v. tell* 527
intimation 527
intimidate 860, 909
intimidation 860
intolerable 830
intolerance *prejudice* 481
  obstinacy 606
  impatience 825
intolerant 481, 489
intomb 363
intonation *sound* 402
  voice 580
intone *sing* 416
intoxicated 959
intoxication 959
intrap 545
intrench 664, 717
intrepid 861
intricacy 533
intricate 59, 248
intrigue *plot* 626
  finesse 702
intrinsic 5, 121
introduce *add* 37
  lead 62
  interpose 228
  precede 280
  admit 296
  insert 300
introduction
  [see introduce]
  preface 64
  reception 296
introductory *precursor* 64
  beginning 66
  receptive 296
introspective 451
intrude
  be inopportune 135
  intervene 228
  trespass 303
intruder 57

intrusion 135, 228
intrusive 228, 706
intrust *commit* 755
  lend 787
  credit 805
INTUITION 477, 490
intwine 43, 248
inundate 348
inure 613, 823
INUTILITY 645
invade 294, 716
invalid, *n.* 655
invalid, *adj. illogical* 477
invalidate *disable* 158
  confute 479
invaluable 644, 648
invariable 16
invasion 294, 716
invective 908, 932
inveigh 932
inveigle *deceive* 545
  seduce 615
invent *imagine* 515
  lie 544
  devise 626
invention 515
inventive *skillful* 698
inventor 164
inventory 86
inverse 14, 218
INVERSION
  contrariety 14
  change 140
  reversion 145
  of position 218
invert 14, 218
  [see inversion]
invertebrate *weak* 945
invest *impower* 157
  clothe 225
  surround 227
  besiege 716
  give 784
  lend 787
  -*in purchase* 795
investigate 461
investment [see invest]
investor 784
inveterate *old* 124
  established 150
invidious 898, 921
invigorate 159, 171
invincible 159
inviolate *permanent* 141
  secret 528
  stainless 939
INVISIBILITY 447
invisible 193, 447, 526
invitation [see invite]
invite *induce* 615
  offer 763
  ask 765
invocation [see invoke]
invoice 86
invoke *address* 586
  implore 765

J

knob 249
knobby 250
knock
  blow 276
  sound 406
  -down *lay flat* 213

knockout 67
knoll 206
knot *ligature* 45
  group 72
  intersection 219
  difficulty 704

knotted *rough* 256
know 484, 490
knowing 702
knowingly 620
KNOWLEDGE 490, 539
known 490
kowtow 308, 725

L

label 550
labor 680, 686
  -in vain 645
laboratory 691
laborer 686, 690
laborious 686
labyrinth 248, 533
labyrinthine 248, 533
lace *stitch* 43
lacerate 378
lack 53, 630, 865
lackey 746
laconic 585
lacquer 223
lad 129
ladder 305
lade *load* 184, 190
ladle 191
lady 374, 875
ladylove 897
lag *linger* 275
  follow 281
laggard 603
lagoon 343
laicize 997
lair *den* 189
laird 875
LAITY 997
LAKE 343
lamb 366
lambent 379
lame 158
lament 839
lamentable 837
LAMENTATION 839
lamp 423
lampoon 934
lampooner 936
lance, *n. spear* 727
lance, *v. pierce* 260
  throw 284
lancer 726
lancet 253, 262
LAND, *n.* 342
land, *v.* 292
landholder 779
landing place 292
landlocked 292
landlord *innkeeper* 637
  possessor 779
landlubber 701
landmark 233, 550

landowner 779
landscape *prospect* 448
  -painting 556
landslide 306
landsman 342
lane 189, 260
LANGUAGE 560
languid *weak* 160
  inert 172
  slow 275
  inactive 683
languish *decrease* 36
  be inactive 683
  repine 828
  affect 855
languishing 855
languor 683
  [see languid]
lanky *tall* 200
lantern *lamp* 423
  -jawed 203
lap, *n. support* 215
  -of *weaves* 405
lap, *v. drink* 298
  circuit 311
lapse, *n. conversion* 144
  fall 306
  relapse 661
  guilt 947
lapse, *v. proceed* 109
  pass 122
  cease 142
  relapse 661
larceny 791
large *quantity* 31
  size 192
  at - *liberated* 750
largehearted 906, 942
lariat 45
lark *bird* 366
  spree 840
larva 193
lash *tie together* 43
  whip 370
  incite 615
  punish 972
lass *girl* 129
lassitude 688
lasso 45
last, *n. model* 22
last, *v. abide* 1
  -in order 67

  endure 106, **110**
  -in time 122
  continue 141
latch 43, 45
late *past* 122
  new 123
  tardy **133**
  dead 360
lately 122, 123
LATENCY 526
LATENESS 133
latent *inert* 172
  concealed 526
  -influence **526**
later 117
lateral 236
latest 118
lath 205
lathe 633
lather 353
Latin deities 979
latitude *breadth* 202
  freedom 748
latter 63, 122
latterly 122, 123
lattice 219
laud *praise* 931
laudable 944
laudatory 931
laugh 838
  -at *ridicule* 856
  sneer 929
laughable 853
LAUGHINGSTOCK 857
laughter 838
launch, *n. boat* 273
launch, *v. begin* 66
  propel 284
  -forth 676
  -into 676
  -out 573
laundress 652
laundry 652
laundryman 652
laurel *glory* 873
lavatory 652
lave *water* 337
  clean 652
lavender *color* 437
lavish, *adj. profuse* 809
lavish, *v. squander* 818
law *regularity* 80

libel *detraction* 934
   accusation 938
libelant 938
libeler 936
liberal *ample* 639
   expending 809
   generous 816
LIBERALITY 784, 816
liberate *disjoin* 44
   deliver 672
   free 748, 750
LIBERATION 750
LIBERTINE 962
liberty *freedom* 748
   permission 760
   right 924
library 593
lice 366
license *laxity* 738
   permission 760
   right 924
lid 223
lie, *n. untruth* 546
lie, *v. be situated* 183
   be present 186
   recline 213
   fib 544
   -*in be* 1
lien *security* 771
   credit 805
lieutenant *officer* 745
   deputy 759
LIFE *essence* 5
   events 151
   vitality 359
   biography 594
   activity 682
   -*to come* 152
lifeboat 273
life-giving 168
lifeless *inert* 172
   dead 360
lifelike 17, 21
lifelong 110
lifetime 108
lift *raise* 307
ligament 45
ligature 45
LIGHT, *n. window* 260
   luminosity 420
   luminary 423
   aspect 448
   knowledge 490
light, *adj. not heavy* 320
   luminous 420
   trivial 643
   unburdened 705
   gay 836
light, *v. arrive* 292
   descend 306
   kindle 384
   illumine 420
light-colored 429
lighten *illume* 420
   facilitate 705
light-fingered 791

light-footed *fleet* 274
   active 682
lightheaded 503
lighthearted 836
lighthouse 550
lightning 420
like, *adj. similar* 17
like, *v. relish* 394
   enjoy 827
   wish 865
   love 897
likely 472
likeness *similarity* 17, 21
   portrait 554
likewise 37
lilac *color* 437
Liliputian 193
limb *member* 51
limber *pliable* 324
LIMIT, *n. end* 67
   boundary 233
limit, *v. circumscribe* 195, 229
   qualify 469
   restrain 751
limitation [*see* limit]
limited 32
limitless 105
limp, *adj. weak* 160
   supple 324
limp, *v.* 275
limpid 425, 570
line, *n. fastening* 45
   row 69
   lineage 69, 167
   length 200
   direction 278
   mark 550
   vocation 625
   armed force 726
line, *v.* 224
lineage *kindred* 11
   series 69
   ancestry 122, 166
   posterity 167
lineament *outline* 230
   appearance 448
linear 200
linen 225
liner 273
linger *delay* 133
   loiter 275, 281, 291
   -*on time* 106
lingo 563
lingua franca 563
lingual 560
linguistic 560
liniment *ointment* 356
LINING 224
link, *n. tie* 9
   vinculum 45
link, *v. connect* 43
lion *animal* 366
   celebrity 873
lion-hearted 861
lionize 873

lip 231
LIQUEFACTION 335
liquefy 335
liquid *fluid* 333
liquidate 807
liquidity 333
liquor 298
lisp 583
LIST, *n. catalogue* 86
   leaning 217
   schedule 611
   arena 728
list, *v. classify* 69
   hear 418
   record 551
listen 418
listless *inactive* 683
   indifferent 866
literal *exact* 516
literally 19
literary 560
literature 490, 560
lithe 324
litigant 938, 969
litigate 969
litigation 969
litigious 713
litter, *n. disorder* 59
litter, *v. derange* 61
   bed cattle 370
little -*in degree* 32
   -*in size* 193
   bigoted 988
LITTLENESS 32, 193
liturgy 998
live *exist* 1, 359
   continue 141
   dwell 186
livelihood 803
liveliness 836 [*see* lively]
livelong 110
lively *frisky* 309
   keen 375
   active 682
   acute 821
   sensitive 822
   sprightly 836
livery 225
livid 431, 437
living *alive* 359
   benefice 995
lizard 366
load, *n. quantity* 31
   cargo 190
   hindrance 706
   anxiety 828
load, *v. fill* 52
   lade 184, 190
loadstar [*see* lodestar]
loadstone *attraction* 288
loaf *dawdle* 683
loafer 268, 927
loan 787
loath 603, 867
loathe *dislike* 867
   hate 898

relinquish 624
lure *charm* 288
　deceive 545
　entice 615
lurid *dark* 421
　dim 422
lurk 526, 528
luscious *savory* 394
luster 420, 873

lustily *loud* 404
lustrous *shining* 420
lusty *strong* 159
　big 192
luxuriant *fertile* 168
　rank 365
luxurious *pleasant* 377
　intemperate 954
luxury

enjoyment 377, 827
　sensuality 954
lying 544
lymphatic *slow* 275
lynch 972
　-law 964
lyncher 975
lyric 597
lyrist 597

M

mace *weapon* 727
　scepter 747
machination 626, 702
machine *automobile* 272
　instrument 633
　party 712
machinery 633
machinist 690
mackintosh 225
mad *violent* 173
　insane 503
　excited 824
madam 374, 877
madden 824
MADMAN 504
madness 503
Madonna 977
maelstrom *whirl* 312
magazine *book* 593
　store 636
magenta 434, 437
magic 992
magician 548, 994
magisterial 878, 885
magistrate 967
magnanimity 942
magnanimous 942
magnate 875
magnet *attraction* 288
　desire 865
magnetic 157, 829
magnetism *power* 157
　influence 175
　attraction 288
magnetize 157, 288
magnificent *fine* 845
　grand 882
magnify *increase* 31, 35
　enlarge 194
　overrate 549
magnitude 25, 31, 192
maharajah 875
mahogany *color* 433
maid *girl* 129
　servant 746
　spinster 904
maiden *first* 66
　girl 129
maidenly 374
mail *post* 270, 534
　armor 717
maim *injure* 659

main, *n. ocean* 341
　land 342
　conduit 350
　in the - *principally* 642
main, *adj principal* 642
　-force strength 159
　violence 173
　compulsion 744
mainland 342
mainspring *cause* 153
mainstay *support* 215
　refuge 666
　hope 858
maintain *keep* 141
　continue 143
　sustain 170
　assert 535
　preserve 670
maintenance
　[see maintain]
majestic *grand* 31
　glorious 873
　stately 882
majesty 745, 873
major, *adj greater* 33
major, *officer* 745
majority *superiority* 33
　plurality 100
　age 131
make *constitute* 54, 56
　render 144
　produce 161
　form 240
　complete 729
　compel 744
　create 976
　-believe 545
　-good
　demonstrate 478
　-out discover 480a
　know 490
　interpret 522
　-up complete 52
maker *inferer* 690
Make-, the - 976
makeshift *substitute* 147
　excuse 617
make-up *composition* 54
makeweight 30
malady 655
malcontent 710, 832
male *man* 373

MALEDICTION 908
malefaction 947
malefactor 975
maleficent 907
MALEVOLENCE 907
malevolent 907
malformation 243
malformed 241
malice *hate* 898
　spite 907
　bear - 907
malign, *adj. malevolent* 907
malign, *v detract* 934
malignant 907
malignity 907
malinger 544
malison 908
malleable *soft* 324
maltreat *injure* 649
　aggrieve 830
　molest 907
mamma 166
mammal 366
Mammon 803
mammoth 192
MAN, *n. mankind* 372
　male 373
　workman 690
　servant 746
　-of action 682
man, *v. prepare* 673
　defend 717
manacle *fetter* 752
manage 175, 693
manageable *easy* 705
management 692, 693
manage *director* 694
mandate *requirement* 630
　command 741
mane 256
manege 370
maneuver *operation* 680
　stratagem 702
manful *strong* 159
　resolute 604
　brave 861
manger 191
mangle *smooth* 255
　injure 659
manhood 131, 861
mania *insanity* 503
　desire 865

maniac 504
manifest, n. list 86
manifest, adj. visible 446
  obvious 525
MANIFESTATION 525
manifold 81
manipulate handle 379
  use 677
MANKIND 372
manly adolescent 131
  strong 159
  male 373
  brave 861
  upright 939
manna food 396
manner kind 75
  style 569
  way 627
  conduct 692
mannerism special 79
  affectation 855
manners breeding 852
man-of-war 726
manse 1000
mansion 189
manslaughter 361
mantle, n. dress 225
mantle, v. redden 434
manual schoolbook 542
  book 593
  -labor 686
manufactory 691
manufacture 161
manufacturer 690
manuscript 590
many 102
many-colored 428, 440
many-sided 81
map 554
mar deface 241
  botch 699
maraud 791
marauder 792
marble ball 249
  sculpture 557
marbled 440
march journey 266
  music 415
  -with 199
marchioness 875
mare 271
margin space 180
  edge 231
marine, n 269, 726
marine, adj 273, 341
MARINER 269
marital 903
maritime 267, 273, 241
mark, n. degree 26
  indication 550
  object 620
  repute 873
mark, v. take cognizance
  450
  attend to 457
  -out choose 609

command 741
-time halt 265
marked [see mark]
  special 79
market consumer 677
  mart 799
marksman 284, 700
maroon, adj. 433, 434
maroon, v 782
marquis 875
marriage 43, 903, 998
marriageable 131
married 903
-man 903
-woman 903
marrow 5, 221, 222
marry combine 43, 48
  wed 903
MARSH 345
marshal, n. auxiliary 711
  officer 745
marshal, v. 60
marshy 345
MART 799
martial 722
martinet 739
martyr 828
  ascetic 955
martyrdom 828, 972
marvel wonder 870
  prodigy 872
marvelous 870
mascot 993
masculine strong 159
  male 373
mash soften 324
  squash 352
mask dress 225
  shade 424
  concealment 528
Masonic 712
masquerade 530, 840
masquerader 528
Mass worship 990
  Eucharist 998
mass quantity 25
  much 31
  whole 50
  heap 72
  size 192
  density 321
massacre 361
massage 324, 331, 379
masses, the 876
masseur 662
massive huge 192
  heavy 319
  dense 321
mast 206
MASTER, n. teacher 540
  ruler 745
  adept 700
  owner 779
master, v. influence 175
  understand 518
  learn 539

succeed, conquer 731
-of the situation 731
masterpiece 650, 698
mastery success 731
masticate 298
mastiff 366
mat 215
match fellow 17
  copy 19
  equal 27
  contest 720
  marriage 903
matchless unequal 28
  supreme 33
mate similar 17
  equal 27
  duality 89
  auxiliary 711
  friend 890
material, n. substance 316
  stuff 635
material, adj.
  important 642
materialism 984
materialist, 316, 984
MATERIALITY 3, 316
materialize 316
MATERIALS 635
materia medica 662
maternal 166
maternity 166
mathematical precise 494
mathematician 85
mathematics 25
matin 125
matinée 892
matrimonial 903
matrimony 903, 998
matrix mold 22
matron 374, 903
matronly 131
matter, n. affair 151
  material world 316
  topic 454
  -of-fact 1
matter, v. signify 642
matter-of-fact prosaic 576
  blunt 703
  dull 843
mature, adj old 124
  adolescent 131
  ripe 678
  -though 451
mature, mellow 144
  perfect 650
  prepare 673
maturity 124
  [see nature]
maul hew 649
maunder prose 573
  mumble 583
mausoleum 363
mauve 437
maw 191
MAXIM 80, 496
maximum supreme 33

fastidious 868
metrical *measured* **466**
metropolis 189, 222
mettle *energy* 171
 spirit 820
 courage 861
mew *cry* 412
microbe 193
microscopic 32
mid 68
MID-COURSE 628
midday 125
MIDDLE *-in degree* 29
 -in order 68
 -in space 222
 -age **131**
middle-aged 131
middle-class 29
middleman 228
middling 736
midmost 68
midnight **126**
midriff 228
midshipman 269
midst 68
midsummer 125
midway **68**
mien 448
might 31, 157
mighty *much* 31
 strong 157, 159
migrate 266
mild *moderate* 174
 warm 382
 lenient 740
 calm 826
MILDNESS 740
mile 200
militant 722
military 722
 soldiers 726
 -authorities **745**
militia 726
milksop *coward* 862
milky 430
mill, *n.* 691
mill, *v. indent* 257
 pulverize 330
millennium *period* 108
 hope 858
millinery *ornament* 847
million 98, 876
millionaire 803
mimic *imitate* 19
mince *step short* 275
 lisp 583
 affect 855
mind, *n. intellect* 450
 will 600
 purpose 620
 desire 865
 bear in - 505
mind, *v. attend to* 457
 dislike 867
mindful 457, 505
mine, *n.* 545, 636

mine, *v. sap* 162, 252, 717
miner 252
 sapper and - 726
mineral 358
mineralize 358
mingle 41
miniature *small* 32
minimize 36
minimum 32, 34
minister *deputy* 759
 clergy 996
 -to help 707, 746
ministerial 995
ministration *aid* 707
ministry *direction* 693
 aid 707
 church 995
 clergy 996
minor *inferior* 34
 infant 129
minority *few* 103
 youth 127
minster 1000
minstrel 416, 597
mint 22
minuend 38
minus *subtracted* 38
 absent 187
minute, *n. period* 108
 record 551
minute, *adj. -in degree* 32
 -in size 193
minutemen 726
minuteness 457, 459
minutiae 32, 643
miracle *exceptional* 83
 prodigy 872
miraculous *wonderful* 870
mirage 443
mire 653
mirror, *n. reflector* 445
mirror, *v. imitate* 19
mirth 836
misadventure 735
misanthrope 911
MISANTHROPY 911
misapply *misinterpret* 523
 misuse 679
 mismanage 699
misapprehend *mistake* 495
 misinterpret 523
misappropriate 679
misbehave 851, 945
misbehavior
 discourtesy 851, 895
 guilt 947
misbelief 485
misbeliever 984
miscalculate 481, 495
miscall 565
miscarry 732
miscellany 41, **72**, 78
mischance *misfortune* 735
mischief 619
mischief-maker 913
mischievous 649

misconceive *mistake* 481, 495
 misinterpret 523
misconception 481, 495
misconduct *guilt* 947
misconstrue 523
miscreant 949
misdate 115
misdeed 947
misdemeanor 947
misdoubt 485
misemploy 679
miser 819
miserable *unhappy* 828
miserably 32
miserly 819
misery 828
misfire 732
misfortune *adversity* **735**
misgiving 485, 860
misguide 495, 538
misguided 699
mishap *failure* **732**
 misfortune 735
misinform 495, 538
misinstruct 538
MISINTERPRETATION
 523
MISJUDGMENT 481, 495
mislay *derange* 61
 lose 776
mislead **495**
mismanage 699
mismatch 15
misname 565
MISNOMER 565
misplace *derange* 61
 displace 185
misprint 495
mispronounce 583
misproportioned *ugly* 846
misreckon 481
misrepresent
 misinterpret **523**
 misteach 538
 lie 544
 distort 555
MISREPRESENTATION
 523, 555
misrule 699, 738
miss, *n. girl* 129
 error 495
miss, *v. neglect* 460
 fail 732
 lose 776
 want 865
misshapen *shapeless* 241
 distorted 243
 ugly 846
missile **284, 727**
missing 2, 187
mission 625, 755
missionary 540
missive 592
misspell 523
misspend 818

mordant *keen* 171
 pungent 392
 vigorous 574
more *superior* 33
 extra 37
moreover 37
moribund *dying* 360
MORNING 125
morose 901a, 911
morris chair 215
morrow 121
morsel 32, 51
mortal, *n. man* 372
mortal, *adj. transient* 111
 fatal 361
mortality *evanescence* 111
 death 360
mortar *cement* 45
 pulverizer 330
 crucible 691
 cannon 727
mortgage *security* 771
 lend 787
 sale 796
 credit 805
mortification
 vexation 830
 humiliation 879
mortify 879
mortise *intersect* 219
mosaic 41, 440
mosque 1000
moss 367
most 31
mote 32
mother *parent* 166
 -tongue 560
motherhood 166
motherland 181, 189
motherly 897, 906
MOTION
 change of place 264
 topic 454
 proposal 763
 request 765
motionless 265
MOTIVE 264, 615
 absence of -615a
 -power 264
motley 41, 81
motor, *n. vehicle* 272
motor, *adj. motion* 264
motor, *v. journey* 266
motor car 272
motorcycle 266, 272
motorist 268
motorize 266
motorman 268
mottled 440
motto *maxim* 496
 device 550
mould [*see* mold]
mound *hill* 206
mount, *n.* 206, 250
mount, *v. increase* 35
 ascend 305

raise 307
mountain 206
mountainous 206
mountebank *quack* 548
 buffoon 844
mourn *grieve* 828
 lament 839
mourner 363, 839
mournful *sad* 837
mourning 839
mouth *entrance* 66
 opening 260, 294
 jaws 298
 estuary 343
mouthful *quantity* 25
 food 298
movable 264, 270
move *begin* 66
 go 264
 propose 514
 induce 615
 offer 763
 excite 824
 -slowly 275
movement 264, 680
movies *theater* 599
moving 185, 264
 -pictures 448, 599
mow *shorten* 201
 -down *destroy* 162
 level 213
much 31
mud 345, 352, 653
muddle *disorder* 59
 derange 61
 blunder 497, 732
muddle-headed 499
muddy *moist* 339
 opaque 426
muff
 dress 225
 bungler 701
muffle *wrap* 225
 silence 403
 deaden 405, 408a
 gag 581
muffler *dress* 225
 silencer 408a
mufti *undress* 225
mug *cup* 191
muggy *moist* 339
mulatto 41
mulct 974
mule 41, 271
mulish 606
multifarious
 diverse 16a
multifold 81
MULTIFORMITY 81
multiplex 81
multiplication
 productiveness 168
multiplicity 102
multiply 163, 168
MULTITUDE 31, 102
mum *mute* 581

mumble *mutter* 583
mummy 362
munch 298
mundane *worldly* 318
 irreligious 989
municipal 965
munificent 816
munition 717
murder 361
murderer 361
murderous 361
murky *dark* 421
murmur 405
muscle 159
muscular 159
muse, *v.* 451
Muse *poetry* 597
Muses, the - 416
mushroom *upstart* 734
MUSIC 415
musical 413, 415, 416
 -instruments 417
 -terms 413
musicale 415
music hall 840
MUSICIAN 416
musing *thought* 451
musket 727
musketeer 726
musketry 727
muss 61
mussy 653
mustache 256
mustang 271
muster 72, 85
muster roll *list* 86
mutable *changeable* 149
mutation 20a 140
mute, *adj. silent* 403
 letter 561
 speechless 581
 sordine 408a
mutescence 408a
mutilate *retrench* 38
 deform 241
mutilated 53
mutilation 38, 619
mutineer 742
mutiny 146, 742
mutter 583
mutual 12, 148
muzzle *silence* 403, 581
 restrain 751
 gag 752
myriad 102
myrmidon 726
mysterious *uncertain* 475
 obscure 519
 concealed 528
mystery
 [*see* mysterious]
 latency 526
 secret 533
mystic 528, 992a
mysticism 992a
mystify *perplex* 519

O

oaf *fool* 501
oar *paddle* 267
  oarsman 269
oarsman 269
oasis 342
oath *assertion* 535
  bad language 908
obdurate *obstinate* 606
  impenitent 951
OBEDIENCE 743
obeisance *bow* 308
  submission 725
obelisk 206, 551
obesity 192
obey 743, 749
object, n. *thing* 3
  matter 316
  intention 620
object, v. disapprove 932
  -to dislike 867
objection 706, 932
objectionable
  inexpedient 647
  wrong 923
objective 6, 316
OBJECTIVENESS 6
oblation 784, 990
obligation *necessity* 601
  promise 768
  debt 806
  duty 926
obligatory 926
oblige *benefit* 707
  compel 744
obliging *helping* 707
  courteous 894
  kind 906
oblique 217
OBLIQUITY 217, 243
obliterate 2, 162, 552
OBLITERATION 552
OBLIVION 506
oblivious 506
obnoxious 898
obscure, adj. *dark* 421
  unseen 447
  unintelligible 519
  ignoble 876
obscure, v. 874
OBSCURITY 421, 571
  [see obscure]
obsequies 363
obsequious 746, 886
OBSERVANCE *rule* 82
  habit 613
  fulfillment 772
  duty 926
observant 772
observation *attention* 457
  assertion 535
observe 457, 772
observer *aviator* 269a

spectator 444
obsess *haunt* 860
obsession 481, 503, 992a
obsolete 122, 124, 851
obstacle 706
OBSTINACY 141, 606
obstinate 606
obstreperous 173
obstruct *close* 261
  hinder 706
obstructionist 710
obstructive 710
obtain 775
obtainable 470
obtrude *interfere* 228
  insert 300
obtrusion 228, 706
obtrusive *interfering* 228
  rude 895
obtuse 254, 499
obverse 234
obviate 706
obvious *visible* 446
  manifest 525
occasion *juncture* 8
  opportunity 134
  cause 153
occasional 134
occasionally 136
occult 526
occultism 526, 992a
occupancy 186, 777
occupant 188, 779
occupation *business* 625
occupier *dweller* 188
  possessor 779
occupy 186, 777
  -oneself with 625
occur *exist* 1
  happen 151
  -to the mind 451
occurrence 151
OCEAN 341
oceanic 341
octave *eight* 98
  period 108
  poetry 597
octopus *mollusk* 366
  monster 913
ocular 441
odd *remaining* 40
  exceptional 83
  single 87
  insane 503
  ridiculous 853
oddity 83, 503
odds *inequality* 28
  chance 156
  discord 713
ode 597
odious *disagreeable* 830
  hateful 898

odium *disgrace* 874
  hatred 898
ODOR 398
of course 478
offend *pain* 830
  anger 900
offense *attack* 716
  anger 900
  guilt 947
offensive *fetid* 401
  foul 653
  displeasing 830
  distasteful 867
  obnoxious 898
OFFER *volunteer* 602
  proposal 763
  give 784
offering *gift* 990
offertory 990
offhand *careless* 460
  spontaneous 612
office 170, 625, 799
officer *director* 694
  soldier 726
  commander 745
official, n. 694, 745
official, adj. *true* 494
  authoritative 737
officiate 625, 680
officious 682
offing *distance* 196
offset 30, 179
offshoot 39, 154
offspring *posterity* 167
often *repeated* 104
  frequent 136
ogle 441, 865
ogre 913, 980
OIL *grease* 355, 356
oily *smooth* 255
  greasy 355
ointment 356, 662
old 124, 128
  -age 128
  -maid *spinster* 904
older 128
old-fashioned 851
oldness 124
oleaginous 355
oligarchy 737
olive *color* 435
olive branch
  pacification 723
olive green 435
OMEN 512
ominous *predicting* 511
  hopeless 859
omission 53, 55, 773
omit [see omission]
omitted *absent* 287
omnibus 272
omnipotence *power* 157

P

burden 706
pack, *v. locate* 184
package 72
packet 72
pact 769
pad *thicken* 194
  line 224
padding *lining* 224
  diffuseness 573
paddle, *n. oar* 267
paddle, *v. walk* 266
paean *rejoicing* 838
PAGAN 984
  -deities 979
paganism 984
page 746
pageant 448, 882
pagoda 206, 1000
pail 191
PAIN *physical* – 378
  moral – 828
  hurt 830
painful 378, 830
PAINFULNESS 830
painless 827
painstaking *active* 682
  laborious 686
paint *coat* 223
  color 428
  delineate 556
  ornament 847
painter *rope* 45
  artist 559
PAINTING 556
pair, *n. similar* 17
  couple 89
  horses 272
pair, *v. combine* 48
pajamas 225
pal *ally* 711
  chum 890
palace 189
palanquin 272
palatable *savory* 394
palate 390
palatial 882
palaver *colloquy* 588
  council 696
pale, *n. inclosure* 232
  limit 233
pale, *adj. dim* 422
  colorless 429
palfrey 271
paling *fence* 232
palisade 717
palisades *cliff* 212
pall, *v. weary* 841
  satiate 869
palliate *moderate* 174
  relieve 834
  extenuate 937
palliative 174
pallid 429
pallor 429
palm *tree* 367
  trophy 733

laurel 877
  -off on 545
palmy *prosperous* 734
  joyous 836
palpable *material* 316
  obvious 446
  manifest 525
palpitate 315, 821
palter 605
paltry *small* 32
  unimportant 643
  mean 940
pampas 344
pamper 954
pan 191
panacea 662
pandemonium 404, 414
pander to 933
panegyric 931
panel *list* 86
  partition 228
  jury 967
pang 378, 828
panic 860
panorama *view* 448
panoramic 78
pant *be hot* 382
  fatigue 688
  be excited 821
pantomimist 599
pantheism 984
Pantheon *gods* 979
  temple 1000
pantomime 550
pantry 191
pap *pulp* 354
papa *father* 166
papacy 995
papal 995
paper 590
  -money 800
par 27
parable 521, 537
parabola *curve* 245
parade *procession* 69
  journey 266
  ostentation 882
Paradise 981
paradox *absurdity* 497
  difficulty 704
paradoxical *uncertain* 475
  absurd 497
paragon *perfect* 650
  glory 873
parallel, *n.* 17
parallel, *adj.* 17, 242
parallel, *v. imitate* 19
  agree 23
  equal 216
PARALLELISM 17, 216, 242
paralysis 158, 376, 823
paralyze 158, 376, 823
paramount *supreme* 33
parapet 717
paraphernalia 780

paraphrase *imitation* 19
  copy 21
  synonym 522
parasite *follower* 65
  puppet 711
  flatterer 935
parasol 223
parboil 384
parcel *divide* 44
  group 72
parch 340, 382
parched 340
parchment 590
pardon 918
pardonable 937
pare *cut* 38
  reduce 195
  peel 204
  divest 226
parent 166
parentage 11, 166
parental 166
parenthesis 198, 228
parenthetical 10, 228
pariah 876, 893
parish 181
parishioner 997
parity 27
park, *n.* 367, 840
park, *v.* 184
parlance 582
parley *talk* 588
  mediation 724
parliament 696
parliamentary 696
parlor 191
parochial *regional* 181
  narrow 481
parody *imitation* 19
  copy 21
  misrepresentation 555
  travesty 856
parole 768
  on - *restraint* 751
paroxysm *violence* 173
  agitation 315
  emotion 825
parquetry 440
parrot *imitation* 19
parrotism 19
parry *confute* 479
  avert 623
  defend 717
parsimonious 819
PARSIMONY 819
parson 996
parsonage 1000
PART, *n. portion* 51, 100a
  role 599
  function 625
  duty 926
part, *v. divide* 44
partake 778
partial *unequal* 28
  part 51
  fractional 100a

pertinent *relative* 9
  congruous 23
perturbation *agitation* 315
  excitation 824, 825
  fear 860
peruse 539
pervade *influence* 175
  extend 186
perverse *reactionary* 283
  obstinate 606
  sulky 901a
perversion *sophistry* 477
  misinterpretation 523
  misteaching 538
  falsehood 544
perversity [*see* perverse]
pervert *quibble* 477
  distort 523
pervious 260
pessimism *dejection* 837,
  859
pessimist 482, 862, 859
pest *bane* 663
pester 830
pestilence 655
pestle 330
pet, *n. favorite* 899
  anger 900
pet, *v. love* 897
  fondle 902
petal 367
petition *ask* 765
  pray 990
PETITIONER 767
pet name 565
petrify *thicken* 321
  harden 323
  organization 357
  thrill 824
  astonish 870
petroleum 356
petticoat 225
pettifogger 968
pettifogging 477
pettish 901
petty 643
  -cash 800
petulance 901
petulant 901
pew 191
pewter 41
phalanx 712, 726
phantasm 443
phantom *unreality* 4
  specter 980a
pharisaical 544, 988
Pharisee 988
pharmacy 662
phase *aspect* 8
  appearance 448
phenomenon *event* 151
  prodigy 872
phial 191
philander 902
philanderer 902
philanthropic 906, 910

philanthropist 906, 910
PHILANTHROPY 906,
  910
Philistine 82
philosopher 500
philosophical
  thoughtful 451
  calm 826
philosophy *intellect* 450
  calmness 826
phlegmatic 823
phonetic *sonant* 402
  tonic 561
  voice 580
  vocal 582
phonograph 418
phonography 402
phosphorescence *light* 420
  luminary 423
phosphorus 423
photograph 554
photographer 554
photography 554, 556
PHRASE 566
phraseology 569
physic *remedy* 662
physical 316
  -pain 378
  -pleasure 377
physician 662, 695
physics 316
physiognomy 234
physiology 357, 359
physique 159, 364
piazza 189
picayune 643
pick, *n. best* 648
pick, *v. select* 609
  -a quarrel 713
  -up *learn* 539
  get better 658
  gain 775
pickaninny 129
picket, *n. fence* 229
  guard 668
picket, *v. join* 43
  locate 184
  restrain 751
pickings *gain* 775
  booty 793
pickle 670
pickpocket 792
picnic 298, 840
pictorial 556
picture *appearance* 448
  representation 554
  painting 556
picture gallery 556
picturesque 556, 845
pie 396
piebald 440
piece, *n. bit* 51
piece, *v.* 140
  cannon 727
  -together 43
piecemeal 51

pied 440
pierce *perforate* 260
  chill 385
  wound 659
  affect 824
piercer 262
piercing *cold* 383
  shrill 410
  acute 821
PIETY 987
pig *animal* 366
  glutton 954a
pigeonhole, *n.* 191
pigeonhole, *v. shelve* 460
piggish 954
pigment 428
pigmy [*see* pygmy]
pike 727
pikestaff 206
pilaster 215
pile *heap* 72
  edifice 161
pilfer *steal* 791
pilferer 792
pilgrim 268, 996
pilgrimage *journey* 266
  undertaking 676
pill 249
pillage *theft* 791
pillar 206, 215
pillory 975
pillow 215
pilot 269, 269a
pimple 250
pin 43,
pinch, *n. emergency* 8
  need 630
  difficulty 704
pinch, *v. contract* 195
  chill 385
pinched [*see* pinch]
  thin 203
pine *mope* 837
  -for 865
pinion *restrain* 751
  fetter 752
pink, *adj.* 434
pink, *v. pierce* 260
pinnace 273
pinnacle 210
pioneer *precursor* 64
pious 987
pipe, *n. tube* 260
pipe, *v. sound* 410
piper 416
piquant *pungent* 392
  impressive 821
pique *excite* 824
  pain 830
  hate 898
piracy 773
pirate, *n.* 792
pirate, *v. plagiarize* 788
pirouette 312
pistol 727
piston 263

pit 208, 252
pitch *degree* 26
  obliquity 217
  descent 306
  musical - 413
pitch, *v. erect* 212
  throw 284
  plunge 310
  reel 314
pitchfork *throw* 284
piteous *painful* 830
PITFALL 667
pith *gist* 5
  meaning 516
pithy *concise* 572
  vigorous 574
pitiable *bad* 649
  painful 830
  contemptible 930
pitiful *bad* 649
  mean 874
  pitying 914
pitiless 914a
PITILESSNESS 914a
pittance *quantity* 25
  dole 640
PITY 914
pivot *junction* 43
  cause 153
pivotal 222
placard 531
placate *pacify* 723
  conciliate 918
PLACE, *n.*
  situation 182, 183
  abode 189
  office 625
place, *v. arrange* 60
  locate 184
  invest 787
placid 826
plagiarism 19, 791
plagiarist 792
plagiarize 788, 791
plague, *n.* 655
plague, *v. worry* 830
plaid 440
PLAIN, *n.* 251, 344
plain, *adj. clear* 446
  manifest 525
  lucid 576
  homely 846
  simple 849
  -speaking
  candor 525
plainly 525
PLAINNESS 576, 849
plaint *cry* 411
  lament 839
plaintiff 938
plaintive 839
plait 219, 258
PLAN *map* 183
  scheme 626
planchette 992a
plane 251, 255

planet 318
plank *platform* 626
PLANT, *n., shrub* 367
  property 780
  management of - 371
plant, *v.* 184, 300
plantation *location* 184
  estate 780
planter 188
plash 348, 408
plaster 45, 223
plastic 240
plate, *n. dish* 191
  coating 204
plate, *v. cover* 223
plateau 251, 344
platform *support* 215
  stage 542
  scheme 626
platitude 843
platoon 726
platter *receptacle* 191
plaudit 931
plausible *probable* 472
  vindicative 937
play, *n. scope* 180
  drama 599
  freedom 748
  amusement 840
play, *v. operate* 170
  music 416
  sport 840
  -truant 623
player *musician* 416
  actor 599
playfellow 890
playful 836
playground 728
playing field 728
playmate 890
plaything *trifle* 643
  toy 840
playwright 599
PLEA *answer* 462
  argument 476
  excuse 617
  vindication 937
plead *answer* 462
  argue 467, 968
  allege 617
  beg 765
pleader *lawyer* 968
pleadings 969
pleasant *agreeable* 829
  amusing 840
pleasantry 842
please 377, 829
  if you - 765
  -oneself 943
pleased 827
pleasing 394, 829
PLEASURABLENESS
  829
PLEASURE *physical* -377
  moral - 827
pleat 258

plebeian 876
plebiscite 480, 609
pledge, *n. promise* 768
  security 771
pledge, *v. borrow* 788
plenipotentiary 758
plenitude 639
plenteous 639
plenty *sufficient* 639
plethora 641
pliable 324
pliant *soft* 324
  irresolute 605
  servile 886
plight *state* 7
  circumstance 8
  promise 768
plinth 211
plod *journey* 266
  be slow 275
  work 682
plodder *worker* 686
plodding 682
plot *-of ground* 181
  scheme 626
plough [see plow]
plow 259
pluck, *n. resolution* 604
  grit 604a
  courage 861
pluck, *v. take* 789
plucky 604, 861
plug, *n.* 263
plug, *v. close* 261, 348
plumage 256
plumb, *adj. vertical* 212
  straight 246
plumb, *v. measure* 466
plume *feather* 256
plummet 208
plump *fat* 192
plumpness 192
plunder, *n. gain* 35
  booty 793
plunder, *v.* 791
PLUNGE *depth* 208
  dive 310
PLURALITY 33, 100
plutocrat 639
pluvial 348
ply *use* 677
  exert 686
pneumatics 334, 338
poach *steal* 791
poacher 792
pocket, *n.* 191
pocket, *v. receive* 785
  take 789
pocketbook 802
pocket money 800
poem 597
poet 597
poetic 597
poetize 597
POETRY 597
poignant 378

point *small* 32
  end 67
  place 182
  sharpness 253
  topic 454
  mark 550
  intention 620
  wit 842
-at *direct attention* 457
  disparage 929
-of view 441
-out *indicate* 79
-to direct 278
  predict 511
point-blank *direct* 278
  plain 576
pointed *sharp* 253
  marked 550
  concise 572
pointedly 620
pointer 550
pointless 254
poise *balance* 27
  weight 319
  inexcitability 826
poison 659, 663
-gas 727
poisonous 657
poke 191
polar 210
-lights 423
polarity 89, 237
pole *pikestaff* 206
  axis 222
  oar 267
polemic 713
polestar *attraction* 288
  luminary 423
  indication 550
police 965
policeman 664
policy 626, 692
polish, n. *smooth* 255
  gloss 332
  taste 850
  politeness 894
polish, v. *rub* 331
  furbish 658
polished *fashionable* 852
  polite 894
polite 894
politeness 894
politic *wise* 498
  cautious 864
politician 694, 700
politics 702
polity 926
poll *count* 85
  list 86
  vote 609
pollute *soil* 653
  corrupt 659
pollution *disease* 655
poltroon 862
pommel, n. 215

pommel, v. *beat* 972
pomp 882
pompom 727
pomposity 878, 882
pompous *inflated* 577
  proud 878
  ostentatious 882
pond 343
ponder 451
ponderous *heavy* 319
poniard 727
pontiff 996
pontificate 995
pony 271
  translation 522
poodle 366
pool, n. *lake* 343
pool, v. *co-operate* 709
poor *feeble* 477
  insufficient 640
  indigent 804
-man 640, 804
poorness [*see poor*]
  inferiority 34
pop *noise* 406
pope 996
popinjay 854
populace 876
popular *choosing* 609
  desirable 865
  celebrated 873
  approved 931
popularize 518
population 188, 372
populous 72, 102, 186
porch 66, 191, 260
pore, n. 260
pore over
  apply the mind 457
  learn 539
porous 252, 295, 322
port *harbor* 189, 666
  left 239
  gait 448
portable 270
portage 270
portal 66, 260
portend 511
portent 512
portentous *prophetic* 511
  fearful 860
porter 263, 271
portfolio *case* 191
  authority 747
  jurisdiction 965
portico 191
portion *part* 51
  allotment 786
portly 192
portmanteau 191
-word 572
portrait 554, 556
portraiture 554
portray 554
pose, n. *situation* 183
  form 240

pose, v. *inquire* 461
  puzzle 475
  affect 855
poser 855
position *circumstances* 8
  situation 183
  post 625
  status 873
positive *real* 1
  great 31
  certain 474
  narrow-minded 481
  assertive 535
posse 72
possess 777, 780
  bedevil 978, 992
POSSESSION 777, 780
POSSESSOR 779
POSSIBILITY *chance* 156
  liability 177
  likelihood 470
possible 177, 470
post, n. *situation* 183
  support 215
  mail 534
  employment 625
post, v. *list* 86
  send 270
  publish 531
  enter accounts 811
postal 592
post card 592
postdate 115
poster 531
posterior *in time* 117
  in space 235
POSTERIORITY 117
POSTERITY 121, 167
posthaste *swiftly* 274
  rash 863
posthumous 117, 133
postilion *rider* 268
postman 271, 534
post-mortem 363
post office 534
postpone 133, 460
postscript 37, 65
posture *situation* 183
  form 240
posy *bouquet* 400
pot *mug* 191
potency 157
potent 157, 159
potentate 745
potential 2, 157
potentiality *power* 157
  possibility 470
potion *beverage* 298
potpourri *mixture* 41
pouch 191
poultry 366
pounce upon *attack* 716
  seize 789
pound *bruise* 330
-the piano 416
pour *emerge* 295

rain 348
pout 250, 901a
POVERTY
  insufficiency 640
  indigence 804
powder 330
  gunpowder 727
POWDERINESS 330
powdery 330
POWER *number* 84
  efficacy 157
  influence 175
  authority 737
powerful 157, 159
powerless 158, 160
practicable *possible* 470
  practical 646
practical *acting* 170
  practicable 646
practically 5
practice, n. *training* 537
  exertion 686
  conduct 692
practice, v. *train* 537
  use 677
  act 680
practiced *skilled* 698
practitioner *general* - 662
  doer 690
pragmatic *practical* 646
pragmatism 646
prairie *space* 180
  plain 344
praise 931, 990
praiseworthy 931
prance *leap* 309
  dance 315
prank *caprice* 608
prate 584
prattle *talk* 582
  chatter 584
pray *beg* 765
  worship 990
prayer *request* 765
  worship 990
preach 537
preacher *teacher* 540
  priest 996
preamble 62, 64
precarious *transient* 111
  dangerous 665
precaution *care* 459
  safety 664
  preparation 673
precede *be superior* 33
  forerun 62, 280
PRECEDENCE 62, 280
  rank 873
precedent *prototype* 22
  habit 613
  legal decision 969
PRECEDING 280
PRECEPT
  requirement 630
  maxim 697
preceptor 540

precinct 181, 227
precious *great* 31
  valuable 814
  beloved 897
  -metals 800
precipice 212
precipitancy *haste* 684
  rashness 863
precipitate, *adj. early* 132
  rash 863
precipitate, *v. sink* 308
precipitous 217
precise 494
precisely 19
preclude 706
preclusive 55
precocious 132, 674
preconception 481
PRECURSOR 64
predatory 789
predecessor 64
predesigned 611
predestinate 976
predestination 611, 976
predestine 976
PREDETERMINATION
  611
predicament 7, 8, 43
predicate 514
predict 507, 511
PREDICTION 511
predilection *bias* 481
  affection 820
predispose 615
predominance 157
predominant 157
predominate 33, 175
pre-eminent *superior* 33
  celebrated 873
pre-exist 116
preface 62, 64
prefer *choose* 609
preference 62
prefix 62
pregnant 642
prehistoric 124
prejudge 481
prejudice 481
prejudicial 649
prelacy 995
prelate 996
preliminary, *n.* 64, 296
preliminary *adj.* 673
prelude 62, 64
premature *early* 132
  unripe 674
premeditate 611
premier 759
premise 62
premises *ground* 182
  evidence 467
  logic 476
premium 810, 973
premonish 668
premonition 668, 992a
premonitory 511, 668

preoccupation 458
PREPARATION 60, 673
  instruction 537
preparatory 673
prepare 537, 673
preparedness 673
preponderance
  superiority 33
  influence 175
prepossessing 829
prepossession
  prejudice 481
preposterous *absurd* 497
  imaginative 515
  ridiculous 853
  improper 925
prerogative 924
prescribe *advise* 695
  order 741
  entitle 924
prescription *decree* 741
  remedy 662
prescriptive 924
PRESENCE 1, 186
  -of mind 864
present, *n. gift* 784
present, *v. offer* 763
  give 784
PRESENT, *adj.*
  -in time 118
  -in space 186
  -events 151
  -time 118
presentable 845
presentment 481, 510
presently 132, 507
PRESERVATION
  continuance 141
  conservation 670
preserve *continue* 143
  keep 670, 976
preserver 670
preside 693
presidency 737
president, 694, 745
press, *n. newspapers* 531
press, *v. crowd* 72
  smooth 255
  weigh 319
  offer 763
  solicit 765
pressing *urgent* 642
pressure
  influence 175
  weight 319
  urgency 642
  adversity 735
presto *instantly* 113
presumable 472
presume 472, 514
presumption *probability*
  472
  rashness 863
  arrogance 885
presumptive 924
presumptuous 885

improving 658
prohibit 761
PROHIBITION 761
exclusion 55
prohibitionist 958
prohibitive 55, 761
project *bulge* 250
impel 284
intend 620
plan 626
projectile 284, 727
projecting 214, 250
projection 250, 283
projector *promoter* 626
proletariat 876
prolific 168
prolix 573
prolixity 573
prologue 64, 599
prolong *protract* 110
delay 133
continue 143
lengthen 200
prolongation 117
[*see* prolong]
prolonged 110
promenade *walk* 266
prominence
[*see* prominent]
prominent *convex* 250
important 642
eminent 873
promiscuous *mixed* 41
indiscriminate 465a
PROMISE 768
promissory 768
-note *security* 771
promontory 206
promote *improve* 658
promoter *planner* 626
promotion 541, 658
prompt, *adj. early* 132
active 682
prompt, *v. remind* 505
tell 527
promulgate 531
prone *horizontal* 213
disposed 820
proneness *tendency* 176
disposition 820
prong 91
pronounce *judge* 480
assert 535
voice 580
speak 582
pronounced 525
pronouncement 531
pronunciation 580
proof *test* 463
demonstration 478
printing 591
-against 664
prop *support* 215
propaganda 673
propagate 161
propel 284

propensity *tendency* 176
inclination 820
proper *individual* 79
due 924
PROPERTY 342, 780
prophecy 511
prophet *seer* 513
prophetic 511
prophylactic *healthful* 656
preventive 706
propinquity 197
propitiate *pacify* 723
mediate 724
atone 952, 976
propitiator 724
propitiatory 952
propitious *timely* 134
prosperous 734
auspicious 858
proportion *relation* 9
symmetry 242
proportions *space* 180
size 192
proposal 763, 765
propose *suggest* 514
offer 763
offer marriage 902
proposition *supposition* 454
reasoning 476
project 626
offer 763
propound *suggest* **514**
proprietor 779
propriety *agreement* 23
elegance 578
fashion 852
duty 926
PROPULSION 284
propulsive 284
prorogue 133
prosaic *sober* 576
dull 843
proscribe *interdict* 761
curse 908
condemn 971
PROSE, *n.* 598
prose, *v.* 584
prosecute *pursue* 622
arraign 969
prosecutor 938
proselyte 144, 607
prospect *destiny* 152
futurity **121**
view 448
expectation 507
prospector 463
prospective 120, 507
prospectus *list* 86
scheme 626
prosper 618, 734
PROSPERITY 734
prostrate, *adj. powerless* 158
low 207
horizontal 213, 251

submissive 725
dejected 837
prostrate, *v. depress* 308
prostration
[*see* prostrate]
sickness 655
prosy *weary* 841
dull 843
protect 664
protection *influence* 175
defense 717
protectionist 751
protective 717
protector 664, 717, 912
protectorate 737
protest *dissent* 489
deprecate 766
not pay 808
protestant
dissenting 489
protoplasm 357
PROTOTYPE 22
protract *prolong* 110
delay 133
lengthen 200
protrude 250
protrusive 250
protuberance 250
proud *dignified* 873
lofty 878
prove *arithmetic* 85
demonstrate 478
indicate 550
proverb 496
proverbial 490
provide *furnish* 637
provided 8, 469
providence 976
provident *careful* 459
prepared 673
providential
opportune 134
fortunate 734
province *department* 75
region 181
office 625
provincial *rural* 189
narrow 481
provincialism 563
PROVISION *food* 298
supply 637
preparation 673
provisional
conditional 8, 770
temporary 111
contingent 134
proviso 469, 770
provocation 900
provoke *cause* 153
excite 824
vex 830
anger 900
prow 234
prowess 861
prowl *walk* 266
lurk 528

Q

R

vehement 825
rampart 717
ramshackle 665
ranch 780
rancid 401, 653
rancor 907
random *casual* 156
  aimless 621
  at - 621
range, *n. extent* 26
  space 180
  freedom 748
range, *v. arrange* 60
  roam 266
rangy *long* 200
rank, *n. order* 58
  row 69
  station 71
  soldiers 726
  glory 873
  nobility 875
rank, *adj. prevalent* 1
  thorough 31
  dense 365
  fetid 401
rank, *v. estimate* 480
rankle 830
ransack *seek* 461
  plunder 791
ransom 672
rant *rave* 825
rap *blow* 276
rapacity 789
rapid 274
rapids 348, 667
rapier 727
rapt 451, 457
rapture *bliss* 827
rapturous 221, 827
rare *unique* 20
  exceptional 83
  few 103
  infrequent 137
  tenuous 322
  choice 648
rarefaction 322
rarefy 322
RARITY 322
  [see rare]
rascal 941, 949
rash *reckless* 863
RASHNESS 863
rasp *rub* 331
rate, *n. degree* 26
  motion 264
  measure 466
  price, tax 812
rate, *v. esteem* 480
  berate 527
rather 32
ratification 467, 488, 762
ratify 488
ratio *relation* 9
  degree 26
  proportion 84
ration *food* 298

rational *judicious* 498
  sane 502
rattle *clatter* 407
rattled *confused* 523
raucous *strident* 410
ravage *destroy* 162
rave *ramble* 503
  rage 824, 825
ravel *disorder* 59
ravenous 865
ravine 198, 350
raving 824
ravish 829
raw *immature* 123
  unprepared 674
  unskilled 699
rawboned 203
ray *light* 420
raze *destroy* 162
  level 213
  -to the ground 308
razor 253
reach, *n. degree* 26
  distance 196
reach, *v.* 292
reaction 145, 277
reactionary 277, 283
read 539
reader 582
readily 705
reading
  interpretation 522
  learning 539
ready *expecting* 507
  willing 602
  prepared 673
  active 682
real *existing* 1
  true 494
  -estate 342, 780
realism 494
realistic 494, 594
reality 1, 494
realize *discover* 480a
  believe 484
  conceive 490
  imagine 515
  acquire 775
  sell 796
realm 181, 737
realty 342, 780
reap 789
reappear 104
REAR, *n.* 65, 67, 235
rear, *v. bring up* 161
  erect 212
  elevate 307
reason, *n. cause* 153
  intellect 450
  wisdom 498
  motive 615
reason, *v. think* 451
  argue 476
reasonable *moderate* 174
  probable 472
  cheap 815

right 922
reasoner 476
REASONING 476
reassemble 72
reassure 858
rebate 38, 40a 813
rebel, *n.* 742
rebel, *v.* 146, 742
rebellion 146, 742
rebellious *defiant* 715
  [see rebellion]
rebirth 660
rebound 277, 325
rebuff, *n. repulse* 732
rebuff, *v.* 764
rebuild 660
rebuke 932
rebut 462, 479
rebuttal [see rebut]
recall *recollect* 505
  cancel 756
recant 950
recapitulate *repeat* 104
  summarize 596
recast 146
recede 283, 287
RECEIPT 807, 810
receive *include* 76
  admit 296
  acquire 775
  take in 785
  take 789
  -money 810
  welcome 892, 894
receiver *vessel* 191
  assignee 785
RECEIVING 785
recent *late* 122
  new 123
RECEPTACLE 191
RECEPTION
  inclusion 76
  admittance 296
  welcome 892, 894
receptive
  [see reception]
recess *receptacle* 191
  corner 244
  vacation 687
recesses *interior* 221
RECESSION
  motion from 287
recipe *remedy* 662
recipient 191, 785
reciprocal 12, 148
reciprocate 12, 148
reciprocity 12, 148
recitation 537, 582
recite *enumerate* 85
  speak 582
  narrate 594
reckless *defiant* 715
  rash 863
reckon *count* 85
reckoning
  numeration 85

revolt *revolution* 146
  rebellion 742
  shock 830
REVOLUTION
  periodicity 138
  change 146
  rotation 312
  rebellion 742
revolutionary 146, 742
revolutionize 140, 146
revolve 138, 312
revolver 727
revulsion *reversion* 145
  recoil 277
REWARD 30, **973**
rhapsody 515
rhetoric *speech* 582
rhetorical 577
rhyme 597
rhythm 104, 138
  verse 597
rhythmic 413, 578
rib 250
ribald 851
ribaldry 908
ribbon 205
rich *abundant* 639
  wealthy 803
  -**man** 639, 803
riches 803
richly *much* 31
rickety *weak* 160
ricochet 277
RIDDANCE 672, 776, 782
riddle, *n. sieve* 260
  secret 533
  enigma 519
ride 266
  -*a horse* 370
rider *appendix* 39
  equestrian 268
ridge 206, 250
ridicule 856
ridiculous *absurd* 497
  foolish 499
  grotesque 853
RIDICULOUSNESS 853
riding
  journey 266
rife 78, 175
riffraff 876, 949
rifle, *n.* 727
rifle, *v. plunder* 791
rift *fissure* 44, 198
rig *dress* 225
  prepare 673
rigging *ropes* 45
right, *n. justness* **922**
  privilege **924**
right, *adj. dextral* 238
  straight 246
  true 494
  proper **924**
  fitting **926**
  virtuous **944**
righteous *virtuous* **944**

rightful **922**
right-handed 238
rigid *regular* 82
  hard 328
  exact 494
rigor 739
rigorous *exact* 494
  severe 739
rile 830
rill 348
rim 231
rind *covering* 223
ring, *n. circle* 247
  clique 712
  arena 728
ring, *v. resound* 408
ringleader 694
ringlet 256
rinse 652
riot *confusion* 59
  violence 173
  mutiny 742
rioter 742
riotous 173
rip *open* 260
ripe 673
ripen *perfect* 650
  prepare 673
ripple 315
  murmur 405
rise *ascend* 35, 305
  begin 66
  revolt 146, 742
  slope 217
rising 305 [*see* rise]
risk, 621, 665
RITE **998**
ritual *ceremony* 882
  worship 990
  rite **998**
ritualism **998**
rival, *n.* 710
rival, *v. emulate* 648
  oppose 708
  compete 720
  outshine 873
rivalry 708
rive 44
RIVER 348
rivet *fasten* 43
rivulet 348
road 278, 627
roadstead 666
roadster 272
roadway 627
roam 266
roan *color* 433
roar *be violent* 173
  sound 404
  bellow 411, 412
  laugh 838
roast 384
rob *plunder* 791
robber 792
robbery 791
robe *dress* 225

robust *strong* 159
  healthy 654
rock, *n.* 342, 667
rock, *v. oscillate* 314
rocket *signal* 550
rocky 323
rod *support* 315
  scourge **975**
rogue 941
roguery 940
roguish *playful* 840
roisterer 887
role *drama* 599
  conduct 692
ROLL, *n. list* 86
  sound 407
  convolution 248
  rotundity 249
  rotate 312
  flow 348
roll, *v. make smooth* 255
  move 264
  wallow 311
roll call 85
roller 255
rollers *billows* 348
rollick 836
romance, *n.*
  imagination 515
  fiction 546, 594
romance, *v.* 497
romantic *imaginative* 515
  descriptive 594
  sentimental 822
romanticism 515
romp 309, 840
Röntgen ray 420
roof *house* 189
  summit 210
  cover 223
rookie 726
rookery *nests* 189
room *space* 180
  chamber 191
roommate 890
roomy 180
roost 189, 215
rooster 366
root *algebraic -* 84
  cause 153
  place 184
  base 211
  -**out** *eject* 297
  -**up** *extract* 301
rooted *old* 124
  firm 150
  located 184
rope *cord* 205
ropy 352
rosary **998**
rose *fragrance* 400
  red 434
roseate *red* 434
  hopeful 858
rosin *resin* 356a
roster

SIMMER INDEX 414

seethe 824
simoom 349
simper *smile* 838
  affect 855
simple *mere* 32
  unmixed 42
  credulous 486
  ignorant 493
  silly 499
  artless 703
  unadorned 849
simple-minded 849
SIMPLENESS 42
simpleton 501
SIMPLICITY 849
  ignorance 499
  [see simple]
simplify 849 [see simple]
simply *little* 32
simulate *resemble* 17
  imitate 19
  cheat 544
simulation 19
simultaneous 120
SIMULTANEOUSNESS 120
sin, n. *guilt* 947
sin, v. *transgress* 945
since *under the circumstances* 8
  after 117
  because 155, 476
sincere *veracious* 543
  ingenuous 703
  earnest 821
sinecure 681
sinew 159
sinewy 159
sinful 945
sing *chant* 416
  rejoice 838
singe 382
singer *musician* 416
single *unmixed* 42
  sole 87
  unmarried 904
single-handed 87
single-minded 703
singleness [see single]
singsong 16
singular *exceptional* 83
  one 87
sinister *left* 239
  bad 649
  adverse 735
sink *disappear* 4
  destroy 162
  lower 308
  submerge 310
  fail 732
sinless 946
sinner 949, 988
Sinn Feiner 712, 742
sinuous 248
sip *drink* 298
sir *man* 373

title 877
sire 166
siren *sea nymph* 341
  tempter 615
  alarm 669
  evil spirit 980
sirocco *wind* 349
sirup 396
sissy *milksop* 158
sister *likeness* 17
  nurse 662
sisterhood 11, 712, 888
sisterly 888
sit 308
site 182, 183
sitting [see sit]
  assembly 696
sitting room 191
situate 183, 184
SITUATION
  circumstances 8
  place 183
  location 184
  business 625
six 98
SIZE *magnitude* 31
  glue 45
  dimensions 192
sizzle 409
skate, n. 272
skate, v. 266
skeleton, *remains* 40
  essential part 50
  outline 626
skeptic *agnostic* 485, 989
skeptical 989
skepticism *doubt* 485
  irreligion 989
sketch *form* 240
  represent 554
  paint 556
  outline 626
sketchy *incomplete* 53
  unfinished 730
ski 225, 272
skid, v. 217, 306
skiff 273
SKILL 698
skillful 698
skim *move* 266
  neglect 460
  summarize 596
skin *tegument* 223
  peel 226
skin-deep 220
skinny *thin* 203
skip *jump* 309
  rejoice 838
skipper *sea captain* 269
  captain 745
skirmish 720
skirt, n. *dress* 225
  edge 231
skirt, v. *environ* 227
  flank 236
skit *ridicule* 856

detraction 934
skittish *excitable* 825
skulk *hide* 528
  sneak 862
skull 450
sky 318
skylight 260
skyscraper 210
slab 251
slack *loose* 47
  inert 172
  slow 275
  unwilling 603
  insufficient 640
  shiftless 674
  lax 738
  nonobservant 773
slacken *loosen* 47
  moderate 174
  retard 275
slacker 623, 927
slake *quench* 174
  satiate 869
slam *shut* 261
slander 934
slanderer 936
slang 563
slant 217
slap 276
slapdash 684
slash 44
slate, n. *schedule* 611
  plan 626
slate, v. *list* 86
slatternly 653
slaughter 361
slave 746
slavery *toil* 686
  subjection 749
slavish *servile* 746, 886
  subject 749
slay 361
slayer 361
sled 272
sledge 272
sleek *smooth* 255
sleep 376, 683
sleepy 683
sleet 383
sleigh 272
sleight *skill* 698
  -of hand *deception* 545
slender 203
sleuth 527
slice, n. 51
slice, v. *cut* 44
  shave 204
slide *elapse* 109
  pass 264
  glide 266
  descend 306
slight, n. 929, 930
slight, adj. *shallow* 209
  rare 322
  feeble 575
slight, v. *neglect* 460

specific, *n. remedy* 662
specific, *adj. special* 79
specification *class* 75
specify *particularize* 79
  tell 527
  name 564
specimen 82
specious *probable* 472
  sophistical 477
  showy 846
speck 32, 193
speckle *variegate* 440
spectacle *show* 599, 882
  appearance 448
  prodigy 872
spectacles 445
spectacular 599, 882
SPECTATOR 197, 444
SPECTER 4, 361, 980a
spectral 980a
spectrum 428
speculate *think* 451
  suppose 514
  chance 621
speculation *chance* 156
  experiment 463
  venture 621
speculative
  thoughtful 451
  experimental 463
speculator 463
SPEECH 582
speechless 581
speed *journey* 266
  velocity 274
speedily *soon* 132
SPELL, *n. period* 106
  influence 175
  exertion 686
  charm 993
spell, *v.* 561
spellbind 586
spellbound 870
spelling 561
spend *waste* 638
  give 784
  expend 809
spendthrift 818
spent *weak* 160
  tired 688
sphere *rank* 26
  class 75
  space 180
  region 181
  ball 249
  function 625
sphinx 513, 520
spice, *n.* 41, 393
spice, *v. season* 392
spicy *fragrant* 400
  exciting 824
spike, *n.* 253, 263
spike, *v. pierce* 260
spill *shed* 297
  waste 638
spin, *n. journey* 266

  aviation 267
spin, *v. rotate* 312
-out *protract* 110
  prolong 200
spindle-shanked 203
spine 253
spineless *weak* 945
spinster 374, 904
spiny 253
spiral 248, 311
spire *height* 206
  peak 253
SPIRIT *essence* 5
  immateriality 317
  intellect 450
  vigorous language 574
  activity 682
  courage 861
  ghost 980a
  evil - 980a
spirited *vigorous* 574
  active 682
  brave 861
spiritism 317, 992a
spiritist 317
spiritual *immaterial* 317
  psychical 450
  divine 976
  pious 987
spiritualism
  immateriality 317
  psychical research 992a
spiritualist 317
spiritualize 317
spit, *n. saliva* 299
spit, *v. pierce* 260
spite 907
spiteful 907
spitfire *shrew* 901
splash 348, 653
splendid 873
splendor *luster* 420
  beauty 845
  glory 873
  display 882
splice *join* 43, 228
  cross 219
splinter, *n.* 205
splinter, *v.* 44, 328
split, *n. quarrel* 713
split, *v. divide* 44
  bisect 91
  break 328
  -hairs 477
spoil, *n. booty* 793
spoil, *v. botch* 699
  hinder 706
spokesman 524, 582
sponge, *n. stopper* 263
  pulpiness 354
  drunkard 959
sponge, *v. moisten* 339
  dry 340
  clean 652
  cringe 886
sponger 886

sponsor *witness* 467
  security 771
spontaneous
  voluntary 600
  willing 602
  impulsive 612
spoon, *n.* 191
spoon, *v. court* 902
spoonerism 495
spoonful 25
spoor 550
sporadic *infrequent* 137
  infectious 657
spore 330
sport *killing* 361
  amusement 840
sportive *gay* 836
  frolicsome 840
sportsman 361, 840
spot, *n. place* 182
  mark 550
  blemish 848
spot, *v. discover* 480a
  soil 653
spotless *perfect* 650
  clean 652
  innocent 946
spotted *variegated* 440
spouse 88, 903
spout, *n.* 295
spout, *v. declaim* 582
sprain 160
sprawl 200, 308
spray, *n. sprig* 51
  foam 353
  flowers 400
spray, *v. atomize* 336
spread, *n. expanse* 180
  meal 298
spread, *v. disperse* 73
  universalize 78
  expand 194
  diverge 291
  publish 531
spree 840
sprig *branch* 51
sprightly *cheerful* 836
  witty 842
spring, *n. early* 125
  source 153
  strength 159
  elasticity 325
  rivulet 348
spring, *v. leap* 309
springy 325
sprinkle *scatter* 73
  wet 337
sprinkler 337
sprint 274
sprout *grow* 365
  expand 194
spruce *neat* 652
  beautiful 845
spur, *n. projection* 250
  prick 253
spur, *v. incite* 370, 615

affect 823, 824
  astonish 870
stunt *shorten* 201
stunted 32, 195
stupefy *stun* 376
  affect 823
  astonish 870
stupendous 31, 192
stupid *unintelligent* 499
  dull 843
stupor *insensibility* 376,
  823
  wonder 870
sturdy *strong* 159
stutter 583
sty *inclosure.* 232
  dirt 653
STYLE *state* 7
  name 564
  diction 569
  fashion 852
stylish 852
suave 894
suavity 894
subaltern 745
subconscious 450, 992a
  -self 450, 992a
subdivide 44
subdivision 44, 51
subdue *calm* 174
  succeed 731
subject, *n. topic* 454
  meaning 516
  servant 746
subject, *adj. liable* 177
  enthrall 749
subject, *v. dominate* 175
SUBJECTION 749
subjective *intrinsic* 5
  immaterial 317
SUBJECTIVENESS 5
subjoin 37, 63
subjugate 731, 749
sublet 787
sublease 787
sublime
  great 31
  high 206
  eminent 873
  magnanimous 942
subliminal 450
  -consciousness 450, 992a
  -self 317, 992a
sublimity [*see* sublime]
submarine, *adj.* 208
submarine, *n. boat* 726
submerge, 310, 337
submergible 310
submersible 310
submersion 310
SUBMISSION 725
  obedience 743
  humility 879
submissive 725, 879
submit *propound* 514·
  yield 725

subordinate 34
subpoena *writ* 960
subscribe *agree to* 769
  give 784
subscriber [*see* subscribe]
subscription *gift* 784
subsequent
  -in order 63
  -in time 117
subserviency 886
subservient
  instrumental 631
  aiding 707
  servile 746
subside *decrease* 36
  sink 306
subsidence 36
subsidiary 707
subsidy *aid* 707
  gift 784
subsist *exist* 1
  continue 141
subsistence *food* 298
substance *thing* 3
  gist 5
  quantity 25
  matter 316
  meaning 516
  wealth 803
substantial *existing* 1, 3
  material 316
  dense 321
  true 494
SUBSTANTIALITY 3,
  316
substantially 5, 50
substantiate
  materialize 316
  verify 467
SUBSTITUTE, *n.* 634,
  759
substitute, *v.* 147
SUBSTITUTION 147
substratum 204
subterfuge *sophistry* 477
  quirk 481
  cunning 702
subterranean 208
subtle *light* 320
  rare 322
  cunning 702
subtlety *rarity* 322
  sophistry 477
  wisdom 498
subtraction 36, 38
subtrahend 38
suburb 197, 227
suburban 227
subversion 14
subvert *destroy* 162
  invert 218
succeed *follow* 63, 117
  triumph 731
  acquire 783
SUCCESS 731
successful 731

succession *sequence* 63,
  117
  continuity 69
  repetition 104
successor 65, 117
succinct 572
succor 707
succulent *nutritive* 298
  juicy 333
succumb *yield* 725
suckle 707
suckling *infant* 129
suction 296
sudden *transient* 111
  instantaneous 113
  soon 132
suds *froth* 353
sue 969
suffer *endure* 151, 826
  ail 378, 655
  allow 760
  feel 821
  ache 828
sufferance 826
suffering 639
SUFFICIENCY 31, 639
sufficient *enough* 639
  satisfactory 831
suffix *adjunct* 39
suffocate *kill* 361
suffocation 361
suffrage 535, 609
sugar 396
sugary 396
suggest *suppose* 514
  inform 527
  advise 695
  -itself 451
suggestion *hint* 527
  plan 626
  advice 695
suggestive 505, 514
suicidal *destructive* 162
suicide 361
suit, *n. clothes* 225
  petition 765
  courtship 902
  lawsuit 969
suit, *v. accord* 23
  befit 646
  -the occasion 134, 646
suitable 23, 134, 646
suite *sequel* 65
  series 69
  retinue 88, 746
suitor *petitioner* 767
  lover 897
sulk 901a
sulkiness [*see* sulky]
sulky *obstinate* 606
  discontented 832
  dejected 837
  sullen 901a
sulks 895
sullen *obstinate* 606
  gloomy 837

swarm, *n. crowd* 72
  multitude 102
swarm, *v. climb* 305
swarthy 431
swath 72
swathe *clothe* 225
sway, *n. power* 157
  influence 175
  agitation 315
  authority 737
sway, *v. influence* 175, 615
  lean 217
  oscillate 314
swear *affirm* 535
  promise 768
sweat, *n. excretion* 299
  fatigue 688
sweat, *v. excretion* 299, 382, 686
sweater 225
sweep, *n. space* 180
  curve 245
sweep, *v. curve* 245
  speed 274
  clean 652
sweeping *whole* 50
  complete 52
  inclusive 76
  general 78
sweepings 645
sweet *saccharine* 396
  melodious 413
  clean 652
  lovely 897
sweeten 396
sweetheart 897
SWEETNESS 396
sweets 396
swell, *n. bulge* 250
  wave 348
  blare 404
  fop 854

swell, *v. increase* 31
  expand 194
swelter 382
swerve *change* 140
  deviate 279
swift 274
swim 267, 320
swindle *cheat* 545
  peculate 791
swindler *cheat* 548
  thief 792
swine 366
swing, *n. operation* 170
  space 180
  freedom 748
swing, *v. hang* 214
  oscillate 314
swirl 348
swish 409
switch, *n. rod* 975
switch, *v. deviate* 279
  flog 972
swollen 194, 250
swoon 158, 688
swoop *descend* 274
  seize 789
sword 727
swordsman 726
Sybarite 954a
sycophant 65, 886
syllable 561
syllabus *list* 86
  compendium 596
sylvan 367
symbol *sign* 550
symbolic *latent* 526
  indicative 550
symbolize *involve* 526
  indicate 550
  represent 554
symmetrical 27, 242

SYMMETRY
  equality 27
  regular form 242
  beauty 845
sympathetic
  [*see sympathy*]
sympathizer 914
sympathize with 906
sympathy
  feeling 821
  love 897
  kindness 906
  pity 914
  condolence 915
symphony *music* 415
symposium 72, 596
symptom 550
synagogue 1000
synchronism 120
syndicate *council* 696
  league 712
synod 696
synodic (al) 696
synonym 522
synonymous 27, 516
synopsis 86, 596
syntax 567
synthesis
  combination 48
  reasoning 476
synthetic 476
syringe, *v.* 337
syrup [*see sirup*]
system *order* 58
  rule 80
  plan 626
systematic 60, 80
systematize *order* 58
  arrange 60
  organize 357
  plan 626

T

tabernacle 189, 1000
table, *n. arrangement* 60
  list 86
  support 215, 251
  repast 298
table, *v. defer* 133, 460
tableau 448, 599
tableland 344
tablet 251, 551
taboo *prohibited* 761
tabular 60
tabulate 60, 69, 86
tabulation 551
tacit *implied* 516
  latent 526
TACITURNITY 585
tack, *n. direction* 278
tack, *v. change course* 140
  turn 279
tackle, *n. fastening* 45
  gear 633

tackle, *v. undertake* 676
  manage 693
tact *discrimination* 465
  wisdom 498
  skill 698
tactful [*see tact*]
  affable 894
tactics *conduct* 692
  warfare 722
tactlessness 895
tactual 379
tag, *n. addition* 37
  sequel 65
  end 67
tag, *v. follow* 63, 235
tail 65, 67, 235
taint, *n. imperfection* 651
  disease 659
  disgrace 874
taint, *v.* 659
take *receive* 785

  appropriate 788, **789**
  -after 17
  -away *subtract* 38
  remove 185
  seize 789
  -from *subtract* 38
  seize 789
  -in *shorten* 201
  admit 296
  understand 518
  deceive 545
  -place 1, 151
  -to *like* 827
  desire 865
  love 897
  -up *pursue* 622
  undertake 676
  use 677
taker 789
TAKING 789
tale *counting* 85

agitate **315**
throe *revolution* **146**
  violence **173**
  agitation **315**
  physical pain **378**
throne **215, 747**
throng **72**
throttle
  render powerless **158**
  close **261**
  kill **361**
through *via* **278**
  by mears of **631**
throughout **52, 106**
throw **284**
  -up *resign* **757**
throwback **145**
thrust *push* **276**
  attack **716**
thud **406, 408a**
thug *murderer* **361, 792**
thumb, *v.* **379**
thump, *n. noise* **406**
thump, *v. beat* **276**
thunder, *n.* **404**
thunder, *v.* **173**
thunderstorm **173**
thunderstruck **870**
thus **8, 233**
thwack *beat* **276**
  punish **972**
thwart *across* **219**
  obstruct **706**
  oppose **708**
tiara *insignia* **747**
  jewelry **847**
tick *sound* **407**
  mark **550**
ticket **550**
  slate **626**
tickle *touch* **380**
  please **829**
ticklish **380**
  dangerous **665**
  difficult **704**
tidbit **298**
tide **52, 348**
  -over **106**
tidings **532**
tidy *orderly* **58**
  clean **652**
tie, *n. relation* **9**
  equality **27**
  fastening **45**
  neckcloth **225**
  obligation **926**
  -s of blood **11**
tie, *v. fasten* **43**
tier *layer* **204**
tiff *quarrel* **713**
  anger **900**
tiger *cheer* **838**
  wild beast **913**
tight *fast* **43**
  closed **261**
tighten **43, 195**

tights **225**
tile *roof* **223**
till, *n. coffer* **191, 802**
till, *v. cultivate* **371**
till, *adv.* **106**
tiller *rudder* **633**
tilt *slope* **217**
  fall **218, 306**
  contention **720**
timber *trees* **367**
TIME, *n.* **106**
  leisure **685**
  in - **109, 152**
time, *v. adjust* **58**
timekeeper **114**
TIMELINESS **134**
timely *early* **132**
  opportune **134**
timepiece **114**
times *present* **118**
  events **151**
timeserver **605, 607, 943**
timeserving **607, 702**
timid *weak* **605**
  fearful **860**
  cowardly **862**
  humble **881**
timidity [*see* timid]
timorous [*see* timid]
tincture *mixture* **41**
  color **428**
tinder *fuel* **388**
tinge *mixture* **41**
  color **428**
tingle **378, 380**
tinker *repair* **660**
tinkle **405, 408**
tinsel *sham* **545**
  ornament **847**
  frippery **851**
tint **428**
tintinnabulation **408**
tiny **193**
tip *end* **67**
  summit **210**
  gift **784, 973**
tipple **298, 959**
tippler **959**
tipsy **959**
tirade *speech* **582**
  censure **932**
tire, *n.* **230**
tire, *v. fatigue* **688**
  bother **841**
  weary **841**
tiresome **830, 841**
tissue *whole* **50**
  texture **329**
titanic **31, 192**
titbit **394**
tit for tat **718**
tithe *tenth* **99**
TITLE *name* **564**
  right to property **780**
  distinction **877**
  right **924**

titter **838**
tittle-tattle *news* **532**
  small talk **588**
titular **564**
to *towards* **278**
  -and fro **12, 314**
toadying **886**
toadyism **933**
toast *roast* **384**
  honor **873**
tobacco **392**
toboggan **272**
tocsin **669**
today **118**
toddle **266, 275**
toe **211**
toga **225**
together *accompanying* **88**
  simultaneously **120**
toil **686**
toilet **225**
token **550**
tolerable *trifling* **643**
  passable **651, 845**
toleration *laxity* **738**
  lenity **740**
  permission **760**
  calmness **826**
toll, *n. tax* **812**
toll, *v. ring* **407**
tomahawk **727**
tomb **363**
tomboy **129**
tombstone **363**
tomfoolery **497**
tomorrow **121**
tone *state* **7**
  sound **402**
  color **428**
tongue *taste* **390**
  language **560**
tonic, *n. medicine* **662**
tonic, *adj. phonetic* **561**
  bracing **656**
tonnage **192**
too *also* **37**
  over and above **641**
tool *instrument* **631, 633**
  cat's-paw **711**
toot **406**
tooth **250, 253**
  taste **390**
toothed **257**
top *summit* **210**
top-heavy **28**
TOPIC **454**
topical **183**
topmost **210**
topography **183**
topple **162**
topsy-turvy **218**
torch **388**
torment *physical* **378**
  moral **828, 830**
tornado **312, 349**
torpedo **727**

torpid *inert* 172
  inactive 683
  insensible 823
torpor 823
torrent 348
torrid 382
tortuous *twisted* 248
torture, *n. physical* 378
  moral 828
  cruelty 907
torture, *v.* **972**
torturer 975
toss *throw* 284
  oscillate 314
  -up 156
tot *child* 129
total, *n. whole* 50
  number 84, 85
total, *adj.* 50
  -abstinence, 953, 955
total, *v. add* 37, **800**
totality 52
totally 52
totter 160
  limp 275
TOUCH, *n. mixture* 41
  sensation 379, 380
  act 680
touch, *v. relate to* 9
  adjoin 199
  feel 379
  excite 824
  excite pity 914
touched *crazy* 503
  tainted 653
  penitent 950
touching 830
touchy 901
tough, *ruffian* 876, 887, 913
tough, *adj. adhesive* 46
  tenacious 327
  difficult 704
tour 266
touring *car* 272
tourist 268
tournament 720
tourniquet 263
tousle 61
tow 285
toward 278
tower, *n.* 150, 191, **206**
tower, *v. loom* 31
  soar 305
towering *great* 31
  high 206
town 189
township 181
toy, *n.* 643, 840
toy, *v. fondle* 902
trace, *n.* 550, 551
trace, *v. follow* 63
  inquire 461
  discover 480a
  delineate 554
tracing 21

track *trace* **461**
  spoor 550
tract *region* 181
  book 593
  dissertation 595
tractable *malleable* 324
  willing 602
  easy 705
tractile 285
TRACTION 285
trade *business* 625
  traffic **794**
trader 797
trademark 550
tradesman 797
trade-union 712
trade wind. 349
tradition 124
traduce 934
traducer 936
traffic 794
tragedian 599
tragedy *drama* 599
  evil 619
tragic *dramatic* 599
tragical 830
trail, *n. sequel* 65
  odor 398
  track 550
  record 551
trail, *v. dawdle* 275
  tow 285
  inquire 461
train, *n. sequence* 63
  sequel 65
  suite 88, 235, 281
  vehicle 272
train, *v. teach* 537
trainer 370
training *education* 537
trait 79, 550
traitor 891, 941
trajectory 627
tram 272
trammel *hinder* 706
  restrain 751
tramp, *n. stroller* 268
  vagabond 876
tramp, *v.* 266
trample upon 649
trance 992a
tranquil *calm* 174
  quiet 265
  peaceful 721
tranquilize *moderate* 174
  quell 265
  pacify 723
  soothe 826
transact 680, 692
transaction 151, 680
transcend 33, 303
transcendency 33
transcendent *superior* 33
  glorious 873
transcendental 450
transcribe 19, 525

transcript *copy* 21
TRANSFER *copy* 21
  -of *things* 270
  -of *property* **783**
transferable 270, 783
TRANSFERENCE 140, 270
transfiguration *change* 140
  divine - 908
transfix 260
transform 140
transformation **140**
transfuse *mix* 41
  transfer 270
transgress *go beyond* 303
  infringe 773
  sin 945
transgression 303, 947
transgressor 949
TRANSIENCE 111
transient 111
transit 144, 270
transition 144, 270
transitional 140, 264
transitory 111
translate *interpret* 522
translation
  transference 270
  interpretation **522**
transmigration 144
transmission 270, 302
transmit 270, 302
transmutation 140
TRANSPARENCY **425**
transparent
  transmitting light **425**
  obvious 518
transpire *appear* 525
  be disclosed 529
transplant 270
transport, *n. ship* 273
  war vessel 726
  delight 827
transport, *v. transfer* 270
  enrapture 829
transportation 270
transposal 270
transpose *invert* 14, 218
  exchange 148
  transfer 270
transubstantiation
  change 140
  sacrament 998
transverse *oblique* 217
  crossing 219
trap *snare* 545
  pitfall 667
trappings *clothes* 225
  equipment 633
trash *trifle* 643
  rubbish 645
  riffraff 876
trashy 517
travel 266
traveler 268
  bagman 758

vacillating 605
precarious 665
unsteady *mutable* 149
unstable 665
unstrung 160
unsubstantial
immaterial 2, 317
baseless 4
weak 160
erroneous 495
imaginary 515
UNSUBSTANTIALITY 4
unsuccess 732
unsuccessful 732
unsuitable
incongruous 24
inexpedient 647
unsullied *clean* 652
honorable 939
unsurpassed 33
unsusceptible 826
unsuspecting *hopeful* 858
unsuspicious
believing 486
artless 703
hopeful 858
unswerving *straight* 246
direct 278
unsymmetrical
shapeless 241
distorted 243
unsympathetic 24
unsystematic 59, 139
untaught *ignorant* 491
untrained 674
unteachable 499
untenable *illogical* 477
undefended 725
unthankful 917
unthinkable 471
unthinking
unconsidered 452
involuntary 601
unthrifty 818
untidy 59, 653
untie *liberate* 750
until 106
UNTIMELINESS 135
untimely 135
untold *countless* 105
secret 528
untoward *ill-timed* 135
unprosperous 735
unpleasant 830
untrained
unaccustomed 614
unprepared 674
unskilled 699
untried 123
untrue *erroneous* 495
false 546
untrustworthy
uncertain 475
erroneous 495
dishonorable 940
UNTRUTH 546

untruthfulness 544
untwine 313
untwist 313
unusual 83
unutterable *great* 31
wonderful 870
unvalued *underrated* 483
unvaried *uniform* 16
monotonous 104
unvarying 16
unveil *disclose* 529
unventilated 261
unwarlike 862
unwarranted 925
unwary *neglectful* 460
unwatchful 460
unwelcome
disagreeable 830
unsocial 893
unwholesome 657
unwieldy *large* 192
heavy 319
cumbersome 647
unwilling 603
UNWILLINGNESS 603
unwind *evolve* 313
unwise 499
unwished 866
unwomanly 373
unwonted *unimitated* 20
unusual 83
unaccustomed 614
unworldly 939
unworthy *shameful* 874
vicious 945
unwritten *old* 124
spoken 582
unyielding
tough 323
obstinate 606
resisting 719
up 206, 305
upbraid 932
upgrade 305
upgrowth 305
upheaval 146, 307
uphill *steep* 217
laborious 686
uphold *continue* 143
support 215
evidence 467
aid 707
upholder 711
upland, *n.* 180
upland, *adj.* 206
uplands 206
uplift *raise* 206, 307
improve 658
upper 206
-hand *influence* 175
success 731
-ten thousand 875
uppermost 210
upraise 206, 307
uprear 206, 307
upright *vertical* 212

straight 246
honest 939
uprising 146, 742
uproar *disorder* 59
violence 173
noise 404
uproarious 173
uproot *extract* 301
upset *destroy* 162
invert 218
throw down 308
disconcert 874
upshot *result* 154
upstart 123, 734, 876
upturn 210, 218
upward 305
urban 189
urbane 894
urchin *child* 129, 167
urge *impel* 276
incite 615
hasten 684
beg 765
urgency *need* 865
[*see urgent*]
urgent
pressing 630
important 642
importunate 765
usage
custom 613
use 677
USE *habit* 613
utility 644
employ 677
useful
instrumental 176, 633
serviceable 644, 677, 746
useless
unproductive 169
futile 645
user 677
usher, *n.*
attendant 263, 746
usher, *v.*
receive 296
-in *begin* 66
herald 116
announce 511
usual *ordinary* 82
customary 613
usurer *lender* 787
miser 819
usurp *assume* 739
violate 925
usurpation [*see usurp*]
usurper 706, 925
usury 806
utensil 633
utilitarian *useful* 677
UTILITY 644
utilize 677
utmost 33
utopia 858
utter, *v. distribute* 73
disclose 529

publish 531
speak 580, 582

money 800
utterance [see utter]

utterly *completely* 52
uttermost 31

V

vacancy [see vacant]
vacant *void* 4
  absent 187
  thoughtless **452**
  scanty 640
vacate *displace* **185**
  depart 293
  resign **757**
vacation 687
vacillate *change* 149
  waver **605**
vacuity 452
vacuous *unsubstantial* 4
  absent 187
vacuum 2, 187, 197
vagabond 268, 876
vagary *fantasy* 515
  whim 608
vagrant, *n.* 268
vagrant, *adj.* 266
vague *unsubstantial* 4
  uncertain 475
  obscure 519
vagueness 475
vain *unprofitable* 645
  conceited **880**
vainglorious 878
vale 252
valediction *adieu* 293
valedictorian 293
valedictory 293, 582
valentine 902
valet 746
valiant 861
valid *powerful* 157
  true **494**
valise 191
valley 252
valor 861
valuable *useful* 644
  good 648
value, *n. color* 428
  importance **642**
  utility 644
  goodness 648
  price 812
value, *v.* 466, 480
valve 263, 350
vampire *evildoer* 913
  demon 980
van *front* 234
  wagon 272
vandal 165, 913
vandalism 851
vane 349
vanguard 234
vanish *disappear* 2, **4**, 449
  be transient 111
VANITY *conceit* **880**

vanquish 731
vapid *insipid* 391
vapor *gas* 334, 353
VAPORIZATION 336
vaporize 336
vaporizer 336
vaporous *unsubstantial* 4
  volatile 336
variable *irregular* 120
  changeable 140, 149
variance *difference* 15
  disagreement 24
  discord **713**
VARIATION
  difference 15
  dissimilarity 18
  diverseness 20a
  chance 140
varied 15, 16a
variegated 428, 440
VARIEGATION 440
variety *difference* 15
  class 75
  multiformity 81
various *different* 15
  many 102
varnish, *n. resin* 356a
varnish, *v. overlay* 223
  decorate 847
vary *differ* 15, **18**, 20a
  change 140
  fluctuate 149
vase 191
vassal 746
vast *great* 31
  spacious 180
  large 192
vat 191
vaudeville 599
vault, *n. cellar* 191, 207
  dome 250
  tomb 363
vault, *v. leap* 309
vaunt 884
veer *change* 140
  deviate 279
  go back 283
VEGETABLE 367
  -kingdom 367
  -life 365
vegetarian 953
vegetarianism 298
vegetate *exist* 1
  grow 365, 367
VEGETATION 365
  inaction 681
vegetative 365, 367
vehemence *violence* 173
  emotion 825

vehement *violent* 173, **825**
  impassioned **574**
VEHICLE *carriage* 272
  instrument 631
veil, *n. covering* 225, 424
veil, *v. shade* **424**
  conceal 528
vein *conduit* 350
  humor 602, 820
  mine 636
VELOCITY
  rate of motion 264
  swiftness **274**
vender 796
vendetta 919
vendor 796
veneer 204, **223**
venerable *old* 124, 128
  sage 500
  respected **928**
veneration *respect* **928**
  piety **987**
vengeance 919
venom *bane* 663
  malignity 907
venomous *bad* 649
  poisonous 657
  rude 895
  maleficent 907
vent, *n. opening* 260, 295
vent, *v. disclose* 529
ventilate *air* 338
  discuss 595
venture, *n. chance* 621
  trial 675
  undertaking 676
venture, *v. experiment* 463
  presume 472
  risk 665
  try 675
  dare 861
venturesome
  enterprising 676
  brave 861
  rash 863
VERACITY 494, 543
veranda 191
verbal 562
verbatim 19, 516
verbiage 562, 573
verbosity *words* **562**
  diffuseness 573
verdant *green* 435
verdict *opinion* 480
  lawsuit 969
verdure *vegetation* 367
  green 435
verge, *n. edge* 231
  limit 233

X

Y

Z

FOREIGN WORDS AND PHRASES

à bas. [F.] Down, down with.

ab initio. [L.] From the beginning.

à bon marché. [F.] Cheap; a good bargain.

ab origine. [L.] From the origin.

ab ovo. [L.] From the egg; from the beginning.

à cheval. [F.] On horseback.

addenda. [L.] Things to be added; list of additions.

ad finem. [L.] To the end.

ad hoc. [L.] To or with respect to this (object); said of a body elected or appointed for a definite work (as a school board for education).

ad infinitum. [L.] To infinity.

ad libitum. [L.] At pleasure; as much as one pleases.

ad nauseam. [L.] To the point of disgust or satiety.

ad rem. [L.] To the purpose; to the point.

adsum. [L.] I am present; here!

ad valorem. [L.] According to the value.

advocatus diaboli. [L.] Devil's advocate; a person chosen to dispute before the papal court the claims of a candidate for canonization.

æquo animo. [L.] With an equable mind; with equanimity.

ære perennius. [L.] More lasting than brass (or bronze).

affaire d'amour. [F.] A love affair.

affaire de cœur. [F.] An affair of the heart.

affaire d'honneur. [F.] An affair of honor; a duel.

a fortiori. [L.] With stronger reason.

Agnus Dei. [L.] Lamb of God.

à haute voix. [F.] Aloud.

à la belle étoile. [F.] Under the stars; in the open air.

à la bonne heure. [F.] In good time; very well.

à la carte. [F.] According to the bill of fare.

à la mode. [F.] According to the custom (or fashion).

al fresco. [It.] In the open air.

alter ego. [L.] Another self.

amende honorable. [F.] Satisfactory apology; reparation.

à merveille. [F.] Admirably; marvelously.

amour propre. [F.] Self-love; vanity.

ancien régime. [F.] The former order of things.

anglice. [NL.] In the English language or fashion.

anguis in herba. [L.] A snake in the grass; an unsuspected danger.

anno urbis conditæ. [L.] In the year (or from the time) of the founded city (Rome).

à outrance. [F.] To the utmost.

aperçu. [F.] A general sketch or survey.

à perte de vue. [F.] Till beyond one's view.

à peu près. [F.] Nearly.

à pied. [F.] On foot.

a posteriori. [L.] From effect to cause; empirical.

a priori. [L.] From cause to effect; presumptive.

arbiter elegantiarum. [L.] A judge or supreme authority in matters of taste.

arcana imperii. [L.] State secrets.

argumentum ad hominem. [L.] An argument to the individual man; *i.e.*, to his interests and prejudices.

arrière-pensée. [F.] Mental reservation.

ars est celare artem. [L.] It is true art to conceal art.

ars longa, vita brevis. [L.] Art is long, life is short.

au contraire. [F.] On the contrary.

au courant. [F.] Fully acquainted with matters.

au désespoir. [F.] In despair.

au fait. [F.] Well acquainted with; expert.

au fond. [F.] At bottom.

au reste. [F.] As for the rest; besides.

au revoir. [F.] Until we meet again.

autant d'hommes, autant d'avis. [F.] So many men, so many minds.

avant-propos. [F.] Preliminary matter; preface.

à votre santé! [F.] To your health!

ballon d'essai. [F.] A trial balloon; a device to test opinion.

bas bleu. [F.] A bluestocking; a literary woman.

beau idéal. [F.] The ideal of perfection.

beau monde. [F.] The world of fashion.

beaux esprits. [F.] Men of wit.

beaux yeux. [F.] Fine eyes; good looks.

bel esprit. [F.] A person of wit or genius; a brilliant mind.

ben trovato. [It.] Well found.

bête noire. [F.] A bugbear; a special aversion; *lit.*, black beast.

bis dat qui cito dat. [L.] He gives twice who gives quickly.

bona fides (bona fide). [L.] Good faith (in good faith).

bon ami. [F.] Good friend.

bon gré, mal gré. [F.] With good or ill grace; willing or unwilling.

bon jour. [F.] Good day; good morning.

bon mot. [F.] A witty saying.

bonne foi. [F.] Good faith.

bon naturel. [F.] Good nature.

bon soir. [F.] Good evening.

bon ton. [F.] Fashionable society; good style.

bon vivant. [F.] A lover of good living; a gourmet.

bon voyage! [F.] A good voyage or journey to you!

campo santo. [It.] A burying-ground; *lit.*, a holy field.

canaille. [F.] Rabble.

carpe diem. [L.] Enjoy the present day; improve the time.

casus belli. [L.] That which causes or justifies war.

catalogue raisonné. [F.] A catalogue arranged according to subjects.

cause célèbre. [F.] A celebrated or notorious case (in law).

caveat emptor. [L.] Let the purchaser beware (*i.e.*, he buys at his own risk).

cave canem. [L.] Beware of the dog.

cela va sans dire. [F.] That goes without saying; that is a matter of course.

c'est-à-dire. [F.] That is to say.

c'est égal. [F.] It's all one.

c'est magnifique, mais ce n'est pas la guerre. [F.] It is magnificent, but it is not war.

c'est autre chose. [F.] That's quite another thing.

ceteris paribus. [L.] Other things being equal.

chacun à son goût. [F.] Every one to his taste.

chef-d'œuvre. [F.] Masterpiece.

cherchez la femme. [F.] Look for the woman (who is at the bottom of the affair).

chère amie. [F.] A dear (female) friend.

chevalier d'industrie. [F.] One who lives by his wits; a swindler.

ci-gît. [F.] Here lies.

circa. [L.] About.

cogito, ergo sum. [L.] I think, therefore I exist.

comme il faut. [F.] As it should be; in good form.

compte rendu. [F.] An account rendered; a report.

con amore. [It.] With love; very earnestly.

confrère. [F.] Colleague.

contretemps. [F.] An unex-

pected or untoward event; a hitch.

coram populo. [L.] Publicly; in public.

corpus delicti. [L.] The body of the crime.

corrigenda. [L.] Things to be corrected; a list of errors.

coup. [F.] A stroke.—**coup d'essai,** a first attempt.—**coup d'état,** a sudden decisive blow in politics; a stroke of policy.—**coup de grâce,** a finishing stroke.—**coup de main,** a sudden attack or enterprise.—**coup de maître,** a master stroke.—**coup d'œil,** a rapid glance of the eye.—**coup de pied,** a kick.—**coup de soleil,** sunstroke.—**coup de théâtre,** a theatrical effect.

coûte que coûte. [F.] Cost what it may.

credat Judæus Apella. [L.] Let Apella, the superstitious Jew, believe it; I won't.

credo quia absurdum. [L.] I believe because it is absurd, or contrary to reason.

cui bono? [L.] For whose advantage?

cul-de-sac. [F.] A blind alley (often used figuratively).

cum grano salis. [L.] With a grain of salt; with some allowance.

d'accord. [F.] In agreement.

débâcle. [F.] The break-up of ice in a river; *hence*, a general, confused rout.

de bonne grâce. [F.] With good grace; willingly.

de facto. [L.] In point of fact; actual or actually.

dégagé. [F.] Free; easy; unconstrained.

de gustibus non est disputandum. [L.] There is no disputing about tastes.

Dei gratia. [L.] By the grace of God.

de jure. [L.] From the law; by right.

delenda est Carthago. [L.] Carthage must be destroyed.

de mortuis nil nisi bonum. [L.] (Say) nothing but good of the dead.

dénoûement. [F.] The issue; the end of a plot.

de novo. [L.] Anew.

Deo gratias. [L.] Thanks to God.

de profundis. [L.] Out of the depths.

de rigueur. [F.] Indispensable; obligatory.

dernier ressort. [F.] A last resort.

de trop. [F.] Too much; more than is wanted; out of place.

deus ex machina. [L.] A god from a machine; used in reference to forced or unlikely events introduced in a drama, novel, etc., to resolve a difficult or awkward situation; derived from the use of deities in the ancient drama.

dies iræ. [L.] Day of wrath.

Dieu et mon droit. [F.] God and my right (British royal motto).

distingué. [F.] Distinguished; of elegant appearance.

dolce far niente. [It.] Sweet doing-nothing; sweet idleness.

Dominus vobiscum. [L.] The Lord be with you.

double entente (or, esp. in English, entendre). [F.] A double meaning; a play upon words.

dramatis personæ. [L.] Characters of the drama or play.

dulce et decorum est pro patria mori. [L.] It is sweet and glorious to die for one's country.

dum spiro, spero. [L.] While I breathe, I hope.

dum vivimus, vivamus. [L.] While we live, let us live.

ecce homo. [L.] Behold the man!

édition de luxe. [F.] A splendid and expensive edition of a book.

editio princeps. [L.] The first printed edition of a book.

ego et rex meus. [L.] I and my king.

élite. [F.] The best part; the pick.

emeritus. [L.] Retired or superannuated after long service.

en avant. [F.] Forward.

en déshabillé. [F.] In undress.

en effet. [F.] In effect; substantially; really.

en famille. [F.] With one's family; in a domestic state.

enfant gâté. [F.] A spoiled child.

enfants perdus. [F.] Lost children; a forlorn hope.

enfant terrible. [F.] A terrible child, that is, one who makes disconcerting remarks.

enfant trouvé. [F.] A foundling.

enfin. [F.] In short; at last; finally.

en masse. [F.] In a mass (*or* body).

en rapport. [F.] In harmony; in agreement.

en route. [F.] On the way.

en suite. [F.] In company; in a set.

entente cordiale. [F.] Cordial understanding, especially between two states.

entourage. [F.] Surroundings; friends, confidants, etc., closely associated with a person.

entre nous. [F.] Between ourselves.

en vérité. [F.] In truth; verily.

e pluribus unum. [L.] One out of many; one composed of many (motto of the United States).

errata. [L.] Errors; list of errors.

esprit de corps. [F.] The animating spirit of a collective body, *as* a regiment.

est modus in rebus. [L.] There is a medium in all things.

et cætera (or **et cetera.**) [L.] And the rest.

et id genus omne. [L.] And everything of the sort.

et tu, Brute! [L.] And thou also, Brutus!

eureka! [Gr.] I have found (it)!

Ewigkeit. [G.] Eternity.

ex cathedra. [L.] From the chair; with high authority.

excelsior. [L.] Higher, *that is*, taller, loftier.

exeunt omnes. [L.] All go out (*or.* retire).

exit. [L.] He goes out.

ex nihilo nihil fit. [L.] Out of nothing, nothing comes.

ex officio. [L.] In virtue of (his) office.

ex parte. [L.] From one party or side.

ex pede Herculem. [L.] From the foot we recognize a Hercules; we judge of the whole from the specimen.

experto crede. [L.] Trust one who has had experience.

exposé. [F.] A statement; a recital.

ex post facto. [L.] After the deed is done; retrospective.

extra muros. [L.] Beyond the walls.

ex uno disce omnes. [L.] From one judge of the rest.

facile princeps. [L.] Easily preeminent; indisputably the first.

facilis est descensus Averni. [L.] The descent to Avernus (*or* hell) is easy.

façon de parler. [F.] Way of speaking.

fait accompli. [F.] A thing already done.

faux pas. [F.] A false step; a slip in behavior.

femme de chambre. [F.] A chambermaid; lady's maid.

festina lente. [L.] Hasten slowly.

feu de joie. [F.] A discharge of firearms as a sign of rejoicing.

fiat justitia, ruat cœlum. [L.] Let justice be done though the heavens should fall.

fiat lux. [L.] Let there be light.

fides Punica. [L.] Punic (*or*

Carthaginian) faith; treachery.

fidus Achates. [L.] Faithful Achates; a true friend.

fin de siècle. [F.] End of the (nineteenth) century.

finis coronat opus. [L.] The end crowns the work.

flagrante delicto. [L.] In the commission of the crime; redhanded.

fons et origo. [L.] The source and origin.

force majeure. [F.] Greater force or strength; overwhelming force; compulsion.

fortiter in re. [L.] With firmness in acting.

fortuna favet fortibus. [L.] Fortune favors the bold.

furor loquendi. [L.] A rage for speaking.

furor scribendi. [L.] A rage for writing.

gaucherie. [F.] Awkwardness.

gaudeamus igitur. [L.] So let us be joyful.

genius loci. [L.] The genius (or guardian spirit) of a place.

gens d'armes. [F.] Men at arms.

gloria in excelsis (Deo). [L.] Glory (to God) in the highest.

gloria Patri. [L.] Glory be to the Father.

goût. [F.] Taste; relish.

grâce à Dieu. [F.] Thanks to God.

habitué. [F.] One in the habit of frequenting a place.

hic et ubique. [L.] Here and everywhere.

hic jacet. [L.] Here lies.

hinc illæ lacrimæ. [L.] Hence these tears.

hodie mihi, cras tibi. [L.] Mine today; yours tomorrow.

hoi polloi. [Gr.] The many; the vulgar; the rabble.

homme d'esprit. [F.] A man of wit or genius.

homo sum; humani nihil a me alienum puto. [L.] I am a man; I count nothing human indifferent to me.

honi soit qui mal y pense. [O. F.] Shamed be he who thinks evil of it (motto of the Order of the Garter).

horribile dictu. [L.] Horrible to relate.

hors de combat. [F.] Out of the combat; disabled.

hors d'œuvre. [F.] A relish.

hôtel de ville. [F.] A town hall.

hôtel-Dieu. [F.] A hospital.

humanum est errare. [L.] To err is human.

ibidem. [L.] At the same place (in a book).

ich dien. [G.] I serve (motto of the Prince of Wales).

ici on parle français. [F.] French is spoken here.

ignotum per ignotius. [L.] The unknown (explained) by the still more unknown.

il n'y a pas de quoi. [F.] Don't mention it; it's not worth speaking of.

il n'y a que le premier pas qui coûte. [F.] It is only the first step that costs.

il penseroso. [It.] The pensive man.

impasse. [F.] A deadlock; an insurmountable difficulty.

impedimenta. [L.] Encumbrances; luggage; baggage.

in æternum. [L.] Forever.

in articulo mortis. [L.] At the point of death; in the last struggle.

index expurgatorius. [L.] A list of prohibited works.

in esse. [L.] In being; in actuality.

in extenso. [L.] At full length.

in extremis. [L.] At the point of death.

infra dignitatem. [L.] Below one's dignity.

in loco. [L.] In the place; in the natural (*or* proper) place.

in loco parentis. [L.] In the place of a parent.

in medias res. [L.] Into the midst of things.

in memoriam. [L.] To the memory of; in memory.

in nomine. [L.] In the name of.

in omnia paratus. [L.] Prepared for all things.

in perpetuum. [L.] Forever.

in posse. [L.] In possible existence; in possibility.

in præsenti. [L.] At the present moment.

in propria persona. [L.] In one's own person.

in puris naturalibus. [L.] Quite naked.

in re. [L.] In the matter of.

in rerum natura. [L.] In the nature of things.

in sæcula sæculorum. [L.] For ages on ages.

in situ. [L.] In its original position.

in statu quo. [L.] In the former state.

inter alia. [L.] Among other things.

inter nos. [L.] Between ourselves.

in terrorem. [L.] As a warning.

in toto. [L.] In the whole; entirely.

intra muros. [L.] Within the walls.

in transitu. [L.] In course of transit.

in vacuo. [L.] In empty space; in a vacuum.

in vino veritas. [L.] There is truth in wine; truth is told under the influence of liquor.

invita Minerva. [L.] Against the will of Minerva; without genius or natural abilities.

ipse dixit. [L.] He himself said it; a dogmatic saying or assertion.

ipsissima verba. [L.] The very words.

ipso facto. [L.] By that very fact.

ipso jure. [L.] By the law itself.

jacquerie. [F.] French peasantry; a revolt of peasants.

je ne sais quoi. [F.] I know not what; a something or other.

jeu de mots. [F.] A play on words; a pun.

jeu d'esprit. [F.] A display of wit; a witticism.

jeunesse dorée. [F.] Gilded youth; rich and fashionable young men.

jubilate Deo. [L.] Rejoice in God; be joyful in the Lord.

jure divino. [L.] By divine law.

jure humano. [L.] By human law.

juste milieu. [F.] The golden mean.

laborare est orare. [L.] To labor is to pray; work is worship.

labor omnia vincit. [L.] Labor conquers everything.

laissez-faire. [F.] Let alone; noninterference.

l'allegro. [It.] The merry man.

lapsus calami. [L.] A slip of the pen.

lapsus linguæ. [L.] A slip of the tongue.

lapsus memoriæ. [L.] A slip of the memory.

lares et penates. [L.] Household gods.

lasciate ogni speranza voi ch'entrate. [It.] All hope abandon ye who enter here (inscription on the entrance to the hell of Dante's Inferno).

laudator temporis acti. [L.] A praiser of past times.

laus Deo. [L.] Praise to God.

l'avenir. [F.] The future.

le beau monde. [F.] The fashionable world.

lebe wohl. [G.] Farewell.

la grand monarque. [F.] The great monarch; Louis XIV of France.

le pas. [F.] Precedence in place or rank.

le roi est mort, vive le roi! [F.] The king is dead, long live the king (his successor)!

le roy le veult. [Norm. F.] The king wills it; the formula used by the sovereign in assenting to a bill.

le roy s'avisera. [Norm. F.] The king will consider; the formula formerly used by the sovereign in rejecting a bill.

lèse-majesté. [F.] High treason.

l'état c'est moi. [F.] It is I who am the state.

le tout ensemble. [F.] The whole (taken) together.

lettre de cachet. [F.] A sealed letter containing private orders; a royal warrant.

lex non scripta. [L.] Unwritten law; common law.

lex scripta. [L.] Statute law.

l'homme propose, et Dieu dispose. [F.] Man proposes, and God disposes.

l'inconnu. [F.] The unknown.

littera scripta manet. [L.] The written word remains.

locum tenens. [L.] One occupying the place of another; a substitute.

longo intervallo. [L.] By *or* at a long interval.

lucus a non lucendo. [L.] Used as typical of an absurd derivation—*lucus*, a grove, having been derived by an old grammarian from *luceo*, to shine—"from not shining."

lusus naturæ. [L.] A sport or freak of nature.

ma chère. [F.] My dear (fem.).

ma foi. [F.] Upon my faith.

magna est veritas, et prevalebit. [L.] Truth is mighty, and will prevail.

magnum opus. [L.] A great work.

maison de santé. [F.] A private asylum *or* hospital.

maître d'hôtel. [F.] A house steward.

mala fide. [L.] With bad faith; treacherously.

mal-à-propos. [F.] Ill-timed; out of place.

mal de mer. [F.] Seasickness.

malgré nous. [F.] In spite of us.

mañana. [Sp.] Tomorrow.

mardi gras. [F.] Shrove Tuesday.

mare clausum. [L.] A closed sea; a sea belonging to a single nation.

mariage de convenance. [F.] Marriage from motives of interest rather than of love.

materfamilias. [L.] Mother of a family.

matériel. [F.] Baggage and munitions of an army; material equipment as opposed to men.

mauvaise honte. [F.] Bashfulness; shamefacedness.

mauvais goût. [F.] Bad taste.

mauvais sujet. [F.] A bad subject; a worthless scamp.

mea culpa. [L.] My fault; by my fault.

me judice. [L.] I being judge; in my opinion.

mêlée. [F.] A confused conflict.

memento mori. [L.] Remember that you must die; a reminder of death.

mens sana in corpore sano. [L.] A sound mind in a sound body.

mens sibi conscia recti. [L.] A mind conscious of rectitude.

meo periculo. [L.] At my own risk.

mésalliance. [F.] A bad match; marriage with one of a lower rank.

meum et tuum. [L.] Mine and thine.

mirabile dictu. [L.] Wonderful to relate.

mirabile visu. [L.] Wonderful to see.

mise en scène. [F.] Stage setting.

modus operandi. [L.] Manner of working.

modus vivendi. [L.] Manner of living; used of a temporary working agreement or compromise.

mon ami. [F.] My friend (masc.).

mon cher. [F.] My dear (masc.).

mont-de-piété. [F.] A public or municipal pawnshop.

monumentum ære perennius. [L.] A monument more lasting than brass.

more majorum. [L.] After the manner of our ancestors.

morituri te salutamus. [L.] We, about to die, salute thee:— said by the Roman gladiators to the emperor.

mot d'ordre. [F.] Watchword.

motu proprio. [L.] Of his own accord.

moyen âge. [F.] Middle Ages.

multum in parvo. [L.] Much in little.

mutatis mutandis. [L.] With the necessary changes.

natura non facit saltum. [L.] Nature does not make a leap.

née. [F.] Born; used in giving

the maiden name of a married woman.

négligé. [F.] Morning dress; an easy loose dress.

nemine contradicente. [L.] No one speaking in opposition; without opposition.

nemine dissentiente. [L.] No one dissenting; with a dissenting voice.

nemo me impune lacessit. [L.] No one assails me with impunity (motto of Scotland).

ne plus ultra. [L.] Nothing further; the uttermost point; perfection.

ne quid nimis. [L.] Avoid excess.

n'est-ce pas? [F.] Isn't that so?

nicht wahr? [G.] Isn't that so?

nil admirari. [L.] To be astonished at nothing.

nil desperandum. [L.] There is no reason for despair.

n'importe. [F.] It matters not.

nisi Dominus, frustra. [L.] Except the Lord (build the house, they labor) in vain (that build it). Ps. cxxvii. (motto of Edinburgh).

noblesse oblige. [F.] Rank imposes obligations.

Noël. [F.] Christmas.

nolens volens. [L.] Unwilling or willing.

noli me tangere. [L.] Touch me not.

nom de guerre. [F.] A war name; a pseudonym; a pen name.

nom de plume. [F.] A pen name. (Incorrect for *Nom de guerre*.)

non Angli sed angeli. [L.] Not Angles but angels.

non compos mentis. [L.] Not of sound mind.

non est. [L.] He (*or* it) is not.

non est inventus. [L.] He has not been found.

non libet. [L.] It does not please (me).

non liquet. [L.] The case is not clear.

non multa, sed multum. [L.] Not many things, but much.

non nobis solum. [L.] Not for ourselves alone.

non omnis moriar. [L.] I shall not wholly die.

non sequitur. [L.] It does not follow.

nosce te ipsum. [L.] Know thyself.

nota bene. [L.] Note well; take notice.

Notre Dame. [F.] Our Lady.

nous avons changé tout cela. [F.] We have changed all that.

nous verrons. [F.] We shall see.

novus homo. [L.] A new man; one who has raised himself from obscurity.

nuance. [F.] Shade; tint.

nulla dies sine linea. [L.] Not a day without a line; no day without something done.

nunc aut nunquam. [L.] Now or never.

obiit. [L.] He (*or* she) died.

obiter dictum. [L.] A thing said by the way.

odi profanum vulgus. [L.] I loathe the profane rabble.

odium theologicum. [L.] The hatred of theologians.

œuvres. [F.] Works.

ohne Hast, ohne Rast. [G.] Without haste, without rest: —motto of Goethe.

omnia vincit amor. [L.] Love conquers all things.

on dit. [F.] They say.

onus probandi. [L.] The burden of proof.

operæ pretium est. [L.] It is worth while.

ora et labora. [L.] Pray and work.

ora pro nobis. [L.] Pray for us.

ore rotundo. [L.] With round full voice; well-turned speech.

O! si sic omnia. [L.] Oh, if all things (were) so; Oh, if he had always so spoken or acted.

O tempora! O mores! [L.] Alas for the times! Alas for the manners (*or* morals)!

otium cum dignitate. [L.] Ease with dignity.

ouï-dire. [F.] Hearsay.

ouvrage de longue haleine. [F.] A work of long breath; a long work *or* one which lasts.

pace. [L.] By leave of; not to give offence to.

palmam qui meruit ferat. [L.] Let him who has won the palm wear it.

pardonnez-moi. [F.] Pardon me; I beg your pardon.

par excellence. [F.] Pre-eminently.

par exemple. [F.] For example.

par hasard. [F.] By chance.

pari passu. [L.] With equal pace; side by side.

par nobile fratrum. [L.] A noble pair of brothers; two just alike.

parole d'honneur. [F.] Word of honor.

particeps criminis. [L.] An accomplice in a crime.

parti pris. [F.] Preconceived opinion.

parvenu. [L.] A person of low origin who has risen suddenly to wealth or position; an upstart.

pas. [F.] A step; precedence.

passim. [L.] Everywhere; throughout; in all parts of the book, chapter, etc.

pâté de foie gras. [F.] Goose-liver pie.

paterfamilias. [L.] Father of a family; head of a household.

pater patriæ. [L.] Father of his country.

pax vobiscum. [L.] Peace be with you.

peccavi. [L.] I have sinned (*or* been to blame).

peine forte et dure. [F.] Strong and severe punishment; a kind of judicial torture.

penchant. [F.] A strong liking.

pensée. [F.] A thought.

per. [L.] For; through; by.— **per contra.** On the contrary. —**per annum.** By the year; annually.—**per capita.** By heads; for each individual.— **per centum.** By the hundred. —**per diem.** By the day; daily.—**per fas et nefas.** Through right and wrong.— **per se.** By itself.

persona non grata. [L.] An unacceptable person.

peu à peu. [F.] Little by little.

peu de chose. [F.] A trifle.

pièce de résistance. [F.] A resistance piece; the main dish of a meal.

pied-à-terre. [F.] A resting-place; a temporary lodging.

pis aller. [F.] The worst or last shift.

place aux dames. [F.] Make room for the ladies.

plebs. [L.] The common people.

poco a poco. [It.] Little by little.

point d'appui. [F.] Point of support; basis.

pons asinorum. [L.] The asses' bridge; a name for the fifth proposition of the first book in Euclid.

poste restante. [F.] To remain in the post office till called for.

post hoc ergo propter hoc. [L.] After this, therefore, on account of this; subsequent to, therefore due to this—an illogical way of reasoning.

pour faire rire. [F.] To excite laughter.

pour le mèrite. [F.] For merit.

pour passer le temps. [F.] To pass the time.

preux chevalier. [F.] A brave knight.

prima donna. [It.] First lady; the chief female singer in an opera, etc.

prima facie. [L.] At first view (*or* consideration).

primo. [L.] In the first place.

primum mobile. [L.] The source of motion; the mainspring.

principia, non homines. [L.] Principles, not men.

pro bono publico. [L.] For the good of the public.

procès-verbal. [F.] An authenticated minute or statement.

pro et contra. [L.] For and against.

profanum vulgus. [L.] The profane herd.

pro forma. [L.] For the sake of form.

pro patria. [L.] For our country.

pro rata. [L.] According to rate or proportion.

pro tanto. [L.] For so much; as far as it goes.

protégé. [F.] One under the protection of another.

Punica fides. [L.] Punic (*or* Carthaginian) faith; treachery.

qualis rex, talis grex. [L.] Like king, like people.

quand même. [F.] Even if; whatever may happen.

quantum libet. [L.] As much as you please.

quantum sufficit. [L.] As much as suffices.

quelque chose. [F.] Something; a trifle.

quid pro quo. [L.] Something in return; an equivalent.

quién sabe? [Sp.] Who knows?

quis custodiet ipsos custodes? [L.] Who shall guard the guards themselves?

qui s'excuse s'accuse. [F.] He who excuses himself accuses himself.

qui va là? [F.] Who goes there?

qui vive? [F.] Who lives? Who goes there? **To be on the qui vive** means to be alert or watchful.

quoad hoc. [L.] To this extent.

quoad sacra. [L.] As far as sacred things are concerned; for ecclesiastical purposes only.

quem Deus vult perdere, prius dementat. [L.] Those whom God wishes to destroy, he first makes mad.

quod erat demonstrandum. [L.] Which was to be proved or demonstrated.

quod vide. [L.] Which see.

quorum pars magna fui. [L.] Of which things, I was an important part.

quot homines, tot sententiæ. [L.] Many men, many minds.

raconteur. [F.] A teller of stories.

raison d'être. [F.] The reason for a thing's existence.

rapprochement. [F.] The act of bringing (*or* coming) together.

rara avis. [L.] A rare bird; a paragon.

réchauffé. [F.] *Lit.*, something warmed up; *hence*, old literary material worked up into a new form.

reductio ad absurdum. [L.] A reducing to the absurd; a method of proof in which a proposition is shown to be true by demonstrating the absurdity of its contradictions.

rencontre. [F.] An encounter; a hostile meeting.

répondez, s'il vous plaît. [F.] Please reply. *R. S. V. P.*

requiescat in pace. [L.] May he rest in peace.

res angusta domi. [L.] Narrow circumstances at home; poverty.

res gestæ. [L.] Things done; exploits; history.

respice finem. [L.] Look to the end.

résumé. [F.] A summary or abstract.

resurgam. [L.] I shall rise again.

revenons à nos moutons. [F.] Let us return to our sheep; let us return to our subject.

rôle. [F.] A character represented on the stage; also other similar meanings.

rouge et noir. [F.] Red and black; a game of chance.

rus in urbe. [L.] The country in town.

salle à manger. [F.] Dining room

sanctum sanctorum. [L.] Holy of holies.

sang froid. [F.] Coolness; indifference.

sans façon. [F.] Without ceremony.

sans peur et sans reproche. [F.] Without fear and without reproach.

sans souci. [F.] Without care.

sartor resartus. [L.] The patcher repatched; the tailor patched (*or* mended).

satis superque. [L.] Enough, and more than enough.

satis verborum. [L.] Enough of words; no more need be said.

sauve qui peut. [F.] Let him save himself who can.

savoir-faire. [F.] The knowing how to act; tact.

savoir-vivre. [F.] Good breeding; refined manners.

scripsit. [L.] Wrote (it).

sculpsit. [L.] Engraved (it).

secundum artem. [L.] According to art (*or* rule).

semper idem. [L.] Always the same.

semplice. [It.] Simple; plain.

seriatim. [L.] In a series; one by one.

sic itur ad astra. [L.] Such is the way to the stars, or to immortality.

sic passim. [L.] So here and there throughout; so everywhere.

sic transit gloria mundi. [L.] Thus passes away the glory of this world.

sicut ante. [L.] As before.

similia similibus curantur. [L.] Like things are cured by like.

simplex munditiis. [L.] Elegant in simplicity.

sine cura. [L.] Without charge or care.

sine die. [L.] Without a day being appointed.

sine qua non. [L.] Without which, not; something indispensable.

siste, viator. [L.] Stop, traveler.

sit tibi terra levis. [L.] Light lie the earth upon thee.

soi-disant. [F.] Self-styled.

sotto voce. [It.] In an undertone.

spero meliora. [L.] I hope for better things.

splendide mendax. [L.] Nobly untruthful; untrue for a good object.

sponte sua. [L.] Of one's (*or* its) own accord.

status quo. [L.] The state in which; the existing condition.

stet. [L.] Let it stand; do not delete.

suaviter in modo, fortiter in re. [L.] Gentle in manner, resolute in execution.

sub judice. [L.] Under consideration.

sub rosa. [L.] Under the rose; confidentially.

succès d'estime. [F.] A partial success, or one based on certain merits.

sui generis. [L.] Of its own peculiar kind; in a class by itself.

summum bonum. [L.] The chief good.

sunt lacrimæ rerum. [L.] There are tears for things; misfortunes call for tears.

suppressio veri. [L.] A suppression of the truth.

sursum corda. [L.] Lift up your hearts.

suum cuique. [L.] Let every one have his own.

tableau vivant. [F.] A living picture; the representation of some scene by a group of persons.

table d'hôte. [F.] A public dinner at an inn or hotel.

tabula rasa. [L.] A smooth or blank tablet.

tant mieux. [F.] So much the better.

tant pis. [F.] So much the worse.

te Deum laudamus. [L.] We praise Thee, O God (*or rather*, as God).

te judice. [L.] You being the judge.

tempus fugit. [L.] Time flies.

terminus ad quem. [L.] The term (*or* limit) to which.

terminus a quo. [L.] The term (*or* limit) from which.

terra firma. [L.] Solid earth; a secure foothold.

terra incognita. [L.] An unknown country.

tertium quid. [L.] A third something; a nondescript.

tiers état. [F.] The third estate; the commons.

timeo Danaos et dona ferentes. [L.] I fear the Greeks, even when they bring gifts.

tot homines, quot sententiæ. [L.] So many men, so many minds.

toto cælo. [L.] By the whole heavens; diametrically opposite.

tour de force. [F.] A notable feat of strength or skill.

tout à fait. [F.] Wholly; entirely.

tout à l'heure. [F.] Instantly.

tout au contraire. [F.] On the contrary.

tout de suite. [F.] Immediately.

tout ensemble. [F.] The whole taken together.

tu quoque. [L.] You also.

ubi supra. [L.] Where above mentioned.

ultima Thule. [L.] Most distant Thule; utmost limit.

una voce. [L.] With one voice; unanimously.

und so weiter. [G.] And so forth.

urbi et orbi. [L.] To the city and to the world.

utile dulci. [L.] The useful with the agreeable.

ut infra. [L.] As below.

ut supra. As above.

væ victis. [L.] Woe to the vanquished.

vale. [L.] Farewell.

valet de chambre. [F.] A personal attendant; a body servant.

varium et mutabile semper femina. [L.] Woman is ever a changeful and capricious thing.

veni, vidi, vici. [L.] I came, I saw, I conquered. (Cæsar's message to the senate when he conquered Pharnaces, king of Pontus.)

verbatim et literatim. [L.] Word for word and letter for letter.

verbum sat sapienti. [L.] A word is enough for a wise man.

via, veritas, vita. [L.] The way, the truth, the life.

vice versa. [L.] The terms of the case being interchanged or reversed; conversely.

videlicet. [L.] Namely (*lit.*, one may see).

vide ut supra. [L.] See what is stated above.

vi et armis. [L.] By force and arms; by main force.

vincit qui se vincit. [L.] He conquers who conquers himself.

virginibus puerisque. [L.] For maidens and boys.

vis a tergo. [L.] A force from behind.

vis-à-vis. [F.] Opposite; face to face.

vis inertiæ. [L.] The power of

inertia; resistance to force applied.

vis medicatrix naturæ. [L.] The healing power of nature.

vis vitæ. [L.] Living force; energy.

vivat regina (rex)! [L.] Long live the queen (king)!

viva voce. [L.] By the living voice; orally.

vive la bagatelle! [F.] Long live trifles (*or* frivolity)!

vive le roi! [F.] Long live the king!

vogue la galère! [F.] Row the galley; come what may!

voilà. [F.] Behold; there is; there are.

voilà tout. [F.] That's all.

vox et præterea nihil. [L.] A voice and nothing more; sound but no sense.

vox populi, vox Dei. [L.] The voice of the people is the voice of God.

vraisemblance. [F.] Probability; apparent truth.

vulgo. [L.] Commonly.

Wanderjahr. [G.] Year of wandering.

Wanderlust. [G.] Passion for traveling (*or* wandering).

Weltanschauung. [G.] World-view; theory or conception of life or of the world in all its aspects.

Weltschmerz. [G.] World sorrow; sentimental pessimism.

Zeitgeist. [G.] Time-spirit; spirit of the age.

zum Beispiel. [G.] For example.

ABBREVIATIONS USED IN WRITING AND PRINTING

A

a. About; acre; adjective; afternoon; answer; are (metric system); at.

A. Academician; Academy; America; American; artillery.

A. A. A. Amateur Athletic Association.

A. A. A. S. American Association for the Advancement of Science.

A. A. of A. Automobile Association of America.

A. A. U. Amateur Athletic Union.

ab. About.

A. B. Artium Baccalaureus (L., Bachelor of Arts); (also l. c.) able-bodied (seaman).

abbr., or abbrev. Abbreviated; abbreviation.

abd. Abdicated.

A. B. F. M. American Board of Foreign Missions.

abl. Ablative.

Abp. Archbishop.

abr. Abridged; abridgment.

abs. Absolutely; abstract.

A. B. S. American Bible Society.

A. C. Alpine Club; ambulance corps; ante Christum (L., before Christ); Army Corps.

Acad. Academy.

acc. Acceptance; account; accusative.

acct. Account.

ad. (pl. ads.) Advertisement.

a. d. After date; ante diem (L., before the day).

A. D. Anno Domini (L., in the year of our Lord).

A. D. C. Aid-de-camp; aide-de-camp.

ad fin. Ad finem (L., at the end).

ad inf. Ad infinitum (L., to infinity).

ad int. Ad interim (L., in the meantime).

adj. Adjective.

Adj., or Adjt. Adjutant.

Adj. Gen. Adjutant General.

ad. lib. Ad libitum (L., at pleasure).

Adm. Admiral; Admiralty.

admix. Administratrix.

admr. Administrator.

admx. Administratrix.

adv. Ad valorem; adverb; advocate.

Adv. Advent.

Adv. Gd. Advance guard.

advt. Advertisement.

æ., æt., ætat. Ætatis (L., of age, aged).

A. E. F. American Expeditionary Forces.

AF. or A.-F. Anglo-French.

aff. Affectionate; affirmative; affirming.

afft. Affidavit.

Afr. Africa; African.

A. G. Adjutant General; Advance guard; Attorney-general.

agr., *or* **agric.** Agriculture; agricultural.

agt. Agent.

A. H. Anno Hegiræ (L., in the year of the Hegira).

A. H. C. Army Hospital Corps.

A. I. American Institute.

Ala. Alabama.

A. L. A. American Library Association; Automobile Legal Association.

ald., *or* **aldm.** Alderman.

Alex. Alexander.

alg. Algebra.

alt. Alternate; altitude; alto.

Alta. Alberta (Canada).

Am. America; American; ammunition.

a. m. Ante meridiem (L., before noon).

A. M. Anno mundi (L., in the year of the world); Annus Mirabilis (L., the Wonderful Year, i.e., 1666); Artium Magister (L., Master of Arts).

A. M. D. Army Medical Department.

Amer. America; American.

A. M. S. Army Medical Staff.

amt. Amount.

anal. Analogous; analogy; analysis; analytic.

anat. Anatomy.

anc. Ancient; anciently.

anon. Anonymous.

ans. Answer.

ant. Antonym; antiquarian.

Ant. Anthony; Antigua.

anthrop. Anthropology; anthropological.

antiq. Antiquities; antiquarian.

A. N. Z. A. C., *or* **Anzac.** Australian and New Zealand Army Corps.

A. O. Army order.

A. O. C. Army Ordnance Corps.

A. O. D. Army Ordnance Department.

A. O. F. Ancient Order of Foresters.

A. O. H. Ancient Order of Hibernians.

aor. Aorist.

A. P. C. Army Pay Corps.

A. P. D. Army Pay Department.

Apoc. Apocalypse; Apocrypha; Apocryphal.

app. Appendix; appointed.

App. Apostles.

approx. Approximately.

Apr. April.

aq., Aq. Aqua (L., water).

Ar. Arabian; Arabic.

A. R. Anno regni (L., in the year of the reign); Army Regulations.

A. R. A. Associate of the Royal Academy (of Arts, London).

Arab. Arabian; Arabic.

arch. Archaic; archaism; archery; archipelago; architect; architecture.

Arch. Archibald.

archaeol. Archæology.

Archd. Archdeacon; Archduke.

arith. Arithmetic.

Ariz. Arizona.

Ark. Arkansas.

Arm. Armenian.

arr. Arranged; arrived; arrivals.

art. Article; artificial; artillery; artist.

Art. or **A.** Artillery.

AS., or **A.-S.** Anglo-Saxon.

A. S. C. Army Service Corps; Army Staff Corps (British Army).

A. S. C. E. American Society of Civil Engineers.

A. S. M. E. American Society of Mechanical Engineers.

assd. Assigned.

assn. Association.

assoc. Associate; association.

asst. Assistant.

A. S. S. U. American Sunday School Union.

astr., astron. Astronomer; astronomy.

astrol. Astrologer; astrology.

Atl. Atlantic.

att., atty. Attorney.

at. wt. Atomic weight.

A. U. C. Ab urbe condita (L., from the founding of the city; i.e., Rome, about 753 B. C.).

Aug. August.

Aus., Aust. Austria; Austrian.

Austral. Australasia; Australia.

Auth. Ver. Authorized Version.

auxil. Auxiliary.

av. Avenue; average.

A. V. Artillery Volunteers; Authorized Version.

A. V. C. Army Veterinary Corps.

A. V. D. Army Veterinary Department.

ave. Avenue.

A. W. L. Absent with Leave.

A. W. O. L. Absent without Leave.

ax. Axiom.

az. Azure.

B

b. Base; bass; battery; bay; book; born; brother.

B. A. Bachelor of Arts; British Academy; British America.

B. Agr. Bachelor of Agriculture.

bal. Balance.

bap. Baptized.

Bapt. Baptist.

bar. Barometer; barometric; barrel.

Barb. Barbados.

barr. Barrister.

Bart. Baronet.

bat., batt., or **bn.** Battalion.

batt. or **b.** Battery.

bbl. (pl. bbls.) Barrel.

B. C. Before Christ; British Columbia.

B. C. L. Bachelor of Civil Law.

bd. Board; bond; bound.

B. D. Bachelor of Divinity.

bdl. (pl bdls.) Bundle.

b. e. Bill of exchange.

B. E. F. British Expeditionary Forces.

Belg. Belgian, Belgium.

Benj. Benjamin.

B. ès L. Bachelier ès Lettres (F. Bachelor of Letters).

bg. (pl. bgs.) Bag.

b. h. p. Brake horse power.

B. I. British India.

Bib. Bible; Biblical.

biog. Biographer; biography.

biol. Biologist; biology.

bk. Bank; book.

bkg. Banking.

bkt. (pl. bkts.) Basket.

b. l. Bill of lading; breech-loading.

B. L. Bachelor of Laws.

bldg. (pl. bldgs.) Building.

B. Litt. Bachelor of Literature, *or* of Letters.

B. L. R. Breech-loading rifle.

b. m. Board measure.

B. M. Bachelor of Medicine; Brigade Major.

B. Mus. Bachelor of Music.

b. o. Branch office; buyer's option.

Boh. Bohemia; Bohemian.

Bol. Bolivia.

bor. Borough.

bot. Botanical; botanist; botany.

Bp. Bishop.

b. p. Below proof; bill of parcels; bills payable.

B. P. O. E. Benevolent and Protective Order of Elks.

br. Brig; brother; brown.

Br. British.

Br. Am. British America.

b. rec. Bills receivable.

brig. Brigade; brigadier.

Brit. Britain; British.

bro. (*pl.* bros.) Brother.

b. s. Balance sheet; bill of sale.

B. S. Bachelor of Surgery.

B. Sc. Bachelor of Science.

bu., bus. Bushel; bushels.

bul. Bulletin.

Bulg. Bulgaria; Bulgarian.

B. V. M. Beata Virgo Maria (L., Blessed Virgin Mary).

Bvt. Brevet; breveted.

Brig. Gen. Brigadier General.

C

c. Carton; cathode; cent; centime; centimeter; century; chapter; child; circa (L., about); cost; cubic; current.

C. Cape; Catholic; centigrade (thermometer); Chancellor; Congress; Conservative; Consul; Corps; Court.

C. A. Chartered Accountant; Chief Accountant; Confederate Army; Controller of Accounts; Court of Appeal.

cal. Calendar; calends; calorie.

Calif. California.

Cam., Camb. Cambridge.

Can. Canada; Canadian.

Cant. Canterbury, Canticles.

Cantab. Cantabrigiensis (L., of Cambridge).

Cantuar. Cantuaria (LL., Canterbury); Cantuariensis (LL., of Canterbury).

cap. Capital; capitalize; capitulum (L., chapter); captain.

Capt. Captain.

car. Carat; carpentry.

Card. Cardinal.

cash. Cashier.

cat. Catalogue; catechism.

cath. Cathedral.

Cath. Catherine; Catholic.

cav. Cavalry.

C. B. Cape Breton; Cavalry Brigade; Chief Baron; Common Bench; Companion of the Bath; Confined to Barracks.

cc. Cubic centimeter, *or* centimeters.

c. c. Compte courant (F., account current); cubic centimeter, *or* centimeters.

C. C. Caius College (Cambridge, Eng.); Circuit Court; Civil Court; County Clerk.

C. C. D. Commander of Coast Defenses.

C. C. P. Court of Common Pleas.

c. d. v. Carte de visite.

C. E. Church of England; Civil Engineer; Corps of Engineers.

cel. Celebrated.

Celt. Celtic.

cen. Central; century.

cent. Centigrade; central; century; centum.

cert. Certificate; certify.

certif. Certificate; certificated.

cf. Confer (i.e., compare).

C. F. A. Chief of Field Artillery.

c. f. & i. or c. f. i. Cost, freight, and insurance.

cg. Centigram.

C. G. Captain General; Captain of the Guard; Coast Guard; Commanding General; Consul General.

C. G. H. Cape of Good Hope.

C. G. S. or c. g. s. Centimeter-gram-second (system of units); Chief of General Staff in the field.

ch. Chapter; chief; child, church.

Ch. Chancery; Charles; China; Church.

C. H. Captain of the Horse; Courthouse; Customhouse.

chanc. Chancellor; chancery.

chap. Chaplain; chapter.

Chas. Charles.

chem. Chemical; chemist; chemistry.

Chin. China; Chinese.

Ch. J. Chief Justice.

Chr. Christ; Christian; Christopher.

chron. Chronological; chronology.

Chron. Chronicles.

chs. Chapters.

c. i. f. Cost, insurance, and freight.

circ. Circa. circiter, circum (L., about).

cit. Citation, cited; citizen.

civ. Civil; civilian.

C. J. Chief Justice.

cl. Centiliter; class; clause; clergyman; cloth.

class. Classic; classical; classification.

cld. Cleared; colored.

clk. Clerk.

cm. Centimeter.

cml. Commercial.

C. M. Certificated Master; common meter; Corresponding Member; court-martial.

C. M. G. Companion of St. Michael and St. George.

cml. Commercial.

Co. Company; county.

c. o. Care of; carried over.

C. O. Colonial Office; Commanding Officer; Crown Office.

coad. Coadjutor.

C. O. D. Cash, or collect, on delivery.

C. of S. Chief of Staff.

cog. Cognate.

col. College; collegiate; colonial; colony; colored; column.

Col. Colonel; Colossians.

coll. Colleague; collection; collector; college.

collat. Collateral; collaterally.

colloq. Colloquial; colloquially.

Colo. Colorado.

Col. Sergt. Color Sergeant.

com. Comedy; commentary; commerce; common; commonly; communication.

Com. Commander; Commission; Commissioner; Committee; Commodore.

comdg. Commanding.

Comdr. Commander.

Comdt. Commandant.

comp. Compare; comparative; composer; compositor; compound; comprising.

Com. Ver. Common Version.

con. Contra (L., against).

Cong. Congregational; Congress; Congressional.

conj. Conjunction.

Conn. Connecticut.

const. Constable; constitution.

cont. Containing; contents; continent; continue; continued.

contemp. Contemporary.

contr. Contracted; contraction; contrary.

cor. Corner; cornet; corrected; correction; correlative; correspondent; corresponding.

Cor. Corinthians.

Corp. Corporal.

cos. Cosine.

cosec. Cosecant.

cot. Cotangent.

cp. Compare.

c. p. Candle power; chemically pure.

C. P. Common Pleas; Common Prayer; Court of Probate.

C. P. A. Certified public accountant.

cps. Coupons.

C. P. S. Clerk of Petty Sessions.

cr. Created; credit; creditor; crown.

cresc. Crescendo.

C. S. Christian Science; Civil Service.

C. S. A. Confederate States Army; Confederate States of America.

C. S. C. Conspicuous Service Cross.

C. S. I. Companion of the Star of India (Brit. order).

C. S. N. Confederate States Navy.

C. S. O. Chief Signal Officer.

ct. Cent; county

cts. Cents; centimes.

cu., cub. Cubic.

cur. Currency; current.

C. V. Common Version.

c. w. o. Cash with order.

cwt. Hundredweight *or* hundredweights.

cyc., *or* **cyclo.** Cyclopedia; cyclopedic.

C. in C. Commander in Chief.

D

d. Date; daughter; day; dead; degree; denarius, *or* denarii (L., penny *or* pence); deputy; died; dime; dollar; dose.

D. Democrat; department; Deus (L., God); Duke; Dutch.

Dan. Danish, Daniel.

D. A. R. Daughters of the American Revolution.

dat. Dative.

dau. Daughter.

D. C. Da capo (It., from the beginning); Dental Corps; District Court; District of Columbia.

D. C. L. Doctor of Civil Law.

d. d. Days after date.

D. D. Divinitatis Doctor (L., Doctor of Divinity).

D. D. S. Doctor of Dental Surgery.

Dea. Deacon.

deb. Debenture.

dec. Declension; declination; decorative.

Dec. December.

def. Defendant; definition.

deft. Defendant.

deg. Degree.

del. Delegate; delineavit (L., he, or she, drew it).

Del. Delaware.

Dem. Democrat; Democratic.

Den. Denmark.

dep. Department; departs; deponent; deputy.

dept. Department; deponent.

der., or **deriv.** Derivation; derivative; derived.

Deut. Deuteronomy.

D. F. Dean of the Faculty; Defensor Fidei (L., Defender of the Faith).

dft. Defendant; draft.

dg. Decigram.

D. G. Dei gratia (L., by the grace of God); Deo gratias (L., thanks to God); Director General; Dragoon Guards.

diam. Diameter.

dict. Dictator; dictionary.

dim., or **dimin.** Diminuendo; diminutive.

dis. Discipline; discount.

disc. Discount; discovered.

disct. Discount.

disp. Dispensatory.

dist. Distant; distinguished; district.

div. Divide; divided; dividend; divine; division; divisor.

dl. Deciliter.

D. Lit. Doctor of Literature.

D. L. O. Dead Letter Office.

dm. Decimeter.

do. Ditto.

dol. (pl. dols.) Dollar; dollars.

dom. Domestic; dominion.

D. O. M. Deo Óptimó Maximo (L., to God, the Best, the Greatest).

D. O. R. C. Dental Officers' Reserve Corps.

dow. Dowager.

doz. Dozen; dozens.

dpt. Department; deponent.

dr. Dram; drawer.

Dr. Debtor; doctor.

dram. pers. Dramatis personæ.

d. s. Dal segno (It., from the sign; — musical direction); day's sight; days after sight.

D. S. Director of Supplies.

D. Sc. Doctor of Science.

D. S. C. Distinquished Service Cross.

D. S. O. Distinquished Service Order (British, Army and Navy).

D T Double Time; "rush." (Signal).

D. T.'s. Delirium tremens. Colloq.

Du. Dutch.

D. V. Deo volente (L., God willing).

D. V. M. Doctor of Veterinary Medicine.

D. V. S. Director of Veterinary Services.

dwt. Pennyweight or pennyweights.

E

E. Earl; Earth; East; Eastern; Engineer; English.

ea. Each.

Ebor. Eboracum (L., York); Eboracensis (L., of York).

E. C. Eastern Central (Postal District, London); Established Church.

eccl., or eccles. Ecclesiastical.

Eccl., or Eccles. Ecclesiastes.

Ecclus. Ecclesiasticus.

Ecua. Ecuador.

ed. Edition; editor.

E. D. Eastern Department; Extra Duty.

Edin. Edinburgh.

edit. Edition.

Edw. Edward.

E. E. Early English; Electrical Engineer; errors expected.

E. E. & M. P. Envoy Extraordinary and Minister Plenipotentiary.

Eg. Egypt; Egyptian.

e. g. Exempli gratia (L., for example).

E. I. East India; East Indies.

elec. Electrical; electrician; electricity.

Eliz. Elizabeth; Elizabethan.

Em. Emmanuel; Emily; Emma.

E. M. F. Electromotive force.

Emp. Emperor; Empress.

ency., or encyc. Encyclopedia.

ENE. East-northeast.

eng. Engineer; engraving.

Eng. England; English.

engin. Engineer; engineering.

entom. Entomology.

E. O. Engineer Officer.

E. O. R. C. Engineer Officers' Reserve Corps.

Eph. Ephesians, Ephraim.

Epiph. Epiphany.

Epis., or Episc. Episcopal.

eq. Equal; equivalent.

ESE. East-southeast.

esp., or espec. Especially.

Esq. Esquire.

est., or estab. Established.

Esth. Esther.

et al. Et alibi (L., and elsewhere); et alii (L., and others).

etc. Et cetera (L., and others, and so forth).

et seq. Et sequens (L., and the following).

et sqq. Et sequentes (L., and the following), masc. & fem. pl., or sequentia, neut. pl.

etym., or etymol. Etymology.

ex. Examined; example; excursion, executed; executive; export; extract.

ex div. Without dividend.

Exod. Exodus.

exp. Export; express.

Expl. Explosives.

exr. Executor.

exrx. Executrix.

ext. External; extinct; extra; extract.

Ezek. Ezekiel.

F

f. Farthing; fathom; feminine; fine; flower; folio; foot; forte; franc.

F. Fahrenheit; French.

F. A. Field Artillery.

fac. Facsimile.

Fahr. Fahrenheit.

F. A. I. A. Fellow of the American Institute of Architects.

fam. Familiar; family.

F. A. M. Free and Accepted Masons.

far. Farriery; farthing.

F. A. R. C. Field Artillery Reserve Corps.

F. B. A. Fellow of the British Academy (scientific society).

F. C. Free Church (of Scotland).
fcap. Foolscap.
fcp. Foolscap.
F. D. Fidei Defensor (L., Defender of the Faith).
Feb. February.
fem. Feminine.
ff. Folios; following (pages); fortissimo.
F. F. V. First Families of Virginia.
f. i. For instance.
fict. Fiction.
fig. Figurative; figuratively; figure.
Fin. Finland; Finnish.
fir. Firkin; firkins.
fl. Florin; flourished; fluid.
Fl. Flanders; Flemish.
Fla. Florida.
Flem. Flemish.
fm. Fathom.
F. M. Field Marshal; Foreign Mission.
fo. Folio.
F. O. Field Officer; Field Order.
f. o. b. Free on board.
fol. Folio; following.
for. Foreign.
fort. Fortification.
fr. Fragment; franc; from.
Fr. Father; France; Frau; French; Friar.
Fred. Frederick.
freq. Frequent; frequentative.
F. R. G. S. Fellow of the Royal Geographical Society (London).
Fri. Friday.
F. R. S. Fellow of the Royal Society (London).
frs. Francs.
F. S. Field Service.
ft. Feet; foot; fort; fortified.

fur. Furlong; further.
fut. Future.

G

g. Gauge; genitive; gram; guide; guinea or guineas; gulf.
G. German.
Ga. Georgia.
G. A. General Assembly.
gal. (pl. gals.) Gallon.
Gal. Galatians.
G. A. R. Grand Army of the Republic.
gaz. Gazette; gazetteer.
G. B. Great Britain.
G. B. & I. Great Britain and Ireland.
G. C. Grand Chancellor (or Chaplain, Chapter, Council, Conclave, etc.).
g. c. d. Greatest common divisor.
g. c. m. Greatest common measure.
G. C. M. General Court Martial.
Gd. Guard.
gen. Gender; general; generic; genitive; genus.
Gen. General; Genesis.
gent. Gentleman.
Geo. George.
geog. Geographer; geographic; geographical; geography.
geol. Geologic; geological; geologist; geology.
geom. Geometry.
ger. Gerund.
Ger. German; Germany.
G. H. Q. General Headquarters.
gi. Gill; gills.
G. L. Grand Lodge.

gm. Gram.

G. M. Grand Master.

G. O. General order.

G. O. C. General Officer Commanding.

gov. Government; governor.

Gov. Gen. Governor General.

govt. Government.

G. P. Gloria Patri (L., Glory to the Father); Graduate in Pharmacy.

G. P. O. General Post Office.

gr. Grain; grand; great; gross.

Gr. Greece; Greek; Grecian.

gram. Grammar.

Gr. Br., Gr. Brit. Great Britain.

G. S. General Secretary; General Service; General Staff; Grand Scribe; Grand Secretary.

gt. Gilt; great; gutta (L., drop).

gtt. Guttæ (L., drops).

gun. Gunnery.

H

h. Harbor; hard; hardness; height; high; hour; husband.

H., HQ., *or* **Hqrs.** Headquarters.

ha. Hectare.

H. A. Horse Artillery.

Hab. Habakkuk.

Hag. Haggai.

H. B. C. Hudson's Bay Company.

H. B. M. His (*or* Her) Britannic Majesty.

H. C. Heralds' College, House of Commons.

h. c. f. Highest common factor.

H. E. High explosive; His Eminence; His Excellency.

Heb. Hebrew; Hebrews.

hectol. Hectoliter.

hectom. Hectometer.

H. E. I. C. Honorable East India Company.

her. Heraldry.

hg. Hectogram; heliogram.

H. G. His (*or* Her) Grace; Horse Guards; High German.

H. H. His (*or* Her) Highness; His Holiness (the Pope).

hhd. Hogshead; hogsheads.

H. I. H. His (*or* Her) Imperial Highness.

H. I. M. His (*or* Her) Imperial Majesty.

Hind. Hindustan; Hindustani.

hist. Historian; historical; history.

H. J. Hic jacet (L., here lies).

hl. Hectoliter.

H. L. House of Lords.

hm. Hectometer.

H. M. His (*or* Her) Majesty.

H. M. S. His (*or* Her) Majesty's Service; *or* Ship.

ho. House.

Hon. Honorable; honorary.

hort. Horticulture.

Hos. Hosea.

Hosp. Hospital.

H. P., *or* **h. p.** Half pay; high pressure; horse power.

hr. (*pl.* hrs.) Hour.

H. R. House of Representatives.

H. R. E. Holy Roman Emperor, *or* Empire.

H. R. H. His (*or* Her) Royal Highness.

H. S. H. His (*or* Her) Serene Highness.

ht. Height.

Hun., Hung. Hungarian; Hungary.

H. W. M. High-water mark.
Hy. Henry.
hyd. Hydrostatics.
hyp. Hypothesis; hypothetical.

I

I. Imperator (L., Emperor); island.
I. A. Indian Army.
ib., *or* **ibid.** Ibidem (L., in the same place).
Ice., Icel. Iceland; Icelandic.
id. Idem (L., the same).
I. D. R. Infantry Drill Regulations.
i. e. Id est. (L., that is).
i. h. p. Indicated horse power.
IHS. A symbol representing Greek IH (ΣΟΥ) Σ Jesus.
ill., illus., illust. Illustrated; illustration.
Ill. Illinois.
imp. Imparted; imperative; imperfect; imperial; impersonal; imported; importer.
in. (*pl.* ins.) Inch.
inc. Including; inclusive; incorporated; increase.
incl. Including; inclusive.
incog. Incognito.
incor. Incorporated.
ind. Independent; indicative; indigo.
Ind. India; Indian; Indiana.
inf. Infantry; infinitive.
I. N. R. I. Iesus Nazarenus, Rex Iudæorum (L., Jesus of Nazareth, King of the Jews).
ins. Inches; inscribed; inspector; insurance.
insp. Inspector.
inst. Instant; institute; institution.

int. Interest; interior; interjection; internal; international; interpreter; intransitive.
interj. Interjection.
intrans. Intransitive.
in trans. In transitu (L., on the way).
introd. Introduction; introductory.
I. O. O. F. Independent Order of Odd Fellows.
I. O. U. I owe you.
I. R. Inland Revenue; Internal Revenue.
I. R. C. Infantry Reserve Corps.
Ire. Ireland.
is. Island; isle.
Isa. Isaiah.
isl. Island; isle.
It. Italian; Italy.
ital. Italic, italics.
Ital. Italian; Italy.
I. W. Isle of Wight.

J

J. Judge; Justice.
J. A. Judge Advocate.
Jam. Jamaica.
Jan. January.
Jap. Japan; Japanese.
Jas. James.
Jav. Javanese.
J. C. Jesus Christ; Julius Cæsar; jurisconsult.
J. C. D. Juris Civilis Doctor (L., Doctor of Civil Law).
Jer. Jeremiah.
JJ. Justices.
Jno. John.
Jon., Jona. Jonathan.
Jos. Joseph.
Josh. Joshua.
Jour. Journal; journeyman

J. P. Justice of the Peace.

Jr. Junior.

Judg. Judges.

Jun., *or* **jun.** Junior.

Junc. Junction.

jus., just. Justice.

K

K. King; Kings; Knight.

Kans. Kansas.

K. B. King's Bench.

K. C. Knights of Columbus.

K. C. B. Knight Commander of the Bath (Brit. order).

kg. Kilogram.

K. G. Knight of the Garter.

Ki. Kings.

kilom. Kilometer.

K. K. K. Ku-Klux Klan.

kl. Kiloliter.

km. Kilometer; kingdom.

K. M. Knight of Malta (European religious order).

knt. Knight.

K. O. Commanding Officer.

K. P. Kitchen Police; Knight *or* Knights of Pythias.

K. T. Knight Templar.

Ky. Kentucky.

L

l. Lake; land; latitude; leaf; league; left; length; libra (L., a pound); line; link; liter.

L. Lady; Latin; Law; Liber (L., book); Liberal; Low.

La. Louisana.

Lab. Labrador.

Lam. Lamentations.

lat. Latitude.

Lat. Latin.

lb. (*pl.* lbs.) Libra *or* libræ (L., pound *or* pounds).

l.c. Loco citato (L., in the place cited); lower case.

L. C. Lord Chamberlain; Lord Chancellor.

L/C Letter of Credit.

L. C. J. Lord Chief Justice.

l. c. m. Least common multiple.

Ld., ld. Lord.

L. D. Lady Day; (*or* LD.) Low Dutch.

Ldp. Lordship.

lea. League.

leg. Legal; legate; legato; legislative; legislature.

Lev. Leviticus.

LG., *or* **L. G.** Low German.

LGr., *or* **L. Gr.** Low Greek.

l. h. Left hand.

L. H. A. Lord High Admiral.

L. I. Light Infantry; Long Island.

lib. Liber (L., book); librarian; library.

Lieut. *or* **Lt.** Lieutenant.

lin. Lineal; linear.

liq. Liquid; liquor.

lit. Liter; literal; literally; literary; literature.

Lit. D. Literarum Doctor (L., Doctor of Letters).

Lith. Lithuanian.

Litt. D. Litterarum Doctor (L., Doctor of Letters).

LL., *or* **L. L.** Late Latin; Low Latin.

L. L. Lord Lieutenant.

LL. B. Legum Baccalaureus (L., Bachelor of Laws).

LL. D. Legum Doctor (L., Doctor of Laws).

log. Logarithm.

lon., *or* **long.** Longitude.

L. S. Licentiate in Surgery.

L. S. D., *or* **£. s. d.,** *or* **l. s. d.**

Libræ, solidi, denarii (L., pounds, shillings, pence).
Lt. *or* Lieut. Lieutenant.
l. t. Long ton.

M

m. Male; manual; married; masculine; measure; medicine; medium; meridian; meter; middle; mile; mill; minute; month; moon; morning; mountain.
M. Majesty; Manitoba; Marshal; Marquis; Monsieur.
M. A. Magister Artium (L., Master of Arts); Military Academy.
Mac., Macc. Maccabees.
mach. Machinery.
Mad. Madam.
mag. Magazine; magnitude.
Maj. Major.
Mal. Malachi.
man. Manège; manual.
Manit. Manitoba.
manuf. Manufactory; manufacture.
mar. Maritime.
Mar. March.
March. Marchioness.
Marq. Marquis.
mas., *or* masc. Masculine.
Mass. Massachusetts.
math. Mathematician; mathematics.
Matt. Matthew.
max. Maximum.
M. C. Medical Corps; Member of Congress.
Md. Maryland.
M. D. Medicinæ Doctor (L., Doctor of Medicine).
mdse. Merchandise.

Me. Maine.
ME., *or* M. E. Middle English.
M. E. Mechanical, Military, *or* Mining Engineer; Methodist Episcopal; Most Excellent.
meas. Measure.
mech. Mechanics; mechanical.
med. Medical; medicine; medieval; medium.
Medit. Mediterranean.
mem. Memento; memoir; memorandum; memorial.
mer. Meridian; meridional.
Messrs. Messieurs.
metal. Metallurgy.
meteor. Meteorology.
Meth. Methodist.
Mex. Mexican; Mexico.
Mf., *or* mf. Mezzo forte (It., moderately loud).
mfg. Manufacturing.
mfr. (*pl.* mfrs.) Manufacturer.
mg. Milligram.
Mgr. Monseigneur; Monsignore.
M. H. G., *or* MHG. Middle High German.
M. H. R. Member of the House of Representatives.
M. I. Mounted Infantry.
Mic. Micah.
Mich. Michaelmas; Michigan.
mid. Middle; midshipman.
mil. Military; militia.
min. Minim; minimum; mining; minister; minor; minute.
Minn. Minnesota.
Min. Plen. Minister Plenipotentiary.
misc. Miscellaneous.
Miss. Mississippi.
ml. Mail; milliliter.
M. L. A. Modern Language Association.

M. L. G., *or* **MLG.** Middle Low German.

Mlle. Mademoiselle.

mm. Millimeter.

MM. Their Majesties; Messieurs.

Mme. (*pl.* Mmes.) Madame (*pl.* Mesdames).

mo. (*pl.* mos.) Month.

Mo. Missouri.

M. O. Medical officer; money order.

mod. Moderate; moderato (It., moderately); modern.

Moham. Mohammedan.

mol. wt. Molecular weight.

Mon. Monastery; Monday.

Monsig. Monseigneur; Monsignor.

Mont. Montana.

Mor. Morocco.

M. O. R. C. Medical Officers' Reserve Corps.

M. P. Member of Parliament.

M. P. C. Member of Parliament, Canada.

m. p. h. Miles per hour.

Mr. Mister.

M. R. C. Medical Reserve Corps.

Mrs. Mistress.

MS., *or* **ms.** Manuscript.

M. S. Master of Science; Master of Surgery.

m. s. l. Mean sea level.

MSS. *or* **mss.** Manuscripts.

mt. (*pl.* mts.) Mount; mountain.

mun. Municipal.

mus. Museum; music; musician.

Mus. B. Musicæ Baccalaureus (L., Bachelor of Music).

Mus. D. *or* **Musc. Doc.** Musicæ Doctor(L., Doctor of Music).

M. W. Most Worshipful; Most Worthy.

myg. Myriagram.

myl. Myrialiter.

mym. Myriameter.

myth. Mythology.

N

n. Natus (L., born); nephew; neuter; new; nominative; note; noun; number.

N. Navy; Noon; Norse; North; Northern.

N. A. National Academy; National Army; North America; North American.

N. A. A. National Automobile Association.

Nah. Nahum.

nat. National; native; natural.

Nath. Nathanael; Nathaniel.

naut. Nautical.

nav. Naval; navigable; navigation.

N. B. New Brunswick; North Britain; North British; nota bene (L., note well, *or* take notice).

N. C. New Church; Nurses' Corps; North Carolina.

N. C. O. Noncommissioned Officer.

n. d. No date.

N. Dak. North Dakota.

N. E. New England.

N. E. A. National Education Association.

Nebr. Nebraska.

N. E. D. New English Dictionary;—better, O. E. D. (which see).

neg. Negative.

Neh. Nehemiah.

Neth. Netherlands.

neut. Neuter.

Nev. Nevada.

N. F. Newfoundland; (*or* NF.) Norman French.

Ng. Norwegian.

N. G. National Guard; New Granada; (*Slang*) no good.

N. Gr., *or* NGr. New Greek.

N. H. New Hampshire.

Nicar. Nicaragua.

N. J. New Jersey.

N. L., *or* NL. New Latin.

N. Lat. North latitude.

N. Mex. New Mexico.

NNE. North-northeast.

NNW. North-northwest.

N. O. Natural order (*Bot.*); New Orleans.

No., *or* no. (*pl.* Nos., nos.) Numero (L., [by] number).

nol. pros. Nolle prosequi (L., to be unwilling to prosecute).

nom. Nominative.

non seq. Non sequitur (L., it does not follow).

Nor. Norman; North.

Norw., *or* Nor. Norway; Norwegian.

Nov. November.

N. P. New Providence; Notary Public.

nr. Near.

N. R. North Riding; North River.

N. S. National Society; New Series; New Style (since 1752); Novia Scotia.

N. S. W. New South Wales.

N. T. New Testament; Northern Territory.

Num. Numbers.

NW. Northwest; Northwestern.

N. W. T. Northwest Territories.

N. Y. New York.

N. Z. New Zealand.

O

O. Old; Ontario; Order.

o/a. On account (of).

ob. Obiit (L., he, *or* she, died).

Obad. Obadiah.

obdt. Obedient.

obj. Object; objection; objective.

obl. Oblique; oblong.

obs. Observation; observatory; obsolete.

obt. Obedient.

oc. Ocean.

Oct. October.

O. D., *or* OD. Old Dutch.

O. E., *or* OE. Old English.

O. E. Omissions excepted.

O. E. D. Oxford English Dictionary.

O. F., *or* OF. Old French.

off. Offered; officer; official; officinal.

O. H. G., *or* OHG. Old High German.

O. H. M. S. On His (*or* Her) Majesty's Service.

O. K., *or* OK. Correct; all right. *Cant.*

Okla. Oklahoma.

ol. Oleum (L., oil).

O. M. Old measurement; Order of Merit.

Ont. Ontario.

O. O. R. C. Ordnance Officer Reserve Corps.

op. Opera; opposite; opus.

opp. Opposed; opposite.

opt. Optative; optics.

Or. Oriental.

O. R. C. Order of the Red Cross; Officers' Reserve Corps.

ord. Ordained; order; ordinance; ordinary; ordnance.

Oreg. Oregon.

orig. Original; originally.

O. S. Old School; Old Series; Old Style; ordinary seaman.

O. T. Old Testament.

O. T. C. Officers' Training Camp.

Oxon. Oxonia (L., Oxford); Oxoniensis (L., Oxonian).

oz. Ounce; ounces.

P

p. Page; part; participle; past; penny; piano (It., softly); pint; pipe; pole; population; professional.

P. Pastor; pater (L., father); père (F., father); post; president; priest; prince.

Pa. Pennsylvania.

p. a. Participial adjective; per annum (L., by the year).

P/A. Power of attorney; private account.

Pac. Pacific.

pam. Pamphlet.

Pan. Panama.

par. Paragraph; parallel; parenthesis; parish.

Para. Paraguay.

parl. Parliament; parliamentary.

part. Participle.

pass. Passive.

P. B. Prayer Book.

p. c. Per cent; postal card; post card.

pd. Paid.

P. E. Presiding Elder; Protestant Episcopal.

P. E. I. Prince Edward Island.

pen. Peninsula.

Pent. Pentecost.

per an. Per annum (L., by the year).

per ct. Per cent.

perf. Perfect.

perh. Perhaps.

pers. Person; personal.

Pers. Persia; Persian.

pert. Pertaining.

Pet. Peter.

pf. Preferred.

Pg. Portugal; Portuguese.

P. G. M. Past Grand Master.

Phar. Pharmacy; Pharmacopœia.

Ph. B. Philosophiæ Baccalaureus (L., Bachelor of Philosophy).

Ph. D. Philosophiæ Doctor (L., Doctor of Philosophy).

Ph. G. Graduate in Pharmacy.

Phil. Philemon; Philip; Philippians; Philippine.

Phila. Philadelphia.

philol. Philology; philologist.

philos. Philosopher; philosophical; philosophy.

physiol. Physiologist; physiology.

P. I. Philippine Islands.

pinx. Pinxit (L., he, *or* she, painted it).

pk. (*pl.* pks.) Peck.

pkg. (*pl.* pkgs.) Package.

pl. Place; plural.

plf., *or* **plff.** Plaintiff.

plup., *or* **plupf.** Pluperfect.

plur. Plural.

pm. Premium.

P. M., *or* **p. m.** Post meridiem.

(L., afternoon); post mortem.

P. M. G. Postmaster-General.

P. O. Post office; Province of Ontario.

P. O. B. Post-office box.

P. O. D. Pay on delivery; Post Office Department.

Pol. Poland; Polish.

pol., polit. Political.

pol. econ. Political economy.

pop. Popular; population.

Port. Portugal; Portuguese.

pos. Positive; possessive.

poss. Possession; possessive.

pp. Pages; past participle; pianissimo.

p. p. Past participle; postpaid.

P. P. C. *or* **p. p. c.** Pour prendre congé (F., to take leave).

pph. Pamphlet.

p. pr. Present participle.

P. Q. Previous question; Province of Quebec.

pr. Pair; present; price; priest; prince.

Pr. Preferred stock.

P. R. Puerto Rico.

prep. Preparatory; preposition.

pres. President; presidency.

Presb. Presbyterian.

pret. Preterit.

prin. Principal.

priv. Privative.

prob. Probably; problem.

Prof. Professor.

pron. Pronominal; pronoun; pronounced; pronunciation.

propr. Proprietor.

pros. Prosody.

Prot. Protestant.

pro tem. Pro tempore (L., temporarily).

prov. Provident; province; provisional.

Prov. Provençal; Proverbs; Provost.

prox. Proximo (L., next, of the next month).

prs. Pairs.

Prus. Prussia; Prussian.

Ps. Psalm; Psalms.

P. S. Postscriptum (L., postscript); Privy Seal.

pseud. Pseudonym.

psychol. Psychologist; psychology.

pt. (*pl.* pts.) Part; payment; pint; point; port.

P. T., *or* **p. t.** Post town.

p. v. Post village.

pwt. Pennyweight; pennyweights.

pxt. See *pinx.*

Q

q. Quart; queen; query; question; quintal; quire.

Q. Quebec (province)

Q. E. D. Quod erat demonstrandum (L., which was to be demonstrated).

Q. F. Quick-Fire, *or* quickfiring.

ql. Quintal.

Q. M. Quartermaster.

Q. M. G. Quartermaster-General.

Q. M. O. R. C. Quartermaster Officers' Reserve Corps.

Q. M. S. Quartermaster-Sergeant.

qr. (*pl.* qrs.) Quadrans (L., a farthing); quarter; quire.

qt. Quantity; (*pl.* qts.) quart.

qu. Quart; quarterly; queen; query; question.

ques. Question.

qy. Query.

R

r. Railroad; railway; rare; received; rector; resides; retired; right; river; rises; road; rod; rood; royal.

R. Rabbi; Radical; Réaumur; Republican; response.

R. A. Rear Admiral; Regular Army; Royal Academy; Royal Artillery.

rad. Radical; radix.

R. C. Red Cross; Roman Catholic.

R. C. A. Reformed Church in America.

Re. Rupee.

R. E. Reformed Episcopal; Right Excellent; Royal Engineers.

Réaum. Réaumur.

rec. Receipt; recipe; record; recorded; recorder.

recd. Received.

rec. sec. Recording secretary.

rect. Receipt; rector; rectory.

ref. Referee; reference; referred; reformation; reformed.

Ref. Ch. Reformed Church.

reg. Regent; region; register; registered; registry; regular.

Reg. Regina (L., queen).

regt. Regiment.

rel. Relating; relative (-ly); religion; religious.

rep. Repeat; report; reporter; representative; republic.

Rep. Republican.

Repub. Republic; Republican.

retd. Returned.

rev. Revenue; reverse; review; revise; revised; revision; revolution.

Rev. Revelation; Reverend.

Rev. Ver. Revised Version.

R. F., or r. f. Rapid-fire.

R. F. D. Rural Free Delivery.

R. G. S. Royal Geographical Society (London).

r. h. Right hand.

R. H. Royal Highness.

rhet. Rhetoric; rhetorical.

R. I. Rhode Island.

R. I. P. Requiescat in pace (L., may he, or she, rest in peace).

riv. River.

rm. Ream.

R. M. Resident Magistrate; Royal Marines.

R. M. S. Royal Mail Steamer.

R. N. Royal Navy.

R. N. R. Royal Naval Reserve.

ro. Rood.

Robt. Robert.

Rom. Roman; Romance; Romans.

Rom. Cath. Roman Catholic.

R. O. T. C. Reserve Officers' Training Corps (or Camp).

R. P. O. Railroad Post Office.

rpt. Report.

R. R. Railroad.

Rs. Rupees.

R. S. Recording Secretary; Revised Statutes.

R. S. V. P. Répondez, s'il vous plaît (F., reply, if you please).

Rt. Hon. Right Honorable.

Rt. Rev. Right Reverend.

Rum. Rumania; Rumanian.

Rus., or Russ. Russia; Russian.

R. V. Revised Version; Rifle Volunteers.

R. W. Right Worshipful; Right Worthy.

Ry. Railway.

R. Y. S. Royal Yacht Squadron.

S

s., *or* S. Section; see; series; shilling; signed; singular; son; stem; sun; surplus.

S. Sabbath; Saint; Saxon; school; senate; Socialist; Society; Socius (L., Fellow); soprano; South; Southern.

S. A. Salvation Army; Small-arms; South Africa; South America; South Australia.

sa. Sable.

Sab. Sabbath.

S. Afr. South Africa; South African.

Salv. Salvador.

Sam. Samaritan; Samuel.

S. Amer., *or* S. Am. South America; South American.

S. & T. Supply and Transport.

Sans. Sanskrit.

S. A. R. South African Republic.

Sar. Sardinia; Sardinian.

Sask. Saskatchewan.

Sat. Saturday.

Sax. Saxon; Saxony.

sb. Substantive.

S. B. Bachelor of Science; South Britain.

sc. Scene; and see sci., scil., scr., sculp.

Sc. Scotch; Scottish.

s. c. Small capitals.

S. C. Signal Corps; South Carolina; Staff Corps; Supreme Court.

Scand. Scandinavia; Scandinavian.

S. caps. Small capitals.

sch. Scholium; schooner.

sci. Science; scientific.

scil. Scilicet (L., namely).

Scot. Scotch; Scotland; Scottish.

scr. Scruple.

Script. Scripture.

sculp. Sculpsit (L., he, *or* she, carved it).

s. d. Sine die (L., without [appointing] a day).

S. Dak. South Dakota.

SE. Southeast.

sec. Secant; second; secretary; section; secundum (L., according to).

Sec. Leg. Secretary of Legation.

sect. Section.

Sem. Seminary; Semitic.

Sen. Senate; Senator; Senior.

Sep., *or* Sept. September; Septuagint.

ser. Series; sermon.

serg., sergt., *or* Sgt. Sergeant.

Serv. Servian.

s. g. Specific gravity.

S. G. Solicitor-general; Surgeon-General.

Sgt. Maj. Sergeant-Major.

Sh., *or* sh. Share; shilling; shillings.

Shak. Shakespeare.

S. I. Sandwich Islands; Staten Island.

Sib. Siberia; Siberian.

Sic. Sicilian; Sicily.

sing. Singular.

S. J. Society of Jesus.

S. J. C. Supreme Judicial Court.

Skr., *or* Skt. Sanskrit.

S. L. Solicitor at Law.

S. Lat. South latitude.

Slav. Slavic; Slavonic.

sld. Sailed.

S. M. Sa Majesté (F., His, *or* Her, Majesty); Sergeant-Major; Society of Mary

sm. c., *or* **sm. caps.** Small capitals.

S. O., *or* **s. o.** Seller's option.

S. O. Staff Officer; Signal Officer; Special Order.

soc. Society.

S. of Sol. Song of Solomon.

sol. Solution.

sop. Soprano.

S. O. R. C. Signal Officers' Reserve Corps.

sov. Sovereign.

sp. Species; specimen; spelling; spirit.

Sp. Spain; Spaniard; Spanish.

s. p. Sine prole (L., without issue).

S. P. C. A. Society for Prevention of Cruelty to Animals.

S. P. C. C. Society for Prevention of Cruelty to Children.

specif. Specifically.

sp. gr. Specific gravity.

S. P. Q. R. Senatus Populusque Romanus (L., the Senate and People of Rome); small profits, quick returns.

spt. Seaport.

sq. Squadron.

sq. Sequens (L., the following [one]); square.

sqq. Sequentes (L., the following [ones]).

Sr. Sir; Senior.

S. R. S. Fellow (L., Socius) of the Royal Society.

ss. Scilicet (L., namely); semis (L., half).

S. S. Steamship; Supply Sergeant.

SSE. South-southeast.

SSW. South-southwest.

st. Stanza; stone; stet (L., let it stand).

St. Saint; Strait; Street.

stat. Statuary; statue; statutes.

S. T. D. Sacræ Theologiæ Doctor (L., Doctor of Sacred Theology).

str. Steamer.

Sub. Subaltern.

subj. Subject; subjunctive.

subst. Substantive; substitute.

suff. Suffix.

Sun. Sunday.

sup. Superior; superlative; supine; supplement; supra (L., above).

Sup. C. Superior Court; Supreme Court.

superl. Superlative.

Sup. O. Supply Officer.

supp. Supplement.

Supt. Superintendant.

surg. Surgeon; surgery.

surv. Surveying; surveyor.

s. v. Sub verbo (L., under the word); sub voce (L., under the title).

S. V. Sancta Virgo (L., Holy Virgin); Sanctitas Vestra (L., Your Holiness).

SW. Southwest.

Sw., *or* **Swed.** Sweden; Swedish.

Switz. Switzerland.

syn. Synonym; synonymous.

Syr. Syria; Syriac.

T

t. Temperature; tenor; time; tome; ton; town; township; transitive.

T. Territory; Testament; trains; Turkish.

tan. Tangent.

tel. Telegram; telegraph; telephone.

Tenn. Tennessee.

ter. Terrace; territory.

Test. Testament.

Teut. Teuton; Teutonic.

Tex. Texas.

Th. Thomas.

Theo. Theodore; Theodosia.

Theoph. Theophilus.

Thess. Thessalonians.

Tho., *or* **Thos.** Thomas.

Thurs. Thursday.

Tim. Timothy.

T. M. True mean.

T. N. T. Trinitrotoluene *or* Trinitrotoluol.

t. o. Telegraph office; turn over.

topog. Topographical; topography.

tp. Township.

tr. Translated; translation; translator; transpose; treasurer; trustee.

trav. Travel; traveler.

treas. Treasurer; treasury.

trig. Trigonometric; trigonometrical; trigonometry.

Trin. Trinity.

trop. Tropic; tropical.

T. S. Transport and Supply.

T. T. Telegraphic transfer; Trinity term.

T. U. Trade Union.

Tues. Tuesday.

Turk. Turkey; Turkish.

typ. Typographer; typographic (-ical); typography.

U

U. Uncle; Unionist; upper.

U. K. United Kingdom.

ult. Ultimately; ultimo.

Unit. Unitarian.

univ. Universally; university.

Univ. Universalist.

U. of S. Afr. Union of South Africa.

U. P. C. United Presbyterian Church.

Uru. Uruguay.

U. S. Uncle Sam; United States.

U. S. A. United States Army; United States of America.

U. S. C. United States of Colombia.

U. S. M. United States Mail; United States Marine.

U. S. M. A. United States Military Academy.

U. S. N. United States Navy.

U. S. N. A. United States Naval Academy.

U. S. N. G. United States National Guard.

U. S. S. United States Senate; United States Ship *or* Steamer.

usu. Usual; usually.

u. s. w. Und so weiter (G., and so forth).

V

v. Verb; verse; version; versus; very; vicar; vice-; vide (L., see); village; vocative; volume; von (G., of).

V. Venerable; Victoria; Viscount; Volunteers.

Va. Virginia.

v. a. Verb active.

V. A. Vicar Apostolic; Vice Admiral.

var. Variant; variation; variety; various.

Vat. Vatican.

vb. n. Verbal noun.

V. C. Veterinary Corps; Vice Chancellor; Victoria Cross.

Ven. Venerable; Venice.

Venez. Venezuela.

ver. Verse; verses.

Vet. Veterinary.

V. G. Vicar-general.

v. i. Verb intransitive.

Vic. Victoria.

vid. Vide (L., see).

vil. Village.

Vis., or Visc. Viscount.

viz. Videlicet (L., namely).

V. M. D. Veterinariæ Medicinæ Doctor (L., Doctor of Veterinary Medicine).

v. n. Verb neuter.

voc. Vocative.

vocab. Vocabulary.

vol. (pl. vols.) Volume; volunteer.

vol. Volcano; volcanic.

V. P. Vice-President.

v. r. Verb reflexive.

V. R. Victoria Regina (L., Queen Victoria).

V. Rev. Very Reverend.

vs. Versus.

v. s. Vide supra (L., see above).

V. S. Veterinary Surgeon.

Vt. Vermont.

v. t. Verb transitive.

Vul. Vulgate.

vv. Verses; violins.

W

w. Wanting; week; wide; wife; with.

W. Wales; Washington; Welsh; West; Western.

W. A. West Africa; Western Australia.

Wash. Washington.

W. C. Wesleyan Chapel; Western Central (Postal District, London).

W. C. T. U. Woman's Christian Temperance Union.

W. D., or War D. War Department.

Wed. Wednesday.

w. f. Wrong font.

w. g. Wire gauge.

W. G. C. Worthy Grand Chaplain.

W. G. M. Worthy Grand Master.

whf. Wharf.

W. I., or W. Ind. West Indies; West Indian.

Wis. Wisconsin.

Wisd. of Sol. Wisdom of Solomon.

wk. Week.

W. long. West longitude.

Wm. William.

W. M. Worshipful Master.

WNW. West-northwest.

W. O. War Office.

wp. Worship.

W. R. Water reserve; West Riding.

WSW. West-southwest.

wt. Weight.

W. Va. West Virginia.

Wyo. Wyoming.

X

X. Χριστος (Gr., Christ).

X-c., or X-cp. Ex coupon.

Xmas [no period] Christmas.

Xn. Christian.

Xnty., or Xty. Christianity.

Xper., or Xr. Christopher.

Xt. Christ.

Y

y. Yard; year.

yd. (*pl.* yds.) Yard.
Y. M. C. A. Young Men's Christian Association.
Y. M. Cath. A. Young Men's Catholic Association.
Y. M. C. U. Young Men's Christian Union.
Y. P. S. C. E. Young People's Society of Christian Endeavor.
yr. (*pl.* yrs.) Year; younger; your.

Y. W. C. A. Young Women's Christian Association.

Z

Zach. Zacharias; Zachary.
Zeb. Zebadiah; Zebedee.
zoogeog. Zoogeography.
zool. Zoological; zoologist; zoology.
Z. S. Zoological Society.
Zech. Zechariah.
Zeph. Zephaniah.

About

ROGET'S INTERNATIONAL THESAURUS

from which

ROGET'S POCKET THESAURUS

is derived

In 1852, Peter Mark Roget, an English doctor, published the first thesaurus. It filled an important need and became an immediate success. That little book with the long title—*Thesaurus of English Words and Phrases Classified and Arranged so as to Facilitate the Expression of Ideas and Assist in Literary Composition*—was the father of all thesauruses. Fortunately, perhaps, his title has been shortened; but that is the only thing about it which has shrunk. Today *Roget's Pocket Thesaurus* and the bigger volume from which it is derived, *Roget's INTERNATIONAL Thesaurus*, are lineal descendants of Roget's *Thesaurus of English Words*. In these two volumes reside not only the genius of Roget himself, but the work of many subsequent compilers and editors who have expanded the original book into one of the largest and certainly one of the most useful word books in the English language.

Peter Roget was surely inspired when he devised his *Thesaurus*. Known as a brilliant physician, a Fellow of the Royal Society, and a founder of the Society for the Diffusion of Knowledge, this amazing and versatile man invented a slide rule, did pioneer work on a calculating machine, and wrote volumes on phrenology, electricity, physiology, and other scientific problems of his time. But today he is best known for his *Thesaurus,* a book which, ironically enough, he always considered a mere side line.

The basic principle of Roget's *Thesaurus,* which has been scrupulously observed in *Roget's Pocket Thesaurus* and in *Roget's INTERNATIONAL Thesaurus,* is the *grouping of words according to their ideas* rather than the listing of words, as the dictionaries do, according to the alphabet. This is the secret of a genuine thesaurus and is the basis for its remarkable usefulness.

Good writing depends on using the exact word; but how often do you have to grope—usually without success— for the exact word to fit the idea you have in mind? A thesaurus solves just that problem. With a thesaurus you start with an idea and find the word or phrase that suits it. A dictionary, on the other hand, is just the reverse: you start with a word and find its definition. It is impossible, because of the very nature of these two basic reference books, to compile a thesaurus in dictionary form, and it was the genius of Roget which saw this first and the wisdom of subsequent editors which has warned them not to tamper with a proved success.

Roget's Pocket Thesaurus and the more complete *Roget's INTERNATIONAL Thesaurus* are arranged in two basic sections. The first, or main text, consists of hundreds of lists of related words and phrases. These lists cover all areas of knowledge. Originally devised by Peter Roget, they represent a famous breakdown of knowledge which, in its own right, was a feat of human intelligence. Within these lists are placed words and phrases of related meanings; the words themselves are clustered into tiny groups of almost synonymous meanings. But these groups grow and spread like animal cells into a network of related meanings so that if, for example, you want to find a word similar in meaning, though not completely synonymous, to "gay," a thesaurus can help you where a dictionary of synonyms cannot. No dictionary of synonyms has been so useful or enjoyed such success as Roget's *Thesaurus.*

The second section is the all-important index. Here are listed in alphabetical order all the words of the first section and the exact places where they appear. "Gay," for example, appears several places in the text: it is listed in its senses of bright, cheerful, and showy. The index tells you this, and shows you where to turn to find the lists of related words and phrases for every one of these basic meanings of "gay." Without this index a thesaurus is useless. It is the quick and efficient key that unlocks the hundreds of lists of related words and phrases—it is the essential key that is lacking in so-called "dictionary thesauruses."

The extraordinary usefulness of *Roget's Pocket Thesaurus* and *Roget's INTERNATIONAL Thesaurus* is attested to by many famous writers. Kenneth Roberts has written: "I can't possibly remember how many copies of this book I've owned and worn to tatters; but ever since the days when I was writing verse for the old *Life*, I have regarded it as the most valuable reference book that an author could have." Mary Roberts Rinehart said that she has "used at least four of these books since I first commenced to write, and even the fourth one is now in poor shape." And Philip Van Doren Stern wrote that "with the exception of the dictionary, it is the reference book I most often use and find indispensable for that elusive word that slips the mind when you want it most. To the professional writer whose everyday job has to do with words the book is an absolute necessity."

Roget's Pocket Thesaurus, then, and *Roget's INTERNATIONAL Thesaurus* derive their extraordinary usefulness from the fidelity with which they adhere to Peter Mark Roget's original concept. Naturally both volumes have been expanded. For example, many new listings have had to be added to Roget's original divisions of knowledge to provide room for the advances in science and technology which even this amazing doctor did not dream of. Altogether, in the larger edition, there are more than 200,000 words and phrases, and in both editions appear contemporary American colloquialisms and slang. Pocket

Pocket Books and the Thomas Y. Crowell Company have taken exceptional pride in bringing this famous reference book to a peak of usefulness for the modern American; it is pre-eminently suitable for the student, teacher, housewife, business and professional man, writer —in short, for everyone who ever has need of writing anything from a letter to a play, from a business report to a scientific treatise.